THE
RHETORIC
OF
BLACK
AMERICANS

MERRILL'S

International Speech Series

Under the Editorship of

John Black

Ohio State University

Paul Moore

University of Florida

THE
RHETORIC
OF
BLACK
AMERICANS

James L. Golden
Ohio State University

Richard D. Rieke
University of Utah

Charles E. Merrill Publishing Co.
A Bell & Howell Company
Columbus, Ohio

International Standard Book Number: 0-675-09283-3

Library of Congress Catalog Card Number: 72-133263

1 2 3 4 5 6 7 8 9 10 — 75 74 73 72 71

Printed in the United States of America

Gratefully dedicated to
our
Wives and Children

PREFACE

The 1969 Summer Conference of the
Speech Communication Association in
Minneapolis was devoted to the study
of rhetorical issues relevant to contemporary America. Participants were
organized into several study groups,
each concerned with a different problem.
One of the largest groups chose as its
theme the needs of black Americans and
the role of communication and persuasion in their struggle. Early in the
conference, many delegates from other
sessions left their own discussions in
order to hear the compelling ideas being
considered by the black rhetoric group.
With enthusiasm and foresight, the
conference concluded with the call for a
comprehensive study of the rhetoric of
black Americans to serve as a comple-
ment to the volumes on the *History and
Criticism of American Public Address.*
Coincidentally, at the time of this
meeting, work on *The Rhetoric of Black
Americans* was more than half completed. We took comfort in knowing that
this work was developing in the mainstream of contemporary rhetorical
interest.

The primary focus of the book is on the
overall analysis of the persuasive
campaign of black Americans and the
competing strategies of *assimilation,
separation,* and *revolution.* While much
space is devoted to the complete texts of
addresses, sermons, essays, interviews,

debates, letters, and the like, it is significant to note that this book is not a collection of speeches. We have tried to gather the primary documents which have been generated by three hundred years of struggle, presenting them from the perspective of rhetorical and communication theory. The works selected are neither restricted to a single theme or era, nor are they intentionally structured to present a particular point of view with regard to the present conflict between black and white Americans. We have sought to keep personal judgments and random speculation to a minimum.

Original essays have been written, developing each of the aspects of the study. The reprinted documents are interwoven into the essays and serve essentially to illustrate the particular concepts. We have decided, however, that readers will be better served if the documents are presented in their full and original form. In this way, our analysis is more completely supported by documentary examples.

The goal of this book is to propose that all Americans have something to learn from discussion of a singular American topic which, for too long, has been a neglected part of our history. Thus, it is our hope that other students of black rhetoric will be able to use this material as the foundation for additional research.

We are grateful to many people for their help in the preparation of this volume. However, we are most indebted to the faculty, administration, and students of Shaw University in Raleigh, North Carolina. Both of the authors learned much that stimulated their interest and understanding of the rhetoric of black Americans while serving temporarily on the faculty at Shaw. This close association with the Shaw University community not only provided many pleasant memories, but also was the principal force which moved us to dedicate ourselves to this task.

Thanks must also be offered to the staff of the Schomburg Collection in the Harlem Branch of the New York Public Library for their cooperation during an extended period of research. Finally, we deeply appreciate the help received from faculty and students at Ohio State University.

James L. Golden
Richard D. Rieke

Columbus, Ohio
Salt Lake City, Utah
September, 1970

CONTENTS

ix

THE
RHETORIC
OF
BLACK
AMERICANS

Chapter 1   BLACK RHETORIC

This volume, spanning more than two hundred years of American history and culture, seeks to tell, either directly or indirectly, the story of the black American's'quest for the "good life." No effort has been made to demonstrate the full scope of the black man's participation in the affairs of society, or to provide a comprehensive picture of his complete rhetorical practices. Rather, these discussions have been designed to show how persuasion became an instrument for attempting to construct a way of life based on human dignity and freedom. The analysis has not included judgmental statements which might reflect the values and perspectives of the authors. The objective, instead, has been to present data from which readers may test for themselves the hypothesis that black rhetoric is best viewed as a single persuasive campaign. Of course, the analysis suggesting that the campaign can be reasonably perceived in terms of the three broad rhetorical strategies of assimilation, separation, and revolution is a function of the authors' judgment. However, an examination of the documents included here should confirm that approach. Against this background of general perspective, this introduction seeks to bring into focus the basic ground that has been covered.

A comprehensive view of the essays and

documents in this study reveals that black Americans from the colonial period to the present have been confronted with a rhetorical situation that demanded a meaningful response. The reality they saw in each era was all too often marked by a pervasive belief in the inferiority of blacks which led, in turn, to suppression. This belief, hardened by years of prejudice, passed on from generation to generation among the whites, produced slavery in the South and discrimination in the North during the antebellum period. It created burdensome black codes in the post-Reconstruction period, and prompted what many people have called "second class citizenship" in the mid-twentieth century.

As the blacks saw an overriding exigency rooted in the prevailing value system of a majority of whites, they took comfort in the view that their potential audiences, if properly motivated, had the basic power and will to alter the status quo. Thus, they accepted the challenge to respond to the rhetorical situation. At the outset they provided the rationale for seeking their goal by constructing arguments designed to prove ethnological equality. These arguments included attacks on the nature and accomplishments of the Anglo-Saxon race, and vivid descriptions of the achievements and the potentials of blacks. By lowering whites from their assumed position of superiority and raising blacks from their relegated situation of inferiority, black leaders hopefully moved the two races to the level of equality.

Once they came to believe that the premise of equality was established to the satisfaction of reasonable and impartial men, they continued their campaign to remove the exigencies and constraints inherent in the listeners. With an inventive process utilizing a remarkable consistency in the selection and development of forms of proof, black speakers with varied orientations and philosophies were alike in two important respects. First, they often equated their cause with either the will of God or the natural rights of man. Second, they preached the value of self- and/or group-reliance, and racial pride. When it became evident, however, that the exigencies persisted despite a well organized and protracted speaking and writing campaign, rhetorical strategies evolved which recommended dramatically different solutions. These strategies ranged from the moderate position of assimilation to the more extreme philosophies of revolution and separatism. Assimilation which rests at one end of a linear attitude scale and separatism which stands in the polar position, constitute goals in themselves. Revolution, however, is a strategy based on means, not ends. It has as its function the ultimate achievement of assimilation or separatism or, indeed, a combination of both within the same society; and if this were to occur, the black man would be expected to play the dominant role.

Several factors related to the black Americans' use of the three major rhetorical strategies are worth noting. Individual speakers, for example, have assumed either rigid or flexible attitudes toward the strategies. Some steadfastly adhered to a particular emphasis, rarely modifying their essential approach. Frederick Douglass, Booker T. Washington, Martin Luther King, Jr. — to name a representative few — never veered from assimilation. In contrast, Marcus Garvey remained loyal to separatism. Others have moved freely from one strategy to another as they sought to adjust their solutions to the pressing exigencies of the moment. Henry Highland Garnet exemplified this type of flexibility. He turned first to assimilation, then to revolution, then to assimilation, then to separatism, and then back again to assimilation. Malcolm X likewise utilized different strategies in order to adapt to what he believed were changing circumstances. After expressing an initial sympathy for assimilation, he became successively a separatist and a revolutionist. Not to be overlooked, moreover, were deviations within a strategy. Although Washington and W. E. B. DuBois, for instance, were loyal assimilationists at the turn of the century, they held widely variant views concerning the educational and social goals for blacks. Similarly, many contemporary separatists derive their inspiration from the unitarian theology of the Muslims, while others are committed to the doctrine of Christianity.

Another significant feature of the strategies is the presence of historical continuity. With almost cyclical regularity the strategies have recurred in order to cope with changing rhetorical situations. All of them were employed from time to time prior to the Civil War. Although revolution faded as a viable option during the Reconstruction and its aftermath, both assimilation and separatism continued to flourish. With the historic Supreme Court decision in 1954, the three emphases gained renewed impetus.

The impact of the rhetoric of black Americans, taken as a whole, is uneven. Standing side by side are positive achievements and observable failures. Among its successes is the body of challenging literature that has developed. The style and thrust of many of the speeches and documents gave to the messages an enduring eloquence and relevance. Here are a few typical specimens of the rhetoric to be covered in this study that may lay claim to permanence: the primitive, rough-hewn, and anguished appeals of David Walker; the disarming and dramatic confessions of Nat Turner; the bold and galvanic call to arms by Henry Garnet; the penetrating and provocative insight into the meaning of the Fourth of July for the Negro by Frederick Douglass; the compassionate and searching *Souls of Black Folk* by W. E. B. DuBois; and the memorable "I Have a Dream Speech" by Martin Luther King, Jr. These sample addresses, along with others by speakers such as Alexander Crummell, Marcus Garvey, Malcolm X, and Stokely Carmichael, are examples of articulate and effective speech. Not only have many of the speeches earned a place in literature, but they have played no minor role in fashioning heroes. Implicit throughout this volume is the premise that eloquence helped make Frederick Douglass the authentic black leader of the nineteenth century; and it was rhetorical excellence that enabled Martin Luther King, Jr. and Malcolm X to stand above so many of their contemporaries.

More important than the literary or ethos impact of the speeches is the fact that these persuasive efforts often effected a needed change. Frequently, they altered the white man's perception of blacks, and gave to him an awareness of the damaging effects of prejudice. Many whites who came under the influence of Douglass and King later supported civil rights legislation which previously they had rejected. Rhetoric also occasionally changed the black man's perception of himself. At its best, it helped instill pride in his race and stimulated a challenge to fulfill himself. It provided a sense of belonging to a noble cause.

Notwithstanding evidences of positive effect, rhetoric, except in a few instances, has not yet produced the "good life." Indeed, the strong conclusion which follows from this study is that the power of rhetoric to effect major change is more limited than many have believed. One of the hypotheses advanced in Chapter II has suggested that the efforts of blacks in this country to launch a mass movement reveal more faith in the capacity of persuasion to yield positive results than has been held by leaders of successful mass movements in the past. Indeed when leaders of mass movements, according to Hoffer, can choose between persuasion and coercion, they typically choose coercion.[1] Black leaders, for the most part, have not chosen similarly. Overwhelmingly perceiving their situation as a rhetorical one, they have, instead, behaved in a way to suggest they were committed to the idea that messages could effect a change in their condition. In short, many of these spokesmen unlike Bitzer, expressed hope in the belief that all exigencies or urgent imperfections are capa-

ble of positive modification through discourse.[2] They often failed
to recognize that the concept is not dichotomous, but that exigencies must be viewed on a continuum ranging from almost totally
rhetorical situations to those which cannot be influenced through
discourse. In many instances black orators, convinced of the ultimate power of words, did not succeed in making this distinction
even when the situation was well along the continuum toward the
point at which rhetoric plays no useful role.

On balance, the failure of black Americans to achieve their
intended goal through rhetoric seems puzzling. For the rhetorical
documents and essays contained in this study tend to show that
the traditional variables of persuasion — message content and
structure, credibility of source, and effective use of media — have
been skillfully employed. Yet, a breakdown often has occurred
when blacks communicate either with whites or members of their
own race. What, then, are the causes of this failure? If applied to
the black man's communicative efforts to the whites, the answer
can be found not in the persuasive procedures utilized, but in
the nature of the task itself. Rokeach observes that the persuader
primarily deals with attitudes found in the most peripheral group
which he calls "inconsequential."[3] The primitive attitudes and
beliefs found at the center of an individual's system concern concepts such as self identity, personal knowledge about self and
the world, which rest on complete consensus, or which are so
much a function of his own world view that they exist apart from
any reference to others. These beliefs, observes Rokeach, tend
to be almost totally resistant to change, and if they do change
they cause alterations throughout the entire belief system. At this
point, the subject seems to be psychiatric and not persuasive. An
individual, for example, might believe that all the people around
him are part of a conspiracy to do him harm. No amount of
rational argument will dissuade him from that idea, for it rests
in his mind, totally apart from reference to other persons. It is
something he, and only he, knows. By the same token, one might
believe he is incapable of intellectual thought in a meaningful
way because all of his life his teachers, friends, and even parents
have told him that he is inferior. Again, it is unlikely that he can
be persuaded to give up that idea when others tell him, no matter
how effectively, that he is indeed intelligent.

In both cases, if the beliefs held are felt to be damaging to
one's ability to function in society, he probably requires psychiatric attention to overcome his attitudes, or learn to cope with
them. This study of the rhetoric of black Americans suggests the

possibility that the rhetorical goal — communicating with white men about their beliefs and attitudes regarding black men — may be more a psychiatric than a persuasive problem. Rokeach observes that one might accomplish persuasion by relating an inconsequential belief with a more central one in a way that will cause a modification of the inconsequential belief. However, if the audience's central beliefs, their self-concepts, their perception of themselves in relation to black persons, their respected authority figures and institutions and the beliefs derived from them, all point to a state of black inferiority, the likely outcome is the continued adjustment of inconsequential beliefs to conform in a direction away from the goal of black persuasion.

Many black speakers and writers show an understanding of this notion when they speak of institutionalized racism, when they charge this nation with being essentially racist, and when they say that most, if not all, white Americans are, in the final analysis, racist. Whites are indignant about the charge largely because they fail to understand what is said. The white says that he is not racist — he believes in racial equality, integrated schools and housing, and in equal employment opportunities. But these concepts, no matter how important they seem, are essentially inconsequential beliefs. When forced to search deep into his own central belief system, the white man discovers he perceives himself as a white man and holds beliefs of a primitive nature, that whites are not only different but better than blacks. Black speakers often use the many little instances of these beliefs that manifest themselves in the language of white men as evidence of prejudice: "white lie," "whitewash," "white paper," "blackball," "blackmail," "blackhearted," "black sheep," "black Friday," and so forth. The white man uses expressions of his white perspective on the world to refer to other peoples as "nonwhite," to talk of the discovery of parts of the world in terms of the first white man to find them, to call parts of the world in which white domination does not exist, primitive or pagan, to patronize the peoples of Asia, Africa, Latin and South America by presuming that in any field of endeavor the white man has more knowledge and expertise. Even teenage whites are presumed to be capable of teaching adults in the "backward" parts of the world about life and work, and American soldiers are viewed as vastly superior to their counterparts in Asia.

Perhaps the most discouraging aspect of this study is the discovery that those whites most responsive to the message seem to share a strong white-orientation. The abolitionists and white liberals of each period seemed to have retained this basic perception of themselves as white, and often are accused of using the black cause as an outlet for their own need of therapy. When the black speaker tells his white audience to look deep inside their own belief systems and purge their racist ideas, he is confronting the most central, the most ego-involving of all attitudes of the listener. The task may require a more intensive effort toward the re-structuring of beliefs, attitudes, and values than can be accomplished through the ordinary channels of communication. As psychiatrists often observe, in these cases the patient may have to purge himself of his damaging beliefs. In the case of black rhetoric, it may be that the white man must deal with himself and others like him.

As perplexing as the problem of black to white communication is, the failure of black to black communication is even more troublesome. The pages of this study are filled with support for the conclusion that black Americans have been singularly ineffective in establishing common premises for action among themselves. There has been no failure to recognize that the primary need of black Americans is organization. Documents from all periods show an awareness of this goal. Yet there has been constant warfare among exponents of the three major strategies and even disabling disagreements within a strategy over the subordinate methods to be used. Eldridge Cleaver described the "archipelago of one-man showcase groups that plagued the black community with division." Stokely Carmichael in a speech to the students at St. Augustine College in November 1968, described the black man as the most aggressive of all in a black-to-black situation. He challenged his audience to go into any black neighborhood on a weekend if they want to see black men fighting, cutting, or otherwise doing damage to their fellow blacks. But vis-a-vis the white man it has been at best non-violent resistance, usually becoming every man for himself in search of the white man's favors.

Many observers of black rhetoric give the impression that the existence of different strategies such as assimilation, separation, and revolution is the product of a systematic progression. They suggest that black men have tried these strategies one-by-one, and the modern emphasis on revolution represents an advanced rhetorical evolution. This study shows rather clearly that such an analysis is not responsive to the evidence. On the contrary, the evidence points out that *all* the strategies used in the modern period have evolved from past efforts, but they have followed independent paths, and continue to reveal the basic differences among blacks. The contempt which Booker T. Washington and W. E. B. DuBois shared was no greater than that which Roy Wilkins and Stokely Carmichael have for each other. The modern black revolutionary reveres the word "together." He speaks of an individual being "together" to suggest that the person has found himself and knows where he wants to go. Groups of blacks are said to be "together" when they have organized for concerted action in their own behalf. But these same individuals speak openly of their hatred for the "Uncle Tom," and include him among white men as the enemy. These same black men cannot form nationwide organizations of any permanence. They soon breakdown over the emergence of rival leaders or ideology.

Stokely Carmichael has shown his awareness of this problem when he argues that any black man who does not hate whites must not have an undying love for his black brethren. Certainly much modern, as well as early persuasion has been aimed at the creation of black pride, identity, and love; yet the rhetoric of black pride and love has existed for two hundred years and little in the way of organization has been accomplished. One must ask again whether or not this is an exigence which can be productively influenced by rhetoric. Can a productive and pervasive black culture be generated in the presence of a white majority and in a nation in which a white perspective is the path to rewards? Can a culture aimed at resisting white supremacy exist in the face of white counter persuasion through messages and the systematic deflating of anti-white action by generous applications of money? The capacity of white Americans to "co-opt" blacks by giving them material and social rewards seems almost unlimited. The evidence of this study points to a systematic process of white counter-action by rewarding black leaders which, in turn, leads them away from their people, and rejecting or disciplining those who refuse to cooperate. The remaining articulate black men seem to be stymied because of their disagreements with other blacks. For whatever reason, the rhetoric of black organization has been noticeably unable to bring black Americans together.

A final conclusion which may be drawn from this study is that a new area of rhetorical emphasis seems to be suggested. Within the general analysis of rhetorical practice, scholars have been inclined to focus on such distinct bodies of discourse as Attic oratory, Roman oratory, Eighteenth Century British oratory, and American public address. The compelling lesson to be drawn from this study, however, is that the rhetoric of black Americans cannot be viewed as simply a part of American oratory. The analysis of black rhetoric is not simply a temporary requirement ultimately to be blended into the broad study of the persuasion of all Americans, or even all agitators, or all revolutionists, or all religious speakers. The evidence strongly suggests that the body of persuasive messages generated by black men to gain their freedom, identity, or "good life" as used here is a singular rhetorical syndrome that deserves study *per se.*

STRATEGIC ANALYSIS

If the essence of humanity is the ability and opportunity to engage in free and enlightened choice, and if rhetoric is the rationale of the discourse through which man achieves humanity, then the study of the rhetoric of black Americans is an extraordinary instance of this process in action.[4] The character of the black experience in the United States is a volatile subject to discuss. To describe it is to overlay the perceptions of the describer, and in the present case, there is a wide variation of perceptions. However, there is probably general agreement that this experience has involved people — black and white — using messages in one form or another to increase their freedom to engage in enlightened decision-making and their freedom to act according to their decisions.

This seeking for increased freedom is not a one-sided process. Certainly, from the point of view of the black American the effort has been rather clearly directed at escape from one or another form of involuntary subservience, whether it is formal slavery or the more informally imposed socioeconomic form, which some individuals have compared to colonialism.[5] The white American has been less likely to perceive the experience as a movement to free himself. Typically playing the dominant role, he has been inclined to feel free to decide as he wishes and act accordingly. But, it is possible to see the white man as much enslaved as the black. First, in relationship to the black man, the average white man has been, and probably still is, relatively unfree to effect change. The following statement develops this idea from an admittedly biased point of view:

> The groups which have access to the necessary resources and the ability to effect change benefit politically and economically from the continued subordinate status of the black community. This is not to say that every single white American consciously oppresses black people. He does not need to. Institutional

racism has been maintained deliberately by the power structure and through indifference, inertia and lack courage [sic.] on the part of white masses as well as petty officials. . . . One way or another, most whites participate in economic colonialism.[6]

One could add, to the last sentence, "whether they want to or not." If, as the above authors argue, racism or colonialism has been institutionalized in American society, then the typical white person is relatively unfree to influence relations with the black people.

Furthermore, the white man can be seen as lacking freedom in his development of attitudes from which decisions flow. The fact of slavery and the subsequent relationships between white and black have generated attitudes and values in whites which cannot be changed easily. The point can be argued this way:

But how fully can white people free themselves from the tug of the group position — free themselves not so much from overt racist attitudes in themselves as from a more subtle paternalism bred into them by the society and, perhaps more important, from the conditioned reaction of black people to their whiteness.[7]

Such a universe of discourse generated within a society for the mutual extension of freedom of the citizens of that society is particularly appropriate for rhetorical analysis.

UNIQUENESS OF BLACK RHETORIC

Several characteristics distinguish black rhetoric from other persuasive situations or movements. Of course, illustrations of the specific distinguishing features of this rhetorical effort will come in later chapters, but it seems useful to suggest a few of the aspects which make the rhetoric of black Americans of particular concern to the rhetorician.

PERSUASIVE CAMPAIGN

The rhetoric of black Americans, when viewed as a campaign, offers an unusual opportunity for the study of persuasion. This is true, first, because most modern critics have come to believe that persuasion is most usefully studied as a process or a campaign rather than as a series of single speeches; and, second, because the persuasion generated by this group of Americans extends over time and space, reveals a variety of strategies, and yet is sufficiently unified to be perceived as a single campaign. Each of these reasons requires some additional development.

A desire to view persuasion in terms of a campaign stems from both the concept of instrumentality and an awareness of the complexity of change in modern society. Fotheringham uses the term "instrumental" to refer to the effects brought about by messages which, in turn, bring about the action-goal sought by the messages.[8] Instrumental effects are contrasted with consummatory effects in this way:

> Immediate effects, such as comprehension, recognition, approval or disapproval, and belief, may be valued as goals in themselves. For other communicators, they are valued for their instrumentality in generating some desired action. Thus responses are, from the source's view, consummatory when they reduce or eliminate his motivated state. The same responses are instrumental when they lead receivers to that further behavior, the source's goal, which satisfies his motivated conditions. Communicators interested in effects primarily for their value in producing further behavior (action) are persuaders.[9]

Because the concept of stimulus-response is viewed as including an important mediating variable which takes place within the organism, the old idea of a single speech yielding audience behavior is felt to be incomplete. A speaker (or source) must not only determine what action goal is wanted from the audience but also must determine what instrumental effects can be aroused as meaning is stimulated in the receivers by his message, which will influence the audience to behave as he would have them. A highly simplified illustration of this kind of analysis might be this:

SOURCE: Malcolm X
AUDIENCE: Members of the black community
INSTRUMENTAL EFFECTS: To generate a belief or meaning that the white man is indeed the Devil and the concomitant belief that the black man is therefore superior to the white man
ACTION-GOAL: To bring black men to join the Nation of Islam and follow the behavior patterns it prescribes

It is, of course, possible that the entire persuasive process can be accomplished in the course of a single speech. A persuasive pattern such as the "motivated sequence" developed by Monroe is consistent with this idea when it advises the speaker first to address himself to instrumental effects, such as, a sense of "need" and its satisfaction, and visualization before moving the audience to action.[10] However, a more realistic assessment of the persuasive process suggests that a series of messages which develop various instrumental effects over a period of time and through various media including mass communication, public speaking, and the interpersonal influence of opinion leaders may be necessary to bring about significant action-goals. Malcolm X observed this in his *Autobiography.*

> I can't remember any black man ever in those living-room audiences . . . who didn't stand up immediately when I asked after each lecture, "Will all stand who *believe* what you have heard?" And each Sunday night, some of them stood while I could see others not quite ready when I asked "How many of you want to *follow* The Honorable Elijah Muhammad ." [author's italics][11]

This speaker was making a clear distinction between the instrumental effect of *believing* what was said, and the action goal of *following* the leader and his organization. The author goes on to observe that after attending a series of his lectures which each time added to the meaning or belief connected with the Muslim movement, many people finally took the action of joining. Until the instrumental effects were strong enough to move the receiver to take action, no persuasion was accomplished.

Fotheringham develops the notion of a persuasive campaign in this way:

> The concept of instrumentality encourages seeing persuasion as a campaign — a structured sequence of efforts to achieve adoption, continuance, deterrence, or discontinuance — rather than as a one-shot effort. Effects established in an earlier phase of a campaign are instrumental to the development of subsequent effects. The first effort to persuade others commonly accomplishes only part of the job; that part, however, is necessary for the success of the next phase and for the ultimate goal.[12]

Much rhetorical criticism has been predicted on a relatively simplistic idea of change in attitude and human behavior. Great speakers have been studied and conclusions have been drawn suggesting that in a single speech, audiences have been moved to take dramatic actions quite contrary to their previous inclinations and behaviors. As more is learned about the way in which changes in human behavior occur, this simplistic approach seems less and less useful. For example, susceptibility to change of beliefs, attitudes, or values may depend upon their centrality in the system of the receiver. Rokeach conceives of belief systems as organized into five levels ranging from primitive beliefs (the most central) to inconsequential beliefs (the most peripheral). He also hypothesizes that the more central a belief, the more it will resist change. If the modification of beliefs is the instrument of persuasion, then the complexity of the persuasive effort must vary with the type of belief that is being addressed.[13] Rokeach suggests that even the advertising man, who deals almost exclusively with inconsequential beliefs, must plan a systematic campaign in which the receiver is confronted with a juxtaposition of inconsequential with primitive beliefs designed to yield change.[14] If a campaign approach to persuasion in advertising is appropriate, then it is even more relevant to the rhetoric which is addressed to more central beliefs concerning authority or reference persons and groups, and the beliefs which are derived from them.

Complexity of change is also illustrated by the concept of ego-involvements and attitudes. Sherif, Sherif, and Nebergall present evidence that as receivers are more ego-involved in their attitudes, they will be more resistant to change. In fact, highly ego-involved persons may react negatively to an effort to persuade which will actually end in reinforcing their previous attitudes in contrast to the instrumental effects sought by the persuader.[15] As in the case of more central beliefs, the complexity of a persuasive effort must vary with the degree of ego-involvement in the attitude under consideration. Again, a campaign analysis may be most useful, even to the extent of suggesting that a modification of the amount of ego-involvement (either increasing or decreasing) may be instrumental to the modification of an attitude which, in turn, may be instrumental to the source desired goal.

CAMPAIGNS AND MOVEMENTS

If, as suggested here, it is useful to base rhetorical analysis upon the campaign idea, the scope of black American rhetoric seems to overflow the limits of the term "campaign." One is immediately inclined to feel that a broader concept, such as "movement", is needed to embrace this subject. Griffin has recommended the rhetorical analysis of historical movements, but he recommends the selection of a smaller, more manageable passage of history than the messages generated by black men since the earliest history of America.[16] He might suggest the selection of a study of the "civil rights" movement, or the "black power" movement, or the "nationalist" movement, or the "abolition" movement, or the "colonization" movement. But all of these so-called movements, while different, are still a part of the same process, whatever it may be called. It would certainly make the scholar's task easier to abstract from the whole a single, relatively unified part. However, if such an abstraction yields misleading conclusions about a broader rhetorical effort, it must not be done.

If, in the study of the overall effort to increase government's social responsibility, one selects a study of child labor legislation or social security legislation, or public medical care, a real service to scholarship might be gained from the ability to focus on detail. There is reason to believe, however, that the rhetoric of black Americans yields different results — when only the "civil rights" movement is studied, it may lead to the altering of messages to fit into the selected mold. Similarly, many efforts to study the "black power" movement have suffered from a tendency to look at speeches of previous centuries and perceive them as being aimed at the same concept of power as speeches of today.

Lester, in his book devoted to the discussion of the black power movement, views Frederick Douglass this way:

> When the Garrisonians made the final break with Douglass in 1852, it was because Douglass "dared differ from the American Anti-Slavery Society and its leaders as to how he should exercise his powers."

> Militant though he was, Frederick Douglass was considered a moderate by many of his black contemporaries. Douglass never firmly resolved in his mind just what tactic should be used against slavery. At times, he was for violence . . ."[17]

The same book suggests that the black power movement was truly implicit in the significant phases of black activity which seemed to precede it.

> The Movement was moving. It was no longer a Friendship Contest. It was becoming a War of Liberation.
> Ideologically, it is a big step to move in six years from We Shall Overcome, Black and White Together, to Black Power. This development has been decried by many observers of SNCC, who now claim that the organization has come to its present position because it is frustrated and, in essence, spiritually bankrupt. These observers have been unaware of what has been transpiring on the psychological level . . . . No black person has been uninvolved on this level, though most have never taken part in a demonstration or carried a picket sign. Nonetheless, they have been in "the movement," often silent and unseen, but affecting the course of events.[18]

Whether a given message is a part of the "civil rights" or the "black power" movement is less a function of the message and more the responsibility of the person making the analysis. Any analyst who is determined to study a particular "movement" can find, in the universe of discourse generated by black Americans, "examples" of what he wants. At the same time, he may ignore messages which do not seem to illustrate his point. The result is a single, selected point of view, which, if left unassisted by other points of view, may lead to dangerous distortions of meaning.

Of course, no analysis can avoid the problem of selective perception. But, there is a unique quality in black rhetoric that suggests the selection of the broadest possible body of communication for rhetorical analysis. Lester's assertion that prior phases of black persuasion may have been instrumental to the effect of black power may be a realistic one. On the other hand, the assertions which he quotes — that black power represents the frustration and spiritual bankruptcy of the civil rights movement — may also be realistic.

Two conclusions may be drawn from this discussion. First, unlike some other phenomena, black rhetoric may suffer serious distortions if only smaller, separate, movements growing out of it are studied. Second, there is a unity of purpose and a potential instrumentality among the various aspects of black rhetoric that demand broad analysis.

The unique character of black rhetoric is further illustrated by a comparison with Hoffer's description of mass movements.[19] He suggests the following requirements:

> For men to plunge headlong into an undertaking of vast change, they must be intensely discontented yet not destitute, and they must have the feeling that by the possession of some potent doctrine, infallible leader or some new technique they have access to a source of irresistible power. They must also have an extravagant conception of the prospects and potentialities of the future. Finally, they must be wholly ignorant of the difficulties involved in their vast undertaking.[20]

Black Americans have certainly met these requirements at one time or another, but they have by no means been general throughout the long-term effort. For instance, although intense discontent has been present, the effectiveness of the white counter-movement has seemingly left black people destitute, with little or no sense of power, constantly reminded of the difficulties involved in their undertaking. While the rhetoric of black Americans is filled with messages addressed to the ideas of hope, power, and disregard for the difficulties, the chapters that follow will reveal the varied effects they have had.

Does the presence of the requirements for a mass movement in the rhetoric of a group mean that a movement exists? Hoffer would not think so. This, he would say, is only the first step.

> . . . the readying of the ground for a mass movement is done best by men whose chief claim to excellence is their skill in the use of the spoken or written word; . . . the hatching of an actual movement requires the temperament and the talents of the fanatic; and . . . the final consolidation of the movement is largely the work of practical men of action.[21]

Hoffer goes on to say that "it also seems that, where a mass movement can either persuade or coerce, it usually chooses the latter."[22] It is the thesis of this book that the black effort in the United States cannot be adequately described in this sequential manner. First, the effort has been consistently inclined toward persuasion rather than coercion, although the latter has certainly appeared from time-to-time. Second, it is not possible to characterize the "movement" in terms of phases such as persuasion, fanatic, and consolidating and stabilizing phases. There has been relatively less fanaticism and consolidating than persuading, and these phases have occurred side-by-side, or, at best, cyclically, rather than in a chronological sequence leading to the present state of activity.

PERSUASION AND COERCION

Persuasion can be distinguished from the other forms of influencing human behavior by its reliance upon a perception of choice in the minds of the individuals who are the objects of the change efforts.[23] Coercion, conversely, implies a conscious effort to influence someone's behavior through means which at least seem to confront him with no other choice than the one indicated. Overt force, however, may not be the only form of coercion. Messages may be used to create the instrumental effect of believing one has no choice. Fotheringham argues that only when a person "approves of his action as the best in given circumstances" and still "perceives himself its chief selector" can the influence be called persuasion.[24] The distinction is tenuous. It would be difficult to measure the precise point in the decision process at which the person concludes that his action choice is the best in the circumstances and that he has been its chief selector. Man's capacity to generate self-justifying beliefs to restore harmonious affective and cognitive states that may have been disrupted by the action of force or authority is vast.

Although Congress persistently claims that the passage of Civil Rights legislation is not related to violent actions in the cities, the positive correlation between rebellious behavior and legislative action is suspicious. Most congressmen will protest loudly that their vote was their own choice of the best action under the circumstances, and reject, out of hand, any suggestion they were coerced. Who can say how or when they came to that perception, or whether Molotov cocktails or persuasive testimony were the primary determinants of Congressional behavior? It seems almost certain that at least with regard to black Americans, both persuasion and coercion have operated to achieve results.

Perhaps a more useful approach, in the light of the extraordinary nature of black rhetoric, is to note the relative emphasis placed on persuasive messages, messages of threat, and overt coercion. First, a characteristic of many movements is the use of terror and fanaticism. Fotheringham discusses the strategy of some totalitarian leaders in the use of waves of terror with in-between periods of relative calm.[25] He says,

> . . . the intervals of calm and the absence of observable tension-producing incidents can be used to good advantage for political persuasion *provided some new wave of terror is anticipated.* The threat is instrumental in establishing persuasive effects during the "breathing spell.[26] (author's italics)

But this relationship between coercion and persuasion hardly seems applicable to black rhetoric. On the contrary, although there have been waves of terror from slave revolts to the urban violence of the present day, it would seem to be more appropriately described as *waves of persuasion with in-between periods of terror.* Until the semi-regularity of the modern "long hot summers", the terror has been intermittent and sufficiently widespread that when it has come, it has usually been unanticipated by the white population which has usually convinced itself that the blacks are contented and unlikely to complain, much less revolt. Even today, with violence occurring more and more regularly, there seem to be enough messages of calm and assurance from persons *perceived* as able to speak with authority that a large portion of the population reconvinces itself that the terror is over and will not return. Thus, the potential instrumental effect of the terror is minimized.

Messages which promise that coercion will be forthcoming have also been utilized. Whether they are more or less frequent than actual force; whether they have consistently proved accurate in the prediction of future terror; and whether these messages are to be judged as more or less desirable than actual coercion must be answered later. It is to be noted here simply that this is a distinguishing characteristic of black rhetoric. Obviously when one speaks of forthcoming violent revolution, he is seeking to modify behavior in a way that will obviate the very force of which he speaks. If he were committed to the successful accomplishment of the violence, he would probably not spend his time publishing books and delivering speeches about the coming terror.

Hoffer distinguishes between men of words and fanatics. It is the man of words who attacks the establishment and threatens it with destruction unless changes are made immediately. This man may, according to Hoffer, be appalled if the destruction actually comes. The fanatic, on the other hand, thrives on destruction. He will not spend his time trying to convince the establishment to change in order to avoid tragedy. He will attack.[27] To the extent this analysis is accurate — that it is unlikely that men of words are also capable of fanaticism — the threatening messages represent a different mode of influence than force itself.

These messages of threat have occurred throughout the history of the black effort. The following was written in 1884:

> I do not indulge in the luxury of prophecy when I declare that the American people are fostering in their bosoms a spirit of rebellion which will yet shake the pillars of popular government as they have never before been shaken, unless a wiser policy is inaugurated and honestly enforced. All the indications point to the fulfilment of such declaration.[28]

In 1968 a similar message appeared.

> The time seems near, however, for the full range of the black masses to put down the broom and buckle on the sword. And it grows nearer day by day. Now we see skirmishes, sputtering erratically, evidence if you will that the young men are in a warlike mood. But evidence as well that the elders are watching closely and may soon join the battle.
>
> One might consider the possibility that, if the national direction remains unchanged, such a conflagration simply might *not* come about. Might not black people remain where they are, as they did for a hundred years during slavery? Such seems truly inconceivable.[29]

While both messages promise that violence is coming, both also clearly include an escape clause: if national direction changes, violence can be avoided. These men are not behaving as Hoffer's fanatics would. They are men of words whose primary tool is still persuasion even though they seek to present the nation with no realistic choice other than change or destruction. It seems remarkable that so many men of words have emerged from the effort of black people and apparently so few fanatics.

Another point to be observed within the discussion of persuasion and coercion is what one man has called the rhetoric of preparation.[30] This involves the carrying through of all realistic motions to prepare for violence by men of persuasive intent rather than fanatics. The goal, in this situation, is to change the behavior of those who see the preparations and believe they are not a bluff. This concept is near the idea of "brinkmanship" associated with the foreign policy of John Foster Dulles. Implicit in this rhetoric is the commitment to peaceful change. The preparations, however, must be real if they are to have the necessary credibility to achieve peaceful change. It follows logically that if the preparations do not generate the desired instrumental effects, violence will occur.

The same problem exists in the rhetoric of preparation as in brinkmanship: if the action comes under the direction of fanatics, the violence may become an end in itself, and once more, as in Hoffer's description, the men of words will watch in horror as their movement takes on a new direction. However, to the extent the rhetoric of black Americans is still aimed toward the use of the threat to persuade, and the effort has not come under the influence of fanatics, it is a relatively unique type of movement.

SITUATIONS AND STRATEGIES

In the effort of the black American to change the white man's perception of him, persuasion seems to have been employed more frequently than other available strategies, and this apparently violates the typical pattern of mass movements. Not only does this decision to emphasize persuasion rather than coercion distinguish the black effort from other movements, but also the fact that there has been a continuous public discourse pursuant to this decision is noteworthy. That is to say, it is one thing to generate rhetoric aimed at the modification of a situation; it is another to generate discourse aimed at deciding whether or not a situation is *susceptible* to change through rhetoric.

Bitzer's discussion of rhetorical situations is useful in explaining this idea.[31] He defines a rhetorical situation this way:

> Rhetorical situation may be defined as a complex of persons, events, objects, and relations presenting an actual or potential exigence which can be completely or partially removed if discourse, introduced into the situation, can so constrain human decision or action as to bring about the significant modification of the exigence.[32]

An exigence is described as "an imperfection marked by urgency". Situations must, according to Bitzer, include audiences of persons capable "of being influenced by discourse and of being mediators of change," and a set of constraints such as persons, events, and objects which can be instrumental to the desired change.[33] The important point here is that there may be situations in need of change for which rhetoric is inappropriate. Exigencies which are unchangeable, such as death and taxes, are clearly of this type. Similarly, exigencies which might be changed only by coercion, either overt force or the application of power as in bargaining, are not rhetorical situations. Or, at least, the nature of the situation has changed and therefore requires a different rhetorical response. Stevens makes this point in his writing on strategy and collective bargaining when he notes that the role of persuasion in a bargaining situation is limited to an effort to modify an opponent's preferences or his perception of the forces operating upon him from outside the negotiation environment.[34] If one is in fact involved in a bargaining situation and responds to it as if it were susceptible to change through ordinary rhetorical appeals, his efforts will almost certainly be fruitless.

Bitzer says that an exigence "is rhetorical when it is capable of positive modification and when positive modification requires discourse or can be assisted by discourse."[35] The exigence, or urgent imperfection, facing the black man in America has been subject to many interpretations. Most of them, however, center on oppressive behavior of one kind or another by white men and directed toward black men. There has been considerably less agreement over whether or not this exigence can be modified by discourse.

At the root of black rhetoric is the debate over the question of whether or not the situation is rhetorical. Even while the rhetorical campaign has proceeded, there have been black men who have argued that persuasion is futile. They have asserted that the differences between these two groups are inherent and cannot be improved, much less resolved, through discourse. Of course, many white men have advanced the same idea. The problem is to determine what kind of relationship exists between white and black. If it is decided that the relationship is one of coordination or common interest, then the role of persuasion will be important in bringing the parties together to see how their interests are essentially the same, and how the groups can structure themselves to maximize the mutual benefits of this shared interest. At the opposite end of the continuum, the parties could determine that their relationship is one of pure conflict and persuasion is irrelevant. Under this circumstance, it would be pointless to attempt to engage the other party in discourse with the goal of changing attitudes and reaching agreement.

If the situation were defined as one of essential conflict, then the relevant audience would be reduced to members of one's own group and no one else. Discourse could be addressed to the members of the group to organize them for winning the game, as a team huddles to plan the next play. If black Americans determined that every gain they were to make would be at the direct expense of the white man and the two groups could not cooperate, then discourse would be addressed only to other black men to exhort them to oppose directly or withdraw from the conflict altogether.

At least a third alternative interpretation of the situation is possible. The relationship could be one in which conflict exists between the parties, but they share enough motives to allow for some behaviors which are mutually rewarding. As in the case of labor and management, where conflict exists within the larger framework of mutual interest and dependence, the black man can perceive himself in competition with the white man for certain rewards available in a society on which both white and black man are dependent.

Persuasion has a limited role in this situation. Stevens' discussion of this has already been mentioned. In the bargaining situation, according to Stevens, persuasion is one tactic that might be used along with the tactics of coercion, bluff, and threat.[36] The black man might address himself to persons who are not parties to the negotiation — in other countries or situations — in order to bring pressure to bear on the particular white group under consideration. Or, the black man might address his rhetoric to his white adversaries in order to change their perception of their own preferences and alternatives. Where the white man might previously have desired a totally segregated society, the black man might persuade him that this is an unreasonable expectation, and he should be satisfied with something less. Where the white man might once have felt the best he could do was stop discriminating against black men because of their color, the black man might convince him he can reasonably consider a plan of positive discrimination in favor of black men to offset the years of segregation. These efforts can be likened to labor convincing management that a plan of supplemental unemployment benefits is a viable alternative for bargaining, when once it would have been considered unthinkable. The parties are not convincing their adversaries that these alternatives are "good" or "proper" or "just" but simply that they fall within a range of acceptable settlements if the bargaining is hard enough.

It is significant that the rhetoric of black Americans has been characterized by this continuing discussion of whether the exigence they face is rhetorical or not. The discussion continues today. Bitzer speaks of "indeterminate exigencies" in which the rhetor's "decision to speak is based mainly upon the urgency of the exigence and the probability that the exigence is rhetorical.[37] Black rhetoric seems to fall within this description, although the probability, when probability is defined as the willingness of the blacks to commit themselves to rhetorical strategies, that the situation is rhetorical has certainly varied from time-to-time and group-to-group.

To suggest that situations are either rhetorical or not rhetorical would be a misleading polarization. The extremes of complete conflict and pure coordination have been described as well as a middle position of bargaining. When dealing with a complex situation such as that facing the black American, however, one must be prepared to analyze a range of relationships at various times and places. With some audiences and exigencies, the situation may approach coordination of motives, while other audiences and times may present a situation much less responsive to change through rhetoric. Moreover, it would be a mistake to presume that in all situations black Americans have perceived themselves as a single group with completely common motives. When black faces black, the question must be asked, "What game are we playing, and to what extent will rhetoric alone yield a resolution of our differences?"

The rhetoric of black Americans includes discourse aimed at answering the question of the relationship of black to black, and the means by which they can come to perceive common values and motives. Whether one attributes it to the conspiracy of the white man or to typical behavior in human groups, black men have divided into groups which perceive themselves in some degree of conflict with each other. Malcolm X, in his "Message to the Grass Roots," characterized this intra-group conflict from this point of view.

> . . . back during slavery, there were two kinds of slaves, the house Negro and the field Negro. The house Negroes — they lived in the house with master, they dressed pretty good, they ate good because they ate his food — what he left.

> And if you came to the house Negro and said, "Let's run away, let's escape, let's separate." the house Negro would look at you and say, "Man, you crazy. What you mean, separate? Where is there a better house than this? . . . That was that house Negro. In those days he was called a "house nigger." And that's what we call them today, because we've still got some house niggers running around here.

> This modern house Negro loves his master. He wants to live near him. He'll pay three times as much as the house is worth just to live near his master, and then brag about "I'm the only Negro out here."

> On that same plantation, there was the field Negro . . . The Negro in the field caught hell. He ate leftovers . . . If someone came to the field Negro and said, "Let's separate, let's run," he didn't say "Where we going?" He'd say, "Any place is better than here.[38]

Differences among black groups are obviously unlike the differences between white and black. While white and black seem in conflict almost because of the nature of the society (recall the discussion of institutionalized racism analyzed earlier), the various black groups, by the same token, must see themselves essentially as sharing a common fate. For this reason, while one black group may seem in conflict with another, their conflict is not as much a question of fundamental goals and values as a question of strategies which ought to be followed in the pursuit of common goals.

Assume, for the moment, that the character of the situation facing the black man in America has been understood to be the desire to achieve the freedom to seek a good life, how ever each man may define that. Assume also that the absence of this freedom is directly a product of the bahavior of white men, whether it is presumed to be conscious, malicious, and conspiratorial or not. Assume further that this audience (white men) is not only able to effect a change in the behavior which denies freedom, but can be influenced to do so through discourse. Even if these assumptions are made, the rhetor or persuader (in this case, the black man) must still determine what instrumental effects, or constraints, or strategies are available, and which of them will be most likely to achieve the goal of increased freedom.

In the earlier discussion of instrumental effects, it was noted that there will probably be several levels of effect sought in a complex campaign. Specific and elemental effects, such as comprehension, may be sought in the course of achieving a more difficult effect, such as attitude change, which, in turn, may yield a minor change in behavior, such as promotion policies in an industry, which may finally bring forth an advancement in freedom. Even the accomplishment of this increase in freedom is likely to be an instrumental effect to an even greater advance in freedom at a later time or in other contexts.

At these various steps in effect, the persuader must decide not only what instrumental effects will be sought, but what rhetorical strategy will be used to achieve the selected effect. The term "strategy" is used in various contexts and deserves some explication. Martin and Andersen give this description in a footnote:

> A word about *strategy* as the term for the means of producing desired effects with communications. Strategy in the original military sense of the word, meant a grand design framed to accomplish stated objectives by means of intelligent deployment of a host of resources. Strategic decisions involved knowledge of available alternatives and the judgment and 'art' to bring all of one's available resources to bear in the most advantageous and economic way. This seems exactly the task of the persuasive speaker or writer.[39]

These authors go on to discuss strategies at the most basic level. They speak of such strategies as the use of variety, climax and anti-climax order, redundancy, familiar language, statistical testimony, and so forth.

Black uses the concept "strategy" in connection with his idea of "rhetorical transactions" which include situations, strategies, and effects. In Black's view, a strategy should be inferred through examination of the situations. In other words, what rhetorical approaches to a specific situation have produced what effect?[40]

Strategy, as a concept, is closely associated with the theory of games, and often is taken to imply a game situation. Rapoport would associate the term with the determination of alternatives open in a given situation, and the selection of one on the basis of predicted consequences in a conflict situation.[41]

If the situation at hand is judged to be a rhetorical one, then the appropriate response should be rhetorical strategies. The alternative strategies, such as coercion, force, aggression, or one of the various possibilities are usually judged to be less socially desirable in our culture, and are considered less effective in producing happy, lasting, and self-perpetuating solutions than rhetoric.[42] If quixotic attempts at persuasion are to be avoided in a non-rhetorical situation, then the employment of force or authority where discourse would serve is equally undesirable. Thus, some distinction must be made between rhetorical and non-rhetorical strategies, or more realistically between those strategies which are more rhetorical than non-rhetorical, and other types of strategies in which rhetoric plays little or no role.

Fotheringham provides a basis for such a distinction in his concept of the dominance of message effect. He characterizes a message as opposed to other stimuli by function instead of properties.

> A message is viewed as a sign or group of signs — signals and/or symbols — intentionally used by a source to arouse significance or symbolization.[43]

A rhetorical strategy, then, would be one in which messages are the major determinant of instrumental effects.

Some thought must be given to the scope of activities which may fall within the category of rhetorical strategies. Can demonstrations, marches, picketing, rallies, and even shooting, looting, and burning, be considered rhetorical? Some writers would be inclined to include most, if not all, of these behaviors within the context of messages. Fotheringham says this:

> As part of the integration campaign, Negroes on Easter Sunday, 1963, sought entrance to all-white churches in Birmingham, Alabama. The participants were not acting the parts of others. Doubtlessly, the event was perceived by observers to involve real, not theatrical, behavior. To the extent to which this event was created to arouse a particular meaning and affect behavior, it was a message. If it was used to arouse the meaning that white people violate the Christian principles they profess even in their churches, then it was an event-message.[44]

The requirements he sets for event-messages or what might be called non-verbal rhetorical strategies should be reiterated. The event must be used *intentionally* to arouse meaning in others who will both perceive the event as *real* and perceive themselves as exercising *choice* over their reactions, and the meaning must be aimed at generating instrumentally some *behavior.*

Haiman would agree that when individuals seek to influence through messages they may be obliged to engage in non-verbal behavior in the form of demonstrations. His concept, "rhetoric of the streets," suggests his point of view.[45] But a question still remains over determining the point at which messages arousing meaning in those perceiving themselves engaging in free choice begin to give way to the use of force and the threat of force to coerce a desired response.

Once more, the question must be asked if college presidents who decide to establish black studies programs after a series of fires, rock throwings, and an occasionally brandished rifle can be said to have been persuaded. They are as able as congressmen to come up with good reasons in support of their decisions after the fact. But the ability to rationalize a decision does not deny that it was coerced.

A few generalizations seem to be in order. First, it seems clear that efforts to draw a clear line between rhetorical and non-rhetorical strategies are destined to frustration. A distinction made along the lines of verbal and non-verbal behavior simply would not be responsive to the data and theory most respected in the field of communications. A distinction based on the perception of choice is much more appealing but almost impossible to put into operation. Therefore, for critics who want to limit their study to those efforts which are mostly or essentially or predominantly rhetorical, an arbitrary distinction must be made. Second, although the efforts of black Americans have certainly included the full spectrum of behaviors, verbal and non-verbal, coercive and supplicatory, they are unusually inclined toward the use of verbal persuasive appeals when compared to other mass movements. Third, and in conclusion, this book will focus on spoken and written discourse because that reflects the particular interest of the authors and still allows for a meaningful study of black rhetorical efforts.

UNIVERSALITY OF BLACK RHETORIC

The study of black rhetoric offers a promise of insights with universal applicability. The discourse that has emerged from black Americans over the past 300 years has meaning today, because the conflict among races is as intense now as it has ever been, because the black-white relationship offers an analogue to other instances of inter-cultural communication, and because it provides an excellent case study in persuasion theory.

CONTEMPORARY CONFLICT

Rhetorical analysis of the black movement as it has progressed over the years is particularly relevant to the contemporary scene. The situation which has faced the black man in America for so long is still present, and it will be for some time to come. Whether "progress" has been made; whether rhetoric has been a primary agent of "improvement" will be discussed later in this book and by many other authors. But, as the situation is faced in the future, and as strategies are evaluated, a thorough understanding of what has led to this juncture is critical to the selection of the best response. Bitzer puts it this way:

> Some situations . . . persist; this is why it is possible to have a body of truly *rhetorical* literature. The Gettysburg Address, Burke's Speech to the Electors of Bristol, Socrates' Apology — these are more than historical documents, more than specimens for stylistic or logical analysis. They exist as rhetorical responses *for us* precisely because they speak to situations which persist — which are in some measure universal.[46]

The conflict, as viewed by some, transcends the United States. Quite probably, the problems facing America are only part of a broader problem involving the old, white, European-oriented people on the one hand and the so-called emerging, non-white people of Africa and Asia. "Black Power," as defined by some of its leading exponents, is taken to mean ". . . that black people see themselves as part of a new force, sometimes called the 'Third World'; that we see our struggle as closely related to liberation struggles around the world."[47]

> We must for example, ask ourselves: when black people in Africa begin to storm Johannesburg, what will be the role of this nation — and of black people here? It seems inevitable that this nation would move to protect its financial interests in South Africa, which means protecting white rule in South Africa. Black people in this country then have the responsibility to oppose . . . the effort by white America.
> This is but one example of many such situations which have already arisen around the world — with more to come.[48]

The universe of discourse which is called black rhetoric has universal application to similar situations which must be dealt with in the time to come.

INTER-CULTURAL COMMUNICATION

Beyond the contemporary and future conflict between the black and white people of the world is a still broader situation in which people of different cultures perceive themselves in conflict with each other and are turning to communication theory to search for responses. Almost certainly the most critical of these situations is that existing between the industrialized, non-communist nations of the West and the Soviet Union, China, and the various so-called communist bloc nations of the East. Perhaps equally important to the future of civilization is the conflict between what is called the "establishment" or the "power structure" in the United States and the rising generation of Americans who associate themselves with movements such as those represented by the Students for a Democratic Society. In these and other cases in which cultural groups seem to be in conflict and a process of evaluating strategies for approaching the situation is underway, the analogy of black rhetoric as a study of ways to evaluate and select strategies may be useful.

A good deal of the literature that has come out of the cold war is concerned with problems and solutions that have a remarkable similarity to those of the black-white confrontation. Possibly the closest analogy is in the process of selecting approaches: dialogue or diatribe; interaction or interposition. Rapoport is concerned with two kinds of thinkers: those concerned with conscience and those concerned with strategy, which is defined in terms of game theory.[49] They are distinguished in three ways.

> First, whereas the strategic thinker conceives of each choice of action primarily ... in terms of its effects on the environment, the conscience-driven thinker conceives actions primarily with regard to their effects on the actor.
> Second, whereas the strategist can begin his work only when values (utilities) are given or assumed, the conscience-driven thinker considers the determination of these values to be the principal problem . . .
> Third, while the strategist frequently recognizes the importance of self-fulfilling assumptions, their role is hardly ever actually taken into account in strategic analysis.[50]

An observer of the black-white struggle illustrated one side of this distinction in this way. He said that he opposed the trend toward hating all white people and doing them violence *not* because of what it might do to the white man if successful, but because of what it might do to his black brothers whether successful or not. He said, "I have seen hate in the white man and what kind of man it makes him. I don't want to see the same thing happen to my brothers and sisters." This man was engaging in what Rapoport would call conscience-driven thinking.

For an example of what might be called the thinking of the strategist observe this:

> Black people are no longer interested in adjudicating the situation, in negotiating the situation, in arbitrating the situation. Their only interest now is in being able to summon up whatever it will take to wreak havoc upon Babylon that will force Babylon to let the black people go. For all other avenues have been closed.[51]

As Rapoport would put it, the strategist's concern is this: "In a conflict, how can I gain an advantage over him?" The conscience-driven thinker, however, asks, "If I gain an advantage over him, what sort of person will I become?[52]

Still writing primarily in terms of the cold war, Rapoport observes that the strategist will argue that he does not approve of violence or the "power game." He will claim that he is simply responding to the world as it is. But Rapoport disagrees.

> But the strategists' conclusions are not mere descriptions. They are frankly recommendations, predominantly recommendations to try to get more power in the power struggle, and so are predicated on the tacit assumption that power is a "pure good." The conscience-driven thinker challenges this assumption.[53]

Examine a further statement of the strategist in the struggle between white and black.

> Let me make myself clear. I don't dig violence. Guns are ugly. People are what's beautiful; and when you use a gun to kill someone, you're doing something ugly. But there are two forms of violence: violence directed at you to keep you in your place and violence to defend yourself against that suppression and to win your freedom. If our demands are not met, we will sooner or later have to make a choice between continuing to be victims or deciding to seize our freedom.[54]

The distinction between the types of thinking is not simply a choice of policies to pursue, or persuasive goals to seek, nor is it simply a question of what kinds of limits should be placed on the range of choices to be considered. Rather, it is a distinction between thinking which focuses upon the achievement of given goals, and thinking which regularly re-examines the goals or values in terms of the means for achieving them, to ascertain whether or not the outcome will be worth what is required to obtain it. In the cold war question, one might ask, "What kind of world will there be if the strategy of deterrence works?" In the other context, it might be asked, "What kind of freedom will exist after it has been violently seized?"

As strategy is defined in this book, that is, in rhetorical terms, the options of both the strategist and the conscience-driven thinker (in Rapoport's definitions) are of concern. The concept of rhetorical strategies includes what is called dialogue, as well as diatribe, even though "rhetoric" is most frequently associated with diatribe by writers with no background in the discipline. Within the concept of rhetorical strategy falls procedures such as public speaking, as well as private discussion; and messages aimed at achieving understanding through interpersonal integration as well as those intended to inflict psychological pain and incite riot. The avenues of adjudication, negotiation, and arbitration, which the strategist claimed had been closed, are rhetorical strategies.

Buber, along with Rapoport, claims that mankind has a tremendous stake in which rhetorical strategy finally emerges in the relationship between East and West. He suggests that hope rests only in the option of dialogue among representatives of the sides in the conflict.

> The representatives of whom I speak will each be acquainted with the true needs of his own people, and on these needs will be willing to state themselves. But they will also turn understandingly to the true need of other peoples, and will know in both cases how to extract the true needs from the exaggerations. Just for that reason they will unrelentingly distinguish between truth and propaganda within what is called the opposition of interests. Only when out of the alleged amount of antagonisms just the real conflicts between genuine needs remain can the consideration of the necessary and possible settlements between them begin. The question one must proceed from will be this . . .: What does man need, every man, in order to live as a man? For if the globe is not to burst asunder, every man must be given what he needs for really human life.[55]

Obviously, the same statement could be made about the possibility of dialogue between white and black. Very much the same stake may reside in the choice of rhetorical approach as resides in the international political scene. This choice seems to be a universal one. Rapoport suggests the universality of the choice between strategy and conscience, or dialogue and diatribe, with this pessimistic conclusion:

> It is imperative to establish avenues of communication between Blacks and Whites and between East and West, because they all must either learn to live with each other or perish. In the case of strategy and conscience, I am not sure. Here, I believe, is essential incompatibility, not merely a result of misunderstanding.[56]

Many specialists in inter-cultural communications have invested considerable effort in the study of international exchanges of one kind or another, and this is undoubtedly worthwhile. But, contained within the limits of the United States, is a microcosm of inter-cultural communication, or the lack of it, which is vitally important. The *Report of the President's Commission on Civil Disorders* is widely quoted as saying that the United States is rapidly moving into two nations, or cultures, or camps, one black and the other white.[57] There can be little question that distinguishable cultures of white and black have existed for some time. The analysis of the rhetoric of black Americans, both as it is addressed to the selection of rhetorical strategies and as it serves to further selected strategies, is relevant not only to this inter-cultural struggle in the United States, but also to problems of inter-cultural communication wherever they occur.

CASE STUDY OF PERSUASION

Communication specialists have also worked at length studying various aspects of persuasion with a view toward assessing the effectiveness of one strategy compared with another. Of course, persuasion cannot be studied apart from an audience or interacting group and a rhetorical situation. The attitudes, values, ego-involvements, social influence, and group polarization of an audience will dramatically influence the impact a given message may have. Many scholars have criticized laboratory experiments in persuasion because they involve students responding to messages on subjects of little importance to them. Yet, the laboratory has the distinct advantage of allowing the study of one variable of persuasion at a time while other variables are eliminated or controlled. The experimentalist can also qualify his observations and employ sophisticated measuring instruments. Thus he often charges the critic with studying messages in isolation — one-shot situations. Since the critic has no way of controlling variables, he must refrain from drawing conclusions which assert a given rhetorical effort has made the effect observed. It may have been the product of any number of other variables not under observation. The critic has also been charged with a failure to use scientific methods when they are available.

Many scholars are beginning to feel that only through the fullest possible use of both the laboratory and the field or case study can productive generalizations about persuasion be made. This idea will be developed in greater detail in the section that follows. At this point, it should only be noted that the study of black American rhetoric provides an unusual opportunity to combine some of the values of both methods of research.

Obviously, this study is derived from a real situation and not a laboratory situation. The rhetoric will be studied as it has occurred and is occurring. The audiences' attitudes and involvements can be observed in relation to an issue of immediate importance to them. There will be no laboratory distortion by putting subjects into a strange environment apart from social influence and applying a variety of measurements to them.

Some of the values of laboratory research pertain to the case of black rhetoric. Since the situation has remained relatively stable for many years, many different rhetorical audiences may exist in different places, but tend to respond to essentially the same stimuli. They could be sometimes described as groups drawn randomly from the same population. Next, a variety of rhetorical strategies has been employed, not in sequence, but at the same time to different audiences. The efforts have been continued concurrently for many years.

While there is, unquestionably, contamination through exposure to many stimuli at once, there is also some opportunity to observe one rhetorical strategy at a time as the primary stimulus, and to compare its effects with those of another strategy which was the primary stimulus for another group. In a very real sense it can be said that black Americans have experimented with a wide range of rhetorical strategies, and a study of their efforts will reveal some useful data on the theory of persuasion.

A CRITICAL APPROACH

From what has been said, it can be inferred that this book falls within the category of scholarship called rhetorical criticism. To accept this label, however, does not necessarily lead to an understanding of what to expect in the pages that follow. On the contrary, a scholarly revolution in rhetorical criticism is now underway, as one writer after another discredits the so-called traditionalist who overlays Aristotelian principles on a piece of discourse to see how they fit.[58] To replace this approach, a number of alternative perspectives have been proposed.[59] At this time, it is not possible to define rhetorical criticism in any specific sense, and that may be a healthy state of affairs. The major problem of past criticism has been its deductive, formulary character. An almost closed system has existed in which men have engaged in an impressive but frustrating process of academic circumlocution. Discourse is compared to a set of theories that have largely been accepted a *priori*, and a report is written stating the extent to which the discourse conformed to the theories. When a researcher goes into the field with an established theoretical bias, it is not surprising to learn that he perceives the world in terms of his theory. The question remains whether he has contributed to man's understanding of himself and his affairs.

The comments that follow are intended to explain the particular approach to rhetorical criticism that will be employed in this book.

RHETORIC-REALITY

Since the word "rhetoric" constitutes a major term in this volume, it is necessary to discuss the meaning suggested by its use. Already in this chapter "rhetoric" and "persuasion" have been used almost interchangeably. "Persuasion" has been characterized as a body of "effects in receivers, relevant and instrumental to source-desired goals, brought about by a process in which messages have been a major determinant of those effects."[60] The following statement carries the concept further:

> Everyone who talks or writes wants something; he would not go to the trouble of communcating if he did not . . . almost all of the talking or gesturing we do in the presence of other people, . . . is directed toward the accomplishment of some goal, in short, is motivated. Therefore, "communication" and "persuasion" are nearly synonymous.[61]

For the purposes of this book, "rhetoric" can be added to that list of nearly synonymous terms.

But rhetoric, by virtue of its age and extensive use, is probably more connotative than either of those other terms. Often, "rhetoric" is used instead of "persuasion" to suggest that the user is of the traditional, non-scientific school of thought. To the extent that this implies that the studies which follow will not be primarily quantitative, or experimental in nature, it is a useful meaning. To the extent that such an association suggests a philosophy in opposition to the scientific method or modern experimental studies in communication and persuasion, it would be a most inappropriate meaning for this book.

Specifically, "rhetoric" in this work will mean the interaction between sources, black Americans, and receivers, white and black, American and otherwise, through the use of messages, written, spoken, and to a lesser extent, non-verbal, that refer to the particular goal of "freedom" or the "good life" for black Americans. The study is presented with the aim of increasing man's understanding of the role of communication, persuasion, or rhetoric in the long term efforts of black Americans; of increasing his ability to predict the future role of rhetoric in relations between men black and white; and of increasing man's understanding of rhetoric generally.

An additional comment must be made before some more specific thoughts on rhetorical criticism can be presented. In typical use, "rhetoric" has a negative connotation, usually suggesting sham, pretense, flattery, empty, flowery language; as opposed to the truth, or the reality of a situation. For many people, a continuum is suggested with rhetoric at one end and reality at the other. If a communicator describes some message as "rhetoric", the receiver can usually interpret it as an epithet and infer that the communicator wishes to dissociate himself from the message. Note the following statement:

> The advocates of Black Power reject the old slogans and meaningless rhetoric of previous years in the civil rights struggle. The language of yesterday is indeed irrelevant: progress, non-violence, integration, fear of "white backlash," coalition. Let us look at the rhetoric and see why these terms must be set aside or redefined.[62]

Although this writer shows a sophistication by using the adjective "meaningless" to show his awareness that some rhetoric may be meaningful, he nevertheless associates the term with ideas he rejects and never describes his own writings and speeches as rhetoric, meaningful or otherwise. This is typical. To each of us, reality is "The world as I perceive it, and those who vigorously disagree with me are probably using mere rhetoric."

When viewing from a distance, however, the scholar must be struck with the thought that one man's reality is another's rhetoric, and *vice versa*. Who is to decide, goes the classic conundrum, what is "real" or "true?" Does internal consistency, majority vote, workability, and so forth determine what is "real?" Or is truth simply that with which one chooses to agree?[63] Is there any reality apart from man's perceptions? Can man have perceptions unaffected by intercommunication with other men? Can there be a clear distinction between rhetoric and reality? It might be more useful to forget the continuum and simply speak of rhetoric-reality.

ORDERLY METHODOLOGY

A more specific discussion of goals and procedures of rhetorical criticism is in order. The first objective of this book will be to demonstrate an orderly methodology. That is, the methods of criticism used should be clear and objective enough to allow the reader to understand the basis of judgments, and the fellow scholar to replicate or build upon the conclusions drawn. Criticism which relies upon the taste-judgments of the writer may make fascinating reading, but it is of little scholarly value. Readers in these situations are asked to accept, *a priori,* the feelings of the critic and not to inquire into the bases for these feelings. Systematic or orderly methodology may not produce more "true" judgments, but it does produce ones which are accountable to a clear set of criteria that others may accept or reject at their pleasure.

Rhetorical criticism, by virtue of the questions it asks and the present state of knowledge, does not achieve the rigor of the laboratory. Thompson expresses the idea this way:

> Scholars should understand that rhetoric inevitably is an art in all of its larger and more fundamental features and that it can be a science only in scattered particulars. Human beings and the situations in which they communicate are so complex that no amount of investigation, no matter how ingenious, is going to reduce the rhetorical act to a wholly predictable state.[64]

Having asserted this, however, the rhetorician does not free himself to go his speculative way without regard to system. Nichols criticizes traditionally oriented rhetoricians for a lack of ". . . an orderly — and . . . demonstrably useful method for the analysis of speeches."[65] Bowers suggests that even in a "pre-scientific" state, rhetorical criticism can serve science by the production of ". . . testable hypotheses which, when verified, will have the status of scientific laws." But to do this, he continues, the critic must ". . . learn the habit of defining his terms operationally." He must inform himself of the results of communication research studies, and he must then specify the variables with which he is concerned, so that other scholars may understand and manipulate the same variables.[66] Bowers may be guilty of the rhetoric-reality syndrome by relegating criticism to a prescientific category because it does not follow precisely his concept of science. In modern society, to be labeled "non-scientific" is almost as bad as to be labeled "rhetoric." Some might feel that if a scholar is defining his terms operationally, objectively identifying his variables, relating his work to scientific literature, and drawing his conclusions from the systematic observation of empirical phenomena, he is behaving scientifically. Others could argue that criticism cooperates with experimentalism in the testing of hypotheses by relating them to specific cases and observing the effects.

Bowers makes the following description of theorizing:

> . . . science proceeds from hunches about functional relationships (first hypotheses), the statements which the rhetorical critic is uniquely qualified to formulate and which I have called pre-scientific, to tests of the predictions made by those hypotheses. Those tests will produce laws, or, at least, systematic observations which lead to new hypotheses (second hypotheses). The synthesis of laws gives birth to theory, statements relating laws, which in turn generate predictions of still higher order (third hypotheses). The entire process is characterized by the precision of its definitions, and the open nature of its methods.[67]

As long as the critic is responsible for the command of precision in definition and the employment of an open and systematic method, he is behaving scientifically, according to this description. The criticism advanced in this book will seek to accomplish that.

INDUCTIVE CRITICISM

No matter how systematic or scientific this work is, it will succeed or fail as criticism and nothing else. That means that the careful observations and descriptions will be accompanied by judgments aimed at providing insight into the rhetorical phenomenon. But unlike some criticism, it will reject two roles: first, it will not serve as an apology for any established rhetorical theory; and second, it will not be pedagogically oriented.

The so-called traditional approach to criticism has already been discussed. It could be called deductive in that a particular theory such as Aristotle's is used as the major premise for all conclusions drawn. The criticism tends to become a test of the scholar's ability to adjust his material to fit his theory. A more useful approach would seem to be one in which the scholar seeks to adjust his theory to fit the material as he finds it. This could be called inductive criticism. With this method, the critic begins with his observations and then searches among available theories or other data to find those which help him understand, describe, or otherwise deal with the product of his observations. When his theory seems inadequate to explain the findings, he may suggest a tentative hypothesis for further scientific testing, as Bowers suggested. In this procedure, the critic performs several roles: he, of course, advances understanding of the particular rhetorical phenomenon under investigation; he also reveals weaknesses in the present theory as well as gives support for some theoretical findings, and he suggests avenues for future research.

In the past, the critic has too readily accepted the role of discoverer of strategies for successful persuasion. Criticism has been oriented around the pedagogical motivation of learning how to train future orators. Klyn suggests that the critic must be freed from this obligation.

> Clearly, in the traditional *modus operandi* of rhetorical criticism, the critic has been imagined primarily as a teacher, concerned less with the illumination of particular works of rhetoric, of speaker, or of movements than with putting his insights to use practically, as generalizations, so that he might teach others to speak well. . . .
>
> This pedagogic compulsion which has dominated rhetorical criticism — making it, in this sense, "sophistic" rather than disinterested — is, again, rooted in a misconception — not of the function of rhetoric but of the nature of criticism. For the *practice* of rhetoric, the emphasis seems quite sound, and it has proved eminently workable. But for the *criticism* of rhetoric, it has generated a severely limiting set of priorities, the limits growing out of the assumption that the job of the critic is essentially to be useful to the practitioner. And this . . . he could only be by producing "technical" criticism concerned basically with the intricacies of rhetorical strategies and the "effects" they are thought to have produced.[68]

Of course, any insight into a rhetorical situation holds some promise of value to future practitioners. The important idea to be noted in Klyn's statement is the set of priorities which become operative when criticism is perceived as primarily pedagogical in purpose. These priorities will be rejected in the criticism that follows, and in their place will be the motivation of discovery or illumination. If observations tend to suggest that persuasion has failed in some case, it will be reported without suggestions of how it might have been made more effective.

What is the value of this inductive process for seeking illumination? Perhaps not all criticism should be so oriented, but the study of the black American rhetoric suggests some particularly important values to be gained from an inductive criticism. Nilsen urges the critics to assume an interpretive role in seeking the meaning of speeches ". . . in the sense of what the speech indirectly implies, for man and the society in which he lives." He suggests that a society can, perhaps, learn more about itself by studying the process by which it makes its decisions than by studying the decisions themselves, and the critic, then necessarily becomes involved in the decision process as rhetoric is inherent to decision-making.[69] Addressing himself more specifically to the critical process, Nilsen says that

> . . . seeking to understand the implications for society embodied in the speech, . . . we should ask what the speech implies about rationality, tolerance and the moral autonomy of the individual; what is implied about the expression of opinions, deliberation and persuasion, free inquiry, free criticism, and free choice; what it implies about discussion and debate, the use of information, the interchange of ideas, the function of opposition, and attitudes toward what is orthodox and unorthodox in thought and action. Only if what the speech implies about these attitudes and procedures is made clear, can we make significant judgments about the ends to which the speech is moving men.[70]

With regard to black rhetoric, one might add that only if these attitudes and procedures are understood can the decision to use or not use speech as opposed to other forms of change be understood. The sweep of black rhetoric from colonial times to the present centers on exactly these questions which Nilsen considers the essence of the rhetorical consideration. A key question for black speakers and writers has always been a judgment of man, ideas, and society with regard to the relationship of black man to white. Black rhetors demonstrate, by their selection of rhetorical strategy, a judgment on this question which can be discovered by the critic. Many black persuaders have proceeded on the assumption of the basic rationality and goodness of man without any test of that hypothesis except their faith and almost 100 percent of their experience rejecting it. What could be a more appropriate case study in rhetorical criticism than this issue which embodies the stuff of which rhetoric is made — the business of men interacting, deciding, judging one another and seeking the best possible way of life?

VALUES AND GOALS

A final comment regarding rhetorical criticism is necessary before moving to an outline of the goals and strategies of black rhetoric. When discussing a conflict situation, the critic faces the difficult task of describing and evaluating values and goals of the opposing parties. He runs a serious risk of being charged with bias or shortsightedness by both sides, unless the criticism is written from the perspective of one side only. Consider the difficulty of criticising the rhetoric of the Cold War in a way to be clear and at least intellectually acceptable to citizens of the United States, the Soviet Union and the Peoples' Republic of China. The citizen of the United States asks, "How can they believe we mean them any harm? We Americans are peace-loving people." To understand the rhetoric of the "other side" the critic must see the Americans from the perspective of the Soviet Union or China; not with the purpose of deciding if their perceptions are "right or wrong," but to answer the question, "How can the Americans be perceived as a threatening, warlike nation which calls forth such rhetoric?"

The task is no less difficult in analyzing black rhetoric. The white American asks, "How can they be so demanding and threatening? Don't they know we are doing all we can?" There is a tendency to criticize black rhetoric, its underlying assumptions, values, and goals, totally from the point of view of a white man's logic. Blau suggests, "In fairness to the speaker these ulterior implications should be analyzed in terms of a logic that he [the speaker] would accept; in practice this requirement is seldom observed."[71] Just as the historian must guard against judging the past in terms of the knowledge, values, and logic of contemporary times, the critic of black rhetoric must establish a basis of judgment which is relevant and acceptable to the speakers and writers being judged. The charge that no white man can ever fully understand the black experience, and, therefore, can never fully appreciate the black man's view of the white world may be correct to some extent. But this must not prevent the white critic from seeking some basis of judgment that is both meaningful to the black persuader and the white listener. It may also be true that no one who has not lived his life as a citizen of China can understand their attitude toward the United States, but again the critic must not be deterred from seeking some *mutually* acceptable basis for judgment. This does not mean that the speakers must be in agreement with every judgment the critic makes about them. Blau argues this way:

> This is a concern for the speaker's assumptions, for what the speaker takes for granted. In most cases, the point is not merely that the speaker fails to defend these positions by argument or evidence; he often does not even realize that there is anything that needs defense. He may never put into words his unargued, undefended substructure of ideas; it may seem to him too obviously "self-evident" to mention. Yet it may well condition every later thing that he says.[72]

Speakers may object to being labeled with one or another underlying assumption, but they must be able to understand how a critic could *legitimately* reach the conclusion. For example, today it is unpopular for black speakers to argue for assimilation of the races, and many who have done so in the past are rapidly trying to change their position in order to retain a position of influence. They may not appreciate a critic saying that they are, or have been, "assimilationist" because it will weaken their present efforts. However, if they can understand intellectually that the critic has made an honest judgment, the critical tools will have been well chosen.

A SCHEME OF BLACK RHETORIC

Analysis of a phenomenon as complex as black rhetoric calls for the construction of a scheme in which the various goals, instrumental effects, and strategies for their accomplishment are set forth. No pretense is made that the plan we advanced is any more "true" than what others might suggest. It merely represents one way to conceptualize the broad development of rhetorical efforts by black Americans, and seems to be a useful plan from which to engage in rhetorical criticism. The labels used in this analysis have been chosen because they seem best able to suggest the meaning of the concept under consideration, and not for their

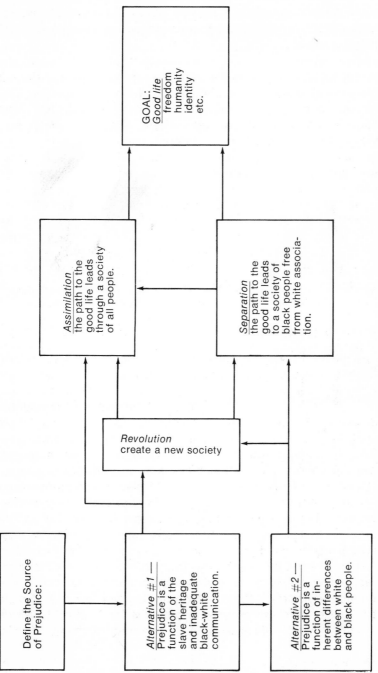

GOAL:
Good life
freedom
humanity
identity
etc.

Assimilation
the path to the good life leads through a society of all people.

Separation
the path to the good life leads to a society of black people free from white association.

Revolution
create a new society

Define the Source of Prejudice:

Alternative #1 —
Prejudice is a function of the slave heritage and inadequate black-white communication.

Alternative #2 —
Prejudice is a function of inherent differences between white and black people.

RHETORICAL STRATEGIES OF BLACK AMERICANS

probable political popularity. Some readers will no doubt quarrel with the choice of words, but that would occur regardless of the language used.

When viewed as a whole, the rhetoric of black Americans seems to have been universally aimed toward the accomplishment of a single ultimate goal, variously described as *freedom; full humanity;* or in a more pragmatic sense, *the good life.* Three relatively distinguishable persuasive campaigns have been pursued toward different goals considered likely to be instrumental to the accomplishment of that ultimate goal: *assimilation, separation, and revolution.* These campaigns have been conducted concurrently, although with varying degrees of emphasis from time-to-time. Each of them has exhibited various rhetorical substrategies which will be described below. Further, alongside the rhetoric of the strategies themselves has been debate concerning which strategy is more likely to yield the desired result. Figure 1 shows schematically the relationship of these elements, and the brief descriptions which follow will serve to explain the diagram as well as introduce the structure of the book.

SELECTING STRATEGIES

Regardless of the point from which measurement begins, the subordinate position of the black man in American society must be taken as fact. The fundamental question from which the black rhetorician then must begin is, "What is the cause of the subordinate position?" The determination of rhetorical strategy to follow rests on the answer to this question. For example, if one assumes that the black man's status in society is the product of an honest, however erroneous, belief that black men are inferior to whites, one might reasonably choose to follow a plan of rhetoric seeking to provide evidence of equality. In the face of contrary evidence, honest men should abandon mistaken beliefs. If one assumes that the previous condition of servitude is the cause of prejudice, then perhaps a two-pronged rhetoric might be used, appealing to fellow black men to educate themselves to overcome their deficiencies, and appealing to whites to keep an open mind, and allow for a fair chance to improve. If, however, one decided that prejudice is the product of color differences, arguments for a return to Africa and a land in which black men are in the majority might be most appropriate.

Whether or not a speaker or writer has consciously considered these and similar alternatives, his use of one rhetorical strategy or another rests upon an assumption about the instrumental effects necessary to overcome the inferior status of black men. In fact, a considerable body of discourse has emerged in which black men have argued the merits of various interpretations of the cause of prejudice.

ASSIMILATION. The primary strategy which has emerged from an assumption that the differences between white and black men are not inherent and thus inevitable, is the seeking of freedom, humanity, and the good life through assimilation into the United States society. This campaign would be predicated upon the notion that black men can find their greatest reward just as other ethnic groups have, in some form of the "melting pot" ideal. The sub-strategies utililized include arguments of ethnological equality with the white man; the brotherhood of man within the Christian church; equality of citizens of the United States as proclaimed in the Declaration of Independence, the Constitution, and the various federal, state, and local laws; equality through intellectual accomplishment and formal education; and equality through responsible and productive citizenship. The character of the assimilation sought has varied from equal opportunity within an essentially segregated society through complete inter-mingling in the cultural, social, and economic life of the United States. This strategy encompasses the concepts of "desegregation" and "integration," and does not necessarily rely upon a literal interpretation of America's "melting pot." The fact that other ethnic groups have not "melted" to form a single "American" population, but have nevertheless achieved full freedom and the good life, could simply be used as a datum in determining the expectations of black men in the same society.

SEPARATION. It also could be decided that the prejudice directed at the black man is derived from the color difference and, therefore, it is futile to engage in rhetoric aimed at convincing the white man of inherent equality of the races. So long as men are black and white, states this reasoning, they will hate each other. Since the black man cannot become white (in spite of the efforts of the assimilationists) both because it is genetically impossible and culturally undesirable, the groups should separate. If this alternative is selected, the rhetoric is aimed primarily at other black men. The only message that needs to be directed to whites is, "Get off our backs."

The message to black men would be first aimed at convincing them of the strategic decision itself: white and black cannot live together as equals. Further, it must be argued that the life of the black man when he lives only with other non-whites would be more desirable than it could ever be in an "integrated society." Beyond this point, a variety of sub-strategies seem to have been developed to create the effects necessary to create some kind of separate society. First, the kind or extent of separation sought varies from actual return or movement to black Africa to semi-autonomous black enclaves within the United States.

The sub-strategies include relatively distinct movements such as colonization and the development of the so-called Black Muslims who preach black superiority over the white "devils." Less distinct rhetorical efforts can be characterized by such concepts as "black is beautiful" and "black power" which signify efforts toward cultural separatism. Appeals against white colonialism, organized on the assumption that the black man in the United States is indentifiable with the nationalistic movements in Asia, Africa, Latin and South America, can be included under the general strategy of separatism. Also, legislative efforts such as those aimed at the passage of bills calling for urban self-determination, or the creation of all-black political-economic units from former ghettos such as Harlem, Watts, or South Chicago, are forms of the separatist strategy.

In the diagram in Figure 1, an arrow can also be seen going from separation to assimilation, and from there to the ultimate goals. This serves to indicate that some of the separatist rhetoric includes the possibility that once black men have gotten together and established some political, economic and cultural identity and power, they might be able to join other ethnic groups forming a kind of assimilated United States society.

REVOLUTION. Some decision making might lead to a conclusion that black men cannot be assimilated into a basically racist society, nor can they obtain their fully deserved freedom, humanity, and a good life by withdrawing into all black communities. This line of reasoning might indicate that black men have built up tremendous credit in America — they have seen a wealthy nation grow out of their labor, and that labor and its accompanying humiliation and injustice have never been compensated. Thus, if the black man cannot reach his goal by leaving this society; and if he cannot reach it by joining this society; he must create a new society. This rhetoric argues that only by removing power from those who have created the racist society, and giving it to those who can use it properly can the black man ever reach his ultimate goals. This means revolution in one form or another.

Once again, the messages fall into two large categories: those directed to whites and those to blacks. The messages to blacks are aimed first at the convincing of blacks that revolution is the only viable strategy for them. Once this idea has been communicated, the persuader can turn to a discussion of the kind of revolution necessary. Primarily, the messages are intended to convince blacks that violence of one form or another, either civil disobedience, or other coercive methods, is legitimate and necessary. The messages are used to organize the black community, to get blacks together, so that they constitute a genuine revolutionary threat to the American society in their eyes and in the thinking of whites. Then, the rhetoric is used to move them into revolutionary acts.

At the same time, a specifically persuasive campaign is directed toward the white population to the effect that it is their choice whether the revolution will be violent or not. It is said that whether or not there must be a revolution is no longer under discussion. It will come. Through what has been called earlier the "rhetoric of preparation," the white man is subjected to persuasion by observing the black man prepare for violent revolution. Messages are used to keep his attention to the preparations, and suggest that he can avoid revolution only by making changes peacefully. Thus, the rhetoric serves a role in an essentially bargaining situation. Again, it will be noticed that in the diagram an arrow also goes from revolution to assimilation, and from there to the ultimate goals. Again, some revolutionary rhetoric allows that if the necessary changes occur, it will be possible for black and white to establish a common society.

SUMMARY

In the first section we attempted to discuss the unique characteristics of black rhetoric in terms of a persuasion theory. To have sought to overlay some theory or combination of theories of persuasion over the efforts of black Americans would not be desirable because the effort is unusual in many respects. It has been a campaign, but not in the typical sense of the term. It is a movement, but it has deviated from the typical pattern of movements by continuing to stress persuasion over coercion. When viewed in terms of the situation confronting black Americans, the uniqueness is most apparent. It is unique both in the relationship of black man to white, and in the fact that the situation has persisted so long. The concept of rhetorical strategies has been discussed in terms of the black movement, and a working, although arbitrary, definition has been set up.

Our discussion has been aimed at the introduction of a rationale and method for the rhetorical criticism of the speaking and writing of black Americans in search of their freedom, humanity, identity, and good life. A number of reasons have been given for making such a study. There are many unique characteristics about black rhetoric that make the work promising. There are universal aspects to this persuasive effort that suggest the conclusions from this analysis will yield general information. The reasons and some of the methods for rhetorical analysis have been given to suggest the potential values to be gained from viewing the black effort in America from a communications perspective. Finally, an analytic scheme has been presented which will constitute the general organization of the remainder of the book.

REFERENCES

[1]Eric Hoffer, *The True Believer* (New York: Harper & Row Publishers, 1951).

[2]For a thoughtful analysis of rhetorical situations and their role in communication, see Lloyd Bitzer, "The Rhetorical Situation," *Philosophy and Rhetoric*, Vol. 1 (January 1968), pp. 1-15.

[3]Milton Rokeach, *Beliefs, Attitudes, and Values* (San Francisco: Jossey-Bass, Inc., Publishers, 1968). The ideas which are summarized briefly here will be developed more fully in the following chapter.

[4]This perception of rhetoric and the humanities is well developed in Marie H. Nichols, *Rhetoric and Criticism* (Baton Rouge: Louisiana State University Press, 1963), pp. 3-18.

[5]See Stokely Carmichael and Charles V. Hamilton, *Black Power* (N.Y.: Random House, Inc., 1967), pp. 2-33 for a full argument of the colonial analysis.

[6]*Ibid.*, p. 22.

[7]*Ibid.*, p. 28.

[8]See Wallace Fotheringham, *Perspectives On Persuasion* (Boston: Allyn & Bacon, Inc., 1966), Chapter 3, for a full discussion of the instrumentality of effects.

[9]*Ibid.*, p. 22.

[10]See Alan H. Monroe, *Principles of Speech* (Chicago: Scott, Foresman and Company, 1958).

[11]Malcolm X and Alex Haley, *The Autobiography of Malcolm X* (N.Y.: Grove Press, Inc., 1964), p. 213. Reprinted with permission of Grove

Press, Inc. Copyrighted © 1964 by Alex Haley and Malcolm X. Copyrighted © 1965 by Alex Haley and Betty Shabazz.

[12]Fotheringham, *op. cit.*, p. 34.

[13]Rokeach, *op. cit.*, Chapters 1 and 2.

[14]*Ibid.*, Appendix A.

[15]Carolyn Sherif, Muzafer Sherif, and Roger Nebergall, *Attitude and Attitude Change* (Philadelphia: W. B. Saunders Company, 1965), p. 243.

[16]Leland M. Griffin, "The Rhetoric of Historical Movements," *Quarterly Journal of Speech*, XXXVIII, No. 2 (April, 1952), 184.

[17]Reprinted from *Look Out Whitey! Black Power's Gon' Get Your Mama!* by Julius Lester. Copyrighted © 1968 by Julius Lester. Used by permission of The Dial Press, pp. 46-47.

[18]*Ibid.*, pp. 24-25.

[19]*Op. cit.*

[20]*Ibid.*, p. 20.

[21]*Ibid.*, p. 120.

[22]*Ibid.*, p. 101.

[23]See Fotheringham, *Perspectives On Persuasion,* Chapter 5.

[24]*Ibid.*, p. 80.

[25]*Ibid.*, p. 36.

[26]*Ibid.*, pp. 36-37.

[27]Hoffer, *The True Believer,* pp. 130-131.

[28]T. Thomas Fortune, *Black and White: Land, Labor, and Politics in the South* (N.Y.: Arno Press and The New York Times, 1968 reprint of 1884 edition).

[29]William H. Grier, and Price M. Cobbs, *Black Rage* (N.Y.: Bantam Books, Inc., 1968), pp. 178-179.

[30]This concept was advanced by Dr. Harland Randolph, President of Federal City College, during a private conversation.

[31]Lloyd F. Bitzer, "The Rhetorical Situation," *Philosophy and Rhetoric,* I, No. 1 (January, 1968), 1.

[32]*Ibid.*, p. 6

[33]*Ibid.*, pp. 6-8.

[34]Carl M. Stevens, *Strategy and Collective Bargaining Negotiation* (N.Y.: McGraw-Hill Book Company, 1963).

[35]Bitzer, *op. cit.*, p. 7.

[36]Stevens, *op. cit.*

[37]Bitzer, *op. cit.*, p. 7.

[38]Malcolm X, "Message to the Grass Roots," in George Breitman, ed., *Malcolm X Speaks* (N.Y.: Grove Press, Inc., 1965), pp. 10-11.

[39]Howard H. Martin and Kenneth E. Andersen, *Speech Communication, Analysis and Readings* (Boston: Allyn & Bacon, Inc., 1968), p. 126.

[40]Edwin B. Black, *Rhetorical Criticism: A Study in Method* (N.Y.: The Macmillan Company, 1965).

[41]Anatol Rapoport, *Fights, Games, and Debates* (Ann Arbor: University of Michigan Press, 1960).

[42]See Fotheringham, *Perspectives On Persuasion,* pp. 144-154 for a comparison of persuasion with non-persuasive methods.

[43]*Ibid.,* p. 54.

[44]*Ibid.,* p. 70.

[45]Franklyn Haiman, "The Rhetoric of the Streets: Some Legal and Ethical Considerations," *Quarterly Journal of Speech,* LII, No. 2 (April, 1967), 99-114.

[46]Bitzer, "The Rhetorical Situation," p. 13.

[47]Carmichael and Hamilton, *Black Power,* p. xi.

[48]*Ibid.*

[49]Anatol Rapoport, "Strategy and Conscience," in Floyd Matson and Ashley Montagu, eds., *The Human Dialogue* (N.Y.: The Free Press, 1967), pp. 79-96.

[50]*Ibid.,* p. 90.

[51]Eldridge Cleaver, "The Land Question and Black Liberation," in Robert Scheer, ed., *Eldridge Cleaver* (N.Y.: Random House, Inc., 1967), p. 75.

[52]Rapoport, "Strategy and Conscience," *op. cit.,* p. 91.

[53]*Ibid.,* pp. 91-92.

[54]Cleaver, *op. cit.,* p. 166.

[55]Martin Buber, "Hope for This Hour," in Matson and Montagu, *op. cit.,* p. 312.

[56]Rapoport, "Strategy and Conscience," *op. cit.,* p. 96.

[57]*Report of the President's Commission on Civil Disorders* (N.Y.: Bantam Books, Inc., 1968).

[58]There is no need to review these attacks here. For discussion of these ideas see Black's *Rhetorical Criticism,* already cited.

[59]The best single collection of these alternatives is Thomas R. Nilsen, ed., *Essays on Rhetorical Criticism* (N.Y.: Random House, Inc., 1968). This collection has been used extensively in preparing this discussion of method.

[60]This definition is the one used by Wallace Fotheringham in his work previously cited, *Perspectives on Persuasion.*

[61]Howard Martin and Kenneth E. Andersen, "Communication Strategies," in Martin and Andersen, *Speech Communication, op. cit.,* p. 126.

[62]Carmichael and Hamilton, *Black Power,* p. 50.

[63]A very thoughtful discussion of this question is given by Douglas Ehninger in "Validity as Moral Obligation," *Southern Speech Journal,* XXXIII, No. 3, (Spring, 1968), 215-222.

[64]Wayne Thompson, *Quantitative Research in Public Address and Communication* (N.Y.: Random House, Inc., 1967), p. 215.

[65]Marie Hochmuth Nichols, *Rhetoric and Criticism, op. cit.,* p. 106.

[66]John Waite Bowers, "The Pre-Scientific Function of Rhetorical Criticism," in Nilsen, *Essays on Rhetorical Criticism, op. cit.,* pp. 127-132.

[67]*Ibid.,* p. 131.

[68]Mark S. Klyn, "Toward a Pluralistic Rhetorical Criticism," in Nilsen, *op. cit.,* p. 150.

[69]Thomas R. Nilsen, "Interpretive Function of the Critic," in Nilsen, *op. cit.*, pp. 87-89.

[70]*Ibid.*, p. 95.

[71]Joseph L. Blau, "Public Address as Intellectual Revelation," in Nilsen, *op. cit.*, p. 20.

[72]*Ibid.*, p. 25.

Chapter 2 THE RHETORIC OF ASSIMILATION

A study of the quest of black Americans for freedom, equality, and the good life rooted in the dignity of man, embraces the full sweep of American history. From the colonial period to the latter part of the twentieth century significant black spokesmen, seeking to blunt the debilitating effects of racism, have used various rhetorical strategies in order to achieve their goal. Of these strategies, none has proved more durable or universal than assimilation. Among those communicators who persistently expressed faith in the "melting pot" concept have been poets, essayists, journalists, lecturers, ministers, lawyers, physicians, teachers, and historians. Some were ex-slaves who had little formal education or money; others were college educated and, occasionally, independently wealthy men. With different backgrounds and a singleness of purpose, they cut across all eras, preaching a varied message of assimilation to both white and black audiences. Richard Allen, Prince Hall, and Phillis Wheatley in the closing years of the eighteenth century; Frederick Douglass, Henry Highland Garnet, and Charles Lenox Remond throughout the antebellum period; Alexander Crummell, William E. B. DuBois, and Booker T. Washington in the reconstruction period and the early 1900's: and Martin Luther King, Jr., Thurgood Marshall, and Roy

51

Wilkins in the mid-twentieth century are only a representative few of those leaders who strove mightily to integrate their fellow man into the mainstream of American life. Often rebuffed and frequently discouraged, they nevertheless remained devoted to the belief that persuasion could effect change.

In developing their persuasive campaign, these speakers and writers used three sub-strategies based upon the following compelling needs confronting black Americans: (1) the need to rely upon the Christian message; (2) the need for personal worth and achievement through education, industry, and temperance; and (3) the need to press for legislative and judicial action which could guarantee equality and freedom under the law. These strategies, designed to produce peer acceptance within a democratic society, derived their principal thrust from the premise that Negroes are ethnologically equal to whites. It is essential, first of all, to turn to a consideration of this argument in order to establish a rationale for the analysis of the three sub-strategies which flowed from it.

THE ETHNOLOGICAL ARGUMENT

One of the most disturbing challenges facing black Americans — especially in the antebellum period — was a convincing refutation to the persistent and troubling claim that Negroes were basically inferior to whites. Failure to meet this issue satisfactorily would, in turn, frustrate any attempt to create a meaningful assimilation of the races. As a result, black spokesmen developed a universe of discourse which recognized the primacy of environment, rather than heredity, in moulding a man. From this position, they could argue with conviction that the subordinate status of the Negro was due not to natural endowments or cultural heritage, but to enforced slavery brought about by unprincipled men. This reasoning led them to the conclusion that one who is free to worship God as he pleases, to live in a locale he cherishes, to work in an occupation he chooses, to have access to knowledge in all areas, and to serve his country in a rewarding capacity can realize his potentials. In short, he has the opportunity to assume a place of full equality in any society. This philosophy found eloquent expression in the poetry of Phillis Wheatley who, at the age of eight in 1761, was forced to leave Africa to become a slave in the household of John Wheatley of Boston.[1] In a poem dedicated *To the Right Honorable William, Earl of Dartmouth* in 1773, she spoke sorrowfully of her past and expressed the hope that other members of her race would not experience the pain of separation and tyranny.

Should you, my Lord, while you peruse my song,
Wonder from whence my love of Freedom sprung,
Whence flow these wishes for the common good,
By feeling hearts alone but understood,
I, young in life, by seeming cruel fate
Was snatched from Afric's fancied happy seat:
What pangs excruciating must molest,
What sorrows labor in my parent's breast!
Steeled was that soul, and by no misery moved,
That from a father seized his babe beloved:
Such, such my case. And can I then but pray
Others may never feel tyrannic sway?[2]

A similar compassionate plea in another poem, entitled *On Being Brought from Africa to America,* challenged her readers to perceive the intrinsic worth of black Americans.

Some view our sable race with scornful eye —
'Their color is a diabolic dye.'
Remember, Christians, Negroes black as Cain
May be refined, and join the angelic train.[3]

Two decades later these views were reinforced by another ex-slave, Richard Allen, a minister who was to become the founder and first Bishop of the African Methodist Episcopal Church.[4] In a brief address "To those Who Keep Slaves and Approve the Practice," he spoke feelingly of the potential power of education to elevate his people:

We believe if you would try the experiment of taking a few black children, and cultivate their minds with the same care and let them have the same prospect in view as to living in the world, as you would wish for your own children, you would find upon the trial, they were not inferior in mental endowments.[5]

Convinced that slavery rather than nature was the cause of existing inequities between blacks and whites, Allen next turned to the Bible to demonstrate God's attitude toward those who willfully oppressed others.

I do not wish to make you angry, but excite your attention to consider how hateful slavery is in the sight of that God who hath destroyed kings and princes for their oppression of the poor slaves. Pharoah and his princes, with the posterity of King Saul, were destroyed by the protector and avenger of slaves. Would you not suppose the Israelites to be utterly unfit for freedom and that it was impossible for them to obtain to any degree of excellence? Their history shows how slavery had debased their spirits. Men must be wilfully blind and extremely partial, that cannot see the contrary effects of liberty and slavery upon the mind of man: I truly confess the vile habits often acquired in a state of servitude, are not easily thrown off; the example of the Israelites shows, who with all that Moses could do to reclaim them from it, still continued in their habits more or less; and why will you look for better from us? why will you look for grapes from thorns, or figs from thistles? It is in our posterity enjoying the same privileges with your own, that you ought to look for better things.[6]

The gentle and indirect persuasion of Phillis Wheatley in 1773 and the pointed refutation of Richard Allen in 1793 gave way to a direct frontal attack in the 1830's against those who failed to appreciate the genuine nature and credentials of black Americans. Buttressed by the rise of the anti-slavery movement in 1831,[7] many spokesman boldly drew comparisons between the physical and intellectual endowments of blacks and whites. Often, these elaborately constructed contrasts sought to prove not only the basic equality of Negroes but also their actual superiority due to an innate ability to transcend unfavorable circumstances. Typical of this approach was *A Treatise on the Intellectual Character, and Political Condition of the Colored People of the United States.* Published in 1837, this document, which was written by a Protestant minister, Hosea Easton,[8] set forth in the introduction the claim that since no "constitutional difference exists in the children of men, which can be said to be established by hereditary laws," one can only conclude that whenever manifestations of physical or intellectual inferiority occur, they are causal or fortuitous.[9] In subsequent arguments Easton traced the history of Europe and Africa and detailed the adverse effects of slavery on one's mind and body. Encouraged by the factual data he had discovered, he confidently predicted that the Africans, particularly the Egyptians, had contributed more to the happiness and welfare of mankind than had all the Europeans "put together."[10]

The ethnological argument which Easton had sketched in 1837, served as a guideline for other speakers and writers. In 1848, Henry Highland Garnet, a former slave who ranked with Frederick Douglass as the most significant black leader and orator in the antebellum era,[11] spoke in glowing terms of the rich cultural heritage of Negro Americans. Addressing the Female Benevolent Society of Troy, New York on its fifteenth anniversary, he graphically described the early splendor of Egypt and Ethiopia. Out of these countries, he boasted, came the wives of Moses, Solomon,

and Mark Antony, and the celebrated general, Hannibal. Taunt-
ingly, he then observed in the blunt and vivid language that was
to become his hallmark:

> At this time when these representatives of our races were filling
> the world with amazement, the ancestors of the now proud and
> boasting Anglo Saxons were among the most degraded of the
> human family. They abode in caves underground, either naked
> or covered with the skins of wild beasts. Night was made hid-
> eous by their wild shouts, and day was darkened by the smoke
> which arose from bloody altars, upon which they offered human
> sacrifice.[12]

Not content to limit his discussion to a past marked by the obser-
able achievements of his race, Garnet turned with bitterness to
the present degraded condition of many black Americans. Like
Easton, he traced the cause of the current inequities to the South's
"peculiar institution." "Our young men," said he, "are brutalized
in intellect, and their manly energies are chilled by the frosts of
slavery."[13]

As northern liberals increased their attacks on the institution
of slavery in the early 1850's, conservative southern leaders, concerned about the threat to their economic and social structure,
felt constrained to reiterate their commitment to the idea that
Negroes were basically inferior to whites. Indeed, as the editor of
the *Richmond Enquirer* observed, unless this fact could be satisfactorily demonstrated, there was no acceptable justification for
the continuation of slavery. He then attempted to show, much to
the delight and relief of his readers, that the Negro was less than
a man.[14] It was against this background that the most celebrated
black leader of the nineteenth century, Frederick Douglass,[15]
received an invitation to deliver the commencement address at
Western Reserve College in Cleveland, Ohio on July 12, 1854.
Although Douglass had spoken freely throughout the North and in
Great Britain, it marked the first time that he was to deliver a
commencement speech before a predominantly white college
audience. He used the occasion to answer the editor of the
Richmond Enquirer and others who turned to the popular pseudo-
science of phrenology to strengthen their claim that Negroes
were physiologically and intellectually lower than whites.

Douglass' partiality for rational discourse was evident
throughout his remarks. He combined narration, causal and ana-
logical reasoning, refutation, and testimony drawn largely from
contemporary works on ethnology to illustrate, first, the manhood

of the Negro, and, second, the need for faith in the concept of the unity of the human race and the brotherhood of man. There arguments and the style used to express them may be seen in the address that follows.

Frederick Douglass
*The Claims of the Negro, Enthnologically Considered**

Gentlemen of the Philozetian Society:

I propose to submit to you a few thoughts on the subject of the Claims of the Negro, suggested by ethnological science, or the natural history of man. But before entering upon that subject, I trust you will allow me to make a remark or two, somewhat personal to myself. The relation between me and this occasion may justify what, in others, might seem an offence against good taste.

This occasion is to me one of no ordinary interest, for many reasons; and the honor you have done me, in selecting me as your speaker, is as grateful to my heart, as it is novel in the history of American Collegiate or Literary Institutions. Surprised as I am, the public are no less surprised, at the spirit of independence, and the moral courage displayed by the gentlemen at whose call I am here. There is felt to be a principle in the matter, placing it far above egotism or personal vanity; a principle which gives to this occasion a general, and I had almost said, an universal interest. I engage to-day, for the first time, in the exercises of any College Commencement. It is a new chapter in my humble experience. The usual course, at such times, I believe, is to call to the platform men of age and distinction, eminent for eloquence, mental ability, and scholarly attainments — men whose high culture, severe training, great experience, large observation, and peculiar aptitude for teaching, qualify them to instruct even the already well instructed, and to impart a glow, a lustre, to the acquirements of those who are passing from the Halls of learning, to the broad theatre of active life. To no such high endeavor as this, is your humble speaker fitted; and it was with much distrust and hesitation that he accepted the invitation, so kindly and perseveringly given, to occupy a portion of your attention here to-day.

I express the hope, then, gentlemen, that this acknowledgment of the novelty of my position, and my unaffected and honest confession of inaptitude,

---

*Frederick Douglass, "The Claims of the Negro, Enthnologically Considered." Speech delivered on July 12, 1854 in Cleveland, Ohio. Published as a pamphlet by Lee, Mann & Company in 1854.

will awaken a sentiment of generous indulgence towards the scattered thoughts I have been able to fling together, with a view to presenting them as my humble contribution to these Commencement Exercises.

Interesting to me, personally, as this occasion is, it is still more interesting to you; especially to such of you as have completed your education, and who (not wholly unlike the gallant ship, newly launched, full rigged, and amply fitted, about to quit the placid waters of the harbor for the boisterous waves of the sea,) are entering upon the active duties and measureless responsibilities incident to the great voyage of life. Before such, the ocean of mind lies outspread more solemn than the sea, studded with difficulties and perils. Thoughts, theories, ideas, and systems, so various, and so opposite, and leading to such diverse results, suggest the wisdom of the utmost precaution, and the most careful survey, at the start. A false light, defective chart, an imperfect compass, may cause one to drift in endless bewilderment, or to be landed at last amid sharp, destructive rocks.

On the other hand, guided by wisdom, manned with truth, fidelity and industry, the haven of peace, devoutly wished for by all, may be reached in safety by all. The compensation of the preacher is full, when assured that his words have saved even one from error and from ruin. My joy shall be full, if, on this occasion, I shall be able to give a right direction to any one mind, touching the question now to be considered.

Gentlemen, in selecting the Claims of the Negro as the subject of my remarks to-day, I am animated by a desire to bring before you a matter of living importance — matter upon which action, as well as thought is required. The relation subsisting between the white and black people of this country is the vital question of the age. In the solution of this question, the scholars of America will have to take an important and controling part. This is the moral battle field to which their country and their God now call them. In the eye of both, the neutral scholar is an ignoble man. Here, a man must be hot, or be accounted cold, or, perchance, something worse than hot or cold. The lukewarm and the cowardly, will be rejected by earnest men on either side of the controversy. The cunning man who avoids it, to gain the favor of both parties, will be rewarded with scorn; and the timid man who shrinks from it, for fear of offending either party, will be despised. To the lawyer, the preacher, the politician, and to the man of letters, there is no neutral ground. He that is not for us, is against us. Gentlemen, I assume at the start, that wherever else I may be required to speak with bated breath, here, at least, I may speak with freedom the thought nearest my heart. This liberty is implied, by the call I have received to be here; and yet I hope to present the subject so that no man can reasonable say, that an outrage has been committed, or that I have abused the privilege with which you have honored me. I shall aim to discuss the claims of the negro, general and special, in a manner, though not scientific, still sufficiently clear and definite to enable my hearers to form an intelligent judgment respecting them.

The first general claim which may here be set up, respects the manhood of the negro. This is an elementary claim, simple enough, but not without question. It is fiercely opposed. A respectable public journal, published in Richmond, Va., bases its whole defence of the slave system upon a denial of the negro's manhood.

The white peasant is free, and if he is a man of will and intellect, can rise in the scale of society; or at least his offspring may. He is not deprived by law of those ' inalienable rights,' 'liberty and the pursuit of happiness,' by the use of it. But here is the essence of slavery — that we do declare the negro destitute of these powers. We bind him by law to the condition of the laboring peasant for ever, without his consent, and we bind his posterity after him. Now, the true question is, have we a right to do this? If we have not, all discussion about his comfortable situation, and the actual condition of free laborers else-where, are quite beside the point. If the negro has the same right to his liberty and the pursuit of his own happiness that the white man has, then we commit the greatest wrong and robbery to hold him a slave — an act at which the sentiment of justice must revolt in every heart — and negro slavery is an institution which that sentiment must sooner or later blot from the face of the earth. — *Richmond Examiner*.

After stating the question thus, the *Examiner* bodly asserts that the negro has no such right — BECAUSE HE IS NOT A MAN!

There are three ways to answer this denial. One is by ridicule; a second is by denunciation; and a third is by argument. I hardly know under which of these modes my answer to-day will fall. I feel myself somewhat on trial; and that this is just the point where there is hestitation, if not serious doubt. I cannot, however, argue; I must assert. To know whether negro is a man, it must first be known what constitutes a man. Here, as well as elsewhere, I take it, that the "coat must be cut according to the cloth." It is not necessary, in order to establish the manhood of any one making the claim, to prove that such an one equals Clay in eloquence, or Webster and Calhoun in logical force and directness; for, tried by such standards of mental power as these, it is apprehended that very few could claim the high designation of *man*. Yet something like this folly is seen in the arguments directed against the human-ity of the negro. His faculties and powers, uneducated and unimproved, have been contrasted with those of the highest cultivation; and the world has then been called upon to behold the immense and amazing difference between the man admitted, and the man disputed. The fact that these intellects, so powerful and so controlling, are almost, if not quite as exceptional to the general rule of humanity, in one direction as the specimen negroes are in the other, is quite overlooked.

Man is distinguished from all other animals, by the possession of certain definite faculties and powers, as well as by physical organization and propor-tions. He is the only two-handed animal on the earth — the only one that laughs, and nearly the only one that weeps. Men instinctively distinguish between men and brutes. Common sense itself is scarcely needed to detect the absence of manhood in a monkey, or to recognize its presence in a negro. His speech, his reason, his power to acquire and to retain knowledge, his heaven-erected face, his habitudes, his hopes, his fears, his aspirations, his prophecies, plant between him and the brute creation, a distinction as eternal as it is palpable. Away, therefore, with all the scientific moonshine that would connect men with monkeys; that would have the world believe that humanity, instead of resting on its own characteristic pedestal — gloriously independent — is a sort of sliding scale, making one extreme brother to the ou-rang-ou-tang, and all the other to angels, and all the rest intermediates! Tried by all the usual, and all the *un*usual tests, whether mental, moral, physical, or psycological, the negro is a MAN — considering him as possessing knowledge, or needing knowledge, his elevation or his degradation, his virtues, or his vices — whichever road you take, you reach the same conclusion, the negro is a MAN. His good and his bad, his innocence and his guilt, his joys and his sorrows, proclaim his manhood in speech that all mankind practically and readily understand.

A very recondite author says, that "man is distinguished from all other animals, in that he resists as well as adapts himself to his circumstances." He does not take things as he finds them, but goes to work to improve them. Tried by this test, too, the negro is a man. You may see him yoke his oxen, harness the horse, and hold the plow. He can swim the river; but he prefers to fling over it a bridge. The horse bears him on his back — admits his mastery and dominion. The barn-yard fowl know his step, and flock around to receive their morning meal from his sable hand. The dog dances when he comes home, and whines piteously when he is absent. All these know that the negro is a MAN. Now, presuming that what is evident to beast and to bird, cannot need elaborate argument to be made plain to men, I assume, with this brief statement, that the negro is a man.

The first claim conceded and settled, let us attend to the second, which is beset with some difficulties, giving rise to many opinions, different from my own, and which opinions I propose to combat.

There was a time when, if you established the point that a particular being is a man, it was considered that such a being, of course, had a common ancestry with the rest of mankind. But it is not so now. This is, you know, an age of science, and science is favorable to division. It must explore and analyze, until all doubt is set at rest. There is, therefore, another proposition to be stated and maintained, separately, which, in other days, (the days before the Notts, the Gliddens, the Agassiz, and Mortons, made their profound discoveries in ethnological science,) might have been included in the first.

It is somewhat remarkable, that, at a time when knowledge is so generally diffused, when the geography of the world is so well understood — when time and space, in the intercourse of nations, are almost annihilated — when oceans have become bridges—the earth a magnificent hall—the hollow sky a dome—under which a common humanity can meet in friendly conclave — when nationalities are being swallowed up — and the ends of the earth brought together—I say it is remarkable—nay, it is strange that there should arise a phalanx of learned men—speaking in the name of *science*—to forbid the magnificent reunion of mankind in one brotherhood. A mortifying proof is here given, that the moral growth of a nation, or an age, does not always keep pace with the increase of knowledge, and suggests the necessity of means to increase human love with human learning.

The proposition to which I allude, and which I mean next to assert, is this, that what are technically called the negro race, are a part of the human family, and are descended from a common ancestry, with the rest of mankind. The discussion of this point opens a comprehensive field of inquiry. It involves the question of the unity of the human race. Much has and can be said on both sides of that question.

Looking out upon the surface of the Globe, with its varieties of climate, soil, and formations, its elevations and depressions, its rivers, lakes, oceans, islands, continents, and the vast and striking differences which mark and diversify its multitudinous inhabitants, the question has been raised, and pressed with increasing ardor and pertinacity, (especially in modern times,) can all these various tribes, nations, tongues, kindred, so widely separated, and so strangely dissimilar, have descended from a common ancestry? That is the question, and it has been answered variously by men of learning. Different modes of reasoning have been adopted, but the conclusions reached may be divided into two — the one YES, and the other NO. *Which* of these answers is most in accordance with facts, with reason, with the welfare of the world, and reflects most glory upon the wisdom, power, and goodness of the Author of all existence, is the question for consideration with us? On which side is the weight of the argument, rather than which side is absolutely proved?

It must be admitted at the beginning, that, viewed apart from the authority of the Bible, neither the unity, nor diversity of origin of the human family, can be demonstrated. To use the terse expression of the Rev. Dr. Anderson, who speaking on this point, says: "It is impossible to get far enough back for that." This much, however, can be done. The evidence on both sides, can be accurately weighed, and the truth arrived at with almost absolute certainty.

It would be interesting, did time permit, to give here, some of the most striking features of the various theories, which have, of late, gained attention and respect in many quarters of our country — touching the origin of mankind — but I must pass this by. The argument to-day, is to the unity, as against that theory, which affirms the diversity of human origin.

THE BEARINGS OF THE QUESTION.

A moment's reflection must impress all, that few questions have more important and solemn bearings, than the one now under consideration. It is connected with eternal as well as with terrestrial interests. It covers the earth and reaches heaven. The unity of the human race — the brotherhood of man — the reciprocal duties of all to each, and of each to all, are too plainly taught in the Bible to admit of cavil. — The credit of the Bible is at stake — and if it be too much to say, that it must stand or fall, by the decision of this question, *it is* proper to say, that the value of that sacred Book — as a record of the early history of mankind — must be materially affected, by the decision of the question.

For myself I can say, my reason (not less than my feeling, and my faith) welcomes with joy, the declaration of the Inspired Apostle, "that God has made of one blood all nations of men for to dwell upon all the face of the earth." But this grand affirmation of the unity of the human race, and many others like unto it, together with the whole account of the creation, given in the early scriptures, must all get a new interpretation or be overthrown altogether, if a diversity of human origin can be maintained. — Most evidently, this aspect of the question makes it important to those, who rely upon the Bible, as the sheet anchor of their hopes — and the frame work of all religious truth. The young minister must look into his subject and settle it for himself, before he ascends the pulpit, to preach redemption to a fallen race.

The bearing of the question upon Revelation, is not more marked and decided than its relation to the situation of things in our country, at this moment. *One seventh* part of the population of this country is of negro descent. The land is peopled by what may be called the most dissimilar races on the globe. The black and the white — the negro and the European — these constitute the American people — and, in all the likelihoods of the case, they will ever remain the principal inhabitants of the United States, in some form or other. The European population are greatly in the ascendant in numbers, wealth and power. They are the rulers of the country — the masters — the Africans, are the slaves — the proscribed portion of the people — and precisely in proportion as the truth of human brotherhood gets recognition, will be the freedom and elevation, in this country, of persons of African descent. In truth, this question is at the bottom of the whole controversy, now going on between the slaveholders on the *one* hand, and the abolitionists on the other. It is the same old question which has divided the selfish, from the philanthropic part of mankind in all ages. It is the question whether the rights, privileges, and immunities enjoyed by some ought not to be shared and enjoyed by all.

It is not quite two hundred years ago, when such was the simplicity (I will not now say the pride and depravity) of the Anglo Saxon inhabitants of the British West Indies, that the learned and pious Godwin, a missionary to the West Indies, deemed it necessary to write a book, to remove what he conceived to be the injurious belief that it was sinful in the sight of God to baptize negroes and Indians. The West Indies have made progress since that time. — God's emancipating angel has broken the fetters of slavery in those islands, and the praises of the Almighty are now sung by the sable lips of eight hundred thousand freemen, before deemed only fit for slaves, and to whom even baptismal and burial rights were denied.

The unassuming work of *Godwin* may have had some agency in producing this glorious result. One other remark before entering upon the argument. It may be said, that views and opinions, favoring the unity of the human family, coming from one of lowly condition, are open to the suspicion, that "*the wish is father to the thought*," and so, indeed, it may be. — But let it be also remembered, that this deduction from the weight of the argument on the one side, is more than counterbalanced by the pride of race and position arrayed on the other. Indeed, ninety-nine out of every hundred of the advocates of a diverse origin of the human family in this country, are among those who hold it to be the privilege of the *Anglo-Saxon* to enslave and oppress the African — and slaveholders, not a few, like the Richmond Examiner to which I have referred, have admitted, that the whole argument in defense of slavery, becomes utterly worthless the moment the African is proved to be equally a man with the Anglo-Saxon. The temptation, therefore, to read the negro out of the human family is exceedingly strong, and may account somewhat for the repeated attempts on the part of Southern pretenders to science, to cast a doubt over the Scriptural account of the origin of mankind. If the origin and motives of most works, opposing the doctrine of the unity of the human race, could be ascertained, it may be doubted whether *one* such work could boast an honest parentage. Pride and selfishness, combined with mental power, never want for a theory to justify them — and when men oppress their fellow-men, the oppressor ever finds, in the character of the oppressed, a full justification for his oppression. Ignorance and depravity, and the inability to rise from degradation to civilization and respectability, are the most usual allegations against the oppressed. The evils most fostered by slavery and oppression, are precisely those which slaveholders and oppressors would transfer from their system to the inherent character of their victims. Thus the very crimes of slavery become slavery's best defence. By making the enslaved a character fit only for slavery, they excuse themselves for refusing to make the slave a freeman. A wholesale method of accomplishing this result, is to overthrow the instinctive consciousness of the common brotherhood of man. For, let it be once granted that the human race are of multitudinous origin, naturally different in their moral, physical, and intellectual capacities, and at once you make plausible a demand for classes, grades and conditions, for different methods of culture, different moral, political, and religious institutions, and a chance is left for slavery, as a necessary institution. The debates in Congress on the Nebraska Bill during the past winter, will show how slaveholders have availed themselves of this doctrine in support of slaveholding. There is no doubt that Messrs. Nott, Glidden, Morton, Smith and Agassiz were duly consulted by our slavery propagating statesmen.

ETHNOLOGICAL UNFAIRNESS TOWARDS THE NEGRO.

The lawyers tell us that the credit of a witness is always in order. Ignorance, malice or prejudice, may disqualify a witness, and why not an author? Now, the disposition everywhere evident, among the class of writers alluded to, to separate the negro race from every intelligent nation and tribe in Africa, may fairly be regarded as one proof, that they have staked out the ground beforehand, and that they have aimed to construct a theory in support of a foregone conclusion. The desirableness of isolating the negro race, and especially of separating them from the various peoples of Northern Africa, is too plain to need a remark. Such isolation would remove stupendous difficulties in the way of getting the negro in a favorable attitude for the blows of scientific christendom.

Dr. Samuel George Morton may be referred to as a fair sample of American Ethnologists. His very able work "*Crania Americana*," published in Philadelphia in 1839, is widely read in this country. — In this great work his contempt for negroes, is ever conspicuous. I take him as an illustration of what had been alleged as true of his class.

The fact that Egypt was one of the earliest abodes of learning and civilization, is as firmly established as are the everlasting hills, defying, with a calm front the boasted mechanical and architectural skill of the nineteenth century — smiling serenely on the assaults and the mutations of time, there she stands in overshadowing grandeur, riveting the eye and the mind of the modern world — upon her, in silent and dreamy wonder — Greece and Rome and through them Europe and America have received their civilization from the ancient Egyptians. This fact is not denied by any body. But Egypt is in Africa. Pity that it had not been in Europe, or in Asia, or better still, in America! Another unhappy circumstance is, that the ancient Egyptians were not white people; but were, undoubtedly, just about as dark in complexion as many in this country who are considered genuine negroes; and that is not all, their hair was far from being of that graceful lankness which adorns the Anglo Saxon head. But the next best thing, after these defects, is a positive unlikeness to the negro. Accordingly, our learned author enters into an elaborate argument to prove that the ancient Egyptians were totally distinct from the negroes, and to deny all relationship between. Speaking of the "Copts and Fellahs," whom every body knows are descendants of the Egyptians, he says, *"The Copts, though now remarkably distinct from the people that surround them, derive from their remote ancestors some mixture of Greek, Arabian, and perhaps even negro blood."* Now, mark the description given of the Egyptians in this same work: *"Complexion brown. The nose is straight, excepting the end, where it is rounded and wide; the lips are rather thick, and the hair black and curly."* This description would certainly seem to make it safe to suppose the presence of *"even* negro blood." A man, in our day, with brown complexion, "nose rounded and wide, lips thick, hair black and curly," would, I think, have no difficulty in getting himself recognized as a negro!!

The same authority tells us that the "Copts are supposed by NEIBHUR, DENON and others, to be the descendants of the ancient Egyptians;" and Dr. Morton adds, that it has often been observed that a strong resemblance may be traced between the Coptic visage and that presented in the ancient mummies and statues. Again, he says, the *"Copts can be, at most, but the degenerate remains, both physically and intellectually, of that mighty people who have claimed the admiration of all ages."* Speaking of the Nubians, Dr. Morton says, (page 26,)—

The hair of the Nubian is thick and black — often curled, either by nature or art, and sometimes *partially frizzled*, but *never woolly*.

Again:—

Although the Nubians occasionally present their national characters unmixed, they generally show traces of their social intercourse with the Arabs, and *even* with the negroes.

  •   •   •   •   •   •   •   •   •   •   •   •

The repetition of the adverb here *"even,"* is important, as showing the spirit in which our great American Ethnologist pursues his work, and what deductions may be justly made from the value of his researches on that account. In everything touching the negro, Dr. Morton, in his "Crania Americana," betrays the same spirit. He thinks that the *Sphinx* was not the representative of an Egyptian Deity, but was a shrine, worshiped at by the degraded *negroes* of Egypt; and this fact he alleges as the secret of the mistake made by Volney, in supposing that the Egyptians were real negroes. The absurdity of this assertion will be very apparent, in view of the fact that the great Sphinx in question was the chief of a series, full two miles in length. Our author again repels the supposition that the Egyptians were related to negroes, by saying there is no mention made of *color* by the historian, in relating the marriage of Solomon with Pharaoh's daughter; and with genuine American feeling, he says, such a circumstance as the marrying of an European monarch with the daughter of a negro would not have been passed over in silence in our day. This is a sample of the reasoning of men who reason from *prejudice* rather than from *facts*. It assumes that a *black skin* in the *East* excites the same prejudice which we see here in the West. Having denied all relationship of the negro to the ancient Egyptians, with characteristic American assumption, he says, "It is easy to prove, that whatever may have been the hue of their skin, they belong to the same race with ourselves."

Of course, I do not find fault with Dr. Morton, or any other American, for claiming affinity with Egyptians. All that goes in that direction belongs to my side of the question, and is really right.

The leaning here indicated is natural enough, and may be explained by the fact, that an educated man in Ireland ceases to be an Irishman; and an intelligent black man is always supposed to have derived his intelligence from his connection with the white race. To be intelligent is to have one's negro blood ignored.

There is, however, a very important physiological fact, contradicting this last assumption; and that fact is, that intellect is uniformly derived from the maternal side. Mulattoes, in this country, may almost wholly boast of Anglo Saxon male ancestry.

It is the province of prejudice to blind; and scientific writers, not less than others, write to please, as well as to instruct, and even unconsciously to themselves, (sometimes,) sacrifice what is true to what is popular. Fashion is not confined to dress; but extends to philosophy as well — and it is fashionable, now, in our land, to exaggerate the differences between the negro and the European. If, for instance, a phrenologist, or naturalist undertakes to represent in portraits, the differences between the two races — the negro and the European — he will invariably present the *highest* type of the European, and the *lowest* type of the negro.

The European face is drawn in harmony with the highest ideas of beauty, dignity and intellect. Features regular and brow after the Websterian mold. The negro, on the other hand, appears with features distorted, lips exaggerated, forehead depressed — and the whole expression of the countenance made to harmonize with the popular idea of negro imbecility and degradation. I have seen many pictures of negroes and Europeans, in phrenological and ethnological works; and all, or nearly all, excepting the work of Dr. Prichard, and that other great work, Comb's Constitution of Man, have been more or less open to this objection. I think I have never seen a single picture in an American work, designed to give an idea of the mental endowments of the negro, which did any thing like justice to the subject; nay, that was not infamously distorted. The heads of A. CRUMMEL, HENRY H. GARNET, SAM'L R. WARD, CHAS. LENOX REMOND, W. J. WILSON, J. W. PENNINGTON, J. I. GAINES, M. R. DELANY, J. W. LOGUIN, J. M. WHITFIELD, J. C. HOLLY, and hundreds of others I could mention, are all better formed, and indicate the presence of intellect more than any pictures I have seen in such works; and while it must be admitted that there are negroes answering the description given by the American ethnologists and others, of the negro race, I contend that there is every description of head among them, ranging from the highest Indoo Caucasian downward. If the very best type of the European is always presented, I insist that *justice*, in all such works, demands that the very best type of the negro should also be taken. The importance of this criticism may not be apparent to all; — to the *black* man it is very apparent. He sees the injustice, and writhes under its sting. But to return to Dr. Morton, or rather to the question of the affinity of the negroes to the Egyptians.

It seems to me that a man might as well deny the affinity of the American to the Englishman, as to deny such affinity between the negro and the Egyptian. He might make out as many points of difference, in the case of one as in that of the other. Especially could this be done, if, like ethnologists, in given cases, only typical specimens were resorted to. The lean, slender American, pale and swarthy, if exposed to the sun, wears a very different appearance to the full, round Englishman, of clear, *blonde* complexion. One may trace the progress of this difference in the common portraits of the American Presidents. Just study those faces, beginning with WASHINGTON; and as you come thro' the JEFFERSONS, the ADAMSES, and the MADISONS, you will find an increasing bony and wiry appearance about those portraits, & a greater remove from that serene amplitude which characterises the countenances of the earlier Presidents. I may be mistaken, but I think this is a correct index of the change going on in the nation at large, — converting Englishmen, Germans, Irishmen, and Frenchmen, into Americans, and causing them to lose, in a common American character, all traces of their former distinctive national peculiarities.

AUTHORITIES AS TO THE RESEMBLANCE OF THE EGYPTIANS TO NEGROES.

Now, let us see what the best authorities say, as to the personal appearance of the Egyptians. I think it will be at once admitted, that while they differ very strongly from the negro, debased and enslaved, that difference is not greater than may be observed in other quarters of the globe, among people notoriously belonging to the same variety, the same original stock; in a word, to the same family. If it shall be found that the people of Africa have an African character, as general, as well defined, and as distinct, as have the people of Europe, or the people of Asia, the exceptional differences among them afford no ground for supposing a difference of race; but, on the contrary, it will be inferred that the people of Africa constitute one great branch of the human family, whose origin may be as properly referred to the families of Noah, as can be any other branch of the human family, from whom they differ. Denon, in his 'Travels in Egypt,' describes the Egyptians, as of full, but "delicate and voluptuous forms, countenances sedate and placid, round and soft features, with eyes long and almond shaped, half shut and languishing, and turned up at the outer angles, as if habitually fatigued by the light and heat of the sun; cheeks round; thick lips, full and prominent; mouths large, but cheerful and smiling; complexion dark, ruddy and coppery, and the whole aspect display-ing — as one of the most graphic delineators among modern travelers has observed — the genuine African character, of which the *negro* is the exagger-ated and extreme representation." Again, Prichard says, (page 152,) —

> Herodotus traveled in Egypt, and was, therefore, well acquainted with the people from personal observation. He does not say any-thing directly, as to the descriptions of their persons, which were too well known to the Greeks to need such an account, but his indirect testimony is very strongly expressed. After mentioning a tradition, that the people of Colchis were a colony from Egypt, Herodotus says, that 'there was one fact strongly in favor of this opinion — the Colchians were *black* in complexion and *woolly* haired.'

These are the words by which the complexion and hair of negroes are described. In another passage, he says that

> The pigeon, said to have fled to Dodona, and to have founded the Oracle, was declared to be *black*, and that the meaning of the story was this: The Oracle was, in reality, founded by a female captive from the Thebaid; she was *black*, being an Egyptian." "Other Greek writers," says Pritchard, "have expressed themselves in similar terms.

Those who have mentioned the Egyptians as a *swarthy* people, according to Prichard, might as well have applied the term *black* to them, since they were doubtless of a chocolate color. The same author brings together the testimony of Eschylus and others as to the color of the ancient Egyptians, all corres-ponding, more or less, with the foregoing. Among the most direct testimony educed by Prichard, is, first that of Volney, who, speaking of the modern Copts, says:

> They have a puffed visage, swollen eyes, flat nose, and thick lips, and bear much resemblance to mulattoes.

Baron Larrey says, in regard to the same people:

> They have projecting cheek bones, dilating nostrils, thick lips, and hair and beard black and *crisp*.

Mr. Ledyard, (whose testimony, says our learned authority, is of the more value, as he had no theory to support,) says:

> I suspect the *Copts* to have been the *origin* of the *negro* race; the nose and lips correspond with those of the negro; the hair, wherever I can see it among the people here, is curled, *not* like that of the negroes, but like the mulattoes.

Here I leave our learned authorities, as to the resemblance of the Egyptians to negroes.

It is not in my power, in a discourse of this sort, to adduce more than a very small part of the testimony in support of a near relationship between the present enslaved and degraded negroes, and the ancient highly civilized and wonderfully endowed Egyptians. Sufficient has already been adduced, to show a marked similarity in regard to features, hair, color, and I doubt not that the philologist can find equal similarity in the structures of their languages. In view of the foregoing, while it may not be claimed that the ancient Egyptians were negroes, — viz: — answering, in all respects, to the nations and tribes ranged under the general appellation, negro; still, it may safely be affirmed, that a strong affinity and a direct relationship may be claimed by the negro race, to THAT GRANDEST OF ALL THE NATIONS OF ANTIQUITY, THE BUILDERS OF THE PYRAMIDS.

But there are other evidences of this relationship, more decisive than those alledged in a general similarity of personal appearance. Language is held to be very important, by the best ethnologists, in tracing out the remotest affinities of nations, tribes, classes and families. The color of the skin has sometimes been less enduring than the speech of a people. I speak by authority, and follow in the footsteps of some of the most learned writers on the natural and ethnological history of man, when I affirm that one of the most direct and conclusive proofs of the general affinity of Northern African nations, with those of West, East and South Africa, is found in the general similarity of their language. The philologist easily discovers, and is able to point out something like the original source of the multiplied tongues now in use in that yet mysterious quarter of the globe. Dr. R. G. LATHAM, F. R. S., corresponding member of the Ethnological Society, New York — in his admirable work, entitled "Man and his Migrations" — says:

> In the languages of Abyssinia, the Gheez and Tigre, admitted, as long as they have been known at all, to be *Semitic,* graduate through the Amharic, the Talasha, the Harargi, the Gafat and other languages, which may be well studied in Dr. Beke's valuable comparative tables, into the Agow tongue, unequivocally indigenous to Abyssinia, and through this into the true negro classes. But, unequivocal as may the Semitic elements of the Berber, Coptic and Galla, their affinities with the tongues of Western and Southern Africa are more so. I weigh my words when I say, not *equally,* but *more*; changing the expression, for every foot in advance which can be made towards the Semitic tongues in one direction, the African philologist can go a yard towards the negro ones in the other.

In a note, just below this remarkable statement, Dr. Latham says:

> A short table of the Berber and Coptic, as compared with the other African tongues, may be seen in the Classical Museum of the British Association, for 1846. In the Transactions of the Philological Society is a grammatical sketch of the Tumali language, by Dr. S. Tutshek of Munich. The Tumali is a truly negro language of Kordufan; whilst, in respect to the extent to which its inflections are

formed, by internal changes of vowels and accents, it is fully equal to the Semitic tongues of Palestine and Arabia.

This testimony may not serve prejudice, but to me it seems quite sufficient.

SUPERFICIAL OBJECTIONS

Let us now glance again at the opposition. A volume, on the Natural History of the Human Species, by Charles Hamilton Smith, quite false in many of its facts, and as mischievous as false, has been published recently in this country, and will, doubtless, be widely circulated, especially by those to whom the thought of human brotherhood is abhorrent. This writer says, after mentioning sundry facts touching the dense and spherical structure of the negro head:

> This very structure may influence the erect gait, which occasions the practice common also to the Ethiopian, or mixed nations, of carrying burdens and light weights, even to a tumbler full of water, upon the head.

No doubt this seemed a very sage remark to Mr. Smith, and quite important in fixing a character to the negro skull, although different to that of Europeans. But if the learned Mr. Smith had stood, previous to writing it, at our door, (a few days in succession,) he might have seen hundreds of Germans and of Irish people, not bearing burdens of "*light* weight," but of *heavy* weight, upon the same vertical extremity. The carrying of burdens upon the head is as old as Oriental Society; and the man writes himself a blockhead, who attempts to find in the custom a proof of original difference. On page 227, the same writer says:

> The voice of the negroes is feeble and hoarse in the male sex.

The explanation of this mistake in our author, is found in the fact, that an oppressed people, in addressing their superiors — perhaps I ought to say, their oppressors — usually assume a minor tone, as less likely to provoke the charge of intrusiveness. But it is ridiculous to pronounce the voice of the negro feeble; and the learned ethnologist must be hard pushed, to establish differences, when he refers to this as one. Mr. Smith further declares, that

> The typical woolly haired races have never discovered an alphabet, framed a grammatical language, nor made the least step in science or art.

Now, the man is still living, (or was but a few years since,) among the Mandingoes of the Western coast of Africa, who has framed an alphabet; and while Mr. Smith may be pardoned for his ignorance of that fact, as an ethnonogist, he is inexcusable for not knowing that the Mpongwe language, spoken on both sides of the Gaboon River, at Cape Lopez, Cape St. Catharine, and in the interior, to the distance of two or three hundred miles, is as truly a grammatically framed language as any extant. I am indebted, for this fact, to Rev. Dr. M. B. ANDERSON, President of the Rochester University; and by his leave, here is the Grammar — [holding up the Grammar.] Perhaps, of all the attempts ever made to disprove the unity of the human family, and to brand the negro with natural inferiority, the most compendious and bare-faced is the book, entitled *"Types of Mankind,"* by Nott and Glidden. One would be well employed, in a series of Lectures, directed to an exposure of the unsoundness, if not the wickedness of this work.

THE AFRICAN RACE BUT ONE PEOPLE.

But I must hasten. Having shown that the people of Africa are, probably, one people; that each tribe bears an intimate relation to other tribes and nations in that quarter of the globe, and that the Egyptians may have flung off the different tribes seen there at different times, as implied by the evident relations of their language, and by other similarities; it can hardly be deemed un-reasonable to suppose, that the African branch of the human species — from the once highly civilized Egyptian to the barbarians on the banks of the Niger — may claim brotherhood with the great family of Noah, spreading over the more Northern and Eastern parts of the globe. I will now proceed to consider those physical peculiarities of form, features, hair and color, which are sup-posed by some men to mark the African, not only as an inferior race, but as a distinct species, naturally and originally different from the rest of mankind, as really to place him nearer to the brute than to man.

THE EFFECT OF CIRCUMSTANCES UPON THE PHY-SICAL MAN.

I may remark, just here, that it is impossible, even were it desirable, in a discourse like this, to attend to the anatomical and physiological argument connected with this part of the subject. I am not equal to that, and if I were, the occasion does not require it. The form of the *negro* — [I use the term *negro,* precisely in the sense that you use the term Anglo Saxon; and I believe, too, that the former will one day be as illustrious as the latter] — has often been the subject of remark. His flat feet, long arms, high cheek bones and retreating forehead, are especially dwelt upon, to his disparagement, and just as if there were no white people with precisely the same peculiarities. I think it will ever be found, that the *well* or *ill* condition of any part of mankind, will leave its mark on the physical as well as on the intellectual part of man. A hundred instances might be cited, of whole families who have degenerated, and others who have improved in personal appearance, by a change of cir-cumstances. A man is worked upon by what *he* works on. He may carve out his circumstances, but his circumstances will carve him out as well. I told a boot maker, in New Castle upon Tyne, that I had been a plantation slave. He said I must pardon him; but he could not believe it; no plantation laborer ever had a high instep. He said he had noticed, that the coal heavers and work people in low condition, had, for the most part, flat feet, and that he could tell, by the shape of the feet, whether a man's parents were in high or low condition. The thing was worth a thought, and I have thought of it, and have looked around me for facts. There is some truth in it; though there are exceptions, in individual cases.

The day I landed in Ireland, nine years ago, I addressed, (in company with Father SPRATT, and that good man who has been recently made the subject of bitter attack; I allude to the philanthropic JAMES HAUGHTON, of Dublin,) a large meeting of the common people of Ireland, on temperance. Never did human faces tell a sadder tale. More than five thousand were assembled; and I say, with no wish to wound the feelings of any Irishman, that these people lacked only a black skin and woolly hair, to complete their likeness to the plantation negro. The open, uneducated mouth — the long, gaunt arm — the badly formed foot and ankle — the shuffling gait — the retreating forehead and vacant expression — and, their petty quarrels and fights — all reminded me of the plantation, and my own cruelly abused people. Yet, *that* is the land of GRATTAN, of CURRAN, of O'CONNELL, and of SHERIDAN. Now, while what I have said is true of the common people, the fact is, there are no more really handsome people in the world, than the educated Irish people. The Irishman educated, is a model gentleman; the Irishman ignorant and degraded, compares in form and feature, with the negro!

I am stating facts. If you go into Southern Indiana, you will see what climate and habit can do, even in one generation. The man may have come from New England, but his hard features, sallow complexion, have left little of New England on his brow. The right arm of the blacksmith is said to be larger and stronger than his left. The ship carpenter is at forty round shouldered. The shoemaker carries the marks of his trade. One locality becomes famous for one thing, another for another. Manchester and Lowell, in America, Manchester and Sheffield, in England, attest this. But what does it all prove? Why, nothing positively, as to the main point; still, it raises the inquiry — May not the condition of men explain their various appearances? Need we go behind the vicissitudes of barbarism for an explanation of the gaunt, wiry, ape like appearance of some of the genuine negroes? Need we look higher than a vertical sun, or lower than the damp, black soil of the Niger, the Gambia, the Senegal, with their heavy and enervating miasma, rising ever from the rank growing and decaying vegetation, for an explanation of the negro's color? If a cause, full and adequate, can be found here, *why seek further?*

The eminent Dr. LATHAM, already quoted, says that nine tenths of the white population of the globe are found between 30 and 65 degrees North latitude. Only about one fifth of all the inhabitants of the globe are white; and they are as far from the Adamic complexion as is the negro. The remainder are — *what?* Ranging all the way from the brunette to jet black. There are the red, the reddish copper color, the yellowish, the dark brown, the chocolate color, and so on, to the jet black. On the mountains on the North of Africa, where water freezes in winter at times, branches of the same people who are *black* in the valley are *white* on the mountains. The Nubian, with his beautiful curly hair, finds it becoming frizzled, crisped, and even woolly, as he approaches the great Sahara. The Portuguese, white in Europe, is brown in Asia. The Jews, who are to be found in all countries, never intermarrying, are white in Europe, brown in Asia, and black in Africa. Again, what does it all prove? Nothing, absolutely; nothing which places the question beyond dispute; but it *does* justify the conjecture before referred to, that outward circumstances *may* have something to do with modifying the various phases of humanity; and that color itself is at the control of the world's climate and its various concomitants. It is the sun that paints the peach — and may it not be, that he paints the *man* as well? My reading, on this point, however, as well as my own observation, have convinced me, that from the beginning the Almighty, within certain limits, endowed mankind with organizations capable of countless variations in form, feature and color, without having it necessary to begin a new creation for every new variety.

A powerful argument in favor of the oneness of the human family, is afforded in the fact that nations, however dissimilar, may be united in one social state, not only without detriment to each other, but, most clearly, to the advancement of human welfare, happiness and perfection. While it is clearly proved, on the other hand, that those nations freest from foreign elements, present the most evident marks of deterioration. Dr. JAMES MCCUNE SMITH, himself a colored man, a gentleman and scholar, alledges — and not without excellent reason — that this, our own great nation, so distinguished for industry and enterprise, is largely indebted to its composite character. We all know, at any rate, that now, what constitutes the very heart of the civilized world — (I allude to England) — has only risen from barbarism to its present lofty eminence, through successive invasions and alliances with her people. The Medes and Persians constituted one of the mightiest empires that ever rocked the globe. The most terrible nation which now threatens the peace of the world to make its will the law of Europe, is a grand piece of Mosaic work, in which almost every nation has its characteristic feature, from the wild Tartar to the refined Pole.

But, gentlemen, the time fails me, and I must bring these remarks to a close. My argument has swelled beyond its appointed measure. What I intended to make special, has become, in its progress, somewhat general. I meant to speak here to-day, for the lonely and the despised ones, with whom I was cradled, and with whom I have suffered; and now, gentlemen, in conclusion, what if all this reasoning be unsound? What if the negro may not be able to prove his relationship to Nubians, Abysinians and Egyptians? What if ingenious men are able to find plausible objections to all arguments maintaining the oneness of the human race? What, after all, if they are able to show very good reasons for believing the negro to have been created precisely as we find him on the Gold Coast — along the Senegal and the Niger — I say, what of all this? — "*A man's a man for a' that.*" I sincerely believe, that the weight of the argument is in favor of the unity of origin of the human race, or species — that the arguments on the other side are partial, superficial, utterly subversive of the happiness of man, and insulting to the wisdom of God. Yet, what if we grant they are not so? What, if we grant that the case, on our part, is not made out? Does it follow, that the negro should be held in contempt? Does it follow, that to enslave and imbrute him is either *just* or *wise?* I think not. Human rights stand upon a common basis; and by all the reason that they are supported, maintained and defended, for one variety of the human family, they are supported, maintained and defended for *all* the human family; because all mankind have the same wants, arising out of a common nature. A diverse origin does not disprove a common nature, nor does it disprove a united destiny. The essential characteristics of humanity are everywhere the same. In the language of the eloquent CURRAN, "No matter what complexion, whether an Indian or an African sun has burnt upon him," his title deed to freedom, his claim to life and to liberty, to knowledge and to civilization, to society and to Christianity, are just and perfect. It is registered in the Courts of Heaven, and is enforced by the eloquence of the God of all the earth.

I have said that the negro and white man are likely ever to remain the principal inhabitants of this country. I repeat the statement now, to submit the reasons that support it. The blacks can disappear from the face of the country by three ways. They may be colonized, — they may be exterminated, — or, they may die out. Colonization is out of the question; for I know not what hardships the laws of the land can impose, which can induce the colored citizen to leave his native soil. He was here in its infancy; he is here in its age. Two hundred years have passed over him, his tears and blood have been mixed with the soil, and his attachment to the place of his birth is stronger than iron. It is not probable that he will be exterminated; two considerations must prevent a crime so stupendous as that — the influence of Christianity on the one hand, and the power of self interest on the other; and, in regard to their dying out, the statistics of the country afford no encouragement for such a conjecture. The history of the negro race proves them to be wonderfully adapted to all countries, all climates, and all conditions. Their tenacity of life, their powers of endurance, their maleable toughness, would almost imply especial interposition on their behalf. The ten thousand horrors of slavery, striking hard upon the sensitive soul, have bruised, and battered, and stung, but have not killed. The poor bondman lifts a smiling face above the surface of a sea of agonies, *hoping on, hoping ever.* His tawny brother, the Indian, dies, under the flashing glance of the Anglo Saxon. *Not* so the negro; civilization cannot kill him. He accepts it — becomes a part of it. In the Church, he is an Uncle Tom; in the State, he is the most abused and least offensive. All the facts in his history mark out for him a destiny, united to America and Americans. Now, whether this population shall, by FREEDOM, INDUSTRY, VIRTUE and INTELLIGENCE, be made a blessing to the country and the world, or whether their multiplied wrongs shall kindle the vengeance of an offended God, will depend upon the conduct of no class of men so much as upon the Scholars of the country. The future public opinion of the land, whether anti-slavery or pro-slavery, whether just or unjust, whether magnanimous or mean, must redound to the honor of the Scholars of the country or cover them with shame. There is but one safe road for nations or for individuals. The fate of a wicked man and of a wicked nation is the same. The flaming sword of offended justice falls as certainly upon the nation as upon the man. God has no children whose rights may be safely trampled upon. The sparrow may not fall to the ground without the notice of his eye, and men are more than sparrows.

Now, gentlemen, I have done. The subject is before you. I shall not undertake to make the application. I speak as unto wise men. I stand in the presence of Scholars. We have met here to-day from vastly different points in the world's condition. I have reached here — if you will pardon the egotism — by little short of a miracle; at any rate, by dint of some application and perseverance. Born, as I was, in obscurity, a stranger to the halls of learning, environed by ignorance, degradation, and their concomitants, from birth to manhood, I do not feel at liberty to mark out, with any degree of confidence, or dogmatism, what is the precise vocation of the Scholar. Yet, this I *can* say, as a denizen of the world, and as a citizen of a country rolling in the sin and shame of Slavery, the most flagrant and scandalous that ever saw the sun, "Whatsoever things are true, whatsoever things are honest, whatsoever things are just, whatsoever things are pure, whatsoever things are lovely, whatsoever things are of good report, if there be any virtue, and if there be any praise, think on these things."

Douglass' well researched address doubtlessly brought together the best available arguments and evidence in support of the Negro's ethnological claims that could be found on the eve of the Civil War. Yet, not only did the message fail to alter opinion in the South, it did little to change prevailing attitudes in the North. With the rise of the anti-slavery Republican Party in 1856 and the nomination of Abraham Lincoln in 1860, several black spokesmen — including Frederick Douglass — were hopeful that the day of their full acceptance would soon arrive. Before long, however, they were disappointed; and this, in turn, led them to reaffirm, with increased vigor, their faith in the potential of their race. What took place in Framingham, Massachussetts on July 4, 1860, exemplifies the black American's refusal, at this time, to accept either the charge or the implication that he was inferior. The principal speaker at this anti-slavery meeting was H. Ford Douglass, a twenty-eight year old activist from Illinois.[16] Armed with facts he had derived from personal experience, interviews, and newspaper sources, and relying upon the colorful delivery he had cultivated on the hustings (political campaigns), he denounced the four major political parties in the campaign[17] on the grounds that their leaders were motivated by both overt and subtle prejudices which prompted them to assign a superior position in society to white men. After indicting Lincoln and Douglas, he asserted in tones reminiscent of Henry Highland Garnet:

> There is a great deal of talk in this country about the superiority of the white race. We often hear, from this very platform, praise of the Saxon race. Now, I want to put this question to those who deny the equal manhood of the negro: What peculiar trait of character do the white men of this country possess, as

a mark of superiority, either morally or mentally, that is not also manifested by the black man, under similar circumstances? (Hear, hear") You may take down the white and black part of the social and political structure, stone by stone and in all the relations of life, where the exercise of his moral and intellectual function is not restricted by positive law, or by the solitary restraints of society, you will find the negro the equal of the white man, in all the elements of head and heart.[18]

If H. Ford Douglass was disillusioned with Lincoln's refusal to acknowledge the Negro's full potential during the contest of 1860, William Wells Brown[19] was also disturbed with Lincoln's initial performance as president. When he learned, therefore, that the President allegedly told a black delegation from the District of Columbia in 1862, "that the whites and the blacks could not live together in peace on account of one race being superior intellectually to the other," he decided to write a definitive study of *The Black Man, His Antecedents, His Genius, and His Achievements.* [20] It was a comprehensive analysis similar to the book by Easton and the speech by Frederick Douglass. But while Easton spoke as a minister and Douglass as a journalist and debater, Brown brought to his task the tools of the historian. As a result, his volume summarizes, with clarity and force, the salient features of the ethnological argument used by blacks in the antebellum period. Brown began his treatise by comparing the richness of African culture with the crudeness and barbarity that often accompanied the early Anglo-Saxon world. To prove that the circumstance of slavery, rather than lack of natural talent, was the major cause of existing inequalities, he eulogized the accomplishments of free Negroes in America, England, and the West Indies. He also pointed out numerous instances of the white man's dependence upon the emancipated Negro.

Brown's thesis was not new, but his work is significant for several reasons. First, his ability to range freely through the pages of history, to assess documents, and to allude to personal experiences at home and abroad made his study a standard source for later writers. Moreover, Brown's sketch constituted an important landmark in the black American's rhetorical campaign to prove that he was a man and not a chattel to be manipulated at a master's will. It was this belief in an ethnology that taught equality of the races which served as a catalyst for black spokesmen to recommend a rhetoric of assimilation.

ASSIMILATION THROUGH RELIANCE UPON GOD

One of the distinguishing characteristics of the early rhetoric of black Americans was a strong preoccupation with the power of religion. It was to the God of the Bible that they often turned for guidance, inspiration, protection, and their belief in the equality of man. This interest in spiritual matters was due, in part, to the loss of a sense of community in other personal areas brought about by the institution of slavery. To perpetuate this economic and social system families were broken, and children, separated from their parents and siblings, became estranged members of a society which viewed them as unassimilable.[21] The only recourse for the slave, therefore, was to turn to a sovereign God who someday would transport him from an unhappy earthly environment to a place of equality in an eternal world. Sensing the power of this appeal, Jupiter Hammon,[22] a slave from Long Island, sent a message to the Negroes of New York in 1787, urging them to focus their attention on the kingdom of heaven. "We have so little time in this world," he said, "that it is no matter how wretched and miserable we are, if it prepares us for heaven. What is forty, fifty, or sixty years, when compared to eternity . . . ."[23] Hammon then advised his colleagues not to concentrate on their bondage. Be patient, he suggested, for "if God designs to set us free, he will do it, in his own time and way . . . ."[24] It is instructive to note that Hammon made his plea at a time when delegates from the thirteen colonies were meeting in Philadelphia to create the formation of the federal government.

This rhetoric of accommodation based on future reward not only became an integral part of religious sentiment for the slave but also gave meaning and direction to the Negro spiritual. Sufferings caused by separation could be endured by those who sharpened their devotion to God, and participated in the cathartic experience of pointing, in song, to an ultimate restoration of the family:

> I've got a mother in the heaven,
>   Outshines de sun,
> I've got a father in de heaven,
>   Outshines de sun,
> I've got a sister in de heaven,
>   Outshines de sun,
> When we get to heaven, we will
>   Outshine de sun,
>   Way beyond de moon.[25]

The Negro spiritual was not limited to a discussion of personal needs. It also dealt with the slave's compelling desire for group association through the church.

> I'm gwine to jine de great 'sociation
> I'm gwine to jine de great 'sociation
> Den my little soul's gwine to shine.[26]

In many instances, the reliance on God as the most efficacious solution to the Negro's lack of freedom and identity held a similar appeal for those who used a rhetoric of revolution. Both Denmark Vesey and Nat Turner, as we shall see in a later chapter, looked toward heaven for their inspiration. Indeed, they perceived themselves as chosen vessels to implement the will of God. In the larger view, however, it was the assimilationist who saw most clearly all the possibilities inherent in the religious argument. Belief in God and the Scriptures gave to him a rationale for the unity of the races within a framework of justice. Moreover, it presented to him an opportunity to realize his potentials as a man. Most of all it provided him, as well as his white counterpart who might occupy a superior position, with a message of love and reconciliation. Many, consciously or unconsciously, came to believe that the teachings of the Bible by giving worth and dignity to the Negro, rendered him more suitable for inclusion in American society, and by stimulating the conscience of the white community it softened, to some degree, hardened attitudes of prejudice.

Nothwithstanding their faith in religion as a pragmatic means of achieving assimilation, these spokesmen were, nevertheless, prepared to meet failure by taking comfort in the conviction that their efforts would be honored in eternity. Richard Allen was one of the first to use this rhetorical strategy. His widely publicized address "To the People of Color," published first in 1793, attracted national attention.

Richard Allen

*To the People of Color**

Feeling an engagement of mind for your welfare, I address you with an affectionate sympathy, having been a slave, and as desirous of freedom as any of you; yet the bands of bondage were so strong that no way appeared for my release; yet at times a hope arose in my heart that a way would open for it; and when my mind was mercifully visited with the feeling of the love of God, then these hopes increased, and a confidence arose that he would make for my enlargement; and as a patient waiting was necessary, I was sometimes favored with it, at other times I was very impatient. Then the prospect of liberty almost vanished away, and I was in darkness and perplexity.

---

*From George A. Singleton, ed., *The Life, Experience, and Gospel Labors of the Rt. Rev. Richard Allen, Written by Himself* (New York: Abingdon Press, 1960), pp. 72-74

I mention experience to you, that your hearts may not sink at the discouraging prospects you may have, and that you may put your trust in God, who sees your condition, and as a merciful father pitieth his children, so doth God pity them that love Him; and as your hearts are inclined to serve God, you will feel an affectionate regard towards your masters and mistresses, so called, and the whole family in which you live. This will be seen by them, and tend to promote your liberty, especially with such as have feeling masters; and if they are otherwise, you will have the favor and love of God dwelling in your hearts, which you will value more than anything else, which will be a consolation in the worst condition you can be in, and no master can deprive you of it; and as life is short and uncertain, and the chief end of our having a being in this world is to be prepared for a better, I wish you to think of this more than anything else; then you will have a view of that freedom which the sons of God enjoy; and if the troubles of your condition end with your lives, you will be admitted to the freedom which God hath prepared for those of all colors that love him. Here the power of the most cruel master ends, and all sorrow and tears are wiped away.

To you who are favored with freedom, let your conduct manifest your gratitude toward the compassionate masters who have set you free; and let no rancour or ill-will lodge in your breast for any bad treatment you may have received from any. If you do, you transgress against God, who will not hold you guiltless. He would not suffer it even in his beloved people Israel; and you think he will allow it unto us? Many of the white people have been instruments in the hands of God for our good even such as have held us in captivity, are now pleading our cause with earnestness and zeal; and I am sorry to say, that too many think more of the evil than of the good they have received, and instead of taking the advice of their friends, turn from it with indifference. Much depends upon us for the help of our color — more than many are aware. If we are lazy and idle, the enemies of freedom plead it as a cause why we ought not to be free, and say we are better in a state of servitude, and that giving us our liberty would be an injury to us; and by such conduct we strengthen the bands of oppression and keep many in bondage who are more worthy than ourselves. I entreat you to consider the obligations we lie under to help forward the cause of freedom. He who knows how bitter the cup is of which the slave hath to drink, O, how ought we to feel for those who yet remain in bondage! Will even our friends excuse — will God pardon us — for the part we act in making strong the hands of the enemies of our color?

Four years after Allen wrote his brief but cogent address, Prince Hall[27] expressed similar sentiments in a charge delivered to the African Lodge in West Cambridge, Massachusetts. Using the metaphor of the "Grand Lodge" to depict a future heavenly fraternity, Hall equated the hopes and aspirations of the members of his race with those of different nationalities who had responded to the Biblical message. Whoever loved God, regardless of his orientation, he argued, would seek communion with his fellowmen. For illustrative, supporting material he, like Allen, turned to the Scriptures. Jethro, an Ethiopian, he pointed out, gave instructions to his son-in-law Moses; Philip communicated side by side with an African eunuch; and the Grand Master Solomon held sessions with the Queen of Sheba. Although Hall's immediate audience was comprised of members of the African Lodge, he envisioned as a part of his larger rhetorical situation, the white residents of Massachusetts. Thus he reminded them that in the name of the Christian tradition they must renounce the oppressive acts against Negroes which were occurring daily in the streets of Boston.[29]

In Chillicothe, Ohio, more than three decades later, Reverend David Nickens, attempting to advance the cause of assimilation, pointed out to his congregation the power of Christianity to reform lives. With this reformation, he said, would come an elimination of the dissonance and divisiveness which served as barriers in human relations. Convinced that one who is true to God would then be true to his neighbor, he called for a unity of the churches, so that Negroes could stand united in their campaign for freedom and acceptance.[30]

As the War Between the States approached, pressure for congressional anti-slavery measures increased. Accompanying this trend was a shift in the religious argument. Appeals to the basic tenets of Christianity were still present, but they moved from a central to a peripheral position in the rhetoric of black Americans. Influential preachers such as Henry Highland Garnet and Samuel Ward remained devout churchmen, throughout this period, but, as we shall observe later, they turned their energies to the public platform where they sought to arouse mass sentiment on behalf of legislative action on slavery. With the close of the war and the adoption of the thirteenth and fourteenth amendments, however, came renewed hope in the appropriateness of a rhetoric of assimilation based on Christianity. The most eloquent champion of this post-war rhetorical strategy was Alexander Crummell, an Episcopalian clergyman whose parish included Africa and America.[31] His impressive appearance and courtly manner have been recorded in the following portrait by W. E. B. DuBois:

I saw Alexander Crummel first at a Wilberforce commencement season, amid its bustle and crush. Tall, frail, and black he stood, with simple dignity and an unmistakable air of good breeding. I talked with him apart, where the storming of the lusty young orators could not harm us. I spoke to him politely, then curiously, then eagerly, as I began to feel the fineness of his character — his calm courtesy, the sweetness of his strength, and his fair blending of the hope and truth of life. Instinctively I bowed before this man, as one bows before the prophets of the world. Some seer he seemed, that came not from the crimson Past or the gray To-come but from the pulsing Now, — that mocking world which seemed to me at once so light and dark, so splendid and sordid. Four-score years had he wandered in this same world of mine, within the Veil.[32]

Crummell's address on "The Race Problem in America," delivered at the Protestant Episcopal Church Congress in Buffalo, New York on November 20, 1888 is one of the most significant documents that appeared in the nineteenth century, utilizing the Christian assimilation argument. A close reading of this speech, which is printed in its entirety below, reveals, Crummell's rhetorical technique of establishing a historical base from which he can construct a logical argument that moves toward a climax. Explicit throughout the analysis is his belief that God's hand is ever present in history. It is the Divine Being Who in the past has enabled different races to live together; and it is He Who commands us through His ordinances to preserve racial identity. To be genuinely Christian, therefore, is to oppose amalgamation because it dilutes an aspect of organic life. Crummell identifies democracy as a divinely ordained system created for the purpose of promoting civil and political amity. Since man has a right to choose his own friends, Crummell had no desire to recommend a policy which would guarantee social intercourse between the races or nationalities. Such a requirement, he held, would interfere with freedom of choice in one's private life. He was content, therefore, to develop a philosophy of assimilation that eliminated race as a criterion for acceptability.

Alexander Crummell
The Race Problem in America*

The residence of various races of men in the same national community, is a fact which has occurred in every period of time and in every quarter of the globe. So well known is this fact of history that the mention of a few special instances will be sufficient for this occasion.

It took place in earliest times on the plains of Babylon. It was seen on the banks of the Nile, in the land of the Pharaohs. The same fact occurred

---

*From Alexander Crummell, *Africa and America* (Springfield, Mass.: Wiley & Company, 1891), pp. 39-57.

again when the barbarian hosts of the North fell upon effete Roman society, and changed the fate of Europe. Once more we witness the like fact when the Moors swept along the banks of the Mediterranean, and seated themselves in might and majesty on the hills of Granada and along the fertile slopes of Arragon and Castile. And now, in the 19th century, we have the largest illustration of the same fact in our own Republic, where are gathered together, in one national community, sixty millions of people of every race and kindred under the sun. It might be supposed that an historical fact so large and multiform would furnish a solution of the great race-problem, which now invites attention in American society. We read the future by the past. And without doubt there are certain principles of population which are invariable in their working and universal in their results. Such principles are inductions from definite conditions, and may be called the laws of population. They are, too, both historical and predictive. One cannot only ascertain through them the past condition of States and peoples, but they give a light which opens up with clearness the future of great commonwealths.

But, singular as it may seem, there is no fixed law of history by which to determine the probabilities of the race-problem in the United States. We can find nowhere such invariability of result as to set a principle or determine what may be called an historical axiom.

Observe just here the inevitable confusion which is sure to follow the aim after historical precedent in this problem.

The descendants of Nimrod and Assur, people of two different stocks, settled in Babylon; and the result was amalgamation.*

The Jews and the Egyptians under the Pharaohs inhabited the same country 400 years; but antagonism was the result, and expulsion the final issue.

The Tartars overran China in the tenth century, and the result has been amalgamation.

The Goths and Vandals poured into Italy like a flood, and the result has been absorption.

The Celts and Scandinavians clustered like bees from the fourth to the sixth centuries in the British Isles, and the result has been absorption.

The Northmen and Gauls have lived side by side in Normandy since the tenth century, and the result has been absorption.

The Moors and Spaniards came into the closest contact in the sixth century, and it resulted in constant antagonism and in final expulsion.

The Caucasian and the Indian have lived in close neighborhood on this continent since 1492, and the result has been the extinction of the Indian.

The Papuan and the Malay have lived side by side for ages in the tropical regions of the Pacific, and have maintained every possible divergence of tribal life, of blood, government, and religion, down to the present, and yet have remained perpetually and yet peacefully separate and distinct.**

---

*"Duties of Higher toward Lower Races." Canon Rawlinson, Princeton Review, No., 1878.
**See "Physics and Politics," by Bagehot, pp. 84, 85.

These facts, circling deep historic ages, show that we can find no definite historical precedent or principle applicable to the race-problem in America.

Nevertheless we are not entirely at sea with regard to this problem. There are certain tendencies, seen for over 200 years in our population, which indicate settled, determinate proclivities, and which show, if I mistake not, the destiny of races.

What, then, are the probabilities of the future? Do the indications point to amalgamation or to absorption as the outcome of race-life in America? Are we to have the intermingling of our peoples into one common blood or the perpetuity of our diverse stocks, with the abiding integrity of race, blood, and character?

I might meet the theory which anticipates amalgamation by the great principle manifested in every sphere, viz: "That nature is constantly departing from the simple to the complex; stating off in new lines from the homogeneous to the heterogeneous;" striking out in divers ways into variety; and hence we are hedged in, in the aim after blood-unity, by a law of nature which is universal, and which excludes the notion of amalgamation.

But I turn from the abstract to history. It is now about 268 years since the tides of immigration began to beat upon our shores. This may be called a brief period, but 268 years is long enough to fix a new type of man. Has such a new type sprung up here to life? Has a new commingled race, the result of our diverse elements, come forth from the crucible of our heterogeneous nationality?

We will indulge in no speculation upon this subject. We will exclude even the faintest tinge of the imagination. The facts alone shall speak for themselves.

First of all is the history of the Anglo-Saxon race in America. In many respects it has been the foremost element in the American population; in largeness of numbers, in civil polity and power, in educational impress, and in religious influence. What has become of this element of our population? Has it been lost in the current of the divergent streams of life which have been spreading abroad throughout the land?

Why, every one knows that in New England, in Virginia, in the Far West, along the Atlantic Seaboard, that fully three-fifths of the whole American population are the offspring of this same hardy, plodding, common-sense people that they were centuries ago, when their fathers pressed through the forests of Jamestown or planted their feet upon the sterile soil of Plymouth.

Some of you may remember the remark of Mr. Lowell, on his return in 1885 from his mission to England. He said that when English people spoke to him of Americans as a people different from themselves, he always told them that in blood he was just as much an Englishman as they were; and Mr. Lowell in this remark was the spokesman of not less than thirty-six millions of men of as direct Anglo-Saxon descent as the men of Kent or the people of Yorkshire.

The Celtic element came to America in two separate columns. The French entered Canada in 1607. They came with all that glow, fervor, gallantry, social aptitudes, and religious loyalty which, for centuries, have characterized the Gallic blood, and which are still conspicuous features on both sides of the Atlantic.

The other section of the Celtic family began their immigration about 1640; and they have almost depopulated Ireland to populate America; and their numbers now are millions.

One or two facts are observable concerning the French and Irish, viz: (1) That, although kindred in blood, temperament, and religion, they have avoided both neighborhood of locality and marital alliance; and (2) so great has been the increase of the Hibernian family that in Church life and political importance, they form a vast solidarity in the nation.

The German, like the Celtic family, came over in two sections. The Batavian stock came first from Holland in 1608, and made New York, New Jersey, and Pennsylvania their habitat. The Germans proper, or High Germans, have been streaming into the Republic since 1680, bringing with them that steadiness and sturdiness, that thrift and acquisitiveness, that art and learning, that genius and acumen, which have given an elastic spring to American culture, depth to philosophy, and inspiration to music and to art.

And here they are in great colonies in the Middle and Western States, and in vast sections of our great cities. And yet where can one discover any decline in the purity of German blood, or the likelihood of its ultimate loss in the veins of alien people?

The Negro contingent was one of the earliest contributions to the American population. The black man came quickly on the heel of the Cavalier at Jamestown, and before the arrival of the Puritan in the east. "That fatal, that perfidious bark" of Sir John Hawkins, that "ferried the slave captive o'er the sea" from Africa, preceded the Mayflower one year and five months.

From that small cargo and its after arrivals have arisen the large black population, variously estimated from 8 to 10,000,000. It is mostly, especially in the wide rural areas of the South, a purely Negro population. In the large cities there is a wide intermixture of blood. This, by some writers, is taken as the indication of ultimate and entire amalgamation. But the past in this incident is no sign of the future. The gross and violent intermingling of the blood of the southern white man cannot be taken as an index of the future of the black race.

Amalgamation in its exact sense means the approach of affinities. The word applied to human beings implies will, and the consent of two parties. In *this* sense there has been no amalgamation of the two races; for the negro in this land has ever been the truest of men, in marital allegiance, to his own race.

Intermixture of blood there has been — not by the amalgamation, which implies consent, but through the victimizing of the helpless black woman. But even this has been limited in extent. Out of 4,500,000 race in the census of 1861, 400,000 were set down as of mixed blood. Thousands of these were the legitimate offspring of colored parents; and the probability is that not more than 150,000 had white fathers. Since emancipation the black woman has gained possession of her own person, and it is the testimony of Dr. Haygood and other eminent Southerners that the base process of intermixture has had a wide and sudden decline, and that the likelihood of the so-called amalgamation of the future is fast dying out.

And now, after this survey of race tides and race life during 268 years, I repeat the question: "Has a *new* race, the product of our diverse elements, sprung up here in America? Or, is there any such a probability for the future?"

Let me answer this question by a recent and striking reference.

Dr. Strong, in his able, startling, striking Tractate, entitled *"Our Country,"* speaks in ch. 4, p. 44, of the Helvetian settlement in southern Wisconsin. He deprecates the preservation of its race, its language, its worship, and its customs in their integrity. In this, you see, he forgets the old Roman adage that "though men cross the seas they do not change their nature." He then protests (and rightly, too) against the perpetuation of race antipathies, and closes his criticism with the suggestion, similar to that of Canon Rawlinson, of Oxford, viz., that the American people should seek the solution of the race-problem by universal assimilation of blood.

Dr. Strong evidently forgets that the principle of race is one of the most persistent of all things in the constitution of man. It is one of those structural facts in our nature which abide with a fixed, vital, and reproductive power.

Races, like families, are the organisms and the ordinance of God; and race feeling, like the family feeling, is of divine origin. The extinction of race feeling is just as possible as the extinction of family feeling. Indeed, a race *is* a family. The principle of continuity is as masterful in races as it is in families — as it is in nations.

History is filled with the attempts of kings and mighty generals and great statesmen to extinguish this instinct. But their failures are as numerous as their futile attempts; for this sentiment, alike subtle and spontaneous, has both pervaded and stimulated society in every quarter. Indeed, as Lord Beaconsfield says, "race is the key to history." When once the race-type gets fixed as a new variety, then it acts precisely as the family life; for, 1st, it propagates itself by that divine instinct of reproduction, vital in all living creatures, and next, 2nd, it has a growth as a "seed after its own kind and in itself," whereby the race-type becomes a perpetuity, with its own distinctive form, constitution, features, and structure. Heredity is just as true a fact in races as in families, as it is in individuals.

Nay, we see, not seldom, a special persistency in the race life. We see families and tribes and clans swept out of existence, while race "goes on forever." Yea, even nations suffer the same fate. Take, for instance, the unification of States now constantly occurring. One small nation after another is swallowed up by another to magnify its strength and importance, and thus the great empires of the world become colossal powers. But it is observable that the process of unification leaves untouched the vitality and the persistency of race. You have only to turn to Great Britain and to Austria to verify this statement. In both nations we see the intensity of race cohesion, and at the same time the process of unification. Indeed, on all sides, in Europe, we see the consolidation of States; and at the same time the integration of race: Nature and Providence thus developing that principle of unity which binds the universe, and yet at the same time manifesting that conserving power which tends everywhere to fixity of type. And this reminds us of the lines of Tennyson:

> Are God and nature, then, at strife,
> That nature lends such evil dreams?
> So careful of the type she seems,
> So careless of the single life.

Hence, when a race once seats itself permanently in a land it is almost as impossible to get rid of it as it is to extirpate a plant that is indigenous to its soil. You can drive out a family from a community. You can rid yourself of a clan or a single tribe by expulsion. You can swallow up by amalgamation a simple emigrant people.

But when a RACE, *i. e.*, a compact, homogeneous population of one blood, ancestry, and lineage — numbering, perchance, some eight or ten millions — once enters a land and settles therein as its home and heritage, then occurs an event as fixed and abiding as the rooting of the Pyrenees in Spain or the Alps in Italy.

The race-problem, it will thus be seen, cannot be settled by extinction of race. No amalgamating process can eliminate it. It is not a carnal question — a problem of breeds, or blood, or lineage.

And even if it were, amalgamation would be an impossibility. How can any one persuade seven or eight millions of people to forget the ties of race? No one could *force* them into the arms of another race. And even then it would take generations upon generations to make the American people homogeneous in blood and essential qualities. Thus take one single case: There are thirty millions of Negroes on the American *continent* (eight or more millions in the United States of America), and constantly increasing at an immense ratio. Nothing but the sheerest, haziest imagination can anticipate the future dissolution of this race and its final loss; and so, too, of the other races of men in America.

Indeed, the race-problem is a moral one. It is a question entirely of ideas. Its solution will come especially from the domain of principles. Like all the other great battles of humanity, it is to be fought out with the weapons of truth. The race-problem is a question of organic life, and it must be dealt with as an ethical matter by the laws of the Christian system. "As diseases of the mind are invisible, so must their remedies be."

And this brings me to the one vast question that still lingers, *i. e.*, the question of AMITY. Race-life is a permanent element in our system. Can it be maintained in peace? Can these races give the world the show of brotherhood and fraternity? Is there a moral remedy in this problem?

Such a state of concord is, we must admit, a rare sight, even in christendom. There is great friction between Celt and Saxon in Britain. We see the violence of both Russ and German against the Jew. The bitterness is a mutual one between Russia on the one hand and Bulgaria and the neighboring dependent principalities on the other, and France and Germany stand facing one another like great fighting cocks.

All this is by no means assuring, and hence we cannot dismiss this question in an off-hand and careless manner.

The current, however, does not set all one way. There is another aspect to this question.

Thus, the Norman and the Frank have lived together harmoniously for centuries; the Welsh, English, and Scotch in England; the Indian, the Spaniard, and Negro in Brazil, and people of very divergent lineage in Spain.

And now the question arises: What are the probabilities of amity in a land where exists such wide divergence of race as the Saxon on the one hand and the Negro on the other?

First of all, let me say that the social idea is to be entirely excluded from consideration. It is absolutely a personal matter, regulated by taste, condition, or either by racial or family affinities; and there it must remain undisturbed forever. The Jews in this land are sufficient for themselves. So are the Germans, the Italians, the Irish, and so are the Negroes. Civil and political freedom trench in no way upon the domestic state or social relations.

Besides, there is something ignoble in any man, any class, any race of men whining and crying because they cannot move in spheres where they are not wanted.

But, beyond the social range there should be no compromise; and this country should be agitated and even convulsed till the battle of liberty is won, and every man in the land is guaranteed fully every civil and political right and prerogative.

The question of equality pertains entirely to the two domains of civil and political life and prerogative.

Now, I wish to show that the probabilities tend toward the complete and entire civil and political equality of all the peoples of this land.

1st. Observe that this is the age of civil freedom. It has not as yet gained its fullest triumphs; neither yet has Christianity.

But it is to be observed in the history of man that, in due time, certain principles get their set in human society, and there is no such thing as successfully resisting them. Their rise is not a matter of chance or hap-hazard. It is God's hand in history. It is the providence of the Almighty, and no earthly power can stay it.

Such, pre-eminently, was the entrance of Christianity in the centre of the world's civilization, and the planting of the idea of human brotherhood amid the ideas in the laws and legislation of great nations. *That* was the seed from which have sprung all the great revolutions in thought and governmental policies during the Christian era. Its work has been slow, but it has been certain and unfailing. I cannot pause to narrate all its early victories. We will take a limited period. We will begin at the dawn of modern civilization, and note the grand achievements of the idea of Christian brotherhood.

It struck at the doctrine of the Divine Right of Kings, and mortally wounded it. It demanded the extinction of Feudalism, and it got it. It demanded the abolition of the Slave Trade, and it got it. It demanded the abolition of Russian Serfage, and it got it. It demanded the education of the masses, and it got it.

In the early part of the eighteenth century this principle of brotherhood sprouted forth into a grander and more consummate growth, and generated the spirit of democracy.

When I speak of the spirit of democracy I have no reference to that spurious, blustering, self-sufficient spirit which derides God and authority on the one hand, and crushes the weak and helpless on the other. The democratic spirit I am speaking of is that which upholds the doctrine of human rights; which demands honor to all men; which recognizes manhood in all conditions; which uses the State as the means and agency for the unlimited progress of humanity. This principle has its root in the Scriptures of God, and it has come forth in political society to stay! In the hands of man it has indeed suffered harm. It has been both distorted and exaggerated, and without doubt it needs to be chastised, regulated, and sanctified. But the democratic principle in its essence is of God, and in its normal state it is the consummate flower of Christianity, and is irresistible because it is the mighty breath of God.

It is democracy which has demanded the people's participation in government and the extension of suffrage, and it got it. It has demanded a higher wage for labor, and it has got it, and will get more. It has demanded the abolition of Negro slavery, and it has got it. Its present demand is the equality of man in the State, irrespective of race, condition, or lineage. The answer to this demand is the solution of the race-problem.

In this land the crucial test in the race-problem is the civil and political rights of the black man. The only question now remaining among us for the full triumph of Christian democracy is the equality of the Negro.

Nay, I take back my own words. It is NOT the case of the Negro in this land. It is the nation which is on trial. The Negro is only the touch-stone. By this black man she stands or falls.

If the black man cannot be free in this land, if he cannot tread with firmness every pathway to preferment and superiority, neither can the white man. "A bridge is never stronger than its weakest point."

> In nature's chain, whatever link you strike,
> Tenth or ten-thousandth, breaks the chain alike.

So compact a thing is humanity that the despoiling of an individual is an injury to society.

This nation has staked her existence on this principle of democracy in her every fundamental political dogma, and in every organic State document. The democratic idea is neither Anglo-Saxonism, nor Germanism, nor Hibernianism, but HUMANITY, and humanity can live when Anglo-Saxonism or any class of the race of man has perished. Humanity anticipated all human varieties by thousands of years, and rides above them all, and outlives them all, and swallows up them all!

If this nation is not truly democratic then she must die! Nothing is more destructive to a nation than an organic falsehood! This nation cannot live — this nation does not deserve to live — on the basis of a lie!

Her fundamental idea is democracy; and if this nation will not submit herself to the domination of this idea — if she refuses to live in the spirit of this creed — then she is already doomed, and she will certainly be damned.

But neither calamity, I ween, is her destiny.

The democratic spirit is of itself a prophecy of its own fulfillment. Its disasters are trivialities; its repulses only temporary. In this nation the Negro has been the test for over 200 years. But see how far the Negro has traveled this time.

In less than the lifetime of such a man as the great George Bancroft, observe the transformation in the status of the Negro in this land. When *he* was a child the Negro was a marketable commodity, a beast of the field, a chattel in the shambles, outside of the pale of the law, and ignorant as a pagan.

Nay, when I was a boy of 13, I heard the utterance fresh from the lips of the great J. C. Calhoun, to wit, that if he could find a Negro who knew the Greek syntax he would then believe that the Negro was a human being and should be treated as a man.

If he were living to-day he would come across scores of Negroes, not only versed in the Greek syntax, but doctors, lawyers, college students, clergymen, some learned professors, and *one* the author of a new Greek Grammar.

But just here the caste spirit interferes in this race-problem and declares: "You Negroes may get learning; you may get property; you may have churches and religion; but this is your limit! This is a white man's Government! No matter how many millions you may number, we Anglo-Saxons are to rule!" This is the edict constantly hissed in the Negro's ear, in one vast section of the land.

Let me tell you of a similar edict in another land:

Some sixty years ago there was a young nobleman, an undergraduate at Oxford University, a youth of much talent, learning, and political ambition; but, at the same time, he was *then* a foolish youth! His patrician spirit rose in bitter protest against the Reform Bill of that day, which lessened the power of the British aristocracy and increased the suffrages of the Commons. He was a clever young fellow, and he wrote a brilliant poem in defense of his order, notable, as you will see, for its rhythm, melody, and withal for its — silliness! Here are two lines from it:

> Let Laws and Letters, Arts and Learning die;
> But give us still our old Nobility.

Yes, let everything go to smash! Let civilization itself go to the dogs, if only an oligarchy may rule, flourish, and dominate!

We have a blatant provincialism in our own country, whose only solution of the race-problem is the eternal subjection of the Negro, and the endless domination of a lawless and self-created aristocracy.

Such men forget that the democratic spirit rejects the factious barriers of caste, and stimulates the lowest of the kind to the very noblest ambitions of life. They forget that nations are no longer governed by races, but by ideas. They forget that the triumphant spirit of democracy has bred an individualism which brooks not the restraints of classes and aristocracies. They forget that, regardless of "Pope, Consul, King," or oligarchy, this same spirit of democracy lifts up to place and power her own agents for the rule of the world; and brings to the front, now a Dane as King of Greece, and now a Frenchman as King of Sweden; now a Jewish D'Israeli as Prime Minister of England, and now a Gallatin and a Schurz as cabinet ministers in America. They forget that a Wamba and a Gurth in one generation, whispering angry discontent in secret places, become, by the inspiration of democracy, the outspoken Hampdens and Sydneys of another. They forget that, as letters ripen and education spreads, the "Sambos" and "Pompeys" of to-day will surely develop into the Touissants and the Christophes, the Wards and the Garnets of the morrow, champions of their race and vindicators of their rights. They forget that democracy, to use the words of De Tocqueville, "has severed every link of the chain" by which aristocracy had fixed every member of the community, "from the peasant to the king."*

They forget that the Church of God is in the world; that her mission is, by the Holy Ghost, "to take the weak things of the world to confound the mighty," "to put down the mighty from their seats, and to exalt them of low degree;" that now, as in all the ages, she will, by the Gospel, break up tyrannies and useless dynasties, and lift up the masses to nobleness of life, and exalt the humblest of men to excellence and superiority.

Above all things, they forget that "the King invisible, immortal, eternal" is upon the throne of the universe; that thither caste, and bigotry, and race-hate can never reach; that He is everlastingly committed to the interests of the oppressed; that He is constantly sending forth succors and assistances for the rescue of the wronged and injured; that He brings all the forces of the universe to grind to powder all the enormities of earth, and to rectify all the ills of humanity, and so hasten on the day of universal brotherhood.

By the presence and the power of that Divine Being all the alienations and disseverances of men shall be healed; all the race-problems of this land easily be solved, and love and peace prevail among men.

In an undated Thanksgiving sermon preserved in the private papers of Crummell, the author reaffirmed his faith in the power of religious sentiment as a remedy to the race problem in the United States. After admonishing his parishioners that an attempt to answer slanderous charges made by bigoted whites would be "a useless expenditure of both your force and your feelings," he reminded them that there would be a "providential advance" of those blacks who were willing to work, pray, and place their trust in God.[33]

Standing squarely in the tradition of Crummell was another preacher Francis J. Grimké, who eulogized his predecessor for his persistent efforts to organize Christian ministers of all denominations into a common union based on the brotherhood of man.[34] Crummell's ecumenical approach appealed to Grimké, and stimulated him to deliver a sermon entitled, "Religion and Race

---

*"DEMOCRACY IN AMERICA," B. 2, Ch. 2.

Elevation."[35] Delivered at least five times before several church groups between 1906 and 1910, this sermon advanced the thesis that religion lies at the root of all racial problems in America. From this basic premise Grimké constructed the following rhetorical syllogism which summarized his logical position:

> Anything which is good for individuals and families is good for races.
>
> Religion is good for individuals and families.
>
> Religion, therefore, is good for races.

As Grimké worked toward his climax, he utilized an argument from the topic of less to greater. He first pointed out the need for industrial and higher education, bank accounts, and property holdings. But the intellectual and physical achievements, he then added, were secondary to religion as a "lever for lifting the race."[36]

Five of the six steps of the Toulmin Model[37] were present in Grimké's argument. Beginning with a statement of evidence, he proceeded to offer a warrant and support drawn from a wide variety of Biblical, historical, literary, and contemporary sources. In his claim that religion could elevate a race, however, he was not inclined to suggest a qualifier. His devotion to Christianity was derived from what he believed to be a self-evident premise that God, the Prime Mover of history, would reward those who placed their faith in him.

With undiminishing force, the religious assimilation arguments remained a vital rhetorical strategy for many black leaders in the first half of the twentieth century. Often, as we shall see in subsequent chapters, it was combined with other strategies. This was especially evident in the non-violent mass movement generated by Martin Luther King, Jr. in the 1950's and 1960's. But the modern spokesman who most nearly resembled Crummell and Grimké in offering Christianity as the overriding solution to problems of race was Howard Thurman, long-time minister of Marsh Chapel at Boston University.[38] Called by *Life Magazine,* in 1953,[39] one of the most impressive Protestant divines in America, Thurman combined searching content and a forceful, elegant, yet simple style with a slow, deliberate, and reverent delivery to captivate his audiences. He spoke as if he were communicating directly not only with his listeners but also God.[40] Consequently, he projected the image — at least to white members of his audience — of a man who had already found the key to race elevation in his own life.

The whole thrust of the strategy outlined in this section is epitomized in Thurman's message, "Good News for the Underprivileged." Presented at Bethune-Cookman College in Daytona Beach, Florida on May 26, 1959, it sought to demonstrate how the doctrine of Christianity fulfills the needs of "the poor, the disinherited, the dispossessed." Crucial to the position which Thurman wished to establish was his analogy of Christ as a poor member of a rejected minority group who understood through experience what it might mean to be a twentieth-century underprivileged man. In Christianity Thurman saw a force which could eliminate fear and insecurity and substitute in their place love and serenity. Observe how this strategy unfolds in the transcript of the address which follows.

Howard Thurman
Good News for the Underprivileged*

There is no more searching question that the individual Christian should ask himself than this: What is the message, the good news, that Christianity has to give to the poor, the disinherited, the dispossessed? In seeking an answer certain basic historical facts must be taken into account. First, Christianity is an historical faith, the result of a movement that was started in time, by an individual located in history. Setting aside for the moment all metaphysical and theological considerations, simply stated, this individual was a Jew. That mere fact is arresting. Did it simply happen that as a result of some accidental collocation of atoms, this human being came into existence so conditioned and organized within himself that he was a perfect instrument for the embodiment of a set of ideals of such alarming potency that they were capable of changing the calendar, redirecting the thought of the world, and placing a new sense of the rhythm of life in a weary nerve-broken civilization? Or was there something basic in the great womb of the people out of which he sprang that made of him the logical founding of a long development of race experience, ethical in quality and spiritual in tone? Doubtless there is widespread agreement with the latter position.

He was a poor Jew — so poor that his family could not afford a lamb for the birth presentation to the Lord, but had to secure doves instead (Leviticus 12.8). Is it too daring to suggest that in his poverty he was the symbol of the masses of men so that he could truly be Son of Man more naturally and accurately than if he had been a rich Jew?

As a poor Jew, Jesus was a member of a minority race, underprivileged and to a great degree disinherited. The Jews were not citizens of the Roman

---

*From Roy Hill, *Rhetoric of Racial Revolt* (Denver: The Golden Bell Press 1964), pp. 258-65. This sermon was delivered on May 26, 1959 in Daytona Beach, Florida.

Empire and hence were denied the rights and privileges such citizenship guaranteed. They were a captive group, but not enslaved.

There were exceptions. The first great creative interpreter of the Christian religion was a Jew, but a Roman citizen. This fact is instructive in enabling us to understand the psychology of this flaming, mystic tent-maker with his amazing enthusiasm. It is demanding too much of human nature to expect that a man who was by blood and ties deeper than blood — religion — a member of a despised group, could overcome that fact and keep it from registering in the very ground of his underlying interpretation of the meaning of existence. No matter where Paul happened to be located within the boundaries of the then all inclusive Roman Empire, he could never escape the consciousness of his citizenship. Whenever he was being beaten by a mere Roman soldier, doubtless hired to be the instrument of discipline and imperialism of the Empire, he knew that in the name of the Emperor he could demand the rights of citizenship of the Empire. He could appeal to Caesar in his own right and be heard. It is to his great credit and a decided tribute to the "fragrance of Christ," of which he called himself the essence, that he did not resort to this more frequently. But there it stands, a distinguishing mark setting him off from his group in no uncertain fashion. Do we wonder then that he could say: "Every subject must obey the government authorities, for no authority exists apart from God, the existing authorities have been constituted of God, hence any one who resists authority is opposing the divine order, and the opposition will bring judgment on themselves . . . If you want to avoid being alarmed at the government authorities lead an honest life, and you will be commended for it; the magistrate is God's servant for your benefit. . . . You must be obedient, therefore, not only to avoid the divine vengeance but as a matter of conscience, for the same reason that you pay taxes. Since magistrates are God's offering bent upon the maintenance of order and authority (Romans 13). Or again: "Slaves, be obedient to those who are your masters, saidth the Lord, with reverence and trembling, with singleness of heart, as to Christ himself" (Ephesians 6.5). Other familiar references could be quoted. Why Paul could feel this way is quite clear, when we remember that he was a Jew — yes, but a free Jew. But Jesus was not a free Jew. If a Roman soldier kicked Jesus into a Galilean ravine, it was merely a Jew in the ravine. He could not appeal to Caesar. Jesus was compelled to expand the boundaries of his citizenship out beyond the paltry political limitations of a passing Empire, and establish himself as a Lord of Life, the Son of God, who caused his sun to shine upon Roman and Jew, free and bond. The implications of his insight had to be worked out on a narrow stage in the agonizing realities of the struggle of his people against an over-arching might power — the Roman Empire. Christianity, in its social genesis, seems to me to have been a technique of survival for a disinherited minority.

The meaning of his public commitment in the little Nazareth synagogue, when he felt himself quickened into dedication by the liquid words of the prophet of Deutero-Isaiah, is much to the point:

The Spirit of the Lord is upon me:
  For he has consecrated me to preach the gospel to
    the poor,
He has sent me to proclaim release for captives
And recovery of sight for the blind, to set free the
    oppressed,
To proclaim the Lord's year of favor. (Moffatt.)

What, then, is the gospel that this underprivileged One would proclaim to the poor and the disinherited? The first demand it makes is that fear should be uprooted and destroyed, so that the genuine power of the dominant group may not be magnified or emphasized. Fear is the lean, hungry hound of hell that rarely ever leaves the track of the dispossessed.

The dispossessed are in minority, sometimes a minority as to numbers, always a minority as to economic power, but even then, it is a matter of playing one element of the powerful over against the other. Because of the insecure political and economic position of the dispossessed, they are least able to protect themselves against violence and coercion on the part of the powerful. The fear of death is ever present. Men with healthy minds and fairly adequate philosophies do not fear death as an orderly process in the scheme of life. But it is exceedingly difficult for individuals to accommodate themselves to cataclysmic death at the hands of other men, not nature, without associating it with some lofty ideal or great cause. This is the lot of the dispossessed. Without a moment's notice any one of them may be falsely accused, tried, sentenced without adequate defense and certainly without hope of justice. This is true because the dispossessed man is without political and economic status as a psychological fact, whatever the idea of the state may specify to the contrary.

Fear becomes, therefore, a safety valve which provides for a release of certain tensions that will ordinarily be released in physical resistance. Physical resistance is almost always suicidal, because of a basic lack in the tools of violence and the numbers to use them. Fear is a natural defense because it acts as a constant check on the activities which may result in clashes and subsequent reprisals. Psychologically, it makes certain costly errors impossible for the individual and thereby becomes a form of normal insurance against violence. But it disorganizes the individual from within. It strikes continually at the basic ground of his self-estimate, and by so doing makes it impossible for him to live creatively and to function effectively even within the zones of agreement.

Religion undertakes to meet this situation in the life of the dispossessed by seeking to establish for the individual a transcending basis of security which locates its center in the very nature of life. Stated in conventional religious terminology, it assures the individual that he is a child of God. This faith, this confidence, this affirmation has a profound effect upon the individual's self-estimate. It assures him of a basic status that his environment cannot quite undermine. "Fear not, those who can kill the body, but rather fear him who can destroy both soul and body," says Jesus. To say that this is merely a defense mechanism is not to render it invalid. Granted that it may be, although I do not think so, the practical results of such a conception are rich and redemptive.

This kind of self-estimate makes for an inner-togetherness, carrying within it the moral obligation to keep itself intact. It gives the inner life a regulation that is not conditioned by external forces. In its most intensified form it makes of men martyrs and saints. Operating on the lower reaches of experience, it gives to them a wholeness, and a simple but terrible security that renders fear of persons and circumstances ridiculous.

Again, this kind of relaxation at the center of life, growing out of a healthy self-estimate, gives to the individual an objectivity and detachment which enable him to seek fresh and unsuspecting ways for defeating his environment. "Behold, I send you out as lambs among wolves, you must be wise as serpents and as harmless as doves." Often these are things on the horizon that point logically to a transformation of society, especially for the underprivileged, but he cannot cooperate with them because he is spiritually and intellectually confused. He mistakes fear for caution and caution for fear. Now, if his mind is free and his spirit unchained, he can work intelligently and courageously for a new day. Yes, with great calmness and relaxation, as sons of God, the underprivileged may fling their defiance into the teeth of circumstances as they work out their salvation with fear and trembling as to God.

Religion also insists upon basic sincerity and genuineness as to attitude and character. Let your words be yes and no; you must be clear and transparent, and of no harm to any one; have your motive so single that your purpose is clear and distinct — such are the demands of religion.

This emphasis in Christianity creates the most difficult problem for the weak. It is even more difficult than the injunction to love your enemies. This is true because it cuts the nerve of the most powerful defense that the weak have against the strong — deception. In the world of nature, the weak survive because in the regular process of natural selection ways of deceiving the enemy have been determined upon and developed. Among some lower animals and birds the techniques are quite uncanny. The humble cuttlefish is supplied with a tiny bag of sepia fluid, and when beset by an enemy he releases the fluid into the water, making it turn murky and cloudy. Under the cover of this smoke screen he disappears, to the utter confusion of his enemy.

Among many American Negroes, self-deception has been developed into an intricate subtle defense mechanism. This deception is often worked out with deliberate unerring calculation. A classic example is to be found in the spiritual, "All God's Chillun." The slave heard his master's minister talk about heaven as the final abode of those who had lived the good life. Naturally, the terror of his present existence made him seek early to become a candidate for a joyous to-morrow, under a very different order of existence. Knowing how hard and fast the lines were drawn between him and his master in this world, he decided that there must be two heavens; but no, for there is but one God. Then an insight occurred to him. While on earth, his master was having his heaven; when he died, he would have his hell. The slave was having his hell now; when he died, he would have his heaven. As he worked the next day chopping cotton, he sang to his fellow-slave: "I got shoes, you got shoes, all God's chillun got shoes (pointing to the rest of the slaves); when we get to heaven we're goin' to put on our shoes, and shout all over God's heaven. (No lines, no slave row there.) But everybody talking 'bout heaven (pointing to the big house where the master lives) ain't goin' there."

There are three possible solutions to the dilemma of genuineness as the underprivileged man faces it. First, deliberate deception and a naive confidence that God will understand the tight place in which the individual is caught and be merciful. It is needless to point out what such a course may do to the very foundation of moral values. Traffic along this avenue leads to the quicksand of complete moral breakdown and ineffectiveness. The second possibility is an open frankness and honesty of life projecting itself in a world-society built upon subterfuge and deceit. It is the way that is taken by the rare spirit in response to the highest demands of his nature without regard to consequences; for the average individual completely outside of the range of his powers as yet developed. It will mean stretching himself out of shape for the sake of ends that are neither clear nor valid. The third means accepting an attitude of compromise. The word is a bad one. No man can live in a society of which he does not approve without some measure of compromise. The good man is one who often with studied reflection seeks to reduce steadily to a vanishing point the areas of compromise without and within. The third attitude stated categorically is, absoluteness as to the ideal; compromise in achievement. This means that the battle must be fought to the limit of one's power in areas not fundamental to one's self-estimate and integrity. A line must be drawn beyond which the underprivileged man cannot go in compromising. Religion, with its cardinal virtue, sincerity, inspires the individual to become increasingly aware of, and sensitive to, the far-reaching significance of many of his simplest deeds, making it possible for him to act, in time, as though his deeds were of the very essence of the eternal. This type of action inspires courage and makes for genuineness at increasingly critical points. He is made to know that out of the heart are the issues of life and that life is its own restraint. With an insight overmastering and transcending, he becomes spiritually and practically convinced that vengeance belongeth to God. It becomes clear to him that there are some things in life that are worse than death.

The third demand that religion makes upon the underprivileged is that they must absorb violence directed against them by the exercise of love. No demand has been more completely misused. The keenest discrimination is quite necessary in the exercise of this prerogative of the spirit. It belongs in the same category as grace, the outpouring of unasked for and unobligated kindness without chartering it on the basis of objective merit. For the under-privileged man this often seems to mean cowardice and treason to his own highest group and personal interest. This particular emphasis of Christianity has many times been used by the exploiters of the weak to keep them submissive and subservient. For the man of power to tell the powerless to love is like the Zulu adage which says: "Full belly child says to empty belly child, be of good cheer!"

In examining the basic roots of the concept there are revealed three elements which are fundamental. Love always implies genuine courage. It is built upon an assumption of individual spiritual freedom that knows not the limitations of objective worthiness and merit. It means acting contrary to the logical demands of objective worthiness and character — hence the exercise of a kind of bold power, vast and overwhelming!

It means the exercise of a discriminatory understanding which is based upon the inherent worth of the other, unpredictable in terms of external achievement. It says, meet people where they are and treat them as if they were where they ought to be. Here we are dealing with something more than the merely formal and discursive, rational demand. It is the functioning of a way of knowing that Paul aptly describes as "having a sense of what is vital." Love of this sort places a crown over the head of another who is always trying to grow tall enough to wear it. In religion's profoundest moments it ascribes to God this complete prerogative.

It widens the foundations of life so that one's concept of self increasingly includes a larger number of other individual units of life. This implies the dramatic exercise of simple, direct, thoroughgoing imaginativeness rooted in an experience of life as one totality. Years ago, I encountered this quotation: "The statement, 'know thyself', has been taken more mystically from the statement, 'thou hast seen thy brother, thou hast seen thy God'."

In this third demand religion gives to the underprivileged man no corner for individual hatred and isolation. In complete confidence it sends him forth to meet the enemy upon the highway; to embrace him as himself, understanding his limitations and using to the limit such discipline upon him as he has discovered to be helpful in releasing and purifying his own spirit.

Only the underprivileged man may bring the message to the underprivileged. No other can without the penalty of the Pharisee. Jesus, the underprivileged One of Palestine, speaks his words of power and redemption across the ages to all the disinherited:

> Come to me, all who are laboring and burdened,
> And I will refresh you.
> Take my yoke upon you and learn from me, for I am
>   gentle and humble in heart, and you will find
>   your souls refreshed,
> My yoke is kindly and my burden light.

ASSIMILATION BASED UPON SELF-RELIANCE

Dependence upon God and church as an effective means of achieving identity, equality, and freedom was not the only rhetorical strategy of assimilation used by black Americans. Equally appealing was another approach based upon the concept of self-reliance. As important as a man's need for divine help may be, the proponents of the philosophy of self-reliance held that it was perhaps less significant than the need for personal morality, education, initiative, and confidence in one's own ability to generate solutions for his problems. With this point of view, they found it easy to turn to the ancient cardinal virtues and to the nineteenth-century doctrine of rugged individualism. They saw in Plato's four canons of virtue — courage, temperance, wisdom, and justice[41] — a source of energy and power that could make the goal of assimilation a reality rather than a mere potentiality. Similarly, they felt that if these virtues were reinforced by boundless personal industry, they could quicken the achievement of the goal.

One of the first people to use, in public, the appeal to self-reliance was the popular lecturer, Maria W. Stewart.[42] In an address presented before the African-American Female Intelligence Society of Boston in April, 1832, she reminded her auditors of their low esteem: "We this day are considered as one of the most degraded races upon the face of the earth."[43] She then suggested that, "under such unfortunate circumstances our women in particular cannot sit on folded hands any longer and view with indifference and cowardice the lack of friendship and love that divides our people. We would do well," she concluded, "to emulate the noble spirit which in earlier years had epitomized the historic struggle for freedom of the Greeks, French, Poles, and Russians."

In February of the following year, Maria Stewart, in a speech delivered at the African Masonic Hall in Boston, spoke with still greater candor about the failure of black Americans to exemplify the cardinal virtues of courage and wisdom.[44] Motivated by what she described as a "holy indignation," she challenged her listeners to seek improvement through knowledge and courage.

> I would ask, is it blindness of mind, or stupidity of soul, or the want of education, that has caused our men who are 60 or 70 years of age, never to let their voices be heard nor their hands be raised in behalf of their color? Or has it been for the fear of offending the whites? If it has, O ye fearful ones, throw off your fearfulness, and come forth in the name of the Lord, and in the strength of the God of Justice, and make yourselves useful and active members in society; for they admire a noble and patriotic spirit in others — and should they not admire it in us?[45]

These initial remarks served only as a preface to the aggressive charges that were to follow. With a finger of blame pointed toward the male members of her race, she depicted their shortcomings in strong terms couched in the form of rhetorical questions.

> Have the sons of Africa no souls? feel they no ambitious desires? shall the chains of ignorance forever confine them? shall the insipid appellation of "clever negroes," or "good

creatures," any longer content them? Where can we find amongst ourselves the man of science, or a philosopher, or an able statesman, or a counsellor at law? . . . Where are our lecturers on natural history, and our critics in useful knowledge? . . . . Where is the man that has distinguished himself in these modern days by acting wholly in the defence of African rights and liberty.[46]

In her closing plea, Mrs. Stewart called for a Spartan life free of the corrupting influences of gambling, dancing, and intemperance. A daily program of self-denial, she observed, not only would please God and ennoble the human spirit, it would enlarge the opportunity of blacks to assimilate into an American society which, for too long, had been controlled by whites.

Maria Stewart's faith in self-reliance and virtue as a method of removing the barriers to integration was shared by other spokesmen who also rejected any practices that might hamper the development of a strong character and dynamic initiative. Of particular concern to many leaders throughout the nineteenth century was the problem of drinking. The evidence these orators and essayists accumulated through observation, experience, and reading convinced them that alcohol weakened man's capacity for reflective thought and impaired his health. They further held that while all excessive drinkers risked these general harms, the black American who practiced intemperance faced three additional dangers. First, he might provide support for prejudiced whites who believed in the stereotype that blacks would happily sacrifice full equality and meaningful labor on the altar of pleasure and leisure. Second, he could destroy his ambition and pride — perhaps the most essential traits needed by any race that seeks to raise its status. Finally, the cost of maintaining such a damaging habit was prohibitive for those who were economically disadvantaged.

These beliefs stimulated considerable interest in the temperance movement that developed in the nineteenth century. Black rhetoricians often joined the temperance societies, carried announcements of the major meetings of these organizations in their journals, and delivered lectures on the subject at various special conferences and conventions. In 1832, for example, one year after the rise of the formal anti-slavery movement, *The Liberator* reprinted an address presented by Alexander Deblois "before the Temperance Society of the people of color, of New Haven, Connecticut."[47]

In subsequent years, the number of these reform speeches increased. As the century drew to a close, the message of temperance had assumed the form of a national crusade. The lecture of Francis Grimké constituted a peak in this trend. During the period from July, 1898 to May, 1902, he delivered a lecture, "Temperance and the Negro Race," to audiences in Virginia, Alabama, South Carolina, and Washington, D.C.[48] Early in this widely publicized speech Grimké set the stage for his attack on alcohol by outlining briefly the poverty, moral degradation, and excessive mortality of the members of his race. In the light of these facts, he then asked: "What attitude should we assume on the subject of temperance?" The answer to this question already had been determined by his largely sympathetic audience. Nevertheless, Grimké painstakingly proceeded to buttress his thesis by citing supporting data derived from the Bible, literature, secular testimony, statistics, and examples. From these appeals directed primarily to the understanding, he moved to an emotional climax, calling for recruits, who would serve the cause "until the principle of total abstinence is inscribed upon the doorposts of every Negro home, church, and school-house throughout the land."[49]

Quite clearly Grimké and his predecessors had seized upon temperance and, at times, abstinence as a strategy to challenge black Americans to cultivate an attitude of self-reliance and an ambition which would be grounded in pride. If the policy seemed overly austere and demanding, it had the liberalizing purpose of attempting to free blacks from those habits which could in any way hinder their quest for freedom.

During the years separating the lectures of Maria Stewart and the temperance sermons of Francis Grimké, other speakers and writers occasionally used the message of self-reliance. Not the least of these communicators were Frederick Douglass and Booker T. Washington. Notwithstanding the fact that Douglass, as we shall note later, was more closely identified with a rhetoric of assimilation based upon legislative and judicial principles of democracy, he strove to help black Americans to see better versions of themselves.[50] He tried to do this by describing their potential and challenging them to test the value of virtues such as personal worth and initiative. As an assimilationist, he acknowledged his appreciation to thoughtful and sympathetic whites, but argued that, in the final analysis, blacks must be primarily responsible for elevating their own condition. He urged blacks to eliminate apathy, seek diligently to strengthen their character, use their large and influential churches located in major northern cities as vehicles to disseminate the doctrine of equality, and plant the seed for future advancement by establishing a program to educate their children. Observe how this theme was developed in 1848 in the following editorial, entitled "What are the Colored People Doing for Themselves?"

Frederick Douglass
*What are the Colored People Doing for Themselves?**

The present is a time when every colored man in the land should bring this important question home to his own heart. It is not enough to know that white men and women are nobly devoting themselves to our cause; we should know what is being done among ourselves. That our white friends have done, and are still doing, a great and good work for us, is a fact which ought to excite in us sentiments of the profoundest gratitude; but it must never be forgotten that when they have exerted all their energies, devised every scheme, and done all they can do in asserting our rights, proclaiming our wrongs, and rebuking our foes, their labor is lost — yea, worse than lost, unless we are found in the faithful discharge of our anti-slavery duties. If there be one evil spirit among us, for the casting out of which we pray more earnestly than another, it is that lazy, mean and cowardly spirit, that robs us of all manly self-reliance, and teaches us to depend upon others for the accomplishment of that which we should achieve with our own hands. Our white friends can and are rapidly removing the barriers to our improvement, which themselves have set up; but the main work must be commenced, carried on, and concluded by ourselves. While in no circumstances should we undervalue or fail to appreciate the self-sacrificing efforts of our friends, it should never be lost sight of, that our destiny, for good or for evil, for time and for eternity, is, by an all-wise God, committed to us; and that all the helps or hindrances with which we may meet on earth, can never release us from this high and heaven-imposed responsibility. It is evident that we can be improved and elevated only just so fast and far as we shall improve and elevate ourselves. We must rise or fall, succeed or fail, by our own merits. If we are careless and unconcerned about our own rights and interests, it is not within the power of all the earth combined to raise us from our present degraded condition.

> *Hereditary bondmen, know ye not*
> *Who would be free, themselves must strike the blow?*

We say the present is a time when every colored man should ask himself the question, What am I doing to elevate and improve my condition, and

---

*Frederick Douglass, "What are the Colored People Doing For Themselves?" *The North Star*, (July 14, 1848).

that of my brethren at large? While the oppressed of the old world are making efforts, by holding public meetings, putting forth addresses, passing resolutions and in various other ways making their wishes known to the world, and the working men of our own country are pressing their cause upon popular attention, it is a shame that we, who are enduring wrongs far more grievous than any other portion of the great family of man, are comparatively idle and indifferent about our welfare. We confess, with the deepest mortification, that out of the five hundred thousand free colored people in this country, not more than two thousand can be supposed to take any special interest in measures for our own elevation; and probably not more than fifteen hundred take, read and pay for an anti-slavery paper. We say this in sorrow, not in anger. It cannot be said that we are too poor to patronize our own press to any greater extent than we now do; for in popular demonstrations of odd-fellowship, free-masonry and the like, we expend annually from ten to twelve thousand dollars. If we put forth a call for a National Convention, for the purpose of considering our wrongs, and asserting our rights, and adopting measures for our mutual elevation and the emancipation of our enslaved fellow-countrymen, we shall bring together about *fifty;* but if we call a grand celebration of odd-fellowship, or free-masonry, we shall assemble, as was the case a few days ago in New York, from *four to five thousand* — the expense of which alone would be from seventeen to twenty thousand dollars, a sum sufficient to maintain four or five efficient presses, devoted to our elevation and improvement. We should not say this of odd-fellowship and free-masonry, but that it is swallowing up the best energies of many of our best men, contenting them with the glittering follies of artificial display, and indisposing them to seek for solid and important realities. The enemies of our people see this tendency in us, and encourage it. The same persons who would puff such demonstrations in the newspapers, would mob us if we met to adopt measures for obtaining our just rights. They see our weak points, and avail themselves of them to crush us. We are imitating the inferior qualities and examples of white men, and neglecting superior ones. We do not pretend that all the members of odd-fellow societies and masonic lodges are indifferent to their rights and the means of obtaining them; for we know the fact to be otherwise. Some of the best and brightest among us are numbered with those societies; and it is on this account that we make these remarks. We desire to see these noble men expending their time, talents and strength for higher and nobler objects than any that can be attained by the weak and glittering follies of odd-fellowship and free-masonry.

We speak plainly on this point, for we feel deeply. We have dedicated ourself, heart and soul, without reserve, to the elevation and improvement of our race, and have resolved to sink or swim with them. Our inmost soul is fired with a sense of the various forms of injustice to which we are daily subjected, and we must and will speak out against anything, within ourselves or our guilty oppressors, which may tend to prolong this reign of injustice. To be faithful to our oppressors, we must be faithful to ourselves; and shame on any colored man who would have us do otherwise. For this very purpose the *North Star* was established — that it might be as faithful to ourselves as to our oppressors. In this respect, we intend that it shall be different from most of its predecessors, and if it cannot be sustained in its high position, its death will be welcomed by us. But to return.

It is a doctrine held by many good men, in Europe as well as in America, that every oppressed people will gain their rights just as soon as they prove themselves worthy of them; and although we may justly object to the extent to which this doctrine is carried, especially in reference to ourselves as a people, it must still be evident to all that there is a great truth in it.

One of the first things necessary to prove the colored man worthy of equal freedom, is an earnest and persevering effort on his part to gain it. We deserve no earthly or heavenly blessing, for which we are unwilling to labor. For our part, we despise a freedom and equality obtained for us by others, and for which we have been unwilling to labor. A man who will not labor to gain his rights, is a man who would not, if he had them, prize and defend them. What is the use of standing a man on his feet, if, when we let him go, his head is again brought to the pavement? Look out of ourselves as we will — beg and pray to our white friends for assistance as much as we will — and that assistance may come, and come at the needed time; but unless we, the colored people of America, shall set about the work of our own regeneration and improvement, we are doomed to drag on in our present miserable and degraded condition for ages. Would that we could speak to every colored man, woman and child in the land, and, with the help of Heaven, we would thunder into their ears their duties and responsibilities, until a spirit should be roused among them, never to be lulled till the last chain is broken. — But here we are mortified to think that we are now speaking to tens where we ought to speak to thousands. Unfortunately, those who have the ear of our people on Sundays, have little sympathy with the anti-slavery cause, or the cause of progress in any of its phases. They are too frequently disposed to follow the beaten paths of their fathers. — The most they aim at, is to get to heaven when they die. They reason thus: Our fathers got along pretty well through the world without learning and without meddling with abolitionism, and we can do the same. — We have in our minds three pulpits among the colored people in the North, which have the power to produce a revolution in the condition of the colored people in this country in three years.

First among these, we may mention the great Bethel Church in Philadelphia. That church is the largest colored church in this Union, and from two to three thousand persons worship there every Sabbath. It has its branches in nearly all parts of the North and West, and a few in the South. It is surrounded by numerous little congregations in Philadelphia. Its ministers and bishops travel in all directions, and vast numbers of colored people belong to its branches all over the country. The Bethel pulpit in Philadelphia may be said to give tone to the entire denomination — "as goes large Bethel, so go the small Bethels throughout the Union." Here is concentrated the talent of the church, and here is the central and ruling power. — Now, if that pulpit would but speak the right word — the word for progress — the word for mental culture — encourage reading, and would occasionally take up contributions to aid those who are laboring for their elevation, as the white churches do to aid the colonization society to send us out of the country — there is no telling the good that would result from such labors. An entire change might soon take place in that denomination; loftier views of truth and duty would be presented; a nobler destiny would be opened up to them, and a deeper happiness would at once be enjoyed through all the ramifications of that church.

Similarly situated is the "Zion Church" in New York. That church exerts a controlling influence over the next largest colored denomination in this country. It, too, is a unit — has its branches in all directions in the North rather than in the South. Its ministers are zealous men, and some of them powerful preachers. There is no estimating the good these men might do, if they would only encourage their congregations to take an interest in the subject of reform.

The next church in importance, is St. Phillip's, in New York. This church is more important on account of the talent and respectability which it comprises, than for its numbers. Now, could the influence of these churches be enlisted in exciting our people to a constant and persevering effort at self-elevation, a joyful change would soon come over us.

What we, the colored people, want, is *character,* and this nobody can give us. It is a thing we must get for ourselves. We must labor for it. It is gained by toil — hard toil. Neither the sympathy nor the generosity of our friends can give it to us. It is attainable — yes, thank God, it is attainable. "There is gold in the earth, but we must dig it" — so with character. It is attainable; but we must attain it, and attain it each for himself. I cannot for you, and you cannot for me. — What matters it to the mass of colored people of this country that they are able to point to their Peningtons, Garnets, Remonds, Wards, Purvises, Smiths, Whippers, Sandersons, and a respectable list of other men of character, which we might name, while our general ignorance makes these men exceptions to our race? Their talents can do little to give us character in the eyes of the world. We must get character for ourselves, as a people. A change in our political condition would do very little for us without this. Character is the important thing, and without it we must continue to be marked for degradation and stamped with the brand of inferiority. With character, we shall be powerful. Nothing can harm us long when we get character. — There are certain great elements of character in us which may be hated, but never despised. Industry, sobriety, honesty, combined with intelligence and a due self-respect, find them where you will, among black or white, must be *looked up to* — can never be *looked down upon.* In their presence, prejudice is abashed, confused and mortified. Encountering this solid mass of living character, our vile oppressors are ground to atoms. In its presence, the sneers of a caricaturing press, the taunts of natural inferiority, the mischievous assertions of Clay, and fine-spun sophisms of Calhoun, are innoxious, powerless and unavailing. In answer to these men and the sneers of the multitude, there is nothing in the wide world half so effective as the presentation of a character precisely the opposite of all their representations. We have it in our power to convert the weapons intended for our injury into positive blessings. That we may sustain temporary injury from gross and general misrepresentation, is most true; but the injury is but temporary, and must disappear at the approach of light, like mist from the vale. The offensive traits of character imputed to us, can only be injurious while they are true of us. For a man to say that sweet is bitter — that right is wrong — that light is darkness — is not to injure the truth, but to stamp himself a liar; and the like is true when they impute to us that of which we are not guilty. We have the power of making our enemies slanderers, and this we must do by showing ourselves worthy and respectable men.

We are not insensible to the various obstacles that throng the colored man's pathway to respectability. Embarrassments and perplexities, unknown to other men, are common to us. Though born on American soil, we have fewer privileges than aliens. The school-house, the work-shop, counting-house, attorney's office, and various professions, are opened to them, but closed to us. This, and much more, is true. A general and withering prejudice — a malignant and active hate, pursues us even in the best parts of this country. But a few days ago, one of our best and most talented men — and he a *lame man,* having lost an important limb — was furiously hurled from a car on the Niagara & Buffalo Railroad, by a band of white ruffians, who claim impunity for their atrocious outrage on the plea that New York law does not protect the rights of colored against a company of white men, and the sequel has proved them right; for the case, it appears, was brought before the grand jury, but that jury found no bill. We cannot at this time dwell on this aspect of the subject.

The fact that we are limited and circumscribed, ought rather to incite us to a more vigorous and persevering use of the elevating means within our reach, than to dishearten us. The means of education, though not so free and open to us as to white persons, are nevertheless at our command to such an extent as to make education possible; and these, thank God, are increasing. Let us educate our children, even though it should us subject to a coarser and scantier diet, and disrobe us of our few fine garments. "For the want of knowledge we are killed all the day." Get wisdom — get understanding, is a peculiarly valuable exhortation to us, and the compliance with it is our only hope in this land. — It is idle, a hollow mockery, for us to pray to God to break the oppressor's power, while we neglect the means of knowledge which will give us the ability to break this power. — God will help us when we help ourselves. Our oppressors have divested us of many valuable blessings and facilities for improvement and elevation; but, thank heaven, they have not yet been able to take from us the privilege of being honest, industrious, sober and intelligent. We may read and understand — we may speak and write — we may expose our wrongs — we may appeal to the sense of justice yet alive in the public mind, and by an honest, upright life, we may at last wring from a reluctant public the all-important confession, that we are men, worthy men, good citizens, good Christians, and ought to be treated as such.

Douglass' views on self respect and self-reliance had a profound effect on Booker T. Washington, who became the most celebrated

black leader in America from 1876 to 1915. John Hope Franklin summarizes Washington's influence in the following passage:

> Despite the fact that there were Negroes who vigorously op-
> posed Washington's leadership and that there were some valid
> exceptions to his program for the salvation of the Negro, he
> was unquestionably the central figure—the dominant person-
> ality—in the history of the Negro down to his death in 1915.
> The vast majority of the Negroes acclaimed him as their leader
> and few whites ventured into the matter of race relations with-
> out his counsel. . . . Washington's influence, sometimes for
> better and sometimes for worse, was so great that there is con-
> siderable justification in calling the period, "The Age of Booker
> T. Washington."[51]

To gain a proper perspective on Washington's philosophy and rhetorical strategy, it is necessary to trace briefly the two ideologies which doubtlessly motivated his thinking. The first ideology found expression in the teachings and practice of John Chavis, an early nineteenth century free Negro who spent most of his career in North Carolina.

Chavis, whose first profession was that of a Presbyterian minister in Virginia, migrated to Raleigh, North Carolina where he became a successful teacher of both blacks and whites. Always zealous for the improvement of his race, he taught them what he believed to be the most up-to-date and practical theories of English grammar and spelling.[52] But his covert desire for full equality and freedom for the slaves was tempered by an overt recognition of the prejudice which permeated his locale. The strategy which he promulgated, therefore, adhered to a two step process. First, he sought to prove to the whites in Raleigh that he was the ablest teacher in the state and thereby worthy to instruct students of any race.[53] Second, he articulated his opposition to those highly controversial ideas which proved to be offensive to large segments of the population in the South. Consequently, he used what Richard Weaver called "the argument from circumstance" rather than "the argument from definition or the essential nature of things."[54] Chavis repudiated slavery in principle. Yet, he feared the doctrine of abolition because it was fraught with danger for the blacks. This fear led him to embrace a policy of accommodation which he expressed to his former pupil, Senator Willie P. Mangum of North Carolina in 1836.

> That slavery is a national evil no one doubts, but what is to be
> done? It exists and what can be done with it? All that can be

done, is to make the best of a bad bargain. For I am clearly of the opinion that immediate emancipation would be to entail the greatest earthly curse upon my brethren according to the flesh that can be conferred upon them especially in a Country like ours....[55]

Chavis knew that these words would produce dissonance in the minds of some of his peers. "I suppose if they knew I said this," he remarked, "they would be ready to take my life, but as I wish them well I feel no disposition to see them any more miserable than they are."[56]

Chavis' support of a doctrine of accommodation in the 1830's was not due to a belief that black Americans should be relegated to a position of second-class citizenship. Rather, it would appear he chose this strategy because he felt the exigencies in the rhetorical situation[57] demanded a response which would move the reactionary elements in the white power structure of North Carolina away from an attitude of extremism and toward an attitude of moderation.[58] He had come to believe that while accommodation might temporarily keep his people in bondage, it provided an appropriate setting in which education could flourish. The end result of this policy of self-reliance, he hoped, would be assimilation.

The recognition by black leaders, in the mid-nineteenth century, of the need for training in the skilled trades and agricultural arts was also significant in forming the political and social philosophy of Booker T. Washington. Frederick Douglass, an early proponent of this view, used his newspaper as a medium for conveying this message. In 1853, he urged: "Make your sons Mechanics and Farmers — not Waiters, Porters, and Barbers."[59] Douglass forcefully argued that it was wrong for parents to keep their children at home to assist in menial tasks, that the present haphazard system of labor led to excessive unemployment, and that unskilled service jobs held little hope for advancement. "Unless this condition is remedied," he added, "we will foster the twin evils that have plagued our race since the establishment of American slavery." In recommending the need for practical study and instruction, therefore, he warned: "He who omits to give his son a trade when he can do so, is guilty of degrading his own blood, and of perpetuating the degradation of his race."[60]

Douglass' conviction that practical education and skilled trades would help promote personal dignity and economic prosperity gained numerous converts. During the early days of the Reconstruction Period there were unmistakable signs pointing to new directions in education and economics which would be initiated on a grand scale. With the passage of the Morrill Act in 1860, the stage was set for the creation of land grant colleges that would instruct students in agriculture and technology. Moreover, successful eastern industrialists who stimulated the era of the gospel of wealth in the 1870's and 1880's saw an opportunity to help build a new South. It was against this background of renewed hope in the potential of free enterprise that Washington, as a young boy of sixteen in 1872, enrolled in Hampton Institute in Virginia. While there, he fell under the influence of the school's founder, General Samuel Chapman Armstrong, who taught his students "the value of acquiring land and homes, vocations and skills."[61] When Washington left Hampton he was convinced that blacks in order to be successful and free must be self-reliant and useful. When he went to Tuskegee in 1881, he built the institute around the concept of industrial education.

Washington, it would appear, was a product of his age. Caught up in a society which gave primacy to economic prosperity, he sought, according to August Meier, to apply the fruits of the gospel of wealth to the race problems of his time. Thus, he became an apostle of conservative pragmatism which stressed the need for blacks to make themselves useful to members of the white community so that they could share equally in the general prosperity and, most of all, secure their constitutional rights.[62] This they could do largely by themselves if they practiced thrift and industry, and demonstrated a Christian character.

On July 16, 1884 Washington defined the role of education in the struggle for improved racial relations. Addressing a meeting of the National Educational Association in Madison, Wisconsin, he argued that education was more important than pending civil rights legislation in integrating the races. There were, he said, enough men of good will in the South to solve the problem from within; therefore, he optimistically asserted that if blacks had good school teachers, an industrial and vocational curriculum, and adequate financial support, they would win acceptance through utility. With pride, he alluded to his students who used their minds and hands to pay for their schooling. This philosophy, expressed three years after he had founded Tuskegee Institute in Alabama, is so essential in understanding Washington's long range rhetorical strategy of self-reliance that the full text of the address follows.

Booker T. Washington

*The Educational Outlook in the South**

Mr. President, Ladies and Gentlemen:

Fourteen years ago it is said that Northern teachers, in the South for the purpose of teaching in colored schools, were frightened away by the whites from the town of Tuskegee, Alabama. Four years ago the Democratic members of the Alabama legislature from Tuskegee voluntarily offered and had passed by the General Assembly a bill, appropriating $2,000 annually to pay the salaries of teachers in a colored normal school to be located at Tuskegee. At the end of the first session of the school the legislature almost unanimously passed a second bill appropriating an additional $1,000 annually, for the same purpose. About one month ago one of the white citizens of Tuskegee who had at first looked on the school in a cold, distant kind of a way said to me, "I have just been telling the white people that the Negroes are more interested in education than we, and are making more sacrifices to educate themselves." At the end of our first year's work, some of the whites said, "We are glad that the Normal School is here because it draws people and makes labor plentiful." At the close of the second year, several said that the Normal School was beneficial because it increased trade, and at the close of the last session more than one said that the Normal School is a good institution, it is making the colored people in this state better citizens. From the opening of the school to the present, the white citizens of Tuskegee have been among its warmest friends. They have not only given of their money but they are ever ready to suggest and devise plans to build up the institution. When the school was making an effort to start a brick yard, but was without means, one of the merchants donated an outfit of tools. Every white minister in the town has visited the school and given encouraging remarks. When the school was raising money to build our present hall, it occurred to one of the teachers that it would be a good idea to call on the white ladies for contributions in the way of cakes etc., toward a fair. The result was that almost every lady, called on, gave something and the fair was made up almost entirely of articles given by these friends. A former slaveholder working on a Negro normal school building under a Negro master carpenter is a picture that the last few years have made possible.

Any movement for the elevation of the Southern Negro, in order to be successful, must have to a certain extent the coöperation of the Southern whites. They control government and own the property — whatever benefits the black man benefits the white man. The proper education of all the whites will benefit the Negro as much as the education of the Negro will benefit the whites. The Governor of Alabama would probably count it no disgrace to

---

*From E. Davidson Washington, *Selected Speeches of Booker T. Washington* (Garden City, N.Y.: Doubleday, Doran & Company, Inc., 1932) pp. 1-11. This speech was delivered on July 16, 1884 in Madison, Wisconsin.

ride in the same railroad coach with a colored man, but the ignorant white man who curries the Governor's horse would turn up his nose in disgust. The president of a white college in Tuskegee makes a special effort to furnish our young men work that they may be able to remain in school, while the miserable unlettered "brother in white" would say, "You can't learn a nigger anything." Brains, property, and character for the Negro will settle the question of civil rights. The best course to pursue in regard to the civil rights bill in the South is to let it alone; let it alone and it will settle itself. Good school teachers and plenty of money to pay them will be more potent in settling the race question than many civil rights bills and investigating committees. A young colored physician went into the city of Montgomery, Alabama, a few months ago to practise his profession — he was the first to professionally enter the ex-Confederate capital. When his white brother physicians found out by a six days' examination that he had brains enough to pass a better examination, as one of them said, than many of the whites had passed, they gave him a hearty welcome and offered their services to aid him in consultation or in any other way possible — and they are standing manfully up to their promise. Let there be in a community a Negro who by virtue of his superior knowledge of the chemistry of the soil, his acquaintance with the most improved tools and best breeds of stock, can raise fifty bushels of corn to the acre while his white neighbor only raises thirty, and the white man will come to the black man to learn. Further, they will sit down on the same train, in the same coach and on the same seat, to talk about it. Harmony will come in proportion as the black man gets something that the white man wants, whether it be of brains or of material. Some of the county whites looked at first with disfavor on the establishing of a normal school in Tuskegee. It turned out that there was no brick yard in the county; merchants and farmers wanted to build, but bricks must be brought from a distance or they must wait for one house to burn down before building another. The Normal School with student labor started a brick yard. Several kilns of bricks were burned; the whites came from miles around for bricks. From examining bricks they were led to examine the working of the school. From the discussion of the brick yard came the discussion of Negro education — and thus many of the "old masters" have been led to see and become interested in Negro education. In Tuskegee a Negro mechanic manufactures the best tinware, the best harness, the best boots and shoes, and it is common to see his store crowded with white customers from all over the county. His word or note goes as far as that of the whitest man.

I repeat for emphasis that any work looking towards the permanent improvement of the Negro South must have for one of its aims the fitting of him to live friendly and peaceably with his white neighbors both socially and politically. In spite of all talks of exodus, the Negro's home is permanently in the South: for coming to the bread-and-meat side of the question, the white man needs the Negro, and the Negro needs the white man. His home being permanently in the South, it is our duty to help him prepare himself to live there an independent, educated citizen.

In order that there may be the broadest development of the colored man and that he may have an unbounded field in which to labor, the two races must be brought to have faith in each other. The teachings of the Negro in various ways for the last twenty years have been rather too much to array him against his white brother than to put the two races in coöperation with each other. Thus Massachusetts supports the Republican party, because the Republican party supports Massachusetts with a protective tariff, but the Negro supports the Republican party simply because Massachusetts does. When the colored man is educated up to the point of reasoning that Massachusetts and Alabama are a long way apart and the conditions of life are very different, and if free trade enables my white neighbor across the street to buy his plows at a cheaper rate it will enable me to do the same thing, then will he be consulted in governmental questions. More than once have I noticed that when the whites were in favor of prohibition the blacks, led even by sober upright ministers, voted against it simply because the whites were in favor of it, and for that reason the blacks said that they knew it was a "Democratic trick." If the whites vote to levy a tax to build a schoolhouse, it is a signal for the blacks to oppose the measure, simply because the whites favor it. I venture the assertion that the sooner the colored man South learns that one political party is not composed of all angels and the other of all devils, and that all his enemies do not live in his own town or neighborhood, and all his friends in some distant section of the country, the sooner will his educational advantages be enhanced many fold. But matters are gradually changing in this respect. The black man is beginning to find out that there are those even among the Southern whites who desire his elevation. The Negro's new faith in the white man is being reciprocated in proportion as the Negro is rightly educated. The white brother is beginning to learn by degrees that all Negroes are not liars and chicken thieves. A former owner of seventy-five or one hundred slaves and now a large planter and merchant said to me a few days ago, "I can see every day the change that is coming about. I have on one of my plantations a colored man who can read and write and he is the most valuable man on the farm. In the first place I can trust him to keep the time of the others or with anything else. If a new style of plow or cotton planter is taken on the place, he can understand its construction in half the time that any of the others can."

My faith is that reforms in the South are to come from within. Southern people have a good deal of human nature. They like to receive the praise of doing good deeds, and they don't like to obey orders that come from Washington telling them that they must lay aside at once customs that they have followed for centuries, and henceforth there must be but one railroad coach, one hotel, and one schoolhouse for ex-master and ex-slave. In proof of my first assertion, the railroads in Alabama required colored passengers to pay the same fare as the whites, and then compelled the colored to ride in the smoking car. A committee of leading colored people laid the injustice of the matter before the railroad commissioners of Alabama, who at once ordered that within thirty days every railroad in the State should provide equal but separate accommodations for both races. Every prominent newspaper in the State pronounced it a just decision. Alabama gives $9,000 annually towards the support of colored normal schools. The last legislature increased the annual appropriation for free schools by $100,000, making the total annual appropriation over $500,000, and nearly half of this amount goes to colored schools, and I have for the first time to hear of any distinction being made between the races by any state offices in the distribution of this fund. Why, my friends, more pippins are growing in the South than crab apples, more roses than thorns.

Now, in regard to what I have said about the relations of the two races, there should be no unmanly cowering or stooping to satisfy unreasonable whims of Southern white men, but it is charity and wisdom to keep in mind the two hundred years' schooling in prejudice against the Negro which the ex-slaveholders are called upon to conquer. A certain class of whites South object to the general education of the colored man on the ground that when he is educated he ceases to do manual labor, and there is no evading the fact that much aid is withheld from Negro education in the South by the states on these grounds. Just here the great mission of

INDUSTRIAL EDUCATION

coupled with the mental comes in. It "kills two birds with one stone," viz.: secures the coöperation of the whites, and does the best possible thing for the black man. An old colored man in a cotton field in the middle of July lifted his eyes toward heaven and said, "De cotton is so grassy, de work is so hard, and de sun am so hot, I believe this darkey am called to preach." This old man, no doubt, stated the true reason why not a few enter school. Educate the black man, mentally and industrially, and there will be no doubt of his prosperity, for a race who has lived at all, and paid, for the last twenty years, twenty-five and thirty per cent interest on the dollar advanced for food, with almost no education, can certainly take care of itself when educated mentally and industrially.

The Tuskegee Normal School, located in the black belt of Alabama, with an ignorant, degraded Negro population of twenty-five thousand within a radius of twenty miles, has a good chance to see the direct need of the people; and to get a correct idea of their conditions one must leave the towns and go far out into the country, miles from any railroad, where the majority of the people live. They need teachers with not only trained heads and hearts, but with trained hands. Schoolhouses are needed in every township and country. The present wrecks of log cabins and bush harbors, where many of the schools are now taught, must be replaced by comfortable, decent houses. In many schoolhouses rails are used for seats, and often the fire is on the outside of the house, while teacher and scholars are on the inside. Add to this a teacher who can scarcely write his name and who is as weak mentally as morally, and you then have but a faint idea of the educational condition of many parts of the South. It is the work of Tuskegee, not to send into these places teachers who will stand off and tell the people what to do, or what ought to be done, but to send those who can take hold and show the people *how* to do. The blacksmiths, carpenters, brickmasons, and tinners, who learned their trades in slavery, are dying out, and slavery having taught the colored boy that labor is a disgrace, few of their places are being filled. The Negro now has a monopoly of the trades in the South, but he can't hold it unless the young men are taught trades while in school. The large number of educated loafers to be seen around the streets of our large cities furnishes another reason in favor of industrial education. Then the proud fop with his beaver hat, kid gloves, and walking cane, who has done no little to injure the cause of education South, by industrial training, would be brought down to something practical and useful. The Tuskegee Normal School, with a farm of five hundred acres, carpenter's shop, printing office, blacksmith's shop, and brick yard for boys, and a sewing department, laundry, flower gardening, and practical housekeeping for girls, is trying to do its part towards furnishing industrial training. We ask help for nothing that we can do for ourselves; nothing is bought that the students can produce. The boys raise the vegetables, have done the painting, made the brick, the chairs, the tables, the desks; have built a stable, a carpenter's shop, and a blacksmith's shop. The girls do the entire housekeeping, including the mending, ironing, and wasihng of the boys' clothes; besides they make many garments to sell.

The majority of the students are poor and able to pay but little cash for board; consequently the school keeps three points before it: first, to give the student the best mental training; secondly, to furnish him with labor that will be valuable to the school, and that will enable the student to learn something from the labor *per se;* thirdly, to teach the dignity of labor. A *chance* to help himself is what we want to give to every student; this is the chance that was given me ten years ago when I entered the Hampton Institute with but fifty cents in my pocket, and it is my only ambition in life to do my part in giving it to every other poor but worthy young man and woman.

As to morals, the Negro is slowly but surely improving. In this he has had no standard by which to shape his character. The masses in too many cases have been judged by their so-called leaders, who are as a rule ignorant, immoral preachers or selfish politicians. The number of these preachers is legion. One church near Tuskegee has a total membership of two hundred, and nineteen of these are preachers.

Poverty and ignorance have affected the black man just as they affect the white man. They have made him untruthful, intemperate, selfish, caused him to steal, to be cheated, and made the outcast of society, and he has aspired to positions which he was not mentally and morally capable of filling. But the day is breaking, and education will bring the complete light. The scales of prejudice are beginning to drop from the eyes of the dominant classes South, and through their clearer and more intelligent vision they are beginning to see and recognize the mighty truth that wealth, happiness, and permanent prosperity will only come in proportion as the hand, head, and heart of both races are educated and Christianized.

The year 1895, marked a historic date in the black American's campaign for identity and human rights. It was the year of Frederick Douglass' death and the widespread acclaim of Washington as the new symbol of freedom and eloquence among his race. Prior to this period, Washington had achieved recognition as the foremost black educator in the South and had attracted attention especially among important segments in the Negro community. But, he had not yet established a sufficient national forum to promulgate his doctrines. In September, he was confronted with an opportunity which was to dramatize his theories and alter his career. After considerable maneuvering among the leaders in charge, Washington received an invitation to speak at the Atlanta Exposition. The setting, the audience, and the speaker combined to produce a memorable event in the history of American public address. The occasion was the opening of the Atlanta Cotton States and International Exposition, and the listeners included members of both races. Washington, however, also spoke to a third group which was not present — the northern whites. The situation, he felt, demanded an address that could help resolve the aspirations, antagonisms, and suspicions of all three classes concerned. In attempting to fulfill what he admitted was "a difficult and at times puzzling task,"[63] he moved, observes C. Van Woodward, "with consummate diplomacy, trading renunciation for concession and playing sentiment against interest."[64] Washington highlighted the theme, "Cast down your bucket where you are," and declaimed, much to the satisfaction of many of his white audience: "In all things that are purely social we can be as separate as the fingers, yet one as the hand in all things essential to mutual progress."

Booker T. Washington
*Atlanta Exposition Address**

Mr. President and Gentlemen of the Board of Directors and Citizens:
    One third of the population of the South is of the Negro race. No enterprise seeking the material, civil, or moral welfare of this section can disregard

---

*From E. Davidson Washington, *Selected Speeches of Booker T. Washington* (Garden City, N.Y.: Doubleday, Doran & Company, Inc., 1932) pp. 169-74. This address was delivered on September, 1895 in Atlanta, Georgia.

this element of our population and reach the highest success. I but convey to you, Mr. President and Directors, the sentiment of the masses of my race when I say that in no way have the value and manhood of the American Negro been more fittingly and generously recognized than by the managers of this magnificent exposition at every stage of its progress. It is a recognition that will do more to cement the friendship of the two races than any occurrence since the dawn of our freedom.

Not only this, but the opportunity here afforded will awaken among us a new era of industrial progress. Ignorant and inexperienced, it is not strange that in the first years of our new life we began at the top instead of at the bottom; that a seat in Congress or the State Legislature was more sought than real estate or industrial skill; that the political convention or stump-speaking had more attraction than starting a dairy farm or truck garden.

A ship lost at sea for many days suddenly sighted a friendly vessel. From the mast of the unfortunate vessel was seen a signal: "Water, water; we die of thirst!" The answer from the friendly vessel at once came back: "Cast down your bucket where you are." A second time the signal, "Water, water; send us water!" ran up from the distressed vessel, and was answered: "Cast down your bucket where you are." And a third and fourth signal for water was answered. "Cast down your bucket where you are." The captain of the distressed vessel, at last heeding the injunction, cast down his bucket, and it came up full of fresh, sparkling water from the mouth of the Amazon River. To those of my race who depend upon bettering their condition in a foreign land, or who underestimate the importance of cultivating friendly relations with the Southern white man who is their next-door neighbor, I would say: "Cast down your bucket where you are" — cast it down in making friends, in every manly way, of the people of all races by whom we are surrounded.

Cast it down in agriculture, mechanics, in commerce, in domestic service, and in the professions. And in this connection it is well to bear in mind that whatever other sins the South may be called to bear, when it comes to business, pure and simple, it is in the South that the Negro is given a man's chance in the commercial world, and in nothing is this Exposition more eloquent than in emphasizing this chance. Our greatest danger is that in the great leap from slavery to freedom we may overlook the fact that the masses of us are to live by the productions of our hands, and fail to keep in mind that we shall prosper in proportion as we learn to dignify and glorify common labor, and put brains and skill into the common occupations of life; shall prosper in proportion as we learn to draw the line between the superficial and the substantial, the ornamental gew-gaws of life and the useful. No race can prosper till it learns that there is as much dignity in tilling a field as in writing a poem. It is at the bottom of life we must begin, and not at the top. Nor should we permit our grievances to overshadow our opportunities.

To those of the white race who look to the incoming of those of foreign birth and strange tongue and habits for the prosperity of the South, were I permitted, I would repeat what I say to my own race, "Cast down your bucket where you are." Cast it down among the eight million Negroes whose habits you know, whose fidelity and love you have tested in days when to have proved treacherous meant the ruin of your firesides. Cast down your bucket among these people who have without strikes and labor wars tilled your fields, cleared your forests, builded your railroads and cities, brought forth treasures from the bowels of the earth, and helped make possible this magnificent representation of the progress of the South. Casting down your bucket among my people, helping and encouraging them as you are doing on these grounds, and, with education of head, hand, and heart, you will find that they will buy your surplus land, make blossom the waste places in your fields, and run your factories. While doing this, you can be sure in the future, as in the past, that you and your families will be surrounded by the most patient, faithful, law-abiding, and unresentful people that the world has seen. As we have proved our loyalty to you in the past, in nursing your children, watching by the sick bed of your mothers and fathers, and often following them with tear-dimmed eyes to their graves, so in the future, in our humble way, we shall stand by you with a devotion that no foreigner can approach, ready to lay down our lives, if need be, in defense of yours, interlacing our industrial, commercial, civil, and religious life with yours in a way that shall make the interests of both races one. In all things that are purely social we can be as separate as the fingers, yet one as the hand in all things essential to mutual progress.

There is no defense or security for any of us except in the highest intelligence and development of all. If anywhere there are efforts tending to curtail the fullest growth of the Negro, let these efforts be turned into stimulating, encouraging, and making him the most useful and intelligent citizen. Effort or means so invested will pay a thousand per cent interest. These efforts will be twice blessed — "Blessing him that gives and him that takes."

There is no escape through law of man or God from the inevitable:

> The laws of changeless justice bind
> Oppressor with oppressed;
> And close as sin and suffering joined
> We march to fare abreast.

Nearly sixteen millions of hands will aid you in pulling the load upward, or they will pull, against you, the load downward. We shall constitute one third and more of the ignorance and crime of the South, or one third its intelligence and progress; we shall contribute one third to the business and industrial prosperity of the South, or we shall prove a veritable body of death, stagnating, depressing, retarding every effort to advance the body politic.

Gentlemen of the Exposition, as we present to you our humble effort at an exhibition of our progress, you must not expect overmuch. Starting thirty years ago with ownership here and there in a few quilts and pumpkins and chickens (gathered from miscellaneous sources), remember, the path that has led from these to the inventions and production of agricultural implements, buggies, steam engines, newspapers, books, statuary carving, paintings, the management of drugstores and banks, has not been trodden without contact with thorns and thistles. While we take pride in what we exhibit as a result of our independent efforts, we do not for a moment forget that our part in this exhibition would fall far short of your expectations but for the constant help that has come to our educational life, not only from the Southern states, but especially from Northern philanthropists, who have made their gifts a constant stream of blessing and encouragement.

The wisest among my race understand that the agitation of questions of social equality is the extremest folly, and that progress in the enjoyment of all the privileges that will come to us must be the result of severe and constant struggle rather than of artificial forcing. No race that has anything to contribute to the markets of the world is long, in any degree, ostracized. It is important and right that all privileges of the law be ours, but it is vastly more important that we be prepared for the exercise of those privileges. The opportunity to earn a dollar in a factory just now is worth infinitely more than the opportunity to spend a dollar in an opera house.

In conclusion, may I repeat that nothing in thirty years has given us more hope and encouragement, and drawn us so near to you of the white race, as this opportunity offered by the Exposition; and here bending, as it were, over the altar that represents the result of the struggles of your race and mine, both starting practically empty-handed three decades ago. I pledge that, in your effort to work out the great and intricate problem which God has laid at the doors of the South you shall have at all times the patient, sympathetic help of my race; only let this be constantly in mind, that while, from representations in these buildings of the product of field, of forest, of mine, of factory, letters, and art, much good will come, yet far above and beyond material benefits will be that higher good, that, let us pray God, will come in a blotting out of sectional differences and racial animosities and suspicions, in a determination to administer absolute justice, in a willing obedience among all classes to the mandates of law. This, coupled with our material prosperity will bring into our beloved South a new heaven and a new earth.

Washington's brief speech, which became known as the "Atlanta Compromise," produced an instantaneous effect. "Nothing has happened since Henry Grady's immortal speech before the New England Society in New York," reported James Creelman in the *World,* "that indicates so profoundly the spirit of the New South."[65] Moderates in the North and South hailed the address as a landmark event in racial relations and industrial development. Most black Americans who studied the message were not dismayed by Washington's rhetoric of accommodation. They seemed to accept the view that the best way to become assimilated in a society controlled by whites was to endorse a gospel of conservatism that stressed the worth of education, material progress, and patience. At least, they appeared content for the moment to remain silent.

The ascendancy of Washington increased steadily in the years following his Atlanta Exposition Address. By 1903 W. E. B. DuBois was able to say:

> Mr. Washington's cult has gained unquestioning followers, his work has wonderfully prospered, his friends are legion, and his enemies are confounded. Today he stands as the one recognized spokesman of his ten million fellows, and one of the most notable figures in a nation of seventy millions.[66]

But despite the warm praise he extended to his contemporary, DuBois cautiously but pointedly discussed the mistakes and limitations in Washington's approach. After criticizing Washington's failure to judge the white South discriminatingly, he questioned the wisdom of his policy that urged black people to give up "political power," "insistence on civil rights," and "higher education of Negro youth."[67] DuBois, in short, believed that Washington's overriding desire to placate the white South had led to a program based on adjustment and submission; and this, he regretfully suggested, was too far removed from the vigorous doctrine of self-assertion preached by Frederick Douglass.

DuBois was not content to present only a negative response to Washington's rhetorical strategy. In fact, he supported, in 1903, the goal of assimilation, and acknowledged the strong need for education. Education, however, held a different meaning for DuBois than it did for Washington. Instead of training men to be useful and subordinate, he felt that it should assist them to become leaders and innovators. From this premise, he concluded that black Americans needed academic college instruction more than vocational training. Only in this way could they be a "talented tenth" who could elevate their race.

DuBois' message of self-reliance and assertiveness featuring higher education stemmed from his own experience as a professor and his knowledge of American history. He had observed his students and saw that they compared favorably with pupils from white colleges. Similarly, he noted that they were better prepared for meeting the exigencies of life than those who had attended technical schools. The black man, he asserted, should therefore be encouraged to enroll in a Negro college which has as its threefold purpose to effect a social regeneration of the Negro, to offer solutions of racial problems, and to develop men. These ideas, expressed in the following essay "Of the Training of Black Men," represent a striking contrast to the philosophy and style of Washington. They contain a careful review of historical data, a tight organizational pattern, and a commitment to the argument from definition. They also reveal a preference for words rich in connotative power and a tendency to soar to the level of the ornate. In all, it is a typical DuBois essay both in content and in style.

W. E. B. DuBois
Of the Training of Black Men*

Why, if the Soul can fling the Dust aside,
And naked on the Air of Heaven ride,
    Were't not a Shame — were't not a Shame for him
In this clay carcase crippled to abide?
        OMAR KHAYYAM (FITZGERALD).

From the shimmering swirl of waters where many, many thoughts ago the slave-ship first saw the square tower of Jamestown, have flowed down to our day three streams of thinking: one swollen from the larger world here and over-seas, saying, the multiplying of human wants in culturelands calls for the world-wide coöperation of men in satisfying them. Hence arises a new human unity, pulling the ends of earth nearer, and all men, black, yellow, and white. The larger humanity strives to feel in this contact of living Nations and sleeping hordes a thrill of new life in the world, crying, "If the contact of Life and Sleep be Death, shame on such Life." To be sure, behind this thought lurks the afterthought of force and domination, — the making of brown men to delve when the temptation of beads and red calico cloys.

The second thought streaming from the death-ship and the curving river is the thought of the older South, — the sincere and passionate belief that somewhere between men and cattle, God created a *tertium quid,* and called it a Negro,—a clownish, simple creature, at times even lovable within its limitations, but straitly foreordained to walk within the Veil. To be sure, behind the thought lurks the afterthought, — some of them with favoring chance might become men, but in sheer self-defence we dare not let them, and we build about them walls so high, and hang between them and the light a veil so thick, that they shall not even think of breaking through.

And last of all there trickles down that third and darker thought, — the thought of the things themselves, the confused, half-conscious mutter of men who are black and whitened, crying "Liberty, Freedom, Opportunity—vouchsafe to us, O boastful World, the chance of living men!" To be sure, behind

*From W. E. DuBois, *The Souls of Black Folk* (Chicago: A. C. McClurg & Co., 1911), pp. 88-109.

the thought lurks the afterthought, — suppose, after all, the World is right and we are less than men? Suppose this mad impulse within is all wrong, some mock mirage from the untrue?

So here we stand among thoughts of human unity, even through conquest and slavery; the inferiority of black men, even if forced by fraud; a shriek in the night for the freedom of men who themselves are not yet sure of their right to demand it. This is the tangle of thought and afterthought wherein we are called to solve the problem of training men for life.

Behind all its curiousness, so attractive alike to sage and *dilettante,* lie its dim dangers, throwing across us shadows at once grotesque and awful. Plain it is to us that what the world seeks through desert and wild we have within our threshold, — a stalwart laboring force, suited to the semi-tropics; if, deaf to the voice of Zeitgeist, we refuse to use and develop these men, we risk poverty and loss. If, on the other hand, seized by the brutal afterthought, we debauch the race thus caught in our talons, selfishly sucking their blood and brains in the future as in the past, what shall save us from national decadence? Only that saner selfishness, which Education teaches men, can find the rights of all in the whirl of work.

Again, we may decry the color-prejudice of the South, yet it remains a heavy fact. Such curious kinks of the human mind exist and must be reckoned with soberly. They cannot be laughed away, nor always successfully stormed at, nor easily abolished by act of legislature. And yet they must not be encouraged by being let alone. They must be recognized as facts, but unpleasant facts; things that stand in the way of civilization and religion and common decency. They can be met in but one way, — by the breadth and broadening of human reason, by catholicity of taste and culture. And so, too, the native ambition and aspiration of men, even though they be black, backward, and ungraceful, must not lightly be dealt with. To stimulate wildly weak and untrained minds is to play with mighty fires; to flout their striving idly is to welcome a harvest of brutish crime and shameless lethargy in our very laps. The guiding of thought and the deft coordination of deed is at once the path of honor and humanity.

And so, in this great question of reconciling three vast and partially contradictory streams of thought, the one panacea of Education leaps to the lips of all: — such human training as will best use the labor of all men without enslaving or brutalizing; such training as will give us poise to encourage the prejudices that bulwark society, and to stamp out those that in sheer barbarity deafen us to the wail of prisoned souls within the Veil, and the mounting fury of shackled men.

But when we have vaguely said that Education will set this tangle straight, what have we uttered but a truism? Training for life teaches living; but what training for the profitable living together of black men and white? A hundred and fifty years ago our task would have seemed easier. Then Dr. Johnson blandly assured us that education was needful solely for the embellishments of life, and was useless for ordinary vermin. To-day we have climbed to heights where we would open at least the outer courts of knowledge to all, display its treasures to many, and select the few to whom its mystery of Truth is revealed, not wholly by birth or the accidents of the stock market, but at least in part according to deftness and aim, talent and character. This programme, however, we are sorely puzzled in carrying out through that part of the land where the blight of slavery fell hardest, and where we are dealing with two backward peoples. To make here in human education that ever necessary combination of the permanent and the contingent — of the ideal and the practical in workable equilibrium — has been there, as it ever must be in every age and place, a matter of infinite experiment and frequent mistakes.

In rough approximation we may point out four varying decades of work in Southern education since the Civil War. From the close of the war until 1876, was the period of uncertain groping and temporary relief. There were army schools, mission schools, and schools of the Freedman's Bureau in chaotic disarrangement seeking system and coöperation. Then followed ten years of constructive definite effort toward the building of complete school systems in the South. Normal schools and colleges were founded for the freedmen, and teachers trained there to man the public schools. There was the inevitable tendency of war to underestimate the prejudices of the master and the ignorance of the slave, and all seemed clear sailing out of the wreckage of the storm. Meantime, starting in this decade yet especially developing from 1885 to 1895, began the industrial revolution of the South. The land saw glimpses of a new destiny and the stirring of new ideals. The educational system striving to complete itself saw new obstacles and a field of work ever broader and deeper. The Negro colleges, hurriedly founded, were inadequately equipped, illogically distributed, and of varying efficiency and grade; the normal and high schools were doing little more than common-school work, and the common schools were training but a third of the children who ought to be in them, and training these too often poorly. At the same time the white South, by reason of its sudden conversion from the slavery ideal, by so much the more became set and strengthened in its racial prejudice, and crystallized it into harsh law and harsher custom; while the marvellous pushing forward of the poor white daily threatened to take even bread and butter from the mouths of the heavily handicapped sons of the freedmen. In the midst, then, of the larger problem of Negro education sprang up the more practical question of work, the inevitable economic quandary that faces a people in the transition from slavery to freedom, and especially those who make that change amid hate and prejudice, lawlessness and ruthless competition.

The industrial school springing to notice in this decade, but coming to full recognition in the decade beginning with 1895, was the proffered answer to this combined educational and economic crisis, and an answer of singular wisdom and timeliness. From the very first in nearly all the schools some attention had been given to training in handiwork, but now was this training first raised to a dignity that brought it in direct touch with the South's magnificent industrial development, and given an emphasis which reminded black folk that before the Temple of Knowledge swing the Gates of Toil.

Yet after all they are but gates, and when turning our eyes from the temporary and the contingent in the Negro problem to the broader question of the permanent uplifting and civilization of black men in America, we have a right to inquire, as this enthusiasm for material advancement mounts to its height, if after all the industrial school is the final and sufficient answer in the training of the Negro race; and to ask gently, but in all sincerity, the ever-recurring query of the ages, Is not life more than meat, and the body more than raiment? And men ask this today all the more eagerly because of sinister signs in recent educational movements. The tendency is here, born of slavery and quickened to renewed life by the crazy imperialism of the day, to regard human beings as among the material resources of a land to be trained with an eye single to future dividends. Race-prejudices, which keep brown and black men in their "places," we are coming to regard as useful allies with such a theory, no matter how much they may dull the ambition and sicken the hearts of struggling human beings. And above all, we daily hear that an education that encourages aspiration, that sets the loftiest of ideals and seeks as an end culture and character rather than bread-winning, is the privilege of white men and the danger and delusion of black.

Especially has criticism been directed against the former educational efforts to aid the Negro. In the four periods I have mentioned, we find first, boundless, planless enthusiasm and sacrifice; then the preparation of teachers for a vast public-school system; then the launching and expansion of that school system amid increasing difficulties; and finally the training of workmen for the new and growing industries. This development has been sharply ridiculed as a logical anomaly and flat reversal of nature. Soothly we have been told that first industrial and manual training should have taught the Negro to work, then simple schools should have taught him to read and write, and finally, after years, high and normal schools could have completed the system, as intelligence and wealth demanded.

That a system logically so complete was historically impossible, it needs but a little thought to prove. Progress in human affairs is more often a pull than a push, a surging forward of the exceptional man, and the lifting of his duller brethren slowly and painfully to his vantage-ground. Thus it was no accident that gave birth to universities centuries before the common schools, that made fair Harvard the first flower of our wilderness. So in the South: the mass of the freedmen at the end of the war lacked the intelligence so necessary to modern workingmen. They must first have the common school to teach them to read, write, and cipher; and they must have higher schools to teach teachers for the common schools. The white teachers who flocked South went to establish such a common-school system. Few held the idea of founding colleges; most of them at first would have laughed at the idea. But they faced, as all men since them have faced, that central paradox of the South, — the social separation of the races. At that time it was the sudden volcanic rupture of nearly all relations between black and white, in work and government and family life. Since then a new adjustment of relations in economic and political affairs has grown up, — an adjustment subtle and difficult to grasp, yet singularly ingenious, which leaves still that frightful chasm at the color-line across which men pass at their peril. Thus, then and now, there stand in the South two separate worlds; and separate not simply in the higher realms of social intercourse, but also in church and school, on railway and street-car, in hotels and theatres, in streets and city sections, in books and newspapers, in asylums and jails, in hospitals and graveyards. There is still enough of contact for large economic and group coöperation, but the separation is so thorough and deep that it absolutely precludes for the present between the races anything like that sympathetic and effective group-training and leadership of the one by the other, such as the American Negro and all backward peoples must have for effective progress.

This the missionaries of '68 soon saw; and if effective industrial and trade schools were impracticable before the establishment of a common-school system, just as certainly no adequate common schools could be founded until there were teachers to teach them. Southern whites would not teach them; Northern whites in sufficient numbers could not be had. If the Negro was to learn, he must teach himself, and the most effective help that could be given him was the establishment of schools to train Negro teachers. This conclusion was slowly but surely reached by every student of the situation until simulultaneously, in widely separated regions, without consultation or systematic plan, there arose a series of institutions designed to furnish teachers for the untaught. Above the sneers of critics at the obvious defects of this procedure must ever stand its one crushing rejoinder: in a single generation they put thirty thousand black teachers in the South; they wiped out the illiteracy of the majority of the black people of the land, and they made Tuskegee possible.

Such higher training-schools tended naturally to deepen broader development: at first they were common and grammar schools, then some became high schools. And finally, by 1900, some thirty-four had one year or more of studies of college grade. This development was reached with different degrees of speed in different institutions: Hampton is still a high school, while Fisk University started her college in 1871, and Spelman Seminary about 1896. In all cases the aim was identical, — to maintain the standards of the lower training by giving teachers and leaders the best practicable training; and above all, to furnish the black world with adequate standards of human culture and lofty ideals of life. It was not enough that the teachers of teachers should be trained in technical normal methods; they must also, so far as possible, be broad-minded, cultured men and women, to scatter civilization among a people whose ignorance was not simply of letters, but of life itself.

It can thus be seen that the work of education in the South began with higher institutions of training, which threw off as their foliage common schools, and later industrial schools, and at the same time strove to shoot their roots ever deeper toward college and university training. That this was an inevitable and necessary development, sooner or later, goes without saying; but there has been, and still is, a question in many minds if the natural growth was not forced, and if the higher training was not either overdone or done with cheap and unsound methods. Among white Southerners this feeling is widespread and positive. A prominent Southern journal voiced this in a recent editorial.

The experiment that has been made to give the colored students classical training has not been satisfactory. Even though many were able to pursue the course, most of them did so in a parrot-like way, learning what was taught, but not seeming to appropriate the truth and import of their instruction, and graduating without sensible aim or valuable occupation for their future. The whole scheme has proved a waste of time, efforts, and the money of the state.

While most fair-minded men would recognize this as extreme and overdrawn, still without doubt many are asking, Are there a sufficient number of Negroes ready for college training to warrant the undertaking? Are not too many students prematurely forced into this work? Does it have the effect of dissatisfying the young Negro with his environment? And do these graduates succeed in real life? Such natural questions cannot be evaded, nor on the other hand must a Nation naturally skeptical as to Negro ability assume an unfavorable answer without careful inquiry and patient openness to conviction. We must not forget that most Americans answer all queries regarding the Negro *a priori,* and that the least that human courtesy can do is to listen to evidence.

The advocates of the higher education of the Negro would be the last to deny the incompleteness and glaring defects of the present system: too many institutions have attempted to do college work, the work in some cases has not been thoroughly done, and quantity rather than quality has sometimes been sought. But all this can be said of higher education throughout the land; it is the almost inevitable incident of educational growth, and leaves the deeper question of the legitimate demand for the higher training of Negroes untouched. And this latter question can be settled in but one way, — by a first-hand study of the facts. If we leave out of view all institutions which have not actually graduated students from a course higher than that of a New England high school, even though they be called colleges; if then we take the thirty-four remaining institutions, we may clear up many misapprehensions by asking searchingly, What kind of institutions are they? what do they teach? and what sort of men do they graduate?

And first we may say that this type of college, including Atlanta, Fisk, and Howard, Wilberforce and Claflin, Shaw, and the rest, is peculiar, almost unique. Through the shining trees that whisper before me as I write, I catch glimpses of a boulder of New England granite, covering a grave, which graduates of Atlanta University have placed there, —

> "IN GRATEFUL MEMORY OF THEIR
> FORMER TEACHER AND FRIEND
> AND OF THE UNSELFISH LIFE HE
> LIVED, AND THE NOBLE WORK HE
> WROUGHT; THAT THEY, THEIR
> CHILDREN, AND THEIR CHIL
> DREN'S CHILDREN MIGHT BE
> BLESSED."

This was the gift of New England to the freed Negro: not alms, but a friend; not cash, but character. It was not and is not money these seething millions

want, but love and sympathy, the pulse of hearts beating with red blood; —
a gift which to-day only their own kindred and race can bring to the masses,
but which once saintly souls brought to their favored children in the crusade
of the sixties, that finest thing in American history, and one of the few things
untainted by sordid greed and cheap vainglory. The teachers in these institutions came not to keep the Negroes in their place, but to raise them out of the
defilement of the places where slavery had wallowed them. The colleges they
founded were social settlements; homes where the best of the sons of the
freedmen came in close and sympathetic touch with the best traditions of
New England. They lived and ate together, studied and worked, hoped and
harkened in the dawning light. In actual formal content their curriculum
was doubtless old-fashioned, but in educational power it was supreme, for
it was the contact of living souls.

From such schools about two thousand Negroes have gone forth with the
bachelor's degree. The number in itself is enough to put at rest the argument
that too large a proportion of Negroes are receiving higher training. If the
ratio to population of all Negro students throughout the land, in both college
and secondary training, be counted, Commissioner Harris assures us "it must
be increased to five times its present average" to equal the average of the land.

Fifty years ago the ability of Negro students in any appreciable numbers
to master a modern college course would have been difficult to prove. To-day
it is proved by the fact that four hundred Negroes, many of whom have been
reported as brilliant students, have received the bachelor's degree from Harvard, Yale, Oberlin, and seventy other leading colleges. Here we have, then,
nearly twenty-five hundred Negro graduates, of whom the crucial query must
be made, How far did their training fit them for life? It is of course extremely
difficult to collect satisfactory data on such a point, — difficult to reach the
men, to get trustworthy testimony, and to gauge that testimony by any generally acceptable criterion of success. In 1900, the Conference at Atlanta
University undertook to study these graduates, and published the results.
First they sought to know what these graduates were doing, and succeeded
in getting answers from nearly two-thirds of the living. The direct testimony
was in almost all cases corroborated by the reports of the colleges where they
graduated, so that in the main the reports were worthy of credence. Fifty-
three percent of these graduates were teachers, — presidents of institutions,
heads of normal schools, principals of city school-systems, and the like.
Seventeen per cent were clergymen; another seventeen per cent were in the
professions, chiefly as physicians. Over six per cent were merchants, farmers,
and artisans, and four per cent were in the government civil-service. Granting
even that a considerable proportion of the third unheard from are unsucess-
ful, this is a record of usefulness. Personally I know many hundreds of these
graduates, and have corresponded with more than a thousand; through others
I have followed carefully the lifework of scores; I have taught some of them
and some of the pupils whom they have taught, lived in homes which they
have builded, and looked at life through their eyes. Comparing them as a
class with my fellow students in New England and in Europe, I cannot hesitate in saying that nowhere have I met men and women with a broader spirit

of helpfulness, with deeper devotion to their life-work, or with more consecrated determination to succeed in the face of bitter difficulties than among Negro college-bred men. They have, to be sure, their proportion of ne'er-do-weels, their pedants and lettered fools, but they have a surprisingly small proportion of them; they have not that culture of manner which we instinctively associate with university men, forgetting that in reality it is the heritage from cultured homes, and that no people a generation removed from slavery can escape a certain unpleasant rawness and *gaucherie,* despite the best of training.

With all their larger vision and deeper sensibility, these men have usually been conservative, careful leaders. They have seldom been agitators, have withstood the temptation to head the mob, and have worked steadily and faithfully in a thousand communities in the South. As teachers, they have given the South a commendable system of city schools and large numbers of private normal-schools and academies. Colored college-bred men have worked side by side with white college graduates at Hampton; almost from the beginning the backbone of Tuskegee's teaching force has been formed of graduates from Fisk and Atlanta. And to-day the institute is filled with college graduates, from the energetic wife of the principal down to the teacher of agriculture, including nearly half of the executive council and a majority of the heads of departments. In the professions, college men are slowly but surely leavening the Negro church, are healing and preventing the devastations of disease, and beginning to furnish legal protection for the liberty and property of the toiling masses. All this is needful work. Who would do it if Negroes did not? How could Negroes do it if they were not trained carefully for it? If white people need colleges to furnish teachers, ministers, lawyers, and doctors, do black people need nothing of the sort?

If it is true that there are an appreciable number of Negro youth in the land capable of character and talent to receive that higher training, the end of which is culture, and if the two and a half thousand who have had something of this training in the past have in the main proved themselves useful to their race and generation, the question then comes, What place in the future development of the South ought the Negro college and college-bred man to occupy? That the present social separation and acute race-sensitiveness must eventually yield to the influences of culture, as the South grows civilized, is clear. But such transformation calls for singular wisdom and patience. If, while the healing of this vast sore is progressing, the races are to live for many years side by side, united in economic effort, obeying a common government, sensitive to mutual thought and feeling, yet subtly and silently separate in many matters of deeper human intimacy, — if this unusual and dangerous development is to progress amid peace and order, mutual respect and growing intelligence, it will call for social surgery at once the delicatest and nicest in modern history. It will demand broad-minded, upright men, both white and black, and in its final accomplishment American civilization will triumph. So far as white men are concerned, this fact is to-day being recognized in the South, and a happy renaissance of university education seems imminent. But the very voices that cry hail to this good work are, strange to relate, largely silent or antagonistic to the higher education of the Negro.

Strange to relate! for this is certain, no secure civilization can be built in the South with the Negro as an ignorant, turbulent proletariat. Suppose we seek to remedy this by making them laborers and nothing more: they are not fools, they have tasted of the Tree of Life, and they will not cease to think, will not cease attempting to read the riddle of the world. By taking away their best equipped teachers and leaders, by slamming the door of opportunity in the faces of their bolder and brighter minds, will you make them satisfied with their lot? or will you not rather transfer their leading from the hands of men taught to think to the hands of untrained demagogues? We ought not to forget that despite the pressure of poverty, and despite the active discouragement and even ridicule of friends, the demand for higher training steadily increases among Negro youth: there were, in the years from 1875 to 1880, 22 Negro graduates from Northern colleges; from 1885 to 1890 there were 43, and from 1895 to 1900, nearly 100 graduates. From Southern Negro colleges there were, in the same three periods, 143, 413, and over 500 graduates. Here, then, is the plain thirst for training; by refusing to give this Talented Tenth the key to knowledge, can any sane man imagine that they will lightly lay aside their yearning and contentedly become hewers of wood and drawers of water?

No. The dangerously clear logic of the Negro's position will more and more loudly assert itself in that day when increasing wealth and more intricate social organization preclude the South from being, as it so largely is, simply an armed camp for intimidating black folk. Such waste of energy cannot be spared if the South is to catch up with civilization. And as the black third of the land grows in thrift and skill, unless skilfully guided in its larger philosophy, it must more and more brood over the red past and the creeping, crooked present, until it grasps a gospel of revolt and revenge and throws its new-found energies athwart the current of advance. Even to-day the masses of the Negroes see all too clearly the anomalies of their position and the moral crookedness of yours. You may marshal strong indictments against them, but their counter-cries, lacking though they be in formal logic, have burning truths within them which you may not wholly ignore, O Southern Gentlemen! If you deplore their presence here, they ask, Who brought us? When you cry, Deliver us from the vision of intermarriage, they answer that legal marriage is infinitely better than systematic concubinage and prostitution. And if in just fury you accuse their vagabonds of violating women, they also in fury quite as just may reply: The rape which your gentlemen have done against helpless black women in defiance of your own laws is written on the foreheads of two millions of mulattoes, and written in ineffaceable blood. And finally, when you fasten crime upon this race as its peculiar trait, they answer that slavery was the arch-crime, and lynching and lawlessness its twin abortion; that color and race are not crimes, and yet they it is which in this land receives most unceasing condemnation, North, East, South, and West.

I will not say such arguments are wholly justified, — I will not insist that there is no other side to the shield; but I do say that of the nine millions of Negroes in this nation, there is scarcely one out of the cradle to whom these arguments do not daily present themselves in the guise of terrible truth. I insist that the question of the future is how best to keep these millions from brooding over the wrongs of the past and the difficulties of the present, so that all their energies may be bent toward a cheerful striving and co-operation with their white neighbors toward a larger, juster, and fuller future. That one wise method of doing this lies in the closer knitting of the Negro to the great industrial possibilities of the South is a great truth. And this the common schools and the manual training and trade schools are working to accomplish. But these alone are not enough. The foundations of knowledge in this race, as in others, must be sunk deep in the college and university if we would build a solid, permanent structure. Internal problems of social advance must inevitably come, — problems of work and wages, of families and homes, of morals and the true valuing of the things of life; and all these and other inevitable problems of civilization the Negro must meet and solve largely for himself, by reason of his isolation; and can there be any possible solution other than by study and thought and an appeal to the rich experience of the past? Is there not, with such a group and in such a crisis, infinitely more danger to be apprehended from half-trained minds and shallow thinking than from over-education and over-refinement? Surely we have wit enough to found a Negro college so manned and equipped as to steer successfully between the *dilettante* and the fool. We shall hardly induce black men to believe that if their stomachs be full, it matters little about their brains. They already dimly perceive that the paths of peace winding between honest toil and dignified manhood call for the guidance of skilled thinkers, the loving, reverent comradeship between the black lowly and the black men emancipated by training and culture.

The function of the Negro college, then, is clear; it must maintain the standards of popular education, it must seek the social regeneration of the Negro, and it must help in the solution of problems of race contact and co-operation. And finally, beyond all this, it must develop men. Above our modern socialism, and out of the worship of the mass, must persist and evolve that higher individualism which the centres of culture protect; there must come a loftier respect for the sovereign human soul that seeks to know itself and the world about it; that seeks a freedom for expansion and self-development; that will love and hate and labor in its own way, untrammeled alike by old and new. Such souls aforetime have inspired and guided worlds, and if we be not wholly bewitched by our Rhine-gold, they shall again. Herein the longing of black men must have respect: the rich and bitter depth of their experience, the unknown treasures of their inner life, the strange rendings of nature they have seen, may give the world new points of view and make their loving, living, and doing precious to all human hearts. And to themselves in these the days that try their souls, the chance to soar in the dim blue air above the smoke is to their finer spirits boon and guerdon for what they lose on earth by being black.

I sit with Shakespeare and he winces not. Across the color line I move arm in arm with Balzac and Dumas, where smiling men and welcoming women glide in gilded halls. From out the caves of evening that swing between the strong-limbed earth and the tracery of the stars, I summon Aristotle and Aurelius and what soul I will, and they come all graciously with no scorn nor condescension. So, wed with Truth, I dwell above the Veil. Is this the life you grudge us, O knightly America? Is this the life you long to change into the dull red hideousness of Georgia? Are you so afraid lest peering from this high Pisgah, between Philistine and Amalekite, we sight the Promised Land?

DuBois' *Souls of Black Folk,* rejecting the traditional self-image theory Washington had consciously or unconsciously nurtured among the Negroes, became a classic example of what Kenneth Boulding has called "a process of image-formation."[68] DuBois, like his disciples, viewed black Americans as part of a movement that sought to alter their perception of themselves and the world. His analysis of the mind of the Negro, designed to create new images, went far to restore self-respect and to give fresh meaning to self-reliance and its role in the campaign for assimilation. The particular message destined to have the greatest long range influence was the call for higher education and the description of guidelines to be used by Negro colleges to implement this challenge.

Benjamin E. Mays,[69] and James E. Cheek,[70] became two of the leading intellectual heirs to DuBois' educational philosophy. Aware of the fact that ninety percent of all Negro college graduates and ninety-five percent of all Negro teachers attended predominantly Negro colleges such as Howard, Lincoln, Fisk, Morehouse, and Shaw,[71] they used their administrative talents to upgrade the quality of these institutions. Despite his retirement from his long-time position as President of Morehouse College, Mays still projects his message of assimilation and self-reliance to appreciative audiences in the North and South. In a typical address, presented at the 101st Founder's Day Convocation at Shaw University in 1965, Mays set forth the philosophy which had motivated his professional career.[72] He warned the students in the audience that when a fully desegregated society eventually comes they must be ready to compete with whites on equal terms. There would be no allowances made, he argued, for shortcomings due to 350 years of discrimination resulting from either enforced slavery or segregation, nor would there be special consideration extended to blacks because of their poverty or faulty training. Indeed, they would be pushed aside with the rationalization, he added, that "no Negro can be found with proper qualifications." The solution which Mays recommended was to make black Americans competitive by striving for excellence in education and initiative. For those who questioned the premise that black students enrolled in Negro colleges could achieve distinction in a prejudiced society, he advised them to examine the accomplishments of Thurgood Marshall, Edward Brooke, John Hope Franklin, Martin Luther King, Jr., James Cheek, Angie Brooks, and Benjamin Quarles. These impressive citations enabled Mays to identify with the needs and aspirations of the audience, and gave him the freedom to establish a hierarchy of values with education at one end of the continuum and materialism at the other. With candor tinged with benevolent paternalism, he said:

> Whether we like it or not, Negroes must read more and socialize less, study more and frolic less, think more and ape the white man less, do more research and play less, write books and articles and become recognized in our respective fields. It is better by far to be known by the articles we write than by the bridge we play; by the books we publish than by the house we live in. It is better to have our students rave about our great teaching than about our beautiful cars and clothes. It is better to have our colleagues envious of our scholarship and research than of our houses and land.[73]

In his closing remarks Mays attempted to put the record of desegregation in proper historical perspective. He confessed that Negroes had not yet "been accepted into the mainstream of American life." Failing to make their mark in politics, business, and education, and often regarded by many as "boys," they have not, he claimed, in most instances, displayed the confidence needed for success in the professional world. But these facts did not prevent Mays from asserting that "the Negro's future in America is brighter than ever before." He concluded his plea by quoting some lines from Tennyson's *Ulysses:*

> Come my friends,
> 'Tis not too late to seek a newer world.[74]

DuBois' faith in Negro colleges and Mays' talent for moving eloquence helped form the rhetorical strategy of James Cheek. As President of Shaw University and Howard University, he constructed a universe of discourse stressing the theme of equality of opportunity for the neglected "one tenth" of American citizens. This problem, he observed, transcended in importance the war in Vietnam and the landing of men on the moon; for the perpetuation of inequality over a period of three centuries had cut so deeply into the fabric of American society that serious ethnic divisions, poverty, and educational disparities had developed. The challenge of the 1970's, therefore, could be stated simply: either black men and white men will come together in an atmosphere of mutual respect, or racial tensions will substantially increase.

Rejecting the "myths" that current practices in integration had led to genuine progress and that inequality of opportunity was due exclusively to the attitudes and actions of a white majority, Cheek called for a new social order under the aegis of the Negro colleges. But the crusade he envisioned could only succeed if these "peculiar institutions" eliminated their mimetic character based on the traditional "pursuit of excellence" and substituted in their place a "pursuit of relevance." By becoming a directional force, Negro colleges could point the way to the meaning of the self-concept. While most of these ideas appear in the principal educational addresses of Cheek,[75] they are perhaps best summarized in the following speech, entitled "From Weakness to Strength."[76] Typically, this message shows an awareness of the exigencies stemming from the racial upheaval in the American scene, and contains a solution that urges Negro colleges to move toward relevance so that they can become the prime force in making assimilation a reality. The message, moreover, seeks to establish student and faculty pride in the accomplishments and potentials of their institutions; at the same time, it strives to demonstrate to the larger American community the significant role that this type of higher education could play in resolving the dilemma of racial conflict. Ethical, logical, and emotional appeals expressed in clear, specific, and vivid language are combined to produce a rhetoric of urgency. With this rhetorical approach, Cheek, like Mays, tends to generate a strong response from both black and white members of his audience.

James Cheek

From Weakness to Strength*

On yesterday, quite by accident, I met with a group of students in the Union lounge just to talk. For almost three hours we shared our views, largely about Shaw—where it *used* to be, where it *now* is, and where it *can* go.

---

*James Cheek, "From Weakness to Strength." An address given at the fall convocation at Shaw University on October 25, 1967. Printed as a brochure. Reprinted with the permission of Dr. James Cheek.

Those moments with a few students served for me as a kind of tonic —
a re-stimulation of the exhilaration and enthusiasm with which this venture
was begun almost four years ago. For the brief period of three hours we
talked, not as President and students, but as partners in a common enterprise,
caught up together in the enthusiasm of a creative moment of expression.

I discovered more in that brief period about what Shaw now is than
I could possibly have learned from reading the flood of memos and reports
which invade my desk daily.

Students, when given the opportunity to express themselves freely, can
be refreshingly honest, but also brutally candid. They voice their feelings
without restraint. They show far keener insight into what education ought to
mean than we assume they are capable of showing, and possess a maturity
and sensitivity about their lives and their future far in excess of what many
of us think.

Our meeting ended abruptly because someone discovered it was time
for lunch, and Shaw students, as I have always observed, will eat no matter
how bad the food.

This accidental and all too brief encounter, with a few of those who
have come to Shaw to learn, served to further confirm for me a feeling I have
always had: that most of our students not only belong to a new generation,
but they belong also to a totally new age and a new world.

The year 1967 will be recalled in years to come as the year when America
passed from James Baldwin's "The Fire Next Time" to Leroi Jones' and
Rap Brown's "The Fire This Time." It will be known also as the year when
America's black citizens ceased to chant "We Shall Overcome" and began to
shout "Burn, Baby, Burn."

It will thus be long remembered as the year when the Negro's struggle
to achieve full equality took a bold and awesome new direction.

The events of the summer past may represent that important moment
in the history of a nation when it rapidly matured and discovered that *it can
happen here,* or they may represent that awful point in a nation's history
when the final curtain began to be lowered, bringing to an end its hopes and
dreams.

To many of us, wrapped in the safe environs of the academic community, there has been a feeling of secure shelter from the shattering events
which are invading our domestic tranquility and peace of mind. To far too
many in colleges like this, there has been the temptation to view ourselves
removed from these struggles and to believe that whatever new madness our
time produces will soon spin itself and wither away.

Our academic pedigrees have set us apart; and our position in the ivory
tower has set us above. We view the new moods with the distant eye of the
astronomer; it is an interesting phenomenon that belongs to another world.

Historians though we are, we have failed to apply the lessons of history
to our own historical experiences. Social behaviorists though we be, we have
not fully comprehended the reason and meaning of this kind of social behavior in our land. And humanists though we claim, we have missed the valuable
insights of tragedy and pain, irony and satire, suffering and despair to which
these events and expressions give testimony.

Our history, our science, our humanism, and our theology now seem no longer to serve us.

Years have been devoted by academicians to analyzing and interpreting the politics of power, but now that power is being modified by the adjective "black," all of a sudden *power* is not understood.

For generations we have taught the anatomy of social revolutions with their inherent expressions of violence, but in our time the demonstration of violence by a people long oppressed is both bewildering and confusing.

All of this adds up to one clear observation: the Negro is indeed, perhaps, America's only real dilemma.

We have long recognized that America's chief domestic problems are: the problem of ethnic divisions, the problem of poverty, and the problem of educational disadvantage. But running through all three of these is the problem of race. If somehow America could rid itself of the black man, the problem of ethnic divisions would be resolved, the problem of poverty could be overcome, and the problem of educational disadvantage could be cured.

We are a pluralistic society, characterized by a multiplicity of ethnic groups; we are the world's richest nation, disposed to use our wealth to eliminate poverty around the world; we are an enlightened nation, wedded to the concept of equal education for all as the only guarantee of an authentic democracy.

But yet these three problems remain, and now they are being propelled toward a position of crisis largely because America cannot resolve the problem of race.

The events of 1967 make clear to me the hard choice that the nation must now make: its hallowed language of the Declaration of Independence; its guarantee of the Constitution and Bill of Rights; and its poetic expressions of hope engraved on the Statue of Liberty must have meaning for all human beings or it will have meaning for none.

Here, on these shores, between the Atlantic and the Pacific, the Gulf of Mexico and the borders of Canada, the ancient quest of man for equality shall in truth become a reality for all or it will not be a reality of any.

In the true spirit of Bunker Hill; in the faithful example of the Boston Tea Party; and in the authentic voice of Jefferson and Patrick Henry, the Negro American in 1967 has summoned the nation to choose: to be what it says it is or not to be at all.

As fantastic as this may seem, it is no fantasy. As mad as this may appear, it is no madness; as traitorous as this may sound, it is no treason.

Those who sailed the stormy seas of the Atlantic in pursuit of freedom and equality in the new world engraved on their coins: "Resistance to tyranny is obedience to God."

Alone, among all nations of modern history, America has for three centuries or more engaged in tyranny over one-tenth of its people. To resist tyranny is no less noble from black men than it is from white men.

The year 1967 was not only the year that established the terms of the survival of the nation. It was also the year that established the terms of the survival of one of its peculiar institutions: *The Negro College.*

This year, the Negro college has been the object of an intensive assault.

It will be remembered as the year of the Riesman-Jencks report, which characterized the Negro college as the "disaster area" of American higher education, and the year of the SREB Commission report on "The Negro and Higher Education in the South," which paints a picture of almost unbelievable weakness against a background of relative strength.

But it will also be remembered as the year of Stokely Carmichael and Nathan Hare whose scathing denunciations and searching analyses revealed how feeble Negro colleges have been, and now are, in coming to terms with the meaning of their past, the strangeness of their present and the possibilities for their future.

These events related to Negro education also make clear to me the hard choice that Negro colleges must now make: change or disappear.

The beginning of this our 103rd year, therefore, takes place in an atmosphere of unparalleled national upheaval, but also in an atmosphere of unparalleled challenge and opportunity.

The response of our nation to the problems of race and ethnic divisions, of poverty and of educational disadvantage will take its shape and substance in the various social institutions of church and state, and it has long been recognized that the meeting ground of these institutions is on the campuses of institutions of higher learning.

For better or worse, institutions of higher learning will set the example that the status-seeking society will emulate. Higher education has within its power to provide the leadership for the fashioning of a higher social order, remaking the best of the old and the discovery of the new.

But among all of the institutions of higher education, the Negro college is in the best position to lead the nation in the direction of a new social order.

Most students of higher education who have examined the question of the role of education in effecting a new social order have expressed the fear that the educational establishment—on the whole—has become conservative out of strength and, therefore, cannot change.

The Negro college, however, I believe, because of its position of weakness, *can* change, and the very "disaster" which Riesman and Jencks see as the picture of our institutions can become the very reason for their strength.

Several years ago John F. Kennedy, while a freshman senator, made the observation on the floor of the Senate that "when it is not necessary to change, it is necessary not to change."

In the context of the events of our time, I should make a similar but contrary observation: *When it is necessary to change, change is a necessity.*

American education during most of this century has characterized itself as being in the pursuit of *excellence.*

For this institution, we begin this year to commit ourselves to the pursuit of relevance, and to perform what we might call a telic function; that is, it is now our goal to become a directional force in our society.

But we will not begin the pursuit of relevance until we begin to develop in our students the consciousness of themselves as a people rather than as a race, and until we begin to teach them to appreciate the music of James Brown and Ray Charles; the poetry of Cullen, Hughes and McKay; the fiction of Chestnutt, Toomer and Wright; and the drama of Leroi Jones; and the history of black men in Africa and America.

We will not be engaged in relevance until we begin to eliminate the bondage of our students to faculty and the deference of our faculty to administrative paternalism, and until we begin to practice here the process of shared authority.

We will not be a relevant institution until we can demonstrate efficiency in administration without unnecessary red tape, and until we rid ourselves of archaic and useless regulations, more designed to keep our students irresponsible rather than to make them free, mature and responsible.

We will not be relevant unless we begin to reward industry and hard work rather than simply brilliance, and truly begin the job of working with our students where they are rather than on the basis of where we think they ought to be.

We will not have relevance here until we begin the job of training leadership for service in the urban community in totally new tasks and endeavors that will truly have an effect upon people's social, economic and personal development.

We will be neither relevant nor a directional force in our society until we become a force in our local community, involved in the problems of the poor in our backyard, the issue of urban renewal which surrounds us, the expressions of prejudice which we confront daily.

For if we hope to have an impact on changing the larger society, we must begin now to change the character and nature of this academic community.

Here, timidity must give way to a prudent boldness. Here, we shall attempt to create a reasoning and action-oriented commitment; the focus of our education, henceforth, will be on our heritage — past and present — as a key to social action, not as a womb to return to in times of distress.

As the Talmud expresses it, "It is not our duty to complete the task; but neither are we free to desist from it."

Not too long ago there was published a report by the Syracuse University Research Corporation entitled: *The United States and The World in 1985.* This work represented a comprehensive effort on the part of physical and social scientists to develop a social prophecy based upon painstaking examination of data. It is a projection of present trends and a studied analysis of those factors combining for and against change in our society.

To me the most significant aspect of this report is embodied in the conclusion that with all the miracles of science and technology, Americans will not yet have come to grips with their basic problems of peace, of government by law, of equality of opportunity, and of a social conscience.

This view of America in the 1985 era is based on the assumption of business as usual — of uneasy peace as usual — and of formal education as usual.

But institutions like ours dare not and cannot continue with business as usual, and neither can our nation.

It becomes incumbent upon us, therefore, to address ourselves forthrightly to the question of whether we shall change and, therefore, live to serve, or whether we shall remain static and, therefore, die to be remembered.

On this decision may rest the question of the survival of our country.

Because we are weak, let us at Shaw begin the task of remaking our institution, not to perpetuate an educational tradition whose obsolescence is reflected daily in its ineffectiveness; but to create a new tradition of educational relevance where the minds and spirits of our students are trained and cultivated to engage and resolve the problems created by a new society.

Let us seek wisdom, not only in the ancient texts of generations past, but in the raw experience of generations present. And let us pursue truth not in the towers of ivory removed from man's struggles, but in the very midst of his endeavors to bring order into a world increasingly characterized by disorder.

Let this institution be reborn — not to give hallow sanction to a heritage it did not create, but to give bold creative direction to a heritage it hopes to forge for this and future generations.

Let us seek new knowledge to confront new problems, and let us together here at Shaw find a way to *unite* these *disunited* states.

We are caught up together — both black and white — in a period of awesome change, and the words of John Stuart Mill, quoted by Franklin D. Roosevelt 35 years ago during another period of change, can serve us well again:

> "The unwise are those who bring nothing constructive to the process of change, and who greatly imperil the future of mankind by leaving great questions to be fought out between ignorant change on the one hand, and ignorant opposition to change, on the other."

Today our generation is given the opportunity to be constructive, and schools like ours can provide for us all a constructive opportunity.

It is my hope and prayer that as we proceed through this year we will be wise in our use of it. For I am convinced that there is truth in Lowell's insight:

> The laws of changeless justice bind oppressor with oppressed.
> And close as sin and suffering joined we march to fate abreast

I thank you.

King V. Cheek, Jr.[77] who succeeded his brother as President of Shaw University in the summer of 1969, also has an abiding faith in the potential power of the predominantly Negro college to function as a center for producing social, political, and economic change. In a convocation address delivered to the administration, faculty, staff, and students at Shaw in the fall of 1969, he defined the goals of a university by setting forth five basic principles in the form of an educational manifesto. A true university, he said, must be a democratic community which recognizes the personal worth of all students, the need for environmental learning, the challenge of serving America at large, the right of dissent, and the importance of ". . . self determination of all black people in a multi-racial society." He then charged his audience to bring themselves together, and through "brain power" turn out future leaders who can point the way to a meaningful integration of the races. The flow of these arguments, revealing the disciplined mind and legal training of the author and a commitment to the goal of liberation, may be seen in the manuscript of the address which follows. Cheek's message, like that of his predecessor, suggests Shaw's continuing role as an innovative institution in search of relevance and involvement.

King V. Cheek, Jr.
*Toward a Redefinition of the University**

Members of the Board of Trustees, administrative and teaching colleagues, fellow students, ladies and gentlemen:

We meet today at a critical time in our nation's history. Whether we survive this decade or this century will depend upon the sincerity of our commitment to create a more humane social and economic order.

For some time, we have listened to rhetoric calling for an emancipation of the human mind and spirit and for the reconstruction of our society in a manner more consistent with real human needs.

We have noted with dismay and alarm the national response to the problems we face. Billions of dollars are spent to place men on the moon to collect rocks we already have — while students, the real life blood of our nation, suffer because funds are not available for their education. Many more inconsistencies reveal the sham and hypocrisy of our national priorities.

The university must not remain silent in the face of these crises. Indeed our failure to be activists in the arena of social, political and economic change is one cause for what critics call the "under thirty" generation rebellion.

Our responsibility as a university is clear and pressing. What Shaw is and proposes to be is of critical concern and importance to all of us as we seek to make our response to the urban crisis.

However, like universities in general, we must first turn our attention inward and promote those internal reforms which are urgently needed if we

---

*King V. Cheek, Jr., "Toward a Redefinition of the University." An address given at the fall convocation at Shaw University on October 10, 1969. Reprinted with the permission of Dr. King V. Cheek, Jr.

are to exist with meaning and relevance. We must first determine our own character and goals and know what we seek to become as one in battle with the foes of humanity.

Five principles which we shall call "The Shaw Manifesto" set our character.

First, we believe in the dignity, personal worth and educability of all Shaw students.

Second, we believe in education which promotes successful living and which prepares our students for a lifetime of learning and inspires them to be active change agents in reconstructing this society.

Third, we believe in the university commitment to serve a larger community and in its efforts to raise the level of hope for the poor and the forgotten.

Fourth, we believe in the right of dissent for all members of this community, in the promotion of individuality and responsibility and in the art of democratic campus citizenship.

Fifth, we believe in the self-determination of all black people so that our destiny in a multi-racial society will be fulfilled and controlled by us.

Our first principle, that of the educability and personal worth of our students, expresses our genuine and firm belief that our students can learn. We do not pay homage to the outmoded and indeed immoral practice of prejudging our students' potential. We recognize that our tools of measurement are defective in that they cannot tell us of your aptitude. At best, they provide a measure of what your precollege environment has offered you.

Therefore, our educational methods and procedures will continue to be unorthodox, and the power structure be damned! Our responsibility and our decision making will be responsive to the needs and preferences of the people who live here, the students, the faculty, the staff, and not the whims of the outside establishment.

Our second commitment, education for successful living, is as vital as the first. Irving Babbett, in his book, *Literature and the American College* wrote:

> The best of the small colleges will render a service to American education if they decide to make a sturdy defense of the humane tradition. . . . The college should remember that its business is to make of its graduates 'men of quality.' Only then can it do its share toward creating that aristocracy of character and intelligence which is needed in a community like ours to take the place of an aristocracy of birth and counteract the tendency toward an aristocracy of money.

The ultimate end of our education must be the greatest possible development of the individual.

We do not exist as a cafeteria designed to transmit bits and pieces of knowledge to our students. Neither will we emphasize narrow vocational and specialized interests.

The public demand is shifting to a need for liberal knowledge. In industry, in business, governmental service, and the urban sciences, there is a pressing need for men and women who know something of human nature, of history, of imaginative literature, and of sciences in its larger meaning.

The focus is shifting from the content mastery to learning to learn as a continuous process throughout life. Occupations are changing so rapidly that the individual who has the capacity to adapt and manage knowledge, conceptualize problems, and pursue information for solutions, will be the one to derive satisfaction and success.

This University must fulfill its role of educating citizens who are committed to providing ethical and intellectual leadership to our society, who are sensitive and critical enough to challenge traditional values and institutions in an effort to create a better moral and social order. Their function will not be to ornament society, but to serve it.

These tasks call for far more innovative techniques than we now employ. We have recognized that our students can learn effectively in working environments. It is not necessary for them to relinquish their income earning power while they are pursuing a college education.

Accordingly, the university will seek to insure, to every student who desires it, employment in an internship position intimately connected to his declared professional and educational goals. The places where our students will work will be considered classrooms in the same sense that study places are in our academic buildings. This concept of environmental learning will provide the unique experiences which are integral to our goals.

In spite of our concepts, we must remember that our goals cannot be achieved without a kind of academic hothouse where ideas are exciting. No paraphernalia of courses or requirements will take the place of an atmosphere where the excitement of learning is electric and contagious.

The university's third resolve is to be a powerful force in this community so that our presence is felt in all aspects of the community's life. As a resident and citizen in an urban community, we intend to use strategic power and our resources to insure that the needs of the poor are met. Our presence here will affect the economy as well as the cultural and political life of the people of southside and of Raleigh.

Our future facilities will represent a process and not a dead sea. Indeed many of our functions will best be performed in buildings which include residential, commercial and other non-academic components . . . This University will be enmeshed and intertwined with the life of its community.

Further, I am happy to announce that the first Urban University — The Urban College of Roxbury-Boston, a satellite campus of Shaw — will soon open in the early 70's. Our resources and commitments will extend beyond this city as we seek to develop black manpower in the urban areas of the north. Not only Raleigh but all of America will come to feel the presence of Shaw University as we seek to live out our commitment.

Our fourth belief is in the right of dissent for all members of this community, in the promotion of individuality and responsibility and in the art of democratic campus citizenship.

It is important in our world that we promote, rather than discourage, activism on all fronts. When I consider the invectives cast upon students and the young, I am moved to defend their efforts to reform our society.

Though, in many instances, strategies are misguided, there is the hope of a better world in the rebellion of today's youth.

For they, through their protest, have sharpened the critique of our society and have, more clearly, enunciated the contradictions which older adults have tolerated for so long.

They see a certain hypocrisy in the allegiance to freedom, law and order taught by patriotic school teachers when they smell the stench of southern justice and the burning of flesh of children napalmed by American bombs in Vietnam.

They have placed in bold perspective the myth of America's commitment to a decent life for all citizens when they challenged the priority of a moon shot over the uplift of 30 million Americans who still live in poverty.

The myth of American liberty stands exposed as we view public support for separate societies — black and white — with blacks systematically and deliberately excluded from the mainstream of American life.

Students recognize that the University is guilty of supporting or covering up many of these basic social evils. The disaffection which they now have for a political, economic and social system, that has lost its ability to be responsive to the needs of ordinary people, is shared by many of us. Their outcries and protests have helped us understand a little more of the reality of America and have sharpened our belief that so long as the least of our brothers and sisters remain exploited and repressed, all of the rest of us are likewise dehumanized by the maintenance of a system which allows their exploitation.

This University will not maintain a safe isolation from these problems. The fact that many universities have maintained an aloofness and have sought to fit students to the system has caused many students to turn their attention and protests inward and to question the legitimacy of their education.

As we seek to respond to the questions which students raise, we must begin at home. For it is here, inside the university, that students see the greatest hypocrisy.

We espouse the concept of community; yet there are some among us, faculty, administrators and staff, who still treat students as if they are children, unwanted customers or vassals.

I strongly believe that young adults — and students are — have a special wisdom to contribute to the life style and character of this university community. There is pervasive evidence that in all of our formal learning systems, students have a more penetrating and enduring educational impact upon each other than their teachers have on them.

For educational, as well as other reasons, we should plan for and facilitate the opportunity for students to teach each other. In this adult world of learning, which a university should be, everybody is a teacher and everybody is a student. That is the true meaning of a community of scholars.

Under no circumstances will we permit this university to be a 7:30 to 5:30 place of work — like a factory — where residence halls are hotels and student government is tokenism — where status differences keep us from talking to each other about problems we jointly define as important. Instead, ours must be an education directed toward the concerns of the people here, organized democratically and conducted in the most open and cooperative fashion.

We do not exist for the employment of a president, staff and teachers, but rather for learning and the nature of the process requires that students be treated as persons and active participants rather than as numbers.

Further, if we are to develop a community — all of us — students, faculty and administrators must recognize that anarchy is destructive of freedom. The rights of all of us can be insured only if our individual freedom to dissent is respected. Freedom of thought or expression is integral to our purpose. The freedom of antipersonal behavior which curtails the freedom of others is not.

We will protect the right of all persons here to peaceful and constructive dissent. We will not tolerate behavior calculated to destroy us or corrode our purpose.

Because we believe in this concept called democracy and because we intend to insure that all who live and work here serve well . . . we are appointing a select faculty-student commission on course and teacher evaluation.

We will no longer maintain a double standard in our university which requires students to perform and exempts the President, the administrative staff and faculty. If students are dropped for their failures so must the rest of us be judged by equitable standards.

For those who feel threatened, let me add a note of caution. The procedures we project are not intimidation, rather, they are fulfillments of our concept of a true community. If we act otherwise, we continue to endorse hypocrisies which we are committed to destroy.

There will be skeptics among us who will question the competency of students to judge a course or a teacher or an administrator. My experience, on the other hand, convinces me that, although students may lack competence in specific subject matter, they are competent judges of good and bad teaching. This is an area where their competence is superior to mine or to any other person in the academic community.

Dull lectures, perfunctory examinations, papers graded without substantive comment, inaccessibility of professors — all rank higher in importance for the student than a professor's decision to teach Hamlet rather than King Lear. Teaching is not there unless someone is learning and the student can distinguish between teaching and the routine exercise of displaying knowledge.

What we seek here is the democratization of the learning process in which the student is not a passive but rather, an active participant.

To my fellow students . . . The time you spend here is a precious part of your life. The wise use of your time will bear its fruit many years from now.

You may succumb to the easy role of the outside critic who sees wrong and doesn't seek to correct it, who rebels by engaging in meaningless activity on the block or who seek to suppress his anxieties through all night card games. If you fall into this trap, remember that the time you lose cannot be recaptured. The expense or cost of your time is not measured in terms of what you pay, but is also represented by opportunities foregone.

If you are disenchanted, join the rest of us who seek to inject meaning and relevance into our environment. The freedom to be creative is a cherished right at Shaw. Our history demonstrates our creativity and innovation. Join with us as we seek new discoveries and new excitements.

Remember that it is easier to lay blame for your failings on your teachers and your peers, because you have not been stimulated to learn. Others may bear the guilt but you must insure that you do not carry the penalty. Our responsibility for learning is jointly shared. If you fail to use the library and other resources which we have . . . if you fail to keep step with the rest of your peers who seek the discovery of new ideas . . . the burden you carry will be heavy and the disservice is to yourself.

If, indeed, you have an undying love for your black brothers and sisters, you must now resolve that your development here will create a cast of character and mind which will fit you for the leadership of our people.

Our battle for liberation must be fought not by rhetoric and oratory but skillfully designed action. Your love for our people will be expressed in what you do and not what you say or when.

Your responsibility, therefore, is clear. "Get Yourselves Together." Black America and the world needs you. If you mean what you say, and I believe you do, then, brain power must be your goal. The future or destiny of our people is in our hands. Let us not forsake this responsibility.

Our fifth manifesto — the self determination of all black people is a charge which is clear and unmistakable. It is not a new role for black universities such as Shaw. Since our founding, we along with others have carried the responsibility for developing the black leadership in this country and we will not now forsake this responsibility.

Our role as a university in this arena is threefold. We must first insure that all of us — students, faculty and administrators alike, develop a concept of ourselves as a people which is wholesome and respectable. Without this concept of ourselves, our cause is hopeless.

The African and Afro-American Studies Program, which we are developing, will join with other programs in our curricula to help us understand the contributions of black people in America and in the world. We must redress the brainwashing which has stripped us of our dignity and restore to ourselves the proper understanding of what we are and intend to be.

Secondly, this university, as well as others, must promote the development of the black managerial and political class so essential to our survival and advancement. If we are to control our destiny, black capitalism and black political power must become a reality.

All of the rhetoric, the oratory and the splinter organizations controlled by pseudo liberal radicals cannot make us free. The revolution in values and the development of economic and political power must be led by us.

We will not tolerate the psuedo liberals who put guns into our hands and retreat behind safe walls to witness the slaughter of our youth. Their tactic is to divide and conquer, for many of them will shave and take their places in the fixed establishments which continue to exploit us.

If we are to be victorious in our quest for true freedom, we must identify our goals and use our own institutions to promote them. Brain power will be our key to liberation, that capacity to develop strategies, analyze problems and devote an effective response.

The necessity for this university commitment is made clear by the analysis of the times. The report of the Kerner Commission is well known to all of us. As the Kerner Commission reported, "Our nation is moving toward two societies . . . one black, one white, separate and unequal."

In a series of reports appearing in the *Washington Post,* "That prediction is rapidly becoming a reality."

We are told, in last week's issue of *Newsweek,* of the growing discontent of America's white middle class . . . the group President Nixon calls, the forgotten Americans.

The middle class white, quotes *Newsweek,* "Is full of wrath against the incendiary black militant and the welfare mother, hedonistic hippie and the campus revolutionary."

Let America be reminded that we did not get the United States into a war in Southeast Asia, which has cost nearly 40,000 American lives and injured 250,000 more.

We are not responsible for the inflation which has eroded the dollar. We recognize that ours is a multi-racial society, but we also know more clearly than ever before, that we cannot await the second coming before we enjoy the fruits of heaven. It is because we live in a multi-racial society that we must enlist the support of all sensitive and clear thinking Americans. Ethnic consciousness, I emphasize, is not racism . . . its goal is spiritual and economic uplift for that group of Americans who no longer will remain the outcasts of our society.

My fellow colleagues, students, faculty and staff alike, our commitment is clear . . . we have a job to do . . . let us not use the generation gap, status differences between faculty and staff, faculty and students and differences in skin color as excuses for not listening to each other.

Together we can build a better world and insure that this university fulfills its purpose of making men good as men and promoting the welfare of our society.

The assimilationists, as we have seen, began with the premise that black Americans are ethnologically equal to whites and should, therefore, have the right to be fully integrated into the American culture. In order to facilitate this goal, numerous Negro spokesmen adopted a rhetorical strategy designed to enhance the appeal of the members of their race. Meaningful assimilation, they argued, could best be obtained by turning to Christianity and/or self-reliance. While general agreement among the speakers existed on the need for man's dependence upon God and the classical virtues of courage, temperance, wisdom, and justice; significant differences of opinion occurred over the type of education required. Frederick Douglass and Booker T. Washington stressed the worth of practical training which would increase earning power, pride, and utility. In contrast, W. E. B. DuBois, Benjamin Mays, James Cheek and King Cheek, felt that the potential inherent in the "talented tenth" must be nurtured, not in technical or apprentice schools, but in higher educational institutions, emphasizing relevance as well as excellence.

Yet to be considered is the still more popular, influential, and pervasive assimilationist argument establishing the claim that the most effective route leading to desegregation is the one which passes through the legislative halls and judicial chambers. How this faith in the democratic process became a dynamic persuasive force for a century and a half is the subject for Chapter III.

REFERENCES

[1]Phillis Wheatley was born in Africa in 1753 and died in 1784. Despite her short life she achieved some stature as a poet. Among those who praised her work was George Washington.

[2]Phillis Wheatley, *Miscellaneous Poems,* in *Memoir and Poems of Phillis Wheatley,* 3rd ed. (Boston: Isaac Knapp, 1838), pp. 83-84.

[3]*Ibid.,* p. 48.

[4]Allen (1760-1831) was converted under the influence of the Methodists, educated largely by his own efforts, and began a career in religious work. He was instrumental in creating a church that had approximately eighty congregations at the time of his death.

[5]George A. Singleton, ed., *The Life, Experience, and Gospel Labors of the Rt. Rev. Richard Allen, Written by Himself* (Tenn.: Abingdon Press, 1960), p. 69.

[6]*Ibid.,* pp. 69-70.

[7]John Hope Franklin has observed: "The militant anti-slavery movement that had developed by 1831 was, in itself, a powerful religious crusade—part of the larger humanitarian movement sweeping Europe and the Northern United States." *From Slavery to Freedom,* 3rd ed. (New York: Alfred A. Knopf, Inc., 1967), p. 244.

[8]Easton was a clergyman in Hartford, Connecticut who was sensitive to the common practice of denigrating Negroes.

[9]Hosea Easton, *A Treatise on the Intellectual Character, and Political Condition of the Colored People of the United States* (Boston: Isaac Knapp, 1837), p. 5.

[10]*Ibid.,* p. 18.

[11]Garnet (1815-1882) escaped from bondage in 1824 and, after attending Oneida Institute in New York, entered the ministry and became active in slavery agitation. Contemporaries ranked him as one of the

foremost abolitionist orators in the 1840's and 1850's. For a thorough discussion of his life, see James McCune Smith, "Sketch of the Life and Labors of Rev. Highland Garnet," in Garnet, *A Memorial Discourse* (Philadelphia: J. M. Wilson, 1865), pp. 17-68.

12Henry Highland Garnet, *The Past and the Present Condition, and the Destiny of the Colored Race* (Troy, New York: J. C. Kneeland and Co., 1848), p. 12.

13*Ibid.*, p. 15.

14*Richmond Examiner,* cited in Frederick Douglass, *The Claims of the Negro, Ethnologically Considered* (Rochester, New York: Lee, Mann, & Co., 1854), p. 7.

15Frederick Douglass (1817-1895) has become through the years a legendary figure in the history of his race. The description of his speeches appearing in *The Liberator, The Frederick Douglass' Paper, The North Star,* and *The New Era,* along with his own *Narrative of the Life of Frederick Douglass, an American Slave,* provide a remarkable portrait of his role in the civil rights struggle.

16Although historians have largely ignored H. Ford Douglass, two scholars in speech have examined in detail one of his most important speeches. See Orville A. Hitchcock and Ota Thomas Reynolds, "Ford Douglass' Fourth of July Oration, 1860," in J. Jeffrey Auer, ed., *Antislavery and Disunion, 1858–1861* (New York: Harper & Row, Publishers, 1963), pp. 133-51.

17The full text of the speech appears in *The Liberator,* July 13, 1860.

18*Ibid.*

19Brown (1816-1884) was not only an antislavery orator but a historian who wrote the following works: *Narrative of William W. Brown, A Fugitive Slave* (1847); *Three Years in Europe* (1852); *The Black Man, His Antecedents, His Genius, and His Achievements* (1863); and *The Rising Son; or the Antecedents and the Advancement of the Colored Race* (1874).

20This volume is strikingly similar to the later work entitled *The Rising Son.*

21Daniel J. Boorstin, *The Americans: The National Experience* (New York: Random House, Inc., 1965), pp. 179-90.

22Hammon, a slave from Long Island, was born about 1720. He was an essayist and versifier who lived until approximately 1800.

23Jupiter Hammon, "An Address to the Negroes of the State of New York," in Carter Woodson, ed., *The Mind of the Negro as Reflected in Letters Written During the Crisis, 1800–1860* (Washington, D.C.: The Associated Publishers, 1926), p. xv.

24*Ibid.*

25Cited in Boorstin, *The Americans: The National Experience,* p. 193.

26*Ibid.*

27Hall came to the mainland from Barbados in 1765 and, as a minister, was a leader of his people. In 1784, he helped establish a chapter of Negro Masons called the Grand Lodge.

144   THE RHETORIC OF ASSIMILATION

28William C. Nell, *The Colored Patriots of the American Revolution* (Boston: Robert F. Wallcutt, 1855), p. 62.

29*Ibid.*, pp. 62-64.

30*The Liberator,* August 11, 1832, p. 126.

31Crummell, an Episcopalian minister who studied in England, went to Liberia in 1853 where he became a leading figure in race relations. In the 1870's he returned to America and assumed the pastorate of an important church in Washington, D.C. His rhetoric embraced from time to time both the strategies of assimilation and separatism.

32W. E. B. DuBois, *The Souls of Black Folk* (Chicago: A. C. McClurg & Co., 1911), p. 216.

33The Alexander Crummell Papers in the Shomburg Collection, New York Public Library, Harlem Branch, New York City.

34Grimké, who was born in 1850 and educated at Lincoln University and Princeton Theological Seminary, became a prominent Presbyterian minister. In this capacity he delivered numerous guest lectures and special occasional sermons.

35Carter Woodson, ed. *The Works of Francis Grimké,* Vol. II (Washington, D.C.: The Associated Publishers, 1942), 566-88.

36*Ibid.,* 580.

37Stephen Toulmin, *The Uses of Argument* (London: Cambridge University Press, 1964), pp. 94-145.

38Thurman was born in Florida, educated at Morehouse College and Colgate-Rochester Theological Seminary. For many years he served as Dean of Marsh Chapel at Boston University.

39"Twelve Great Preachers," *Life Magazine,* xxxiv, No. 14 (April 6, 1953), pp. 126-33.

40One of the authors studied his unique rhetorical style when Thurman was a guest minister at the First Methodist Church in Pasadena, California on July 15, 1956.

41These cardinal virtues constitute a major emphasis in *The Republic.*

42Not much is known about Mrs. Stewart's background. That she was in demand as a speaker for important occasions is clear from the pages of *The Liberator* in the early 1830's.

43*The Liberator,* April 28, 1832, p. 66.

44This speech is published in two parts. One appears in *The Liberator,* April 27, 1833; the other in the same source on May 4, 1833.

45*Ibid.*

46*Ibid.*

47*Ibid.,* June 9, 1832, p. 92.

48Woodson, *The Works of Francis J. Grimké,* Vol. II, pp. 482-94.

49*Ibid.,* 491.

50This philosophy is often expressed in his editorials appearing in the *Frederick Douglass' Paper, The North Star,* and *The New Era.*

51Franklin, *From Slavery to Freedom,* p. 397.

52For informative discussions of Chavis, see E. W. Knight, "Notes on John Chavis," *North Carolina Historical Review,* VII (July, 1930), pp. 326-45; John Hope Franklin, *The Free Negro in North Carolina, 1790-1860* (Chapel Hill: University of North Carolina Press,, 1943), pp. 169-74; and Clement Eaton, *The Mind of the Old South,* rev. ed. (Baton Rouge: Louisiana State University Press, 1967), pp. 176-79.

53John Chavis to Willie P. Mangum, Raleigh, N.C., July 9, 1832, in Henry T. Shanks, ed., *The Papers of Willie Person Mangum,* Vol. I (Raleigh, N.C.: State Department of Archives and History, 1952), p. 563.

54Weaver treats this concept in *The Ethics of Rhetoric* (Chicago: Henry Regnery Co., 1953).

55Chavis to Mangum, April 4, 1836, in Shanks, *The Papers of Willie Person Mangum,* Vol. II, p. 419.

56*Ibid.*

57Bitzer defines the nature of a rhetorical exigency in his essay on "The Rhetorical Situation," *Philosophy and Rhetoric,* Vol. I (January, 1968), pp. 1-14.

58The South in general had reacted violently against the insurrections of Denmark Vesey and Nat Turner. Thus, the pulpit in the early 1830's was closed to free Negroes in North Carolina. This meant that Chavis was free to teach but could no longer be an active minister.

59*Frederick Douglass' Paper,* March 18, 1853, p. 2.

60*Ibid.*

61Franklin, *From Slavery to Freedom,* p. 396.

62August Meier, "Booker T. Washington: An Interpretation," in Meier, *Negro Thought in America, 1880–1915* (Ann Arbor: University of Michigan Press, 1963), pp. 100-18.

63Booker T. Washington, *My Larger Education; Being Chapters from My Experience* (Garden City, N.Y: Doubleday, Page & Co., 1911), pp. 24-25.

64C. Vann Woodward, *Origins of the New South, 1877–1913* (Baton Rouge: Louisiana State University Press, 1951), p. 357.

65Cited in Booker T. Washington, *Up From Slavery* (New York: Doubleday, Page & Co., 1901), p. 238.

66*The Souls of Black Folk,* p. 43.

67*Ibid.,* pp. 43-59.

68Kenneth E. Boulding, *The Image* (Ann Arbor: The University of Michigan Press, 1966).

69The following citation presented to Dr. Mays upon being awarded an honorary Doctor of Humane Letters Degree in 1965 reveals his impact on his times: "In consent with Luther, 'A Christian individual is perfectly free, Lord of all and subject to none—and yet—he is the perfectly dutiful servant of all.' Mr. President, in the Life, the Learning and Leadership of Benjamin Elijah Mays, Luther's faith is justified through works both good and great. . . . As an orator, speaking on the things dearest to the hearts of men: freedom, liberty, faith and life, equality and human dignity, Benjamin Elijah Mays has motivated men to think and moved them to act in reverence for their God and in respect for their fellow man."

70Dr. James Cheek has had a remarkable career which began as a minister. He came to Shaw University in the 1960's at a time when the institution was experiencing serious financial difficulties. His success in lifting Shaw to national prominence enabled him to win an appointment in 1969 as President of Howard University.

71Benjamin E. Mays, "Desegregation: An Opportunity and a Challenge." An address presented at the 101st Founder's Day Convocation at Shaw University in 1965.

72*Ibid.*

73*Ibid.*

74*Ibid.*

75Consider, for example, the following unpublished manuscript addresses: "To Achieve Full Equality," Founder's Day Address delivered at Bennett College in 1968; and "Address to the Eastern Piedmont District Teacher's Association.

76One of the authors was present to hear Dr. Cheek deliver this address at Shaw University on October 25, 1967.

77King Cheek, who became the 8th President of Shaw University on July 1, 1969, received a Master's degree in Economics and a Doctor of Laws degree from the University of Chicago. After joining the staff at Shaw as an Assistant Professor of Economics and Business in 1964, he was appointed Vice President for Academic Affairs. For further views concerning the educational philosophy of King Cheek, see "The System," in *Shawensis* I, No. 2 (Summer, 1969), 17-21.

Chapter 3   ASSIMILATION THROUGH DEMOCRACY

Much has been written about the legislative and judicial process as it developed in America from 1789 to the mid-twentieth century. Regrettably, the Negro's role in this development has been largely ignored or at least tangential. When he is featured, the analysis is drawn almost exclusively from white sources with the result that the descriptions are often blurred and distorted. Frequently, the typical black American emerges from these studies either as a docile man who stood idly by while reactionary whites chipped away at his freedom, or as a patient and optimistic man who waited contentedly while white liberals represented him in governmental and judicial agencies. Recent research, however, has tended to show that there is a large body of evidence created and preserved by blacks showing their activist role in pressing for civil rights through democratic means.

This chapter will trace the rhetorical strategies of those assimilationists who held that local, state, and national legislatures and courts of law had an obligation to produce and enforce regulations guaranteeing equality and freedom. To provide unity and continuity and to illuminate the long-range campaign strategy which evolved in major historical periods, a chronological pattern will be used. Before proceeding

with this analysis, however, it is necessary to make two preliminary observations. First, the assimilationists discussed in this section not only strongly advocated legislative and judicial action
in the area of human rights but also believed in the importance
of Christianity and self-reliance as necessary tools in the struggle
for deliverance. Second, those, as we saw in the last chapter,
who constructed the major thrust of their rhetoric around this
approach also fully endorsed the concept that governments must
foster integration. The unifying principle, then, for all of the
assimilationists was the theory that racial discrimination and
separatism could not be condoned in a society comprised of
people who were potentially equal in intellect, morality, and
physique.

THE ANTEBELLUM PERIOD

The central issue in America during the antebellum period was
slavery. At the time of the establishment of the federal government in 1789, there were 700,000 slaves; by 1860, however, there
were approximately four million who constituted one-third of the
entire population of the South. In addition, the number of free
Negroes had grown from 59,000 to 488,070.[1] It is instructive to
note that black immigrants arriving in the colonies in the 17th
century were not at first relegated to the status of slaves. This
did not occur, observes Boorstin, until "the demand for labor
increased and the cost of labor rose . . . ."[2] Concerned with their
economy, Southern political leaders gradually reduced the immigrants to the level of slaves. The immigrant, therefore, could
not be considered as a candidate for assimilation into the community.[3] Free Negroes, as might be expected, held a higher status
but even they, as the slavery controversy enlarged, were viewed
as dangerous elements. Therefore, they were, as Franklin suggests, only "quasi-free."[4]

From time to time the South initiated stringent "black codes"
designed to perpetuate slavery. These became especially harsh
following an insurrection such as that of Denmark Vesey or Nat
Turner.[5] For the most part, however, the South maintained control
over its "peculiar institution" through the concept of the unwritten
law.[6] With an uncompromising rigidity, the leaders refused to
bend, despite the fact that less than five percent of the white
southerners in 1860 owned slaves. They answered attacks on
slavery with idealized, unrealistic arguments depicting the slave
as a willing partner in a mutually beneficial economic system.

They pointed with some justification, to the depressed conditions facing the free Negroes in the North who worked in industrial plants. While the unwritten law "tyrannized the South,"[7] a stream of federal legislation flowed from Congress protecting the institution of slavery. Buffeted by southern ultras on one side and northern abolitionists on the other, Congressional moderates held a balance of power which enabled them to pass the compromise measures of 1820 and 1850. These policies of circumstances and expediency went far to delay the Civil War but they did little to solve the compelling moral issue.[8]

Black Americans during the antebellum period responded in different ways to the problems of slavery and segregation. For three decades preceding the War, many slaves, in search of freedom, escaped to the North and West. At the same time, numerous free Negroes, hoping to discover improved opportunities, followed similar courses. This mass migration inevitably led to racial tensions and riots in the North;[9] and this, in turn, delayed progress in civil rights legislation. Against this background of deprived freedom, black Americans began to organize a campaign to eliminate slavery in the South and to secure rights in the North.

Before 1800, orators like Prince Hall and Richard Allen supported the doctrine of abolition, and organizations such as the Free African Society of Philadelphia, passed resolutions calling for the elimination of slavery. By 1830, at least fifty separate Negro groups had been created for the purpose of applying pressure against the system of slavery, and producing a climate conducive to civil rights legislation.[10] Typical of these societies was the General Colored Association of Boston. At its first semi-annual meeting in December, 1828, David Walker, who was soon to gain fame for his provocative *Appeals,* spoke for many when he said:

> Do not two hundred and eight years of very intolerable sufferings teach us the actual necessity of a general union among us? Do we not know indeed, the horrid dilemma into which we are, and from which, we must exert ourselves, to be extricated? Shall we keep slumbering on, with our arms completely folded up, exclaiming every now and then, against our miseries, yet never do the least thing to ameliorate our condition, or that of posterity? Shall we not by such inactivity leave, or rather entail a hereditary degradation on our children, but a little, if at all, inferior to that which our fathers, under all their comparative disadvantages and privations, left on us? In fine, shall we, while

almost every other people under Heaven are making such mighty efforts to better their condition, go around from house to house, inquiring what good associations and societies are going to do to us? Ought we not to form ourselves into a general body to protect, aid, and assist each other to the utmost of our power. . . .[11]

This trend toward civil rights made it easy for blacks to help form the American Anti-Slavery Society, and to provide the financial assistance needed to launch Garrison's *The Liberator*.[12]

Blacks took advantage of the varied communication opportunities made possible by the rise of the abolitionist movement and the establishment of Negro organizations. They spoke freely at biracial conferences and their own conventions, and served as journalists for the newspapers they had created.[13] Moreover, leading white abolitionists never tired of introducing Negro orators — particularly the ex-slaves — to audiences in the United States, the British Isles, France, and Germany. In putting the eloquence of articulate blacks on display, sympathetic whites hoped to demonstrate that their competence was equal to that of the most impressive Anglo-Saxons.

From this general view of the antebellum rhetorical situation, let us now turn to the structure of the arguments and universe of discourse that characterized the speaking practices of leading, representative black Americans who pressed for assimilation through the channel of democracy. In the vanguard of the abolition movement was Nathaniel Paul, pastor of the African Baptist Society in Albany.[14] His contributions to the cause of human rights led him to be selected as a principal speaker at the tenth anniversary celebrating the abolition of slavery in New York.[15] Paul used this occasion to tell the biracial audience that the humane action taken by New York in 1817 would ultimately be repeated in all states and foreign countries where men still were held in bondage by legal sanction. Expressing full confidence in the United States and in the divine wisdom of God, Paul, nevertheless, warned that if it were to become clear in the future that universal abolition could never materialize, he would then be ready to renounce his country and the Bible and become a disloyalist and an atheist. This militant claim in no way suggested that Paul's life-long faith in the justice and power of democracy had diminished. Indeed, it demonstrated instead an optimism which was shared by many liberal thinkers in Europe and Latin America. To Paul, emancipation was more than a probability; it was on the level of apodeictic certainty.[16]

The year 1817 not only marked the date of the emancipation of slaves in New York but also the year of the founding of the American Colonization Society for Liberia. During the next twenty years this organization attracted occasional support from prominent whites and blacks who viewed the prospects of integration with forlorn hope. It made little impact, however, upon those who steadfastly believed that Negroes must remain in America and fight for their democratic rights. Typical of the opposition to the colonization movement was that voiced by Theodore S. Wright, a scholarly assimilationist and clergyman from New York.[17] In an address delivered at the New York State Anti-Slavery Society of Utica in October, 1837, he eulogized James Forten and other Negro leaders in Philadelphia for their immediate opposition to separatism when it was proposed in 1817. "Let us," observed Wright, "imitate their wisdom and courage by repeating their words: 'This is my country, here I was born, here I have toiled and suffered, and here I will die.' "[18]

The argument was geared to blacks both in the primary and the secondary audience. But Wright was not content to let an opportunity pass which might enable him to influence the attitudes of the white abolitionists. He urged that the standards for membership in the Society at Utica be tightened. He suggested that a test should be administered to ascertain whether or not a prospective member fully believed in the dignity and equality of all men. Wright concluded with a plea that all present should examine their hearts and minds through reflection and prayer, and then "rejoice and bless God for this first institution which has combined its energies for the overthrow of the system of slavery."[19]

These two ministers — Nathaniel Paul and Theodore Wright — were the type of mature and scholarly orators the white anti-slavery leaders wished to cultivate. There were, however, a group of youthful black spokesmen who also received invitations to address important conferences and conventions. On January 27, 1841, for example, a student at Dartmouth College, Thomas Paul, journeyed to Boston to deliver a speech before the Massachusetts Anti-Slavery Society.[20] Displaying a remarkable grasp of Biblical literature, European and American history, Paul established a philosophical framework for a strong attack against slavery. After associating the cause he represented with that of a moral reformation, praising Garrison as a genuine reformer in the best historical tradition, and discussing the advantages which both blacks and whites would accrue from emancipation, he dramatically pinpointed what he believed to be the evils of slavery and the challenges awaiting the Massachusetts Society.

> It is, then, to stay this torrent of vice that is rushing over us, and threatening to sweep away every vestige of that edifice the revolutionary fathers constructed with so much care and art, that we have formed the anti-slavery society. It is to lift up our perishing countrymen from the horrible state into which they are plunged by a despotism unparalleled in the history of nations. It is to give opportunity for the development of the moral and intellectual powers of man, to save woman from the bloody lash that is raised above her shrinking form, and to restore the babe to its bereaved mother. It is to save our churches and ministers from the awful charge of fostering and maintaining a sin, against which the great Author of our religion has denounced the most fearful penalties. It is to wipe a foul blot from our country, that her guilty, cowering form may stand erect, no longer the butt of merited ridicule and sarcasm, to save her from the horrors of a servile war, and render her more secure against the foreign harpies who are ready to pounce upon her. And call you this treason? And do the friends of the slave deserve hanging for such motives and purposes?[21]

As an assimilationist who saw salvation in enlightened democracy, Paul advised his listeners to scorn demagogues and "designing politicians," and vote only for those legislators who stood on the side of liberty. In this way, he concluded, we can "make the government what the great Solon would call the most perfect — where an injury done to one individual is the concern of all."[22]

The 1840's and 1850's were years of increased rhetorical activity on the part of black assimilationists who sought to mould public opinion. Among the free Negroes and ex-slaves who delivered special, occasional orations on the government's responsibility for guaranteeing human rights were James W. C. Pennington, Jermin W. Loguen, James McCune Smith, Robert Purvis, William Wells Brown, and Sojourner Truth.[23] By common consent, however, the four most eloquent and influential antebellum black speakers were Charles Lenox Remond, Henry Highland Garnet, Frederick Douglass, and Samuel Ward.[24] Most observers agreed with the following description included in an address by Alexander Crummell in 1882.

> There was the fiery and impulsive Remond, as true and gallant a knight as ever, with unsheathed sword rushed into the thickest of battle fray, and did right noble service. There was our celebrated neighbor [Frederick Douglass], then a youthful re-

cruit, but now 'the old man eloquent,' of Anacostia, who some of our young graduates seem to think a mere bagatelle, but of whom a scholar and divine of my own church told me the other day that he was the only man in America who reminded him, in his eloquence, of the great Prime Minister of England, William Ewart Gladstone. There was Samuel Ward, that mighty master of speech, that giant of intellect, called in his day 'the ablest thinker on his legs,' whom Charles T. Torry declared was only second in his day to Daniel Webster in logical power. And last, but by no means least, was Henry Highland Garnet.[25]

Remond was the first member of his race to become a regular lecturer in the anti-slavery cause. Born and reared in Massachusetts, he was a genteel and urbane man of New England who often boasted that "not a drop of slave blood coursed through his veins." He took pride in the fact that he was the representative of "the educated free man of color."[26] Remond's small stature and lack of originality were more than balanced by his impeccable dress, pleasing voice, and cultivated manner. His impressive appearance, combined with a talent for condensing meaning into concise and forceful terms, rendered him a popular speaker in New England and the British Isles in the early 1840's.[27]

From 1837 through 1840, Remond held the center stage among black speakers in the North. When the organizers of the first World Anti-Slavery Convention meeting in England in 1840, decided to invite one Negro representative from America, they turned logically to Remond. In his maiden speech, the fiery little speaker from Massachusetts ingratiated himself with his partisan audience when he observed that for the first time in his life he stood "on the soil which a slave had but to tread to become free."[28] For the next two years, Remond addressed anti-slavery and temperance groups throughout the British Isles. In these discourses he praised his listeners for their liberal and humane views, eulogized their celebrated reformers, condemned the atrocities inherent in slavery, and described the discourtesies extended to black tourists who travel on steamships and in carriages. Because of Remond's need for immediate feedback from his audience and his confidence in his impromptu and extemporaneous speaking ability, he spoke without manuscript and with few notes. The audible responses and interruptions which frequently occurred served only to trigger additional remarks from the speaker. Remond's British campaign, in short, had all the elements of a genuine rhetorical situation. There was a qualified speaker participating in an occasion that demanded an immediate and appropriate response. Moreover, there was an audience, largely free from constraints, that had the power — not to abolish slavery in America — but to pass resolutions calling for a world-wide moral crusade against the practice of enforced servitude.

Remond's speech before the Hibernian Anti-Slavery Society in Dublin, Ireland typified his approach. The following extended summary of this address, which appeared in *The Liberator* on November 19, 1841, is an important document revealing the rhetorical strategy of a pre-war assimilationist who believed that persuasion could be a meaningful force in rallying public opinion, causing voters, in turn, to pass legislation to emancipate slaves and eliminate segregation.

Charles Lenox Remond
From *Slavery and the Irish**

In rising to make some remarks on the great cause which has brought us together, I wish to preface them with one request : it is, that those by whom I am surrounded will do me the favor of listening to me as attentively and as noiselessly as they may — partly in consideration of my own health, and partly for their own sake. [Hear.] If I rise for one thing more than another, on the present occasion, it is to utter a few sentiments which are founded on the truth, and nothing but the truth, and such being the broad and immutable principle on which are grounded the doctrines I would propound, and the facts to which I would direct attention, I trust that you will not consider that anything which may fall from me is meant to be directed to any one sect or portion of the oppressed, but that my words are designed to have a general and unbounded application to all who suffer under persecution or sorrow, under the bondage of the enthraller. [Cheers.]

There is not a single individual, of all who surround me in this assembly, who may not have it in his power to promote and forward the glorious cause, to the advocacy of which I have devoted myself; nor is there one, the effect and benefit of whose exertions in behalf of the unhappy slave will not be felt and appreciated even in the remote land from which I have traveled hither. It is not the lack of friends, nor of means, nor of publications devoted to our interests which prevents our progressing as rapidly in this holy work as we would wish to progress; but I know from long experience that there is wanting, on the part of the people of Ireland, England, and Scotland, a strong and thorough conviction of the service and benefit which each individual man

---

*Address delivered before the Hibernian Anti-Slavery Society in Dublin, Ireland. Printed in *The Liberator,* November 19, 1841, p. 185.

may, in his own person, render to the cause of liberty, by his own adhesion to our ranks. [Hear! Hear!]

I mean not to deny that in your enlightened and intellectual land, my friends, there are many wise and good men who sympathize most cordially with us, and whose hearts bleed as they think of the heartless cruelty by which the slave is victimized; but keenly though they feel his wrongs, and deeply though they regret his sorrows, they are deterred from taking an active part in the efforts now making to restore him to the life of liberty, from the mistaken and most infatuated idea, that their assistance and cooperation could be but of little service. This is a fatal error, and one against which I cannot too emphatically forewarn you. [Hear! and cheers.]

It is the proud prerogative of all men — even of the most lowly and unobtrusive — to conduce in their own persons to the furtherance of the sacred cause of liberty and tolerance. Nor is it in words only that we should testify our love of freedom, and detestation of oppression. It is very easy to come here and pass resolutions laudatory of the one, and condemnatory of the other; but little advance will be made towards freedom's goal, by our resolving, unless we take care that the tone, tenor, and practice of our lives shall keep pace with our professions. How fondly do I hope that all in this meeting — yea more, in this city, and even throughout the wide extent of your country — may be induced to regard the subject in this light, and to model the practice of their lives accordingly!

I stand here to advocate a cause which, above all others, should be, and ever has been, dear to the Irish heart — the cause of liberty. Nor do I pretend to ask from any Irishman that which I would not always most willingly and delightfully concede to him, if the occasion should ever arise. [Loud cheers.] The request which I would make of you is the request of suffering humanity — the observations I would direct to you are the observations of justice and of truth; and, such being the case, surely there is no Irishman, worthy the name, who will consider that my request is unreasonable, or my observations ill-timed or out of place. The request which I now make, and have often made, is, that those who hear me will forget complexion, and that when the hateful truth is naked to their ears, that slavery exists in America, they will be inclined to consider the subject not as one of color, but of kind—not as one, the merits of which are to be decided by the hue of the skin, but rather one the test whereof should be the nature and character of the being who is enslaved. Enough! he is a man, and so are ye. [Cheers.]

Our love of freedom, our execration of tyrants and tyranny, are founded not merely upon our own individual principles, but also upon a grand and heavenly principle which we draw from the source whence all we have of noble and of good is derived — the source of holy writ. This is the principle which sways the mind of the society which I represent — such, too, I feel assured is the principle of the society I address; and while we can, with truth, make such an averment, there is not a slaveholder in America — there is not a slaveholder in Cuba — there is not a slaveholder in India, but must admit our principle to be good. They acknowledge that principle in their words, but act in defiance of it by their promotion of slavery. We, too, recognize the same heavenly principle, but be it ours to act in accordance with it, by loathing, condemning, and trampling under foot the unholy cause of bondage, meet it where we may.

Many there are, I grieve to say, who are deterred from the consideration of this subject through a vain and silly thought that the question is an elaborate and complicated one, and that in the discussion of it they would become bewildered and mentally blinded, as it were. 'Tis false, most corruptly false, to say so. There is no complication in the matter. The road lies before us, clear, straight, and unwarped as is the path of truth and justice. The question is resolved into two words only — liberty or slavery? And all men who acknowledge and reverence the one as pure and holy, and who loathe and execrate the other as hateful and infamous, ought to come forward and speak the sentiments of their hearts.

These are the few things I had intended to give utterance to as prefatory to the facts I will briefly lay before you in seconding the resolution commended to my charge — after which I will take ocasion to make another motion in connexion with that brought forward by my friend Allen.

The question now before us — namely, that of slavery as it exists in the United States — is probably of greater moment and importance than that of the same evil as it may exist in any other land. This I say, not merely because there are in the United States a vast number of slaves, but also because I know that there are very many countries which, in this as in other respects, take their cue (so to use the word) from America; and of this I feel assured, that while the eyes of the whole world are directed to my own guilty country, the fingers of the wise and of the good in all lands are also pointed ignominiously at that glorious charter which she pretends to have adopted as the rule of her life, but which, day by day, desecrates and dishonors — therefore it is that I consider the behavior of America on the slavery question is looked upon with greater attention, and she exercises in this respect a more paramount influence by her example than does any other country.   [Hear! hear!]

I know that in the pictures which I have drawn of the atrocities to which America in witness, and in the descriptions I have given of the horrors of the slave trade is that country, I am said to have been too severe and rather exaggerated. This, too, was said of the first man who ever mooted the question; but in my own case, as in his, my own breast tells me the charge is unfounded, and the accusation will only have the effect of making me more zealous and energetic in the vindication of truth and humanity.   [Cheers.]

Some there are who are prevented from joining in the great struggle wherein we are engaged from a false and corrupt pride, for they consider (or feign to consider) that the vindication of the slaves' rights is an undignified employment; but I tell them it is an employment more dignified, more noble, more exalted than any other whatsoever in which man can be engaged. [Cheers.]   It is not because the slave is a poor man, nor an ignorant man, nor a lowly man, that I profess myself his friend — it is because he is a despised man, an outraged man, a trampled man, a brutified man — one who, being a man as the best of you are men, is yet herded with the things that crawl and the beasts that grovel.   [Loud cheers.]   It is because I know that He who has promulgated to us all truth — who is Himself the fountain of justice — the source of truth — the perfection of loveliness — has announced from the hill of Sinai, that man cannot attempt the bondage of his fellowman without being guilty of a deadly crime. [Loud cheering.]

I mean not to draw an afflicting picture of the tortures to which the slave is subjected in the United States, and thus, by harrowing your feeling, enlist your sympathies. Sufficient to say he is a man. You are yourselves of his nature, feelings, and character — in his sufferings you are tortured — in his indignities you are insulted. [Hear! hear! and cheers.]   What care I how a man is murdered? — whether he be drowned, strangled, shot, stabbed, or beheaded, is to me indifferent. I only know that he is murdered, and it little boots to him or me whether the wretch be prostrated dead upon the plain in a moment of time — or whether he is murdered piecemeal in being condemned to a hateful, lingering existence, from which man would be relieved by death, and whereof the only solace is the hope of the grave. [Great applause.]

It has been said that for slavery as it exists in British India there is "Balm in Gilead," and it is with pleasure I assent to the proposition. [Hear! hear!] You have learned from my friend, Mr. Allen, how you in this country are situated with respect to British India. He has described to you in vivid and forcible language the position and capabilities of this latter country, and he has proved in the clearest manner how incalcuable are the benefits which the people of Ireland, England, and Scotland have it in their power to confer not merely on those who suffer beneath the yoke of bondage in that fine colony, but even upon themselves, at home, by resolving on having recourse to the fertility of the British Indian soil, and the ingenuity of its population, for those tropical products which are now derived from other climes. [Hear! hear!]

Such, my friends, being the case. I ask you, are we looking for more than we ought to expect from the honor, virtue, and magnanimity of the British people, in expressing a strong and fervent hope that when they shall have considered the horrible nature and fatal tendency of slavery, they will unite as one man in adopting a measure which will at once promote their own interests, and exterminate that inhuman mode of traffic which pours forth human blood like mountain streams, and the continuing of which gives a death-stab to the high renown and glory of England? If you will not consent to do this, you avow yourselves part and parcel of that class of men who whirl the whip and bear the branding-iron. Ah! believe me, my friends, it is a noble work, that in which we are now engaged. [Hear! hear!]   No reproaches of conscience — my inward chidings — no sighing after lost time can embitter the remembrance of this evening's proceedings; and I hope that, if the clock chimes ten ere we shall have concluded, there is none amongst us who will regret that we have devoted so much of our time to a noble task, the aim and object whereof is to raise the lowly, to exalt the afflicted, and strike the ignoble fetter from the dusky limbs of our fellowmen.

My bosom swells with pride and pleasure when I reflect that I am standing before Irishmen — men who in the year 1841 have the name of philanthropists. [Hear! hear! and loud cheers.]   Be it yours, my friends, to retain the lofty title, conditioned as you are as to your political influences, rather than having the name of republicans and democrats, to nurture slavery, and to countenance oppression. [Loud cheers.] Give me a monarchy — give me an oligarchy — give me an autocracy — yea, or even give me a despotic and tyrannical government, if, despite the pride of place and the "proud man's contumely," I see the living spirit of liberty blowing bright and imperishable in the people's breast, rather than a republicanism whose watchwords are, "Equality to all, and mastery to none," but whose deeds belie their splendid promises, and whose actions are those of oppression and persecution. [Cheers.] "Despotism" is a fearful scourge; but there is no delusion in the word. "Despotism" is not a sound which wins softly but deceptively on the ear, lulling it to ruin: it closes no man's mouth — it steals not away the sense — it blinds not the victim : stern and detestable in itself, it falls strongly and detestably on the ear; but give it to me, with all its horrors, rather than that which is in itself, a lie — professing, indeed, to be all that is sweet and goodly, but doing such deeds as, to think of, makes men's blood to freeze. [Immense applause.]

Flattering though this applause cannot but prove to my feelings, I will, however, experience a sentiment of far greater rapture, if, in some six or eight months hence, when in my own country, I shall learn that the call which I this evening make upon you has been responded to, not in words merely, but in deeds: then, indeed, will I feel great delight in having visited your Hibernian country; for I will know that I stood before men who have not merely professed their love and devotion for liberty, but whose life and actions are testimonials of the sincerity of the words they have uttered in witness thereof. [Cheers.]

One word more with reference to British India. It has been my high privilege, for the last few years, to have been associated with George Thompson, the eloquent advocate of the slave in the West Indies. He has been successful in his noble enterprise as regards the West Indies; and never have I listened to him for half an hour upon this subject that I did not feel the truth of what Mr. Allen avers, that if Great Britain would strike the chains off the slaves in America and elsewhere, it must be by giving encouragement to India. In British India is to be found the instrument which will put to death American slavery. If British India may produce, in as great excellence and abundance, those things which are now imported from America at the expense of slave toil, why should not Britain give the preference to the former country? It is only consistent with her well-known love of liberty that she should do so. Look to the confessions of the slaveholders themselves, and you will find it there avowed that the people of England, Ireland, and Scotland, have this power vested in their own hands. Many worthy persons in my own country are deterred from giving their aid and co-operation to the antislavery cause, from an apprehension which, to my mind, is exceedingly silly and unfounded. [Hear!] Their objection to do so is, that they imagine the slaveholders have, in their own hands, the means of putting down all abolitionists, for that they (the slaveholders) have threatened that, in case an effort were made to emancipate the slaves they would dissolve the American Union. Very many good and well-intentioned men in America would have lent us their assistance long ago, were it not for this threat, that the slaveholders would dissolve the American Union. Now, if in this assertion there was or could be one iota of truth — the smallest particle of rationality — I would grant that the objection should have some weight; but the thing is preposterous; beyond all parallel. [Hear! hear!] Why, the very thought is absurdity. What does the American Union mean? Nothing more than this, that the twenty-six States of America are joined together in government and civil rights. The Union is but a parchment document, and as there is no hill so lofty that it may not be surmounted, no space of ocean so boundless that it may not be traversed, there is nothing more possible than that the Union might be dissolved. But is it probable? Suppose that the Union were dissolved to-morrow, by what power or agency, let me ask, would it be possible for the holders to retain their slaves greater in number than themselves? [Loud cries of "hear! hear!"] To whom should the slaveholders look for sympathy, co-operation, and support, in their endeavors to keep these wretches in bondage? Will they look to the free States? Certainly not, for the very deed of dissolution precludes the possibility of that. Will they look to Mexico? No; for the Mexicans regard them with an eye of the rankest jealousy. Will they look to Canada? The thought is absurd. Will they look to the West Indies? What! ask men who are themselves but just liberated to aid in forging chains for other wretches! Who will believe it? Spain is the only land to which they can turn their eyes; but Spain has her own foes to trouble her, and the demon of slavery lurks within her own confines. Where, then, will they look for sympathy, and whither will they fly for aid? [Hear!] Every door is shut against them. Ah, Sir, believe me, the moment when the American Union is dissolved, that instant the power of the slaveholder is prostrated in the dust. Hopeless, helpless, friendless, they become an isolated class of beings, having nothing to depend on but their own strength, and that is weakness indeed. Then will rouse the crushed worm, turning on its torturer, and, in the fierce indignation of outraged men, the slaves will demand the right of measuring arms with their masters. [Immense cheering.] (A voice from the gallery — "Heaven speed the day!")

I do not think I shall myself live to see that day, but that such would be the effect of a dissolution of the American Union I feel confidently assured. [Hear!] Where is the man, who, if asked to become a slave, would not hurl back the offer indignantly in the teeth of the oppressor? — Nay, where is the woman — where is the child? The slaves of the United States are men, women, and children; and that they are as worthy this appellation, nay, worthier, perhaps, than the denizens of more favored lands, is amply testified by their patient and enduring conduct under contumely and outrage, for they, like yourselves, have preferred rather to suffer wrong than to do wrong. [Loud cheers.] I care not, then, for the insolent threat of those contumacious masters, for if the slaveholders of our country were to dissolve the Union sometime next year — if it were to be dissolved at twelve o'clock in the day, it is my firm conviction that before one o'clock (and that is but a single hour) there could not be found a solitary slave throughout the wide dominion of our land. [Cheers.] To suppose, therefore, that the slaveholders are serious in their haughty threat, bears absurdity on its very front: they'll never do it. They would not be so foolish—so thoroughly destitute of common sense as to dissolve the American Union, because forsooth it might be forbidden them to expose their slaves for sale, whip them with thongs, or brand them with iron within the confines of the land.

Is there amongst yourselves, think you, a single man who would be so detestably cruel, so utterly heartless, as to brand his sheep, his oxen, or his horse? For the sake of human nature, I trust there is not one; yet in the guilty land from which I have travelled hither, you will find men calling themselves republicans and patriots, who, with professions of universal equality for ever in their mouths, and the words of liberty ever on their lips, can yet find in their hearts to stand unmoved and unaffected by, while the sleeve is turned up of the wretched helot's garment, and the noise of the red-hot iron, branding the word "slave" in the flesh of his fellowman is hissing in his ears (sensation). I ask of you are you men? and, being men, will you acknowledge or endure such a system as this? [No, no.] Who is there that can visit the Egyptian Hall in London, and having seen there the picture of a slave-market, will not turn away in disgust and indignation, and vow himself from that moment out the inveterate and implacable enemy of that atrocious system which brings ruin, infamy, and disgrace on human nature, and which can have first originated only in motives unearthly and infernal? Look at this state of things, and, freemen as you are yourselves, say will you suffer your fellowmen thus to be trampled on, and insulted with impunity?—Forget the past, but dwell with minds, calm as the intensity of your honest indignation will suffer them to be calm, on the present condition of the slave, and prove that you are worthy of the freedom you yourselves enjoy by aiding to unshackle him. [Loud applause.] Only picture to your mind's eye one man presuming in the face of high heaven, and before the civilized world to spread such wild havoc among his fellowmen as that which I have seen spread by a single slaveholder! When I see a woman condemned to wear such a collar as it were cruelty to bind around the neck of a dog, working in that collar, eating in it, aye, even sleeping in it, for no other crime than merely that of having asked permission to visit her child in an adjoining plantation — when, I repeat, I look on sights like these, my frame shudders with disgust — my blood freezes, and my heart bursts with indignation as I exclaim, "If these things be the result of Christianity or of patriotism, may heaven deliver me from the influence of either!" [Loud cheers.] Such is the system which prevails in many districts of the United States — such the hateful system that I beg of you to aid me in destroying. Who, sir, that looks around and views such scenes as have met my eye full often, could believe that we have the authority of heaven itself for averring "that God has made of one blood the nations of men to dwell on all the face of the earth"? Yet, so it is. What I now demand of all Irishmen is, not merely that they should assent to the resolutions we may here propose, nor be content in merely promising that they will further my plans, but that their whole lives will be a system of unceasing warfare against the inhuman principles of slavery. And, in the name of truth and of justice — in the name of Him who is the God of truth and justice — in the name of dishonored humanity, and of the unhappy slave, whatever be the hue of the skin he wears, whether white or black, blue (if such might be) or red — I call upon you, Irishmen, to extend to the oppressed and enthralled man, under whatsoever sun he may be found, that aid and co-operation, that sympathy and affection, which you would wish, were you in similar circumstances, should be extended to yourselves. [Cheers.]

I regret not, my friends, having made allusion to the brandings and other inhuman cruelties practised by the slaveholders on their unhappy victims — for, as soon will I believe the school-boy's wild and idle tale of the phantom who affrighted him, as believe that anything I have uttered can shock the delicacy of any around me. The recital will, I know, have a salutary effect upon the well organised mind. It may shock the sensibility, but it will inspirit you the rather to use your best exertions to annihilate this cruel system. I mean not here to be understood as saying that every slaveholder in America brands his slaves — I care not, though there be but one branded slave, it is enough for me. That one, so disfigured and disgraced, is a man, and it behoves not those, who are of the same kind, to stand quiescently by, and suffer such an outrage on their fellowman.   [Cheers.]   Yet such an outrage is actually attempted under the American laws. Oh, let such laws be disowned and repudiated by all who love liberty and abhor oppression. Let Irishmen shun a land, however goodly, however fair, where deeds are done which call to heaven for vengeance — let them say to the Americans, "Long have we wished to visit your country; but never will we soil a foot by planting it on your shore until such enormities as now disfigure your national character shall have been done away with and atoned for." — [Cheers.]   Let them tear the flag of freedom down, which flaunts absurdly over a recreant land which has nurtured oppression and makes liberty a mockery, while she pretends to extol its sacred cause.

When Mr. O'Connell — and now, that I have mentioned his name, let me take occasion to say how deply I venerate that good and mighty man, who has put himself forth the undaunted and fearless champion of liberty and the rights of man in every clime the sun adorns. [A peal of applause here burst from the whole assembly which almost made the walls to shake, and which continued for several minutes.]   I could wish, my friends, that if you consider me worthy the honor of your approbation, you would do me the favor of applauding with somewhat more of discretion and good judgment. I was about to say something with reference to a man who is justly dear to all your hearts, but you interrupted me in the middle of my sentence, and I am not sure that I have not forgotten all that I intended to utter.   [Laughter and cheers.]

When, not many months ago, Mr. O'Connell, in the discharge of his duty as a public man and the advocate of liberty, asserted in his place in the House of Commons that there were to be found in Virginia many men who were not merely slaveholders, but even slave-breeders, and furthermore, that the gentleman who discharged the office of American ambassador at the English court, was himself a slaveholder, this latter person, instead of disproving the averment, challenged Mr. O'Connell to fight a duel. [Laughter.]   As soon as he did so, and that the fact of his being a slaveholder had become known, that instant all Ireland should have raised her voice against him, and he should have been politely requested to pack up and return to his own estates, for that Irishmen were not in the habit of being called out to fight for having told the truth. [Cheers and laughter.] What a pretty fellow was this to represent a great nation at the court of St. James's! — a man who felt himself so troubled and scandalized by the truth, that the fighting of a duel was the only device he could have recourse to for healing his wounded honor. Such a man was not fit to have had a local habitation amid a free people. He ought to have been ashamed to have visited free and happy England. Can any more eloquent evidence be adduced of the state of things in my own guilty land than that which is comprised in this fact, that America despatches as her ambassador to the Court of St. James's, not the representative of human liberty — not a man whose life bore evidence of the zeal and faithfulness wherewith he obeyed the doctrine of republicanism, but a man who is himself actually one of the greatest slaveholders in the United States! Should the words which I now utter chance to reach the ears of Mr. Stevenson, it may be, perhaps, that he will challenge me, too, to fight a duel with him, but he should wait until I had learned the art of doing so first, and I fear that so long a postponement might be considered inconvenient.   [Laughter.]

But perhaps I am wandering from my subject. I hold in my hand a resolution, which I will now read for you, and for which I am anxious for your assenting voices. It is this —

"That we receive in the fullest acceptation the Scripture declaration 'that God has made of one blood all nations of men to dwell on the face of the earth': and that to attach any stamp of inferiority or degradation to any portion of the human family, however the Creator has dyed their skins of a deeper hue, is, in our deliberate opinion, at once wicked and anti-Christian."

(Mr. Remond continued at considerable length, and having animadverted in fluent and forcible language on the sinful and infamous prejudice against color, as also on the absurdity of the arguments used by certain of the slaveholders against the amalgamation of the white and negro populations, he concluded his eloquent appeal.)

And now my friends, in resuming my seat, I have nothing further to say unless it be to express my unfeigned gratitude, and that of the Antislavery Society, to the proprietor of this house, who, in the most generous manner, has laid it gratuitously at our disposal.   [Cheers.]   It is a new edifice, and if I were asked to what purpose a structure intended for the service of the Irish public should on the first night of its opening be devoted, I would unhesitatingly say that the project which would most ennoble it and that which would be dearest to the Irish heart, would be such an one as we who are here assembled within these walls are now engaged in — a project which derives its origin from the best and purest feelings of our nature, and whose object is none other than that holy and godlike one of elevating to the station and glorious dignity of a man, him who is degraded and dishonored almost beyond the level of the beast. If in the course of the remarks which I have this evening offered, I may have said anything in reference to my native country — America — which may perhaps be looked upon as severe and unmitigated in its tone — I regret that I cannot make amends — I grieve to think, not that I should have so spoken, but that I should have been compelled so to speak.

[Hear! hear! and cheers.]   I have testified only to that which I have seen —
I have borne evidence solely to that which I have witnessed. With all her
faults and follies, I cannot but regard my native land with feelings of the
proudest affection, and I adopt with pleasure, as wholly consonant with my
own sentiments, the beautiful lines of an American poet, once resident in
England:

> "I love thee — witness Heaven above
> That I, that land — that people love;
> And, rail thy slanders as they will,
> Columbia, I will love thee still.
> Nor love thee less when I do tell,
> Of crimes which in thy bosom dwell.
> Oh! that my weakest words might roll,
> Like Heaven's own thunder through thy soul.
> There is oppression in thy hand
> A sin corrupting all the land;
> There is within thy gates a pest,
> Gold and a Babylonish vest,
> Not hid in shame's concealing shade,
> But broad against the sun displayed.
> Repent thee, then, and quickly bring
> Forth from the camp the accursed thing;
> Consign it to remorseless fire,
> Watch till the latest sparks expire —
> Then, strew its ashes on the wind,
> Nor leave an atom wreck behind.
> Then shall thy wealth and power increase —
> Then shall thy people dwell in peace,
> On thee the Almighty's glory rest,
> And all on earth in thee be blest!"

Remond had cause to be pleased with the response he generated abroad. At the close of one of his addresses, the chairman
announced that those who had had doubts concerning the manhood of the Negro would have had them dispelled upon hearing
a speech from Remond. Similarly, after observing him speak in
Belfast, a journalist published a poem eulogizing the American
orator for the eloquent manner in which he had advocated a
Christian cause.[29] Not all of his experiences, however, were favorable. Some questioned the wisdom of his campaign; others including church groups, refused to make their facilities available
for public anti-slavery meetings. Despite this occasional opposition, Remond returned to the United States sanguine about the
prospects of achieving his goals. It did not take him long, however, to realize that the freedom and accord given to him in
Britain was still unobtainable in the United States, even in a
Northern city like Boston. Partly because of his race and partly
because of his rhetoric, he came to know the meaning of equality

when mingling with the British. But upon his return to his native state he again felt the pangs of prejudice as he attempted to integrate into American society. It was particularly evident in the areas of public and private transportation and housing facilities. Restricted by code and custom from travelling as an equal on railroads and ships and from living as a first class citizen in hotels, the Negro, charged Remond, was humiliated and degraded. The relatively favorable conditions he had experienced abroad prompted Remond to compare the treatment received by blacks in England, Ireland, and Scotland with the treatment they received in the North. This message showing the comparative disadvantage of being an American became a significant aspect of Remond's rhetoric during the next two decades. He developed this particular theme as a witness before the Legislative Committee in the House of Representatives of Massachusetts, respecting the rights of black citizens in travelling. The transcript of his testimony appears below in the February 25, 1842 edition of *The Liberator.*

Charles Lenox Remond

Remarks to the House of Representatives, Respecting the Rights of Colored Citizens in Travelling . . .

Mr. Chairman, and Gentlemen of the Committee:

In rising at this time, and on this occasion, being the first person of color who has ever addressed either of the bodies assembling in this building, I should, perhaps, in the first place, observe that, in consequence of the many misconstructions of the principles and measures of which I am the humble advocate, I may in like manner be subject to similar misconceptions from the moment I open my lips in behalf of the prayer of the petitioners for whom I appear, and therefore feel I have the right at least to ask, at the hands of this intelligent committee, an impartial hearing; and that whatever prejudices they may have imbibed, be eradicated from their minds, if such exist. I have, however, too much confidence in their intelligence, and too much faith in their determination to do their duty as the representatives of this Commonwealth, to presume they can be actuated by partial motives. Trusting, as I do, that the day is not distant, when, on all questions touching the rights of the citizens of this State, men shall be considered *great* only as they are *good* — and not that it shall be told, and painfully experienced, that, in this country, this State, ay, this city, the Athens of America, the rights, privileges and immunities of its citizens are measured by complexion, or any other physical peculiarity or

---

*Address delivered before the Legislative Committee in the House of Representatives of Massachusetts. Printed in *The Liberator,* February 25, 1842, p. 30.

conformation, especially such as over which no man has any control. Complexion can in no sense be construed into crime, much less be rightfully made the criterion of rights. Should the people of color, through a revolution of Providence, become a majority, to the last I would oppose it upon the same principle; for, in either case, it would be equally reprehensible and unjustifiable — alike to be condemned and repudiated. It is Justice I stand here to claim, and not favor for either complexion.

And now, sir, I shall endeavor to confine my remarks to the same subject which has occupied the attention of the Committee thus far, and to stand upon the same principle which has been so ably and so eloquently maintained and established by my esteemed friend, Mr. Phillips.

Our right to citizenship in this State has been acknowledged and secured by the allowance of the elective franchise and consequent taxation; and I know of no good reason, if admitted in this instance, why it should be denied to any other.

With reference to the wrongs inflicted and injuries received on railroads, by persons of color, I need not say they do not end with the termination of the route, but, in effect, tend to discourage, discourage and depress this class of citizens. All hope of reward for upright conduct is cut off. Vice in them becomes a virtue. No distinction is made by the community in which we live. The most vicious is treated as well as the most respectable, both in public and private.

But it is said, we all look alike. If this is true, it is not true that we all behave alike. There is a marked difference; and we claim a recognition of this difference.

In the present state of things, they find God's provisions interfered with in such a way, by these and kindred regulations, that virtue may not claim her divinely appointed rewards. Color is made to obscure the brightest endowments, to degrade the fairest character, and to check the highest and most praiseworthy aspirations. If the colored man is vicious, it makes but little difference; if besotted, it matters not; if vulgar, it is quite as well; and he finds himself as well treated, and received as readily into society, as those of an opposite character. Nay, the higher our aspirations, the loftier our purposes and pursuits, does this iniquitous principle of prejudice fasten upon us, and especial pains are taken to irritate, obstruct and injure. No reward of merit, no remuneration for services, no equivalent is rendered the deserving. And I submit, whether this unkind and unchristian policy is not well calculated to make every man disregardful of his conduct, and every woman unmindful of her reputation.

The grievances of which we complain, be assured, sir, are not imaginary, but real — not local, but universal — not occasional, but continual — every day matter of fact thing — and have become, to the disgrace of our common country, matter of history.

Mr. Chairman, the treatment to which colored Americans are exposed in their own country, finds a counterpart in no other; and I am free to declare that, in the course of nineteen months' travelling in Engand, Ireland and Scotland, I was received, treated and recognized, in public and private society, without any regard to my complexion. From the moment I left the American packet ship in Liverpool, up to the moment I came in contact with it again. I was never reminded of my complexion; and all that know any thing of my usage in the American ship will testify that it was unfit for a brute, and none but one could inflict it. But how unlike that afforded in the British steamer Columbia! Owing to my limited resources, I took a steerage passage. On the first day out, the second officer came to inquire after my health, and finding me the only passenger in that part of the ship, ordered the steward to give me a berth in the second cabin; and from that hour until my stepping on shore at Boston, every politeness was shown me by the officers, and every kindness and attention by the stewards; and I feel under deep and lasting obligations to them, individually and collectively.

In no instance was I insulted, or treated in any way distinct or dissimilar from other passengers or travellers, either in coaches, railroads, steampackets, or hotels; and if the feeling was entertained, in no case did I discover its existence.

I may with propriety here relate an incident illustrative of the subject now under consideration. I took a passage ticket at the steam packet office in Glasgow, for Dublin; and on going into the cabin to retire, I found the berth I had engaged occupied by an Irish gentleman and merchant. I enquired if he had not mistaken the number of his berth? He thought not. On comparing tickets, we saw that the clerk had given two tickets of the same number; and it appeared I had received mine first. The gentleman at once offered to vacate the berth, against which I remonstrated, and took my berth in an opposite state room. Here, sir, we discover treatment just, impartial, reasonable; and we ask nothing beside.

There is a marked difference between social and civil rights. It has been well and justly remarked by my friend Mr. Phillips that we all claim the privilege of selecting our society and associations; but in civil rights one man has not the prerogative to define rights for another. For instance, sir, in public conveyances, for the rich man to usurp the privileges to himself, to the injury of the poor man would be submitted to in no well regulated society. And such is the position suffered by persons of color. On my arrival home from England, I went to the railway station, to go to Salem, being anxious to see my parents and sisters as soon as possible — asked for a ticket, paid 50 cents for it, and was pointed to the American designation car. Having previously received information of the regulations, I took my seat peaceably, believing it better to suffer wrong than do wrong. I felt then, as I felt on many occasions prior to leaving home, unwilling to descend so low as to bandy words with the superintendents, or contest my rights with conductors, or any others in the capacity of servants of any stage or steamboat company, or railroad corporation; although I never, by any means, gave evidence that, by my submission, I intended to sanction usages which would derogate from uncivilized, much less long and loud professing and high pretending America.

Bear with me, while I relate an additional occurrence. On the morning after my return home, I was obliged to go to Boston again, and on going to the Salem station, I met two friends, who enquired if I had any objection to their taking seats with me. I answered, I should be most happy. They took their seats accordingly, and soon afterwards one of them remarked to me —

'Charles, I don't know if they will allow us to ride with you.' It was some time before I could understand what they meant, and on doing so, I laughed — feeling it to be a climax to every absurdity I had heard attributed to Americans. To say nothing of the wrong done those friends, and the insult and indignity offered me by the appearance of the conductor, who ordered the friends from the car in a somewhat harsh manner — they immediately left the carriage.

On returning to Salem some few evenings afterwards, Mr. Chase, the superintendent on this road, made himself known to me, by recalling by-gone days and scenes, and then enquired if I was not glad to get home, after so long an absence in Europe. I told him I was glad to see my parents and family again, and this was the only object I could have, unless he thought I should be glad to take a hermit's life in the great pasture; inasmuch as I never felt to loathe my American name so much as since my arrival. He wished to know my reasons for the remark. I immediately gave them, and wished to know of him, if, in the event of his having a brother with red hair, he should find himself separated while travelling because of this difference, he should deem it just. He could make no reply. I then wished to know if the principle was not the same; and if so, there was an insult implied by his question. In conclusion, I challenged him, as the instrument inflicting the manifold injuries upon all not colored like himself, to the presentation of an instance in any other christian or unchristian country, tolerating usages at once so disgraceful, unjust and inhuman. What if some few of the West or East India planters and merchants should visit our liberty-loving country, with their colored wives — how would he manage? Or, if R.M. Johnson, the gentleman who has been elevated to the second office in the gift of the people, should be travelling from Boston to Salem, if he was prepared to separate him from his wife or daughters (involuntary burst of applause, instantly restrained).

Sir, it happens to be my lot to have a sister a few shades lighter than myself; and who knows, if this state of things is encouraged, whether I may not on some future occasion be mobbed in Washington street, on the supposition of walking with a white young lady! (Suppressed indications of sympathy and applause)

Gentlemen of the Committee, these distinctions react in all their wickedness — to say nothing of their concocted and systematized odiousness and absurdity — upon those who instituted them and particularly so upon those who are illiberal and mean enough to practise them.

Mr. Chairman, if colored people have abused any rights granted them, or failed to exhibit due appreciation of favors bestowed, or shrunk from dangers or responsibility, let it be made to appear. Or if our country contains a population to compare with them in loyalty and patriotism, circumstances duly considered, I have it yet to learn. The history of our country must ever testify in their behalf. In view of these and many additional considerations, I unhesitatingly assert their claim, on the naked principle of merit, to every advantage set forth in the Constitution of this Commonwealth.

Finally, Mr. Chairman, there is in this and other States a large and growing colored population, whose residence in your midst has not been from choice, (let this be understood and reflected upon,) but by the force of circumstances, over which they never had control. Upon the heads of their oppressors and calumniators be the censure and responsibility. If to ask at your hands redress for injuries, and protection in our rights and immunities, as citizens, is reasonable, and dictated alike by justice, humanity and religion, you will not reject, I trust, the prayer of your petitioners.

Before sitting down, I owe it to myself to remark that I was not appraised of the wish of my friends to appear here until passing through Boston, a day or two since; and having been occupied, with other matters, I have had no opportunity for preparation on this occasion. I feel much obliged to the Committee for their kind, patient and attentive hearing. (Applause)

In retrospect, Remond's British campaign was the peak of his career. He had left the United States in 1840 as the first spokesman of American blacks and won new laurels as an international leader in the world anti-slavery movement. Yet even with his early prestige and successes, he soon was overshadowed by two former slaves — Henry Highland Garnet and Frederick Douglass — who identified more closely with the liberal elements among the white communities and the black masses. Garnet cannot be easily categorized as a rhetorical strategist. He began and ended his colorful career as an assimilationist preaching the power of democracy to institute social reform. At times, however, during the interim period of his life, as we will later note, he grew impatient and advocated revolution and separatism as the most productive solutions. Whatever strategy he used, he brought to his task a vibrant, well honed extemporaneous speech that often led to a galvanic response. Alexander Crummell, who heard Garnet speak in his prime, penned the following laudatory sketch:

He had a voice of vast compass and of the sweetest tones. His presence, his scrupulous neatness, his gentlemanly address, his deferential attitude, his fine enthusiasm always won his audience from the start. And then, when he became thoroughly warmed up to his subject and brought his hearers into full accord with himself, he carried them whithersoever he pleased. Now he convulsed them with laughter and filled them with delight; and then by a sudden turn his entire audience would be bathed in tears. At one moment you would be carried away by the terse statement, pointed and accurate, as if from the lips of a Webster, and soon your reason would be addressed by argument as solid and weighty as the utterances of a judge. Anecdote, incisive, sparkling, and convulsive, would be, perchance, the very next turn of the meandering stream; and then, like sunlight breaking on the scene, there would be the sudden bursting forth of a sublime and magnificent passage, carrying the entire audience beyond themselves, and eliciting equal astonishment and applause. The whole effort would generally close with a brief finished, touching peroration, in which pathos and beauty would equally combine. Not unfrequently, at the close of some such grand oration, amid universal plaudits, grand ladies, as well as the humble women of his own race, would shower him with flowers.[30]

In contrast to Remond, Garnet was tall and commanding and proud of his slave ancestry and his unadulterated blood. He was quick to remind his auditors of his close kinship with his oppressed brothers in the South. He was, in all, a representative of all segments of his race.

Garnet launched his rhetorical career in a major address before the annual meeting of the American Anti-Slavery Society in New York in May, 1840. In his maiden speech Garnet presented evidence showing how Negroes had assisted whites in the defense of their country, in the exercise of their religion, in the development of agriculture, and in the advancement of science and literature. He reminded his predominantly white audience that their forefathers "crossed the ocean in search of the freedom now denied to us." From this statement of evidence, warrant, and support, he moved to the unqualified claim that all slaves must be emancipated, and all blacks should be redressed for the wrongs they had suffered. The arguments and the style used to convey this message may be seen in the following transcript of the address reported in *The Liberator,* May 22, 1840.

Henry Highland Garnet

An Address

Resolved, That all the rights and immunities of American citizens are justly due to the people of color, who ever have been, and still are willing to contribute their full share to enrich and to defend our common country.

In rising, Mr. President, to bespeak the passage of the resolution which I have just read, I cannot hope to express all the feelings of my heart. I would

---

*Speech delivered at the anniversary of the American Anti-Slavery Society on May, 1840 in New York. Printed in *The Liberator,* May 22, 1840, p. 82.

point this assembly to the early history of our country. I would invite Americans to examine anew the foundations of our republican institutions. I would remind you, sir, of dear-bought privileges said to be held out to all, but which are notwithstanding denied to immortal millions. I would hold up before you covenants written with blood, that might have been placed in the ark of the nation's glory, but which have been seized by the oppressor's hand and torn to pieces by his scourage. I would call you to listen to the shrill sound of the plantation horn, that comes leaping from the South, and finding an echo even among our northern hills. In a word, I would direct your attention to a pile of wrong, and national disgrace, and shame, as high as heaven.

Sir, the foundation of this government was formed of the most solid materials. Those who first laid their hands to the work of building up in this new world an edifice within whose walls the most extensive liberty should abide, were men who had no communion with tyranny and oppression. It must ever animate and cheer the bosom of the true American patriot to dwell upon the moral sublimity of the spirit of the pilgrims, — a spirit which led them to break asunder the ties that bound them to kindred and country, and to fix their dwellings, and to throw their destinies in the midst of the trackless wilderness. While speaking of those men, the tongue of the orator will never become ineloquent. The strains of the poet that shall entwine their deeds in song shall never vex the ear of patriotism. As they launched into the deep, their very sails were swelled by the breath of liberty. As pure in motive and as resistless in spirit as the waves that bore them thither, they laid the broad foundation of republican institutions. It was then, sir, that new and astonishing truths in regard to the principles of liberty were developed. Acting under the influence of these truths, our fathers pressed forward with holy and patriotic zeal in the road to that national independence which the revolution of seventy-six opened to them. Of the wonderful perseverance — of the ceaseless love of liberty, religious, political, and social, which regulated their actions, who is so base as to complain?

Of the principles laid down in the Declaration of Independence, we find no fault. For that instrument declares, 'that all men are created equal.' We would not question the sincerity of purpose, and devotion to freedom, which seemed to wield the swords of most of the fathers of the revolution. But we complain, in the most unqualified terms, of the base conduct of their degenerate sons. If, when taking into consideration the circumstances with which the revolutionists were surrounded, and the weakness of human nature, we can possibly pardon them for neglecting our brethren's rights — if, in the first dawning of the day of liberty, every part of the patriot's duty did not appear plain — now that we have reached the mid-day of our national career — now that there are ten thousand suns flashing light upon our pathway, this nation is guilty of the basest hypocrisy in withholding the rights due to millions of American citizens.

It is not necessary, Mr. President, for me to attempt to mark out the grounds upon which is built the right of American citizenship. Let it be what it may, upon it the colored inhabitants of this country stand.

It is with pride that I remember that in the earliest attempts to establish democracy in this hemisphere, colored men stood by the side of your fathers and shared with them the toils of the revolution. When freedom, that had been chased over half the world, at last thought she had here found a shelter, and held out her hands for protection, the tearful eye of the colored man, in many instances, gazed with pity upon her tattered garments, and ran to her relief. Many fell in her defence. The grateful soil received them affectionately into its bosom. No monumental piles distinguish their 'dreamless beds.' Scarcely an inch on the page of history has been appropriated to their memory. Yet truth will give them a share of the fame that was reaped upon the field of Lexington and Bunker Hill. Truth will affirm that they participated in the immortal honor that adorned the brow of the illustrious Washington.

In the last war, also, colored citizens rendered signal service to the country. So anxious were they to defend their native shores from invasion, at the batttle of New Orleans, that they did not stop to consult the safety of General Jackson's cotton bags. In order to show to you their ardor in that struggle, permit me to recite to you the words of the late President of the United States. 'I knew well how you loved your native country, and that you had, as well as ourselves, to defend what man holds most dear, parents, relations, wives, children and property. You have done more than I expected. In addition to those previous qualities I before knew you to possess, I found, moreover, among you a noble enthusiasm which leads to the performance of great things.' Such is the language of slaveholders when they would have colored men stand in the front of battle. If they are forgotten by history — if they are not mentioned in the halls of Congress — if prejudice denies them a place in the grateful recollections of Americans in general, I trust they will at least be remembered amid the cloister of the Hermitage.

Sir, in consideration of the toils of our fathers in both wars, we claim the right of American citizenship. We claim it, but shall we ever enjoy it? Our ancestors fought and bled for it, but I will leave it with this assembly to decide whether they fought and bled as wise men or as fools. They have gone to their rest, many of them with their brows all marked with wounds received in fighting the battles of Liberty, while their backs were furrowed by the cruel scourage. Unfortunate men! They knew not that their children were to be immolated upon the altars of slavery — altars erected upon their very graves. They little thought that the Power against which they were fighting would one day emancipate all its slaves, while their own country would muster all her power, and make her mightiest effort to blot out the few scattering stars that linger in the horizon of their posterity's hopes.

But what shall be said? shall we blame these men, and say that they slew their own interests? No, sir, if the revolution was right, they have done nobly, and will stand approved of heaven in the last great day. For, seeing this self same soil which now yields the bitter fruits of slavery in such abundance, in days that have passed, yielded other fruits, 'we ought to blame the culture, not the soil.'

In the exercise of religion, Mr. President, which is the salt that has kept the nation from moral putrefaction, the people of color have rendered their fellow-citizens some small assistance. Our religion truly has taught us to cling to that charity which suffereth long, and endureth all things. The truthfulness of the words of the British statesman, that religion is the basis of civil society, is almost universally acknowledged. And the spirit of our institutions lays it down as a primary duty of Americans to acknowledge the moral government of God in all our affairs. The greatest blessings which we have received as a nation have been given to us on account of the little piety that has been found among us. And no one will say that there has not been now and then a pious soul among our people, although there is enough sin among us to excite the tears of the Christian world. The spirit of Christianity, while it is as extensive as the universe in the desire to do good to man, is also as impartial as the light of heaven. It does not stop to consider the complexion of its adorers. No fervent prayer of the righteous has ever fallen to the earth. No stone brought up to build altars to God, by hands however humble, has ever been rejected. He who heareth the ravens when they cry, and feedeth the young lion when he roars for lack of food, most assuredly forgets not the petitions of his chosen people.

Religion, then, is the preservation of our institutions. It is the mighty pillar which holds up the well-begun structure of this government, which I trust it will ultimately finish. Colored men have been with you in this labor. We are with you still, and will be with you forever. We even hope to worship in the earthly temples of our Lord. If they finally fall, as did the churches of Asia, on account of their sins, without being guilty of contributing to their destruction, let us be buried beneath their ruins. We wish not to survive their overthrow.

Sir, the slaveholder looks upon his victim as though he were not an heir of immortality. The apologists of oppression disregard his tears and blood. Church and State, the one holding up a Christianity, falsely so called, immersed in blood and the other endeavoring to shield itself behind law, have united in platting a scourage with which they have whipped him away from the highest privileges, and driven him into the most hopeless darkness. But from the gloom of the dungeon, prayers, fervent, righteous prayers, have ascended, in answer to which are the blessings that we now enjoy. Among the slaves of the South have been found some of the Lots, in consideration of whose supplications the Lord of Hosts has turned back the fiery waves of the vengeance which a disregard of His law in high places has justly merited.

Sir, if the privilege of American citizenship is granted in return for services done in contributing to the agricultural prosperity of the country, what class of Americans stands above the colored inhabitants of the soil? Who is it that will deny that they here stand pre-eminently entitled to the blessings of life and liberty? Let America blush with eternal shame, and hang her guilty head, when it is fearlessly asserted, that many of our poor, unfortunate females, bleeding under the lash of monsters, have been and still are the tillers of the land. From the Chesapeake Bay to the Sabine River, there is not a foot of cultivated ground that has not smiled beneath the hard hand of the dark American. In the middle States also, we have contributed our proportionate share in tilling the soil. But the South, that points to her cotton fields and sugar plantations, that luxuriates in her orange groves fanned by her spicy breezes, that exults in the pride of her mighty rivers — the South that boasts of her slave supported hospitality, and manages to scare half the world by the blaze of her chivalry, and who in her turn is frightened into hysterics at the appearance of that awful raw-head-and-bloody-bones that is continually groaning 'can't take care of themselves,' she is indebted to us for every breath of agricultural prosperity that she draws. Hear slaveholders themselves on the subject. If we emancipate our slaves, say they, we are undone. Without stopping to show the fallacy of a part of their doctrine, I would have you notice the bare fact set forth in this language, that so far as the agricultural interests of the South are concerned, the slave is her all in all. And, indeed, not only in the labor of the field are the people of color her bone and sinew, her life and blood, for we are told by one who knows all about the wholesome and industrious influence of slavery, that southern republicans, in case emancipation should take place, would be put to their wit's ends as to how their boots should be blacked.

If the dwellers beyond the Potomac have any thing to boast of, it is the wealth of their fields. It is here among the rocks and valleys of the North that the trades display their ten thousand implements. The very clothing in which these dealers in the souls of men are dressed, and the carriages in which they ride, are made at the North. The bowie knives which they flourish in Quixotic glory are manufactured in New York, or somewhere else among innocent northerners. The whips that they bury in the quivering flesh of their prostrate victims are platted on the banks of Passaic. Since the first captive was landed on the old Dominion, colored men have been toiling to make the South what she is today.

Not only in war, and in the exercise of religion, and in promoting the agricultural interests of the country, have colored men assisted you, but they have also contributed greatly in supporting the science and literature of the South. For poor Tom and Dick are sold far away in order that my young lord Frederick William may be sent to college.

Sir, it has been shown, that we assisted you in the days that tried men's souls. We have knelt with you on the footstool of our Heavenly Father, and have supplicated with you for blessings civil, religious, and political. And may God grant that we may never be behind any class of our fellow-citizens in this respect. In slavery we have greatly aided in turning your wildernesses into fruitful fields. Give us our freedom, remunerate us for our labor, and protect our family altars, and, by the blessings of Heaven, we will help make those fruitful fields to blossom and bloom as Eden.

With every fibre of our hearts entwined around our country, and with an indefensible determination to obtain the possession of the natural and inalienable rights of American citizens, we demand redress for the wrongs we have suffered, and ask for the restoration of our birth-right privileges. But we would not look to man alone for these things. The Lord is our strength.

> Avenge thy plundered poor, oh Lord!
> But not with fire, but not with sword;
> Avenge our wrongs, our chains, our sighs,
> The misery in our children's eyes!
> But not with sword, — no, not with fire,

Chastise our country's locustry;
Nor let them feel thine heavier ire;
Chastise them not in poverty;
Though cold in soul as coffined dust,
Their hearts are tearless, dead, and dry,
Let them in outraged mercy trust,
And find that mercy they deny.

I speak in the behalf of my enslaved brethren and the nominally free. There is, Mr. President, a higher sort of freedom which no mortal can touch. That freedom, thanks be unto the Most High, is mine. Yet I am not, nay, cannot be entirely free. I feel for my brethren as a man — bound with them as a brother. Nothing but emancipating my brethren can set me at liberty. If that greatest of all earthly blessings, 'prized above all price," cannot be found in my own native land, than I must be a stranger to it during my pilgrimage here below. For although I were dwelling beneath the bright skies of Asia, or listening to the harp-like strains of the gentle winds that whisper of freedom among the groves of Africa — though my habitation were fixed in the freest part of Victoria's dominions, yet it were vain, and worse than vain for me to indulge the thought of being free, while three millions of my countrymen were wailing to the dark prison-house of oppression.

In submitting the resolution, sir, I would again call upon Americans to remember, that but a few years ago their fathers crossed the ocean in search of the freedom now denied to us. I would beseech them to remember that the great day of God's final reckoning is just before us, remember his eternal justice and then remember the outcast bondman, and let him go forth free in the presence of God, in whose image he was created.

During the next decade Garnet continued to deliver anti-slavery speeches in America and in Europe. With the exception of his most famous and militant address, delivered in New York in 1843,[31] he employed the strategy of assimilation. In January, 1844, he addressed the New York State Legislature on behalf of equal suffrage; and four years later he gave one of his best known lectures entitled, "The Past and the Present Condition, and the Destiny of the Colored Race."[32] In 1850, he went to England as a guest lecturer for the Free Labor Movement. He remained there for two and a half years, speaking in churches and on public platforms.

Despite the eminence he achieved as an orator, Garnet fell short of the accomplishments of Frederick Douglass who was lionized by his contemporaries. Shortly after Douglass' death, Francis Grimké captured the prevailing sentiment of his colleagues when he said:

On the twentieth day of February, 1895, there passed from the stage of action the greatest representative of the colored race that this country has yet produced; one of the most illustrious citizens of the Republic; and one of the most remarkable men of the last century.[33]

Douglass first gained national recognition following his introduction to the abolitionists in 1841. He quickly became a celebrity because of his ability to relate, in compelling form, his experiences as a slave. "Tell your story, Frederick," Garrison would whisper to his protegé, whenever Douglass took the platform.[34] Few speakers were more active than Douglass during the pre-Civil War period. In 1843 alone, he participated in one hundred conventions and countless special assignments.[35] As his rhetorical opportunities expanded, he grew weary of telling the story of his life. He began to use a broader based rhetoric which put the black American's struggle for freedom into historical perspective. In meticulous detail, *The Liberator,* the *North Star,* and the *Frederick Douglass Paper* reported the activities of Douglass. Together, they have preserved an account of the chronological narrative of a major participant in the anti-slavery movement.

Of the antebellum speeches delivered by Douglass, none surpassed in range of power and originality his July 5, 1852 Rochester, New York address entitled, "The Meaning of July Fourth for the Negro."[36] In his remarks Douglass chose not to follow the standard pattern of a celebration speech in which the orator is expected to praise the historical events being commemorated, describe in optimistic terms their relevance for the present, and predict future triumphs. Instead, he startled his audience by demonstrating that the spirit of freedom epitomized by the founding fathers apparently did not apply to Negroes. To dramatize the isolation his people continued to feel seventy-six years after the signing of the Declaration of Independence, he repeatedly substituted the pronoun "your" for "our." Moreover, he drew heavily upon his past personal experiences to depict the suffering and degradation of the four million slaves who could not, in their present condition understand the white man's interpretation of July Fourth. Throughout the major portion of his address, Douglass consciously presented a depressing picture of the status quo and warned of the consequences of a policy based on dual standards. Yet in the end, he remained committed to the belief that the democratic system of government would ultimately provide justice for all men. In making the concluding observation that he did not "despair of this country," Douglass was reflecting his hope that the liberal trend sweeping the world would inevitably change the attitudes of reluctant American citizens who had become accustomed to the institution of slavery.

This speech, presented in its entirety below, explains in part the persistent popularity Douglass has enjoyed with black Americans for the past one hundred and twenty-five years.

Frederick Douglass
The Meaning of July Fourth for the Negro*

Mr. President, Friends and Fellow Citizens:

He who could address this audience without a quailing sensation, has stronger nerves than I have. I do not remember ever to have appeared as a speaker before any assembly more shrinkingly, nor with greater distrust of my ability, than I do this day. A feeling has crept over me quite unfavorable to the exercise of my limited powers of speech. The task before me is one which requires much previous thought and study for its proper performance. I know that apologies of this sort are generally considered flat and unmeaning. I trust, however, that mine will not be so considered. Should I seem at ease, my appearance would much misrepresent me. The little experience I have had in addressing public meetings, in country school houses, avails me nothing on the present occasion.

The papers and placards say that I am to deliver a Fourth of July Oration. This certainly sounds large, and out of the common way, for me. It is true that I have often had the privilege to speak in this beautiful Hall, and to address many who now honor me with their presence. But neither their familiar faces, nor the perfect gage I think I have of Corinthian Hall seems to free me from embarrassment.

The fact is, ladies and gentlemen, the distance between this platform and the slave plantation, from which I escaped, is considerable — and the difficulties to be overcome in getting from the latter to the former are by no means slight. That I am here to-day is, to me, a matter of astonishment as well as of gratitude. You will not, therefore, be surprised, if in what I have to say I evince no elaborate preparation, nor grace my speech with any high sounding exordium. With little experience and with less learning, I have been able to to throw my thoughts hastily and imperfectly together; and trusting to your patient and generous indulgence, I will proceed to lay them before you.

This, for the purpose of this celebation, is the Fourth of July. It is the birthday of your National Independence, and of your political freedom. This,

---

*Frederick Douglass, "The Meaning of July Fourth for the Negro." Delivered on July 5, 1852 in Rochester, New York. Published as a pamphlet by Lee, Mann & Co. in 1852.

to you, is what the Passover was to the emancipated people of God. It carries your minds back to the day, and to the act of your great deliverance; and to the signs, and to the wonders, associated with that act, and that day. This celebration also marks the beginning of another year of your national life; and reminds you that the Republic of America is now 76 years old. I am glad, fellow-citizens, that your nation is so young. Seventy-six years, though a good old age for a man, is but a mere speck in the life of a nation. Three score years and ten is the allotted time for individual men; but nations number their years by thousands. According to this fact, you are, even now, only in the beginning of your national career, still lingering in the period of child-hood. I repeat, I am glad this is so. There is hope in the thought, and hope is much needed, under the dark clouds which lower above the horizon. The eye of the reformer is met with angry flashes, portending disastrous times; but his heart may well beat lighter at the thought that America is young, and that she is still in the impressible stage of her existence. May he not hope that high lessons of wisdom, of justice and of truth, will yet give direction to her destiny? Were the nation older, the patriot's heart might be sadder, and the reformer's brow heavier. Its future might be shrouded in gloom, and the hope of its prophets go out in sorrow. There is consolation in the thought that America is young. — Great streams are not easily turned from channels, worn deep in the course of ages. They may sometimes rise in quiet and stately majesty, and inundate the land, refreshing and fertilizing the earth with their mysterious properties. They may also rise in wrath and fury, and bear away, on their angry waves, the accumulated wealth of years of toil and hardship. They, however, gradually flow back to the same old channel, and flow on as serenely as ever. But, while the river may not be turned aside, it may dry up, and leave nothing behind but the withered branch, and the unsightly rock, to howl in the abyss-sweeping wind, the sad tale of departed glory. As with rivers so with nations.

Fellow-citizens, I shall not presume to dwell at length on the associations that cluster about this day. The simple story of it is, that, 76 years ago, the people of this country were British subjects. The style and title of your "sovereign people" (in which you now glory) was not then born. You were under the British Crown. Your fathers esteemed the English Government as the home government; and England as the fatherland. This home government, you know, although a considerable distance from your home, did, in the exercise of its parental prerogatives, impose upon its colonial children, such restraints, burdens and limitations, as, in its mature judgment, it deemed wise, right and proper.

But your fathers, who had not adopted the fashionable idea of this day, of the infallibility of government, and the absolute character of its acts, presumed to differ from the home government in respect to the wisdom and the justice of some of those burdens and restraints. They went so far in their excitement as to pronounce the measures of government unjust, unreasonable, and oppressive, and altogether such as ought not to be quietly submitted to. I scarcely need say, fellow-citizens, that my opinion of those measures fully accords with that of your fathers. Such a declaration of agreement on my part would not be worth much to anybody. It would certainly prove noth-

ing as to what part I might have taken had I lived during the great controversy of 1776. To say now that America was right, and England was wrong,
is exceedingly easy. Everybody can say it; the dastard, not less than the noble
brave, can flippantly discant on the tyranny of England towards the American
Colonies. It is fashionable to do so; but there was a time when, to pronounce
against England, and in favor of the cause of the colonies, tried men's souls.
They who did so were accounted in their day plotters of mischief, agitators
and rebels, dangerous men. To side with the right against the wrong, with the
weak against the strong, and with the oppressed against the oppressor! here
lies the merit, and the one which, of all others, seems unfashionable in our
day. The cause of liberty may be stabbed by the men who glory in the deeds
of your fathers. But, to proceed.

Feeling themselves harshly and unjustly treated, by the home government, your fathers, like men of honesty, and men of spirit, earnestly sought
redress. They petitioned and remonstrated; they did so in a decorous, respectful, and loyal manner. Their conduct was wholly unexceptionable. This, however, did not answer the purpose. They saw themselves treated with sovereign
indifference, coldness and scorn. Yet they persevered. They were not the men
to look back.

As the sheet anchor takes a firmer hold, when the ship is tossed by the
storm, so did the cause of your fathers grow stronger as it breasted the chill-
ing blasts of kingly displeasure. The greatest and best of British statesmen
admitted its justice, and the loftiest eloquence of the British Senate came to
its support. But, with that blindness which seems to be the unvarying characteristic of tyrants, since Pharaoh and his hosts were drowned in the Red
Sea, the British Government persisted in the exactions complained of.

The madness of this course, we believe, is admitted now, even by England; but we fear the lesson is wholly lost on our present rulers.

Oppression makes a wise man mad. Your fathers were wise men, and
if they did not go mad, they became restive under this treatment. They felt
themselves the victim of grievous wrongs, wholly incurable in their colonial
capacity. With brave men there is always a remedy for oppression. Just here,
the idea of a total separation of the colonies from the crown was born! It was
a startling idea, much more so than we, at this distance of time, regard it.
The timid and the prudent (as has been intimated) of that day were, of
course, shocked and alarmed by it.

Such people lived then, had lived before, and will, probably, ever have
a place on this planet; and their course, in respect to any great change (no
matter how great the good to be attained, or the wrong to be redressed by it),
may be calculated with as much precision as can be the course of the stars.
They hate all changes, but silver, gold and copper change! Of this sort of
change they are always strongly in favor.

These people were called Tories in the days of your fathers; and the
appellation, probably, conveyed the same idea that is meant by a more modern, though a somewhat less euphonious term, which we often find in our
papers, applied to some of our old politicians.

Their opposition to the then dangerous thought was earnest and power-ful; but, amid all their terror and affrighted vociferations against it, the alarming and revolutionary idea moved on, and the country with it.

On the 2d of July, 1766, the old Continental Congress, to the dismay of the lovers of ease, and the worshipers of property, clothed that dreadful idea with all the authority of national sanction. They did so in the form of a resolution; and as we seldom hit upon resolutions, drawn up in our day, whose transparency is at all equal to this, it may refresh your minds and help my story if I read it.

> "Resolved, That these united colonies are, and of right, ought to be free and Independent States; that they are absolved from all alle-giance to the British Crown; and that all political connection be-tween them and the State of Great Britain is, and ought to be, dissolved."

Citizens, your fathers made good that resolution. They succeeded; and to-day you reap the fruits of their success. The freedom gained is yours; and you, therefore, may properly celebrate this anniversary. The 4th of July is the first great fact in your nation's history — the very ringbolt in the chain of your yet undeveloped destiny.

Pride and patriotism, not less than gratitude, prompt you to celebrate and to hold it in perpetual remembrance. I have said that the Declaration of Independence is the ringbolt to the chain of your nation's destiny; so, indeed, I regard it. The principles contained in that instrument are saving principles. Stand by those principles, be true to them on all occasions, in all places, against all foes, and at whatever cost.

From the round top of your ship of state, dark and threatening clouds may be seen. Heavy billows, like mountains in the distance, disclose to the leeward huge forms of flinty rocks! That bolt drawn, that chain broken, and all is lost. Cling to this day — cling to it, and to its principles, with the grasp of a storm-tossed mariner to a spar at midnight.

The coming into being of a nation, in any circumstances, is an interesting event. But, besides general considerations, there were peculiar circumstances which make the advent of this republic an event of special attractiveness.

The whole scene, as I look back to it, was simple, dignified and sublime. The population of the country, at the time, stood at the insignificant number of three millions. The country was poor in the munitions of war. The popula-tion was weak and scattered, and the country a wilderness unsubdued. There were then no means of concert and combination such as exist now. Neither steam nor lightning had then been reduced to order and discipline. From the Potomac to the Delaware was a journey of many days. Under these, and innumerable other disadvantages your fathers declared for liberty and inde-pendence and triumphed.

Fellow Citizens, I am not wanting in respect for the fathers of this republic. The signers of the Declaration of Independence were brave men. They were great men, too — great enough to give frame to a great age. It does not often happen to a nation to raise, at one time, such a number of truly great men. The point from which I am compelled to view them is not, certainly, the most favorable; and yet I cannot contemplate their great deeds with less than admiration. They were statesmen, patriots and heroes, and for the good they did, and the principles they contended for, I will unite with you to honor their memory.

They loved their country better than their own private interests; and, though this is not the highest form of human excellence, all will concede that it is a rare virtue, and that when it is exhibited it ought to command respect. He who will, intelligently, lay down his life for his country is a man whom it is not in human nature to despise. Your fathers staked their lives, their fortunes, and their sacred honor, on the cause of their country. In their admiration of liberty, they lost sight of all other interests.

They were peace men; but they preferred revolution to peaceful submission to bondage. They were quiet men; but they did not shrink from agitating against oppression. They showed forbearance; but that they knew its limits. They believed in order; but not in the order of tyranny. With them, nothing was "settled" that was not right. With them, justice, liberty and humanity were "final"; not slavery and oppression. You may well cherish the memory of such men. They were great in their day and generation. Their solid manhood stands out the more as we contrast it with these degenerate times.

How circumspect, exact and proportionate were all their movements! How unlike the politicians of an hour! Their statesmanship looked beyond the passing moment, and stretched away in strength into the distant future. They seized upon eternal principles, and set a glorious example in their defence. Mark them!

Fully appreciating the hardships to be encountered, firmly believing in the right of their cause, honorably inviting the scrutiny of an on-looking world, reverently appealing to heaven to attest their sincerity, soundly comprehending the solemn responsibility they were about to assume, wisely measuring the terrible odds against them, your fathers, the fathers of this republic, did, most deliberately, under the inspiration of a glorious patriotism, and with a sublime faith in the great principles of justice and freedom, lay deep, the corner-stone of the national super-structure, which has risen and still rises in grandeur around you.

Of this fundamental work, this day is the anniversary. Our eyes are met with demonstrations of joyous enthusiasm. Banners and pennants wave exultingly on the breeze. The din of business, too, is hushed. Even mammon seems to have quitted his grasp on this day. The ear-piercing fife and the stirring drum unite their accents with the ascending peal of a thousand church bells. Prayers are made, hymns are sung, and sermons are preached in honor of this day; while the quick martial tramp of a great and multitudinous nation, echoed back by all the hills, valleys and mountains of a vast continent, bespeak the occasion one of thrilling and universal interest—a nation's jubilee.

Friends and citizens, I need not enter further into the causes which led to this anniversary. Many of you understand them better than I do. You could instruct me in regard to them. That is a branch of knowledge in which you feel, perhaps, a much deeper interest than your speaker. The causes which led to the separation of the colonies from the British crown have never lacked for a tongue. They have all been taught in your common schools, narrated at your firesides, unfolded from your pulpits, and thundered from your legislative halls, and are as familiar to you as household words. They form the staple of your national poetry and eloquence.

I remember, also, that, as a people, Americans are remarkably familiar with all facts which make in their own favor. This is esteemed by some as a national trait — perhaps a national weakness. It is a fact, that whatever makes for the wealth or for the reputation of Americans and can be had cheap! will be found by Americans. I shall not be charged with slandering Americans if I say I think the American side of any question may be safely left in American hands.

I leave, therefore, the great deeds of your fathers to other gentlemen whose claim to have been regularly descended will be less likely to be disputed than mine!

My business, if I have any here to-day, is with the present. The accepted time with God and His cause is the ever-living now.

> Trust no future, however pleasant
> Let the dead past bury its dead;
> Act, act in the living present,
> Heart within, and God overhead.

We have to do with the past only as we can make it useful to the present and to the future. To all inspiring motives, to noble deeds which can be gained from the past, we are welcome. But now is the time, the important time. Your fathers have lived, died, and have done their work, and have done much of it well. You live and must die, and you must do your work. You have no right to enjoy a child's share in the labor of your fathers, unless your children are to be blest by your labors. You have no right to wear out and waste the hard-earned fame of your fathers to cover your indolence. Sydney Smith tells us that men seldom eulogize the wisdom and virtues of their fathers, but to excuse some folly or wickedness of their own. This truth is not a doubtful one. There are illustrations of it near and remote, ancient and modern. It was fashionable, hundreds of years ago, for the children of Jacob to boast, we have "Abraham to our father," when they had long lost Abraham's faith and spirit. That people contented themselves under the shadow of Abraham's great name, while they repudiated the deeds which made his name great. Need I remind you that a similar thing is being done all over this country to-day? Need I tell you that the Jews are not the only people who built the tombs of the prophets, and garnished the sepulchers of the righteous? Washington could not die till he had broken the chains of his slaves. Yet his monument is built up by the price of human blood, and the traders in the bodies and souls of men shout — "We have Washington to *our father*." — Alas! that it should be so; yet so it is.

> The evil that men do, lives after them,
> The good is oft interred with their bones.

Fellow-citizens, pardon me, allow me to ask, why am I called upon to speak here to-day? What have I, or those I represent, to do with your national independence? Are the great principles of political freedom and of natural justice, embodied in that Declaration of Independence, extended to us? and am I, therefore, called upon to bring our humble offering to the national altar, and to confess the benefits and express devout gratitude for the blessings resulting from your independence to us?

Would to God, both for your sakes and ours, that an affirmative answer could be truthfully returned to these questions! Then would my task be light, and my burden easy and delightful. For *who* is there so cold, that a nation's sympathy could not warm him? Who so obdurate and dead to the claims of gratitude, that would not thankfully acknowledge such priceless benefits? Who so stolid and selfish, that would not give his voice to swell the halleujahs of a nation's jubilee, when the chains of servitude had been torn from his limbs? I am not that man. In a case like that, the dumb might eloquently speak, and the "lame man leap as an hart."

But such is not the state of the case. I say it with a sad sense of the disparity between us. I am not included within the pale of this glorious anniversary! Your high independence only reveals the immeasurable distance between us. The blessings in which you, this day, rejoice, are not enjoyed in common. — The rich inheritance of justice, liberty, prosperity and independence, bequeathed by your fathers, is shared by you, not by me. The sunlight that brought light and healing to you, has brought stripes and death to me. This Fourth July is *yours,* not *mine. You* may rejoice, *I* must mourn. To drag a man in fetters into the grand illuminated temple of liberty, and call upon him to join you in joyous anthems, were inhuman mockery and sacrilegious irony. Do you mean, citizens, to mock me, by asking me to speak to-day? If so, there is a parallel to your conduct. And let me warn you that it is dangerous to copy the example of a nation whose crimes, towering up to heaven, were thrown down by the breath of the Almighty, burying that nation in irrevocable ruin! I can to-day take up the plaintive lament of a peeled and woe-smitten people!

"By the rivers of Babylon, there we sat down. Yea! we wept when we remembered Zion. We hanged our harps upon the willows in the midst thereof. For there, they that carried us away captive, required of us a song; and they who wasted us required of us mirth, saying, Sing us one of the songs of Zion. How can we sing the Lord's song in a strange land? If I forget thee, O Jerusalem, let my right hand forget her cunning. If I do remember thee, let my tongue cleave to the roof of my mouth."

Fellow-citizens, above your national, tumultuous joy, I hear the mournful wail of millions! whose chains, heavy and grievous yesterday, are, to-day, rendered more intolerable by the jubilee shouts that reach them. If I do forget, if I do not faithfully remember those bleeding children of sorrow this day, "may my right hand forget her cunning, and may my tongue cleave to the roof of my mouth!" To forget them, to pass lightly over their wrongs, and to chime in with the popular theme, would be treason most scandalous and shocking, and would make me a reproach before God and the world. My subject, then, fellow-citizens, is American slavery. I shall see this day and its popular characteristics from the slave's point of view. Standing there identified with the American bondman, making his wrongs mine, I do not hesitate to declare, with all my soul, that the character and conduct of this nation never looked blacker to me than on this 4th of July! Whether we turn to the declarations of the past, or to the professions of the present, the conduct of the nation seems equally hideous and revolting. America is false to the past, false to the present, and solemnly binds herself to be false to the future. Standing with God and the crushed and bleeding slave on this occasion, I will, in the name of humanity which is outraged, in the name of liberty which is fettered, in the name of the constitution and the Bible which are disregarded and trampled upon, dare to call in question and to denounce, with all the emphasis I can command, everything that serves to perpetuate slavery — the great sin and shame of America! "I will not equivocate; I will not excuse"; I will use the severest language I can command; and yet not one word shall escape me that any man, whose judgment is not blinded by prejudice, or who is not at heart a slaveholder, shall not confess to be right and just.

But I fancy I hear some one of my audience say, "It is just in this circumstance that you and your brother abolitionists fail to make a favorable impression on the public mind. Would you argue more, and denounce less; would you persuade more, and rebuke less; your cause would be much more likely to succeed." But, I submit, where all is plain there is nothing to be argued. What point in the anti-slavery creed would you have me argue? On what branch of the subject do the people of this country need light? Must I undertake to prove that the slave is a man? That point is conceded already. Nobody doubts it. The slaveholders themselves acknowledge it in the enactment of laws for their government. They acknowledge it when they punish disobedience on the part of the slave. There are seventy-two crimes in the State of Virginia which, if committed by a black man (no matter how ignorant he be), subject him to the punishment of death; while only two of the same crimes will subject a white man to the like punishment. What is this but the acknowledgment that the slave is a moral, intellectual, and responsible being? The manhood of the slave is conceded. It is admitted in the fact that Southern statute books are covered with enactments forbidding, under severe fines and penalties, the teaching of the slave to read or write. When you can point to any such laws in reference to the beasts of the field, then I may consent to argue the manhood of the slave. When the dogs in your streets, when the fowls of the air, when the cattle on your hills, when the fish of the sea, and the reptiles that crawl, shall be unable to distinguish the slave from a brute, *then* will I argue with you that the slave is a man!

For the present, it is enough to affirm the equal manhood of the Negro race. Is it not astonishing that, while we are ploughing, planting, and reaping, using all kinds of mechanical tools, erecting houses, constructing bridges, building ships, working in metals of brass, iron, copper, silver and gold; that, while we are reading, writing and ciphering, acting as clerks, merchants and secretaries, having among us lawyers, doctors, ministers, poets, authors, editors, orators and teachers; that, while we are engaged in all manner of enterprises common to other men, digging gold in California, capturing the whale in the Pacific, feeding sheep and cattle on the hill-side, living, moving, acting, thinking, planning, living in families as husbands, wives and children, and, above all, confessing and worshipping the Christian's God, and looking hopefully for life and immortality beyond the grave, we are called upon to prove that we are men!

Would you have me argue that man is entitled to liberty? that he is the rightful owner of his own body? You have already declared it. Must I argue the wrongfulness of slavery? Is that a question for Republicans? Is it to be settled by the rules of logic and argumentation, as a matter beset with great difficulty, involving a doubtful application of the principle of justice, hard to be understood? How should I look to-day, in the presence of Americans, dividing, and subdividing a discourse, to show that men have a natural right to freedom? speaking of it relatively and positively, negatively and affirmatively. To do so, would be to make myself ridiculous, and to offer an insult to your understanding. — There is not a man beneath the canopy of heaven that does not know that slavery is wrong *for him.*

What, am I to argue that it is wrong to make men brutes, to rob them of their liberty, to work them without wages, to keep them ignorant of their relations to their fellow men, to beat them with sticks, to flay their flesh with the lash, to load their limbs with irons, to hunt them with dogs, to sell them at auction, to sunder their families, to knock out their teeth, to burn their flesh, to starve them into obedience and submission to their masters? Must I argue that a system thus marked with blood, and stained with pollution, is *wrong?* No! I will not. I have better employment for my time and strength than such arguments would imply.

What, then, remains to be argued? Is it that slavery is not divine; that God did not establish it; that our doctors of divinity are mistaken? There is blasphemy in the thought. That which is inhuman, cannot be divine! *Who* can reason on such a proposition? They that can, may; I cannot. The time for such argument is passed.

At a time like this, scorching irony, not convincing argument, is needed. O! had I the ability, and could reach the nation's ear, I would, to-day, pour out a fiery stream of biting ridicule, blasting reproach, withering sarcasm, and stern rebuke. For it is not light that is needed, but fire; it is not the gentle shower, but thunder. We need the storm, the whirlwind, and the earthquake. The feeling of the nation must be quickened; the conscience of the nation must be roused; the propriety of the nation must be startled; the hypocrisy of the nation must be exposed; and its crimes against God and man must be proclaimed and denounced.

What, to the American slave, is your 4th of July? I answer; a day that reveals to him, more than all other days in the year, the gross injustice and cruelty to which he is the constant victim. To him, your celebration is a sham; your boasted liberty, an unholy license; your national greatness, swelling vanity; your sounds of rejoicing are empty and heartless; your denunciation of tyrants, brass fronted impudence; your shouts of liberty and equality, hollow mockery; your prayers and hymns, your sermons and thanksgivings, with all your religious parade and solemnity, are, to Him, mere bombast, fraud, deception, impiety, and hypocrisy — a thin veil to cover up crimes which would disgrace a nation of savages. There is not a nation on the earth guilty of practices more shocking and bloody than are the people of the United States, at this very hour.

Go where you may, search where you will, roam through all the monarchies and despotisms of the Old World, travel through South America, search out every abuse, and when you have found the last, lay your facts by the side of the everyday practices of this nation, and you will say with me, that, for revolting barbarity and shameless hypocrisy, America reigns without a rival.

Take the American slave-trade, which we are told by the papers, is especially prosperous just now. Ex-Senator Benton tells us that the price of men was never higher than now. He mentions the fact to show that slavery is in no danger. This trade is one of the peculiarities of American institutions. It is carried on in all the large towns and cities in one-half of this confederacy; and millions are pocketed every year by dealers in this horrid traffic. In several states this trade is a chief source of wealth. It is called (in contradistinction to the foreign slave-trade) *"the internal slave-trade."* It is, probably, called so, too, in order to divert from it the horror with which the foreign slave-trade is contemplated. That trade has long since been denounced by this government as piracy. It has been denounced with burning words from the high places of the nation as an execrable traffic. To arrest it, to put an end to it, this nation keeps a squadron, at immense cost, on the coast of Africa. Everywhere, in this country, it is safe to speak of this foreign slave-trade as a most inhuman traffic, opposed alike to the laws of God and of man. The duty to extirpate and destroy it, is admitted even by our doctors of divinity. In order to put an end to it, some of these have consented that their colored brethren (nominally free) should leave this country, and establish themselves on the western coast of Africa! It is however, a notable fact that while so much execration is poured out by Americans upon all those engaged in the foreign slave-trade, the men engaged in the slave-trade between the states pass without condemnation, and their business is deemed honorable.

Behold the practical operation of this internal slave-trade, the American slave-trade, sustained by American politics and American religion. Here you will see men and women reared like swine for the market. You know what is a swine-drover? I will show you a man-drover. They inhabit all our Southern States. They perambulate the country, and crowd the highways of the nation, with droves of human stock. You will see one of these human flesh jobbers, armed with pistol, whip, and bowie-knife, driving a company of a hundred men, women, and children, from the Potomac to the slave market at New Orleans. These wretched people are to be sold singly, or in lots, to suit purchasers. They are food for the cotton-field and the deadly sugar-mill. Mark the sad procession, as it moves wearily along, and the inhuman wretch who drives them. Hear his savage yells and his blood-curdling oaths, as he hurries on his affrighted captives! There, see the old man with locks thinned and gray. Cast one glance, if you please, upon that young mother, whose shoulders are bare to the scorching sun, her briny tears falling on the brow of the babe in her arms. See, too, that girl of thirteen, weeping, *yes!* weeping, as she thinks of the mother from whom she has been torn! The drove moves tardily. Heat and sorrow have nearly consumed their strength; suddenly you hear a quick snap, like the discharge of a rifle; the fetters clank, and the chain rattles simultaneously; your ears are saluted with a scream, that seems to have torn its way to the centre of your soul! The crack you heard was the sound of the slave-whip; the scream you heard was from the woman you saw with the babe. Her speed had faltered under the weight of her child and her chains! that gash on her shoulder tells her to move on. Follow this drove to New Orleans. Attend the auction; see men examined like horses; see the forms of women rudely and brutally exposed to the shocking gaze of American slave-buyers. See this drove sold and separated forever; and never forget the deep, sad sobs that arose from that scattered multitude. Tell me, citizens, where, under the sun, you can witness a spectacle more fiendish and shocking. Yet this is but a glance at the American slave-trade, as it exists, at this moment, in the ruling part of the United States.

I was born amid such sights and scenes. To me the American slave-trade is a terrible reality. When a child, my soul was often pierced with a sense of its horrors. I lived on Philpot Street, Fell's Point, Baltimore, and have watched from the wharves the slave ships in the Basin, anchored from the shore, with their cargoes of human flesh, waiting for favorable winds to waft them down the Chesapeake. There was, at that time, a grand slave mart kept at the head of Pratt Street, by Austin Woldfolk. His agents were sent into every town and county in Maryland, announcing their arrival, through the papers, and on flaming *"hand-bills,"* headed cash for Negroes. These men were generally well dressed men, and very captivating in their manners; ever ready to drink, to treat, and to gamble. The fate of many a slave has depended upon the turn of a single card; and many a child has been snatched from the arms of its mother by bargains arranged in a state of brutal drunkenness.

The flesh-mongers gather up their victims by dozens, and drive them, chained, to the general depot at Baltimore. When a sufficient number has been collected here, a ship is chartered for the purpose of conveying the forlorn crew to Mobile, or to New Orleans. From the slave prison to the ship, they are usually driven in the darkness of night; for since the anti-slavery agitation, a certain caution is observed.

In the deep, still darkness of midnight, I have been often aroused by the dead, heavy footsteps, and the piteous cries of the chained gangs that passed our door. The anguish of my boyish heart was intense; and I was often consoled, when speaking to my mistress in the morning, to hear her say that the custom was very wicked; that she hated to hear the rattle of the chains and the heart-rending cries. I was glad to find one who sympathized with me in my horror.

Fellow-citizens, this murderous traffic is, to-day, in active operation in this boasted republic. In the solitude of my spirit I see clouds of dust raised on the highways of the South; I see the bleeding footsteps; I hear the doleful wail of fettered humanity on the way to the slave-markets, where the victims are to be sold like *horses, sheep,* and *swine,* knocked off to the highest bidder. There I see the tenderest ties ruthlessly broken, to gratify the lust, caprice and rapacity of the buyers and sellers of men. My soul sickens at the sight.

> *Is this the land your Fathers loved,*
> *The freedom which they toiled to win?*
> *Is this the earth whereon they moved?*
> *Are these the graves they slumber in?*

But a still more inhuman, disgraceful, and scandalous state of things remains to be presented. By an act of the American Congress, not yet two years old, slavery has been nationalized in its most horrible and revolting form. By that act, Mason and Dixon's line has been obliterated; New York has become as Virginia; and the power to hold, hunt, and sell men, women and children, as slaves, remains no longer a mere state institution, but is now an institution of the whole United States. The power is co-extensive with the star-spangled banner, and American Christianity. Where these go, may also go the merciless slave-hunter. Where these are, man is not sacred. He is a bird for the sportsman's gun. By that most foul and fiendish of all human decrees, the liberty and person of every man are put in peril. Your broad republican domain is hunting ground for *men.* Not for thieves and robbers, enemies of society, merely, but for men guilty of no crime. Your law-makers have commanded all good citizens to engage in this hellish sport. Your President, your Secretary of State, your *lords, nobles,* and ecclesiastics enforce, as a duty you owe to your free and glorious country, and to your God, that you do this accursed thing. Not fewer than forty Americans have, within the past two years, been hunted down and, without a moment's warning, hurried away in chains, and consigned to slavery and excruciating torture. Some of these have had wives and children, dependent on them for bread; but of this, no account was made. The right of the hunter to his prey stands superior to the right of marriage, and to *all* rights in this republic, the rights of God included! For black men there is neither law nor justice, humanity nor religion. The Fugitive Slave *Law* makes mercy to them a crime; and bribes the judge who tries them. An American judge gets ten dollars for every victim he consigns to slavery, and five, when he fails to do so. The oath of any two villains is sufficient, under this hell-black enactment, to send the most pious and exemplary black man into the remorseless jaws of slavery! His own testimony is nothing. He can bring no witnesses for himself. The minister of American justice is bound by the law to hear but *one* side; and *that* side is the side of the oppressor. Let this damning fact be perpetually told. Let it be thundered around the world that in tyrant-killing, king-hating, people-loving, democratic, Christian America the seats of justice are filled with judges who hold their offices under an open and palpable *bribe,* and are bound, in deciding the case of a man's liberty, *to hear only his accusers!*

In glaring violation of justice, in shameless disregard of the forms of administering law, in cunning arrangement to entrap the defenceless, and in diabolical intent this Fugitive Slave Law stands alone in the annals of tryrannical legislation. I doubt if there be another nation on the globe having the brass and the baseness to put such a law on the statute-book. If any man in this assembly thinks differently from me in this matter, and feels able to disprove my statements, I will confront him at any suitable time and place he may select.

I take this law to be one of the grossest infringements of Christian Liberty, and, if the churches and ministers of our country were not stupidly blind, or most wickedly indifferent, they, too, would so regard it.

At the very moment that they are thanking God for the enjoyment of civil and religious liberty, and for the right to worship God according to the dictates of their own consciences, they are utterly silent in respect to a law which robs religion of its chief significance and makes it utterly worthless to a world lying in wickedness. Did this law concern the *"mint, anise, and cummin"* — abridge the right to sing psalms, to partake of the sacrament, or to engage in any of the ceremonies of religion, it would be smitten by the thunder of a thousand pulpits. A general shout would go up from the church demanding *repeal, repeal, instant repeal!* — And it would go hard with that politician who presumed to solicit the votes of the people without inscribing this motto on his banner. Further, if this demand were not complied with, another Scotland would be added to the history of religious liberty, and the stern old covenanters would be thrown into the shade. A John Knox would be seen at every church door and heard from every pulpit, and Fillmore would have no more quarter than was shown by Knox to the beautiful, but treacherous, Queen Mary of Scotland. The fact that the church of our country (with fractional exceptions) does not esteem "the Fugitive Slave Law" as a declaration of war against religious liberty, implies that that church regards religion simply as a form of worship, an empty ceremony, and *not* a vital principle, requiring active benevolence, justice, love, and good will towards man. It esteems sacrifice above mercy; psalm-singing above right doing; solemn meetings above practical righteousness. A worship that can be conducted by persons who refuse to give shelter to the houseless, to give bread to the hungry, clothing to the naked, and who enjoin obedience to a law forbidding these acts of mercy is a curse, not a blessing to mankind. The Bible addresses all such persons as "scribes, pharisees, hypocrites, who pay tithe of *mint, anise, and cummin,* and have omitted the weightier matters of the law, judgment, mercy, and faith."

But the church of this country is not only indifferent to the wrongs of the slave, it actually takes sides with the oppressors. It has made itself the bulwark of American slavery, and the shield of American slave-hunters. Many of its most eloquent Divines, who stand as the very lights of the church, have shamelessly given the sanction of religion and the Bible to the whole slave system. They have taught that man may, properly, be a slave; that the relation of master and slave is ordained of God; that to send back an escaped bondman to his master is clearly the duty of all the followers of the Lord Jesus Christ; and this horrible blasphemy is palmed off upon the world for Christianity.

For my part, I would say, welcome infidelity! welcome atheism! welcome anything! in preference to the gospel, *as preached by those Divines!* They convert the very name of religion into an engine of tyranny and barbarous cruelty, and serve to confirm more infidels, in this age, than all the infidel writings of Thomas Paine, Voltaire, and Bolingbroke put together have done! These ministers make religion a cold and flinty-hearted thing, having neither principles of right action nor bowels of compassion. They strip the love of God of its beauty and leave the throne of religion a huge, horrible, repulsive form. It is a religion for oppressors, tyrants, man-stealers, and *thugs*. It is not that *"pure and undefiled religion"* which is from above, and which is *"first pure, then peaceable, easy to be entreated,* full of mercy and good fruits, *without partiality,* and *without hypocrisy."* But a religion which favors the rich against the poor; which exalts the proud above the humble; which divides mankind into two classes, tyrants and slaves; which says to the man in chains, *stay there;* and to the oppressor, *oppress on;* it is a religion which may be professed and enjoyed by all the robbers and enslavers of mankind; it makes God a respecter of persons, denies his fatherhood of the race, and tramples in the dust the great truth of the brotherhood of man. All this we affirm to be true of the popular church, and the popular worship of our land and nation — a religion, a church, and a worship which, on the authority of inspired wisdom, we pronounce to be an abomination in the sight of God. In the language of Isaiah, the American church might be well addressed, "Bring no more vain oblations; incense is an abomination unto me: the new moons and Sabbaths, the calling of assemblies, I cannot away with; it is iniquity, even the solemn meeting. Your new moons, and your appointed feasts my soul hateth. They are a trouble to me; I am weary to bear them; and when ye spread forth your hands I will hide mine eyes from you. Yea! when ye make many prayers, I will not hear. Your hands are full of blood; cease to do evil, learn to do well; seek judgment; relieve the oppressed; judge for the fatherless; plead for the widow."

The American church is guilty, when viewed in connection with what it is doing to uphold slavery; but it is superlatively guilty when viewed in its connection with its ability to abolish slavery.

The sin of which it is guilty is one of omission as well as commission. Albert Barnes but uttered what the common sense of every man at all observant of the actual state of the case will receive as truth, when he declared that "There is no power out of the church that could sustain slavery an hour, if it were not sustained in it."

Let the religious press, the pulpit, the Sunday School, the conference meeting, the great ecclesiastical, missionary, Bible and tract associations of the land array their immense powers against slavery, and slave-holding; and the whole system of crime and blood would be scattered to the winds, and that they do not do this involves them in the most awful responsibility of which the mind can conceive.

In prosecuting the anti-slavery enterprise, we have been asked to spare the church, to spare the ministry; but *how,* we ask, could such a thing be done? We are met on the threshold of our efforts for the redemption of the slave, by the church and ministry of the country, in battle arrayed against us; and we are compelled to fight or flee. From *what* quarter, I beg to know, has proceeded a fire so deadly upon our ranks, during the last two years, as from the Northern pulpit? As the champions of oppressors, the chosen men of American theology have appeared — men honored for their so-called piety, and their real learning. The Lords of Buffalo, the Springs of New York, the Lathrops of Auburn, the Coxes and Spencers of Brooklyn, the Gannets and Sharps of Boston, the Deweys of Washington, and other great religious lights of the land have, in utter denial of the authority of *Him* by whom they professed to be called to the ministry, deliberately taught us, against the example of the Hebrews, and against the remonstrance of the Apostles, *that we ought to obey man's law before the law of God.*

My spirit wearies of such blasphemy; and how such men can be supported, as the "standing types and representatives of Jesus Christ," is a mystery which I leave others to penetrate. In speaking of the American church, however, let it be distinctly understood that I mean the *great mass* of the religious organizations of our land. There are exceptions, and I thank God that there are. Noble men may be found, scattered all over these Northern States, of whom Henry Ward Beecher, of Brooklyn; Samuel J. May, of Syracuse; and my esteemed friend (Rev. R. R. Raymond) on the platform, are shining examples; and let me say further, that, upon these men lies the duty to inspire our ranks with high religious faith and zeal, and to cheer us on in the great mission of the slave's redemption from his chains.

One is struck with the difference between the attitude of the American church towards the anti-slavery movement, and that occupied by the churches in England towards a similar movement in that country. There, the church, true to its mission of ameliorating, elevating and improving the condition of mankind, came forward promptly, bound up the wounds of the West Indian slave, and restored him to his liberty. There, the question of emancipation was a high religious question. It was demanded in the name of humanity, and according to the law of the living God. The Sharps, the Clarksons, the Wilberforces, the Buxtons, the Burchells, and the Knibbs were alike famous for their piety and for their philanthropy. The anti-slavery movement *there* was not an anti-church movement, for the reason that the church took its full share in prosecuting that movement: and the anti-slavery movement in this country will cease to be an anti-church movement, when the church of this country shall assume a favorable instead of a hostile position towards that movement.

Americans! your republican politics, not less than your republican religion, are flagrantly inconsistent. You boast of your love of liberty, your superior civilization, and your pure Christianity, while the whole political power of the nation (as embodied in the two great political parties) is solemnly pledged to support and perpetuate the enslavement of three millions of your countrymen. You hurl your anathemas at the crowned headed tyrants of Russia and Austria and pride yourselves on your Democratic institutions, while you yourselves consent to be the mere *tools* and *body-guards* of the tyrants of Virginia and Carolina. You invite to your shores fugitives of oppression from abroad, honor them with banquets, greet them with ovations, cheer them, toast them, salute them, protect them, and pour out your money to them like water; but the fugitives from your own land you advertise, hunt, arrest, shoot, and kill. You glory in your refinement and your universal education; yet you maintain a system as barbarous and dreadful as ever stained the character of a nation — a system begun in avarice, supported in pride, and perpetuated in cruelty. You shed tears over fallen Hungary, and make the sad story of her wrongs the theme of your poets, statesmen, and orators, till your gallant sons are ready to fly to arms to vindicate her cause against the oppressor; but, in regard to the ten thousand wrongs of the American slave, you would enforce the strictest silence, and would hail him as an enemy of the nation who dares to make those wrongs the subject of public discourse! You are all on fire at the mention of liberty for France or for Ireland; but are as cold as an iceberg at the thought of liberty for the enslaved of America. You discourse eloquently on the dignity of labor; yet, you sustain a system which, in its very essence, casts a stigma upon labor. You can bare your bosom to the storm of British artillery to throw off a three-penny tax on tea; and yet wring the last hard earned farthing from the grasp of the black laborers of your country. You profess to believe "that, of one blood, God made all nations of men to dwell on the face of all the earth," and hath commanded all men, everywhere, to love one another; yet you notoriously hate (and glory in your hatred) all men whose skins are not colored like your own. You declare before the world, and are understood by the world to declare that you *"hold these truths to be self-evident, that all men are created equal; and are endowed by their Creator with certain inalienable rights; and that among these are, life, liberty, and the pursuit of happiness;* and yet, you hold securely, in a bondage which, according to your own Thomas Jefferson, *"is worse than ages of that which your fathers rose in rebellion to oppose," a seventh part* of the inhabitants of your country.

Fellow-citizens, I will not enlarge further on your national inconsistencies. The existence of slavery in this country brands your republicanism as a sham, your humanity as a base pretense, and your Christianity as a lie. It destroys your moral power abroad: it corrupts your politicians at home. It saps the foundation of religion; it makes your name a hissing and a bye-word to a mocking earth. It is the antagonistic force in your government, the only thing that seriously disturbs and endangers your *Union.* It fetters your progress; it is the enemy of improvement; the deadly foe of education; it fosters pride; it breeds insolence; it promotes vice; it shelters crime; it is a curse to the earth that supports it; and yet you cling to it as if it were the sheet anchor of all your hopes. Oh! be warned! be warned! a horrible reptile is coiled up in your nation's bosom; the venomous creature is nursing at the tender breast of your youthful republic; *for the love of God, tear away,* and fling from you the hideous monster, and *let the weight of twenty millions crush and destroy it forever!*

But it is answered in reply to all this, that precisely what I have now denounced is, in fact, guaranteed and sanctioned by the Constitution of the United States; that, the right to hold, and to hunt slaves is a part of that Constitution framed by the illustrious Fathers of this Republic.

Then, I dare to affirm, notwithstanding all I have said before, your fathers stooped, basely stooped

> *To palter with us in a double sense:*
> *And keep the word of promise to the ear,*
> *But break it to the heart.*

And instead of being the honest men I have before declared them to be, they were the veriest impostors that ever practised on mankind. This is the inevitable conclusion, and from it there is no escape; but I differ from those who charge this baseness on the framers of the Constitution of the United States. It is a slander upon their memory, at least, so I believe. There is not time now to argue the constitutional question at length; nor have I the ability to discuss it as it ought to be discussed. The subject has been handled with masterly power by Lysander Spooner, Esq., by William Goodell, by Samuel E. Sewall, Esq., and last, though not least, by Gerrit Smith, Esq. These gentlemen have, as I think, fully and clearly vindicated the Constitution from any design to support slavery for an hour.

Fellow-citizens! there is no matter in respect to which the people of the North have allowed themselves to be so ruinously imposed upon as that of the pro-slavery character of the Constitution. In that instrument I hold there is neither warrant, license, nor sanction of the hateful thing; but interpreted, as it ought to be interpreted, the Constitution is a glorious liberty document. Read its preamble, consider its purposes. Is slavery among them? Is it at the gateway? or is it in the temple? it is neither. While I do not intend to argue this question on the present occasion, let me ask, if it be not somewhat singular that, if the Constitution were intended to be, by its framers and adopters, a slaveholding instrument, why neither slavery, slaveholding, nor slave can anywhere be found in it. What would be thought of an instrument, drawn up, legally drawn up, for the purpose of entitling the city of Rochester to a tract of land, in which no mention of land was made? Now, there are certain rules of interpretation for the proper understanding of all legal instruments. These rules are well established. They are plain, common-sense rules, such as you and I, and all of us, can understand and apply, without having passed years in the study of law. I scout the idea that the question of the constitutionality of slavery, is not a question for the people. I hold that every American citizen has a right to form an opinion of the constitution, and to propagate that opinion, and to use all honorabe means to make his opinion the prevailing one. Without this right, the liberty of an American citizen would be as insecure as that of a Frenchman. Ex-Vice-President Dallas tells us that the constitution is an object to which no American mind can be too attentive, and no American heart too devoted. He further says, the Constitution, in its words, is plain and intelligible, and is meant for the home-bred, unsophisticated understandings of our fellow-citizens. Senator Berrien tells us that the Constitution is the fundamental law, that which controls all others. The charter of our liberties, which every citizen has a personal interest in understanding thoroughly. The testimony of Senator Breese, Lewis Cass, and many others that might be named, who are everywhere esteemed as sound lawyers, so regard the constitution. I take it, therefore, that it is not presumption in a private citizen to form an opinion of that instrument.

Now, take the Constitution according to its plain reading, and I defy the presentation of a single pro-slavery clause in it. On the other hand, it will be found to contain principles and purposes, entirely hostile to the existence of slavery.

I have detained my audience entirely too long already. At some future period I will gladly avail myself of an opportunity to give this subject a full and fair discussion.

Allow me to say, in conclusion, notwithstanding the dark picture I have this day presented, of the state of the nation, I do not despair of this country. There are forces in operation which must inevitably work the downfall of slavery. "The arm of the Lord is not shortened," and the doom of slavery is certain. I, therefore, leave off where I began, with hope. While drawing encouragement from "the Declaration of Independence," the great principles it contains, and the genius of American Institutions, my spirit is also cheered by the obvious tendencies of the age. Nations do not now stand in the same relation to each other that they did ages ago. No nation can now shut itself up from the surrounding world and trot round in the same old path of its fathers without interference. The time was when such could be done. Long established customs of hurtful character could formerly fence themselves in, and do their evil work with social impunity. Knowledge was then confined and enjoyed by the privileged few, and the multitude walked on in mental darkness. But a change has now come over the affairs of mankind. Walled cities and empires have become unfashionable. The arm of commerce has borne away the gates of the strong city. Intelligence is penetrating the darkest corners of the globe. It makes its pathway over and under the sea, as well as on the earth. Wind, steam, and lightning are its chartered agents. Oceans no longer divide, but link nations together. From Boston to London is now a holiday excursion. Space is comparatively annihilated. — Thoughts expressed on one side of the Atlantic are distinctly heard on the other.

The far off and almost fabulous Pacific rolls in grandeur at our feet. The Celestial Empire, the mystery of ages, is being solved. The fiat of the Almighty, "Let there be Light," has not yet spent its force. No abuse, no outrage whether in taste, sport or avarice, can now hide itself from the all-pervading light. The iron shoe, and crippled foot of China must be seen in contrast with nature. Africa must rise and put on her yet unwoven garment. "Ethiopia shall stretch out her hand unto God." In the fervent aspirations of William Lloyd Garrison, I say, and let every heart join in saying it:

> God speed the year of jubilee
>   The wide world o'er!
> When from their galling chains set free,
> Th' oppress'd shall vilely bend the knee,
> And wear the yoke of tyranny
>   Like brutes no more.
> That year will come, and freedom's reign,
> To man his plundered rights again
>   Restore.
>
> God speed the day when human blood
>   Shall cease to flow!
> In every clime be understood,
> The claims of human brotherhood,
> And each return for evil, good,

Not blow for blow;
That day will come all feuds to end,
And change into a faithful friend
    Each foe.

God speed the hour, the glorious hour,
    When none on earth
Shall exercise a lordly power,
Nor in a tyrant's presence cower;
But to all manhood's stature tower,
    By equal birth!
That hour will come, to each, to all,
And from his prison-house, to thrall
    Go forth.

Until that year, day, hour, arrive,
With head, and heart, and hand I'll strive,
To break the rod, and rend the gyve,
The spoiler of his prey deprive —
So witness Heaven!
And never from my chosen post,
Whate'er the peril or the cost,
Be driven.

As Douglass spoke, the members of his audience who had known him since his escape to freedom in 1838, were impressed with the observable changes in his appearance and manner. When he first joined the Anti-Slavery Movement in Massachusetts in 1841, he was hesitant and insecure and often could not convince his auditors that the anecdotal experiences he related were true. Now, eleven years later, he had been conditioned by the hustings in 1843, by his two year visit to Europe, and by his work as the editor of the *North Star* — a newspaper he had established in 1847. In 1852, he was an imposing and confident figure who stood "over six feet in height, with brown skin, frizzly hair, leonine head, strong constitution, and a fine voice."[37] Many compared him favorably with the great triumvirate of antebellum orators — Clay, Calhoun, and Webster.[38]

Of the three most prominent assimilationists in the 1840's — Remond, Garnet, and Douglass — only Douglass continued to expand his influence as a spokesman for anti-slavery in the 1850's. Remond's sensitivity[39] made it difficult for him to accept racial prejudice in any form, and because Douglass had usurped his position as the foremost black spokesman, he could not view Douglass' meteoric rise with objectivity. He became progressively more petulant and militant.[40] Garnet's diminishing influence, which proved to be temporary, stemmed from other causes. Sent to

Jamaica as a United Presbyterian missionary in 1852, he remained there for three years before returning to the United States as the pastor of the Shiloh Church in New York City. For the next few years, he focused on the task of restoring this church to its former position of power and prestige. To fill this vacuum other black speakers — including H. Ford Douglass, John Mercer Langston, and Dr. John Rock — began to emerge.[41] In many respects Rock's career was unparalleled by that of his contemporaries. Due to his broad interests, Rock became successively a teacher, physician, dentist, and lawyer. The versatility he demonstrated in choosing professions was also evident in his use of rhetoric. He could lecture with insight on a wide range of topics such as, the "Unity of the Human Races" and the "Character and Writings of Madame De Stael."[42] What he liked most, however, was to speak on the adverse effects of slavery and discrimination.

Rock's appearance before the Committee on Federal Relations in the hall of the House of Representatives in Massachusetts, February 24, 1860 was representative of his anti-slavery address. In this setting, he spoke on behalf of a petition to strike out the word "white" in the Militia Law of the State. With telling sarcasm he ridiculed segregationists for their unconvincing practice of comparing "the highest grade of Anglo-Saxon intellect to the lowest form of Negro sensuality." He reminded his audience that a benevolent and just God could never approve the blessings of citizenship only for those men "who have white skins and straight hair!" Rock next sketched his specific grievance against his adopted state of Massachusetts.

> You say to him [the Negro], you shall be free here in this old Puritan Commonwealth; but the moment he begins to walk about as though he could exercise those God-given rights which he feels are common to this country and to humanity, you (surprised at his impudence) say, "You can't go there." You give us the right of citizenship in this Commonwealth, and yet the jury boxes are closed against us; and when we ask you for the right to take up arms to defend a Commonwealth which professes to protect us, you won't. Let us be wise or ignorant, brutes or men, our color is our crime, and oppression the penalty.[43]

Rock further sought to shame his listeners by describing the low esteem with which America was regarded by enlightened Europeans and by expressing the hope that they would not follow a policy of fear dictated by the expedient demands of the forthcoming presidential contest. "In the name of your present interests, your posterity, and your sense of fair play," he asserted in the conclusion, "you should adopt the pending amendment."

On August 1, 1862 — seventeen months after Lincoln's election and more than a year after the outbreak of the Civil War — Rock was still pessimistic about the status of civil rights for the Negro. In an address to the people of the Commonwealth, he scolded northern political leaders for discussing the possibility of compensating slave owners and for treating the blacks of Liberia and Haiti with greater consideration than their counterparts in Boston. Similarly, he rebuked southern slave masters for publicly and legally oppressing blacks while privately practicing enforced amalgamation. Rock's greatest attack was reserved for the Massachusetts men who paid lip service to equality and freedom, yet denied educated and talented blacks the right to find suitable employment and to defend their state and country in time of war.[44] Rock personified the impatience black Americans displayed toward Lincoln's reluctance to sign the Emancipation Proclamation. Yet he, like Douglass, never relinquished his faith in the efficacy of persuasion and the democratic process as means of producing change.

Rock's strategy during the war was to pressure the legislators of Massachusetts, hoping to prod them into action in the area of civil rights. Douglass, on the other hand, used this crisis period to reiterate his political and social philisophy and to translate his theories into action. "He thundered against slavery," observed DuBois, "as the principal cause of the war; he offered black men as soldiers and pleaded with black men to give their services. He assisted in recruiting the celebrated 54th and 55th Massachusetts colored regiments, giving his own sons as first recruits."[45]

Meanwhile, in 1864, Garnet left New York to accept an appointment as pastor of the Fifteenth Street Presbyterian Church in Washington, D.C. On February 12, 1865, he delivered a memorial discourse in the House of Representatives commemorating the passage of the Thirteenth Amendment. Employing the aggressive oratory which characterized his style in the 1840s', he urged the members of Congress to become instrumental in moving their northern voters from a conservative to a liberal position in their attitude toward slavery and civil rights. Armed with testimony drawn from Biblical and historical literature and personal experience, he decried the brutalizing effect of slavery and the hypocrisy of those who defended it. Garnet was conscious of the persistent charge that demands of the reformers were endless. He met this challenge with the assertion that demands in the future would cease only

. . . when all unjust and heavy burdens shall be moved from every man in the land. When all invidious and proscriptive distinctions shall be blotted out from our laws, whether they be constitutional, statute, or municipal laws. When emancipation shall be followed by enfranchisement, and all men holding allegiance to the government shall enjoy every right of American citizenship. When our brave and gallant soldiers shall have justice done unto them. When the men who endure the sufferings and perils of the battlefield in the defense of their country, and in order to keep our rulers in their places, shall enjoy the well-earned privilege of voting for them. When in the army and navy, and in every legitimate and honorable occupation, promotion shall smile upon merit without the slightest regard to the complexion of a man's face. When there shall be no more class legislation, and no more trouble concerning the black man and his rights, than there is in regard to other American citizens. When, in every respect, he shall be equal before the law, and shall be left to make his own way in the social walks of life.[46]

With this presentation and the surrender of Lee's Army two months later came the end of the Civil War. Garnet was prophetic in predicting the persistent pressure for social reform from black assimilationists during the Reconstruction Period and the modern era.

RECONSTRUCTION AND ITS AFTERMATH: 1865-1915

The period following the Civil War was one of the dramatic episodes in American history. Four million blacks who had been slaves were suddenly free and needed to be assimilated into the political, social, and economic system of a country torn by hate. To assist this process, Congress passed the Fourteenth and Fifteenth Amendments, created a Freedmen's Bureau, disfranchised numerous white voters in the South, and established five military districts in the South to maintain law and order. The Reconstruction Era, from approximately 1868 to 1877, dealt with problems of both races but, as Samuel Eliot Morison has pointed out, "the Negro was the central figure."[47] For the first time in the history of the South, blacks became local, state, and national legislators. By 1870, the future in race relations appeared so promising that some Negro leaders welcomed the dawning of a new age. In a sermon delivered at the Zion Church in Boston, W. H. Abbott enthusiastically observed: "We now stand free and untrammeled; the world with its advantages and privileges is now freely offered to us, and we are elevated to a platform loftier, broader, nobler; on an equality with all, second to none."[48] A few months later John Mercer Langston,[49] in an address celebrating the passage of the Fifteenth Amendment, trumpeted the virtues of democracy. This speech which follows is typical of the confidence displayed by black Americans during the early months of Reconstruction.

John M. Langston

The Passage of the Fifteenth Amendment*

Fellow Citizens: In the presence of this occasion and the fact it honors, eloquence itself stands abashed. We celebrate today the triumph of genuine democracy, that democracy which asks nothing but what it concedes, and concedes nothing but what it demands; destructive of despotism, it is the sole conservator of liberty, labor and property. It is the law of nature pervading the law of the land. (Applause)

We celebrate the triumph of that democracy which was affirmed by the founders of our Government in the words, 'We hold these truths to be self-evident, that all men are created equal, and endowed by their Creator with certain inalienable rights, among which are life, liberty, and the pursuit of happiness. To secure these ends governments are instituted among men, deriving their just powers from the consent of the governed.'

We celebrate the triumph of that democracy which was subsequently defined and declared in the language of the preamble and body of the United States Constitution: 'We, the people of the United States, in order to form a more perfect union, establish justice, insure domestic tranquility, provide for the common defence, promote the general welfare, and secure the blessings of liberty to ourselves and our posterity, do ordain and establish this Constitution for the United States of America.' 'No person shall be deprived of life, liberty, or property without due process of law.' And 'the citizens of each State shall be entitled to all the privileges and immunities of the citizens of the several States.' (Applause)

We celebrate the triumph of that democracy which, forgetful of nationality, unmindful of birth-place, oblivious of complexional peculiarities or former condition of servitude, sees in every son of humanity a child of God, and imposes by a stern decree, with solemn sanctions, the obligations and the duty of recognizing and respecting this sonship and fatherhood. (Applause)

We celebrate the triumph of that democracy whose surest protection and support are found in free thought, free speech and a free press, and whose truest and sublimest expression and definition are found in the work-

---

*From the *New National Era,* May 26, 1870, p. 1.

ings and results of self-government. (Applause) In a single word, we celebrate in the demonstrations of this magnificent occasion the triumph of that
democracy, the comprehensive and far-reaching definition of which is given
in the terse and matchless words of the New Testament, 'Whatsoever ye
would that men should do to you do ye even so to them. (Applause)

Standing in the presence of this triumph and regaling ourselves upon the
future glories promised in the yet grander triumphs of our untrammeled and
vigorous democracy, we are able to answer negatively in the full assurance
of an intelligent faith the questions propounded by the silver-tongued orator
of New England when he asked: 'Is liberty to die in this country? Has God
Almighty scooped out the Mississippi Valley for its grave? Has He lifted up
the Rocky Mountains for its monument? And has he set Niagara to hymn
its requiem?' Nay, verily. The Mississippi Valley is to be the theater of the
highest achievements of our freedom and democracy — the Rocky Mountains the monuments upon which are engraved the records of these achievements, and Niagara is set to hymn not the death-dirge, but to swell the chorus
of their song of victory. (Applause) Moses, the great Jewish leader, and
Miriam, the prophetess, sang a song unto the Lord upon the deliverance of
the children of Israel. If they could sing a song saying: 'Sing ye to the Lord,
for he has triumphed gloriously' when three millions of their countrymen
were delivered, how shall we shout for joy and gladness, making utterance
of the liveliest and most profound sentiments of gratitude and thanksgivings
when we remember that forty millions of our countrymen have been emancipated and our whole country disenthralled! The words of the Psalmist befit
our lips: 'O sing unto the Lord a new song; for He hath done marvellous
things; His right hand and His holy arm hath gotten Him the victory.'
(Applause)

First, we meet to celebrate at once the abolition of slavery and the
enfranchisement of the colored men of our country. (Applause)

Second. In order to appreciate suitably these two great facts, so full of
significance and interest, so pregnant of national moment and far-reaching
consequences, we must, at least, briefly consider what slavery was, the interests destroyed by it, the utter shipwreck it made of American liberty itself.
(Applause)

Third. It is necessary, too, would we rejoice intelligently, in view of
our best dispensation of freedom, that we consider well the promise made,
in the good Providence which has wrought so grandly and gloriously in our
behalf. (Applause)

Fourth. And because slavery, while it chattelized the negro, stripped
the white American of freedom of thought, freedom of speech, freedom of
locomotion, thus showing itself the enemy of all, it is well for us, forgetting
now our complexion, our former condition, and our nationality, to join in
the celebration of a triumph upon the field of battle as well as in the field of
politics and morals, which presages and promises us all a free home, and a
Government which is, indeed, a democracy, and rejoice together as citizens
of a common country, to whose welfare and destiny we make a cordial pledge
of 'our lives, our property and our sacred honor.' (Applause)

Fifth. As showing the condition of American liberty in the days of slavery and fugitive slave laws, there are three facts connected with our history, and to be written yet in the biographies, of three Americans who justly claim a pure Anglo-American lineage. (Applause)

And allusion here is made to no obscure and insignificant men, but to men of large and unusual ability, by means of which they have been lifted into high places in the country and State, from which they have gained wide reputation and extended influence, indeed, two of them have made for themselves a reputation and influence as wide as the world, and as enduring as the principles of liberty and equalty which they have so ably and fearlessly advocated.

And, first of Hoar and South Carolina; second, of Charles Sumner; third. of Wm. Lloyd Garrison, forbidden to visit the Capital city of his native country. These cases are but specimens, and indicate the condition of the dominant class in our country — the class representing the intelligence, the wealth and power under the regime of slavery.

And where, then, was the slave and the negro nominally freed? The former was a chattel, numbered with beasts and creeping things, while the latter led a miserable life in disappointed expectation of that freedom denied him under the black laws of the country. But through the dread arbitrament of war, sanctioned and sanctified in the thirteenth amendment of the United States Constitution, we enjoy while we celebrate our emancipation, which is truly national. (Applause)

But more still, we rejoice today in that enfranchisement under the fourteenth and fifteenth amendments of the United States Constitution, which signifies the possession of all civil rights and the enjoyment of all political powers. (Applause)

Thus endowed, under the laws of our country, God and Humanity, as well as duty to both, bid us go forward in life, meeting all its responsibilities in the spirit of true men and patriotic citizens, cultivating among us all those things which are made for the peace and prosperity of our countrymen and the glory and perpetuity of our Union, and the free institutions which, under the fostering folds of our national flag, and in the sunlight of our national freedom, are of natural and abundant growth. (Applause)

General Howard's efforts to educate the negro, not to speak of the work first accomplished in feeding, clothing, and protecting the emancipated millions. Four million negroes, children and adults, are to be educated and fitted to live under democratic institutions, the destiny of which, to a great extent, is controlled by each individual citizen. The means by which the work can be done is by furnishing the primary, grammar, and high school and college; by establishing normal schools to supply the immense demand for teachers; by affording the freedmen, as far as possible, the same advantages offered by a Massachusetts school system, thus affording opportunities through a system of common schools for one class to all the people of the South. The work was begun in Government barracks, furnished by the Bureau, as fast as the Union forces vacated them and retired from the South.

Fortunate has it been for the negroes of the country that we have had a man with views broad enough to comprehend the present and future educational wants of our brethren of the South, and who dared to spend the funds in his hands in furnishing permanent educational facilities. Unfortunate only that the Government (which has performed the great act of justice calling us together today) has not entrusted to this brave and good man fifty millions to be expended in rendering us justice educationally. The nation will yet thank him for the small investment that he has made. The negroes of the South will always be grateful to him, and they will not hesitate to denounce any who may oppose his efforts in their behalf.

Do you know the President of the United States? He is the only man who gave to the negro the vote and official position under the Government! (Three cheers for Grant) Do you know the Postmaster General of the United States? He is the only man who seconded the proposition of the President, and gave the negro official place in his Department! (Cheers for Creswell) When I forget the flaxen hair of these men I sometimes find myself wondering if they are purely white — if they have not some portion of negro blood in their composition. (Laughter) Let the colored race ever go forward, with the motto 'Perpetua' inscribed on their banners. (Great applause)

Obviously, Langston was unduly optimistic about the practical implications of the Fifteenth Amendment and other Reconstruction measures. Despite their decisive defeat on the battlefield, southerners of European descent were united in their effort to keep their area "a white man's country."[50] They harrassed elected Negro political officials, often challenging their right to serve as representatives in the state legislatures and in Congress. They questioned the legality of congressional action in the field of civil rights. When this form of resistance involving white leaders in the state of Georgia became an issue on the Senate floor in March, 1870, the scene was set for Hiram Revels' maiden speech.[51] Revels, the first member of his race to hold such high political office in the United States, was sensitive to the recurring and bitter charges that blacks had betrayed their trust and misused their power. He therefore devoted the first half of his address to a spirited defense of his brethren. Speaking first to the white South, he developed an argument from sign. The fact that slaves remained loyal to their masters throughout the war was a true index of the humane feelings and remarkable restraint that characterized them in a moment of enormous potential power. How then, Revels asked, could such a compassionate people who refused to take advantage of the badly defeated planters be guilty of the unfair acts ascribed to them now? Using a similar line of reasoning, he reminded his northern listeners that the contributions blacks made while fighting on the Union side was a sign of their courage and humanity. Revels turned, in the second half of his remarks, to a detailed account of what he perceived to be the facts in the Georgia situation. He concluded with a plea to Congress to protect the duly elected representatives to the Georgia legislature and to bring that state back into the Union on constitutional terms.[52]

Although Revels did not have a noteworthy record in his short stay in Congress,[53] he had established an important precedent, paving the way for his colleagues who also wanted to hold national office. In 1874, Blanche K. Bruce was elected to the Senate from Mississippi. In all, during the period from 1869 through 1901, two Negroes served in the Senate and twenty in the House of Representatives.[54] Of these, perhaps the spokesman who most impressed his contemporaries with his persuasive power and refutation ability was Robert Brown Elliott of South Carolina.[55] Elliott's restless and impatient temperament made the state legislature and Congress too confining and uninspiring for him, and he resigned at various intervals in his political career. When the issue and the occasion captured his attention, however, he liked the challenge of debate — especially when the subject encompassed human rights. One of these moments occurred in the House discussion on civil rights early in January, 1874. A pending bill sought to eliminate discrimination in traveling, hotel accommodations, restaurants, and public education. Southern leaders immediately opposed the recommendation on the grounds that it was an unwarranted federal intervention into the affairs of state governments. The General Assembly of Virginia, for example, passed a resolution instructing its congressmen to vote against the bill and to work for its defeat.[56] In this setting, Alexander H. Stephens, former Democratic Congressman from Georgia and Vice President of the Confederacy, rose to reaffirm the states' right argument he had developed throughout the antebellum period. In a calm and deliberate manner "Little Alex," as he was affectionately called by his sympathizers, constructed the rationale that was to be used by opponents of federal civil rights legislation for generations to come. It was a rationale that found its base in the constitutional provision: "The powers not delegated to the United States by the Constitution, nor prohibited by it to the States, are reserved to the State respectively, or to the people."

On the following day Congressman Durham of Kentucky, supporting Stephens' strict interpretation of the Constitution, employed a rhetoric of fear designed to stimulate the overt and latent prejudices of his constituency.

Mr. Speaker, I desire to say a few words as to the effect of the passage of this bill will have upon the people I represent. As before said, the slave has been made a freedman — been made a citizen and enfranchised. These are political rights. The State which I in part represent protects him in the enjoyment of these rights, and I do not know of any man in my district who desires to interfere with those rights. But, sir, when you undertake to legislate as to the civil and social relations of the races, then you will have aroused and embittered the feelings of the Anglo-Saxon race to such an extent that it will be hard to control them. The poorest and humblest white person in my district feels and knows that he or she belongs to a superior race morally and intellectually, and nothing is so revolting to them as social equality with this inferior race. They will treat the freedman kindly, but socially hold aloof from him, as belonging to an inferior race. You may say these are not social relations provided for in this bill; but, sir, if I am compelled to sit side by side with him in the theater, the stage-coach, and the railroad car, to eat with him at the same table at the hotels, and my child to be educated at the same schools with his child — if these are not social relations I do not understand them.[57]

What was most objectionable to Durham were the provisions requiring integrated education. He was content to have equal facilities so long as they were separate.

This emotionally charged rhetorical situation challenged Elliott who eagerly entered the debate determined to weaken the case of his opponents and to build a constructive argument of his own. Observe in the following transcript of his address, how he attempted to refute the evidence cited by Stephens and Durham, to prove the loyalty of Negroes to the Constitution and their right to political and social equality, and to show that the antecedent image of Stephens as an apologist for racial discrimination and secession could not be easily ignored.

Robert Brown Elliott
*The Civil Rights Bill**

While I am sincerely grateful for this high mark of courtesy that has been accorded to me by this House, it is a matter of regret to me that it is necessary

*From the *Congressional Record*, Vol. II, Part I, 43rd Congress, First Session, pp. 407-10.

at this day that I should rise in the presence of an American Congress to advocate a bill which simply asserts equal rights and equal public privileges for all classes of American citizens. I regret, sir, that the dark hue of my skin may lend a color to the imputation that I am controlled by motives personal to myself in my advocacy of this great measure of national justice. Sir, the motive that impels me is restricted by no such narrow boundary, but is as broad as your Constitution. I advocate it, sir, because it is right. The bill, however, not only appeals to your justice, but it demands a response from your gratitude.

In the events that led to the achievement of American Independence the Negro was not an inactive or unconcerned spectator. He bore his part bravely upon many battle-fields, although uncheered by that certain hope of political elevation which victory would secure to the white man. The tall granite shaft, which a grateful State has reared above its sons who fell in defending Fort Griswold against the attack of Benedict Arnold, bears the name of Jordan, Freeman, and other brave men of the African race who there cemented with their blood the corner-stone of the Republic. In the State which I have the honor in part to represent the rifle of the black man rang out against the troops of the British crown in the darkest days of the American Revolution. Said General Greene, who has been justly termed the Washington of the North, in a letter written by him to Alexander Hamilton, on the 10th day of January, 1781, from the vicinity of Camden, South Carolina:

"There is no such thing as national character or national sentiment. The inhabitants are numerous, but they would be formidable abroad rather than at home. There is a great spirit of enterprise among the black people, and those that come out as volunteers are not a little formidable to the enemy."

At the battle of New Orleans, under the immortal Jackson, a colored regiment held the extreme right of the American line unflinchingly, and drove back the British column that pressed upon them, at the point of the bayonet. So marked was their valor on that occasion that it evoked from their great commander the warmest encomiums, as will be seen from his dispatch announcing the brilliant victory.

As the gentleman from Kentucky, (Mr. Black), who seems to be the leading exponent on this floor of the party that is arrayed against the principle of this bill, has been pleased, in season and out of season, to cast odium upon the negro and to vaunt the chivalry of his State, I may be pardoned for calling attention to another portion of the same dispatch. Referring to the various regiments under his command, and their conduct on that field which terminated the second war of American Independence, General Jackson says:

At the very moment when the entire discomfiture of the enemy was looked for with a confidence amounting to certainty, the Kentucky reënforcements, in whom so much reliance had been placed, ingloriously fled.

In quoting this indisputable piece of history, I do so only by way of admonition and not to question the well-attested gallantry of the true Kentuckian, and to suggest to the gentleman that it would be well that he should not flaunt his heraldry so proudly while he bears this bar-sinister on the military escutcheon of his State — a State which answered the call of the Republic in 1861, when treason thundered at the very gates of the capital, by coldly declaring her neutrality in the impending struggle. The Negro, true to that patriotism and love of country that have ever characterized and marked his history on this continent, came to the aid of the Government in its efforts to maintain the Constitution. To that Government he now appeals; that Constitution he now invokes for protection against outrage and unjust prejudices founded upon caste.

But, sir, we are told by the distinguished gentleman from Georgia (Mr. Stephens) that Congress has no power under the Constitution to pass such a law, and that the passage of such an act is in direct contravention of the rights of the States. I cannot assent to any such proposition. The constitution of a free government ought always to be construed in favor of human rights. Indeed, the thirteenth, fourteenth, and fifteenth amendments, in positive words, invest Congress with the power to protect the citizen in his civil and political rights. Now, sir, what are civil rights? Rights natural, modified by civil society. Mr. Lieber says:

> By civil liberty is meant, not only the absence of individual restraint, but liberty within the social system and political organism — a com-bination of principles and laws which acknowledge, protect, and favor the dignity of man.* * * Civil liberty is the result of man's two-fold character as an individual and social being, so soon as both are equally respected. — Leiber on *Civil Liberty*, Page 25.

Alexander Hamilton, the right-hand man of Washington in the perilous days of the then infant Republic, the great interpreter and expounder of the Constitution, says:

> Natural liberty is a gift of the beneficent Creator to the whole human race; civil liberty is founded on it; civil liberty is only natural liberty modified and secured by civil society. — Hamilton's *History of the American Republic,* vol. 1, page 70.

In the French constitution of June, 1793, we find this grand and noble declaration:

> Government is instituted to insure to man the free use of his natural and inalienable rights. These rights are equality, liberty, security, property. All men are equal by nature and before the law. * * * Law is the same for all, be it protective or penal. Freedom is the power by which man can do what does not interfere with the rights of another; its basis is nature, its standard is justice, its protection is law, moral boundary is the maxim: 'Do not unto others what you do not wish they should do unto you.

Are we then, sir, with the amendments to our Constitution staring us in the face; with these grand truths of history before our eyes; with innu-merable wrongs daily inflicted upon five million citizens demanding redress, to commit this question to the diversity of State legislation? In the words of Hamilton —

Is it the interest of the Government to sacrifice individual rights to preservation of the rights of an artificial being, called States? There can be no truer principle than this, that every individual of the community at large has an equal right to the protection of Government. Can this be a free Government if partial distinctions are tolerated or maintained?

The rights contended for in this bill are among "the sacred rights of mankind, which are not to be rummaged for among old parchments or musty records; they are written as with a sunbeam, in the whole volume of human nature, by the hand of the Divinity itself, and can never be erased or obscured by mortal power."

But the Slaughter-house cases! — the Slaughter-house cases!

The honorable gentleman from Kentucky, always swift to sustain the failing and dishonored cause of proscription, rushes forward and flaunts in our faces the decision of the Supreme Court of the United States in the Slaughter-house cases, and in that act he has been willingly aided by the gentleman from Georgia. Hitherto, in the contests which have marked the progress of the cause of equal civil rights, our opponents have appealed sometimes to custom, sometimes to prejudice, more often to pride of race, but they have never sought to shield themselves behind the Supreme Court. But now, for the first time, we are told that we are barred by a decision of that court, from which there is no appeal. If this be true we must stay our hands. The cause of equal civil rights must pause at the command of a power whose edicts must be obeyed till the fundamental law of our country is changed.

Has the honorable gentleman from Kentucky considered well the claim he now advances? If it were not disrespectful I would ask, has he ever read the decision which he now tells us is an insuperable barrier to the adoption of this great measure of justice?

In the consideration of this subject, has not the judgment of the gentleman from Georgia been warped by the ghost of the dead doctrines of State-rights? Has he been altogether free from prejudices engendered by long training in that school of politics that well-nigh destroyed this Government?

Mr. Speaker, I venture to say here in the presence of the gentleman from Kentucky, and the gentleman from Georgia, and in the presence of the whole country, that there is not a line or word, not a thought or dictum even, in the decision of the Supreme Court in the great Slaughter-house cases which casts a shadow of doubt on the right of Congress to pass the pending bill, or to adopt such other legislation as it may judge proper and necessary to secure perfect equality before the law to every citizen of the Republic. Sir, I protest against the dishonor now cast upon our Supreme Court by both the gentleman from Kentucky and the gentleman from Georgia. In other days, when the whole country was bowing beneath the yoke of slavery, when press, pulpit, platform, Congress, and courts felt the fatal power of the slave oligarchy, I remember a decision of that court which no American now reads without shame and humiliation. But those days are past. The Supreme Court of today is a tribunal as true to freedom as any department of this Government, and I am honored with the opportunity of repelling a deep disgrace which the gentleman from Kentucky, backed and sustained as he is by the gentleman from Georgia, seeks to put upon it.

What were these Slaughter-houses cases? The gentleman should be aware that a decision of any court should be examined in the light of the exact question which is brought before it for decision. That is all that gives authority to any decision.

The State of Louisiana, by act of her Legislature, had conferred on certain persons the exclusive right to maintain stock-landings and slaughter-houses within the city of New Orleans, or the parishes of Orleans, Jefferson, and Saint Bernard, in that State. The corporation which was thereby chartered were invested with the sole and exclusive privilege of conducting and carrying on the livestock, landing, and slaughter-house business within the limits designated.

The supreme court of Louisiana sustained the validity of the act conferring these exclusive privileges, and the plaintiffs in error brought the case before the Supreme Court of the United States for review. The plaintiffs in error contended that the act in question was void, because, first, it established a monopoly which was in derogation of common right and in contravention of the common law; and, second, that the grant of such exclusive privileges was in violation of the thirteenth and fourteenth amendments of the Constitution of the United States.

It thus appears from a simple statement of the case that the question which was before the court was not whether a State law which denied to a particular portion of her citizens the rights conferred on her citizens generally, on account of race, color, or previous condition of servitude, was unconstitutional because in conflict with the recent amendments, but whether an act which conferred on certain citizens exclusive privileges for police purposes was in conflict therewith, because imposing an involuntary servitude forbidden by the thirteenth amendment, or abridging the rights and immunities of citizens of the United States, or denying the equal protection of the laws, prohibited by the fourteenth amendment

On the part of the defendants in error it was maintained that the act was the exercise of the ordinary and unquestionable power of the State to make regulation for the health and comfort of society — the exercise of the police power of the State, defined by Chancellor Kent to be "the right to interdict unwholesome trades, slaughter-houses, operations offensive to the senses, the deposit of powder, the application of steam-power to propel cars, the building with combustible materials, and the burial of the dead in the midst of dense masses of population, on the general and rational principle that every person ought so to use his own property as not to injure his neighbors, and that private interests must be made subservient to the general interests of the community."

The decision of the Supreme Court is to be found in the 16th volume of Wallace's Reports, and was delivered by Associate Justice Miller. The court holds, first, that the act in question is a legitimate and warrantable exercise of the police power of the State in regulating the business of stock-handling and slaughtering in the city of New Orleans and the territory immediately contiguous. Having held this, the court proceeds to discuss the question whether the conferring of exclusive privileges, such as those conferred by the act in question, is the imposing of an involuntary servitude, the abridging of the rights and immunities of citizens of the United States, or the denial to any person within the jurisdiction of the State of the equal protection of the laws.

That the act is not the imposition of an involuntary servitude the court holds to be clear, and they next proceed to examine the remaining questions arising under the fourteenth amendment. Upon this question the court holds that the leading and comprehensive purpose of the thirteenth, fourteenth, and fifteenth amendments was to secure the complete freedom of the race, which, by the events of the war, had been wrested from the unwilling grasp of their owners. I know no finer or more just picture, albeit painted in the neutral tints of true judicial impartiality, of the motives and events which led to these amendments. Has the gentleman from Kentucky read these passages which I now quote? Or has the gentleman from Georgia considered well the force of the language therein used? Says the court on page 70:

"The process of restoring to their proper relations with the Federal Government and with the other States those which had sided with the rebellion, undertaken under the proclamation of President Johnson in 1865, and before the assembling of Congress, developed the fact that, notwithstanding the formal recognition by those States of the abolition of slavery, the condition of the slave race would, without further protection of the Federal Government, be almost as bad as it was before. Among the first acts of legislation adopted by several of the States in the legislative bodies which claimed to be in their normal relations with the Federal Government, were laws which imposed upon the colored race onerous disabilities and burdens, and curtailed their rights in the pursuit of life, liberty and property to such an extent that their freedom was of little value, while they had lost the protection which they had received from their former owners from motives both of interest and humanity.

"They were in some States forbidden to appear in the towns in any other character than menial servants. They were required to reside on and cultivate the soil, without the right to purchase or own it. They were excluded from any occupations of gain, and were not permitted to give testimony in the courts in any case where a white man was a party. It was said that their lives were at the mercy of bad men, either because the laws for their protection were insufficient or were not enforced.

"These circumstances, whatever of falsehood or misconception may have been mingled with their presentation, forced upon the statesmen who had conducted the Federal Government in safety through the crisis of rebellion, and who supposed that by the thirteenth article of amendment they had secured the result of their labors, the conviction that something more was necessary in the way of constitutional protection to the unfortunate race who had suffered so much. They accordingly passed through Congress the proposition for the fourteenth amendment, and they declined to treat as restored to their full participation in the Government of the Union the States which had been in insurrection until they ratified that article by a formal vote of their legislative bodies.

"Before we proceed to examine more critically the provisions of this amendment, on which the plantiffs in error rely, let us complete and dismiss the history of the recent amendments, as that history relates to the general purpose which pervades them all. A few years' experience satisfied the thoughtful men who had been the authors of the other two amendments that, notwithstanding the restraints of those articles on the States and the laws passed under the additional powers granted to Congress, these were inadequate for the protection of life, liberty, and property, without which freedom to the slave was no boon. They were in all those States denied the right of suffrage. The laws were administered by the white man alone. It was urged that a race of men distinctively marked as was the Negro, living in the midst of another and dominant race, could never be fully secured in their person and their property without the right of suffrage.

"Hence the fifteenth amendment, which declares that 'the right of a citizen of the United States to vote shall not be denied or abridged by any State on account of race, color, or previous condition of servitude.' The Negro having, by the fourteenth amendment, been declared to be a citizen of the United States, is thus made a voter in every State of the Union.

"We repeat, then, in the light of this recapitulation of events almost too recent to be called history, but which are familiar to us all, and on the most casual examination of the language of these amendments, no one can fail to be impressed with the one pervading purpose found in them all, lying at the foundation of each, and without which none of them would have been even suggested: we mean the freedom of the slave race, the security and firm establishment of that freedom, and the protection of the newly-made freeman and citizen from the oppressions of those who had formerly exercised unlimited dominion over him. It is true that only the fifteenth amendment in terms mentions the Negro by speaking of his color and his slavery. But it is just as true that each of the other articles was addressed to the grievances of that race, and designed to remedy them, as the fifteenth."

These amendments, one and all, are thus declared to have as their all-pervading design and end the security to the recently enslaved race, not only their nominal freedom, but their complete protection from those who had formerly exercised unlimited dominion over them. It is in this broad light that all these amendments must be read, the purpose to secure the perfect equality before the law of all citizens of the United States. What you give to one class you must give to all; what you deny to one class you shall deny to all, unless in the exercise of the common and universal police power of the State you find it needful to confer exclusive privileges on certain citizens, to be held and exercised still for the common good of all.

Such are the doctrines of the Slaughter-house Cases — doctrines worthy of the Republic, worthy of the age, worthy of the great tribunal which thus loftily and impressively enunciates them. Do they — I put it to any man, be he lawyer or not; I put it to the gentleman from Georgia — do they give color even to the claim that this Congress may not now legislate against a plain discrimination made by State laws or State customs against that very race for whose complete freedom and protection these great amendments were elaborated and adopted? Is it pretended, I ask the honorable gentleman from Kentucky or the honorable gentleman from Georgia — is it pretended anywhere that the evils of which we complain, our exclusion from the public inn, from the saloon and table of the steamboat, from the sleeping-coach on the railway, from the right of sepulture in the public burial-ground, are an exercise of the police power of the State? Is such oppression and injustice nothing but the exercise by the State of the right to make regulations for the health, comfort, and security of all her citizens? Is it merely enacting that one man shall so use his own as not to injure another's? Are the colored people to be assimilated to an unwholesome trade or to combustible materials, to be interdicted, to be shut up within prescribed limits? Let the gentleman from Kentucky or the gentleman from Georgia answer. Let the country know to what extent even the audacious prejudice of the gentleman from Kentucky will drive him, and how far even the gentleman from Georgia will permit himself to be led captive by the unrighteous teaching of a false political faith.

If we are to be likened in legal view to "unwholesome trades," to "large and offensive collections of animals," to "noxious slaughter-houses," to "the offal and stench which attend on certain manufactures," let it be avowed. If that is still the doctrine of the political party to which the gentlemen belong, let it be put upon record. If State laws which deny us the common rights and privileges of other citizens, upon no possible or conceivable ground save one of prejudice, or of "taste," as the gentleman from Texas termed it, and as I suppose the gentleman will prefer to call it, are to be placed under the protection of a decision which affirms the right of a State to regulate the police of her great cities, then the decision is in conflict with the bill before us. No man will dare maintain such a doctrine. It is as shocking to the legal mind as it is offensive to the heart and conscience of all who love justice or respect manhood. I am astonished that the gentleman from Kentucky or the gentleman from Georgia should have been so grossly misled as to rise here and assert that the decision of the Supreme Court in these cases was a denial to Congress of the power to legislate against discriminations on account of race, color, or previous condition of servitude, because that court has decided that exclusive privileges conferred for the common protection of the lives and health of the whole community are not in violation of the recent amendments. The only ground upon which the grant of exclusive privileges to a portion of the community is ever defended is that the substantial good of all is promoted; that in truth it is for the welfare of the whole community that certain persons should alone pursue certain occupations. It is not the special benefit conferred on the few that moves the legislature, but the ultimate and real benefit of all, even of those who are denied the right to pursue those specified occupations. Does the gentleman from Kentucky say that my good is promoted when I am excluded from the public inn? Is the health or safety of the community promoted? Doubtless his prejudice is gratified. Doubtless his democratic instincts are pleased; but will he or his able coadjutor say that such exclusion is a lawful exercise of the police power of the State, or that it is not a denial to me of the equal protection of the laws? They will not so say.

But each of these gentlemen quote at some length from the decision of the court to show that the court recognizes a difference between citizenship of the United States and citizenship of the States. That is true, and no man here who supports this bill questions or overlooks the difference. There are privileges and immunities which belong to me as a citizen of the United States, and there are other privileges and immunities which belong to me as a citizen of my State. The former are under the protection of the Constitution and laws of the United States, and the latter are under the protection of the constitution and laws of my State. But what of that? Are the rights which I now claim — the right to enjoy the common public conveniences of travel on public highways, of rest and refreshment at public inns, of education in public schools, of burial in public cemeteries — rights which I hold as a citizen of the United States or of my State? Or, to state the question more exactly, is not the denial of such privileges to me a denial to me of the equal protection of the laws? For it is under this clause of the fourteenth amendment that we place the present bill, no State shall "deny to any person within this jurisdiction the equal protection of the laws." No matter, therefore, whether his rights are held under the United States or under his particular State, he is equally protected by this amendment. He is always and everywhere entitled to the equal protection of the laws. All discrimination is forbidden; and while the rights of citizens of a State as such are not defined or conferred by the Constitution of the United States, yet all discrimination, all denial of equality before the law, all denial of the equal protection of the laws, whether State or national laws, is forbidden.

The distinction between the two kinds of citizenship is clear, and the Supreme Court have clearly pointed out this distinction, but they have nowhere written a word or line which denies to Congress the power to prevent a denial of equality of rights, whether those rights exist by virtue of citizenship of the United States or of a State. Let honorable members mark well this distinction. There are rights which are conferred on us by the United States. There are other rights conferred on us by the States of which we are individually the citizens. The fourteenth amendment does not forbid a State to deny to all its citizens any of those rights which the State itself has conferred, with certain exceptions, which are pointed out in the decision which we are examining. What it does forbid is inequality, is discrimination, or, to use the words of the amendment itself, is the denial "to any person within its jurisdiction the equal protection of the laws." If a State denies to me rights which are common to all her other citizens, she violates this amendment, unless she can show, as was shown in the Slaughter-house Cases, that she does it in the legitimate exercise of her police power. If she abridges the rights of all her citizens equally, unless those rights are specially guarded by the Constitution of the United States, she does not violate this amendment.

This is not to put the rights which I hold by virtue of my citizenship of South Carolina under the protection of the national Government; it is not to blot out or overlook in the slightest particular the distinction between rights held under the United States and the rights held under the States; but it seeks to secure equality, to prevent discrimination, to confer as complete and ample protection on the humblest as on the highest.

The gentleman from Kentucky, in the course of the speech to which I am now replying, made a reference to the State of Massachusetts which betrays again the confusion which exists in his mind on this precise point. He tells us that Massachusetts excludes from the ballot-box all who cannot read and write, and points to that fact as the exercise of a right which this bill would abridge or impair. The honorable gentleman from Massachusetts (Mr. Dawes) answered him truly and well, but I submit that he did not make the best reply. Why did he not ask the gentleman from Kentucky if Massachusetts had ever discriminated against any of her citizens on account of color, or race, or previous condition of servitude? When did Massachusetts sully her proud record by placing on her statute-book any law which admitted to the ballot the white man and shut out the black man? She has never done it; she will not do it; she cannot do it so long as we have a Supreme Court which reads the Constitution of our country with the eyes of justice; nor can Massachusetts or Kentucky deny to any man, on account of his race, color, or previous condition of servitude, that perfect equality of protection under the laws so long as Congress shall exercise the power to enforce, by appropriate legislation, the great and unquestionable securities embodied in the fourteenth amendment to the Constitution.

But, sir, a few words more as to the suffrage regulation of Massachusetts. It is true that Massachusetts in 1857, finding that her illiterate population was being constantly augmented by the continual influx of ignorant emigrants, placed in her constitution the least possible limitation consistent with manhood suffrage to stay this tide of foreign ignorance. Its benefit has been fully demonstrated in the intelligent character of the voters of that honored Commonwealth, reflected so conspicuously in the able Representatives she has today upon this floor. But neither is the inference of the gentleman from Kentucky legitimate, nor do the statistics of the census of 1870, drawn from his own State, sustain his astounding assumption. According to the statistics we find the whole white population of that State is 1,098,692; the whole colored population 222,210. Of the whole white population who cannot write we find 201,077; of the whole colored population who cannot write, 126,048; giving us, as will be seen, 96,162 colored persons who can write to 897,615 white persons who can write. Now, the ratio of the colored population to the white is as 1 to 5, and the ratio of the illiterate colored population to the whole colored population is as 1 to 2; the ratio of the illiterate white population is to the whole white population as 1 is to 5. Reducing this, we have only a preponderance of three-tenths in favor of the whites as to literacy, notwithstanding the advantages which they have always enjoyed and do now enjoy of free-school privileges, and this, too, taking solely into account the single item of being unable to write; for with regard to the inability to read, there is no discrimination in the statistics between the white and colored population. There is, moreover, a peculiar felicity in these statistics with regard to the State of Kentucky, quoted so opportunely for me by the honorable gentleman; for I find that the population of that State, both with regard to its white and colored populations, bears the same relative rank in regard to the white and colored population of the United States; and, therefore, while one Negro would be disfranchised were the limitation of Massachusetts put in force, nearly three white men would at the same time be deprived of the right of suffrage — a consummation which I think would be far more acceptable to the colored people of that State than to the whites.

Now, sir, having spoken as to the intention of the prohibition imposed by Massachusetts, I may be pardoned for a slight inquiry as to the effect of this prohibition. First, it did not in any way abridge or curtail the exercise of the suffrage by any person who at that time enjoyed such right. Nor did it discriminate between the illiterate native and the illiterate foreigner. Being enacted for the good of the entire Commonwealth, like all just laws, its obligations fell equally and impartially upon all its citizens. And as a justification for such a measure, it is a fact too well known almost for mention here that Massachusetts had, from the beginning of her history, recognized the inestimable value of an educated ballot, by not only maintaining a system of free schools, but also enforcing an attendance thereupon, as one of the safeguards for the preservation of a real republican form of government. Recurring then, sir, to the possible contingency alluded to by the gentleman from Kentucky, should the State of Kentucky, having first established a system of common schools whose doors shall swing open freely to all, as contemplated by the provisions of this bill, adopt a provision similar to that of Massachusetts, no one would have cause justly to complain. And if in the coming years the result of such legislation should produce a constituency rivaling that of the old Bay State, no one would be more highly gratified than I.

Mr. Speaker, I have neither the time nor the inclination to notice the many illogical and forced conclusions, the numerous transfers of terms, or the vulgar insinuations which further incumber the argument of the gentleman from Kentucky. Reason and argument are worse than wasted upon those who meet every demand for political and civil liberty by such ribaldry as this — extracted from the speech of the gentleman from Kenutcky:

> I suppose there are gentlemen on this floor who would arrest, imprison, and fine a young woman in any State of the South if she were to refuse to marry a Negro man on account of color, race, or previous condition of servitude, in the event of his making her a proposal of marriage, and her refusing on that ground. That would be depriving him of a right he had under the amendment, and Congress would be asked to take it up and say, "This insolent white woman must be taught to know that it is a misdemeanor to deny a man marriage because of race, color, or previous condition of servitude"; and Congress will be urged to say after a while that that sort of thing must be put a stop to, and your conventions of colored men will come here asking you to enforce that right.

Now, sir, recurring to the venerable and distinguished gentleman from Georgia (Mr. Stephens), who has added his remonstrance against the passage of this bill, permit me to say that I share in the feeling of high personal regard for that gentleman which pervades this House. His years, his ability, and his long experience in public affairs entitle him to the measure of consideration which has been accorded to him on this floor. But in this discussion I cannot and I will not forget that the welfare and rights of my whole race in this country are involved. When, therefore, the honorable gentleman from Georgia lends his voice and influence to defeat this measure, I do not shrink from saying that it is not from him that the American House of Representatives should take lessons in matters touching human rights or the joint relations of the State and national governments. While the honorable gentleman contented himself with harmless speculations in his study, or in the columns of a newspaper, we might well smile at the impotence of his efforts to turn back the advancing tide of opinion and progress; but, when he comes again upon this national arena, and throws himself with all his power and influence across the path which leads to the full enfranchisment of my race, I meet him only as an adversary; nor shall age or any other consideration restrain me from saying that he now offers his Government, which he has done his utmost to destroy, a very poor return for its magnanimous treatment, to come here and seek to continue, by the assertion of doctrines obnoxious to the true principles of our Government, the burdens and oppressions which rest upon five millions of his countrymen who never fail to lift their earnest prayers for the success of this Government when the gentleman was seeking to break up the Union of those States and to blot the American Republic from the galaxy of nations. [Loud applause.]

Sir, it is scarcely twelve years since that gentleman shocked the civilized world by announcing the birth of a government which rested on human slavery as its corner-stone. The progress of events has swept away that pseudo-government which rested on greed, pride, and tyranny; and the race whom he then ruthlessly spurned and trampled on are here to meet him in debate, and to demand that the rights which are enjoyed by their former oppressors — who vainly sought to overthrow a Government which they could not prostitute to the base uses of slavery — shall be accorded to those who even in the darkness of slavery kept their allegiance true to freedom and the Union. Sir, the gentleman from Georgia has learned much since 1861; but he is still a laggard. Let him put away entirely the false and fatal theories which have so greatly marred an otherwise enviable record. Let him accept, in its fullness and beneficence, the great doctrine that American citizenship carries with it every civil and political right which manhood can confer. Let him lend his influence, with all his masterly ability, to complete the proud structure of legislation which makes this nation worthy of the great declaration which heralded its birth, and he will have done that which will most nearly redeem his reputation in the eyes of the world, and best vindicate the wisdom of that policy which has permitted him to regain his seat upon this floor.

To the diatribe of the gentleman from Virginia (Mr. Harris), who spoke on yesterday, and who so far transcended the limits of decency and propriety as to announce upon this floor that his remarks were addressed to white men alone, I shall have no word of reply. Let him feel that a Negro was not only too magnanimous to smite him in his weakness, but was even charitable enough to grant him the mercy of his silence. [Laughter and applause on the floor and in the galleries.] I shall, sir, leave to others less charitable the unenviable and fatiguing task of sifting out of that mass of chaff the few grains of sense that may, perchance, deserve notice. Assuring the gentleman that the Negro in this country aims at a higher degree of intellect than that exhibited by him in this debate, I cheerfully commend him to the commiseration of all intelligent men the world over — black men as well as white men.

Sir, equality before the law is now the broad, universal, glorious rule and mandate of the Republic. No State can violate that. Kentucky and Georgia may crowd their statute-books with retrograde and barbarous legislation; they may rejoice in the odious eminence of their consistent hostility to all the great steps of human progress which have marked our national history since slavery tore down the stars and stripes on Fort Sumter; but, if Congress shall do its duty, if Congress shall enforce the great guarantees which the Supreme Court has declared to be the one pervading purpose of all the recent amendments, then their unwise and unenlightened conduct will fall with the same weight upon the gentlemen from those States who now lend their influence to defeat this bill, as upon the poorest slave who once had no rights which the honorable gentlemen were bound to respect.

But, sir, not only does the decision in the Slaughter-house Cases contain nothing which suggests a doubt of the power of Congress to pass the pending bill, but it contains an express recognition and affirmance of such power. I quote now from page 81 of this volume:

> " 'Nor shall any State deny to any person within its jurisdiction the equal protection of the laws.'
>
> In the light of the history of these amendments, and the pervading purpose of them, which we have already discussed, it is not difficult to give a meaning to this clause. The existence of laws in the States where the newly emancipated Negroes resided, which discriminated with gross injustice and hardship against them as a class, was the evil to be remedied by this clause, and by it such laws are forbidden.
>
> If, however, the States did not conform their laws to its requirements, then, by the fifth section of the article of amendment, Congress was authorized to enforce it by suitable legislation. We doubt very much whether any action of a State not directed by way of discrimination against the Negroes as a class, or on account of their race, will ever be held to come within the purview of this provision. It is so clearly a provision for that race and that emergency, that a strong case would be necessary for its application to any other. But as it is a State that is to be dealt with, and not alone the

validity of its laws, we may safely leave that matter until Congress shall have exercised its power, or some case of State oppression, by denial of equal justice in its courts shall have claimed a decision at our hands."

No language could convey a more complete assertion of the power of Congress over the subject embraced in the present bill than is here expressed. If the States do not conform to the requirements of this clause, if they continue to deny to any person within their jurisdiction the equal protection of the laws, or as the Supreme Court had said, "deny equal justice in its courts," then Congress is here said to have power to enforce the constitutional guarantee by appropriate legislation. That is the power which this bill now seeks to put in exercise. It proposes to enforce the constitutional guarantee against inequality and discrimination by appropriate legislation. It does not seek to confer new rights, nor to place rights conferred by State citizenship under the protection of the United States, but simply to prevent and forbid inequality and discrimination on account of race, color, or previous condition of servitude. Never was there a bill more completely within the constitutional power of Congress. Never was there a bill which appealed for support more strongly to that sense of justice and fair-play which has been said, and in the main with justice, to be a characteristic of the Anglo-Saxon race. The Constitution warrants it; the Supreme Court sanctions it; justice demands it.

Sir, I have replied to the extent of my ability to the arguments which have been presented by the opponents of this measure. I have replied also to some of the legal propositions advanced by gentlemen on the other side; and now that I am about to conclude, I am deeply sensible of the imperfect manner in which I have performed the task. Technically, this bill is to decide upon the civil status of the colored American citizen; a point disputed at the very formation of our present Government, when by a short-sighted policy, a policy repugnant to true republican government, one Negro counted as three-fifths of a man. The logical result of this mistake of the framers of the Constitution strengthened the cancer of slavery, which finally spread its poisonous tentacles over the southern portion of the body-politic. To arrest its growth and save the nation we have passed through the harrowing operation of internecine war, dreaded at all times, resorted to at the last extremity, like the surgeon's knife, but absolutely necessary to extirpate the disease which threatened with the life of the nation the overthrow of civil and political liberty on this continent. In that dire extremity the members of the race which I have the honor in part to represent — the race which pleads for justice at your hands today, forgetful of their inhuman and brutalizing servitude at the South, their degradation and ostracism at the North — flew willingly and gallantly to the support of the national Government. Their sufferings, assistance, privations, and trials in the swamps and in the rice-fields, their valor on the land and on the sea, is a part of the ever-glorious record which makes up the history of a nation preserved, and might, should I argue the claim, incline you to respect and guarantee their rights and privileges as citizens of our common Republic. But I remember that valor, devotion, and loyalty are not always rewarded according to their just deserts, and that after the battle some who have borne the brunt of the fray may, through neglect or contempt be assigned to a subordinate place, while the enemies in war may be preferred to the sufferers.

The results of the war, as seen in reconstruction, have settled forever the political status of my race. The passage of this bill will determine the civil status, not only of the Negro, but of any other class of citizens who may feel themselves discriminated against. It will form the cap-stone of that temple of liberty, begun on this continent under discouraging circumstances, carried on in spite of the sneers of monarchists and the cavils of pretended friends of freedom, until at last it stands in all its beautiful symmetry and proportions, a building the grandest which the world has ever seen, realizing the most sanguine expectations and the highest hopes of those who, in the name of equal, impartial, and universal liberty, laid the foundation stones.

The Holy Scriptures tell us of an humble hand-maiden who long, faithfully and patiently gleaned in the rich fields of her wealthy kinsman; and we are told further that at last, in spite of her humble antecedents, she found complete favor in his sight. For over two centuries our race has "reaped down your fields." The cries and woes which we have uttered have "entered into the ears of the Lord of Sabaoth," and we are at last politically free. The last vestiture only is needed — civil rights. Having gained this, we may, with hearts overflowing with gratitude, and thankful that our prayer has been granted, repeat the prayer of Ruth: "Entreat me not to leave thee, or to return from following after thee; for whither thou goest, I will go; and where thou lodgest, I will lodge; thy people shall be my people, and thy God my God; where thou diest, will I die, and there will I be buried; the Lord do so to me, and more also, if aught but death part thee and me." (Great applause.)

The response to Elliott's reply to Stephens was enthusiastic. "I cannot describe the House," noted one eyewitness, "when the two men addressed it, especially when the African answered the Caucasian. Here we have a new history — a history that may, indeed, be repeated, but which stands alone in the novelty of all its surroundings, and in the eloquence of its lessons. . . ."[58] So pleased were the people of South Carolina with Elliott's performance that they held a meeting in his honor in March. In acknowledging his pleasure with the support he had received, Elliott confessed:

It is gratifying to know that my utterances on that memorable occasion have been endorsed, not only by the five millions of people that are most directly concerned in the result of the issue, but by a vast majority of the dominant race.[59]

Elliott then reminisced about what took place in the congressional cloakroom before he delivered the most celebrated speech of his career. His colleagues, after hearing Stephens' attack on the civil rights bill, specifically designated Elliott to deliver the major refutation. With such a responsibility before a crowded gallery, he said, "I trembled for the result." It was this memorable confrontation with Stephens that caught the fancy of blacks and northern liberals, giving to them dramatic proof to help counter the persistent claim of the Negro's alleged intellectual inferiority. The significance of this point did not escape Elliott.

> Friends have been delighted, and enemies have been forced to concede that the Vice President of the Southern Confederacy — a man acknowledged to be of the greatest intellectual force, and long public experience — has been met in debate; and that his sophistries have been exposed, and his constitutional arguments overthrown, by one of that race, which, twelve years ago, he described as fit only to be "hewers of wood and drawers of water" to the dominant white race. This triumph I do not chiefly value as a personal one. If it be a triumph, it is a triumph for you as well as for me — a triumph for our whole race.[60]

Encouraged by the momentary success of his endeavors in Congress, Elliott, like many of his colleagues in the mid-1870's, could not altogether grasp the strong prejudice and dissonance that still lingered in the minds of white southerners. Defeat in war and frustration caused by Carpetbagger rule only served to make them look with nostalgia at the society they had known when the planter was king and the slave subservient to his master's will. Soon, redemptionists, preaching a philosophy of retrenchment and reaction in order to blunt the effects of reconstruction, made the doctrine of laissez faire, according to Vann Woodward, "almost a test of Southern patriotism."[61] These redemptionists succeeded in enacting statutes that enforced segregation and restored whites to their earlier dominant position of political power. Consequently, intimidated blacks once again were denied equal opportunities in voting and in earning a living.[62] These developments prompted John Hope Franklin to say:

> The period that we know as Radical Reconstruction had no significant or permanent effect on the status of the Negro in American life. . . . Neither the Civil War nor the era of Reconstruction made any significant steps toward the permanent elimination of racial barriers."[63]

In a still more pessimistic vein, DuBois viewed this period as an era when "the planters, having lost the war for slavery, sought to begin again where they left off in 1860, merely substituting for the individual ownership of slaves, a new state serfdom of black folk."[64] This general indictment against the South for its obstructionist and reactionary policies in the post-war period may be noted in the following statement from Morison: "The North may have won the war, but the white South won the peace. It preserved the essence of slavery — a pool of cheap, subservient labor — but escaped the capital outlays and social obligations that slavery imposed on the masters."[65]

But the South was not the only impediment to the progress of civil rights. Many northerners, including former abolitionists, appeared content with their achievements in the antebellum period and with the passage of the Thirteenth, Fourteenth, and Fifteenth Amendments. Many of these former radicals, now perceived as prophets in 1870, were ready to enjoy the fruits of their labor. Moreover, they had come to believe that a majority of whites were weary of the Negro problem. This tendency to misjudge the effect of the amendments and to accede to the popular will in the North contributed significantly to the failure of the human rights movement in the latter part of the century. James McPherson has correctly observed that

> . . . many of the equalitarian achievements of the Civil War and Reconstruction were built on a foundation of sand. The freedom and equality of the Negro were based in part on the idealistic traditions of the abolitionist movement, but in greater part on the military and political exigencies of war and reconstruction. The North's conversion to emancipation and equal rights was primarily a conversion of expediency rather than one of conviction. The South was converted only by force. A policy based on "military necessity" may be abandoned when the necessity disappears, and this is what happened in the 1870's. It became expedient for northern political and business interests to conciliate southern whites, and an end to federal enforcement of Negro equality in the South was the price of conciliation. The mass of northern people had never loved the Negro, were tired of the "everlasting negro question," and were glad to see the end of it.[66]

Few black Americans in the 1880's studied more closely the exigencies stemming from the Reconstruction and post-Reconstruction eras than Frederick Douglass. As an active participant in the triumphs and failures of the Negro's search for freedom and equality, he had disciplined himself through the years to balance hard times with good times and to analyze troubling events from a broad historical stance. In short, even in the twilight period of his career, he was an elder statesman who blended the old with the new, refusing to be victimized either by major disappointments or by noteworthy successes. Those who perceived him in this manner invited him to deliver an address in the Congregational Church in Washington, D.C. on April 16, 1883, commemorating the twenty-first anniversary of emancipation in the District of Columbia. The speech, contained in full below, reveals the rhetorical strategy Douglass had used consistently since enlisting in the Anti-Slavery Society. He spoke of a serious need in the field of civil rights but rejected the premise that the problems were inherent in the democratic system. If enough men of goodwill would combine their efforts, he held, the needs could be repaired, thereby enabling blacks to assimilate freely into society. Douglass, it would appear, had lost none of his early zeal for the American form of government and his faith in the power of rhetoric to effect change.

Frederick Douglass
The Address*

Friends and Fellow Citizens: I could have wished that some one from among the younger men of Washington, some one with a mind more fruitful, with a voice more eloquent, with an oratorical ambition more lofty, more active, and more stimulating to high endeavor than mine, had been selected by your Committee of Arrangements, to give suitable utterance to the thoughts, feelings, and purposes, which this 21st anniversary of Emancipation in the District of Columbia is fitted to inspire. That such an one could have been easily found among the aspiring and promising young colored men of Washington, I am happy to know and am proud to affirm. They are the legitimate children of the great act we are met to celebrate. They have been reared in the light of its *new* born freedom, qualified by its education, and by the elevating spirit of liberty, to speak the wise and grateful words befitting the occasion. The presence of one such, as your orator to-night, would be a more brilliant illustration of the wisdom and beneficence of the act of Emancipation, than any words of mine, however well chosen and appropriate. I represent the past, they the present. I represent the downfall of slavery, they the glorious triumphs of liberty. I speak of deliverance from bondage, they speak of concessions to liberty and equality. Their mission begins where my mission ends.

Nevertheless, while I would have gladly given place to one of these rising young men, I could not well decline the duty and the honor of ap-

---

An Address by the Hon. Frederick Douglass, Delivered in the Congregational Church, Washington, D.C., April 16, 1883 on the Twenty-First Anniversary of Emancipation in the District of Columbia (Washington, D.C., 1883).

pearing here to-night. It may, after all, be well to have something of the past mingled with the present, well that one who has had some share in the conflict should share also in the public joy of the victory.

At the outset, as an old watchman on the walls of liberty, eagerly scanning the social and political horizon, you naturally ask me, What of the night? It is easy to break forth in joy and thanksgiving for Emancipation in the District of Columbia. It is easy to call up the noble sentiments and the startling events which made that grand measure possible. It is easy to trace the footsteps of the negro in the past, marked as they are all the way along with blood. But the present occasion calls for something more. How stands the negro to-day? What are the relations subsisting between him and the powerful people among whom he lives, moves, and has his being? What is the outlook, and what is his probable future?

You will readily perceive that I have raised more questions than I shall be able for the present to answer. My general response to these inquiries is a mixed one. The sky of the American Negro is dark, but not rayless; it is stormy, but not cheerless. The grand old party of liberty, union, and progress, which has been his reliance and refuge so long, though less cohesive and strong than it once was, is still a power and has a future. I give you notice, that while there is a Democratic party there will be a Republican party. As the war for the Union recedes into the misty shadows of the past, and the Negro is no longer needed to assault forts and stop rebel bullets, he is in some sense, of less importance. Peace with the old master class has been war to the Negro. As the one has risen, the other has fallen. The reaction has been sudden, marked, and violent. It has swept the Negro from all the legislative halls of the Southern States, and from those of the Congress of the United States. It has, in many cases, driven him from the ballot box and the jury box. The situation has much in it for serious thought, but nothing to cause despair. Above all the frowning clouds that lower about our horizon, there is the steady light of stars, and the thick clouds that now obscure them, will in due season pass away.

In fact, they are already passing away. Time and events which have done so much for us in the past, will, I trust, not do less for us in the future. The moral government of the universe is on our side, and co-operates, with all honest efforts, to lift up the down-trodden and oppressed in all lands, whether the oppressed be white or black.

In whatever else the Negro may have been a failure, he has, in one respect, been a marked and brilliant success. He has managed by one means or another to make himself one of the most prominent and interesting figures that now attract and hold the attention of the world.

Go where you will you will, meet with him. He is alike present in the study of the learned and thoughtful, and in the play house of the gay and thoughtless. We see him pictured at our street corners, and hear him in the songs of our market places. The low and the vulgar curse him, the snob and the flunky affect to despise him, the mean and the cowardly assault him, because they know that his friends are few, and that they can abuse him with impunity, and with the applause of the coarse and brutal crowd. But, despite of it all, the Negro remains like iron or granite, cool, strong, imperturbable and cheerful.

Men of all lands and languages make him a subject of profound thought and study. To the statesman and philosopher he is an object of intense curiosity. Men want to know more of his character, his qualities, his attainments, his mental possibilities, and his probable destiny. Notwithstanding their black faces, the Jubilee singers, with their wild and plaintive music, thrill and charm the most refined and cultivated of the white race, both here and in Europe. Generous and brave men like Andrew Jackson, Benjamin F. Butler, and General Grant, have borne ample testimony to the courage of the negro, to his gallantry, and to his patriotism. Of the books, pamphlets, and speeches concerning him, there is, literally, no end. He is the one inexhaustible topic of conversation at our firesides and in our public halls.

Great, however, as is his advantage at this point, he is not altogether fortunate after all, as to the manner in which his claims are canvassed. His misfortune is that few men are qualified to discuss him candidly and impartially. They either exalt him too high or rate him too low. Americans can consider almost any other question more calmly and fairly than this one. I know of nothing outside of religion which kindles more wrath, causes wider differences, or gives force and effect to fiercer and more irreconcilable antagonisms.

It was so in the time of slavery, and it is so now. Then, the cause was interest, now, the cause is pride and prejudice. Then, the cause was property. He was then worth twenty hundred millions to his owner. He is now worth uncounted millions to himself. While a slave there was a mountain of gold on his breast to keep him down — now that he is free there is a mountain of prejudice to hold him down.

Let any man now claim for the Negro, or worse still, let the Negro now claim for himself, any right, privilege or immunity which has hitherto been denied him by law or custom, and he will at once open a fountain of bitterness, and call forth overwhelming wrath.

It is his sad lot to live in a land where all presumptions are arrayed against him, unless we except the presumption of inferiority and worthlessness. If his course is downward, he meets very little resistance, but if upward, his way is disputed at every turn of the road. If he comes in rags and in wretchedness, he answers the public demand for a negro, and provokes no anger, though he may provoke derision, but if he presumes to be a gentleman and a scholar, he is then entirely out of his place. He excites resentment and calls forth stern and bitter opposition. If he offers himself to a builder as a mechanic, to a client as a lawyer, to a patient as a physician, to a university as a professor, or to a department as a clerk, no matter what may be his ability or his attainments, there is a presumption based upon his color or his previous condition, of incompetency, and if he succeeds at all, he has to do so against this most discouraging presumption.

It is a real calamity, in this country, for any man, guilty or not guilty, to be accused of crime, but it is an incomparably greater calamity for any colored man to be so accused. Justice is often painted with bandaged eyes.

She is described in forensic eloquence, as utterly blind to wealth or poverty, high or low, white or black, but a mask of iron, however thick, could never blind American justice, when a black man happens to be on trial. Here, even more than elsewhere, he will find all presumptions of law and evidence against him. It is not so much the business of his enemies to prove him guilty, as it is the business of himself to prove his innocence. The reasonable doubt which is usually interposed to save the life and liberty of a white man charged with crime, seldom has any force or effect when a colored man is accused of crime. Indeed, color is a far better protection to the white criminal, than anything else. In certain parts of our country, when any white man wishes to commit a heinous offence, he wisely resorts to burnt cork and blackens his face and goes forth under the similitude of a Negro. When the deed is done, a little soap and water destroys his identity, and he goes unwhipt of justice. Some Negro is at once suspected and brought before the victim of wrong for identification, and there is never much trouble here, for as in the eyes of many white people, all Negroes look alike, and as the man arrested and who sits in the dock in irons is black, he is undoubtedly the criminal.

A still greater misfortune to the Negro is that the press, that engine of omnipotent power, usually tries him in advance of the courts, and when once his case is decided in the newspapers, it is easy for the jury to bring in its verdict of "guilty as indicted."

In many parts of our common country, the action of courts and juries is entirely too slow for the impetuosity of the people's justice. When the black man is accused, the mob takes the law into its own hands, and whips, shoots, stabs, hangs or burns the accused, simply upon the allegation or suspicion of crime. Of such proceedings Southern papers are full. A crime almost unknown to the colored man in the time of slavery seems now, from report, the most common. I do not believe these reports. There are too many reasons for trumping up such charges.

Another feature of the situation is, that this mob violence is seldom rebuked by the press and the pulpit, in its immediate neighborhood. Because the public opinion which sustains and makes possible such outrages, intimidates both press and pulpit.

Besides, nobody expects that those who participate in such mob violence will ever be held answerable to the law, and punished. Of course, judges are not always unjust, nor juries always partial in cases of this class, but I affirm that I have here given you no picture of the fancy, and I have alleged no point incapable of proof, and drawn no line darker or denser than the terrible reality. The situation, my colored fellow citizens, is discouraging, but with all its hardships and horrors, I am neither desperate nor despairing as to the future.

One ground of hope is found in the fact referred to in the beginning, and that is, the discussion concerning the Negro still goes on.

The country in which we live is happily governed by ideas as well as by laws, and no black man need despair while there is an audible and earnest assertion of justice and right on his behalf. He may be riddled with bullets, or roasted over a slow fire by the mob, but his cause cannot be shot or burned or otherwise destroyed. Like the impalpable ghost of the murdered Hamlet, it is immortal. All talk of its being a dead issue is a mistake. It may for a time be buried, but it is not dead. Tariffs, free trade, civil service, and river and harbor bills, may for a time cover it, but it will rise again, and again, and again, with increased life and vigor. Every year adds to the black man's numbers. Every year adds to his wealth and to his intelligence. These will speak for him.

There is a power in numbers, wealth and intelligence, which can never be despised nor defied. All efforts thus far to diminish the Negro's importance as a man and as a member of the American body politic, have failed. We are approaching a momentous canvass. If I do not misread the signs of the times, he will play an important part in the politics of the nation during the next Presidential campaign, and will play it well.

When the crisis shall come, neither of the great political parties will fail to appreciate the influence of his voice and his vote. It would not be strange or surprising, if even the Democratic party should be seized with an appetite of unusual intensity for these colored votes. From present indications, too, I apprehend that his vote will be employed in such manner as to more fully open the gates of progress, and secure for himself a better position among his fellow countrymen than heretofore.

Without putting my head to the ground, I can even now hear the anxious inquiry as to when this discussion of the Negro will cease. When will he cease to be a bone of contention between the two great parties? Speaking for myself I can honestly say I wish it to cease. I long to see the Negro utterly out of the whirlpool of angry political debate. No one will rejoice more heartily than I shall when this consummation is reached. I want the whole American people to unite with the sentiment of their greatest captain, U. S. Grant, and say with him on this subject, "Let us have peace." I need it; you need it; the Negro needs it; and every lover of his country should endeavor to withdraw the Negro from this angry gulf. But it is idle, utterly idle to dream of peace anywhere in this world, while any part of the human family are the victims of marked injustice and oppression.

In America, no less than elsewhere, purity must go before tranquility. Nations, no more than individuals, can reverse this fundamental and eternal order of human relations. There is no modern Joshua who can command this resplendent orb of popular discussion to stand still. As in the past, so in the future, it will go on. It may be arrested and imprisoned for a while, but no power can permanently restrain it.

If you wish to suppress it, I counsel you, my fellow citizens, to remove its cause. The voice of popular complaint, whether it is heard in this country or in other countries, does not and can not rest upon dreams, visions, or illusions of any kind. There must be solid ground for it.

The demand for Negro rights would have ceased long since but for the existence of a sufficient and substantial cause for its continuance.

Fellow citizens, the present hour is full of admonition and warning. I despise threats, and remembering as I do the depths from which I have come, and the forlorn condition of those for whom I speak, I dare not assume before the American people an air of haughtiness, but on the other hand I can not forget that the Negro is now, and of right ought to be, an American citizen in the fullest sense of the word. This high position, I take it, was not accorded him in sport, mockery or deception. I credit the American people with sincerity.

No matter what the Democratic party may say; no matter what the old master class of the South may say; no matter what the Supreme Court of the United States may say, the fact is beyond question that the loyal American people, in view of the services of the Negro in the national hour of peril, meant to make him, in good faith and according to the letter and spirit of the Constitution of the United States, a full and complete American citizen.

The amendments to the Constitution of the United States mean this, or they are a cruel, scandalous and colossal sham, and deserve to be so branded before the civilized world. What Abraham Lincoln said in respect of the United States is as true of the colored people as of the relations of those States. They cannot remain half slave and half free. You must give them all or take from them all. Until this half-and-half condition is ended, there will be just ground of complaint. You will have an aggrieved class, and this discussion will go on. Until the public schools shall cease to be caste schools in every part of our country, this discussion will go on. Until the colored man's pathway to the American ballot box, North and South, shall be as smooth and as safe as the same is for the white citizen, this discussion will go on. Until the colored man's right to practice at the bar of our courts, and sit upon juries, shall be the universal law and practice of the land, this discussion will go on. Until the courts of the country shall grant the colored man a fair trial and a just verdict, this discussion will go on. Until color shall cease to be a bar to equal participation in the offices and honors of the country, this discussion will go on. Until the trades-unions and the workshops of the country shall cease to proscribe the colored man and prevent his children from learning useful trades, this discussion will go on. Until the American people shall make character, and not color, the criterion of respectability, this discussion will go on. Until men like Bishops Payne and Campbell shall cease to be driven from respectable railroad cars at the South, this discussion will go on. In a word, until truth and humanity shall cease to be living ideas, and mankind shall sink back into moral darkness, and the world shall put evil for good, bitter for sweet, and darkness for light, this discussion will go on. Until all humane ideas and civilization shall be banished from the world, this discussion will go on.

There never was a time when this great lesson could be more easily learned than now. Events are transpiring all around us that enforce consideration of the oppressed classes. In one form or another, by one means or another, the ideas of a common humanity against privileged classes, of common rights against special privileges, are now rocking the world. Explosives are heard that rival the earthquake. They are causing despots to tremble, class rule to quail, thrones to shake and oppressive associated wealth to turn pale.

It is for America to be wise in time. For the present our institutions are not likely to be shaken by dynamite or daggers. We have free speech and a free press.

"Weapons of war we have cast from the battle." With us there is no apology for violence or crime. Happily we are in a position to win by peaceful means those victories more renowned than any secured by war.

The gates of reason are still open to us; and, while we may speak and vote, we need not despair.

When the nation was in peril; when the country was rent asunder at the center; when rebel armies were in the field, bold, defiant and victorious; when our recruiting sergeants were marching up and down our streets from early morn till late at night, with drum and fife, with banner and badge, footsore and weary; when the fate of the Republic trembled in the balance, and the hearts of loyal men were failing them for fear; when nearly all hope of subduing the rebellion had vanished, Abraham Lincoln called upon the colored men of this country to reach out their iron arms and clutch with their steel fingers the faltering banner of the Republic; and they rallied, and they rallied, full two hundred thousand strong. Ah! then, my friends, the claims of the Negro found the heart of the nation a little more tender and responsive than now. But I ask Americans to remember that the arms that were needed then may be needed again; and it is best that they do not convert the cheerful and loyal brows of six millions into a black Ireland.

A nation composed of all classes should be governed by no one class exclusively. All should be included, and none excluded. Thus aggrieved classes would be rendered impossible.

The question is sometimes asked, when, where and by whom the Negro was first suspected of having any rights at all? In answer to this inquiry it has been asserted that William Lloyd Garrison originated the Anti-slavery movement, that until his voice was raised against the American slave system, the whole world was silent. With all respect to those who make this claim I am compelled to dissent from it. I love and venerate the memory of William Lloyd Garrison. I knew him long and well. He was a grand man, a moral hero, a man whose acquaintance and friendship it was a great privilege to enjoy. While liberty has a friend on earth, and slavery an earnest enemy, his name and his works will be held in profound and grateful memory. To him it was given to formulate and thunder against oppression and slavery the testimonies of all ages. He revived, but did not originate.

It is no disparagement to him to affirm that he was preceded by many other good men whom it would be a pleasure to remember on occasions like this. Benjamin Lundy, an humble Quaker, though not the originator of the Anti-slavery movement, was in advance of Mr. Garrison. Walker, a colored man, whose appeal against slavery startled the land like a trump of coming judgment, was before either Mr. Garrison or Mr. Lundy.

Emancipation, without delay, was preached by Dr. Hopkins, of Rhode Island, long before the voice of either Garrison, Lundy or Walker was heard in the land. John Wesley, a hundred years before, had denounced slavery as the sum of all villainies. Adam Clark had done the same. The Society of

Friends had abolished slavery among themselves and had borne testimony against the evil, long before the modern Anti-slavery movement was inaugurated.

In fact, the rights of the Negro, as a man and a brother, began to be asserted with the earliest American Colonial history, and I derive hope from the fact, that the discussion still goes on, and the claims of the Negro rise higher and higher as the years roll by. Two hundred years of discussion has abated no jot of its power or its vitality. Behind it we have a great cloud of witnesses, going back to the beginning of our country and to the very foundation of our government. Our best men have given their voices and their votes on the right side of it, through all our generations.

It has been fashionable of late years to denounce it as a product of Northern growth, a Yankee device for disturbing and disrupting the bonds of the Union, and the like, but the facts of history are all the other way. The Anti-Slavery side of the discussion has a Southern rather than a Northern origin.

The first publication in assertion and vindication of any right of the Negro, of which I have any knowledge, was written more than two hundred years ago, by Rev. Morgan Godwin, a missionary of Virginia and Jamaica. This was only a plea for the right of the Negro to baptism and church membership. The last publication of any considerable note, of which I have any knowledge, is a recent article in the *Popular Science Monthly,* by Prof. Gilliam. The distance and difference between these two publications, in point of time, gives us a gauge by which we may in good degree measure the progress of the Negro. The book of Godwin was published in 1680, and the article of Gilliam was published in 1883. The space in time between the two is not greater than the space in morals and enlightenment. The ground taken in respect to the Negro, in the one, is low. The ground taken in respect to the possibilities of the Negro, in the other, is so high as to be somewhat startling, not only to the white man, but also to the black man himself.

The book of Morgan Godwin is a literary curiosity and an ethical wonder.

I deem myself fortunate in being the owner of a copy of it. I met with it while in White Haven, England, thirty-seven years ago. I was then abroad for safety rather than for health, for at that time there was no place of safety for me anywhere under the American flag or on American soil. An Irish Number 1 is safer here now, than I was then. Our Government then had no tenderness for refugees, however innocent of crime, if their skins happened to be slightly tanned or their hair a trifle wooly. But to return to Dr. Godwin and his book. He very evidently was not a Negro worshiper, nor what in our day would be called an abolitionist. He proposed no disturbance of the relation of master and slave. On the contrary, he conceded the right of the master to own and control the body of the Negro, but insisted that the soul of the Negro belonged to the Lord. His able reasoning on this point, it is true, left the Negro for himself neither soul nor body. When he claimed his body, he found that belonged to his earthly master, and when he looked around for his soul, he found that that belonged to his master in Heaven. Nevertheless the ground taken in this book by Dr. Godwin was immensely important. It was, in fact, the starting point, the foundation of all the grand concessions yet made to the claims, the character, the manhood and the dignity of the Negro. In the light of his present acknowledged position among men, here and elsewhere, a book to prove the Negro's right to baptism seems ridiculous, but so it did not seem two hundred years ago. Baptism was then a vital and commanding question, one with which the moral and intellectual giants of that day were required to grapple.

The opposition to baptizing and admitting the Negro to membership in the Christian church, was serious, determined and bitter. That ceremony was, in his case, opposed on many grounds, but especially upon three. First, the Negro's unfitness for baptism; secondly, the nature of the ordinance itself; and thirdly, because it would disturb the relation of master and slave. The wily slaveholders of that day were sharp-eyed and keen-scented, and snuffed danger from afar. They saw in this argument of Godwin the thin edge of the wedge which would sooner or later rend asunder the bonds of slavery. They therefore sought in piety to heaven security for their possessions on earth; in reverence to God contempt for man. They sought in the sacredness of baptism the salvation of slavery.

They contended that this holy ordinance could only be properly administered to free and responsible agents, men who, in all matters of moral conduct, could exercise the sacred right of choice; and this proposition was very easily defended. For, plainly enough, the Negro did not answer that description. The laws of the land did not even know him as a person. He was simply a piece of property, an article of merchandise, marked and branded as such, and no more fitted to be admitted to the fellowship of the saints than horses, sheep or swine.

When Chief Justice Taney said that Negroes in those early days had no rights which white men felt bound to respect, he only uttered an historical truth. The trouble was that it was uttered for an evil purpose, and made to serve an evil purpose. The slave was solely answerable for his conduct to his earthly master. To thrust baptism and the church between the slave and his master was a dangerous interference with the absolute authority of the master. The slave-holders were always logical. When they assumed that slavery was right, they easily saw that everything inconsistent with slavery was wrong.

But deeper down than any modification of the master's authority, there was a more controlling motive for opposing baptism. Baptism had a legal as well as a religious significance. By the common law at that time, baptism was made a sufficient basis for a legal claim for emancipation. I am informed by Hon. A. B. Hagner, one of the Judges of the Supreme Court of this District, that there is now an old law in the State of Maryland, reversing the common law at this point.

Had I lived in Maryland before that law was enacted, I should have been baptized if I could have gotten anybody to perform the ceremony.

For in that day of Christian simplicity, honest rules of Biblical interpretation were applied. The Bible was thought to mean just what it said. When a heathen ceased to be a heathen and became a Christian, he could no longer be held as a slave. Within the meaning of the accepted word of God it was the heathen, not the Christian, who was to be bought and sold, and held as a bondman forever.

This fact stood like a roaring lion ready to tear and devour any Negro who sought the ordinance of baptism.

In the eyes of the wise and prudent of his times, Dr. Godwin was a dangerous man, a disturber of the peace of the church. Like our ever-faithful friend, Dr. Rankin, he was guilty of pressing religion into an improper interference with secular things, and making mischief generally.

In fact, when viewed relatively, low as was the ground assumed by this good man two hundred years ago, he was as far in advance of his times then as Charles Sumner was when he first took his seat in the United States Senate. What baptism and church membership were for the Negro in the days of Godwin, the ballot and civil rights were for the Negro in, the days of Sumner. Though standing two centuries apart these two men are, nevertheless, conspicuous links in the great chain of causes and events which raised the Negro to his present level of freedom in this and other lands. Here, tonight on the twenty-first anniversary of Emancipation in the District of Columbia, the capital of the grandest Republic of freedom on the earth, I kneel at the grave, amid the dust and shadows of bygone centuries, and offer my gratitude, and the gratitude of six millions of my race, to Morgan Godwin, as the grand pioneer of Garrison, Lundy, Goodell, Phillips, Henry Wilson, Gerrit Smith, Joshua R. Giddings, Abraham Lincoln, Thaddeus Stevens, and the illustrious host of the great men who have since risen to plead the cause of the negro against those who would oppress him.

Fellow-citizens — In view of the history now referred to, the low point at which he started in the race of life on this continent, and the many obstacles which had to be surmounted the Negro has reasons to be proud of his progress, if not of his beginning. He is a brilliant illustration of social and anthropological revolution and evolution.

His progress has been steady, vast and wonderful. No people has ever made greater progress under similar conditions. We may trace his rise from Godwin contending for his right to baptism, to Garrison with abolitionism, and later on to Gilliam alarmed at the prospect of negro supremacy. His progress is marked with three G's, Godwin, Garrison, Gilliam. We see him changed from a heathen to a christian by Godwin, from a slave to a freeman by Garrison, from a serf to a sovereign by Gilliam.

I am not a disciple of Professor Gilliam, and have neither hope nor fear of black supremacy. I have very little interest in his ethics or his arithmetic. It may or it may not come to pass. Sufficient unto the day is both the evil and the good thereof. A hundred years is a little further down the steps of time than I care to look, for good or for evil.

When father Miller proved by the Bible, from whose pages so many things have been proved, that the world would come to an end in 1843, and proved it so clearly that many began to make their robes in which they were to soar aloft above this burning world, he was asked by a doubting Thomas, "But father Miller, what if it does not come?" "Well," said the good old man, "then we shall wait till it does come."

The colored people of the United States should imitate the wisdom of father Miller, and, wait. But we should also work while we wait. For after all, our destiny is largely in our own hands. If we find, we shall have to seek. If we succeed in the race of life, it must be by our own energies, and our own exertions. Others may clear the road, but we must go forward, or be left behind in the race of life.

If we remain poor and dependent, the riches of other men will not avail us. If we are ignorant, the intelligence of other men will do but little for us. If we are foolish, the wisdom of other men will not guide us. If we are wasteful of time and money, the economy of other men will only make our destitution the more disgraceful and hurtful. If we are vicious and lawless, the virtues and good behavior of others will not save us from our vices and our crimes.

We are now free, and though we have many of the consequences of our past condition to contend against, by union, effort, co-operation, and by wise policy in the direction and the employment of our mental, moral, industrial and political powers, it is the faith of my soul, that we can blot out the handwriting of popular prejudice, remove the stumbling-blocks left in our way by slavery, rise to an honorable place in the estimation of our fellow-citizens of all classes, and make a comfortable way for ourselves in the world.

I have referred to the vast and wonderful changes which have taken place in the condition of the colored people of this country. We rejoice in those changes to-day, and we do well. We are neither wood nor stone, but men. We possess the sentiments common to right-minded men.

But do we know the history of those vast and marvellous changes and the means by which they were brought about? Do we comprehend the philosophy of our progress? Do we ever think of the time, the thought, the labor, the pain, the self-sacrifice, by which they were accomplished? Have we a just and proper conception of the noble zeal, the inflexible firmness, the heroic courage, and other grand qualities of soul, displayed by the reformers and statesmen through whose exertions these changes in our conditions have been wrought out and the victory won?

Mr. Williams, in his History of the Negro, tells his readers that it was the dissolution of the Union that abolished slavery. He might as well have told them that Charles Sumner was a slaveholder; that Jeff Davis was an abolitionist; that Abraham Lincoln was disloyal, and that the devil founded the Christian church. Had the Union been dissolved you and I would not be here this evening. Had the Union been dissolved, the colored people of the South would now be in the hateful chains of slavery. No, no, Mr. Williams, it was not the destruction but the salvation of the Union that saved the slave from slavery and the country to freedom, and the Negro to citizenship.

The abolition of slavery in the District of Columbia was one of the most important events connected with the prosecution of the war for the preservation of the Union, and, as such, is worthy of the marked commemoration we have given it to-day. It was not only a staggering blow to slavery throughout the country, but a killing blow to the rebellion, and was the beginning of the end to both. It placed the National dignity and the National power on the side of emancipation. It was the first step toward a redeemed and regenerated nation. It imparted a moral and human significance to what at first seemed to the outside world, only a sanguinary war for empire.

This great step in National progress, was not taken without a violent struggle in Congress. It required a large share of moral courage, large faith in the power of truth, and confidence in the enlightenment and loyalty of the people, to support this radical measure.

I need not tell you it was bitterly opposed on various grounds by the Democratic members of Congress. To them it was a measure of flagrant bad faith with the slaveholders of the District; and calculated to alienate the border States, and drive them completely into the Confederate States, and make the restoration of the Union impossible. There was much more force in such arguments then than now. The situation was critical. The rebellion was in the fullness of its strength, bold, defiant, victorious, and confident of ultimate success. The great man on horseback had not then become visible along the Western horizon. Sherman had not begun his triumphant march to the sea. But there were moral and intellectual giants in the councils of the Nation at that time. We saw in the Senate Chamber the towering form of the lamented Sumner, the earnest and practical Henry Wilson, the honest and courageous Benjamin F. Wade, the strong and fearless Zachary Chandler, the man who took the unsuccessful General from the head of the Army of the Potomac. In the House we had an army of brilliant men such as Thaddeus Stevens, Owen Lovejoy, and A. G. Riddle, the first to advocate in Congress the arming of the Negro in defence of the Union. There, too was Thomas D. Elliot, Henry Winter Davis, William D. Kelley, Roscoe Conkling, than whom there has appeared in the Senate of the nation no patriot more pure, no orator more brilliant, no friend to liberty and progress more sincere. I speak all the more freely of him since he is now out of politics and in some sense under the shadow of defeat. I cannot forget that these brave men, and others just as worthy of mention, fully comprehended the demands of the hour, and had the courage and the sagacity to meet those demands. They saw that slavery was the root, the sap, the motive, and mainspring of the rebellion, and that the way to kill the rebellion was to destroy its cause.

Among the great names which should never be forgotten on occasions like this, there is one which should never be spoken but with reverence, gratitude and affection, the one man of all the millions of our countrymen to whom we are more indebted for a United Nation and for American liberty than to any other, and that name is Abraham Lincoln, the greatest statesman that ever presided over the destinies of this Republic. The time is too short, his term of office is too recent to permit or to require extended notice of his statesmanship, or of his moral and mental qualities. We all know Abraham Lincoln by heart. In looking back to the many great men of twenty years ago, we find him the tallest figure of them all. His mission was to close up a chasm opened by an earthquake, and he did it. It was his to call back a bleeding, dying and dismembered nation to life, and he did it. It was his to free this country from the crime, curse, and disgrace of slavery, and to lift millions to the plane of humanity, and he did it. Never was statesman surrounded by greater difficulties, and never were difficulties more ably, wisely and firmly met. Friends and fellow-citizens, in conclusion I return to the point from which I started, namely: What is to be the future of the colored people of this country? Some change in their condition seems to be looked for by thoughtful men everywhere; but what that change will be, no one yet has been able with certainty to predict.

Three different solutions to this difficult problem have been given and adopted by different classes of the American people. 1. Colonization in Africa; 2. Extinction through poverty, disease and death; 3. Assimilation and unification with the great body of the American people.

Plainly it is a matter about which no man can be very positive. In scanning the social sky he may fall into mistakes as great as those which vexed the souls of Wiggins and Vennor and other weather prophets. Appearances are deceptive. No man can see the end from the beginning.

It is, however, consoling to think that this limitation upon human foresight has helped us in the past and may help us in the future. Could William the Silent have foreseen the misery and ruin he would bring upon his country by taking up the sword against the Spanish Inquisition, he might have thought the sacrifice too great. Had William Lloyd Garrison foreseen that he would be hated, persecuted, mobbed, imprisoned, and drawn through the streets of his beloved Boston with a halter about his neck, even his courage might have quailed, and the native hue of his resolution been sicklied o'er with the pale cast of thought. Could Abraham Lincoln have foreseen the immense cost, the terrible hardship, the awful waste of blood and treasure involved in the effort to retake and repossess the forts and arsenals and other property captured by the Confederate States; could he have foreseen the tears of the widows and orphans, and his own warm blood trickling at the bidding of an assassin's bullet, he might have thought the sacrifice too great.

In every great movement men are prepared by preceding events for those which are to come. We neither know the evil nor the good which may be in store for us. Twenty-five years ago the system of slavery seemed impregnable. Cotton was king, and the civilized world acknowledged his sway. Twenty-five years ago no man could have foreseen that in less than ten years from that time no master would wield a lash and no slave would clank a chain in the United States.

Who at that time dreamed that Negroes would ever be seen as we have seen them to-day marching through the streets of this superb city, the Capital of this great Nation, with eagles on their buttons, muskets on their shoulders and swords by their sides, timing their high footsteps to the Star Spangled Banner and the Red, White and Blue? Who at that time dreamed that colored men would ever sit in the House of Representatives and in the Senate of the United States?

With a knowledge of the events of the last score of years, with a knowledge of the sudden and startling changes which have already come to pass, I am not prepared to say what the future will be.

But I will say that I do not look for colonization either in or out of the United States. Africa is too far off, even if we desired to go there, which we do not. The navy of all the world would not be sufficient to remove our natural increase to that-far off country. Removal to any of the territories is out of the question.

We have no business to put ourselves before the bayonets of the white race. We have seen the fate of the Indian. As to extinction, the prospect in that direction has been greatly clouded by the census just taken, in which it is seen that our increase is ten per cent. greater than that of the white people of the South.

There is but one destiny, it seems to me, left for us, and that is to make ourselves and be made by others a part of the American people in every sense of the word. Assimilation and not isolation is our true policy and our natural destiny. Unification for us is life: separation is death. We cannot afford to set up for ourselves a separate political party, or adopt for ourselves a political creed apart from the rest of our fellow citizens. Our own interests will be subserved by a generous care for the interests of the Nation at large. All the political, social and literary forces around us tend to unification.

I am the more inclined to accept this solution because I have seen the steps already taken in that direction. The American people have their prejudices, but they have other qualities as well. They easily adapt themselves to inevitable conditions, and all their tendency is to progress, enlightenment and to the universal.

> "Its comin' yet for a' that,
>   That man to man the warld o'er
> Shall brothers be for a' that."

Three days after Douglass delivered his address, he received a letter from twenty black leaders asking him to publish his speech so that it "could be placed in the hands of every voter in the country. . . ." Included in the request for publication was warm praise of Douglass' presentation, but also concern about the white man's lack of appreciation for the Negro's plight.

It is not easy for our fellow white citizens to understand how, with personal freedom and the ballot, we still have a cause that is worth hearing and patiently considering, but you have stated the difficulties that yet environ the colored American with such precision and clearness that no man, who reads your masterly effort can fail to see that the Negro's way is still a rough and thorny one.[67]

Douglass' speech was instructive but it could do little to slow the southern trend toward white supremacy that was developing in the latter part of the nineteenth century. Even while white industrialists and black workers formed an alliance for the purpose of projecting a new South image, southern states revised suffrage provisions and made it increasingly difficult for Negroes to vote.[68]

To broaden its influence, the industrial establishment in the South enlisted the support of the eloquent Georgia orator and journalist, Henry W. Grady, and won at least the tacit approval of Booker T. Washington. However, it failed to meet the demands of the discontented small farmers and the liberal elements in the black community. This agrarian and racial unrest led to the rise of Tom Watson, a white reformer from Georgia, who was elected to Congress in 1890. Watson strove to initiate an agrarian rebellion which would weaken the appeal of the industrialists and strengthen civil rights. Both of the groups Watson represented responded warmly to his message. Negroes "thronged to his rallies by the thousands and stood side by side with white farmers listening to him speak from the same platform with speakers of their own race."[69] The raging controversy generated by Watson and other Populist candidates proved to be dangerous to the sympathetic black speakers who supported them on the hustings. In the 1892 state election campaign in Georgia, an estimated fifteen Negro Populists were killed.[70] Yet, they continued to press their cause. H. S. Doyle, "a young Negro preacher of intelligence and courage," delivered "sixty-three speeches in behalf of Watson's candidacy for Congress during the campaign of 1892," notwithstanding the fact that he faced repeated threats on his life.[71]

Tom Watson made some progress toward his goal of uniting the masses of both races in an agrarian crusade designed to offer a meaningful alternative to the dominating Democratic party of the South. By the middle of the decade, he had forced many of his contemporaries to come to grips with the subject of political and social reform. Two dramatic events, however, suddenly altered this trend. The first was the 1896 Supreme Court decision in *Plessy v. Ferguson,* arguing that the Fourteenth Amendment did not forbid segregated schools provided that they were equal. This action gave legal sanction to many of the Jim Crow laws then being instituted.[72] The second event, which also had far-reaching significance, was the advent of the Spanish American War. The United States policy of Manifest Destiny that ensued gave international affairs precedence over domestic issues. When the political leaders launched a new program of progressivism in the early 1900's, it was "For Whites Only."[73]

As social upheaval continued to build, some Negro leaders were willing to compromise and adjust whenever they thought this action might lead to an improved status in economics and politics. Education based on utility and separatism became a recommended approach for aspiring young blacks who hoped to move up the assimilation ladder. Nevertheless, W. E. B. DuBois was unyielding in his opposition to this form of conciliation and submission. Taking advantage of the favorable image he had developed through the publication of *The Souls of Black Folk,* he asked a group of young Negro intellectuals to meet in Ontario, Canada, in 1905. Here, the delegates initiated a protest organization called the Niagara Movement which, four years later, became the germinal seed for the creation of the National Association for the Advancement of Colored People.[74] One of the distinguishing characteristics of the movement was its recognition that racial discrimination was not limited to the South. Rather, they realized that it was a national problem with strong economic, political, and social implications. It was against this background that DuBois, in 1910, carried his message of the harmful effects of prejudice to the citizens of New York. His speech, which follows, contains many of the rhetorical elements present in the antebellum abolition speeches of Douglass and Garnet.

W.E.B. DuBois

*Race Prejudice**

The more or less theoretical problem of race prejudice today enters largely into the domain of practical politics, and has become of increasing importance in the United States not only because it involves to the Negro in large sections of the country a denial of the principles of democracy, thus engendering passionate feelings against such discrimination, but on account of the unwisdom from an economic standpoint of repressing the colored races.

We have in the United States today a series of rotten boroughs or districts, the political power of which is tremendously and unfairly increased

---

*W.E.B. DuBois, "Race Prejudice," An address delivered on March 5, 1910 in New York City. Published as a pamphlet by the New York Republican Club in 1910.

by the wholesale disfranchisment of their voters, until one man in Georgia or Mississippi often exercises as much power in the counsels of the National government as seven men in Massachusetts. Moreover, these Southern voters have had their political power increased so enormously, not because of political efficiency (since they are the most illiterate part of the Nation), but because strong racial prejudice has led them to deny the right to vote to black men. There has been some pretense of letting a few competent blacks vote, but as the new Senator from Mississippi says boldly, "There is today no such thing as Negro suffrage in Mississippi and never will be as long as the white men of the State stand together." Thus a second political complication enters. The all-powerful rump of the voting population of the South cannot today consider the merits of any political question presented to them. They must vote always and simply to keep negroes down. Outside of all questions of party such a denial of the fundamental principles of democracy is dangerous to the Nation. It means that there are certain parts of the country where reason cannot be applied to the settlement of great political questions. Such weak spots in the political body are sure to become the seat of disease, and so long as the race prejudice in the South shows its result in such disorganization of government and disfranchisement of a large part of the working class and in an unequal balance of political power, as compared with the rest of the Nation, just so long race prejudice is bound to be a burning question of practical politics.

The question, however, is not simply political, it is not simply the old question of the negro's right to vote, — a problem which has been with us so long that we are disposed to give it up in despair. Today the problem is becoming more and more economic. We are seeing arise in the South two great groups of laborers: one white and one black, one with the power of the ballot and one disfranchised. That the disfranchisement of the black workingmen is practically complete there can be no reasonable doubt. These two groups of workingmen are coming more and more into economic competition, and the industrial education of the negro is bound to increase this competition. The result is a situation which is being taken advantage of by two different kinds of selfish interests. The politician in the South who is out of a job finds it more and more to his interest to stir up the passions of the white workingman who has the ballot by appealing to the grossest and worst instincts of race prejudice, and by representing all the present and possible economic ills of the white workingman as due to his black competitor. We have already seen in the South instance after instance of demagogues arising with wide-spread political power by these means and we have known the horror of the Atlanta riot as a sort of first-fruits of this newer economic race danger.

On the other hand, the exploiting capitalist is also tempted to transmute race prejudice in the coin of the realm. He says to his white laborers, "I am not in business for my health; I seek the cheapest competent labor. Larger and larger number of blacks are demanding work at low wages; if you are dissatisfied and continue to make trouble and demand too much I will replace you by black men." He turns to his black laborers, "You are lazy and incompetent — unless you work harder and stop complaining I will replace you with white men." This again leads each class to regard the other as the chief cause of low wages and unfair treatment; and the situation in the South affects the labor problem over the whole nation, and is destined to affect it more and more. The high level of wages in the North cannot entirely withstand the competition of the lower level of wages in the South, and fight as the white laborer may at once to keep up wages and to exclude the black man from his union, he is bound to lose for he is fighting black men, while black men are fighting starvation and must consequently fight harder. So that here again we have a result of race prejudice which is bringing us face to face with a great labor problem.

But the results of race prejudice do not stop even here. The United States is today going through a great economic crisis. It is changing from being a country which raises and exports food stuffs and imports its manufactured articles, into a country which largely consumes its own food stuffs and exports its manufactures. Now the export of food from the United States brought us into contact with European civilization, but the export of manufactured articles is bringing us into contact with the darker world; with Asia, Africa, the West Indies and South America. In our endeavor, however, to open markets for trade in these countries and with these peoples we are being brought face to face with the unpleasant fact that America is not liked in the darker world; she has gone out of her way to insult many of these people. She has enslaved "Niggers," sneered at "Dagos," insulted Chinese and Japanese, and found no words too contemptuous to express her feeling for the "mongrel" races of Central and Southern America. Under such circumstances our invasion of the world market must be under a great moral handicap. There can be no doubt but that a large part of our difficulty in getting South American trade is because of our free exhibition of racial prejudice. In China and the East our prejudices have not helped our economic campaign, and the future is ominous.

Viewing then the situation calmly and judicially, it must frankly be confessed that race prejudice is costing the United States heavily: it is costing us certain fundamental principles of democratic government, peace and development in the labor world, and enhanced difficulty of getting a world market for our goods.

Facing now such a cost, it is reasonable to ask, Why are we paying it? What return are we getting out of it? Is it really worthwhile? Most people when asked about their prejudices as to race say simply: it is a matter of personal like or dislike; some people like one kind of people and some another, similar to a preference for one sort of food over another. The difficulty is, however, that human antipathies between men and men seldom remain at this comparatively harmless stage. The preferences take on vitality and warmth, a value and importance that makes us not satisfied to indulge our likes and dislikes, but to wish to force them on our neighbors and to this end we are nearly always driven, or think we are driven, to use three weapons of offence, which are in the world history of tremendous import. They are: personal insult, persecution and repression.

We forcibly keep certain men from occupying certain positions or entering certain careers. We deliberately persecute some people by means, for instance, of Jim-Crow cars or other discriminations, or we heap personal insult and ridicule upon them. It may be admitted that there are perhaps times in this world when it is necessary and defensible to take a human being by the throat, slowly choke his life out and throw his dead carcass to one side; or if we are not prepared personally to go to that extreme, it is, I am told, at times justifiable to render the life of certain persons so uncomfortable that they will eliminate themselves; and finally it certainly seems to many as though personal insult was now and then necessary to repress some sorts of undesirable men; but despite all this, every civilized being hesitates and shudders at the use of these three awful weapons; and they hesitate because these weapons are dangerous things, not simply deadening, corroding, fatal to the victims, but doubly dangerous to those who get into the habit of using them; from the use of insult grows the arrogant, overbearing nation which so often blindly misses the way of truth; from the bigotry of persecution grows the dead rot of mental death, and from war and murder comes national as well as individual death. Worse than that, these weapons of race prejudice often fail to effect their object. Doubtless objectionable individuals and groups have been persecuted and insulted out of existence or simply massacred. But not always. Often with fierce persistence they have lived, directly or indirectly — consciously or unconsciously to avenge their wrongs. At least these weapons of offense are so despicable and their efficiency so questionable that before we continue their use, ought we not to ask ourselves frankly: just what it is that we really want to accomplish in this matter of racial prejudice.

I think that most people would say upon first thought that they want to be able to live in a world which is in most respects according to their liking and according to their idea of fitness, both in persons and in things; but so soon as such a desire is expressed, it must be said plainly, without further argument, that such a consummation is largely impossible. The simplest and most exclusive club cannot in its membership suit all the people included. We must always come more or less in contact, even in intimate contact, with people whom we do not like. This is true of all ages, but it is especially true in the modern world. A few centuries ago the world existed in such air-tight compartments that groups could isolate themselves and live to themselves. Today we are demanding vociferously the policy of the Open Door. We are demanding, now chiefly for economic reasons, but also in part for political and social reasons, a world-wide contact of men with men. It is expressed today in the right of white men to go anywhere they choose and be treated with consideration and respect. It will be expressed tomorrow in the right of the colored races to return the visits. Under no easily conceivable circumstances can the future world be peopled simply with one of the present social groups or with one of the existing races. Some people, to be sure, dream of a future white world. A glance at any map or newspaper will prove that this is, to say the least, highly improbable. Today the human race throughout the world contains a vast numerical preponderance of colored peoples and the population among these colored races is probably increasing faster than among the whites, so that in the future the aggregate of the Black and Yellow races may outnumber the white race.

Many people would frankly acknowledge this. They would expect a future world of Black and Yellow and White men. But they say: we wish these several races to be kept in their places.

Here again there arise difficulties. What are the respective places of these races? Is the easily assumed hierarchy composed by Ruling White, Servile Black and Docile Yellow men really the last word in social evolution? History is not reassuring on this point, present tendencies are disconcerting, and Science is helplessly spreading its hands. Wise men acknowledge that it is perfectly possible that Black and Yellow men may yet reach and surpass white civilization. This may not seem probable, but in human history the Improbable has often happened.

But let all this be as it may, certain it is that if by natural constitution the great races of men arrange themselves in a hierarchy of ability, efficiency and development, then no such social weapons as are now used by racial prejudice are necessary to reinforce natural law. Education will keep the superior races from degeneracy by intermarriage far better than organized insult; persecution will be quite unnecessary to eliminate such races as are unable to survive under civilized conditions; and Repression of ambition and ability will be attended to by the law of social gravity much more effectively than by "Jim-Crow" legislation. In fine, why should we threaten the efficiency of government, the development of industry and the peace of the world by imperfect and questionable human devices?

So soon as the prejudiced are forced into this inevitable dilemma, then the real bitterness and indefensibleness of their attitude is apt to be revealed; they say bluntly that they do not care what "Niggers," "Dagos," "Chinks," or "Japs" may be capable of — they do not like them and they propose to keep such folk in a place of permanent inferiority to the white race — by peaceful policy if possible, but brute force if necessary. And when a group, a nation or a world assumes this attitude, it is handling dynamite. *There is in this world no such force as the force of a man determined to rise.* The human soul cannot be permanently chained.

Is it not then of supreme importance that here in America we refuse to aid and abet any such attempt and that we refuse to try to hold back by insult, persecution and repression those dark masses of human beings who, though beaten to their knees and bloody with blows, are still doggedly determined to be men?

In view of all this it is a matter not simply of politics but of the widest and broadest statesmanship, of economic foresight and deepest religious thought to see that race prejudice in the United States is combatted and corrected and lessened.

THE MODERN ERA

As DuBois spoke, other developments were taking place which would provide a different dimension to the subject of race relations. In the decade of World War I, approximately a half-million Negroes moved from rural settlements to large southern and northern cities. Especially attractive to these migrants were the major industrial centers in the North such as Chicago, Pittsburgh, and Cleveland.[75] These Negroes at first were pleased with their improved status and self-respect, but, before long, they felt the hostility of a threatened white majority who had, for more than a century, dominated the urban areas of the country. This resistance led to discrimination in the Armed Forces and civilian life during the war years, and culminated in the summer riots of 1919. The rejection of the Negro following the war and the revival of the Ku Klux Klan helped to spawn the Garvey Movement which will be discussed in Chapter V.[76]

With the election of Franklin D. Roosevelt in 1932, many blacks thought the time had come for a new assault on racism by responsible leaders. There were unmistakable signs of progress in the early days of the New Deal. Federal agencies gave grants to Negro colleges, the National Labor Relations Board permitted Negroes to vote in labor disputes, and the W.P.A. paid equal salaries to workers of both races who performed similar services.[77] These gains ingratiated Roosevelt to the black community, but they did not produce equality. Assimilationist orators, therefore, kept reminding black Americans that they had not yet secured full citizenship, nor would they without applying increased pressure on the controlling majority. In 1939 — seven years after Roosevelt assumed office — D. O. W. Holmes, a leading Negro educator who never wavered in his belief in the virtues of democracy, symbolized this new militancy and self-assertiveness.[78] In a dedicatory address delivered at Talladega College in Alabama on April 16, he described the nature of the contemporary racial conflict, defined objectives, and offered a solution based on communication. Part of the problem, he argued, arose from complacency on the part of blacks who confused progress with equality. Another contributing cause was the white man's stereotype of the Negro as a "story-telling Uncle Remus, a pan-cake-cooking Aunt Jemima, a banjo-picking stevedore, a dancing porter or the hammer-swinging John Henry who boastingly pits his strength against a steam drill."[79]

Negro complacency and the white stereotype, Holmes continued, helped to maintain a segregated society which produced separate but unequal facilities in education, prevented accomplished singers like Marian Anderson from singing in Constitution Hall in Washington, D.C. and denied blacks admission into hotels and restaurants. Holmes, anxious to help his audience, presented logical and convincing reasons for rejecting segregation and suggested three arguments that could be used in rhetorical situations. "We can answer our critics who charge us with wishing 'to escape from our own people,' " he said, "with the response that segregation is wrong because it never means equality of status; it fails to provide equal accommodations; and it prevents the two races from knowing each other."[80] Holmes recommended in conclusion a four-part rhetorical strategy to be employed by blacks.

(1) In the first place, we must make the white man know us, so that he may have the facts about us before he decides the degree of equality with himself that we have already attained. Remember that the Caucasian considers himself as belonging to a superior race, a conclusion based upon his logic and his experiences, just as would any other individual in the same circumstances.

(2) The second fact that we must use in our offensive is the white man's natural human fear of being looked upon as an abuser of the weak. He has little objection to exploiting or despoiling the weak so long as he does it under the guise of respectable commerce. But, like the bully in the boys' gang, he indignantly denies that he beats up the little fellows and picks on the cripples.

(3) The third fact that dictates our course is that, not only the American white man, but very few other people in human history have given anything substantial without being asked several times to do so. This suggests the importance of dedicating ourselves here and now to the task of making our wants and wishes known.

(4) The fourth line of attack is through the white man's reverence for his own laws that he has struggled thousands of years to establish and which, in the last analysis, he looks upon as holy signs of his rise from savagery to civilization.[81]

The philosophy of Holmes foreshadowed the rhetorical strategy used by A. Philip Randolph who helped to bring about a civil rights renaissance in the North in the 1940's. Aware of black resentment toward segregation in the Armed Forces and discriminatory practices in employment during World War II, Randolph used a militant yet legal strategy, hoping to move Roosevelt to a more liberal position on civil rights. Threatening to lead a demonstration in the streets of Washington, he succeeded in forcing the President "to issue the first executive order compelling fair employment of Negroes. . . ."[82] The successful confrontation between Randolph and Roosevelt kindled new hopes for black Americans who saw in democracy a slow but efficient means of promoting integration.

In the 1940's, the assimilationists were not content to simply exert pressure on state and national legislatures and on the Chief Executive. They challenged the judicial branch of government by asking the courts on all levels to review specific cases, considering civil rights in light of the constitutional amendments and contemporary evidence advanced by social and behavioral scientists. The Supreme Court responded by declaring segregation illegal in interstate commerce in 1944 and ruling against Democratic primaries in 1947. When Lloyd Gaines was denied admission in the Law School at the University of Missouri in 1936, the Supreme Court declared in 1938 that a state must provide, within its boundaries, education for all its citizens. In 1949, G. W. McLaurin, through legal procedures, forced the University of Oklahoma to accept him as a graduate student. Later, after learning of his segregation in the classroom, he filed an additional suit. The following year the Supreme Court ended discriminatory practices in higher educational institutions.[83] These decisions, which caused the greatest alarm in the South, pertained to the rights of Negroes in higher educational institutions.

As leaders in the South lost their right to maintain segregation in the colleges and universities, they anticipated similar legal challenges to their educational system at the elementary and secondary level. Hurriedly, they began to construct new public schools for Negroes with the hope that equal facilities would thwart enforced integration. Meanwhile the National Association for the Advancement of Colored People, drawing upon its Legal Defense and Educational Fund, inaugurated a campaign to democratize education in the public schools. With the purpose of testing the validity of segregation in education, they took cases arising in various states to the Supreme Court in 1952 and 1953. Thurgood Marshall, for years a major legal counsel for the Association, was the principal judicial rhetorician in these encounters.[84] In 1953 he represented a group of appellants in Virginia and South Carolina who argued that the doctrine of separate but equal facilities violated the Fourteenth Amendment. After filing the brief stating his clients' position and analyzing the opposing brief of the appellees, he went before the Warren Court in December to present his closing oral argument. The outline of his constructive speech, followed by an extended excerpt from his rebuttal, is included here to show how Marshall prepared the way for the historic Brown v. Board of Education decision in 1954.

Thurgood Marshall
From *Oral Argument on Behalf of the Appellants, December 7, 1953**

INTRODUCTION

I. "We are requested to direct our attention to the specific question as to whether or not the Court — this Court — has judicial power in construing the Fourteenth Amendment to abolish segregation in the public schools. And our answer to that question is a flat 'Yes.' "

II. *Specific Purpose:* To demonstrate that the Court not only has the right but the duty to interpret the Fourteenth Amendment as being opposed to the doctrine of separate but equal facilities in education and related areas.

DISCUSSION

I. An examination of legal precedents supports the claim that the Fourteenth Amendment rejects separatism in education and cognate fields.

    A. Two groups of Supreme Court decisions have maintained this concept.

        1. Decisions interpreting the Fourteenth Amendment which were handed down shortly after the ratification of the Amendment concluded that any form of caste and class legislation was unconstitutional.

            (a) The Slaughter House cases refuted the argument that Negroes should be treated differently from Whites.

            (b) *Strauder v. West Virginia* expressed a similar philosophy.

        2. Recent decisions of the Supreme Court with respect to the Fifth and Fourteenth Amendments have also rejected the idea that

---

*Oral Argument: In the Supreme Court of the United States (October Term, 1953), Briggs v. Elliott and Davis v. County School Board, December 7 and 8, 1953. Reprinted in Jayme Coleman Williams, "A Rhetorical Analysis of Thurgood Marshall's Arguments Before the Supreme Court in the Public School Segregation Controversy," Ph.D. dissertation presented in Speech at Ohio State University, 1959. The rebuttal section presented here covers pp. 312-16 in the dissertation. These arguments were transcribed by Ward and Paul, Official Reporters, Washington, D.C.

federal or state governments have the power to use race, class, or national origin for classification purposes.

3. "We believe that a review of these two groups of cases will show that during these two periods, this Court uniformly gave to the Amendment the broad scope which the framers intended."

B. The precedents, cited by the appellees, which are reputed to establish the legality of the separate but equal facilities arguments are not convincing.

1. The appellees have misinterpreted the full implications of the McLaurin case.

2. They have failed to understand that their favorite decision — *Plessy vs. Ferguson* — recognized that the Fourteenth Amendment did indeed cover education.

II. The Court, not the states, has the power to deal with segregation.

A. "The state is deprived of any power to make any racial classifications in any governmental field."

B. After analyzing the two briefs submitted to this Court we must answer the following questions:

1. Should the public policies, customs and mores of the states prevail?

2. Should the avowed intent of the Constitution as expressed in the Fourteenth Amendment prevail?

CONCLUSION

The appellees have attempted to buttress their case in defense of separate but equal facilities by relying on the term "substantial." Although they do not claim that "absolute equality" exists in the predominantly Negro elementary and high schools in Virginia and South Carolina, they suggest that "substantial equality" does exist and that that is the only thing required by *Plessy vs. Ferguson*. But it is instructive to note that "substantial" is "a word that was put into the Fourteenth Amendment by *Plessy vs. Ferguson*, and . . . it cannot be found in any place in the debates."

Further refutation will be offered for the appellants during the rebuttal period.

From *Marshall's Rebuttal Argument, December 8, 1953*

And it follows that with education, this Court has made segregation and inequality equivalent concepts. They have equal rating, equal footing, and if segregation thus necessarily imports inequality, it makes no great difference whether we say that the Negro is wronged because he is segregated, or that he is wronged because he received unequal treatment.

We believe that what we really ask this Court is to make it explicit what they think was inevitably implicit in the McLaurin case, that the two are together. But most certainly I do not agree, and I want to make it clear, that the McLaurin case is under the one-way, and I think that with this understanding, the Court has no difficulty in our position at least.

And finally, I would like to say that each lawyer on the other side has made it clear as to what the position of the State was on this, and it would be all right possibly but for the fact that this is so crucial. There is no way you can repay lost school years.

These children in these cases are guaranteed by the States some twelve years of education in varying degrees, and this idea, if I understand it, to leave it to the States until they work it out — and I think that is a most ingenious argument — you leave it to the States, they say, and then they say that the States haven't done anything about it in a hundred years, so for that reason this Court doesn't touch it.

The argument of judicial restraint has no application in this case. There is a relationship between Federal and State but there is no corollary or relationship as to the Fourteenth Amendment.

The duty of enforcing, the duty of following the Fourteenth Amendment is placed upon the States. The duty of enforcing the Fourteenth Amendment is placed upon this Court, and the argument that they make over and over again to my mind is the same type of argument they charge us with making, the same argument Charles Sumner made. Possibly so.

And we hereby charge them with making the same argument that was made before the Civil War, the same argument that was made during the period between the ratification of the Fourteenth Amendment and the Plessy v. Ferguson case.

And I think it makes no progress for us to find out who made what argument. It is our position that whether or not you base this case solely on the intent of Congress or whether you base it on the logical extension of the doctrine as set forth in the McLaurin case, on either basis the same conclusion is required, which is that this Court makes it clear to all of these States that in administering their governmental functions, at least those that are vital not to the life of the State alone, not to the country alone, but vital to the world in general, that little pet feelings of race, little pet feelings of custom — I got the feeling on hearing the discussion yesterday that when you put a white child in a school with a whole lot of colored children, the child would fall apart or something. Everybody knows that is not true.

Those same kids in Virginia and South Carolina — and I have seen them do it — they play in the streets together, they play on their farms together, they go down the road together, they separate to go to school, they come out of school and play ball together. They have to be separated in school.

There is some magic to it. You can have them voting together, you can have them not restricted because of law in the houses they live in. You can have them going to the same State university and the same college, but if they go to elementary and high school, the world will fall apart. And it is the exact same argument that has been made to this Court over and over again, and we submit that when they charge us with making a legislative argument, it is in truth they who are making the legislative argument.

They can't take race out of this case. From the day this case was filed until this moment, nobody has in any form or fashion, despite the fact I made it clear in the opening argument that I was relying on it, done anything to distinguish this statute from the Black Codes, which they must admit, because nobody can dispute, say anything anybody wants to say, one way or the other, the Fourteenth Amendment was intended to deprive the States of power to enforce Black Codes or anything else like it.

We charge that they are Black Codes. They obviously are Black Codes if you read them. They haven't denied that they are Black Codes, so if the Court wants to very narrowly decide this case, they can decide it on that point.

So whichever way it is done, the only way that this Court can decide this case in opposition to our position, is that there must be some reason which gives the State the right to make a classification that they can make in regard to nothing else in regard to Negroes, and we submit the only way to arrive at this decision is to find that for some reasons Negroes are inferior to all other human beings.

Nobody will stand in the Court and urge that, and in order to arrive at the decision that they want us to arrive at, there would have to be some recognition of a reason why of all of the multitudinous groups of people in this country you have to single out Negroes and give them this separate treatment.

It can't be because of slavery in the past, because there are very few groups in this country that haven't had slavery some place back in the history of their groups. It can't be color because there are Negroes as white as the drifted snow, with blue eyes, and they are just as segregated as the colored man.

The only thing can be is an inherent determination that the people who were formerly in slavery, regardless of anything else, shall be kept as near that stage as is possible, and now is the time, we submit, that this Court should make it clear that that is not what our Constitution stands for.

Thank you, sir.

The N.A.A.C.P. legal cases, under the leadership of Marshall, provided the rationale for the Brown decision announced in May, 1954. Speaking for a unanimous Court, Chief Justice Earl Warren, echoing the message of Marshall, observed:

We conclude that in the field of public education the doctrine of 'separate but equal' has no place. Separate educational facilities are inherently unequal. Therefore, we hold that the plaintiffs and others similarly situated for whom the actions have been brought are, by reason of the segregation complained of, deprived of the equal protection of the laws guaranteed by the Fourteenth Amendment.[85]

Not since the famed Dred Scott decision in 1857 had the Supreme Court provoked such strong and varied reactions. Angry and frightened at the prospects of seeing their social system crumble, white southerners passed hasty legislation attempting to negate the ruling, precipitated violence in Alabama and Mississippi, and accused the N.A.A.C.P. of seeking to control public schools in the South. This volatile situation brought forth a rhetorical response from Roy Wilkins, Executive Secretary of the N.A.A.C.P., at a regional meeting of the organization held in Charleston, South Carolina on February 24, 1956.[86]

Standing on southern soil where he had been denounced by political leaders and journalists, Wilkins hurled a challenge to his critics early in his address. "Here," he said, "is the big basic question for Southerners: Shall we obey the law as to our race relations, or shall we defy the law and insist that our 1856 philosophy be the pattern of 1956? Specifically, shall we comply with the Court's opinion on public schools?"[87] Wilkins proceeded to refute the claim that Negroes were scholastically deficient by offering two arguments: (1) inferiority, if it exists, is due to eighty years of unequal educational opportunities; and (2) the question of relative academic achievements is irrelevant to the Supreme Court ruling which is concerned only with the rights of full citizenship for men regardless of race. He concluded with a statement that set the direction of the assimilationists' approach to the contemporary civil rights movement. "We ask the acknowledgement of our status as citizens. We ask the rights and privileges and responsibilities of citizenship. We ask equality with other citizens under the law."[88]

If the Brown v. Board of Education ruling brought consternation to many southern whites, it heralded good tidings for blacks throughout the country. Now convinced that a united campaign could change personal attitudes on racial prejudice and influence the federal government to take positive action, they organized other civil rights groups with similar goals but different strategies.[89] One of these was the Southern Christian Leadership Conference, the only organization on race relations begun in the South. The inspiration for the movement came from Martin Luther King, Jr.[90] as he led a bus boycott in Montgomery, Alabama in 1955. Cata-

pulted into national fame following his role in this incident, King
began a distinguished career as an advocate of human rights.
It was clear from the outset that King, a disciple of Mahatma
Ghandi, felt non-violence was the key to social change. What
he saw in the remarkable successes of the N.A.A.C.P. legal cases
and the Montgomery bus boycott simply reinforced his faith in
this philosophy. With renewed spirit, therefore, he expressed the
hopes and aspirations of his race in a speech to the First Annual
Institute on Non-Violence and Social Change, meeting in Montgomery in December, 1956. This address, printed below as it
appears in *Phylon* magazine, anticipates the "I Have A Dream"
speech delivered seven years later. It clearly shows the first steps
in the creation of a universe of discourse that marked the rhetorical practice of one of the most popular and persuasive orators
in the modern civil rights struggle.

Martin Luther King, Jr.
From *Facing the Challenge of A New Age**

Those of us who live in the Twentieth Century are privileged to live in one
of the most momentous periods of human history. It is an exciting age filled
with hope. It is an age in which a new social order is being born. We stand
today between two worlds — the dying old and the emerging new.

Now I am aware of the fact that there are those who would contend
that we live in the most ghastly period of human history. They would argue
that the rhythmic beat of the deep rumblings of discontent from Asia, the
uprisings in Africa, the nationalistic longings of Egypt, the roaring cannons
from Hungary, and the racial tensions of America are all indicative of the
deep and tragic midnight which encompasses our civilization. They would
argue that we are retrogressing instead of progressing. But far from representing retrogression and tragic meaninglessness, the present tensions represent
the necessary pains that accompany the birth of anything new. Long ago the
Greek philosopher Heraclitus argued that justice emerges from the strife of
opposites, and Hegel, in modern philosophy, preached a doctrine of growth
through struggle. It is both historically and biologically true that there can
be no birth and growth without birth and growing pains. Whenever there is
the emergence of the new we confront the recalcitrance of the old. So the

*Martin Luther King, Jr., "Facing the Challenge of a New Age." An address
delivered on December, 1956 in Montgomery, Alabama. Reprinted in *Phylon,*
Vol. XVIII (First Quarter, 1957), pp. 25-34. © 1957 by Martin Luther King Jr.
Reprinted by permission of the estate of Martin Luther King, Jr., and *Phylon.*

tensions which we witness in the world today are indicative of the fact that a new world order is being born and an old order is passing away.

We are all familiar with the old order that is passing away. We have lived with it for many years. We have seen it in its international aspect, in the form of colonialism and imperialism. There are approximately two billion four hundred million (2,400,000,000) people in this world, and the vast majority of these people are colored — about one billion six hundred million (1,600,000,000 of the people of the world are colored. Fifty years ago, or even twenty-five years ago, most of these one billion six hundred million people lived under the yoke of some foreign power. We could turn our eyes to China and see there six hundred million men and women under the pressing yoke of British, Dutch, and French rule. We could turn our eyes to Indonesia and see a hundred million men and women under the domination of the Dutch. We could turn to India and Pakistan and notice four hundred million brown men and women under the pressing yoke of the British. We could turn our eyes to Africa and notice there two hundred million black men and women under the pressing yoke of the British, the Dutch and the French. For years all of these people were dominated politically, exploited economically, segregated and humiliated.

But there comes a time when people get tired. There comes a time when people get tired of being trampled over by the iron feet of oppression. There comes a time when people get tired of being plunged across the abyss of exploitation where they experience the bleakness of nagging despair. There comes a time when people get tired of being pushed out of the glittering sunlight of life's July and left standing in the piercing chill of an Alpine November. So in the midst of their tiredness these people decided to rise up and protest against injustice. As a result of their protest more than one billion three hundred million (1,300,000,000) of the colored peoples of the world are free today. They have their own governments, their own economic systems, and their own educational systems. They have broken loose from the Egypt of colonialism and imperialism, and they are now moving through the wilderness of adjustment toward the promised land of cultural integration. As they look back they see the old order of colonialism and imperialism passing away and the new order of freedom and justice coming into being.

We have also seen the old order in our own nation, in the form of segregation and discrimination. We know something of the long history of this old order in America. It had its beginning in the year 1619 when the first Negro slaves landed on the shores of this nation. They were brought here from the soils of Africa. And unlike the Pilgrim Fathers who landed at Plymouth a year later, they were brought here against their wills. Throughout slavery the Negro was treated in a very inhuman fashion. He was a thing to be used, not a person to be respected. He was merely a depersonalized cog in a vast plantation machine. The famous Dred Scott Decision of 1857 well illustrates the status of the Negro during slavery. In this decision the Supreme Court of the United States said, in substance, that the Negro is not a citizen of the United States; he is merely property subject to the dictates of his owner. Then came 1896. It was in this year that the Supreme Court of this nation, through the *Plessy V. Ferguson* Decision, established the doctrine of separate-but-equal as the law of the land. Through this decision segregation gained legal and moral sanction. The end result of the Plessy Doctrine was that it lead to a strict enforcement of the "separate," with hardly the slightest attempt to abide by the "equal." So the Plessy Doctrine ended up making for tragic inequalities and ungodly exploitation.

Living under these conditions, many Negroes came to the point of losing faith in themselves. They came to feel that perhaps they were less than human. The great tragedy of physical slavery was that it lead to mental slavery. So long as the Negro maintained this subservient attitude and accepted this "place" assigned to him, a sort of racial peace existed. But it was an uneasy peace in which the Negro was forced patiently to accept insult, injustice and exploitation. It was a negative peace. True peace is not merely the absence of some negative force — tension, confusion, or war; it is the presence of some positive force — justice, goodwill and brotherhood. And so the peace which existed between the races was a negative peace devoid of any positive and lasting quality.

Then something happened to the Negro. Circumstances made it necessary for him to travel more. His rural plantation background was gradually being supplanted by migration to urban and industrial communities. His economic life was gradually rising to decisive proportions. His cultural life was gradually rising through the steady decline of crippling illiteracy. All of these factors conjoined to cause the Negro to take a new look at himself. Negro masses began to reevaluate themselves. The Negro came to feel that he was somebody. His religion revealed to him that God loves all of His children, and that every man, from a bass black to a treble white, is significant on God's keyboard. So he could now cry out with the eloquent poet:

> Fleecy locks and black complexion
> Cannot forfeit nature's claim.
> Skin may differ, but affection
> Dwells in black and white the same.
> And were I so tall as to reach the pole
> Or to grasp the ocean at a span,
> I must be measured by my soul.
> The mind is the standard of the man.

With this new self respect and new sense of dignity on the part of the Negro, the South's negative peace was rapidly undermined. And so the tension which we are witnessing in race relations today can be explained, in part, by the revolutionary change in the Negro's evaluation of himself, and his determination to struggle and sacrifice until the walls of segregation have finally been crushed by the battering rams of surging justice.

Along with the emergence of a "New Negro," with a new sense of dignity and destiny, came that memorable decision of May 17, 1954. In this decision the Supreme Court of this nation unanimously affirmed that the old Plessy Doctrine must go. This decision came as a legal and sociological death blow to an evil that had occupied the throne of American life for several decades. It affirmed in no uncertain terms that separate facilities are inherently unequal and that to segregate a child because of his race is to deny him equal protection of the law. With the coming of this great decision we could gradually see the old order of segregation and discrimination passing away, and the new order of freedom and justice coming into being. Let nobody fool you, all of the loud noises that you hear today from the legislative halls of the South in terms of "interposition" and "nullification," and of outlawing the NAACP are merely the death groans from a dying system. The old order is passing away, and the new order is coming into being. We are witnessing in our day the birth of a new age, with a new structure of freedom and justice.

Now as we face the fact of this new, emerging world, we must face the responsibilities that come along with it. A new age brings with it new challenges. Let us consider some of the challenges of this new age.

First, we are challenged to rise above the narrow confines of our individualistic concerns to the broader concerns of all humanity. The New World is a world of geographical togetherness. This means that no individual or nation can live alone. We must all learn to live together, or we will be forced to die together. This new world of geographical togetherness has been brought about, to a great extent, by man's scientific and technological genius. Man through his scientific genius has been able to dwarf distance and place time in chains; he has been able to carve highways through the stratosphere. And so it is possible today to eat breakfast in New York City and dinner in Paris, France. Bob Hope has described this new jet age in which we live. It is an age in which we will be able to get a non-stop flight from Los Angeles, California to New York City, and if by chance we develop hiccups on taking off, we will "hic" in Los Angeles and "cup" in New York City. It is an age in which one will be able to leave Tokyo on Sunday morning and, because of time difference, arrive in Seattle, Washington on the preceding Saturday night. When your friends meet you at the airport in Seattle inquiring when you left Tokyo, you will have to say, "I left tomorrow." This, in a very humorous sense, says to us that our world is geographically one. Now we are faced with the challenge of making it spiritually one. Through our scientific genius we have made of the world a neighborhood; now through our moral and spiritual genius we must make of it a brotherhood. We are all involved in the single process. Whatever affects one directly affects all indirectly. We are all links in the great chain of humanity. This is what John Donne meant when he said years ago:

> No man is an island, entire of it selfe; every man is a piece of the Continent, a part of the maine; if a clod bee washed away by the Sea, Europe is the lesse, as well as if a Promontorie were, as well as if a Mannor of thy friends or of thine owne were; any mans' death diminishes me, because I am involved in Mankind; And therefore never send to know for whom the bell tolls; it tolls for thee.

A second challenge that the new age brings to each of us is that of achieving excellency in our various fields of endeavor. In the new age many doors will be opening to us that were not opened in the past, and the great challenge which we confront is to be prepared to enter these doors as they open. Ralph Waldo Emerson said in an essay back in 1871:

> If a man can write a better book, or preach a better sermon, or make a better mouse trap than his neighbor, even if he builds his house in the woods the world will make a beaten path to his door.

In the new age we will be forced to compete with people of all races and nationalities. Therefore, we cannot aim merely to be good Negro teachers, good Negro doctors, good Negro ministers, good Negro skilled laborers. We must set out to do a good job, irrespective of race, and do it so well that nobody could do it better.

Whatever your life's work is, do it well. Even if it does not fall in the category of one of the so-called big professions, do it well. As one college president said, "A man should do his job so well that the living, the dead, and the unborn could do it no better." If it falls your lot to be a street sweeper, sweep streets like Michelangelo painted pictures, like Shakespeare wrote poetry, like Beethoven composed music; sweep streets so well that all the host of Heaven and earth will have to pause and say, "Here lived a great street sweeper, who swept his job well." As Douglas Mallock says:

> If you can't be a pine on the top of the hill
> Be a scrub in the valley — but be
> The best little scrub by the side of the hill,
> Be a bush if you can't be a tree.
>
> If you can't be a highway just be a trail
> If you can't be the sun be a star;
> It isn't by size that you win or fail —
> Be the best of whatever you are.

A third challenge that stands before us is that of entering the new age with understanding goodwill. This simply means that the Christian virtues of love, mercy and forgiveness should stand at the center of our lives. There is the danger that those of us who have lived so long under the yoke of oppression, those of us who have been exploited and trampled over, those of us who have had to stand amid the tragic midnight of injustice and indignities will enter the new age with hate and bitterness. But if we retaliate with hate and bitterness, the new age will be nothing but a duplication of the old age. We must blot out the hate and injustice of the old age with the love and justice of the new. This is why I believe so firmly in non-violence. Violence never solves problems. It only creates new and more complicated ones. If we succumb to the temptation of using violence in our struggle for justice, unborn generations will be the recipients of a long and desolate night of bitterness, and our chief legacy to the future will be an endless reign of meaningless chaos.

We have before us the glorious opportunity to inject a new dimension of love into the veins of our civilization. There is still a voice crying out in terms that echo across the generations, saying:

Love your enemies, bless them that curse you, pray for them that despitefully use you, that you may be the children of your Father which is in Heaven.

This love might well be the salvation of our civilization. This is why I am so impressed with our motto for the week, "Freedom and Justice through Love." Not through violence; not through hate; no, not even through boycotts; but through love. It is true that as we struggle for freedom in America we will have to boycott at times. But we must remember as we boycott that a boycott is not an end within itself; it is merely a means to awaken a sense of shame within the oppressor and challenge his false sense of superiority. But the end is reconciliation; the end is redemption; the end is the creation of the beloved community. It is this type of spirit and this type of love that can transform opposers into friends. It is this type of understanding goodwill that will transform the deep gloom of the old age into the exuberant gladness of the new age. It is this love which will bring about miracles in the hearts of men.

Now I realize that in talking so much about love it is very easy to become sentimental. There is the danger that our talk about love will merely be empty words devoid of any practical and true meaning. But when I say love those who oppose you I am not speaking of love in a sentimental or affectionate sense. It would be nonsense to urge men to love their oppressors in an affectionate sense. When I refer to love at this point I mean understanding goodwill. The Greek language comes to our aid at this point. The Greek language has three words for love. First it speaks of love in terms of *Eros*. Plato used this word quite frequently in his dialogues. *Eros* is a type of esthetic love. Now it has come to mean a sort of romantic love. I guess Shakespeare was thinking in terms of *Eros* when he said:

Love is not love which alters when it alteration finds, or bends with the remover to remove. It is an ever fixed mark that looks on tempest and is never shaken. It is a star to every wandering bark. . . .

This is *Eros*. And then the Greek talks about *philia*. *Philia* is a sort of intimate affectionateness between personal friends. It is a sort of reciprocal love. On this level a person loves because he is loved. Then the Greek language comes out with another word which is the highest level of love. It speaks of it in terms of *agape*. *Agape* means nothing sentimental or basically affectionate. It means understanding, redeeming goodwill for all men. It is an overflowing love which seeks nothing in return. It is the love of God working in the lives of men. When we rise to love on the *agape* level we love men not because we like them, not because their attitudes and ways appeal to us, but because God loves us. Here we rise to the position of loving the person who does the evil deed while hating the deed that the person does. With this type of love and understanding goodwill we will be able to stand amid the radiant glow of the new age with dignity and discipline. Yes, the new age is coming. It is coming mighty fast.

Now the fact that this new age is emerging reveals something basic about the universe. It tells us something about the core and heartbeat of the cosmos. It reminds us that the universe is on the side of justice. It says to those who struggle for justice, "You do not struggle alone, but God struggles with you." This belief that God is on the side of truth and justice comes down to us from the long tradition of our Christian faith. There is something at the very center of our faith which reminds us that Good Friday may occupy the throne for a day, but ultimately it must give way to the triumphant beat of the drums of Easter. Evil may so shape events that Caesar will occupy a palace and Christ a cross, but one day that same Christ will rise up and split history into AD and BC, so that even the life of Caesar must be dated by His name. There is something in this universe that justifies Carlyle in saying, "No lie can live forever." There is something in this universe which justifies William Cullen Bryant in saying, "Truth crushed to earth will rise again." There is something in this universe that justifies James Russell Lowell in saying:

> Truth forever on the scaffold
> Wrong forever on the throne
> Yet that scaffold sways the future
> And behind the dim unknown stands God
> Within the shadows keeping watch above his own.

And so here in Montgomery, after more than eleven long months, we can walk and never get weary, because we know there is a great camp meeting in the promised land of freedom and justice.

Before closing I must correct what might be a false impression. I am afraid that if I close at this point many will go away misinterpreting my whole message. I have talked about the new age which is fastly coming into being. I have talked about the fact that God is working in history to bring about this new age. There is the danger, therefore, that after hearing all of this you will go away with the impression that we can go home, sit down, and do nothing, waiting for the coming of the inevitable. You will somehow feel that this new age will roll in on the wheels of inevitability, so there is nothing to do but wait on it. If you get that impression you are the victims of a dangerous optimism. If you go away with that interpretation you are the victims of an illusion wrapped in superficiality. We must speed up the coming of the inevitable.

Now it is true, if I may speak figuratively, that old man segregation is on his death-bed. But history has proven that social systems have a great last minute breathing power, and the guardians of a status quo are always on hand with their oxygen tents to keep the old order alive. Segregation is still a fact in America. We still confront it in the South in its glaring and conspicuous forms. We still confront it in the North in its hidden and subtle forms. But if Democracy is to live, segregation must die. Segregation is a glaring evil. It is utterly unchristian. It relegates the segregated to the status of a thing rather than elevate him to the status of a person. Segregation is nothing but slavery covered up with certain niceties of complexity. Segregation is a blatant denial of the unity which we all have in Christ Jesus.

So we must continue the struggle against segregation in order to speed up the coming of the inevitable. We must continue to gain the ballot. This is one of the basic keys to the solution of our problem. Until we gain political power through possession of the ballot we will be convenient tools of unscrupulous politicians. We must face the appalling fact that we have been betrayed by both the Democratic and Republican parties. The Democrats have betrayed us by capitulating to the whims and caprices of the southern Dixiecrats. The Republicans have betrayed us by capitulating to the blatant hypocrisy of right-wing reactionary Northerners. This coalition of Southern Democrats and Northern right-wing Republicans defeats every proposed bill on civil rights. Until we gain the ballot and place proper public officials in office this condition will continue to exist. In communities where we confront difficulties in gaining the ballot, we must use all legal and moral means to remove these difficulties.

We must continue to struggle through legalism and legislation. There are those who contend that integration can come only through education, for no other reason than that morals cannot be legislated. I choose, however, to be dialectical at this point. It is neither education nor legislation; it is both legislation and education. I quite agree that it is impossible to change a man's internal feelings merely through law. But this really is not the intention of the law. The law does not seek to change one's internal feelings; it seeks rather to control the external effects of those internal feelings. For instance, the law cannot make a man love — religion and education must do that — but it can control his efforts to lynch. So in order to control the external effects of prejudiced internal feelings, we must continue to struggle through legislation.

Another thing that we must do in pressing on for integration is to invest our finances in the cause of freedom. Freedom has always been an expensive thing. History is a fit testimony to the fact that freedom is rarely gained without sacrifice and self-denial. So we must donate large sums of money to the cause of freedom. We can no longer complain that we do not have the money. Statistics reveal that the economic life of the Negro is rising to decisive proportions. The annual income of the American Negro is now more than sixteen billion dollars, almost equal to the national income of Canada. So we are gradually becoming economically independent. It would be a tragic indictment on both the self respect and practical wisdom of the Negro if history reveals that at the height of the Twentieth Century the Negro spent more for frivolities than for the cause of freedom. We must never let it be said that we spend more for the evanescent and ephemeral than for the eternal values of freedom and justice.

Another thing that we must do in speeding up the coming of the new age is to develop intelligent, courageous and dedicated leadership. This is one of the pressing needs of the hour. In this period of transition and growing social change, there is a dire need for leaders who are calm and yet positive, leaders who avoid the extremes of "hot-headedness" and "Uncle Tomism." The urgency of the hour calls for leaders of wise judgment and sound integrity — leaders not in love with money, but in love with justice; leaders not in love with publicity, but in love with humanity; leaders who can subject their particular egos to the greatness of the cause. To paraphrase Holland's words:

> God give us leaders!
> A time like this demands strong minds, great hearts,
>   true faith and ready hands;
> Leaders whom the lust of office does not kill;

Leaders whom the spoils of life cannot buy;
Leaders who possess opinions and a will;
Leaders who have honor; leaders who will not lie;
Leaders who can stand before a demagogue
    and damn his treacherous flatteries without winking!
Tall leaders, sun crowned, who live above the fog
    in public duty and private thinking.

Finally, if we are to speed up the coming of the new age we must have the moral courage to stand up and protest against injustice wherever we find it. Wherever we find segregation we must have the fortitude to passively resist it. I realize that this will mean suffering and sacrifice. It might even mean going to jail. If such is the case we must be willing to fill up the jail houses of the South. It might even mean physical death. But if physical death is the price that some must pay to free their children from a permanent life of psychological death, then nothing could be more honorable. Once more it might well turn out that the blood of the martyr will be the seed of the tabernacle of freedom.

Someone will ask, how will we face the acts of cruelty and violence that might come as results of our standing up for justice? What will be our defense? Certainly it must not be retaliatory violence. We must find our defense in the amazing power of unity and courage that we have demonstrated in Montgomery. Our defense is to meet every act of violence toward an individual Negro with the facts that there are thousands of others who will present themselves in his place as potential victims. Every time one school teacher is fired for standing up courageously for justice, it must be faced with the fact that there are four thousand more to be fired. If the oppressors bomb the home of one Negro for his courage, this must be met with the fact that they must be required to bomb the homes of fifty thousand more Negroes. This dynamic unity, this amazing self respect, this willingness to suffer, and this refusal to hit back will soon cause the oppressor to become ashamed of his own methods. He will be forced to stand before the world and his God splattered with the blood and reeking with the stench of his Negro brother.

There is nothing in all the world greater than freedom. It is worth paying for; it is worth losing a job; it is worth going to jail for. I would rather be a free pauper than a rich slave. I would rather die in abject poverty with my convictions than live in inordinate riches with the lack of self respect. Once more every Negro must be able to cry out with his forefathers: "Before I'll be a slave, I'll be buried in my grave and go home to my Father and be saved."

If we will join together in doing all of these things we will be able to speed up the coming of the New World — a new world in which men will live together as brothers; a world in which men will beat their swords into ploughshares and their spears into pruning-hooks; a world in which men will no longer take necessities from the masses to give luxuries to the classes; a world in which all men will respect the dignity and worth of all human personality. Then we will be able to sing from the great tradition of our Nation:

My Country 'tis of thee,
Sweet land of liberty,
Of thee I sing;

Land where my fathers died;
Land of the pilgrim's pride;
From every mountain side
Let Freedom ring!

This must become literally true. Freedom must ring from every mountain side. Yes, let it ring from the snow-capped Rockies of Colorado, from the prodigious hilltops of New Hampshire, from the mighty Alleghenies of Pennsylvania, from the curvaceous slopes of California. But not only that. Let Freedom ring from every mountain side—from every mole hill in Mississippi, from Stone Mountain of Georgia, from Lookout Mountain of Tennessee, yes, and from every hill and mountain of Alabama. From every mountain side let freedom ring. When this day finally comes "The morning stars will sing together and the sons of God will shout for joy."

With the official organizing of the Southern Christian Leadership Conference in 1957, King symbolized the black American's quest for freedom. Boycotts, sit-ins, and mass demonstrations in the streets — strategies consistent with the philosophy of non-violence — began first in the South and then in the North. These new forms of protest led to large scale arrests and fines, and occasional violence. By 1960, Thurgood Marshall, representing the N.A.A.C.P., argued that this expression of freedom was consistent with the First and Fourteenth Amendments and should be continued notwithstanding the consequences. Speaking at a mass rally in Charlotte, North Carolina in March, he summarized the illegal punishment meted out by southern law enforcement agencies, and then instructed his auditors on how to present a rhetorical response to these acts.

Each of these instances can be cited in state after state wherever the protests have been made. To all of this, we have but one reply, even one word and the word is SHAME. Whenever you read about it — whenever you hear about it — whenever you hear it discussed — say SHAME — SHAME on those who under the guise of states' right or state law seek to throttle young people lawfully protesting. Say SHAME on the white people of the South, the good white people, the so-called moderates who sit idly by and allow young people to be persecuted solely because of their race or color. And when you hear a Negro who has been adequately brainwashed say that this is too much to do just to get a hamburger or a frankfurter, to him say SHAME. For this that the young people are doing is for the best interest of all of us and indeed for the country itself.[91]

The message of King and Marshall reached large segments of the black community who marshalled their forces for the greatest single assault on segregation and discrimination in American history. On the centennial anniversary of the Emancipation Proclamation, in 1963, the Negro grew weary as he gazed at the world from his slums. One hundred years after he had supposedly received his freedom, he still did not have equal rights in education, housing, work opportunities, voting privileges, and entertainment facilities. As he brooded over his status, he could see on his television screen leaders from the newly emerging countries in Africa take their place in the United Nations; he could see them voting on crucial world issues. Now, he had become aware that twenty-three African nations had declared their independence since 1960. This progress, though often accompanied with instability, impressed the black American and made him restless. Against this background of discontent and turmoil, he was aroused, and all America felt the reverberations. Hundreds of cities trembled as the Negroes marched in the streets, sat on the sidewalks and in the cafés. Mass demonstrations had become their new weapon of power, and the jail their badge of courage. Not since the French Revolution of 1789, observed Martin Luther King, had so many people used the streets as a battleground. Those who saw them on August 28, 1963 as they came to the nation's capital 200,000 strong, watched them pass on Constitution Avenue waving their banners in the warm summer breeze. They stopped at the monument grounds and chanted the word "freedom," then marched in unison toward the Lincoln Memorial.[92] It was, in short, a revolution of nonviolent resistance that dramatized the Negro's serious intent to assimilate as an equal into the American society. What Martin Luther King, as principal speaker, said on this occasion already has gained a permanent place in literature. Yet, despite its familiarity, it is included here as an integral part of the rhetoric of black Americans.

Martin Luther King, Jr.

I Have A Dream*

I am happy to join with you today in what will go down in history as the greatest demonstration for freedom in the history of our nation.

---

*Martin Luther King, Jr., "I Have A Dream." An address delivered on August 28, 1963 in Washington, D.C. © 1963 by Martin Luther King, Jr. Reprinted by permission of The New York Times and the estate of Martin Luther King, Jr.

Five score years ago a great American in whose symbolic shadow we stand today signed the Emancipation Proclamation. This momentous decree is a great beacon light of hope to millions of Negro slaves who had been seared in the flames of withering injustice. It came as a joyous daybreak to end the long night of their captivity. But one hundred years later the Negro still is not free. One hundred years later the life of the Negro is still badly crippled by the manacles of segregation and the chains of discrimination. One hundred years later the Negro lives on a lonely island of poverty in the midst of a vast ocean of material prosperity. One hundred years later the Negro is still languished in the corners of American society and finds himself in exile in his own land. So we've come here today to dramatize a shameful condition.

In a sense we've come to our nation's capital to cash a check. When the architects of our Republic wrote the magnificent words of the Constitution and the Declaration of Independence, they were signing a promissory note to which every American was to fall heir. This note was a promise that all men — yes, black men as well as white men — would be guaranteed the unalienable rights of life, liberty and the pursuit of happiness. It is obvious today that America has defaulted on this promissory note insofar as her citizens of color are concerned. Instead of honoring this sacred obligation, America has given the Negro people a bad check, a check which has come back marked "insufficient funds."

But we refuse to believe that the bank of justice is bankrupt. We refuse to believe that there are insufficient funds in the great vaults of opportunity of this nation. So we've come to cash this check, a check that will give us upon demand the riches of freedom and the security of justice.

We have also come to this hallowed spot to remind America of the fierce urgency of now. This is no time to engage in the luxury of cooling off or to take the tranquilizing drug of gradualism. Now is the time to make real the promises of democracy. Now is the time to rise from the dark and desolate valley of segregation to the sunlit path of racial justice. Now is the time to lift our nation from the quicksands of racial injustice to the solid rock of brotherhood.

Now is the time to make justice a reality for all of God's children. It would be fatal for the nation to overlook the urgency of the moment. This sweltering summer of the Negro's legitimate discontent will not pass until there is an invigorating autumn of freedom and equality — 1963 is not an end but a beginning. Those who hope that the Negro needed to blow off steam and will now be content will have a rude awakening if the nation returns to business as usual.

There will be neither rest nor tranquility in America until the Negro is granted his citizenship rights. The whirlwinds of revolt will continue to shake the foundations of our nation until the bright days of justice emerges. And that is something that I must say to my people who stand on the worn threshold which leads into the palace of justice. In the process of gaining our rightful place we must not be guilty of wrongful deeds. Let us not seek to satisfy our thirst for freedom by drinking from the cup of bitterness and hatred.

We must forever conduct our struggle on the high plane of dignity and discipline. We must not allow our creative protests to degenerate into physical violence. Again and again we must rise to the majestic heights of meeting physical force with soul force. The marvelous new militancy which has engulfed the Negro community must not lead us to distrust all white people, for many of our white brothers, as evidenced by their presence here today, have come to realize that their destiny is tied up with our destiny.

They have come to realize that their freedom is inextricably bound to our freedom. We cannot walk alone. And as we walk we must make the pledge that we shall always march ahead. We cannot turn back. There are those who are asking the devotees of civil rights — "When will you be satisfied?" We can never be satisfied as long as the Negro is the victim of the unspeakable horrors of police brutality.

We can never be satisfied as long as our bodies, heavy with the fatigue of travel, cannot gain lodging in the motels of the highways and the hotels of the cities.

We cannot be satisfied as long as the Negro's basic mobility is from a smaller ghetto to a larger one. We can never be satisfied as long as our children are stripped of their adulthood and robbed of their dignity by signs stating "For Whites Only".

We cannot be satisfied as long as the Negro in Mississippi cannot vote and the Negro in New York believes he has nothing for which to vote.

No, no, we are not satisfied, and we will not be satisfied until justice rolls down like waters and righteousness like a mighty stream.

I am not unmindful that some of you have come here out of great trials and tribulation. Some of you have come fresh from narrow jail cells. Some of you have come from areas where your quest for freedom left you battered by the storms of persecution and staggered by the winds of police brutality. You have been the veterans of creative suffering.

Continue to work with the faith that unearned suffering is redemptive. Go back to Mississippi, go back to Alabama, go back to South Carolina, go back to Georgia, go back to Louisiana, go back to the slums and ghettos of our Northern cities, knowing that somehow this situation can and will be changed. Let us not wallow in the valley of despair.

I say to you today, my friends, though, even though we face difficulties of today and tomorrow, I still have a dream. It is a dream deeply rooted in the American dream. I have a dream that one day this nation will rise up, live out the true meaning of its creed: "We hold these truths to be self-evident, that all men are created equal."

I have a dream that one day on the red hills of Georgia, sons of former slaves and sons of former slave-owners will be able to sit down together at the table of brotherhood. I have a dream that one day even the state of Mississippi, a state sweltering with the heat of injustice, sweltering with the heat of oppression, will be transformed into an oasis of freedom and justice.

I have a dream that my four little children will one day live in a nation where they will not be judged by the color of their skin but by the content of their character. I have a dream. . . . I have a dream that one day in Alabama, with its vicious racists, with its governor having his lips dripping with words of interposition and nullification, one day right there in Alabama little black boys and black girls will be able to join hands with little white boys and white girls as sisters and brothers.

I have a dream today. . . . I have a dream that one day every valley shall be exalted, every hill and mountain shall be made low. The rough places will be made plain, and the crooked places will be made straight. And the glory of the Lord shall be revealed, and all flesh shall see it together. This is our hope. This is the faith that I go back to the South with. With this faith we will be able to hew out of the mountain of despair a stone of hope. With this faith we will be able to transform the jangling discords of our nation into a beautiful symphony of brotherhood. With this faith we will be able to work together, to pray together, to struggle together, to go to jail together, to stand up for freedom together, knowing that we will be free one day!

This will be the day when all of God's children will be able to sing with new meaning, "My country, 'tis of thee, sweet land of liberty, of thee I sing. Land where my fathers died, land of the pilgrim's pride, from every mountain side, let freedom ring." And if America is to be a great nation, this must become true. So let freedom ring from the prodigious hilltops of New Hampshire. Let freedom ring from the mighty mountains of New York. Let freedom ring from the heightening Alleghenies of Pennsylvania. Let freedom ring from the snowcapped Rockies of Colorado. Let freedom ring from the curvaceous slopes of California.

But not only that. Let freedom ring from Stone Mountain of Georgia. Let freedom ring from Lookout Mountain of Tennessee. Let freedom ring from every hill and molehill of Mississippi, from every mountain side. Let freedom ring!

When we allow freedom to ring — when we let it ring from every city and every hamlet, from every state and every city, we will be able to speed up that day when all of God's children, black men and white men, Jews and Gentiles, Protestants and Catholics, will be able to join hands and sing in the words of the old Negro spiritual, "Free at last, Free at last, Great God a-mighty We are free at last."

King is perhaps best remembered for his "I Have A Dream" speech and his "Letter from Birmingham Jail."[93] Through these messages and the thrust of his forceful personality and graphic style, he identified with the masses of his race and won the respect of the enlightened members of the white community. Later, as he was attacked by more militant leaders in the civil rights movement, he modified his attitudes on "black power" but refused to alter his basic strategy of non-violence. Shortly after his tragic death the *New York Times,* in capsuling his career, spoke the sentiments of the majority of Americans.

Martin Luther King was a preacher, a man from Georgia and a Negro who became a golden-tongued orator, a spokesman for the Deep South and the Ghetto North, a symbol above color of undying yearnings and imperishable rights. He was an American in the truest sense: for he had a dream. . . . It was said of Dr. King that he had a naive optimism in nonviolence. But his militant nonviolence accomplished more in his short lifetime than all the violence of the racists, black or white. He set the civil rights movement on a new course in the United States; and it will yet prevail. He helped to unify the races by showing what one man could do by believing in brotherhood; others will continue the work of this fallen martyr. He was a Negro who made Americans aware that the better angels of our nature could dominate the struggle of the United States and its people. The dream of true equality of rights and opportunities without regard to race is nearer because in our lifetime there lived an American named Martin Luther King.[94]

The assimilationists, as King regretfully learned in the last five years of his life, were not completely successful in uniting all groups engaged in the campaign for civil rights. Some "black power" advocates, as we shall observe in Chapters IV and V, moved in the direction of revolution and separatism.[95] To offset this trend, the assimilationists mounted a counter-attack designed to reduce its impact. In 1962, James Farmer went to Cornell University to preach the doctrine of integration in a debate with Malcolm X on the subject of separatism.[96] Roy Wilkins, in a keynote address delivered at the 57th annual convention of the N.A.A.C.P. in Los Angeles in July, 1966, indicted the slogan "black power" as a disruptive influence seeking refuge under the dangerous concept of "protective violence." No matter how the term was explained, he argued, it conveyed the meaning of "anti-white power" and separatism. He then concluded with a reaffirmation of the policy of his organization.

We of the NAACP will have none of this. We have fought it too long. It is the ranging of race against race on the irrelevant basis of skin color. It is the father of hatred and the mother of violence. It is the wicked fanaticism which has swelled our tears, broken our bodies, squeezed our hearts and taken the blood of our black and white loved ones. It shall not now poison our forward march.

We seek, therefore, as we have sought these many years, for the inclusion of Negro Americans in the nation's life, not their exclusion. This is our land, as much as it is any American's — every square foot of every city and town and village. The task of winning our share is not the easy one of disengagement and flight, but the hard one of work, of short as well as long jumps, of disappointments and of sweet success.[97]

In a similar but more subdued tone, Channing E. Phillips, Democratic National Committeeman for the District of Columbia,[98] compared "the real black power" with the mythical black power which asserts that a monolithic black community exists and that black power is by definition more virtuous and humane than white power. The "melting pot" goal, Phillips added, "is written too deeply in the rhetoric of this country's creeds, and I think etched too deeply in the spirit of man to view separatism as a viable option for blacks — except as a tactical approach."[99] What, then, is genuine "black power"? Phillips observed that it is a recognition on the part of Negroes of the importance of diversity within solidarity. Further, it is the use of economic and political power for the purpose of upsetting the white "comfort equation" and thereby winning acceptance as peers.[100] Channing's interpretation of "black power" won support from other influential integrationists. In a lecture on "The Black Revolution" presented at North Carolina State University in February, 1969, James Farmer told his predominantly white audience: "Today we find black people confidently asserting blackness and telling their oppressors that 'We are somebody!' " He warned that blacks would at least checkmate, if not eliminate, racism by uniting to produce political, economic, and educational power.[101]

As the decade of the 1960's drew to a close, the assimilationists took pride in their achievements. They had played no small part in the passage of the Civil Rights Acts of 1964 and 1965, and had helped black political candidates win key positions in their parties, gain seats in the United States Senate, and take control of the mayor's office in cities such as, Cleveland, Ohio and Gary, Indiana and a small town in Mississippi. These victories, though painfully slow in coming and requiring enormous energy, justified their confidence in the "melting pot" concept which had become a part of the folklore of American democracy. The spokesmen who participated in these successes were in no mood, therefore, to contemplate a change in their fundamental rhetorical strategy. They were especially displeased with speakers who advocated separatism. Upholding this traditional assimilationist view was Dr. Kenneth W. Clement when he appeared before the Urban League Conference in St. Louis in April, 1969. A nationally known physician and the former director of Carl B. Stokes' mayoral campaign in Cleveland, Clement saw assimilation actually work in a large, industrial northern city. Similarly, his knowledge of history convinced him that a separatist philosophy was the product of despair. The speech published here equates black separatism with white racism and segregation. Observe, moreover, how Clement describes this goal as impractical, unattainable, and undesirable.

Kenneth W. Clement
Will the New Separatism Work?*

There are times in the affairs of men, and races of men, when introspective evaluation of goals and purposes are imperative — in fact, inevitable. In such times old values are deservedly scrutinized, and to the extent that they have been associated with human failure or inadequate achievement in enhancing human relations, these values are exposed to the vulnerability of rejection. We live in such times!

For not only are the purposes and goals of the black man's fight for freedom being properly questioned, but the very values that formed the foundation of our democracy are under attack.

The Judeo Christian ethic which undergirded the nation is being held up for ridicule and scorn — as never before — because of the disparity between principle and practice.

The frustration experienced by Negroes in America is understandable — and the confrontation of the last decade allow few whites to claim ignorance of this fact.

Once again, Black Americans are being offered leadership thought and action which call for voluntary withdrawal from the main segment of society as a final and ultimate answer. The New Separatism envisions political, economic and social divisions based solely on race, exclusive in character.

In practice, many who espouse this New Separatism tolerate no other option for blacks. They make the sole test of loyalty to their newly rediscovered history of black men a pledge to separate from white America.

In the name of the New Separatism some insist that only a black nation will suffice; others drive whites from Negro organizations, schools and communities. Black students insist on black history courses taught by blacks with only black enrollees. Some insist on government supported black dormitories and a few hold other men hostages to insure that their demands for racially segregated facilities and learning situations are met.

The common refrain heard in all of these actions is that white racism is so permanent and pervasive in the American society that only withdrawal

---

*Kenneth W. Clement, "Will the New Separatism Work?" *St. Louis Globe Democrat,* April 18, 1968, p. 17A. Reprinted by permission of the *St. Louis Globe.*

by black men from this society is likely to provide any protection from it. They say only by voluntary segregation — segregation of blacks by blacks for blacks — will allow for one's personality development to bloom in pride and dignity, and insulate us from the dehumanizing hostility of white institutionalized racism.

There can be no argument that white racism has been too slow to yield; that the dehumanizing effects are great; that the country we love is devitalized thereby, and our black children are robbed from birth of their inherent dignity and rightful pride!

However, is the New Separatism really new? Is not this form of separatism really surrender, not victory; surrender to the very tyranny we fight? Is it not an extension of an expressed hopelessness for the white man, to an unexpressed lack of confidence in ourselves as well?

Are we forced to ask, will this New Separatism work? I believe it will not!

Bayard Rustin observes that separation in one form or another has been proposed and widely discussed among American Negroes in three different periods. Each time it was put forward in response to an identical combination of economic and social factors that induced despair among Negroes. The syndrome consists of three elements: great expectations, followed by dashed hopes, then despair and discussions of separatism.

The basic arguments of the neo-segregationists of the black community have not basically changed from those formerly espoused in the post Civil War and the post World War I eras. In fact, the major arguments put forth, including the desire not to be assimilated and protection of biological racial integrity, are not significantly different from those espoused by Bilbo, Talmadge and Eastland, except in one difference. The importance of the difference may be more illusory than real.

Both the white racist and the black separatist say that the Negro is culturally different from the white American (because of this blackness); that no change in his socio-economic, educational, and political life can make him in even these respects equal to his white American counterparts.

The new black separatist rejects, appropriately so, the doctrine of inherent inferiority of blacks and supplants it with the assertion that "black is beautiful." With this I fully agree, with the added reservation that all black is beautiful sometimes and some blacks are beautiful all of the time.

Nothing more and nothing less can be said for white, yellow, red, or brown, when you apply color to people.

Many separatists argue that separation is necessary to develop properly black intellect and to free the black spirit. Doubtless, self-identity is necessary for all men to develop their personality and their sense of personna. Doubtless the historic hostility of white America to the black man has made the development of an appropriate self-image or self-esteem difficult.

As blacks have become more mobile in our society, including job mobility, blacks functioning in positions of greater responsibility in America, and many other ways that reduce the isolation and separation of the races — it has been much easier to successfully assail the old doctrine and stereotype of black inferiority.

There has been significant racial progress despite the self-serving use of statistics on both sides of the argument.

As Desirable as it is, as necessary as it is, to know our own racial identity to help in achieving self-identification, the intellectual process is not necessarily improved by racial separation.

It is important to have that sense of identity that Dr. Howard Thurman speaks of when he says, "I know that a man must be at home somewhere before he can feel at home everywhere."

It is desirable that the self-identification conferred by family and race be positive and affirmative if the best relatedness and adjustments are to be achieved with other men of other races.

While separatism may furnish a basis for the attainment of this kind of racial identity, it does significantly obstruct the realization of one of man's other great needs and yearnings — a sense of belonging; not only to the layer community that is the nation, but the largest community of all, the community of mankind.

It is reasonable to expect that the best minds of black men should always be available to serve the legitimate needs of the race, but it is not reasonable to expect that they should serve the race alone.

The needs of mankind are too great, and even a chance solution of problems involving disease, famine, ignorance and poverty cannot be left to such simple notions that whites solve theirs and blacks solve theirs.

That separatism which calls for a separate state is not only impractical, it is essentially unattainable.

That kind of separatism which calls for a separate state should be opposed, not only because it is impractical and unattainable, but because it is also highly undesirable. It is destructive of that kind of belonging which is the essence of membership in the American society.

Robert Frost, certainly an authentic and wise American poet, describes and probes this mystery of belongingness with a story:

> When the merely seasonal hired man comes back to the farm sick unto death, the farmer's wife says: "He has come home to die: You needn't be afraid he'll leave you this time." The farmer is amused "Home," he mocked gently. The wife replies: "Yes, what else but home?" It all depends on what you mean by home. And so they try, these wise, simple, classically American people, to define "home." The farmer says: "Home is the place where when you have to go there, they have to take you in." His wife adds: "I should have called it, something you somehow haven't to deserve."

The poet does not, be it observed, say anything about what the hired man has first to be in order to be taken in, but emphasizes that home is home because you need do nothing to deserve it.

All of America is indeed, the black man's home. All that the intellect and psyche can span, and every inch of the ground, air and water that man can traverse.

The idea that we must leave the larger society, either physically or psychologically, in order to find our way back to relatedness suggests becoming or being more deserving when we return and frustrates the basic sense of belonging.

The proponents of segregation, black-style, conveniently misunderstand the view of America that black men and white hold who are labeled integrationists. (Labels are inadequate for the separatist and the integrationist, but the latter suffers more from his inadequacy.) They hold that integrationists, of necessity, want to abandon black institutions and effuse through the society, like chocolate through a marble cake, mixed sparsely in the upper vanilla layer and the remainder of the chocolate consolidated on the bottom.

Or, they suggest that we are aiming for a coffee-colored society. Obviously, these straw men are easy to ridicule by even the untutored mind.

This is an old story, and varying versions have been going around to illustrate a basic idea.

A Negro went into an "integrated" restaurant to get a meal after the passage of a law in a southern state that gave him access to a previously segregationist restaurant. The waitress brought him the menu. After he had read it carefully, he looked up at her to say, "Do you have any collard greens?" "No sir." "Do you have any pig's feet or pig's tails?" "No sir." "Well," he said, "You folks aren't ready for integration."

This is out of the culture of the integrationist's fight and clearly indicates that much of white America has been known for a long time not to be ready for the kind of integration which in fact holds that it is as appropriate for whites to join us in strengthening our own black institutions as it is for us to seek out, enjoy and improve white institutions.

The view of men, both black and white, who furnish the preponderant drive towards racial equality and racial justice is that America should be a free and open society where no man or any group of men need deny any past cultural loyalty or give up any cherished fellowship, racial or religious, in order to enjoy all the rights, privileges and benefits of being at home.

Yes, there is an America that nurtures the idea of a free society, a society which knows, as John Stuart Mills wrote in his classical treatise, that its test is, "the freedom and variety of situation." If there is such an America, and I believe there is, where men are not required to give up any cherished ethnic or racial institution or proper loyalty in order to enjoy all the rights and privileges of being Americans, it can thrive and grow; it can be maintained and extended to all, only with one common goal for all of its people, namely, "the freedom and variety of situation" of which Mr. Mills speaks.

Those who seek a separatist society of blacks must ignore the weight of history and they must disregard the failure of other such movements in past eras. If the black extremists of our times, misdirected and exaggerated racial chauvinists of our day, engaged only in rhetoric and philosophy, this part of my address might have been indefinitely deferred. But the separatist movement, the high priests of the black-style segregation of today, promise to "confer" dignity and bring racial unity as a result of this doctrinal retrogression. And, more importantly, there is abundant evidence of actions inimicable to racial progress and individual rights, and actions that retard the development of racial dignity and the realization of racial unity. It is impossible to unify a race on the lowest common denominator or intellectual, ethical and spiritual behavior.

I have already referred to some of the actions of black students who embrace the separatist view.

Time does not permit discussion of the merits of the protean demands. Some are wholly legitimate; others are totally lacking in merit. Some demands are difficult to understand in their lateness in being addressed by administration and faculty at universities. But, rather, it is my purpose to examine these actions in the light of history; their goals, the rule of law, and the ultimate result.

I understand and agree with the black youth's drive to unshackle his mind from the negative brainwashing of the white racist, and opportunistic blacks who serve them, for it is indeed the mind of man which shall make him free!

A mind unfettered by ignorance, unimpoverished by a diseased body, undiminished by a bleakness of spirit.

Yes, A Mind unfettered by ignorance — not only ignorance of black history, but also a mind rescued from that ignorance which denies him productive and marketable skills.

A mind free of that kind of boomeranging hate which leads to so many self destructive acts! A mind free of that kind of hate which is a heavier burden for the possessor than the intended object.

Those of us in medicine, concerned with the public health, know that homicide is one of the ten leading causes of death for black men of all ages. It is understandable then that we should want minds untainted by a philosophy that defines manliness in terms of violence and destruction.

I understand and sympathize with those black students who are disenchanted with some black universities, and with some black leaders who disappoint them when they seem to have a insatiable yearning and need for white confirmation of their inherent worth. They contemplate no thought, they dare no action, lest it be subject to white approval. The answer to this frustration, however, cannot be a cult of slogans or a mystique of swaggering assertiveness. It is as important for the adults to realize, as the young, unless substance is added to the slogans and ability to the assertiveness, the costumed dress and other ephemeral and transient trappings and fads, we are far more likely to produce arrogant, empty-headed, black bullies than beautiful black men of genuine pride and dignity.

This kind of pride needs no mob to sustain its vitality, no initiated violence to confer validity and no force of destruction to win admiration and command respect.

Those in administrative positions of responsibility, governmental, educational and otherwise, who respond to these acts of intimidation and destruction with hyperindulgent tolerance and submissiveness should not escape comment.

It is a sickening spectacle to witness college presidents and administrators, many professed "liberals," confirm the allegations of Bilbo and Eastland and other white racists that black men are so inherently inferior that little or less should be expected of them. And make no mistake, this is what is being said when total amnesty is ubiquitously given for such acts of intimidation, violence and destruction.

The Institutionally unmet needs that represent legitimate grievances should be corrected — but it is no bargain to offer such unwarranted amnesty, either to avoid appropriate social change or to expiate guilt for past historic wrongs.

Although some in the last election used law and order as code phrases for keeping the Negro down (some will use it again and mean the same thing), law and order have been known to have meaning for our side. You will say, "yes, but in this instance justice was served" and I will agree. But I will ask you how just is it to intimidate and threaten, to physically detain persons against their will, to imperil life and destroy in pursuit of "demands"? How just is it for a few, of whatever color, to stop other students from legitimate pursuits?

And when this is done to reinforce a demand for segregation and separation, how much difference is there really between these blacks at that moment and the white racists who stood in the schoolhouse doorways and chanted that familiar and repugnant refrain, "2-4-6-8, we ain't gonna integrate."

It is our task as adults to say to these blacks that, like it or not, inadvertent and even perhaps unintended, they have integrated! They have integrated not with the best that is America, but with its worst. Its worst, both in terms of race and racial attitudes, in thought and action.

Much is said today about self-determination for blacks and legitimately so. Control of our own destiny is desirable. It is a must. It must be understood that the control of our own destiny means not only more control of black institutions, it also means more control of American institutions by black men.

It means also more control of our own legitimate self-interests, and it means satisfactory resistance to false allies who tangentially "join" our fight but publicly profess goals such as total destruction of the total fabric of our society.

No Useful purpose can be served by allowing misguided zealots to use the black man's plight as a pawn in their own inane and failure-doomed misadventure.

In conclusion, I have explored the reasons I believe the New Separatism is doomed to failure. Despite the chaos and confusion, the conflict that the New Separatism creates will be resolved.

White Americans must accelerate progress toward a racially just society. White Americans must cease to demand that the Negro give up any racial pressure that is a part of our cultural past in order to become fully equal, fully American.

And blacks must increasingly yield to no such demand.

As a result, America will strengthen its black institutions, both old and new, and, at the same time, remove all obstructions to free movement of blacks in the total society.

Black Americans who used the rhetoric of assimilation in their search for the good life derived their strategy from two major premises. First was the belief that through their accomplishments and heritage they deserved the status of full citizenship. They had fought in the country's defense, helped to farm the soil and furnish labor for the industrial plants, and upheld the constitutional laws of the land. Similarly, they had proof to demonstrate their ethnological equality. From these premises came the desire to be accepted as peers in the American society. The difficulty in reaching the level of complete assimilation, however, was compounded by the Anglo-Saxon's conviction of his innate superiority and the Negro's feeling of despair resulting from years of oppression. In addressing themselves to this problem, the assimilationists, convinced that communication is the most viable means of effecting change, sought to mount a persuasive campaign to alter the black man's perception of himself and his country, and the white man's attitude toward human rights. They constructed a message to the blacks attempting to show that they could become more worthy as individuals if they drew upon the resources of Christianity and self-reliance. They further argued that America, despite its long history of promoting two worlds of race, held the greatest promise for attaining the good life. Most of these orators in varying degrees shared the optimistic appraisal of the United States expressed by the popular soul singer James Brown in his song "America Is My Home." In the verses which follow, Brown combines praise for his country with an attack on separatism.

> Huh, huh, talking about me leaving America, you got to be crazy.
> Man, I like all the nice things, yeh, Continental suits and things. ,
> Look-a-here, now I'm sorry for the man who don't love this land.
> Now, black and white, they may fight, huh, but if the enemy comes we'll get together and run them out of sight.
>
> Now, look-a-here, the sun don't come out in rainy weather.
> But when you boil it down, they're still together.
> Now let's not overlook the fact that we're still in reach.
> You got a chance to make it, and you got a freedom of speech.
>
> Say what you want to; tell them how you feel.
> There may be a lot of places, a lot of places that you'd like to go.

But believe me, if you get an education you can't blow; you
can't hardly blow.
Now dig this. Now you tell me if I'm wrong.
America is still the best country, and that's without a doubt.
America is still the best country without a doubt.
And if anybody says it ain't, you just try to put him out.
They ain't going nowhere; you got a good fight.[102]

The message presented to the whites by the assimilationists was
both informative and persuasive. It was designed first to instruct
the listeners that their stereotypes of the Negro had little basis
in fact. They needed, therefore, a better understanding of the
black American's true nature and potential. Second, their messages utilized persuasion by appealing to the Anglo-Saxon respect for law and fair play. Whites were told that as the ruling
majority they should democratize the executive, legislative, and
judicial branches of government. If these appeals to the cognitive
and affective behavior of the audience did not gain the full
equality blacks hoped to obtain, they contributed importantly
to a steady improvement in race relations. Success encouraged
the assimilationists but, as we will observe in subsequent chapters, failed to placate the separatists and revolutionists.

REFERENCES

[1]John Hope Franklin, *From Slavery to Freedom,* 3rd ed. (New York:
Alfred A. Knopf, Inc., 1967), p. 186; and James M. McPherson, *The
Negro's Civil War* (New York: Random House, Inc., 1965), p. 317.

[2]Daniel Boorstin, *The Americans: The National Experience* (New
York: Random House, Inc., 1965), p. 182.

[3]*Ibid.,* pp. 180-82.

[4]Franklin, *From Slavery to Freedom,* p. 214.

[5]*Ibid.,* pp. 187-90.

[6]Boorstin, *The Americans: The National Experience,* pp. 200-06.

[7]*Ibid.,* p. 206.

[8]See James L. Golden, "The Speaking of the Southern Unionists,
1850-1860," in Waldo Braden, ed., *Oratory in the Old South* (Baton Rouge:
Louisiana State University Press, 1970), pp. 252-90.

[9]Franklin, *From Slavery to Freedom,* pp. 234-35.

[10]*Ibid.,* pp. 250-51.

[11]*Freedom's Journal,* December 19, 1828.

[12]Franklin, *From Slavery to Freedom,* p. 251.

13The following representative Negro newspapers and the date of their formation provide some clue to the use of the mass media as a tool for advancing the cause of abolition and civil rights during the antebellum period: *Freedom's Journal,* 1827; *The North Star,* 1847; *Frederick Douglass' Paper,* 1850. In the first issue of the *Freedom's Journal,* the editors observed: "We (the blacks) wish to plead our own cause. Too long have others spoken for us." March 16, 1827, p. 1.

14For a brief description of Paul's philosophy and rhetorical technique, see Carter G. Woodson, ed., *Negro Orators and Their Orations* (Washington, D.C.: The Associated Publishers, 1925), p. 63.

15An extract of Paul's address appears in *Freedom's Journal,* August 10, 1827, p. 85.

16Aristotle makes a distinction between probability which is in the province of rhetoric and apodeictic certainty which exists only in the realm of scientific knowledge.

17Wright was a minister for a number of years in New York. He graduated from Princeton Theological Seminary and later pastored the Shiloh Presbyterian Church. He, like his disciple Henry Highland Garnet, combined preaching with anti-slavery activities.

18*The Liberator,* October 13, 1837, p. 165.

19*Ibid.*

20*The Liberator,* February 19, 1841.

21*Ibid.*

22*Ibid.*

23For pen portraits of many of these speakers, see William Wells Brown, *The Black Man, His Antecedents, His Genius, and His Achievements* (New York: Thomas Hamilton, 1863); William Wells Brown, *The Rising Son; or, The Antecedents and Advancement of the Colored Race* (Boston: A. G. Brown & Co., 1874). *The Liberator* also reports many of their anti-slavery presentations.

24Samuel Ward will be treated primarily as a revolutionist because of his violent opposition to the Compromise of 1850.

25"Eulogium on Henry Highland Garnet," in Alexander Crummell, *Africa and America* (Springfield, Mass.: Wiley & Co., 1891), p. 291.

26Brown, *The Rising Son,* p. 403.

27Brown, *The Black Man,* p. 248.

28*The Liberator,* July 31, 1840, p. 121.

29Brown, *The Black Man,* pp. 246-47.

30Crummell, *Africa and America,* pp. 292-93. For similar tributes to Garnet's effectiveness as a speaker, see Brown, *The Black Man,* pp. 149-64; and James McCune Smith, "Sketch of the Life and Labors of Rev. Henry Highland Garnet," in Henry Highland Garnet, *A Memorial Discourse* (Philadelphia: J. M. Wilson, 1865).

31This speech, entitled "An Address to the Slaves of the United States of America," will be analyzed in Chapter V.

32For a description of this address, see Chapter II.

[33]Carter G. Woodson, ed., *The Works of Francis Grimké,* Vol. 1, (Washington, D.C.: The Associated Publishers, 1942), 34.

[34]Frederick Douglass, *The Life and Times of Frederick Douglass* (New York: The Crowell-Collier Publishing Company, 1962), p. 217.

[35]*Ibid.,* pp. 226-31.

[36]When Julian Bond spoke on the campus at Ohio State University in the Spring of 1969 he alluded to Douglass' speech, praising it warmly in his introduction.

[37]W. E. B. DuBois, "Frederick Douglass," in Allen Johnson, ed., *Dictionary of American Biography,* (New York: Charles Scribner's Sons, 1946), p. 407.

[38]*Frederick Douglass' Paper,* August 5, 1853.

[39]Brown, *The Black Man,* p. 247.

[40]*Ibid.,* pp. 248-49.

[41]Langston (1829–1897) was born on a slave plantation in Virginia and graduated from Oberlin College. After being admitted to the bar, he was active in both law and politics as well as education and diplomacy. He served as Director General of the Freedmen's Bureau, Dean of the Law School at Howard University, and American Diplomat in Haiti and Santo Domingo. He was elected to Congress in 1890 as a Republican. In 1894 he wrote *From the Virginia Plantation to the National Capitol* (Hartford, Conn.: American Publishing Company, 1894). Contemporaries praised him for his eloquence. Rock, who was born in 1825, was especially active as a dynamic spokesman for civil rights during the 1860's.

[42]Brown, *The Black Man,* pp. 266-70.

[43]*The Liberator,* March 2, 1860, p. 342.

[44]*The Liberator,* August 15, 1862, pp. 130-35.

[45]DuBois, "Frederick Douglass," *Dictionary of American Biography,* p. 407.

[46]Garnet, *A Memorial Discourse*

[47]S. E. Morison, *The Oxford History of the American People* (New York: Oxford University Press, 1965), p. 711.

[48]*The New National Era,* April 14, 1870, p. 1.

[49]Langston by now was active in Republican politics and had confidence in the national leaders.

[50]Morison, *The Oxford History of the American People,* p. 707. Expressing a similar view, Carl N. Degler has observed: "Throughout most of the nineteenth century the South was at odds with the rest of the nation, first in its defense of slavery, then in its dissatisfaction with, and secession from the Union, and, still later, in its rejection of the Radical Republican solution to the question of the Negro." Degler, "The Peculiar Dissent of the Nineteenth Century South," in Alfred Young, ed., *Dissent: Explorations in the History of American Radicalism* (Dekalb, Ill.: Northern Illinois University Press, 1968), p. 111.

[51]Revels (1822–1901) was born in North Carolina and educated in his native state and in Indiana. Following the war he went to Mississippi

to take part in the affairs of the Freedmen's Bureau. In 1870, he was elected to fill an unexpired term to the United States Senate from Mississippi. Throughout his career he served both as a political leader and as a minister.

[52]*Congressional Globe*, 41st Congress, *Second Session*, Part III, pp. 1886-88.

[53]*New National Era*, January 2, 1873, p. 2.

[54]Franklin, *From Slavery to Freedom*, p. 319.

[55]Elliott was born in Boston, Massachusetts in 1842. After receiving an education in England he entered local politics in South Carolina. He was elected to the 42nd and 43rd Congresses, but in both instances he resigned before completing his term.

[56]*Congressional Record*, Vol. II, Part 1, 43rd Congress, *First Session*, p. 405.

[57]*Ibid.*, 406.

[58]Cited in W. E. B. DuBois, *Black Reconstruction* (New York: Harcourt, Brace, and Company, 1935), p. 628.

[59]*New National Era*, March 19, 1874, p. 1.

[60]*Ibid.*

[61]C. Vann Woodward, *Origins of the New South* (Baton Rouge: Louisiana State University Press, 1951), p. 65.

[62]*Ibid.*, p. 79.

[63]Franklin, *From Slavery to Freedom*, pp. 54-55.

[64]DuBois, *Black Reconstruction*, p. 128.

[65]Morison, *The Oxford History of the American People*, p. 707.

[66]James M. McPherson, *The Struggle for Equality* (Princeton, N.J.: Princeton University Press, 1964), pp. 430-31.

[67]This statement is contained in the preface of Douglass' published speech.

[68]Franklin, *From Slavery to Freedom*, p. 56. C. Vann Wodward expresses a similar view in "Tom Watson and the Negro," *Journal of Southern History*, Vol. IV (February, 1938), pp. 14-33.

[69]Van Woodward, "Tom Watson and the Negro," p. 347.

[70]*Ibid.*, p. 349.

[71]*Ibid.*, p. 348.

[72]Morison, *The Oxford History of the American People*, p. 1086.

[73]Vann Woodward, *Origins of the New South*, pp. 369-95.

[74]Talcott Parsons and Kenneth B. Clark, eds., *The Negro American* (Boston: Beacon Press, 1966), pp. 59, 598.

[75]John Hope Franklin, "The Two Worlds of Race," in Parsons and Clark, *The Negro American*, p. 59.

[76]*Ibid.*, pp. 59-60.

[77]Harry Golden, *Mr. Kennedy and the Negroes* (New York: The World Publishing Co., 1964), pp. 72-73.

[78]Holmes was born in 1877 and educated at Howard University and Columbia University where he received his Ph.D. in 1934. For years he was President of Morgan State College in Maryland.

[79]D. O. W. Holmes, "The Negro Chooses Democracy," *The Journal of Negro Education,* Vol. VIII (October, 1939), p. 623.

[80]*Ibid.,* p. 627.

[81]For a discussion of these points see *ibid.* pp. 629-33.

[82]Kenneth Clark, "The Civil Rights Movement: Momentum and Organization," in Parsons and Clark, *The Negro American,* p. 596.

[83]Franklin, *From Slavery to Freedom,* pp. 553-55.

[84]For a comprehensive analysis of the life and speaking career of Thurgood Marshall, see Harland L. Randolph, "A Rhetorical Study of Persuasion in the Integration Movement," M.A. Thesis, presented in Speech at Ohio State University, 1959.

[85]*Brown v. Board of Education of Topeka* (Kansas) 347 U.S., 483, 1954.

[86]Born in 1901 and educated at the University of Minnesota, Wilkins became editor of *The Crisis* in 1934, succeeding W. E. B. DuBois, and Executive Secretary of the N.A.A.C.P. in 1955.

[87]Roy Wilkins, "Desegregation and Racial Tensions," *The Crisis,* Vol. LXIII (April, 1956), p. 198. Wilkins delivered a similar address in Chicago in 1958. See "Dixie Challenge to Democracy," *ibid.,* Vol. LXV (October, 1958), pp. 471-76.

[88]*Ibid.,* 254.

[89]Clark has an informative discussion of the Urban League, the Congress of Racial Equality, the Southern Christian Leadership Conference, the Student Nonviolent Coordinating Committee, and other groups. "The Civil Rights Movement," in Parsons and Clark, *The Negro American,* pp. 604-25.

[90]King (1929–1968) received his B.A. degree from Morehouse College and his Ph.D. from Boston University. He became co-pastor with his father of Ebenezer Baptist Church in Atlanta in 1957. In 1964, he became the youngest man ever to receive the Nobel Peace Prize.

[91]Thurgood Marshall, "The Cry for Freedom," *The Crisis,* Vol. LXVII (May, 1960), p. 289.

[92]One of the authors was present on this occasion.

[93]The "Letter from Birmingham Jail" may be found in Martin Luther King, Jr., *Why We Can't Wait* (New York: Harper & Row, Publishers, 1964), pp. 77-100.

[94]*The New York Times,* April 7, 1968, p. 12E © 1968 by the New York Times Company. Also see Herbert Mitgang, "A Non-violent Man is Martyred," *ibid.,* p. E-1; and Tom Wicker, "Tragedy of the Living," *ibid.,* p. E-13.

[95]The slogan of "black power" apparently was first used by Stokely Carmichael.

[96]This debate, which will be analyzed in Chapter IV, is printed in full in *Dialogue Magazine*, Vol. II (May, 1962), pp. 13-18.

[97]Roy Wilkins, "Whither 'Black Power'?," *The Crisis,* Vol. LXXIII (September, 1966), pp. 353-54.

[98]During the 1968 National Democratic Convention in Chicago Mr. Phillips was the fourth major presidential candidate. Although a minister, he "has emerged among black people as a new champion in politics, often mentioned in the same breath with Julian Bond. . . ." *The Washington Post,* October 6, 1968, p. A 16.

[99]Channing E. Phillips, "The Real Black Power," *The Washington Post,* November 17, 1968, p. B 4.

[100]*Ibid.*

[101]James Farmer, "The Black Revolution," Unpublished manuscript address delivered at Raleigh, N.C. on February 25, 1969.

[102]James Brown, "America Is My Home" (Starday*King Recording and Publishing Companies Inc.).

Chapter 4   SEPARATION

One of the ideas most closely associated
with the culture of the United States
suggests that no disagreement is
so great that it cannot be resolved once
communication is established. "If we
could only sit down and talk it over,"
goes the long-held belief, "we could
surely come to a mutually agreeable
understanding." This concept is
strongly involved in the "melting pot"
image of the United States. As people
live together, develop a common
language and a common culture, their
former distinctions gradually wither
away and the "American people"
emerge. General semanticists and
teachers of interpersonal communication
have done much to perpetuate this
notion by urging their students to resist
being victimized by language behavior,
to establish a dialogue, and thus, to
reach consensus. It follows logically
that if communication and its products
of mutual understanding and agreement
are held up as the ideal goals of
American society, the opposite — the
end of communication and the
acknowledgment of an inability to
discover even the most fundamental
grounds for dialogue — must be
considered the ultimate failure.

Another apparently strong characteristic
of the American culture is an
unshakable conviction that no matter
how happy are the inhabitants of other

277

nations, if they had the chance to live in the United States, they would seize it. Certainly with some justification, the citizens of the United States are convinced that their country is much better than any other country on earth. They feel that it must be accepted *a fortiori* that anyone who has had the opportunity to live in the United States for a time would prefer to remain than to move to another country. Again, the logical conclusion is this: if the opportunity to dwell in America is the highest aspiration of man, the voluntary decision to live elsewhere, having been born in this country, must be taken as a serious insult.

Both of these attitudes, central to the American belief structure, are involved in the rhetoric of separation. In the first place, most citizens of the United States, particularly the white ones, probably believe that separatist rhetoric has its origins in the Black Muslim movement. They are very likely to think that it is a relatively recent phenomenon. Moreover, if one were to judge by the space allotted in the national press, the American people believe black separatists constitute only a small portion of the black community. A survey by the National Opinion Research Center of the University of Chicago, conducted late in 1964, found a strong antipathy for the Black Muslims in general and Malcolm X in particular.[1] Writing a foreword to the report of that study, Bayard Rustin said, ". . . consistent support for the Muslims was an infinitesimal ripple in the Negro community. Then and now, the overwhelming majority of Negroes were committed to integration: Not separatism, but integration in its profoundest sense. . . ."[2] Without seeking to challenge the results of this survey, it should be noted that the separatist movement is spoken of as identical to the Black Muslims, and the only individual separatist included in the study was Malcolm X, then a Muslim minister who had only recently established a national reputation. The results may not be surprising, for if the survey had asked the typical black man to name another separatist organization, or another separatist leader past or present, he might have been unable to recall any. As this and the following chapter will show, the lack of popular awareness of separatism should not be taken as evidence of its non-existence. For example, the Muslims certainly are not the only separatist organization of any scope that has emerged in the United States. Furthermore, even the Muslims, although well along toward solid establishment in the early 1940's, were not discovered by the nation at large until mid-1959 when a television documentary and a series of magazine articles provided the "exposé" of what was called a "hate organization" and suspected of being subversive and un-American.

Other contemporary observers now doubt that black nationalism or separatism has had only a minor impact. They argue that the two great issues which black men have considered from early slave days to the present have been separation and assimilation as alternative and mutually exclusive paths to the good life.[3] The arguments further state that the alternative of separation has been and still is the equal of integration in importance in the minds of black Americans. While the proponents of assimilation have received more attention in the white press, the advocates of separation have launched the ". . . greatest mass movement yet achieved in American Negro history,"[4] the Universal Negro Improvement Association of Marcus Garvey.

Perhaps the key to an initial understanding of the rhetorical strategy of separation is found in the two basic American values discussed previously. Messages of hope for the ultimate assimilation of blacks into the American culture have a positive valence in this country. They are words of hope for ultimate understanding and mutual accommodation, and they are consistent with the values most Americans hold. Even though white men may not personally look forward to close association with blacks, they want to believe in the "melting pot" ideal. Black Americans, who have also been filled with the American dream, respond favorably to these communications — they want to believe that if whites and blacks establish a true dialogue, consensus will emerge. In these cases messages that argue the futility of dialogue and propose the incompatibility of the two races, have a negative valence as they are inconsistent with the predominant desire. Whites tend to adjust their perceptions and hear separatist messages as actually calling for integration; or, they may simply refuse to perceive the existence of separatist ideologies.

The same analysis might be applied to the perception of proposals to depart from the continental United States. Americans, both white and black, resist the idea that anyone seriously believes a better life can be found elsewhere. Messages to that effect may be perceived as exaggerations, bluffs, as not actually proposing separation, or, at least, not seriously proposing it.

Another explanation of the relative ignorance about separatism may be found in the rhetorical character of the strategy. First, earlier chapters have demonstrated that assimilationist persuasion must have two audiences — white and black. Blacks must be convinced that the assimilationist route is the most promising; whites must be persuaded to take the social, political, legal, economic, steps (which only they can take because of their concentration of power) that would allow assimilation to occur. Separation, however, requires, almost exclusively, persuasion of black audiences. Even more, the strategy of separation calls for the concealment of information from the white man. He must be kept ignorant of plans for separation lest "Berlin walls" of one kind or another are formed, symbolized by the efforts of white southerners to prevent the emigration of needed labor in the late nineteenth century. The message of "leave us alone" is a difficult one to communicate to ignorant but well-intentioned white liberals and even more difficult to communicate to those bent on exploitation. It may be easier to tell the white man what he wants to hear — "We are working toward integration" — than to explain the idea of separating. Since anyone — white or black — who is associated with what is called the "establishment" or the "power structure" is considered committed to assimilationist ideas, the message of separation might be withheld from any discussion in which they were included. Newsmen, surveyors of opinion, politicians, and intellectuals, whether white or black, may be systematically confronted with a misleading preponderance of pro-assimilationist messages.

For whatever reason, the rhetoric of separation has not been as thoroughly studied as the rhetoric of assimilation. We will present evidence to show that an understanding of the rhetoric of black Americans must necessarily include the strategy of separation. The remainder of this chapter will include a detailed discussion of the strategy of separation, and a close examination of two sub-movements. First, we will consider black efforts toward moderate separation within the concept of race unity and self-help. Second, the black reaction to the white-dominated colonization movement will be discussed. In Chapter VI, the study of the rhetoric of separation will be continued with the analysis of black-dominated movements.

THE STRATEGY

For this study, the concept "separation," has been chosen over the other words which are frequently used to describe the same rhetorical effort. Probably the concept most closely associated with the ideas here under discussion is that of nationalism. Essien-Udom, in his book *BLACK NATIONALISM, A Search for an Identity in America,* gives this definition:

> The concept of nationalism . . . may be thought of as the belief
> of a group that it possesses, or ought to possess, a country;
> that it shares, or ought to share, a common heritage of lan-

guage, culture, and religion; and that its heritage, way of life, and ethnic identity are distinct from those of other groups. Nationalists believe that they ought to rule themselves and shape their own destinies, and that they should therefore be in control of their social, economic, and political institutions.[5]

Black nationalism is the term designed to describe the efforts of "American Negroes, particularly among the followers of Muhammad. . . . " The author further states that "although black nationalism shares some characteristics of all nationalisms, it must be considered a unique type of separatist nationalism seeking an actual physical and political withdrawal from existing society."[6]

Malcolm X, as a follower of Elijah Muhammad and particularly after his rejection of Muhammad, conceived of black nationalism in terms of intra-black solidarity. Intra-black solidarity included a separate territory in America for black people, and an international closing of ranks for all non-white people of the world. Even when he considered the possibility of peace among all men regardless of color he said:

> I kept having all kinds of troubles trying to develop the kind of Black Nationalist organization I wanted to build for the American Negro. Why Black Nationalism? Well, in the competitive American society, how can there ever be any white-black solidarity before there is first some black solidarity?[7]

Of course, the idea of nationalism implies a related rhetoric of anti-colonialism. In the case of black Americans, the messages of black nationalism describe black people in the United States as a subjugated people, little different from those in Africa, Asia, and Latin and South America, who have been or still are under the domination of a colonial government. Malcolm X proposed taking the case of black Americans before the United Nations, while Stokely Charmichael and Charles Hamilton, discussed in Chapter I, describe the work of the black American Nationalist in terms of the "politics of liberation in America."

The concept of "nationalism" is somewhat more positive than the concept "separatism" as it suggests the uniting of a given people, rather than separation from another people or peoples. For this reason, it might have been a more desirable term to use. However, "nationalism" also has a propaganda connotation which seems to restrict its usefulness in a scholarly study. Its very association with the anti-colonial movements around the world, and the frequent association of them, in the mind of Americans, with pro-communist activities, whether true or not, causes the word "nationalism" to be less valuable than the term "separatism." Finally, separatism seems to be a more universal term, within which the nationalistic aspects can be included as well as other phases of rhetorical behaviors that are properly related.

As a strategy for achieving the ultimate goal of a good life — freedom, liberty, identity, etc. — the idea of separation from white racist people and institutions can be viewed in three different ways. First, separation can be advocated as the only viable alternative in the face of the failure of assimilation. Second, it can be advanced as a positive good for the preservation of black culture and racial identity; and third, it can be held as an instrumentality to the eventual accomplishment of some form of integration, if not assimilation.

THE FUTILITY OF ASSIMILATION

The most compelling reason for supporting separation is the black American's conviction that full integration or assimilation is impossible. Cruse argues that the charge of separation as a utopian ideal is answered with the charge ". . . that the idea of the eventual acceptance of the Negro as a full-fledged American without regard to race, creed, or color, is also utopian and will never be realized."[8] Cruse goes on to make this assertion:

> Negroes have never been equal to whites of any class in economic, social, cultural, or political status, and very few whites of any class have ever regarded them as such. The Negro is not really an integral part of the American nation beyond the convenient formal recognition that he lives within the borders of the United States. From the white's point of view, the Negro is not related to the "we," the Negro is the "they." This attitude assumes its most extreme expression in the Southern states and spreads out over the nation in varying modes of racial mores. The only factor which differentiates the Negro's status from that of a pure colonial status is that his position is maintained in the "home" country in close proximity to the dominant racial group.[9]

With this analysis, the author concludes that it is not surprising that a nationalistic philosophy has developed.

If both integration and separation are seen as almost utopian goals, then black men have been forced to debate two unlikely alternatives. Thus, the question regarding separation becomes more reasonable when it is viewed as a course of action which may be an improvement over subjugated status. In the analysis to follow, many of the speeches will deal with this question: will separation to another place be any *less* desirable than continued existence as second-class citizens? Separation does not have to be proved to be totally workable to be accepted. If it can be shown to involve an acceptable risk in comparison with remaining in the present state and seeking assimilation, the idea may be persuasive to many.

THE NEED FOR RACIAL INTEGRITY

Separatist rhetoric does not need to advance practical arguments for physical separation from all white Americans to be persuasive. A cultural or psychological separation, designed to develop a sense of group identity or blackness, is another basis for this rhetoric. Since the black man's first appearance on this continent, he has been subordinated to the white. His group identity has been attacked, his values have been rejected, his concepts of good and evil have been re-defined to accord with those of the white man. Many black leaders recognized, even before the Civil War, the need to reject white orientation and develop a sense of self-sufficiency, black pride, and group identity. In both abolition and colonization, the white man was inclined to take control, define goals, plan rhetorical campaigns, and use black men only as exhibits. The arguments for assimilation imply a dilution of blackness until black men have indistinguishably merged into white society. The white man's religion, dress, language, social customs, economic values, and patriotism will be adopted if only the white man will permit it.

Those who valued their blackness; those who felt there was a need to retain the unique customs and values of the black American, if not the African, generated a rhetoric aimed at uniting the black community. Essentially, it involves a re-definition of the ultimate goal of a good life. These separatists are saying that inherently the black man cannot achieve the good life as a synthetic white man. Only as a part of the community of black people in the United States and even, in many cases, the world, can the black American find fulfillment. The rhetoric rests less on charges of evil in the white society, and more on a constructive development of the qualities of blackness. Whites often find it surprising to learn that black men are not ashamed of their racial identity. In fact, some whites are even shocked to discover black men who are convinced that they are superior to whites. Elijah Muhammad professes not to hate white people, but his religious convictions tell him the white man is the devil, and the black man is necessarily superior. To people with these beliefs, the rhetoric of separation is a logical choice.

A STEP TO INTEGRATION

Even men who agree with the assimilationist may be advocates of separation. In this situation, the period or state of separation is intended to be the instrument through which a satisfactory working relationship between black and white communities can be evolved. This moderate form of separatism is based upon the idea that the black man cannot move from a state of second-class dependency to full and equal participation without passing through a period of independence. Power, economic, political, or otherwise, is viewed as the basis of operation in the United States. Moral suasion is rejected as a means of gaining in society, for people seem unlikely to relinquish power simply because it is the proper thing to do. If the black community can unite and form a power base from which to negotiate, however, they can meet white men on their own terms and establish a partnership based upon mutual capability, not a one-sided dependency.

This power base could range from one extreme, the establishment of a black nation composed of several former states of the Union, through a moderate position of semi-autonomous black urban and rural enclaves composed of former ghettos such as Harlem, to an American black community mutually dedicated to the well-being of each other vis-a-vis the white citizen. The moderate position regarding semi-autonomous enclaves is expressed in the preamble to the Community Self-Determination Act proposed to Congress.

> . . . programs . . . should . . . aim to restore to the people of local communities the power to participate directly and meaningfully in the making of public policy decisions on issues which affect their everyday lives. Such programs should aim to free local communities from excessive interference and control by centralized governments in which they have little or no effective voice; . . . order, stability, and progress can be achieved only when the people of a community actively participate in, and are responsible for, their own affairs in such areas as education, neighborhood planning, economic development, recreation and beautification, and social services and welfare;
>
> . . . to achieve these ends, the people of a community must organize for responsible action, in such a way as to reduce fragmentation, create order and stability, make optimum

use of community resources, and maximize the opportunity for creative leadership and self-determination. . . .[10]

An important point to note about this aspect of separation is the premise that black Americans cannot seriously consider integration or any form of assimilation in their present position. They must first establish a cohesive and powerful black community. Then, the debate can proceed over the alternatives of remaining separate or seeking some relationship with the white man. If this message is persuasive, obviously, it will cause all integration activity to cease at least for the time being.

Finally, in this analysis of separatist rhetoric, Booker T. Washington becomes the patron of all contemporary black nationalists. Cruse, in his book *Rebellion Or Revolution* devotes considerable space to this argument.[11] Washington's apparent submissiveness, discussed in Chapter II, is perceived as nothing more that a necessary strategy in nineteenth-century Alabama to hold off destruction until blacks could gather enough expertise, organization, and a capitalistic power base to negotiate with the white man. While many contemporary black spokesmen reject this interpretation of one of the most noted of all black Americans, the discussion of Marcus Garvey (considered the father of black nationalism) will reveal Garvey's acknowledgement of Washington's leadership. The following section will develop the essential characteristics of the messages of racial unity and self-help.

RACE UNITY AND SELF-HELP

On the surface, the words "segregation" and "separation" seem to have a common definition, but in the history of black Americans, there is a difference to those who examine the terms carefully. When one looks at separate churches, schools, and social organizations for black people in terms of outward appearance or from a white man's perspective, it can appear that blacks have been driven away from the white counterpart of these groups. Of course, in many instances and in many ways this is an accurate analysis. The prominence given to assimilationist rhetoric calling for an end to all segregation gives support to this interpretation. Not often is an argument from a black citizen favoring separate churches or schools or social clubs heard. But, occasionally it does occur.

Richard Allen was a man who believed in setting up separate institutions for black people so that they might maintain their self-respect and work for their mutual benefit. Born in 1760, he became, at the age of twenty-two, a Methodist preacher. When he was twenty-seven he established the first Benevolent Society of Colored Persons ". . . for the grand purpose of relieving one another in time of distress."[12] By 1828 there were about forty African Benevolent Societies. Between 1787 and 1816, while America was developing its values of liberty and equality for all men, a practice grew in the churches to seat colored members in the back or in a balcony. By 1816, black resentment of this discrimination had grown, and when Allen was reportedly pulled from his knees during prayer and ordered to take a back seat in the church, he separated from the parent church and established the African Methodist Episcopal Church in spite of strong opposition from other members both white and black. On the celebration of his sixty-ninth birthday, one supporter said of him,

> We all remark, that Bishop Allen was the first person that formed a Religious Society among the People of Colour in the United States of America; . . . He was also the founder of the first African Church in the United States . . ., whereby we were enabled to worship Almighty God, under our own vine and fig-tree, with none to harm, nor yet make us afraid. . . . We are thankful that Almighty God still spares him for the good of the African Race. . . .[13]

In 1887, leaders of the A.M.E. Church proposed a celebration for the centennial of the foundation of their institution with these words about Allen:

> This [establishment of a separate church] is the most decisive act of the religious colored people in the United States, and we know of none like it of the descendants of Africa in the world; if we except the resolve of the Haitians under Toussaint, Christophe Petiou and Boyer. These men were to Hayti and San Domingo, in a civil and political sense, what Allen, Jones, Tapisco and others were to the colored Christians of America; their act was manhood, freedom, and manhood Christianity. To resist oppression in Church or State is manly. . . . The success of Allen and his compeers is demonstrated, for it has given us the largest colored organization in the world.[14]

While Allen was a strong opponent of the colonization movement, he was an effective advocate of the idea of racial unity. He argued that the black men should take care of themselves, identify with their fellow black man, and assume the initiative in the abolition effort.

Alexander Crummell, already introduced in Chapter II, was not only in favor of racially separate institutions such as churches, but also a supporter of colonization in Africa. Considered by his peers to be the most scholarly black man of his time, Crummell studied as a child with such promising persons as Ira Aldridge who was to become a noted actor, and Henry Highland Garnet. He also attended Oneida Institute, did theological study in Massachusetts, having been refused admission to the General Theological Seminary of the Episcopal church, because of his color, and finally studied in Queen's College, Cambridge, England.[15]

Crummell, who claimed his father was of a royal family in Africa, was proud of his race. He spoke in public and private against black people who sought to integrate with whites, adopt their culture, and rid themselves of every possible vestige of their blackness. He used his pulpit in St. Luke's Church, Washington, D.C. to speak to his black brothers and sisters on topics not intended for white ears. A contemporary using language similar to that earlier cited by DuBois, described Crummell this way:

> In personal appearance the doctor is slender, very neat and trim. He is a true African in color, and his intellectual development is of the highest order. His retiring disposition, his earnest enthusiasm and kindly demeanor are all very noticeable and give him a commanding presence. One feels like venerating his frost-white hair and patriarchal style, to the extent that he would rather stand than sit in his presence, not because he overawes one by his sternness, but because you wish to honor him.[16]

This description was made toward the end of Crummell's career, and the sermon which is published here was delivered shortly after his formal retirement. In the sermon, Crummell develops his points in a way that was characteristic of many of his sermons to the people of Washington, D.C. His Christian devotion is clear and strong; he puts full faith in God to control his destiny and that of his people. As suggested in Chapter II, it is possible to interpret his message as simply one of Christian devotion — suffer the evils done to you on this earth, for you will receive your reward later. By accepting, and even leading, segregated institutions such as churches, and schools, Crummell could be categorized with Booker T. Washington as an accommodationist. But a careful reading of his sermons throughout his lifetime, combined with the knowledge that Crummell lived, preached, and taught for many years in Africa, suggests strongly that his rhetoric was oriented towards racial pride and even black supremacy.

Observe in the sermon that follows how carefully Crummell develops his claim that God has selected the black race for superior status. He notes that while other races equally down-trodden as the blacks at one time had become weak and even extinct, the black man has increased in physical, mental, and moral capacity. The use of population figures was a favorite device of Crummell's. By observing the greater rate of repro-duction among black people when compared with whites, he concluded that by the mid-twentieth century, blacks would out-number whites in the United States. His proof of the superior vitality of black people is one used by many other orators: to have been subjected for hundreds of years to the most severe repression and to have survived and even increased is surely a sign of a superior race. Furthermore, Crummell employed another popular line of argument when he recounts the military effective-ness of black men. Finally, in agreement with Washington, the minister advocates patient development of useful skills and trades, and provision for a gradual and thus more effective development of the race so that it will be ready to perform the great deeds for which the Almighty is preparing it.

Alexander Crummell

Sermon*

Ps. cvii; Vs. 13-16

13. Then they cried unto the Lord in their trouble, and he saved them out of their distresses.
14. He brought them out of darkness and the shadow of death and brake their bands in sunder.
15. Oh that *men* would praise the Lord *for* his goodness, and *for* his wonderful works to the children of men!
16. For he hath broken the gates of brass, and cut the bars of iron in sunder.

The Psalms of David are, for the most part, songs of praise and thanks-giving for the gifts and mercies of the Almighty. The special peculiarity of

*Alexander Crummell, unpublished sermon delivered in Washington, D.C. Reprinted from the Schomburg Collection of Alexander Crummell Papers, Harlem Branch of the New York Public Library, New York City, New York.

this 107th Psalm is, that it is a continuous utterance of adoration for the deliverance of the children of Israel from the land of bondage; for their protection from their enemies in the wilderness; for their rescue from divers dangers and misfurtunes, by flood and field; from drought and famine.

The sense of gratitude was so vivid and so glowing that the Psalmist bursts forth, not once or twice, but over and over again, into the exclamation — "O that men would praise the Lord for His goodness, and declare the wonder that he doeth for the children of men."

So similar, in several ways, has been the providence of the Almighty in the history of our race in this country that I have chosen the text just announced, as the base of remarks pertaining to the future prospects stretching out before us. My subject today is — "INCIDENTS OF HOPE FOR THE NEGRO RACE IN AMERICA."

The trials and sufferings of this race have been great for centuries. They have not yet ceased. They are not likely to cease for a long time to come. It may take two or three generations for the race to get a firm and assured status in the land.

Nevertheless there are, I maintain, underlying all the past, present and future attritions and tribulations of our condition certain large and important incidents, which are pregnant with hope, and which are fitted to serve as stimulants to high ambition and indomitable energy.

There is need, just now, for such encouragements. For, in some quarters, there seems to be despondency; as though the car of progress was tardy in its movements; many forgetting that it is impossible to extemporize a full civilization for any people; impossible to leap, at a spring, into a lofty elevation. Hence the dark cloud of despair which overhangs a moody group, leading almost to repudiation of their race. And then, from another section, come the insensate screeching and screaming tones which call upon us to flee to Africa.

For my own part I regret these views as idle and unreasoning. Not blind, indeed, to numerous difficulties, I see, nevertheless, gracious providences in our case; and I am anxious to set before you what I deem some sound and solid grounds of Hope.

1. Consider, first of all, the fact of Negro vitality as an important factor in his destiny. There must be a physical basis, a material substratum for the mental and moral life of man. "A sound mind in a sound body" is an old adage, applied to a promising individual. The adage recognizes the relation of mind to body; the correlation of flesh and spirit; the connection of the soul of man with animal conditions; which shows itself in all the masterful peoples in human history. Grand intellectuality in the races of men, has been generally connected, more or less, with robustness, life-tenacity, and strong vital forces. Weak people, for the most part, are weak in both body and mind; run a short race; have but a slight hold upon life, and soon vanish away.

It is characteristic of the Negro race that it seems, everywhere, to have a smack of the immortal. Amid the rude conditions of the fatherland, shut out for ages from the world's civilization, fecundity and vital powers were immemorial qualities. Never, until the ravages of the slave-trade, was there a known disturbance of this vital feature.

During the last two hundred or more years, a large section of the race has been in a captive state, on the continent and the islands of America. But not even the severest conditions of bondage have been able to bar out this quality. The Negro, everywhere, is a productive factor on American soil. The slave-trade was, for the most part, put an end to, in 1809. The slave populations of the West Indies, of the American States, of Brazil, and the other South American States, at the time of the great Emancipations which have taken place in this century, were less than half of their present numbers under freedom; and hence our increase, under the British, American, and Brazilian flags, cannot be attributed to the supplies and reinforcements of the slave-trade.

And yet here is the fact, that this race, under the unsettled and abnormal conditions of a new freedom, has gone on increasing, at, at least, as rapid a rate as any people on the continent.[2]

In the West Indies, the white race, in many quarters, decreases. By the census of 1880 the rate of *our* increase, i.e. in the United States, was said to be fully 6 percent greater than that of the whites. That census report has since been repudiated as incorrect. Nevertheless the last returns of the Census Bureau, though placing us considerably below that of the white population of the land, sets forth the fact of an *actual* increase of our numbers; though, relatively, less than that of white Americans. The disparity, however, can easily be accounted for by the unsettled conditions of a newly emancipated and antagonized people.[3]

Here then is the fact of persistent vitality, under the difficulties of poverty, bitter repulsion, and political suffering. It is not a fact which stands separate and apart from ideas. Vital force has always some potent underlying principles. There must be thrift, or economy, or a measure of family virtue; or conscious, or unconscious Hope; some, or most of these; or otherwise, a people, — any people, — will die out. Spiritual ideas do, more or less, attend the persistent life of the humblest classes. The Negro lives and grows; because vitality, in his case, springs from internal sources.

The averment may be made — "Your increase is only an evidence of the sheerest animality. It has no relation to the *inner* life, which is the true criterion of manhood, the only promise of futurity."

2.   But this taunt is easily refuted. It is refuted first, by a view of its *intellectual* aspect; and I will take up its spiritual phase later on.

---

[2]Two facts may be noticed under this head (a) That the Negro has supplanted the aboriginal populations, in several quarters, on the American Continent and its Isles; (b) That there is not a spot on which he has been placed but what there he lives and thrives.

[3]I must leave it to each reader to judge for himself the census reports of 1880 and 1890:

PERCENTAGE OF INCREASE

1870 to 1880	(White) 29.22	(Negro) 34.85
1880 to 1890	26.68	13.51

Now I maintain that the mental progress of the Negro has run parallel with its persistent and vital continuity.

The special point to be considered, just here, is the fact that in all the places of our servitude every effort has been put forth, by legislation, to shut out the light of letters from the intellectual eye of the black man. The Statute books, in every State and Nation, on this Western Continent, bristle with the laws which interdict the teaching of the Negro; which forbid, with severe penalties, his instruction in letters. And yet intellectual aspiration has characterized the race in all the lands of their servitude. The laws themselves testify the fact. And, thus, for two hundred years there has been a struggle for the Alphabet: the Primer; the Newspaper, and the Bible.[4]

"Put out the light: and then put out the light" has been the common cry of slavery; in Virginia, in the Carolinas; in Mexico, in Peru, and in Brazil; in Jamaica and in Bermuda.

But the answering cry has gone up from multitudious plantations, during the entire reign of slavery—"Light! Light!" And so, through murky darkness, despite law and penalties, in cane brake, in slave hut, in the seclusion of the forest, in the deep of night by the embers of dying firelight; thousands of slaves have clandestinely groped, and stumbled, and plodded on; struggling to emerge from the darkness of ignorance, to attain, if possible, the ability to read, and the illumination of letters.

Thus it came to pass that even in the darkest days of slavery, not seldom, whole groups of men reached, dimly, to light of letters. Right from the gloomiest precincts of servitude sprung such geniuses as Phillis Wheatley, Banneker, Ward, and Garnett and others. Some, without doubt, were encouraged in their intellectual desires by generous, liberal-minded masters and mistresses. But even thus, the proffer of a gift is a nullity if there be no glad receptivity in the taker. The receptive, yearning faculty was in the Negro; and hence the anxiousness which constantly disclosed itself, in the domain of slavery, for light; and which everywhere met with the effort to reach it!

Just go back with me, a moment, to the year 1620. Stand up beside me, and look at that unfortunate captive! He is the *first* victim of the slave-trade; just landed on American soil. He is a naked pagan! For thousands of years, his ancestors, on the soil of Africa, have lived in a land of ignorance and benightedness; their intellectual life, never, during the ages, stirred by a breeze or a breath of mental inspiration from the world of letters. Through him, the race he represents, is now for the first time, brought into the neighborhood of cultivation, placed in juxtaposition with enlightened civilization.

It is two hundred years and more since this civilizing influence began; and you must remember that it has been only incidental; it has been unintentional; always tardy and reluctant; that it has been carried on under the severest and narrowest limitations.

Join to this another fact. It is indeed a fact of contrast, but it has its special significance.

---

[4]See "Stroud's Slave Laws."

At the time when the black man came in contact with the civilization of the Western World, there was a large group of nations, tribes, and peoples, on the Continent and in the Pacific and Atlantic seas, mostly, in precisely the same semi-barbarous condition as the Negro; with not a few, however, on a higher plane of elevation. There were the American Indians. There were the aboriginal Mexicans and Peruvians, south of the States. There were the Maoris of New Zealand. There were the Gauches of the Canaries. There were the divers tribes of Australia. All these peoples were, nevertheless, crude and uncivilized peoples at the time of the discovery of America.

All were then, touched, for the first time, with the rising rays of civilization. And so it happens that we, with them, have run the same difficult course of enlightenment, which has been so grudgingly given the ruder peoples of the world.

How do we stand today, relatively, in the problem of attainment and of progress? I challenge any man to the comparison.

Go back again with me to that untrained, mind-shrouded and naked African, a captive and a stranded slave on these shores.

Turn back again, on the instant, to his descendants, in the West Indies, and on this American soil. What is the sight which meets your eyes?

Here, remote from the land of their forefathers, is a race, numbering nigh thirty millions of people;[5] a people to a large extent lettered and enlightened; thousands of them cultured persons; in some of the lands of their captivity, merchants, planters, scholars, authors, magistrates, rulers. And in two of the provinces of their former servitude, masters of the situation; having driven out their former owners; and wresting from them the staff of authority, have become, in their own race and blood, Rulers of the land.[6]

Within the period of these two hundred years this same Negro race, despised, trodden upon, sold as beasts and cattle, oft-times murdered by overwork and cruelty, has, nevertheless, by almost superhuman energy, risen above their crushing servitude; and in the very lands of their oppression, produced historic names and characters. Out from the very limitations and agonies of slavery have come cultured civilians, accomplished gentlemen, Physicians, Lawyers, Linguists, Mathematicians, Generals, Philosophers; and from the Coast of Africa men eminent in attainments, in great Universities; not seldom holding professorships in the great schools of Europe. Among these — Henry Diaz, an experienced and commanding officer in Brazil; Hannibal, Lieutenant-General, in Russia; Don Juan Lateno, Latin Professor, at Saville; Anthony William Arno, Doctor of Philosophy of University of Wittenburg.

How stands the case with the divers races and peoples, living in Pagan isolation at the time of the discovery of America? Why, the breath of Euro-

---

[5]The following may be regarded as a fair estimate of the American Continent, and Islands.

United States	8,000,000	Hayti	3,000,000
Brazil	6,500,000	British Possessions	1,500,000
Cuba	1,500,000	Dutch, Danish and	
South and Central		Mexican	400,000
American Republics	2,500,000	French	350,000

[6]Hayti and St. Domingo

pean civilization seemed too strong for nearly all of them! Down they went, tribe after tribe, race after race, to utter oblivion! Some of them are utterly extinct! Once I was shown a Bible in the Library of Andover Seminary, translated, by Elliott, into the tongue of a New England tribe of Indians. There is not a man living on earth who can read it! The tribe has utterly perished!

Not so with the Negro. Not one of the then humbler races has stood the ordeal as he has. Terrible as has been that ordeal, through the murderous invasion of slavetraders, on the coast of Africa; by the horrors of the Midpassage; and through the sufferings of slavery in the lands of our exile; still the Negro lives!

Neither have these other peoples surpassed this race in progress! Not one of them has pressed through direful agonies, up to the hopeful attainments and the promising destiny which seems clearly opening before us.

3.   Allied to this intellectual outgrowth, is another incident of hope for the race — *its moral and spiritual perception.*

I do not pretend angelic qualities for our race. Such a claim would be ludicrous. The common human depravity is our heritage with all the rest of humanity. Moreover, slavery has brought forth its fruitful progeny of special enormities for the depravation of the Negro.

But it is a difficult thing to obliterate aboriginal qualities. The history of man shows how innate tendencies abide in a people, notwithstanding the most adverse, and even deteriorating circumstances. It is thus, through this peculiarity, that the Negro has held on to those special moral qualities, to those high spiritual instincts which were recognized by ancient Pagan writers as qualities of the Hamitic family; and which have been noticed by discerning Christian philosophers and philanthropists in all subsequent times.

Back of all the moral infirmities of nature and of the special vices bred of ignorance and servitude, there are certain constitutional tendencies in the race which are, without doubt, unique and special. A high moral attitude is a primitive quality, antecedent to the coming of Christianity; and which has developed into more positive forms, in Christian lands, under the inspiration of Christian teaching.[7]

The race is essentially religious. Even in his pagan state the spiritual instinct always has had the ascendency. Homer perceived this quality; for he speaks of the Gods visiting and feasting with "Ethiopia's blameless race."

The great African travellers of modern times speak of the same moral characteristic. The testimony of Adamson who visited Senegal in 1754 chimes in with that of Homer. "The Negroes," he says, "are sociable, humane, obliging and hospitable; and they have generally preserved an estimable simplicity of domestic manners. They are distinguished by their tenderness for their

---

[7]The religious growth of the race is closely shown by the following statistics: Dr. H. K. Carroll, in "The Independent," says that the aggregate of colored church members in the United States is, in round numbers, 2,674,000, distributed as follows: Baptists, 1,403,559; Methodists, 1,190,638; Presbyterians, 30,000; Disciples of Christ, 18,578, and Protestant Episcopal, and Reformed Episcopal together, somewhat less than 5,000. According to the census there has been an increase of 1,150,000 colored church members during the last thirty years, which Dr. Carroll thinks is unparalleled in the history of the Christian Church. The value of Negro church property is $26,626,000, and the number of edifices is 22,770.

parents, and great respect for the aged." In similar terms speaks the other great travellers into Africa; Mungo Park, Livingston; the great Stanley of our own day; that extraordinary personage, Mrs. Sheldon French, and others. Kinmont, in his "lectures on Man," says "that the sweet graces of the Christian religion appear almost too tropical and tender plants, to grow in the soil of the Caucassian mind; they require a character of human nature of which you can see the rude lineaments in the Ethiopian." Dr. Wm. Ellery Channing, many years ago, declared — "We are holding in bondage one of the best races of the human family. *** His nature is affectionate, easily touched; and hence he is more open to religious impressions than the white man. *** When I cast my eyes over our Southern region, the land of bowie knives, lynch law and duels — of chivalry, honor and revenge — and when I consider that Christianity is declared to be 'charity, which seeketh not her own, is not easily provoked, thinketh no evil and endureth all things' — can I hesitate in deciding to which of the races in that land, Christianity is most adapted, and in which its noblest disciples are most likely to be reared?"

It will be a great mistake to regard these native qualities of the race as merely *negative* qualities, divorced from strength and robustness. It was first here, if I mistake not, our friend, Dr. Blyden, erred in his learned and interesting Lecture, the other evening. He seemed to think that *passivity* is the normal, aboriginal quality of the race. The Negro, however, is brave as well as gentle; courageous as well as amiable; a gallant soldier as well as a patient sufferer and an enduring martyr. The quiet and submissive qualities of the race have been, not seldom, the butt of ridicule and the sneer of the jester. How constant, down to the present day, is the purpose, in the common American mind, to make the term Negro the equivalent of a ludicrous *Simian!* One instance is quite conspicuous. If you visit the east corridor of the Capitol, on the Senate side, you will see there a noted picture of the naval battle on Lake Erie. That picture is one of the most disgraceful prostitutions of Art in modern times: It is an attempt to stamp a libel and a lie on the dark brow of an innocent, a suffering, but a brave race.[8] There, the Negro is represented as a frightened grimace and coward; whereas we have the record of his prowess, and the eulogy of his bravery, in this very battle, in the archives of this Government. This picture is not only disgraceful to the vulgar creature who painted it; but it is disreputable to a nation which fastens, emblazons and perpetuates a gross mendacity upon the very walls of its National Capitol!

Moreover the fact is historic that, in the Revolutionary war, and in every conflict of this Nation with a foreign or domestic foe, the black man, whether as soldier or sailor, has been a hero; eulogized by Generals and commodores

---

[8]Commodore Perry was the great Hero in the great naval battles on Lake Erie and Lake Champlain. A goodly number of Negroes were sent to the Commodore to reinforce his marines. He took umbrage, and complained at the sending of so many Negroes to his ships! But such was their bravery and efficiency in the engagements, that, in his reports, he afterward speaks of these black naval heroes in the warmest and most enthusiastic manner.

for his prowess.[9] General Lord Wolsely, next to Von Moltke, the greatest Captain of the age, declares that "the Negro makes one of the bravest soldiers in the world."

No one who has read the history of St. Domingo and the grand struggle of the brave Haytiens, under Touissant, can do otherwise than concur with Lord Wolseley's opinion. Where, elsewhere, in the annals of War, a grander martial spirit can be discerned, than under the mighty chief of Hayti, I know not. Nobody will deny the burning, blazing prowess of the black troops in our late civil war in the South. That prowess led to the enrolment of Negroes in the standing army of the Nation: and, year by year, we are receiving the reports of American Generals, of the grand qualities of the Negro Cavalry, whether in action, in conflict with the Indians; or in the camp, in order, or discipline, and high soldierly bearing.

These moral and manly qualities are indications of a noble future. Moral qualities are prophecies. Their predictive elements are strengthened by the facts of progress and of mental advancement which I have brought to your notice; and by the persistent vitality which itself reaches over to the future.

I say therefore that we have every reason to thank God and to take courage. That we have not gone up like sky-rockets, at once, to the highest Empyrean, in the brief period of a generation, is no cause for surprise in our own ranks, nor for the carpings of unthinking critics who delight in disparagement of the Negro. Every thoughtful reader of history knows, thoroughly well, the almost universal fact that the *first,* the almost immediate result of any great revolution, or, any large Emancipation is the decadence of a people. Freedom does not generate a spontaneous elevation, a prompt and extemporaneous development. It always takes an emancipated people TIME to draw themselves together; to get to know themselves, to learn to know their powers and their responsibilities. The children of Israel, after their deliverance from Egypt, went down, down, down for four hundred years; and never became anything until the times of David and Solomon. The modern Greeks, after their bloody severance from Turkish oppression, have had, down to the present, stagnant and unprogressive existence; and today are almost nobodies!

---

[9]The Honorable C. C. [P]inckney of South Carolina, in his day, celebrated as an Orator and Statesman, in the memorable debate on the Missouri question, made the following statement: "In the Northern States, numerous bodies of them (the Negroes) were enrolled, and fought, side by side with the whites, the battles of the Revolution." "*Numerous* bodies!" The statement is literally true. In many cases they fought, in the ranks with whites: but, aside from this, regiments were enlisted, in Massachusetts, New Hampshire, Rhode Island, Connecticut, New York, who fought and died for the independence of the Colonies. History assures us of the conspicuous valor of these men, at Bunker Hill, Fort Griswold, Red Bank, Valley Forge, Saratoga, &c., &c.

So much for the Revolutionary War.

In the war of 1812, they showed the greatest gallantry. At the conclusion of the war General Jackson issued a proclamation in which he spoke in glowing terms of their bravery, declaring — "I *expected much of you.*** You have done *more than I expected.*"

See these petty South American Republics! What wonderful things have they done since their Emancipation?

And now I ask — Why should the Negro-haters of America demand a miraculous, a superhuman development in us? *Contrary* to the general trend of history we do show progress; and that should suffice, for just and reasonable men.[10]

At the same time we must remember that we have reached no place where we can say — "Rest and be thankful!" Nor should we forget that our heritage, for an age or more, is repulse and opposition. Great trials are, without doubt, yet before us as a people; long vistas of thorny roadways, we have yet to travel; many wounds, sore lacerations; and the sufferings of many martyrdoms!

For a long time you will have to meet the assaults of that large brutal class which would fain sweep us out, as remorsely as they would trample out a nest of ants! And then you will have to resist the insidious influences of that weak *pious* class, which is ever prophesying the failure of the Negro; and then, Jesuitically, strive, by sneers, limitations, and cruel neglects to fulfil their own atheistic prophecy!

But you must never listen to the tones of discouragement, come from whatever quarter they may. Least of all may we give heed to the despairing tones of hopeless men in our own ranks, nor to the scepticism of those who confidently assert the narrowest limitations of Negro capacity.

They may tell you — "You have indeed made progress. We admit that you stand on a higher plane than your ancestors; — but you have gone as far as you *can* go! You are incapable of reaching the higher platforms of human achievement. The place of the Negro is, forever, a secondary and inferior one."

But don't you listen, for a moment, to the delusive dictum of finality. It is all a folly and a snare. You have risen from a most prostrate condition, to freedom. That was *one* step. You have pushed forward from freedom to manhood. That was another and a higher step. You have advanced somewhat from manhood to culture and monetary assurance. And now I ask — "Where in what section of your constitution has been planted the law of belittling limitation? Into what cell of the Negro's brain has Almighty God dropt the stagnant atom of finality?

My friends, there are no ascertained bounds to the growth of any active, energetic, hopeful and ambitious race. In the world of Art, Science, Philosophy and letters, there is no pent up monopoly, which excludes *any* section of the great human family. And no spell has fallen upon the intellect of the Negro which confines *his* capacity to narrow and contracted grooves.

I am drawn to these suggestions by certain oblique tendencies of the day. Just now we are in danger of being hoodwinked by specious, but unreal

---

[10]The simple contrast of a homeless, houseless unlettered race, thirty years ago; with the growth of this people into some 3,000 Teachers, nigh 2,000,000 pupils; many Academies and Colleges, and Seminaries, *since* the day of Emancipation; should satisfy any one of the onward march of the race.

teachings, pertaining to the education of the race. Certain pseudo-phil-anthropists who pity the Negro, but cannot learn to love and to uplift him, are endeavoring to fasten upon his brain the "cordon of narrowness." Their counsel is, in substance, this: — "Keep the Negro in a narrow groove! His brain *is* narrow. Give him but a little learning! Then bind him down to the merest manual exercises! Keep him, perpetually, a clown in the fields!"

No such limitations, however, are suggested for the miserable, ofttimes brutalized immigrants, who, by tens of thousands, are landed upon our shores!

"No pent-up Utica may contract *their* powers." They, debased, not seldom half-paganized as they are, are to enter every avenue of culture in the land; to reach forth for the grandest acquisitions of both erudition and ambi-tion! But the Negro must be kept in the humblest places; must be restrained to the narrowest systems of training!

For my own part I utterly repudiate all this specious policy. It is nothing but CASTE, and that of the most injurious character! I ask indeed that there shall be "common sense, in common schooling;" that there shall be no waste of money, or, of means, upon Incapacity; that a whole host of noodles shall not be sent to Universities or Colleges; that manual labour shall be the duty and the destiny of the ordinary and unaspiring.

But when you fall upon a Scholar, an Artist, or a Genius, in any line, if even he be black as mid-night, open wide the gates; clear the pathways, for his noblest gait and his swiftest career! He has the right, by virtue of his endowments, to mount to the highest rounds of the ladder! Cheer him on his way! Give him every possible encouragement to reach the levels; and to rival, if possible, the most ambitious intellects of his age, be they as white as snow!

In the world of mind we are to tolerate neither exclusiveness nor caste. In all humanity and with self-restraint we are, as a people, to find our own place in the scale of nature, in the ranks of society, and in the order of the State.

But *we* must find it ourselves; not be forced into it by others! Hence we should resist the arrogance of that whole class of Americans, both in Church and State, who think they have a divine commission to thrust the Negro into a special place, as an underling, in American society.

Meanwhile we must study the situation in all quietness, soberness, with non-disturbance of soul, yea, even with a goodly quantum of stoicism. Withal, however, we must cultivate the spirit of Hope, perseverence, high self-reliance, and unfailing trust in God.

> "Zealous, yet modest, innocent, tho 'free,
> Serene amidst alarms, inflexible in faith!"

The great need of our race in this generation is sobriety, a deep sense of imperfection, diligence in all pursuits, simplicity in manners, and a deep and pervasive influence of the religious sentiment.

If this people get crazed by the possession of a little liberty; if they be-come intoxicated by inebriating and destructive politics; if they get carried away by the attainment of dazzling learning; if they are soon puffed up and made pompous by the grasp of a little wealth of property; and then begin to exaggerate their importance, to disgust their friends, to forget God, and so become blind to the high virtues — all hope for the future departs!

The race, in this country, is still at school. If they can learn to put away lightness, the love of pleasure, and the mere gratification of sense;

> "If they can scorn delights, and live
> Laborious days;"

if they can bring themselves to see that the life of a race, is the same as the life of a family, or the life of a man; — that is, that it is a trust from God, for the noblest purposes of humanity, and for the glory of God; they are sure to run a glad and a glorious career, if even it be a trying one; to attain the highest excellence of man; to achieve the grandest results in the majestic work which God has committed to the care of his creatures on earth.

Alongside the separate churches, separate social organizations for black people also emerged. As with the churches, it is difficult to make a clear determination of the initiative in organizing these institutions. Of course, they were in large part the result of the exclusivity of white organizations, but they also met a need of black people to associate with persons who shared their culture. For this study, it is only necessary to indicate that no matter what motives led to the formation of exclusively black social organizations, once they were formed, they constituted forums for communication among blacks, which would have been less likely to occur in integrated groups. While they could serve as places in which black people would strive to be as much like white people as possible, they could also function as a dissemination for pro-black messages.

Even before these social organizations began, Maria W. Stewart was an early advocate of black pride. In the speech included here, she remarks that she wishes only to express her views and then "... sink into oblivion, and let my name die in forgetfulness." Apparently her wish was granted, for histories of black Americans make no mention of her. However, her messages in the early 1830's are retained in the pages of the *Liberator,* and they illustrate from time to time, not only a philosophy of assimilation based on self-reliance but also a moderately separatist rhetoric.

Like most speakers of the time, Mrs. Stewart was primarily motivated by her Christian dedication, and her persuasion includes a call for black support of abolition. But she clearly aims causes the word "nationalism" to be less valuable than the term "separatism." Finally, separatism seems to be a more universal term, within which the nationalistic aspects can be included as well as other phases of rhetorical behaviors that are properly related.

As a strategy for achieving the ultimate goal of a good life — freedom, liberty, identity, etc. — the idea of separation from white racist people and institutions can be advocated as the only viable alternative in the face of the failure of assimilation. Second, it can be advanced as a positive good for the preservation of black culture and racial identity; and third, it can be held as an instrumentality to the eventual accomplishment of some form of integration, if not assimilation.

THE FUTILITY OF ASSIMILATION

The most compelling reason for supporting separation or assimilation is the black American's conviction that the charge "..." that the idea of black American, is answered with the charge "..."; that the idea of black American will not really an integral recognition that he lives within the borders convenient formal acceptance of the Negro as a full-fledged American and will of the United States. From the white's point of view, the "they." This attitude is most extreme expression in the Southern is not related to the "we," the Negro is the nation in varying modes of tude assumes its most extreme the nation differentiates the Negro's states and spreads out over the nation which differentiates that his position racial mores. The only factor status is that his proximity to the status from that of a pure colonial in close proximity to the is maintained in the "home" country dominant racial group.'

Negroes have never been equal to whites of any class in economic, social, cultural, or political status, and very few whites of any class have ever regarded them as such. Beyond the borders of the American nation the Negro is utopian ideal is answered with this assertion: the eventual acceptance, creed, or color, is also utopian and will without regard to race, Cruse goes on to make this assertion: never be realized."[8] Cruse goes on to make this assertion:

With this analysis, the author concludes that it is not surprising that a nationalistic philosophy and separation have been developed.

If both integration and separation are seen as almost two unlikely goals, then black men have been forced to debate two unlikely alternatives. Thus, the question regarding separation becomes more reasonable when it is viewed as a course of action which may be an improvement over subjugated status. In the analysis

---

on the white man (although she does
o his own advancement) and exhorta-
e and work for their own good. She
833 speech to the African Masonic
is frequently heard in speeches of
or of the black man has formed the
ccess of White America:

> k as far as you can see — all,
> , except here and there a lowly
> r, midst deprivation, fraud and
> le to procure. Like king Solo-
> hammer to the temple, yet
> the white Americans gained
> s of the great men that are
> have been their principal
> pursued the shadow, they
> have performed the labor,
> have planted the vines,

e with this analysis of the
wealth and prominence of
particularly appealing to
ences are strongly inclined
inclusion in a speech should foster a
identity and pride, and facilitate the agreement
other ideas contained in the speech.

In the address included below, Mrs. Stewart carefully seeks to establish identification with her audience, implicitly through her strong pro-Christian statements and explicitly when she says,

> I am a strong advocate for the cause of God, and for the cause of freedom. I am not your enemy, but a friend both to you and to your children."

Notice also how, in this speech, she seeks to convince the audience of the need for self-help without seeming to be inconsistent with reliance on God:

> God has said that Ethiopia shall stretch forth her hands unto him. True, but God uses means to bring about His purposes; and unless that rising generation manifest a different temper and disposition towards each other from what we have manifested, the generation following will never be an enlightened people.[18]

Maria W. Stewart

*An Address**

Delivered before the Afric-American Female Intelligence Society of Boston. By Mrs. Maria W. Stewart.

The frowns of the world shall never discourage me, nor its smiles flatter me; for with the help of God I am resolved to withstand the fiery darts of the devil, and the assaults of wicked men. The righteous are as bold as a lion, but the wicked flee where no man pursueth. I fear neither men nor devils; for the God in whom I trust is able to deliver me from the rage and malice of my enemies, and from them that rise up against me. The only motive that has prompted me to raise my voice in your behalf, my friends, is because I have discovered that religion is held in low repute amongst some of us; and purely to promote the cause of Christ and the good of souls, in the hope that others more experienced, more able and talented than myself, might go forward and do likewise. I expect to render a strict, a solemn, and an awful account to God for the motives that have prompted me to exertion, and for those with which I shall address you this evening.

What I have to say, concerns the whole of us as Christians and as a people; and if you will be so kind as to give me a hearing this once, you shall receive the incense of a grateful heart.

The day is coming, my friends, and I rejoice in that day, when the secrets of all hearts shall be manifested before saints and angels, men and devils. It will be a great day of joy and rejoicing to the humble following of Christ, but a day of terror and dismay to hypocrites and unbelievers. Of that day and hour knoweth no man, no not even the angels in heaven, but the Father only. The dead that are in Christ shall be raised first. Blessed is he that shall have a part in the first resurrection. Ah, methinks I hear the finally impenitent crying, "Rocks and mountains! fall upon us, and hide us from the wrath of the Lamb, and from him that sitteth upon the throne!

> High on a cloud our God shall come,
>   Bright thrones prepare his way;
> Thunder and darkness, fire and storm,
>   Lead on the dredful day.

Christ shall descend in the clouds of heaven, surrounded by ten thousand of his saints and angels, and it shall be very tempestous round about him; and before him shall be gathered all nations, and kindred, and tongues, and people; and every knee shall bow, and every tongue confess — they also that pierced him shall look upon him, and mourn. Then shall the King separate the righteous from the wicked, as a shepherd divideth the sheep from the goats, and shall place the righteous on his right hand, and the wicked upon

---

*Maria W. Stewart, an address delivered in Boston, Massachusetts. *The Liberator,* April 28, 1832, pp. 66-67.

...ver of Muhammad, ...drawal from existing society, seeking an ...tion of intra-black solidarity, conceived of black nationalism a separate territory in America. Intra-black nationalism national closing of ranks for black solidarity included Even when he considered the possibility of peace among all men regardless of color he said:

I kept having all kinds of troubles trying to develop the kind of Black Nationalist organization I wanted to build for the American Negro. Why Black Nationalism? Well, in the com- petitive American society, how can there ever be any white- black solidarity before there is first some black solidarity?

Of course, the idea of nationalism implies a related rhetoric of anti-colonialism. In the case of black Americans, the messages of black nationalism describe black people in the United States as a subjugated people, little different from those in Africa, Asia, and Latin and South America, who have been or still are under the domination of a colonial government. Malcolm X proposed taking the case of black Americans before the United Nations, while Stokely Charmichael and Charles Hamilton, discussed in Chapter I, describe the work of the black American Nationalist in terms of the "politics of liberation in America."

The concept of "nationalism" is somewhat more positive than the concept of "separatism" as it suggests the uniting of a given people, rather than separation from another people or peo- ples. For this reason, it might have been a more desirable term to use. However, "nationalism" also has a propaganda connota- tion which seems to restrict its usefulness in a scholarly study. Its very association with the anti-colonial movements around the world, and the frequent association of them, in the mind of Americans, with pro-communist activities, whether true or not,

his left. Then, says Christ, shall be weeping, and wailing, and gnashing of teeth, when ye shall see Abraham and the prophets sitting in the Kingdom of heaven, and ye yourselves thrust out. Then shall the righteous shine forth in the Kingdom of their Father as the sun. He that hath ears to hear, let him hear. The poor despised followers of Christ will not then regret their sufferings here; they shall be carried by angels into Abraham's bosom, and shall be comforted; and the Lord God shall wipe away their tears. You will then be convinced before assembled multitudes, whether they strove to promote the cause of Christ, or whether they sought for gain or applause. "Strive to enter in at the strait gait; for many, I say unto you, shall seek to enter in, and shall not be able. For except your righteousness shall exceed the righteousness of the Scribes and Pharisees, ye shall in no wise enter into the Kingdom of Heaven."

Ah, methinks I see the people lying in wickedness; and as the Lord liveth, and as your souls live, were it not for the few righteous that are to be found amongst us, we should become as Sodom, and like unto Gomorrah. Christians have too long slumbered and slept; sinners stumbled into hell, and still are stumbling, for the want of Christian exertion; and the devil is going about like a roaring lion, seeking whom he may devour. And I make bold to say, that many who profess the name of Christ at the present day, live so widely different from what becommeth the Gospel of our Lord Jesus Christ, that they cannot and they dare not reason to the world upon righteousness and judgment to come.

Be not offended because I tell you the truth; for I believe that God has fired my soul with a holy zeal for his cause. It was God alone who inspired my heart to publish the Meditations thereof; and it was done with pure motives of love to your souls, in the hope that Christians might examine themselves, and sinners become pricked in their hearts. It is the word of God, though men and devils may oppose it. It is the word of God; and little did I think that any of the professed followers of Christ would have frowned upon me, and discouraged and hindered its progress.

Ah, my friends, I am speaking as one who expects to give account at the ear of God; I am speaking as a dying mortal to dying mortals. I fear there are many who have named the name of Jesus at the present day that strain a gnat and swallow a camel; they neither enter into the kingdom of heaven themselves, nor suffer others to enter in. They would pull the motes out of their brother's eye, when they have a beam in their own eye. And were our blessed Lord and Saviour, Jesus Christ, upon the earth, I believe he would say of many that are called by his name, "O ye hypocrites, ye generation of vipers, how can you escape the damnation of hell."

I have enlisted in the holy warfare, and Jesus is my captain; and the Lord's battle I mean to fight, until my voice expire in death. I expect to be hated of all men, and persecuted even unto death for righteousness and the truth's sake.

A few remarks upon moral subjects, and I close. I am a strong advocate for the cause of God, and for the cause of freedom. I am not your enemy, but a friend both to you and to your children. Suffer me, then, to express my sentiments just this once, however severe they may appear to be, and then hereafter let me sink into oblivion, and let my name die in forgetfulness.

Had the ministers of the gospel shunned the very appearance of evil; had they faithfully discharged their duty, whether we would have heard them or not; we should have been a very different people from what we now are; but they have kept the truth as it were hid from our eyes, and have cried, "Peace! Peace!" when there was no peace; they have plastered us up with untempered morter, and have been as it were blind leaders of their blind.

It appears to me that there are no people under the heavens, so unkind and so unfeeling towards their own, as are the descendants of fallen Africa. I have been something of a traveller in my day; and the general cry amongst the people is, "Our own color are our greatest opponents;" — and even the whites say that we are greater enemies towards each other, than they are towards us. Shall we be a hissing and a reproach among the nations of the earth any longer! Shall they laugh us to scorn forever? We might become a highly respectable people; respectable we now consider ourselves, but we might become a highly distinguished and intelligent people. And how? In convincing the world, by our own efforts, however feeble, that nothing is wanting on our part but opportunity. Without these efforts, we shall never be a people, nor our descendants after us.

But God has said that Ethiopia shall stretch forth her hands unto him. True, but God uses means to bring about His purposes; and unless the rising generation manifest a different temper and disposition towards each other from what we have manifested, the generation following will never be an enlightened people. We this day are considered as one of the most degraded races upon the face of the earth. It is useless for us any longer to sit with our hands folded, reproaching the whites; for that will never elevate us. All the nations of the earth have distinguished themselves, and have shown forth a noble and a gallant spirit. Look at the suffering Greeks. Their proud souls revolted at the idea of serving a tyrannical nation, who were no better than themselves, and perhaps not so good. They made a mighty effort and arose; their souls were knit together in the holy bonds of love and union; they were united, and came off victorious. Look at the French in the late-revolution! no traitors amongst them, to expose their plans to the crowned heads of Europe! "Liberty or Death!" was their cry. And the Haytians, though they have not been acknowledged as a nation, yet their firmness of character and independence of spirit have been greatly admired and highly applauded. Look at the Poles, a feeble people! They rose against three hundred thousand mighty men of Russia; and though they did not gain the conquest, yet they obtained the name of gallant Poles. And even the wild Indians of the forest are more united than ourselves. Insult one of them, and you insult a thousand. They also have contended for their rights and privileges, and are held in higher repute than we are.

And why is it, my friends, that we are despised above all the nations upon the earth? Is it merely because our skins are tinged with a sable hue? No, nor will I ever believe that it is. What then is it? Oh, it is because that we and our fathers have dealt treacherously one with another, and because many of us now possess that envious and malicious disposition, that we had rather die than see each other rise an inch above a beggar. No gentle methods are used to promote love and friendship amongst us, but much is done to destroy it. Shall we be a hissing and a reproach amongst the nations of the earth any longer? Shall they laugh us to scorn forever?

Ingratitude is one of the worst passions that reigns in the human breast: it is this that cuts the tender fibers of the soul; for it is impossible for us to love those who are ungrateful towards us. "Behold," says that wise man Solomon, counting one by one, "a man have I found in a thousand, but a woman among all these have I not found."

I have sometimes thought, that God had almost departed from among us. And why? Because we hate our brother, we are liars, and the truth is not in us; and certainly if we were the true followers of Christ, I think we could not show such a disposition towards each other as we do — for God is all love.

A lady of high distinction among us, observed to me, that I might never expect your homage. God forbid! I ask it not. But I beseech you to deal with gentleness and godly sincerity towards me; and there is not one of you, my dear friends, who has given me a cup of cold water in the name of the Lord, or soothed the sorrows of my wounded heart, but God will bless, not only you, but your children for it. Cruel indeed, are those that indulge such an opinion respecting me as that.

Finally, I have exerted myself both for your temporal and eternal welfare, as far as I am able; and my soul has been so discouraged within me, that I have almost been induced to exclaim, "Would to God that my tongue hereafter might cleave to the roof of my mouth, and become silent forever!" and then I have felt that the Christian has no time to be idle, and I must be active, knowing that the night of death cometh, in which no man can work — and my mind has become raised to such as extent, that I will willingly die for the cause that I have espoused — for I cannot die in a more glorious cause than in the defence of God and his laws.

O woman, woman! upon you I call; for upon your exertions almost entirely depends whether the rising generations shall be any thing more than we have been or not. O woman, woman! your example is powerful, your influence great; it extends over your husbands and over your children, and throughout the circle of your acquaintance. Then let me exhort you to cultivate among yourselves a spirit of Christian love and unity, having charity one for another, without which all our goodness is as sounding brass, and as a tinkling cymbal. And O, my God, I beseech thee to grant that the nations of the earth may hiss at us no longer! O suffer them not to laugh us to scorn forever!

In Chapter II it was observed that the 1954 decision of the Supreme Court, Brown v. Board of Education of Topeka, Kansas, reversed the decision made in the 1895, Plessey v. Ferguson case, which allowed separate but equal schools for white and black children. Outwardly, the voluminous discussion of the 1954 decision would suggest that the black community was unanimous in its opposition to separate schools. This was not the case. The impression probably comes from the fact that for most black children in this country, from the earliest time to the present, separate school systems were the status quo, and any rhetoric concerning segregated education would be that aimed at changing the status quo. For the most part, those who approved of separation in education had no need of persuasion — there was little likelihood of it coming to an end, and thus little need to argue in its favor.

Early in this century, however, shortly after the Supreme Court published its 1895 decision making separation constitutionally acceptable, some debate among black people did occur. The author of the essay printed here, John Henry Smyth,[19] was one of the pro-separatist advocates. Smyth was born in 1844 in Richmond, his father a slave and his mother free.[20] His education came in Quaker schools, the Academy of Fine Arts of Philadelphia, Pennsylvania, and Howard University Law School. He was politically active, spent seven years as the United States resident minister and consul-general to Liberia, and practiced law in Washington, D.C. His thesis in the essay that follows is a clear call for racial integrity and pride. Education, particularly at the elementary level, he states, is the place for children to learn of their cultural heritage and prepare themselves to become active and effective members of their group. Once they have become adults, they will be able to mingle with members of other races without feeling threatened and without weakening their personal effectiveness. His major premise, although unstated, is clearly the assertion that the maintenance of racial identity is the most desirable path to the highest goals of man. "Our position," Smyth continues, "as a distinct race, liberated and enfranchised, has advantages, which if appreciated will make our future enviable." In a style used successfully by John F. Kennedy and disastrously by Barry M. Goldwater, Smyth says, ". . . all this must impress us that commingling may not be growth, and separation may not be sterility." If one accepts the idea that the black race has inherently superior characteristics, which Smyth and other separatists suggest, then the thesis in favor of segregated schools becomes compelling.

John H. Smyth

From *The Color line in Ohio**

Genesis, Ch. XIII, paragraph 9

"Is not the whole land before *thee?* Separate thyself, I pray thee, from me! If thou wilt take the left hand, then I will go to the right, or if thou depart to the right hand, then I will go to the left."

The Cincinati [*sic.*] Commercial Gazette in its article upon the troubles of the whites and blacks in Felicity and Chilicothe [*sic.*], Ohio arising from the attempted exclusion of Negro pupils from the public schools in common with the whites says: 'This movement has gone so far that there is at present a petition being circulated widely through out the country, which is being signed by almost everybody, asking the legislature to repeal the present law respecting colored schools, and that separate schools be again declared legal. Excitement is even running a little higher than that, and there is a good deal of talk going around now to the effect that all colored people in the city, and especially those in the "shoe string" district, be boycotted and refused employment of all kinds.'

The Atlanta Constitution in its comment upon the matter makes this statement, which reflects the *real sentiment* of the white people of the country: "Anglo Saxon human nature is very much the same everywhere, and the race problem is bound to receive the same treatment in the North that it receives in the South. The just settlement of the whole business is to give the whites and blacks *separate* but *equal privileges* and accomodations in all public places, schools, cars and all buildings and conveyances intended for the convenience of the people. This system works satisfactorily in Georgia and there is no reason why it should not suit other sections. It does not work any injustice to either race, and it is impossible to see how any self-respecting colored man can be against it. The separate system is just as fair to one race as it is to the other. Justice is its very essence."

Now in our reflections upon this matter of the desire of the colored people in Ohio to have their children taught in mixed schools, the common schools of the state which are supported by the taxes paid by the citizens of the state without reference to race; and the opposition of the white people to their admission to the same schools, we shall be governed by common sense, and the reason for which the Negro Children should be sent to school, and the result ultimately expected to come from school training.

The issue is made up; the Negroes want the right protected by enforcement of *the law,* and the whites want the right abrogated by repeal of the law. That any act on the part of any citizen or citizens which obstructs the exer-

---

*John H. Smyth, "The Color line in Ohio," apparently delivered in Washington, D.C. Reprinted from the Schomburg Collection of the John E. Bruce Papers, Harlem Branch of the New York Public Library, New York City, New York.

cise of *the right* of the colored people is wrongful and illegal no law abiding and intelligent citizen will question. The failure of the courts to punish the whites who interfered with the Negroes, is an evidence that white public sentiment in the locality-Felicity, is opposed to the law, and the actions of the whites in Chillicothe shows their sympathy with the white obstructionists in Felicity. The absence of protest from the leading papers of the country, edited by whites is an implied indication of sympathy with the whites of Ohio in this matter, or of indifference to it altogether. The view of the "Constitution" is clearly defined in opposition to the mixing of the races, and in opposition to the rights guaranteed under the law.

But aside from this, ought the Negro race in the United States thing [sic] beyond equality of rights, rather than identy [sic] of rights. We think that the colored people should insist upon equality but not the same rights: that is, the appropriation of an equal amount of money arising from taxation for the education of black children regulated by numbers as is given for white children, the construction in convenient localities to the black pupils homes of as good school buildings as are given the whites convenient to their homes; and the supply of as competent black teachers for black children, as white teachers employed to teach white children; that the the [sic] compensation for teachers of the same grade should be as much for black teachers as white teachers, in short; that there be no difference made in the expenditure of the public money for one class in favor of the other. With rare exceptions, a black teacher in schools in which the children are of both races is very rare in Ohio and throughout the country.

The education of the children and youth of a race, ought first to be in the interest of the progress moral, intellectual and religious of that race, and secondary to this, the good of the state of which they are citizens, the nation of which they constitute a part. Now the education of the blacks and whites *in common* is not a necessity to the attainment of these objects.

If this were not true then up to eighty seven the separate education of the Negro Children and youth would have produced inferior scholarship, inferior character and inferior citizens to those who have been taught in common, with the whites since that time. Look around you, look behind you, and look before you, and determine by what you see and know whether the black men and the black women who received their rudimentary training from their black parents at home, and . . . [manuscript indecipherable] teachers at school, or white teachers in school where there were only black pupils, and answer the question, are they inferior in moral character, in mental achievements, and in citizenship as those who have been taught in mixed schools. The answer, if made, must be — "that they are not!" No pretension is made that such results have flown from the mixed system and opposite results from the unmixed custom. Is it contended anywhere that the men and women of the race who have been trained in mixed schools, that their learning has accomplished *better results* for their race than those who have been separately trained? Has not their training, in too many instances, removed them, in their sympathies and concern for their race, further from it than the training of those who from first to last in schools and out of them have been constantly in contact with their own people? As an evidence of the more beneficial effect of the training of the race by the race, we beg to call attention to the fact of the education of native Africans and Haitian children in Europe. The censensus of opinion in both countries upon this subject is, that the *children* taken from Africa and Haiti to Europe for training, are less useful and loyal Africans and Haitians than those who tho' possessed of less erudition and polish show greater ability . . . [manuscript indecipherable], are more manly, and womanly, and self respecting, more conscious of their man and womanhood than those who went from home to be educated, and returned learned but out of harmony with those whose interests their learning was designed to conserve.

Of the young men and women of the race in the United States, without fear of successful denial, we are of opinion that, those who even with restricted opportunities have done most in the upbuilding of the masses, are they who have been educated in separate schools and by teachers of their own race, rather than those who have the learning of the Universities, and have required the vices and follies of white gentlemen's sons, without their means and opportunity in life, and without their hereditary tendencies, which are a restraining force to acquired license.

All successful mental work for the individual as well as the masses should take into account, personality, individuality. Now races have individuality, and are distinguished by difference just as individuals, and the training that conduces to the evolving and developement [sic.] of the best in character, is the best and wisest system of education.

"The teacher is, or should be, first, last and always, a developer. If he sees no further than methods as set before him by others; if he assumes that one method will suit all his pupils equally well; if he believes that there is any one invariably best method, he will become a machine. [Manuscript indecipherable]. To him the knowledge of the development of man from more primitive conditions is the study of all studies. His great aim should be to carry on in some measure this progress, this evolution or unfolding, for we know as yet but indifferently the possibilities for mankind." Equally important is the study of the individual, and it is the neglect of this that constitutes perhaps the greatest danger of modern education. We adapt our methods to human nature as we conceive of it, but is the individual as much considered as he was?

The tendency of the age is to aggregation of men, to concerted action, to adaptation of methods to the masses, to the average man or boy, or girl, while John Smith and Eliza Brown are apt to be regarded as simply units and nothing more. If I were asked to state what I considered the greatest evil threatening education or actually existing in education; if not in our entire civilization today, I should reply that in my opinion it was just what I have referred to — not recognizing the individual as such in the masses."

There are races, as there are individuals. [Manuscript indecipherable] . . . [T]here is a nearness of all white races to each other, and a corresponding remoteness of the Negro race from them. The admission of the existence of races carries with it the idea of difference. The educator in the mixed schools, if he be capable, and conscientious, must conform his instruction with due reference to difference of race. Can he successfully do it, in the presence and surrounding of both races, and the great preponderance of the one race over the other?

If it be conceded that race individuality is an element to be accounted with in school training, think you that a Celtic father as a rule would, as a matter of preference, send his child to be taught by a Saxon teacher rather than a Celtic one, all things be equal as to the teacher's capacities? Certainly not. Germany is, perhaps, as learned as France. She points to a more illustrious line of savants, but French parents do not send their children to Heidelburg and Leipsic for schooling, but they school them at home, because they mean that their children shall be French, and by education shall develop the best in Frankish character.

We know how natural it is for a people who have known common schools, high schools, colleges and universities for just thrity [sic.] years; and who for life times of fifty, sixty and four score years have looked upon the progress of a magnificent civilization which is misnamed American, to conclude that contact close and intimate with such a comingling of Aryan races is likely to produce better results than reliance upon themselves, and those of their race as educators who have drank of the Pierian waters . . . [manuscript indecipherable].

"In the world of letters at least, the Southern states have shone by reflected light, nor is it too much to say, that mainly by their connection with the North, the Carolinas have been saved from sinking to the level of Mexico and the Antillies. [Manuscript indecipherable].

"Orphaned of the solemn inspiration of antiquity", they gain in surface what they have lost in age; in hope what they have lost in memory."

"That untravelled world whose margin fades Forever and forever when they move," is all their own, and they have the arena and expectations of a continent to set against the culture and the ancestral voices of a thousand years. Where Englishmen remember, Americans anticipate. In thought and action they are ever rushing into empty spaces. The habit of instability, fostered by the rapid vicissitudes of their commercial life and the melting of one class into another, drifts away all land marks but that of temporary public opinion; and where there is little time for verification and study of details, men satisfy their curiosity by crude generalizations." Bred in English habits of thought as most of us are, we have not yet modified our instincts to the necessities of our new modes of life. Our philosophers have not yet taught us what is best, nor have our poets sung to us what is most beautiful in the kind of life that we must lead, and therefore, we still read the old English wisdom, and harp upon the ancient strings. Bancroft's statements of matters of fact are generally reliable, but his comments are moulded even more than is usual by the foregone theories of a political partisan." Nine tenths of their literary performances will prove ephemeral, less from lack of ability in the writers than from an utterly inadequate sense of the time and toil that every true muse demands of her voteries. [Manuscript indecipherable].

Our position as a distinct race, liberated and enfranchised, has advantages, which if appreciated will make our future enviable.

In moral stamina we are equals of the American whites, in Christian force — faith, we by reason of that race peculiarity, we are more Godly; as a consequence of our political opportunity, we are the unnamed legatees of the civilizations dimmed by time, and of those existent.

A rightful comprehension of the fact that, we have more interest in ourselves than it is reasonable to expect others to have in us, and that sympathy in training of the young, next to capacity, and likenesses of the teacher to the taught rather than unlikeness, are effective of the best results, and are inspiratioms [sic.]

Benjamin Bannaker, Bishop Allen, Henry Highland Garnett, Robert Brown Elliott, Oscar J. Dunn, William Whipper, Bishops Moore and Payne, and Professor J. C. Price, did herculian race work in isolation. They might have been lost in contact, to themselves and to the race.

Now, if this course were pursued, separation with equal opportunities are contended for under republican forms of government, according to the natural capacities of the black children, there would be developed as fully as school training is capable of developing the mind, the best there is in the black pupils.

(signed) John H. Smyth

1448 Pierea Place
Washington, D. C.

A good summary for this section on the moderate separatism developed in rhetoric of racial pride, cohesiveness, and advancement, is provided in an article by the Reverend Charles E. Lord, first published in the New York *Observer,* and republished by Frederick Douglass in his *New Era* on June 30, 1870. Lord uses an enthymeme similar to that of Crummell when he sets out as a major premise the theory that any race that persists and thrives in the face of adversity must possess extraordinary characteristics worthy of preservation. Lord relies more on evidence from comparisons of the black race with other races that failed, and less on a religious conviction that God has marked the race for special position. Since the "African race" has survived and prospered under the restraints of slavery, Lord concludes that it has special merit:

> I believe that the African race does possess peculiar traits of character, that under suitable cultivation will give to it a high position in the world. How could any race have borne better the embarrassment and the injustice of slavery, than the black race?[21]

Certainly, states this author, it cannot be said the black man is incapable of self-defense or lacks courage — too much evidence of his participation in past wars exists to support the charge. What, then, are the special characteristics of this group?

But the possibilities of the African race are great, when we reflect upon their emotional and sympathetic nature as related to their religious susceptibilities. This race does have a peculiar type of religious sensibility. It does carry, in the very framework of their mind and hearts, something that every intelligent observer sees to be essentially different from the character of the white population of our country. There is an African idiosyncrasy impossible to imitate, and peculiarly characteristic of the black race; not more sharply defined is the Jewish mind than is the universal stamp of the African mind. Their very civilization belongs to the tropics; and it is a civilization far more favorable to Christianity than that which often appears in the white race. Who that has been a resident of the South, has mingled freely in their religious congregations and listened to their melodies, so true to nature and so destitute of art — who that has observed their soul for music, and yet noticed their perfect simplicity, that has not been struck with the wide contrast between the blacks and the whites?"

Having established the conclusion that the race has characteristics worthy of perpetuation — especially the claim that the black man is more suited to Christianity than the white — Lord proceeds to an appeal for separation of the races.

Now, are all the African race traits to be merged in other races, so that they shall lose all that distinguishes them from the white class? Rather is not the African for Africa just as truly as the Anglo-Saxons are for the temperate zone? May not the tropics yet reveal a civilization not more unique in its nature than luxuriant, and beautiful as that vegitation, which blooms with a perpetual green and is fragrant with the incense of perpetual flowers. Is this diversity of civilization to be worked upon as a determent, to be viewed as reflecting upon that fair Anglo-Saxon type? Rather as we view the stars, so different, shining down upon us from the blue sky; rather as the telescope tells us of suns revolving around suns, and worlds each unique with their peculiar color, forms, motion, climate and distances, so also on this earth God intends to be glorified with endless diversity of mental, moral and physical development, and involve from the mighty whole a nobler beauty than would appear in that sameness which would grow from one universal type of manhood.

Is it not evident that the colored race have a destiny of their own? Should they not be encouraged to emulate the white race, not by a service [sic.] imitation, not by being ashamed of the color God has given to them, not by ignoring those race traits that will always distinguish them from the whites; but by respecting their own race and color, their own peculiar idiosyncrasy of body, mind, and heart? As the great wheel of time turns around and the ages roll on from earth's infancy to its full grown stature, the day may come for an African civilization, diverse indeed, but, for aught we know, as that which has ever visited most favored nations of the Anglo-Saxon, Norman, or Celtic race.

The slogan, "Black is beautiful," appearing one hundred years later, is very much an off-spring of this moderate separatism.

PRO-COLONIZATION

If the end of all persuasion is action, then the goal of separatist rhetoric is the physical removal of the black man from the white and *vice versa*. This action was proposed as early as 1714 by white men, and by 1815, Paul Cuffe, a black ship owner, had traveled to Africa to discover a promising site for colonization and returned to Sierra Leone with thirty-eight other black men to settle the country.[22] The establishment of the American Colonization Society in 1816 under the sponsorship of governmentally powerful white men, created considerable controversy within the black community. Once the society was in existence, the debate could no longer continue along the clear lines of assimilation-separation. As before, the existence of black men, both slave and free in the same country, caused dissonance in the minds of the free blacks. They could do little to advance their own position *vis-a-vis* the white society without feeling as if they were deserting their enslaved brothers. Yet, they were unwilling to stop all progress pending the abolition of slavery. Colonization, with its obvious motivations on the part of slaveholders to rid the nation of free blacks who challenged the continuance of slavery, merely increased the dissonance among the free blacks. Even pro-separatist leaders such as Richard Allen found themselves unable to support the movement because of its potential to assist slaveholders. The pro-integrationist black men would certainly oppose colonization but, as it developed, so did the pro-separatists. The incongruity of motives, according to Franklin, doomed colonization.[23]

No matter how repugnant the American Colonization Society, the idea on which it was based was appealing to a number of black Americans, and it was inevitable that some of them would feel moved to speak in favor of the plan to return to Africa.

Franklin records that shortly after the formation of the Colonization Society, a group of "free Negroes . . . met in Richmond
and mildly approved of the idea of colonization. . . .[24] Reportedly,
six hundred dollars was donated by black citizens of Dayton,
Ohio in 1845 to support colonization after they heard a white
speaker read a letter allegedly written by two black men, William
and Thomas Abney. The letter said the black men asked to go
to Africa because of their

> . . . unhappiness at viewing the white man's privileges which
> were unattainable for the Negro. They were discouraged at
> the fruitless efforts for these privileges in America so they ex-
> pressed a desire to go to Africa where, beside these privileges,
> they could aid in supressing the slave trade and bring the
> 'blessings of civilization and Christianity to Africa.'[25]

Unfortunately, there is some reason to believe the letter was, in
fact, a piece of rhetorical fiction created by white men.[26]

In many places in the North, conventions of black men met
to debate the colonization proposal. Ohio was a significant state
in this effort, for many conventions were held there involving the
black population that had come to the state from the South. In
July of 1849, a group met in Cincinnati and declared that they
despaired of seeing the prejudice of the whites against their
people eliminated for two reasons; first, blacks are all the descendants of slaves and the vain whites would never give social
equality; and second, the blacks have neither the numbers nor
intelligence to enforce political equality.[27] The convention decided to form an association for the purpose of emigrating to the
coast of Africa.

While most of the conventions concluded with resolutions
opposing colonization, an examination of the debate which led
to these conclusions is instructive. First, it must be noted that
there was probably some argument in favor of colonization at
each convention, although it may have constituted no more than
a fraction of the total arguments. Second, as will be seen, some
of those speaking for colonization were men of significance.
Third, the evidence of one debate suggests that some of the
anti-colonization sentiment was prompted more from fear of
retaliation by abolitionist whites than non-separatist conviction.
As suggested earlier, the separation-integration debate is one
that must be conducted largely out of the hearing of white men,
if it is to allow an honest examination of the merits. The colonization movement at this time was a national black-white phenomenon which necessarily precluded this factor.

The State Convention of The Colored Citizens of Ohio convened in Columbus, Ohio on January 10 through 13, 1849 and
considered thirty-three resolutions, one of which concerned the
colonization plan.[28] At the fourth session of the convention, a
motion rejecting colonization was considered. This excerpt from
the minutes gives the secretary's report of the debate.

Mr. Jenkins was opposed to the resolution, thought there were
circumstances under which it would be beneficial to emigrate.

L. Dow Taylor rose to correct Mr. Jenkins, thought he did
not understand the true import of the resolution. Mr. Jenkins
did not stand corrected. He said he was in favor of a scheme
whereby we all might move out of the United States. He said
he thought "there was a great change going on in the minds
of the people." He prayed God that it would go on faster. We
never can be anything in the United States. Mr. J. said that,
two years ago while traveling in the State of New York, he
always had the benefit of two seats. Why was it? said he. So
far as he was concerned, he would always be found battling
for his people.

J. L. Watson of Cuyhoga [Cleveland], said he was in
favor of the resolution, and he was ready and willing to contest every point with any and all of its friends. He said our
"Pilgrim Fathers," who first came to this country, were *not*
colonized. But what was it sir, that brought them here? Their
indomitable love of liberty. Their unabated hatred to tyranny,
and firm resolve to be freemen. Go to Liberia, said Mr. W.,
become President, Senator, Judge, or what not. Come to this
country and see how the founders of this scheme will treat
you. I hope the resolution will pass.

Mr. Williams thought the resolution ought to be discussed
with great care, as it affected not only this State, but every
State in the Union. He said that he did not want to look up to
the white man for every thing. We must have nationality. I am
for going any where, so we can be an independent people.

Mr. Depp said he never would favor any scheme of colonization, he believed that God created all men free and equal.
We have come here for our rights, and our rights we will
have. His motto should be, *"Fight on, fight ever.'*

Mr. J. S. Thompson said he was in favor of the resolution.
The principle of it was correct. He hoped it would pass.

Mr. J. Mercer Langston [see Chapter III], here addressed
the Convention as follows:

Mr. President, I regret exceedingly that this question
has been forced upon the Convention. But trusting as we do,
in the omnipotence of truth, we are willing and ready to "battle
on and battle ever." The resolution goes against the emigration

of the colored people, free and bond, of the United States. I for one, sir, am willing, dearly as I love my native land, (a land which will not protect me however,) to leave it, and go wherever I can be free. We have already drank too long the cup of bitterness and woe, and do gentlemen want to drink it any longer? The spirit of our people must be aroused, they must feel and act as men. Let them proclaim from hill-top and valley, the memorable sentence given birth to by a Roman slave, *"Homo sum atque nihil humani a me alienum puto."* The prejudices, he said, were strong in this country, against the colored man, and he was fearful that they would remain so. He thought we must have a nationality, before we can become any body. Why sir, the very fact of our remaining in this country, is humiliating, virtually acknowledging our inferiority to the white man; I hope sir, that gentlemen, will vote down the Resolution.

Mr. Wilson and several others took part in the discussion, but the Secretary being obliged to leave, can not report what they said.[29]

The motion was referred to a committee consisting of John L. Watson of Cuyahoga County, William H. Burnham of Muskingum County, and John Mercer Langston, who later was to become the Dean of the Howard University Law School and an eloquent spokesman for legal measures to achieve equal rights. By the next morning, the committee reported a two-to-one split, with the following majority report submitted by Burnham and Langston:

Whereas, the question of colonization in the United States, is being greatly agitated, and whereas, certain colored men, together with whites, in the United States, have taken a position relatively to the matter which we deem incorrect, detrimental and destructive to our interest; and whereas, we deem it expedient for us to define our position on this point, determined at any hazard whatever, never to submit to any scheme of colonization, in any part of the world, in or out of the United States, while a vestige of slavery lasts; therefore,

Resolved, That in the event of universal emancipation, taking our freed brother as our coadjutor and helper in the work, prompted by the spirit of the fathers of '76, and following the light of liberty yet flickering in our minds, we are willing, it being optional, to draw out from the American government, and form a separate and independent one, enacting our own laws and regulations, trusting for success only in the God of Liberty and the Controller of human destiny.

The minority report suggested by Watson, said this:

GENTLEMEN OF THE CONVENTION: —
The undersigned, a minority of the committee to which was
referred the following resolution, would respectfully recommend
its adoption.
   Resolved, That we will never submit to the system of
colonization to any part of the world, in or out of the United
States; and we say, once for all, to those soliciting us, that all
of their appeals to us are in vain. Our minds are made up to
remain in the United States, and contend for our rights at all
hazards.[30]

John M. Langston led off the debate which followed the committee's report.

Mr. J. Mercer Langston hoped the report of the minority would
not be adopted. The gentleman in his private opinion is with
us, but he is afraid to express himself. But sir, if I have a
private opinion I will speak it out. If you ask a white man
whether you may associate with his daughter, or whether you
may marry her, he will tell you, *no!* I want to separate myself
from such a government. Gentlemen, if you go to Oberlin,
there you will find a colored school, brought into existence
on account of prejudice even *there.* Will any gentleman deny
this?
   Mr. Day arose and said, "I deny it." Mr. L. asked for the
proof. Mr. Day called on Mr. Thomas Brown, Vice President
of the Convention, and one of the trustees of the school in
question, and who had in his possession the original papers
for founding the school. Mr. Brown arose, and was about to
speak in denial of Mr. Langston's assertion when Pres. Langston decided the whole matter out of order.
   Mr. Watson of Cuyahoga said that the gentleman, (Mr.
J. M. Langston,) had misrepresented him. He was not with
him. He was opposed to colonization. He was unwilling that a
single sentiment should emanate from him in favor of the
scheme.
   Elder Shelton said that there never was a nation situated
like ourselves. We are free-born Americans, but are robbed
of our rights by our American-born brethren. A portion of
us have the elective franchise, and exercising that right in
common with others, love the soil upon which we were born.
I would say to gentlemen, stay where you are, and never
think of leaving this land as long as one chain is to be heard
clanking, or the cry of millions is to be heard floating on every
breeze. He felt that he but reiterated the sentiments that burned

in every bosom present. And when Hallelujah! Hallelujah! shall resound from every hill-top and vale, when the shouts of the ransomed shall be heard reverberating louder than the roar and din of conflicting elements, then gentlemen, I feel assured that you will never regret that you have remained in this country.[31]

The minority report, absolutely rejecting the colonization scheme, was adopted by the convention. The report which was published to the nation at large merely indicated that the Ohio Convention had gone on record as opposing colonization. It did not reveal the substantial debate from which it emerged.

Martin Robinson Delany, while an opponent of the Colonization Society, was one of the leading advocates of emigration to either Africa, or to other parts of the western hemisphere. A comment by Frederick Douglass suggests Delany's devotion to his race: "I thank God," said Douglass, "for making me a man simply; but Delany always thanks him for making him a 'black man.' "[32] His education was varied, but it included the completion of studies in medicine at Harvard College. Much of his life was spent outside the United States in Central America, Canada, and Africa, but he was largely responsible for the establishment of black military units in the Civil War, and he held the rank of Major in the United States Army. Simmons gives this description of Delany:

In personal appearance he was remarkable. He was of medium height, compactly and strongly built, with broad shoulders upon which rested a head seemingly inviting by its bareness, attention to the well developed organs; with eyes sharp and piercing, while will, energy, and fire are alive in every feature; the whole surmounted on a groundwork of most defiant blackness. In speaking, he was most effective when in his loftiest flights.[33]

Delany was probably the prime mover of a series of meetings under the title *National Emigration Convention Of Colored Men.* The published announcement told of a convention to be held in Cleveland, Ohio in August of 1854. A second convention was held two years later, and at an Executive Council meeting in September, 1858 a motion was adopted that Delany should lead an expedition to explore Africa. His official report of *The Niger Valley Exploring Party* was published in 1861, and included a discussion of the political difficulties connected with launching the exploration, and a detailed description of the relevant characteristics of the parts of Africa explored. However, the report also included Delany's philosophy underlying his commitment to find a way for the black man to separate from white Americans. These parts of his report are published below.

Martin R. Delany

From *the Report*
of
*The Niger Valley Exploring Party**

SECTION I.

POLITICAL MOVEMENTS.

On or about the latter part of July, 1853, the following document was sent on, and shortly appeared in the columns of "FREDERICK DOUGLASS' PAPER," Rochester, N. Y., and the "ALIENED AMERICAN," published and edited by William Howard Day, Esq., M. A., at Cleveland, Ohio, U. S., which continued in those papers every issue, until the meeting of the Convention:

CALL FOR A NATIONAL EMIGRATION CONVENTION OF
COLORED MEN,

To be held in Cleveland, Ohio, on the 24th, 25th, and 26th of August, 1854.

"MEN AND BRETHREN: The time has fully come when we, as an oppressed people, should do something effectively, and use those means adequate to the attainment of the great and long desired end — do something to meet the actual demands of the present and prospective necessities of the rising generation of our people in this country. To do this, we must occupy a position of entire *equality,* of *unrestricted* rights, composing in fact, an acknowledged *necessary* part of the *ruling element* of society in which we live. The policy *necessary* to the *preservation* of this *element* must be *in our favor,* if ever we expect the enjoyment, freedom, sovereignty, and equality of rights anywhere. For this purpose, and to this end, then, all colored men in favor of Emigration out of the United States, and *opposed* to the American Colonization scheme of leaving the Western Hemisphere, are requested to meet in CLEVELAND, OHIO, TUESDAY, the 24th day of AUGUST, 1854, in a great NATIONAL CONVENTION, then and there to consider and decide upon the great and important subject of Emigration from the United States.

---

*From Martin R. Delany, *Official Report of the Niger Valley Exploring Party* (New York: Thomas Hamilton, 1861), pp. 6-8, 52-55.

"No person will be admitted to a seat in the Convention, who would introduce the subject of Emigration to the Eastern Hemisphere — either to Asia, Africa, or Europe — as our object and determination are to consider our claims to the West Indies, Central and South America, and the Canadas. This restriction has no reference to *personal* preference, or *individual* enterprise; but to the great question of national claims to come before the Convention.

"All persons coming to the Convention must bring credentials properly authenticated, or bring verbal assurance to the Committee on Credentials — appointed for the purpose — of their fidelity to the measures and objects set forth in this call, as the Convention is specifically by and for the friends of Emigration, and none others — and no opposition to them will be entertained.

"The question is not whether our condition can be bettered by emigration, but whether it can be made worse. If not, then, there is no part of the wide-spread universe, where our social and political condition are not better than here in our native country, and nowhere in the world as here, proscribed on account of color.

"We are friends to, and ever will stand shoulder to shoulder by our brethren, and all our friends in all good measures adopted by them for the bettering of our condition in this country, and surrender no rights but with our last breath; but as the subject of Emigration is of vital importance, and has ever been shunned by all delegated assemblages of our peoples as heretofore met, we cannot longer delay, and will not be farther baffled; and deny the right of our most sanguine friend or dearest brother, to prevent an intelligent inquiry into, and the carrying out of these measures, when this can be done, to our entire advantage, as we propose to show in Convention — as the West Indies, Central and South America — the majority of which are peopled by our brethren, or those identified with us in race, and what is more, *destiny,* on this continent — all stand with open arms and yearning hearts, importuning us in the name of suffering humanity to come — to make common cause, and share one common fate on the continent.

"The Convention will meet without fail at the time fixed for assembling, as none but those favorable to Emigration are admissible; therefore no other gathering may prevent it. The number of delegates will not be restricted — except in the town where the Convention may be held — and there the number will be decided by the Convention when assembled, that they may not too far exceed the other delegations.

"The time and place fixed for holding the Convention are ample; affording sufficient time, and a leisure season generally — and as Cleveland is now the centre of all directions — a good and favorable opportunity to all who desire to attend. Therefore, it may reasonably be the greatest gathering of the colored people ever before assembled in a Convention in the United States.

"Colonizationists are advised, that no favors will be shown to them or their expatriating scheme, as we have no sympathy with the enemies of our race.

"All colored men, East, West, North, and South, favorable to the measures set forth in this Call will send in their names (post-paid) to M. R. Delany, or Rev. Wm. Webb, Pittsburgh, Pa., that there may be arranged and attached to the Call, *five* names from each State.

"We must make an issue, create an event, and establish a position *for* ourselves. It is glorious to think of but far more glorious to carry out.

"Rev. Wm. Webb, M. R. Delany, H. G. Webb, Thos. A. Brown, John Jones, R. L. Hawkins, Samuel Venerable, John Williams, A. F. Hawkins, S. W. Sanders, Jefferson Miller, *Pittsburgh, Pa.;* Rev. A. R. Green, P. L. Jackson, J. H. Mahoney, G. Harper, Jonathan Green, H. A. Jackson, E .R. Parker, Samuel Bruce, *Alleghany City;* J. J. Gould Bias, M.D., Rev. M. M. Clark, A. M. Sumner, Johnson Woodlin, *Philadelphia;* James M. Whitfield, John N. Still, Stanley Matthews, *New York*."

This Call was readily responded to by the addition of names from other States which appeared in subsequent issues.

At the Convention, which according to the Call sat in Cleveland successively on Thursday, 24th, Friday, 25th, and Saturday, 26th of August, 1854, the following States were represented: Rhode Island, New York, Pennsylvania, Ohio, Michigan, Wisconsin, Indiana, Missouri, Kentucky, Tennessee, Louisiana, Virginia, and the Canadas; the great body consisting of nearly sixteen hundred persons. W. H. DAY, Esq., editor of the *Aliened American,* entered the Convention, and the Chairman invited him forward, offering him the privileges of the Convention, stating that wherever colored people were, William Howard Day was free — whether or not he altogether agreed in sentiment on minor points; and the Convention unanimously concurred in the invitation given.

Mr. Day subsequently proffered to the Convention any books or documents at his command for the use of that body.

The following permanent Institution was established:

ORGANIZATION OF THE NATIONAL BOARD OF COMMISSIONERS.

Central Commissioner, Pittsburgh, Pennsylvania — M. R. DELANY, President; WM. WEBB, Vice-President; THOS. A. BROWN, Treasurer; EDW. R. PARKER, Auditor; CHAS. W. NIGHTEN, Secretary; PROFESSOR M. H. FREEMAN, A. M. Special For. Sec.; SAMUEL VENERABLE, ALFRED H. JOHNS, SAMUEL BRUCE, PARKER SORRELL.

DEPARTMENTS.

Committee on Domestic Relations. — SAMUEL BRUCE, Chairman; SAMUEL VENERABLE, CHARLES W. NIGHTEN. *Financial Relations.* — THOMAS A. BROWN, Chairman; PARKER SORRELL, ALFRED H. JOHNS. *Foreign Relations.* — REV. WM. WEBB, Chairman; M. R. DELANY, EDW. R. PARKER.

Special Foreign Secretary. — PROF. MARTIN H. FREEMAN, A.M. *State Commissioners.* — *Massachusetts* — WM. C. NELL, Boston; C. L. REMOND, Salem. *New York, Buffalo.* — JAMES M. WHITFIELD, J. THEODORE HOLLY. *Ohio, Cincinnati.* — AUGUSTUS R. GREEN, PHILIP TOLIVAR, Jun. *Michigan, Detroit.* — WILLIAM C. MUNROE, WILLIAM LAMBERT. *Kentucky, Louisville.* — CONAWAY BARBOUR, JAMES H. GIPSON. *Missouri, St. Louis.* — REV. RICH'D ANDERSON, REV. JORDAN BROWN. *Virginia, Richmond.* — RICHARD HENDERSON, JOHN E. FERGUSON. *Tennessee, Nashville.* — ELDER PETER A. H. LOWRY, CHARLES BARRATT. *Louisiana, New Orleans.* — JORDAN B. NOBLE, REV. JOHN GARROW. *California, San Francisco.* — HENRY M. COLLINS, ORANGE LEWIS.

SECTION II.

SUCCEEDING CONVENTIONS.

The Second Convention, pursuant to a call, was held in Cleveland, in August, 1856, when some modification and amendments were made in the Constitution, and some changes in the officers of the Board; but the president was unanimously re-elected, and continued in office until the close of the Third Convention, which met pursuant to a call in the town of Chatham, Canada West, in August, 1858, when, resigning his position in the Board, the following officers succeeded to the

GENERAL BOARD OF COMMISSIONERS.

CENTRAL COMMISSIONERS. — CHATHAM, CANADA.

WILLIAM HOWARD DAY, President.
MATISON F. BAILEY, Vice-President.
GEORGE WASH. BRODIE, Secretary.
JAMES MADISON BELL, Treasurer.
ALFRED WHIPPER, Auditor.
MARTIN R. DELANY, Foreign Secretary.

NOTE.—The names only of the Central Commissioners are here given, the others being re-elected as chosen in 1856, at Cleveland.

OTHER MEMBERS.

ABRAM D. SHADD.
J. HENRY HARRIS.
ISAAC D. SHADD.

At an Executive Council Meeting of the Board, September 1st, 1858, the following resolution, as taken from the Minutes, was adopted: That Dr. Martin R. Delany, of Chatham, Kent County, Canada West, be a Commissioner to explore in Africa, with full power to choose his own colleagues.

SECTION XI.

WHAT AFRICA NOW REQUIRES.

From the foregoing, it is very evident that missionary duty has reached its *ultimatum.* By this, I mean that the native has received all that the missionary was sent to teach, and is now really ready for more than he can or may receive. He sees and knows that the white man, who first carried him the Gospel, which he has learned to a great extent to believe a reality, is of an entirely different race to himself; and has learned to look upon everything which he has, knows and does, which has not yet been imparted to him (especially when he is told by the missionaries, which frequently must be the case, to relieve themselves of the endless teasing enquiries which persons in their position are subject to concerning all and every temporal and secular matter, law, government, commerce, military, and other matters foreign to the teachings of the gospel; that these things he is not sent to teach, but simply the gospel) as peculiarly adapted and belonging to the white man. Of course, there are exceptions to this. Hence, having reached what he conceives to be the *maximum* of the black man's or African's attainments, there must be a re-action in some direction, and if not progressive it will be retrogressive.

The missionary has informed him that the white man's country is great. He builds and resides in great houses; lives in great towns and cities, with great churches and palaver-houses (public and legislative halls); rides in great carriages; manufactures great and beautiful things; has great ships, which go to sea, to all parts of the world, instead of little canoes such as he has pad-dling up and down the rivers and on the coast; that the wisdom, power, strength, courage, and wealth of the white man and his country are as much greater than him and his, as the big ships are larger and stronger than the little frail canoes; all of which he is made sensible of, either by the exhibition of pictures or the reality.

He at once comes to a stand. "Of what use is the white man's religion and 'book knowledge' to me, since it does not give me the knowledge and wisdom nor the wealth and power of the white man, as all these things belong only to him? "Our young men and women learn their book, and talk on paper (write), and talk to God like white man (worship), but God no hear 'em like He hear white man! Dis religion no use to black man." And so the African *reasonably* reasons when he sees that despite his having yielded up old-established customs, the laws of his fathers, and almost his entire social authority, and the rule of his household to the care and guardianship of the missionary, for the sake of acquiring his knowledge and power — when, after having learned all that his children can, he is doomed to see them sink right back into their old habits, the country continue in the same condition, without the beautiful improvements of the white man — and if a change take place at all, he is doomed to witness what he never expected to see and dies regret-ting — himself and people entangled in the meshes of the government of a people foreign in kith, kin, and sympathy, when he and his are entirely shoved aside and compelled to take subordinate and inferior positions, if not, indeed, reduced to menialism and bondage. I am justified in asserting that this state of things has brought missionary efforts to their *maximum* and native progress to a pause.

Religion has done its work, and now requires temporal and secular aid to give it another impulse. The improved arts of civilized life must now be brought to bear, and go hand in hand in aid of the missionary efforts which are purely religious in character and teaching. I would not have the standard of religion lowered a single stratum of the common breeze of heaven. No, let it rather be raised, if, indeed, higher it can be. Christianity certainly is the most advanced civilization that man ever attained to, and wherever propagated in its purity, to be effective, law and government must be brought in harmony with it — otherwise it becomes corrupted, and a corresponding degeneracy ensues, placing its votaries even in a worse condition than the primitive. This was exemplified by the Author of our faith, who, so soon as he began to teach, commenced by admonishing the people to a modification of their laws — or rather himself to condemn them. But it is very evident that the social must keep pace with the religious, and the political with the social relations of society, to carry out the great measures of the higher civilization.

Of what avail, then, is advanced intelligence to the African without improved social relations — acquirements and refinement without an opportunity of a practical application of them — society in which they are appreciated? It requires not the most astute reformer and political philosopher to see.

The native sees at once that all the higher social relations are the legitimate result and requirements of a higher intelligence, and naturally enough expects, that when he has attained it, to enjoy the same privileges and blessings. But how sadly mistaken — what dire disappointment!

The habits, manners, and customs of his people, and the social relations all around him are the same; improvements of towns, cities, roads, and methods of travel are the same; implements of husbandry and industry are the same; the methods of conveyance and price of produce (with comparative trifling variation) are the same. All seem dark and gloomy for the future, and he has his doubts and fears as to whether or not he has committed a fatal error in leaving his native social relations for those of foreigners whom he cannot hope to emulate, and who, he thinks, will not assimilate themselves to him.

It is clear, then, that essential to the success of civilization, is the establishment of all those social relations and organizations, without which enlightened communities cannot exist. To be successful, these must be carried out by proper agencies, and these agencies must be a *new element* introduced into their midst, possessing all the attainments, socially and politically, morally and religiously, adequate to so important an end. This element must be *homogenous* in all the *natural* characteristics, claims, sentiments, and sympathies — the *descendants of Africa* being the only element that can effect it. To this end, then, a part of the most enlightened of that race in America design to carry out these most desirable measures by the establishment of social and industrial settlements among them, in order at once to introduce, in an effective manner, all the well-regulated pursuits of civilized life.

That no mis-step be taken and fatal error committed at the commencement, we have determined that the persons to compose this new element to be introduced into Africa, shall be well and most carefully selected in regard to moral integrity, intelligence, acquired attainments, fitness, adaptation, and, as far as practicable, religious sentiments and professions. We are serious in this; and, so far as we are concerned as an individual, it shall be restricted to the letter, and we will most strenuously oppose and set our face against any attempt from any quarter to infringe upon this arrangement and design. Africa is our fatherland and we its legitimate descendants, and we will never agree nor consent to see this — the first voluntary step that has ever been taken for her regeneration by her own descendants—blasted by a disinterested or renegade set, whose only object might be in the one case to get rid of a portion of the colored population, and in the other, make money, though it be done upon the destruction of every hope entertained and measure introduced for the accomplishment of this great and prospectively glorious undertaking. We cannot and will not permit or agree that the result of years of labor and anxiety shall be blasted at one reckless blow, by those who have never spent a day in the cause of our race, or know nothing about our wants and requirements. The descendants of Africa in North America will doubtless, by the census of 1860, reach five millions; those of Africa may number two hundred millions. I have outgrown, long since, the boundaries of North America, and with them have also outgrown the boundaries of their claims. I, therefore, cannot consent to sacrifice the prospects of two hundred millions, that a fraction of five millions may be benefitted, especially since the measures adopted for the many must necessarily benefit the few.

Africa, to become regenerated, must have a national character, and her position among the existing nations of the earth will depend mainly upon the high standard she may gain compared with them in all her relations, morally, religiously, socially, politically, and commercially.

I have determined to leave to my children the inheritance of a country, the possession of territorial domain, the blessings of a national education, and the indisputable right of self-government; that they may not succeed to the servility and degradation bequeathed to us by our fathers. If we have not been born to fortunes, we should impart the seeds which shall germinate and give birth to fortunes for them.

The report of the first convention in 1854, over which Delany had considerable influence, stated clearly the logical basis of the separatist position.

When the condition of the inhabitants of any country is fixed by legal grades of distinction, this condition can never be changed except by express legislation. And it is the height of folly to expect such express legislation, except by the force of some irresistible internal political pressure. The force necessary to this imperative demand on our part we can never obtain, because of our numerical feebleness. . . . The rights of no oppressed people have ever yet been obtained by a voluntary act of justice on the part of the oppressors. . . . Where, then, is our hope of success in this country? Upon what is it based? Upon what principle of political policy and sagacious discernment do our political leaders and acknowledged great men — colored men we mean — justify themselves in telling us — and *insisting that we shall believe them, and submit to what they say* — to be patient, remain where we are; that there is a 'bright prospect and glorious future before us in this country'?[34]

Upon his return from the Niger Valley expedition, Delany traveled to various parts of the United States to explain his philosophy of separation, and persuade others to join him. Frederick Douglass, who was not in sympathy with him, reported on his speaking in Rochester. Douglass notes that the most fashionable churches opened their doors to Delany, and "the most intelligent audiences assembled to hear him."[35] Even though he disagreed with the plea to emigrate, Douglass was obviously impressed with the speaking of his former colleague in publishing. The speeches were described as having much warmth, much enthusiasm, "a little hyperbole," but for the most part, concluded Douglass, truthful. Of Delany's race consciousness, Douglass said this:

He cannot speak or write without speaking and writing up the race to which he belongs whether they be found in Africa or in America.[36]

While Delany's concern was almost certainly to speak only to black audiences, Douglass — the assimilationist — could not help noticing the effect the speaker made upon whites. Delany's coming to Rochester helped the black community, Douglass noted, by letting the white population see a black man who is brave, self-conscious, and ". . . who does not cringe and cower at the thought of his hated color. . . ." In his speeches, Delany announced he spoke only of ". . . pure black uncorrupted by Caucasian blood."[37]

But, Douglass did accuse Delany of being too black-conscious. Delany seemed to Douglass to have gone as far in pro-blackness as the white man had gone in the other direction. "He stands up so straight that he leans back a little." But in spite of this criticism, Douglass could not help but make these admiring comments:

Nevertheless, we can say we have been deeply interested in Dr. Delany's lectures, and filled with admiration of the man. He himself, is one of the very best arguments that Africa has to offer. Fine looking, broad chested, full of life and energy, shining like polished black Italian marble, and possessing a voice which when exerted to its full capacity might cause a whole troop of African Tigers to stand and tremble, he is just the man for the great mission of African civilization to which he is devoting his life and powers. We gather from his lectures and conversation that he is fully determined to emigrate in the course of the present year with a company of chosen spirits to settle in Africa, upon territory duly ceded to him by treaty during his stay in Abbeokuta, one of the finest cotton and coffee growing countries in the world. Health, long life, and success to M. R. Delany. If we were going to Africa we should unhesitatingly enroll ourselves under his leadership for we should know, that the race would receive no detriment in his presence — He is the intensest embodiment of black Nationality to be met with outside the valley of the Niger.[38]

These affirmative comments from a philosophical opponent suggest the strength of Delany's persuasiveness.

Douglass himself came under attack by one of his readers who objected to the editor's arguments in favor of ultimate assimilation. John W. Menard, a resident of Washington, D.C., contended that the approaching end of the war and the necessary change of status of the black population called for serious examination of the future. Menard's argument was based on economic and psychological grounds. He noted that the essentially republican character of American society demanded a homogeneous populace, for a republic is "a nation of laborers." To seek to force a mixed nationality from assimilation of whites and blacks would, the writer said, simply hasten the inevitable conflict between black and white laborers competing for the same jobs, and this could not have a favorable result for the powerless and minority black man. In a style similar to that which would be used a hundred years later against black participation in the Vietnam War, Menard said,

> It is clear, then, if we take up arms to perpetuate a *white* nationality or a *natural* antagonistic element, we would be knocking against our own heads and sealing the doom of posterity.[39]

Driving specifically at Douglass' assimilationist arguments, the writer shows a remarkable perception of the white man's potential for hatred for the black:

> Negro regiments fare very well in the old Bay State, but I fear down here in Dixie they would be as soon favored with an attack from the 'Red, White, and Blue' as from the ragged representatives of Jeff Davis. Because, (according to your own

words), the only objection white people have to us is when we appear like *ladies* and *gentlemen*. On this same principle, then, Uncle Sam's uniform on a negro would be a *rival* objection with the doughface soldier. There is already a boiling hatred in the bosom of the Northern people, which, like the burning lava of a sleeping volcano, only awaits a small pretext to explode in restless thunders at our, defenceless race here in this country.

The final two paragraphs of the letter develop the separatist idea in direct contrast with the integrationist position.

Sir, the prosperity and happiness of our race and their posterity lay in a separation from the white race. This is a fact that cannot be controverted by history, experience, or any mathematical demonstration. Oh, that an eternal ocean rolled between the two races!

And now, sir, in closing, let me say to you with due respect, your abolition teachings, if put into operation, will seal the doom of our destiny. We had no hand in bringing on this war; it is a war between white men, and if we want eternal peace in the future, let us go to Africa or some other sea-port, and leave the American people alone in the settlement of their own little family affairs.[40]

In June, 1862, a Presbyterian minister, Edward Wilmot Blyden formerly a citizen of the United States and then a resident of Liberia, spoke to the annual meeting of the Maine Colonization Society. The speaker ridiculed the arguments of the white abolitionists:

Many of the advocates of the abolition of slavery do not desire to see the negroes form themselves into an independent commonality; they believe them fitted only for a subordinate position. They expect them, when the country is delivered from slavery, to find their way among the free laborers, there to remain, pitied and patronized, held up — not allowed to stand alone. They do not realize that the words *Nationality* and *Independence* possess a charm and music for the negro as for them.[41]

He felt that even the white colonizationists demonstrated a greater understanding of humanity than the abolitionists. He argued that when men found themselves in a land surrounded by others of their own people who were taking the lead in every human endeavor, it aroused their manliness, enlarged their mind and ennobled their souls. He went on to say that the abolitionists argued that Christian sentiment would eventually eradicate the intolerant prejudice against the black men that prevented their attainment of true manhood in the United States. This may indeed be true, he said, ". . . but by that time the negro will have passed away, victimized and absorbed by the Caucasian."

The speaker wondered whether it was charitable to advise the black man to stay and fight without any weapons. It was understandable that white men should so advise, for they could not fully comprehend the situation, but it was painful to hear that black men also opposed separation. The speaker then resorted to a rhetorical device which was frequently used by a later, illustrious separationist — Marcus Garvey. The true black man, he said, does not oppose separation: "But he would say that he had not yet found in this land one black man of standing and intelligence who opposed colonization. All the bitter and unrelenting opposition comes from the half-white men." This question-begging device put the opposition in a dilemma: either admit to being half-white, or support colonization.

A final argument was presented to the colonizationists of Maine which bears a resemblance to the black nationalism of the twentieth century. The speaker suggested that the development of the African homeland was a necessary prerequisite to advancement of black people in America. As long as Africa remained degraded and uncivilized, the argument went, it would reflect on black people across the ocean and encourage continued disrespect for them by the other citizens. "Africa is the appropriate home of the black man, and he cannot rise above her."[42]

Edward Wilmot Blyden, who delivered this speech in 1862, was a master of many languages, oriental scholar, one-time Liberian Ambassador to the Court of St. James, candidate for the Presidency of Liberia, and President of Liberia College.[43] Blyden was born in St. Thomas, Danish West Indies, in 1832, and lived in the United States for some time prior to departing to Liberia in 1851. He was, perhaps, a fore-runner of the modern Black Muslim movement with his advocacy of the Mohammedan religion as more suitable for black people than Christianity.

Although a resident of Liberia, Blyden spent a good deal of his time traveling to inform others of the values of emigrating to Africa. A description of him given by a fellow Liberian, Kwamankra, at Hampton Institute in the United States, reveals that he was an effective speaker. The analysis of Blyden is presented here in detail as it not only informs the reader of Blyden, but also gives the views of another separationist as well. Kwamankra, a professor at Liberia College who advocated a return to African dress, language, and manners for black men everywhere, characterized Blyden's claim to greatness as resting on his work, not for any particular group of African people, but for the race as a whole. Booker T. Washington, he claimed,

> . . . seeks to promote the material advancement of the black man in the United States, and W. E. Burghart DuBois his social enfranchisement amid surroundings and in an atmosphere uncongenial to racial development, Edward Wilmot Blyden has sought for more than a quarter of century to reveal everywhere the African unto himself . . . to lead him back unto self-respect.[44]

Kwamankra continued,

> Apart from the magnetism of his personality, the great influence of Dr. Blyden over the rising thinking youth of the race, lies in the fact that he has revealed in his writings and utterances the true motive power which shall carry the race on from victory unto victory. And all he has to say to his people, summing up his teaching in one word, is: man, know thyself.[45]

This description of Blyden, given in 1907, was presented at a time when his entire lifetime could be examined. An example of his rhetoric forms an appropriate summary of this section on the colonization concept. Speaking in 1883, in Washington, D.C. before the sixty-sixth anniversary meeting of the American Colonization Society, Blyden felt that he could give a sympathetic assessment of the Society without the dissonance-arousing factors of anti-slavery and internal political fighting which characterized the earlier days of the organization. His speech gives a calm, if pro-colonization, analysis of the development of the American Colonization Society — an analysis rarely heard from the mouth of a black man. The steps in the growth of the movement are clearly detailed, and a scholar's commitment to evidence is noticeable.

Perhaps a key concept in this speech is that of the "instinct to race" of which Blyden speaks. As other separatists before and after him, he compares the black man with the Jew in terms of the constant motivation to return to the Promised Land. He makes a gently sardonic comment about the accusations that talk of colonization stirs up the black inhabitants of other countries, notably the United States. He claims that with the instinct to race the black man does not need outsiders or "agitators" to stir him up — he motivates himself. This line of reasoning brings to mind the twentieth century charge that Communists go into the black ghettos to foment racial strife. Modern spokesmen are also inclined to be sardonic as they observe that after hundreds of years of white racism, the black man does not require an agitator to stir him up.

Blyden's speech, then, provides the summary to this discussion of the colonziation movement.

Edward W. Blyden
The Origin and Purpose of African Colonization*

THE LORD OF HOSTS HATH SWORN, SAYING, SURELY AS I HAVE THOUGHT, SO SHALL IT COME TO PASS; AND AS I HAVE PURPOSED, SO SHALL IT STAND." — *Isaiah xiv-24.*

Perhaps it would satisfy the evolutionist or agnostic if the passage were read as follows: — "Surely as it has been conceived so shall it come to pass; and as it has been purposed, so shall it stand." For there is not a thinking being, whatever his religious belief, who does not at once recognize the fact that everything in the physical and moral world proceeds according to some plan or order. That some subtle law, call it by whatever name you please, underlies and regulates the movements of the stars in their courses and the sparrows in their flight. It is also the belief of all healthy minds that that law or influence is always tending towards the highest and best results — that its prerogative and design are to make darkness light, crooked things straight and rough places smooth; or, in the misty phraseology of modern criticism, it is the "Eternal not ourselves that makes for righteousness." — that its fiats are irrevocable and their outcome inevitable. With this understanding, men are now constructing the science of history, the science of language, the science of religion, the science of society, formulating dogmas to set aside dogma, and consoling themselves that they are moving to a higher level and solving the problems of the ages.

Among the conclusions to which study and research are conducting philosophers, none is clearer than this — that each of the races of mankind has a specific character and a specific work. The science of Sociology is the science of race.

In the midst of these discussions, Africa is forcing its claims for consideration upon the attention of the world, and science and philanthropy are bringing all their resources to bear upon its exploration and amelioration.

---

*Edward W. Blyden, "The Origin and Purpose of African Colonization." An address delivered on January 14, 1883, in Washington, D.C.

There is hardly an important city in Europe where there is not an organization formed for the purpose of dealing with some of the questions connected with this great continent.

There is "The International African Association," founded at Brussels, in 1876, of which the King of the Belgians is the patron. "The Italian National Association for the exploration and civilization of Africa." The "Association Espanola para la Esploracion del Africa." The King of Spain has taken great practical interest in this Society. "The German Society for the Exploration of Africa," founded in 1872 by the German Geographical Associations. It receives assistance from the government. The "Afrikanische Gesellschaft," in Vienna, founded in 1876, also under royal patronage. "The Hungarian African Association," founded in 1877. "The National Swiss Committee for the Exploration of Central Africa." The French Government and the French Chamber of Commerce have made large grants of money to aid in African exploration. Then there is an African Association at Rotterdam, besides the great Royal Geographical Society of England, which has a special fund for African researches, and has recently sent Thomson to explore the snow covered mountains of eastern Africa.

This anxiety to penetrate the mysteries of Africa, this readiness to turn from the subtleties of philosophy and the fascinations of science, to deal with the great physical fact of an unexplored continent, is not a new experience in the world. The ancients were equally concerned. With a zealous curiosity overcoming the promptings of the finer sentiments and the desire for military glory, Cæsar proposed to abandon his ambitious exploits for the privilege of gazing upon the source of the Nile.

The modern desire for more accurate knowledge of Africa is not a mere sentiment; it is the philanthropic impulse to lift up the millions of that continent to their proper position among the intellectual and moral forces of the world; but it is also the commercial desire to open that vast country to the enterprises of trade. Europe is overflowing with the material productions of its own genius. Important foreign markets, which formerly consumed these productions, are now closing against them. Africa seems to furnish the only large outlet for them, and the desire is to make the markets of Soudan easily accessible to London, Manchester and Liverpool. The depressed factories of Lancashire are waiting to be inspired with new life and energy by the development of a new and inexhaustible trade with the millions of Central Africa; so that Africa, as frequently in the past, will have again to come to the rescue and contribute to the needs of Europe. Emergencies drove homeless wanderers to the shores of Libya: —

> Defessi Æneadae, quae proxima litora, cursu
> Contendunt petere, et Libyae, vertuntur ad oras.*

But the plans proposed by Europeans for opening up Africa, as far as they can be carried out by themselves, are felt to be inadequate. Many feel that commerce, science, and philanthropy may establish stations and trace

---

*Virgil's Æneid.

out thoroughfares, but they also feel that these agencies are helpless to cope fully with the thousand questions which arise in dealing with the people.

Among the agencies proposed for carrying on the work of civilization in Africa, none has proved so effective as the American Colonization enterprise. People who talk of the civilizing and elevating influence of mere trade on that continent, do so because they are unacquainted with the facts. Nor can missionaries alone do this work. We do not object to trade, and we would give every possible encouragement to the noble efforts of missionaries. We would open the country everywhere to commercial intercourse. We would give everywhere hospitable access to traders. Place your trading factories at every prominent point along the coast, and even let them be planted on the banks of the rivers. Let them draw the rich products from remote districts. We say, also, send the missionary to every tribe and every village. Multiply throughout the country the evangelizing agencies. Line the banks of the rivers with the preachers of righteousness—penetrate the jungles with those holy pioneers—crown the mountain tops with your churches, and fill the valleys with your schools. No single agency is sufficient to cope with the multifarious needs of the mighty work. But the indispensable agency is the colony. Groups of Christian and civilized settlers must, in every instance, bring up the rear, if the results of your work are to be widespread, beneficial and enduring.

This was the leading idea that gave birth to the Society whose anniversary we have met to celebrate. To-day we have the Sixty-Sixth Annual Report of the American Colonization Society. This fact by itself would excite no feeling, and perhaps no remark. But when we consider that although this is but the sixty-sixth year of its existence, it has been successful in founding a colony which has now been for thirty-five years an independent nation, acknowledged by all the Powers of the earth, we cannot but congratulate the organization upon an achievement which, considering the circumstances, is unparalleled in the history of civilization; and which must be taken as one of the most beautiful illustrations of the spirit and tendency of Christianity.

When the Society began its work, its programme was modest, and in the early declaration of its policy it was found expedient to emphasize the simplicity of its pretensions and the singleness of its purpose. In describing its objects, one of the most eloquent of its early supporters — Dr. Leonard Bacon — said, "The Colonization Society is not a missionary society, nor a society for the suppression of the slave trade, nor a society for the improvement of the blacks, nor a society for the abolition of slavery; it is simply a society for the establishment of a colony on the coast of Africa."

But in pursuance of its legitimate object, its labors have been fruitful in all the ways indicated in Dr. Bacon's statement. It has not only established a colony, but it has performed most effective missionary work; it has suppressed the slave trade along six hundred miles of coast; it has improved the condition of the blacks as no other means has; and it is abolishing domestic slavery among the Aborigines of that continent.

Like all great movements which are the outcome of human needs, and have in view the amelioration of the condition of large masses of people, it attracted to its support at the opening of its career, men of conflicting views and influenced by divers motives. Some of its adherents gave one reason for their allegiance, others gave another; and sometimes to the superficial observer or to the captious opponent, these different reasons furnished grounds for animadversions against the Society. Though it owed its origin to the judicious heads and philanthropic hearts of some of the best men that ever occupied positions of prominence and trust in this nation, yet there were those who ridiculed the scheme as wild and impracticable. Some opposed it because they loved the Negro; others discountenanced it because they hated the Negro. Some considered that the Society in wishing to give him an opportunity for self-government, placed too high an estimate upon his ability; others thought that the idea of sending him away to a barbarous shore was a disparaging comment upon his capacity, and robbing him of his rights to remain and thrive in the land of his birth. To not a few who neither loved nor hated the Negro — but were simply indifferent to him — the idea of transporting a few emancipated slaves to Africa with the hope of bringing about a general exodus of the millions in this country, or of building up a nation in that far-off land of such materials, seemed absurd and ridiculous.

The Society was hardly fifteen years in operation when it met with organized opposition in the American Anti-Slavery Society, the founders of which looked upon the work of Colonization as an attempt to evade the duty and responsibility of emancipation. At this time Mr. William Lloyd Garrison, a leader of the abolition movement, was the most eloquent and persistent of the assailants of the Society. He carried the war against it into England, and pursued with unrelenting scorn and invective Mr. Elliott Cresson, who was then representing the cause before the British public. In the interesting life of the great anti-slavery reformer, by Oliver Johnson, it is said that when Mr. Garrison returned to this country from England in 1833, he brought with him a "Protest" against the Colonization scheme, signed by Wilberforce, Macaulay, Buxton, O'Connell and others of scarcely less weight.*

But Mr. Garrison ought to have known, and probably did know, that it was not the Colonization scheme as conceived by its founders that these philanthropists opposed, for they were men of a spirit kindred to that which animated Samuel J. Mills, and the Finleys and Caldwells, whose labors brought the Society into being. What they did oppose was the scheme as they saw it under the representations of Mr. Garrison, who, himself, benevolent at heart, had been influenced by personal reasons and by the injudicious utterances of certain advocates of Colonization. They opposed it as they saw it through the glasses of such good old Negroes as Father Snowden of Boston, who, in those days, offered a prayer for the Colonization Society so striking in its eloquence as to have deserved a place, in the judgment of Mr. Oliver Johnson, in a serious narrative of the doings of the great anti-slavery leader— "O God," said the simple and earnest old man, "we pray that that seven-headed, ten-horned monster, the Colonization Society, may be smitten through and through with the fiery darts of truth, and tormented as the whale between the sword-fish and the thresher."‡

---

*William Lloyd Garrison and his Times, by Oliver Johnson, p. 130.

‡*Garrison and his Times, p. 72.* Mr. Oliver Johnson, throughout his work, shows his own conception of the status and functions of the Negro, by never using a capital letter in writing the word that describes the race.

I say that the friends of Africa in England did not oppose African Colonization in itself, for just about the time of Mr. Garrison's visit to England, or very soon after, they adopted, under the lead of Sir Thomas Fowell Buxton, a scheme for the regeneration of Africa by means of her civilized sons, gathered from the countries of their exile; and at great expense sent out an expedition to the Niger, for the purpose of securing on that river a hundred square miles of territory on which to settle the returning exiles. Capt. William Allen, who commanded the first Niger expedition, on his return in 1834, when describing the advantages of a civilized colony, used these words:

"The very existence of such a community, exalted as it would be in its own estimation, and in the enjoyment of the benefits of civilization, would excite among its neighbors a desire to participate in those blessings, and would be at once a normal or model society, gradually spreading to the most remote regions, and, calling forth the resources of a country rich in so many things essential to commerce, might change the destinies of the whole of Western Central Africa."*

In a letter addressed by Stephen Lushington and Thomas Fowell Buxton to Lord John Russell, August 7, 1840, all the arguments used by the American Colonization Society for colonizing civilized blacks in Africa, are reproduced.

Thomas Clarkson, writing to a friend under date Sept. 12, 1842, says: "I am glad to find that in the *Friend of Africa* you lay such stress upon native agency, or the agency of the black people themselves to forward their own cause. Good sense would have dictated this; but God seems to point it out as one of His plans. He has raised up a people by the result of emancipation, qualified both in intellect and habitation to a hot climate, to do for us the grand works in Africa. You know well that we can find among the emancipated slaves people with religious views and with intellectual capacity equal to the whites, and from these, principally, are we to pick out laborers for the African vineyard. * * * You cannot send two or three only to a colony. In the smallest colony there must be more; there must be enough to form a society, both for the appearance of safety and for that converse for which man was fitted by the organs of speech to pass the time usefully to himself and others."†

The experience of years and the progress of Liberia have only served to illustrate the soundness of these views. European workers for Africa feel more and more the importance of such agencies as the Colonization Society has been instrumental in establishing for civilizing Africa. A writer in the London *Times* for May 31st, 1882, says:

"As I have recently returned from Zanzibar, and can speak from some personal experience, may I be allowed to draw the attention of your readers to an attempt to bring about these results, viz.: — the abolition of the slave trade and civilization of the people — with remarkable success? It is the formation of self-sustaining communities of released slaves in the countries whence they were originally brought by the slave dealers, in order that by their example and influence they may teach to the surrounding people the advantages of civilization. The sight of a body of men of the same race as

---

*Narrative of the Expedition to the Niger. Vol. II, p. 434.
†*African Repository,* Vol. XVI, p. 397.

themselves, living in their midst, but raised to a higher level by the influence of Christianity and civilization, has naturally produced in them a desire of raising themselves also."

In an able article on "The Evangelization of Africa," in the Dublin *Review,* January, 1879, written by a Roman Catholic Prelate, the writer asks — "Why should not the example given by the American Colonization Society in founding Liberia, be followed by us in other parts of Africa?"

In a lecture, delivered in 1872, in New York, by the same distinguished author, he says:

"We have come to evangelize the colored people in America. But our mission does not terminate with them. We are travelling through America to that great unexplored, unconverted continent of Africa. We have come to gather an army on our way, to conquer Africa for the Cross. God has His designs upon that vast land. * * * * The branch torn away from the parent stem in Africa, by our ancestors, was brought to America — brought away by divine permission, in order that it might be engrafted upon the tree of the Cross. It will return in part to its own soil, not by violence or deportation, but willingly, and borne on the wings of faith and charity,"

It is sometimes supposed and asserted that the efforts of the Colonization Society stir up a feeling of unrest among the colored population, and make them dissatisfied with their condition in this country. But this charge is brought only by those who have no idea of the power of race instincts. The descendants of Africa in this country have never needed the stimulus of any organization of white men to direct their attention to the land of their fathers. Just as the idea of a departure from the house of bondage in Egypt was in the minds of the Hebrews long before Moses was born, even when Joseph gave commandment concerning his bones; so long before the formation of the Colonization Society there were aspirations in the breasts of thinking Negroes for a return to the land of their fathers. The first practical Colonizationist was not a white man but a Negro, Paul Cuffee. This man took thirty Negro emigrants from New Bedford in his own vessel to Africa in 1815. The law of God for each race is written on the tablets of their hearts, and no theories will ever obliterate the deep impression or neutralize its influence upon their action; and in the process of their growth they will find or force a way for themselves. Those who are working with or for the race, therefore, should seriously consider in any great movement in their behalf, the steps which the proper representatives deem it wise to take. "March without the people," said a French deputy, "and you walk into night; their instincts are a finger pointing of providence, always turning toward real benefit."

The Colonization Society was only the instrument of opening a field for the energies of those of the Africans who desired to go and avail themselves of the opportunities there offered. Mr. Boswell, in his life of Samuel Johnson, tells us that when the sale of Thrales' Brewery was going forward, Johnson was asked what he really considered to be the value of the property which was to be disposed of. He replied, "We are not here to sell a parcel of boilers and vats, but the potentiality of growing rich beyond the dreams of avarice." So the founders of this Society looked to the "potentiality" of the few seeds they were planting on the coast of Africa. In their reply to opponents they said: "We are not here simply to send a few Negroes to Africa and to occupy with them a few swampy regions on the margin of a distant country, but we are endeavoring to stimulate for a race and a continent their potentiality of unlimited development."

They assisted a few courageous men to go and plant a colony on those distant and barbarous shores, in days when nearly every body doubted the wisdom and expediency of such a step. Who then could have divined the results? Considering the circumstances of those pioneer settlers and the darkness of the outlook when they started, no man could have believed until he learned it as a matter of history, that those few men could have established an independent nation on that coast. The story of their trials and struggles and conquests would furnish the material for an exciting novel — many portions of it would resemble chapters not from Froude or Hallam but from Thackeray or Scott. The string of episodes in the first thirty years of their history would form the basis of an interesting epic.

Now what is the work thus far accomplished and being accomplished on that coast? If, when those colonists landed on those shores, inexperienced and uneducated ex-slaves as they were, they had had to contend with simple barbarism or the absence of civilization, their task would have been comparatively easy. But they had to deal with tribes demoralized by ages of intercourse with the most abandoned of foreigners—slave traders and pirates, who had taken up their abode at various points of the coast, and had carried on for generations, without interruption, their work of disintegration and destruction. When, therefore, the colonists found themselves in possession of a few miles of territory, they very soon perceived that they had more to do than simply to clear up the land, build and cultivate. They saw that they had to contend not with the simple prejudices of the Aborigines but with the results of the unhallowed intercourse of European adventurers. But they were brave men. Their spirits, though chastened by the burden of slavery and the sorrows of oppression were never clouded by any doubt in their destiny. They felt themselves able to build up a State, and they set themselves cheerfully to deal with the new and difficult problems which confronted them. Fierce were the struggles in which they had to engage before they succeeded in expelling the pirates from the neighborhood of their settlements. And after they had dislodged these demons in human form, the mischievous consequences of their protracted residence in the land continued and still, to a great extent, continue. In his last message to the Liberian Legislature, the President of the Republic referring to the difficulties at Cape Mount says: "The native wars which have been going on in the vicinity of Cape Mount have now nearly exhausted themselves. These periodical wars are, for the most part, the results of long standing feuds arising from the horrible slave-trade, that dreadful scourge which distinguished the intercourse of the European world with Africa for more than ten generations."

Having secured an undisturbed footing in the land of their fathers, the next step on the part of the colonists was to conciliate the Aborigines and to enlarge the borders of the Colony by purchase from the native lords of the soil. In this way the Colony increased in power and influence, until 1847, when it became a sovereign and independent State. As such it has been acknowledged by all the Powers of Europe and by the United States.

The special work which at this moment claims the attention of the Republic is to push the settlements beyond the sea-board to the elevated and salubrious regions of the interior, and to incorporate the Aborigines, as fast as practicable, into the Republic. Native chiefs are summoned to the Legislature from the different counties and take part in the deliberations; but as yet only those Aborigines who conform to the laws of the Republic as to the tenure of land, are allowed to exercise the elective franchise. All the other questions which press upon independent nations, questions of education, of finance, of commerce, of agriculture, are receiving the careful attention of the people. They feel the importance of making provisions by judicious laws and by proper executive, legislative and judicial management, for the preservation and growth of the State.

In educational matters there is daily noticeable encouraging improvement. We are developing a system of common schools, with a College at the head as a guarantee for their efficiency. The educational work is felt to be of the greatest possible importance; education not only in its literary and religious forms, but also in its industrial, mechanical, and commercial aspects.

The effort now is to enlarge the operations and increase the influence of the College. The faculty has just been added to by the election of two new Professors in this country, young men of learning and culture, who will sail for their field of labor in a few weeks.

It will be gratifying to the people of Liberia as well as to their friends on this side, to observe how heartily the press of this country, both secular and religious, has endorsed and commended this new move for the advancement of education in that land. The College now contains fifty students in the two departments, and it is hoped that the number will soon increase to hundreds, if we can only get the needed help. We have application for admission to its advantages from numerous youths in various institutions of learning in this country, who wish, on the completion of their course, to labor in Africa. Influential chiefs on the coast and in the interior are also anxious to send their sons; and we shall, before very long, have young men from the powerful tribes in our vicinity — Mandingoes, Foulahs, Veys, Bassas, Kroos, Greboes.

A female department has also lately been established in connection with this institution, and a Christian lady of education and culture, in this country, longing to labor in the land of her fathers, has been appointed as first Principal. She will sail in a few months.

In financial matters the Republic is hopeful. The public debt is not so large that it cannot, by the reforms now contemplated, be easily managed and placed under such control as to give no inconvenience to the State. There are evidences of an abundance of gold in the territory of the Republic. The precious metal is brought to the coast from various points in the interior. But the government is not anxious to encourage the opening of gold mines. We prefer the slow but sure, though less dazzling process of becoming a great nation by lapse of time, and by the steady growth of internal prosperity — by agriculture, by trade, by proper domestic economy.

In commercial matters there is also everything to encourage. Three lines of steamers from England and Germany, and sailing vessels from the United States visit the Liberian ports regularly for trading purposes. And the natural resources of the Republic have in various portions of it hardly yet been touched. Palm oil, cam-wood, ivory, rubber, gold-dust, hides, beeswax, gum copal, may be produced in unlimited quantities. For the enterprising merchants of this country — colored or white — there is no better field for the investment of pecuniary capital.

The agriculture of the country is rapidly on the increase. Liberia has been supplying the coffee planters of Ceylon and Brazil with a new and superior kind of coffee for their agricultural industry. The Liberian coffee is considered among the best in the world, and the people are now turning their attention largely to its cultivation. As immigrants arrive from this country, extensive farms under their persevering industry are taking the place of the dense forests. The new settlements pushing out to the rich valleys and fertile slopes of the interior are a marvel to those who a few years ago saw the country in its primitive condition; and to the Negro newcomer from this country in search of a field for his energy and enterprise, there is no picture which, for inspiration and grandeur, can ever equal the sight of these new proprietors of land and these new directors of labor engaged in their absorbing and profitable pursuits. When he sees the thriving villages, the comfortable dwellings, the increasing agriculture, all supervised and controlled by men just like himself, who had only been more fortunate in preceding him by a few years, a feeling of pride and gratification takes possession of him. Like Aeneas, when he witnessed the enterprise of the Tyrian colonists in the building of Carthage, he exclaims

*"O fortunati, quorum jam moenia surgunt."

But, unlike the mythical author of that exclamation, he feels that he has a part in the rising fortunes of the settlements; that what he beholds is not only what he himself may accomplish, but is the promise and pledge of the future greatness of his adopted country.

The nations of the earth are now looking to Liberia as one of the hopeful spots on that continent. The President of the United States in his last message, referred to the interest which this Government feels in that youngest sister of the great international family. To a deputation from the Colonization Society, which called upon him a year ago, President Arthur said that he "had always taken great interest in the work of the Colonization Society, which was, in his judgment, eminently practical."

President Gardner, who has for the last five years presided over that little nation, expresses the views entertained by its most enlightened citizens as follows:

---

*Aenead I, 437.

"The ship of state which, in 1847, we launched in fear and trembling, is still afloat, with timbers sound, and spars unharmed. The Lone Star of Liberia untarnished is pushing its way eastward, successfully achieving victories of peace even to the slopes of the Niger, gathering willing thousands under its elevating and hopeful folds. The American Colonization Society must feel greatly strengthened in its work. It has achieved what no other philanthropic agency in modern times has accomplished, and what, perhaps, no nation could have effected, viz: giving to the Negro an independent home in the land of his fathers, where he has unlimited scope for development and expansion. Had Liberia been the colony of a powerful government, political and commercial jealousies, and the purposes of party spirit, might have prevented the surrender of the colony to the absolute control of the colonists. Hayti had to fight for her independence. It is not practicable for Great Britain to give up Jamaica, or Barbadoes, or Sierra Leone, or Lagos. But the American Colonization Society founded a nation, and continues to strengthen it. So God takes the weak things of the earth to confound the things that are mighty."

In a letter dated at the Palace of Madrid, February 11, 1882, King Alfonso XII, of Spain, writes to the President of Liberia as follows:

"Great and Good Friend,

Desiring to give to you a public testimony of my Royal appreciation and my particular esteem, I have had special pleasure in nominating you Knight of the Grand Cross of the Royal Order of Isabel the Catholic. I am pleased by this action also to furnish new proof of the desire which animates me to strengthen more and more, the friendly relations which happily exist between Spain and the Republic of Liberia; and with this motive I repeat to you the assurance of the affection which I entertain towards you, and with which I am, Great and Good Friend,

Your Great and Good Friend,

ALFONSO."

Palace at Madrid, February 11, 1882.

The Republic of Liberia now stands before the world — the realization of the dreams of the founders of the American Colonization Society, and in many respects more than the realization. Its effect upon that great country is not to be estimated solely by the six hundred miles of coast which it has brought under civilized law. A sea of influence has been created, to which rivulets and large streams are attracted from the distant interior; and up those streams, for a considerable distance, a tide of regeneration continually flows. Far beyond the range of the recognized limits of Liberia, hundreds of miles away from the coast, I have witnessed the effects of American civilization; not only in the articles of American manufacturers which I have been surprised to see in those remote districts, but in the intelligible use of the English language, which I have encountered in the far inland regions, all going out from Liberia. None can calculate the wide-spreading results of a single channel of wholesome influence. Travellers in Syria tell us that Damascus owes its fertility and beauty to one single stream, the river Abana.

Without that little river the charm and glory of Damascus would disappear. It would be a city in a desert. So the influence of Liberia, insignificant as it may seem, is the increasing source of beauty and fertility, of civilization and progress, to West and Central Africa.

As time has gone on and the far reaching plans of the Society have been developed, its bitterest opponents among the whites have relaxed their opposition. They see more and more that the idea which gave rise to it, had more than a temporary or provisional importance; that as long as there are Christian Negroes in this land who may do a civilizing work in Africa, and who desire to go thither, so long will this colonization enterprise be a necessary and beneficent agency.

Colored men of intelligence are also taking a more comprehensive view of the question. The colored people in various parts of the country are not only asserting their independence of party trammels but are taking higher ground with regard to their relations to Africa. The Colonization Society no longer stands between them and the land of their fathers as a dividing agency; no longer the gulf that separates, but for many the bridge that connects. Liberia is producing the elements, which, if they do not to the minds of the thinking colored people, vindicate the methods of some colonizationists in days gone by, amply justify the policy of the Colonization Society. The leading men of color are recognizing the distinction between Liberia as an independent nation, claiming their respect and support, and the Colonization Society, which, from their stand-point, contemplated their expatriation.

Your speaker has had the honor of being listened to on the various occasions on which, recently, he has spoken in this city, by full houses composed of the most intelligent classes of the colored population, who a few years ago would not have thought of attending any meeting which had the remotest connection with Liberia. He has also had the gratifying privilege of being the guest for several days at Uniontown of the leading colored man of the United States, better known than any other Negro in both hemispheres; and this address was written under his hospitable roof and, perhaps, on the same table on which, in years gone by, had been forged those thunderbolts which he hurled with so much power and effect against Colonization; but, *tempora mutantur et nos mutamur in illis.* The times are changed and we are changed with them.

The dawn of a new day in the history of the colored people is not only inspiring them with new views, but bringing forward new actors or leaders. It is not that those who are coming forward are superior to those who have passed away or are passing away. No; the giants of former years — the Wards and Garnets and Douglasses — can never be surpassed or even reproduced. They were the peculiar product of their times. But it is, that the present times require different instruments, and leaders are arising with different purposes and different aspirations. I saw in large letters in a prominent part of Mr. Frederick Douglass's residence the scriptural injunction, "Live peaceably with all men;" a fitting motto, I thought, for the soldier who, after the hard fought battle and the achievement of the victory, has laid down his arms. The motto in the days of Douglass's greatest activity was, "Fight the good fight." Now the days of peace have come. The statesman's office comes after the soldier's. *Cedant arma togae.* The Negro youth as a result of the training which he is now so generously receiving in the schools, will seek to construct States. He will aspire after feats of statesmanship, and Africa will be the field to which he will look for the realization of his desires. Bishop Turner, of the African M. E. Church, who enjoys exceptional opportunities for knowing the feelings of the colored people of this country, said in a newsaper article published a few days ago:

"There never was a time when the colored people were more concerned about Africa in every respect, than at present. In some portions of the country it is the topic of conversation, and if a line of steamers were started from New Orleans, Mobile, Savannah or Charleston, they would be crowded to density every trip they made to Africa. There is a general unrest and a wholesale dissatisfaction among our people in a number of sections of the country to my certain knowledge, and they sigh for conveniences to and from the Continent of Africa. Something has to be done, matters cannot go on as at present, and the remedy is thought by tens of thousands to be a NEGRO NATIONALITY. This much the history of the world establishes, that races either fossilized, oppressed or degraded, must emigrate before any material change takes place in their civil, intellectual or moral status; otherwise extinction is the consequence." *

The general practice among superficial politicians and irresponsible colored journalists in this country is to ignore and deprecate the craving for the fatherland among the Negro population. But nothing is clearer to those who know anything of race instincts and tendencies than that this craving is a permanent and irrepressible impulse. For some reason the American Government has never seen its way clear to give any practical recognition to these aspirations. In vain, apparently, does the American Colonization Society from year to year present the cries and petitions of thousands and hundreds of thousands who yearn for a home in the land of their fathers. Individual philanthropists may admit that such cries deserve respectful sympathy, but the Government takes no note of them. It must be stated, however, that the Government is ever ready to extend assistance to Liberia, and on the ground, partly, as often urged in their diplomatic correspondence, that Liberia is to be the future home of thousands of American citizens of African descent.

Has not the time now come when an earnest and united effort should be made by all sections of this great country to induce the Government to assist the thousands who are longing to betake themselves to those vast and fertile regions to which they are directed by the strongest impulses that have ever actuated the movements of humanity? While it is true that there are causes of dissatisfaction with his position in this country on the part of the Negro, still he will be carried to Africa by a higher impulse than that which brings millions to this country from Europe. Mr. Bright has said: "There are streams of emigration flowing towards America, and much of this arises from the foolishness of European peoples and European governments," and he quotes from

---

*Christian Recorder, Jan. 4, 1883.

Mr. Bancroft the statement that "the history of the colonization of America is the history of the crimes of Europe."

No natural impulses bring the European hither — artificial or external causes move him to emigrate. The Negro is drawn to Africa by the necessities of his nature.

We do not ask that all the colored people should leave the United States and go to Africa. If such a result were possible it is not, for the present at least, desirable, certainly it is not indispensable. For the work to be accomplished much less than one-tenth of the six millions would be necessary. "In a return from exile, in the restoration of a people," says George Eliot, "the question is not whether certain rich men will choose to remain behind, but whether there will be found worthy men who will choose to lead the return. Plenty of prosperous Jews remained in Babylon when Ezra marshalled his band of forty thousand, and began a new glorious epoch in the history of his race, making the preparation for that epoch in the history of the world, which has been held glorious enough to be dated from forevermore."

There are Negroes enough in this country to join in the return — descendants of Africa enough, who are faithful to the instincts of the race, and who realize their duty to their fatherland. I rejoice to know that here where the teachings of generations have been to disparage the race, there are many who are faithful, there are men and women who will go, who have a restless sense of homelessness which will never be appeased until they stand in the great land where their forefathers lived; until they catch glimpses of the old sun, and moon and stars, which still shine in their pristine brilliancy upon that vast domain; until from the deck of the ship which bears them back home they see visions of the hills rising from the white margin of the continent, and listen to the breaking music of the waves — the exhilarating laughter of the sea as it dashes against the beach. These are the elements of the great restoration. It may come in our own life time. It may be our happiness to see those rise up who will formulate progress for Africa — embody the ideas which will reduce our social and political life to order; and we may, before we die, thank God that we have seen His salvation; that the Negro has grasped with a clear knowledge his meaning in the world's vast life — in politics — in science — in religion.

I say it is gratifying to know that there are Negroes of this country who will go to do this great work — cheerfully go and brave the hardships and perils necessary to be endured in its accomplishment. These will be among the redeemers of Africa. If they suffer they will suffer devotedly, and if they die, they will die well. And what is death for the redemption of a people? History is full of examples of men who have sacrificed themselves for the advancement of a great cause — for the good of their country. Every man who dies for Africa — if it is necessary to die — adds to Africa a new element of salvation, and hastens the day of her redemption. And when God lets men suffer and gives them to pain and death, it is not the abandoned, it is not the worst or the guiltiest, but the best and the purest, whom He often chooses for His work, for they will do it best. Spectators weep and wonder; but the sufferers themselves accept the pain in the joy of doing redemptive work, and rise out of lower levels to the elevated regions of those nobler spirits—the glorious army of martyrs — who rejoice that they are counted worthy to die for men. The nation now being reared in Africa by the returning exiles from this country will not be a reproduction of this. The restoration of the Negro to the land of his fathers, will be the restoration of a race to its original integrity, to itself; and working by itself, for itself and from itself, it will discover the methods of its own development, and they will not be the same as the Anglo-Saxon methods.

In Africa there are no physical problems to be confronted upon the solution of which human comfort and even human existence depend. In the temperate regions of the earth there are ever recurring problems, first physical or material, and then intellectual, which press for solution and cannot be deferred without peril.

It is this constant pressure which has developed the scientific intellect and the thoughtfulness of the European. Africa can afford to hand over the solution of these problems to those who, driven by the exigencies of their circumstances, must solve them or perish. And when they are solved we shall apply the results to our purposes, leaving us leisure and taste for the metaphysical and spiritual. Africa will be largely an agricultural country. The people, when assisted by proper impulse from without — and they need this help just as all other races have needed impulse from without — will live largely in contact with nature. The Northern races will take the raw materials from Africa and bring them back in such forms as shall contribute to the comfort and even elegance of life in that country; while the African, in the simplicity and purity of rural enterprises, will be able to cultivate those spiritual elements in humanity which are suppressed, silent and inactive under the pressure and exigencies of material progress. He will find out, not under pressure but in an entirely normal and natural way, what his work is to be.

I do not anticipate for Africa any large and densely crowded cities. For my own taste I cannot say that I admire these agglomerations of humanity. For me man has marred the earth's surface by his cities. "God made the country and man made the town."

It is the cities which have furnished the deadliest antagonisms to prophets and reformers. The prophets and apostles are nurtured in the Nazareths and Bethlehems of the world. I cherish the feeling that in Africa there will never be any Jerusalem or Rome or Athens or London; but I have a strong notion that the Bethlehems and Nazareths will spring up in various parts of the continent. In the solitudes of the African forests, where the din of western civilization has never been heard, I have realized the saying of the poet that the "Groves were God's first temples." I have felt that I stood in the presence of the Almighty; and the trees and the birds and the sky and the air have whispered to me of the great work yet to be achieved on that continent. I trod lightly through those forests, for I felt there was "a spirit in the woods." And I could understand how it came to pass that the prophets of a race — the great reformers who have organized states and elevated peoples, received their inspiration on mountains, in caves, in grottoes. I could understand something of the power which wrought upon Sakya Muni under the trees of India,

upon Numa Pompilius in the retreat of the Nymph Egeria, upon Mohammed
in the silent cave; upon Martin Luther, Xavier and Ignatius Loyola in the
cloisters. One of the sweetest of American poets — Whittier — in his poem
on the Quaker Meeting, pictures the beauty and instructive power of un-
broken stillness —

> And so I find it well to come
> For deeper rest to this still room,
> For here the habit of the soul
> Feels less the outer world's control.
>
> And from the silence multiplied
> By these still forms on either side,
> The world that time and sense have known
> Falls off and leaves us God alone,
>
> So to the calmly gathered thought
> The innermost of truth is taught,
> The mystery, dimly understood,
> That love of God is love of good.

It is under such circumstances that the African will gather inspiration
for his work. He will grow freely, naturally, unfolding his powers in a completely healthy progress.

The world needs such a development of the Negro on African soil. He
will bring as his contribution the softer aspects of human nature. The harsh
and stern fibre of the Caucasian races needs this milder element. The African
is the feminine; and we must not suppose that this is of least importance in
the ultimate development of humanity. "We are apt," says Matthew Arnold,
"to account amiability weak and hardness strong," but even if it were so, there
are forces, as George Sands says truly and beautifully, "there are forces of
weakness, of docility, of attractiveness or of suavity, which are quite as real
as the forces of vigor, of encroachment, of violence, of brutality."*

I see that Michelet claims for France this feminine character among the
nations. Speaking of Jeanne d'Arc, he says: "It was fit that the savior of
France should be a woman. France herself is a woman. She has the fickleness
of the sex but also its amiable gentleness, its facile and charming pity, and the
excellence of its first impulses."

The beauty of woman is not in cowardly yielding or careless servility.
An English poet has embodied in a few striking and beautiful lines, a description of woman's sphere and power;

> I saw her upon nearer view
> A spirit, yet a woman too;
> Her household motions light and free,
> And steps of virgin liberty;
> A countenance in which did meet
> Sweet records, promises as sweet;
> A perfect woman nobly planned

---

*Nineteenth Century, June, 1881.

To warn, to comfort, to command,
And yet a spirit still, and bright
With something of an angel light.

Such will be the African's place when he rises to the proper sphere of his work. France does not occupy that place. That nation may at times wear woman's dress, and go about with light and sportive air, but beneath those charming habiliments beats the same stern and masculine heart that we discern in other European races.

It was a proof of the great confidence felt by Mrs. Stowe in the idea of African Colonization — in the mighty results to be achieved through its means for Africa and for humanity — that she sends two of the most striking characters in Uncle Tom's Cabin to Africa; one, the bright, the enlightened, the cultivated George Harris, goes to Liberia. And never were more forcible reasons given for the emigration of persons of color from this country to that Republic than are presented in the able and eloquent letter which she makes him write to set forth his reasons for emigrating. His arguments are pathetic and unanswerable.

George Harris's letter at least shows what a cultivated Anglo-Saxon and an abolitionist feels ought to be the views of an educated and cultivated colored American; and supplies a hint to those colored writers and speakers who amuse themselves with agitating questions of amalgamation.

Mrs. Stowe speaks of Liberia as "the refuge which the providence of God has provided in Africa." But she does not approve an indiscriminate emigration to Africa. In arguing against it she says wisely,

"To fill up Liberia with an ignorant, inexperienced, half-barbarized race, just escaped from the chains of slavery, would be only to prolong, for ages, the period of struggle and conflict which attend the inception of new enterprises. Let the church of the north receive these poor sufferers in the spirit of Christ; receive them to the educating advantages of Christian republican society and schools, until they have attained to somewhat of a moral and intellectual maturity, and then assist them in their passage to those shores, where they may put in practice the lessons they have learned in America."

Mrs. Stowe's idea does not seem to be that after they have risen to a certain stage of progress they should be absorbed into the great American nation. Her plan is exactly that of the American Colonization Society — to "assist them in their passage to those shores, where they may put in practice the lessons they have learned in America." The attention of those who look to an ultimate American destiny for the American Negro should be called to these utterances of an acknowledged friend and able defender of the race. Mrs. Stowe's wonderful novel was not only the harbinger of emancipation, but the harbinger also of the vast colonization which will sooner or later take place. And that friends of the African should have seized upon her words in the one capacity and not in the other, can only be explained by the fact that as an angel of Abolition the nation was ready for her; but to receive her as an angel of Colonization, it is only now in the process of preparation.

Soon after the close of the war it was the favorite cry of some that the Colonization Society had done its work and should be dropped. But that cry has been effectually hushed by the increasing light of experience, and under the louder cries of the thousands and tens of thousands, who in various parts of the country are asking for aid to reach the land of their fathers. Both white and colored are now recognizing the fact that the Society with its abundant knowledge, with its organized plans, is an indispensable machinery for the diffusion of that special information about Africa of which the American people are so generally destitute, and for the inoffensive creation among the Negro portion of the population of those enlightened opinions about the land of their fathers, and their duty to that land which will lead some at least of the anxious thousands to enter upon it with intelligence and efficiency.

There is evidently, at this moment, no philanthropic institution before the American public that has more just and reasonable claims upon private and official benevolence than the American Colonization Society. And the Christian sentiment of the country, as I gather it from the east and from the west, from the north and from the south, is largely in favor of giving substantial and generous aid to that struggling Christian Republic in West Africa, the power of which, it is conceded, it should be the pride of this nation, as it is its commercial interest, to increase and perpetuate.

REFERENCES

[1]Gary T. Marx, *Protest and Prejudice* (New York: Harper & Row, Publishers, 1967).

[2]*Ibid.*, p. xvi.

[3]The most thorough development of this idea is by Harold Cruse, *Rebellion Or Revolution* (New York: William Morrow & Co., Inc., 1968).

[4]*Ibid.*, p. 78.

[5]E. U. Essien-Udom, *Black Nationalism* (Chicago: The University of Chicago Press, 1962), p. 6.

[6]*Ibid.*, p. 7.

[7]Malcolm X and Alex Haley, *The Autobiography of Malcolm X* (N.Y.: Grove Press, Inc., 1964), p. 374. Reprinted with permission of Grove Press. Copyrighted © 1964 by Alex Haley and Malcolm X. Copyrighted © 1965 by Alex Haley and Betty Shabazz.

[8]Cruse, *op. cit.*, p. 95.

[9]*Ibid.*, p. 77.

[10]S. 33, Community Self-Determination Act of 1969, 91st Congress, 1st Session, pp. 3-4.

[11]See Cruse, *Rebellion Or Revolution,* Chapters 6, 11, 13.

[12]*The Liberator,* February 22, 1828, p. 191.

[13]*Ibid.*

[14]William J. Simmons, *Men Of Mark* (New York: Arno Press, Inc., and *The New York Times,* 1968 reprint of 1887 edition), p. 492.

[15]Biographical information and manuscripts of sermons were obtained in the Crummell Papers held in the Schomburg Collection, Harlem

Branch of the New York Public Library, New York; cited hereafter as Schomburg Collection.

[16]Simmons, *op. cit.,* p. 535.

[17]*The Liberator,* April 27, 1833, p. 68.

[18]*The Liberator,* April 28, 1832, pp. 66-67.

[19]Simmons' biography, op. cit., p. 872, shows the name spelled "Smythe," but the manuscript of the essay printed here bore his signature with the "Smyth" spelling. Simmons' spelling of names throughout his book is often at variance with that generally accepted today. Future references, when a conflict occurs, will reject Simmons' spelling.

[20]Simmons, *Men Of Mark,* p. 872; and Richard Bardolph, *The Negro Vanguard* (N.Y.: Vintage Books, 1959), pp. 95, 97.

[21]*New Era,* June 30, 1870, p. 1.

[22]John Hope Franklin, *From Slavery to Freedom* (New York: Alfred A. Knopf, Inc., 1965), p. 235; Simmons, *op. cit.,* p. 339.

[23]Franklin, *op. cit.,* p. 237.

[24]*Ibid.*

[25]Edward Wesley Shunk, "The Negro Colonization Movement in Ohio Prior to the Civil War," (Master's Thesis, Ohio State University, 1941), pp. 27-28.

[26]*Ibid.,* p. 28.

[27]*African Repository,* Vol. XXVI, p. 219.

[28]*Minutes and Address of the State Convention of Colored Citizens of Ohio,* convened in Columbus, Ohio, January 10th, 11th, 12th, and 13th, 1849 (Oberlin: J. M. Fitch, 1849).

[29]*Ibid.*

[30]*Ibid.*

[31]*Ibid.*

[32]Simmons, *Men Of Mark,* p. 1007.

[33]*Ibid.,* pp. 1007-1008.

[34]*African Repository,* Vol. 31, January, 1855, p. 22.

[35]*Douglass Monthly,* V, No. 3, August, 1862, p. 695.

[36]*Ibid.*

[37]*Ibid.*

[38]*Ibid.*

[39]John W. Menard, *Douglass Monthly,* V, No. 4 (April, 1863), p. 821.

[40]*Ibid.*

[41]Address of Reverend E. W. Blyden at the Annual Meeting of the Maine Colonization Society, June, 1862 (pamphlet).

[42]*Ibid.*

[43]Biographical data on Blyden was found in Casely Hayford (Edra-Agiman), *Ethiopia Unbound: Studies in Race Emancipation* (London: C. M. Phillips, 1911) and in Simmons, *op cit.,* pp. 916-21.

[44]*Ibid.,* p. 163.

[45]*Ibid.,* pp. 164-65.

Chapter 5   SEPARATION: THE BLACK INITIATIVE

For the casual student of American history, and this includes most citizens of the United States, the work of the American Colonization Society constituted the beginning and the end of the efforts of black Americans to separate themselves from whites. The fact that this effort was largely motivated by the action of white men may help explain this. But while public attention was directed at efforts toward assimilation, a *black-motivated* campaign of separation emerged. That campaign will be examined in this chapter. The key movements within this campaign are efforts toward emigration to black dominated lands outside Africa, Marcus Garvey's program of Africa for the Africans, Elijah Muhammad's work through the Nation of Islam, and more modern efforts to establish two Americas.

One way for the pro-separatist to resolve his conflict between his desire to encourage departure from the United States and his disapproval of the American Colonization Society was to advocate emigration to some place other than Africa. If one could reason that the United States was unique among white-dominated nations in its desire to persecute black men, then life in one of the neighboring countries could provide a solution without the difficulty of a long trip to Africa. Moreover,

347

consideration of the West Indies, Haiti, and Central and South America revealed populations with a black majority, even though they were, for the most part, dominated by white colonial powers. Even moving to the western part of the United States, where one could live almost in isolation, and certainly outside the reach of former slave masters in the South, promised much to the black man seeking separation.

Rising United States imperialism during the years following the end of the Civil War created some doubts about this kind of emigration plan. Real possibilities seemed to exist that the United States might colonize many of these prospective refuges. It would be most unfortunate if a black community were established away from the previously oppressive whites in this country, only to have them move in as new masters a few years later.

Therefore, the emigration debate concerned less interaction with the pro-assimilationist group, and more intra-separatist dialogue over the selection of locations to which to emigrate, and the prospects for future independence. Persuasion from the separationist to the uncommitted black population, however, continued in full force.

Samuel Ringgold Ward, a tough and eloquent abolitionist speaker who will be introduced in greater detail in Chapter VI, was, for a time, minister to a white congregation in Cortlandville, New York and an early emigrant to Canada. From his haven in the North, Ward wrote to his black brothers and sisters still in the United States, and in 1852, he offered his beliefs on the matter of emigration. When viewed from the modern era, his ideas seem extraordinarily practical, for his first contention was, "I do not believe, that fear or favor, with or without your consent, will ever remove you from the American continent."[1] Basically, he argued that there were too many people living under too many different circumstances such as slavery and freedom, North and South, for any mass migration to be effective. In logical form, Ward listed his lines of reasoning in support of his assertion that most blacks in the United States should never expect to escape. His first point was every attempt at general emigration on the part of black people had failed. "It was so with emigration to Hayti, in 1832, and it was so with the emigration to Trinidad, in 1839." Second, he observed that history has shown, that once a people is spread throughout an area, and intertwined with the majority population even through blood, no detachment from that majority population is possible. Third, unlike the American Indian, the black man had not drawn back from civilization and refused to mingle and relate to the white population. The black man has not remained as distinct from the rest of the nation as the Indians or Jews have.

Fourth, ". . . the destiny of any people is almost invariably wrought out, for weal or for woe, on *their native soil.* This is true even where that destiny is extermination."

Only once, said Ward, had a people escaped from such circumstances — the Jews from Egypt — and that, he claimed, ". . . was by direct Divine interposition — an agency which I believe is not relied on in this case, by even such *models of piety* as Clay, and Webster, and Hunt, and Greeley." Even if a substantial emigration movement were started, Ward said, people could probably not be removed fast enough to keep ahead of the rate of increase in population.

Having fulfilled his duties as a responsible speaker by refusing to lead his receivers to a state of false hope, Samuel Ward proceeded to consider the prospects for emigration for those few who could reasonably expect it. He first strongly rejected the idea of going to Liberia. He said,

> I think no more of the Government of Liberia, than I do of that of the United States. I have no evidence that the constitution of the former is any better than that of the latter, nor as good; it certainly is not as impartial; and I have no sort of reason to confide in its officers carrying it out a whit better than their Yankee master do theirs.[2]

It would be better, he urged, to live under an impartial and experienced government such as that of the British in Canada. Canada was in no danger of being annexed to the United States, Ward asserted, because none in Canada desired it, particularly after seeing the evil passage of the Fugitive Slave Act. Once again viciously attacking the Liberian government, he said,

> Now, to go to distant Liberia, to become citizens of a country yet in its infancy, *and like to stay so,* and subjects of a Government, whose principles are untried, and whose founding and peopleing, has gone on at the expense of your constant and perservering desparagement, the denial of your rights and the questioning of your very manhood, were as wanting in good sense, as in self-respect. Men who, like His Excellency, President Roberts, allow the wholesale and indiscriminate abuse of Free Blacks, from the lips of the abominable Clay, the deceitful Cresson, and the blasphemer Orcott, (who peddles colonizationism in Connecticut,) without a word of remonstrance, or rebuke, or protest, though he himself knows what it is to have been an American Black Man, are but little better to be trusted with our liberties in Africa, than Fillmore and Clay are in America.[3]

Having argued in favor of emigration to Canada, and against association with Liberia, Ward presents a conclusion which today seems prophetic — he sees nothing in store for the black man in the United States but more suffering, and no resort to turn to but faith in God:

> But I said the great mass of you will remain where you are. I do not say I desire it to be so. I am simply speaking of facts and probabilities. It were much more acceptable to me, to see you all leave the guilty land that gave you birth and come to our shores, where you could be permitted to see, as doubtless you soon will, the judgment of Jehovah descend upon what Gerrit Smith too truthfully calls "a doomed and damned nation." But that you will not do so, I am quite convinced. I am quite satisfied, too that there are other and greater sufferings in store for you.[4]

He offered only one resort — a last one to be sought only after all possible struggle:

> This resort is not to the sword nor to any physical force, right enough in itself when it can be successfully wielded, but unwise and suicidal in the case of so few, against so many, nor is it to cringing nor fawning nor to despairing despondency, nor to a wholesale emigration. What is it? What is it? It is to look above and beyond man, to God.[5]

The separatist, by nature, becomes committed to reliance upon Christian redemption through the force of circumstances.

Samuel R. Ward's ambivalence in calling for trust in God while wishing to separate was rejected by a writer to *Frederick Douglass' Paper* in the following issues. J. W. Adams of Philadelphia said that Ward's advice to look beyond man to God was a step backward to the old slave advice. "Our old fathers," said Adams, "were told to pray on and stand still, but they were dragged from their knees while in prayer and sent to the back of the church" — an obvious reference to the experience of Richard Allen. "They," meaning Allen, "tried to correct this by forming a separate church," Adams continued.

> Unfortunately for them, however, they used similar materials in rearing their fabric, as that from which they isolated themselves, instead of taking (as they ought) the clay and moulding a system for themselves more enlarged and progressive.[6]

As far as Adams was concerned, the system of religion was a failure.

> "Christianity is a failure" because the *Bible* says that Christianity removes evil, . . . yet we see that these, whose systems

of creeds put together, has failed to remove that root of all bitterness to us, *viz.:* prejudice, from the hearts of our . . . *lords and masters.*

Even the Quakers or Friends, who presume to declare themselves our chief protectors, said Adams, have ". . . an especial proviso excluding *"black men"* from an equal privilege in *their* communion." In closing, Adams said he and others like him would reject Ward's advice. Instead, he said, "We must adopt the motto, 'Who would be free, HIMSELF must STRIKE the blow.' "

Bishop Henry MacNeal Turner of the AME Church agreed with this reasoning. Turner, who was described as one of the most forceful personalities among black Americans during the last half of the nineteenth century, felt there was little hope for improvement in the black man's position in the United States, and he argued for a return to Africa. Although Turner was particularly successful within American society — he was the first black army chaplain, chancellor of Morris Brown College, and the recipient of an honorary degree from the University of Pennsylvania — he nevertheless was a particularly effective spokesman for the idea of emigration.[7]

Martin R. Delany, had fully developed his emigrationist ideas by 1852 when he published his book, *The Condition, Elevation, Emigration, and Destiny of the Colored People of the United States, Politically Considered.* At that time, as can be seen from the portion of the volume included here, Delany was committed to emigration within the Western Hemisphere. The book details the kinds of occupations and the places to pursue them that would be most advantageous to the black men of the United States. Admitting that the prime need was knowledge about Africa, Delany noted three objections to Liberia as the place for emigration. First, it was in an undesirable geographical location; second, "it originated in a deep laid scheme of the slaveholders of the country, to *exterminate* the free colored of the American continent;" and third,

Liberia is not an Independent Republic: in fact, *it is not* an independent nation at all; but a poor *miserable mockery* — a *burlesque* on a government — a pitiful dependency on the American Colonizations. . . .[8]

Delany proceeded to discuss possible locations in detail, with apologies to Africa for his criticisms. His concluding chapter, published here, gives the essence of his position.

Martin R. Delany

Chapter XXIV
*A Glance at Ourselves — Conclusion**

> With broken hopes — sad devastation;
> A race *resigned* to DEGRADATION!

We have said much to our young men and women, about their vocation and calling; we have dwelt much upon the menial position of our people in this country. Upon this point we cannot say too much, because there is a seeming satisfaction and seeking after such positions manifested on their part, unknown to any other people. There appears to be, a want of a sense of propriety or *self-respect,* altogether inexplicable; because young men and women among us, many of whom have good trades and homes, adequate to their support, voluntarily leave them, and seek positions, such as servants, waiting maids, coachmen, nurses, cooks in gentlemens' kitchen, or such occupations, when they can gain a livelihood at something more respectable, or elevating in character. And the worse part of the whole matter is, that they have become so accustomed to it, it has become so "fashionable," that it seems to have become second nature, and they really become offended, when it is spoken against.

Among the German, Irish, and other European peasantry who come to this country, it matters not what they were employed at before and after they come; just so soon as they can better their condition by keeping shops, cultivating the soil, the young men and women going to night-schools, qualifying themselves for usefulness, and learning trades — they do so. Their first and last care, object and aim is, to better their condition by raising themselves above the condition that necessity places them in. We do not say too much, when we say, as an evidence of the deep degradation of our race, in the United States, that there are those among us, the wives and daughters, some of the *first ladies,* (and who dare say they are not the "first," because they belong to the "first class" and associate where any body among us can?) whose husbands are industrious, able and willing to support them, who voluntarily leave home, and become chamber-maids, and stewardesses, upon vessels and steamboats, in all probability, to enable them to obtain some more fine or costly article of dress or furniture.

We have nothing to say against those whom *necessity* compels to do these things, those who can do no better; we have only to do with those who can, and will not, or do not do better. The whites are always in the advance, and we either standing still or retrograding; as that which does not go forward, must either stand in one place or go back. The father in all probability is a farmer, mechanic, or man of some independent business; and the wife, sons and daughters, are chamber-maids, on vessels, nurses and waiting-maids, or

*From Martin R. Delany, *The Condition, Elevation, Emigration, and Destiny of the Colored People of the United States Politically Considered* (New York: Arno Press and The New York Times, 1968, reprint of 1852 edition), pp. 197-208.

coachmen and cooks in families. This is retrogradation. The wife, sons, and daughters should be elevated above this condition as a necessary consequence.

If we did not love our race superior to others, we would not concern ourself about their degradation; for the greatest desire of our heart is, to see them stand on a level with the most elevated of mankind. No people are ever elevated above the condition of their *females;* hence, the condition of the *mother* determines the condition of the child. To know the position of a people, it is only necessary to know the *condition* of their *females;* and despite themselves, they cannot rise above their level. Then what is our condition? Our *best ladies* being washerwomen, chamber-maids, children's traveling nurses, and common house servants, and menials, we are all a degraded, miserable people, inferior to any other people as a whole, on the face of the globe.

These great truths, however unpleasant, must be brought before the minds of our people in its true and proper light, as we have been too delicate about them, and too long concealed them for fear of giving offence. It would have been infinitely better for our race, if these facts had been presented before us half a century ago — we would have been now proportionably benefitted by it.

As an evidence of the degradation to which we have been reduced, we dare premise, that this chapter will give offence to many, very many, and why? Because they may say, "He dared to say that the occupation of a *servant* is a degradation." It is not necessarily degrading; it would not be, to one or a few people of a kind; but a *whole race of servants* are a degradation to that people.

Efforts made by men of qualifications for the toiling and degraded millions among the whites, neither gives offence to that class, nor is it taken unkindly by them; but received with manifestations of gratitude; to know that they are thought to be, equally worthy of, and entitled to stand on a level with the elevated classes; and they have only got to be informed of the way to raise themselves, to make the effort and do so as far as they can. But how different with us. Speak of our position in society, and it at once gives insult. Though we are servants; among ourselves we claim to be *ladies* and *gentlemen,* equal in standing, and as the popular expression goes, "Just as good as any body" — and so believing, we make no efforts to raise above the common level of menials; because the *best* being in that capacity, all are content with the position. We cannot at the same time, be domestic and lady; servant and gentleman. We must be the one or the other. Sad, sad indeed, is the thought, that hangs drooping in our mind, when contemplating the picture drawn before us. Young men and women, "we write these things unto you, because ye are strong," because the writer, a few years ago, gave unpardonable offence to many of the young people of Philadelphia and other places, because he dared tell them, that he thought too much of them, to be content with seeing them the servants of other people. Surely, she that could be the mistress, would not be the maid; neither would he that could be the master, be content with being the servant; then why be offended, when we point out to you, the way that leads from the menial to the mistress or the master. All this we seem to reject with fixed determination, repelling with anger, every effort on the part of our intelligent men and women to elevate us, with true Israelitish degradation, in reply to any suggestion or proposition that may be offered, "Who made thee a ruler and judge?"

The writer is no "Public Man," in the sense in which this is understood among our people, but simply an humble individual, endeavoring to seek a livelihood by a profession obtained entirely by his own efforts, without relatives and friends able to assist him; except such friends as he gained by the merit of his course and conduct, which he here gratefully acknowledges; and whatever he has accomplished, other young men may, by making corresponding efforts, also accomplish.

We have advised an emigration to Central and South America, and even to Mexico and the West Indies, to those who prefer either of the last named places, all of which are free countries, Brazil being the only real slaveholding State in South America — there being nominal slavery in Dutch Guiana, Peru, Buenos Ayres, Paraguay, and Uraguay, in all of which places colored people have equality in social, civil, political, and religious privileges; Brazil making it punishable with death to import slaves into the empire.

Our oppressors, when urging us to go to Africa, tell us that we are better adapted to the climate than they — that the physical condition of the constitution of colored people better endures the heat of warm climates than that of the whites; this we are willing to *admit,* without argument, without adducing the physiological reason why, that colored people can and do stand warm climates better than whites; and find an answer fully to the point in the fact, that they also stand *all other* climates, cold, temperate, and modified, that white people can stand; therefore, according to our oppressors' own showing, we are a *superior race,* being endowed with properties fitting us for *all parts* of the earth, while they are only adapted to *certain* parts. Of course, this proves our right and duty to live wherever we may *choose;* while the white race may only live where they *can.* We are content with the fact, and have ever claimed it. Upon this rock, they and we shall ever agree.

Of the West India Islands, Santa Cruz, belonging to Denmark; Porto Rico, and Cuba with its little adjuncts, belonging to Spain, are the only slaveholding Islands among them — three-fifths of the whole population of Cuba being colored people, who cannot and will not much longer endure the burden and the yoke. They only want intelligent leaders of their own color, when they are ready at any moment to charge to the conflict — to liberty or death. The remembrance of the noble mulatto, PLACIDO, the gentleman, scholar, poet, and intended Chief Engineer of the Army of Liberty and Freedom in Cuba; and the equally noble black, CHARLES BLAIR, who was to have been Commander-in-Chief, who were shamefully put to death in 1844, by that living monster, Captain General O'Donnell, is still fresh and indelible to the mind of every bondman of Cuba.

In our own country, the United States, there are *three million five hundred thousand slaves;* and we, the nominally free colored people, are *six hundred thousand* in number; estimating one-sixth to be men, we have *one hundred thousand* able bodied freemen, which will make a powerful auxiliary in any country to which we may become adopted — an ally not to be despised by any power on earth. We love our country, dearly love her, but she don't love us — she despises us, and bids us begone, driving us from her embraces; but we shall not go where she desires us; but when we do go, whatever love we have for her, we shall love the country none the less that receive us as her adopted children.

For the want of business habits and training, our energies have become paralyzed; our young men never think of business, any more than if they were so many bondmen, without the right to pursue any calling they may think most advisable. With our people in this country, dress and good appearances have been made the only test of gentleman and ladyship, and that vocation which offers the best opportunity to dress and appear well, has generally been preferred, however menial and degrading, by our young people, without even, in the majority of cases, an effort to do better; indeed, in many instances, refusing situations equally lucrative, and superior in position; but which would not allow us much display of dress and personal appearance. This, if we ever expect to rise, must be discarded from among us, and a high and respectable position assumed.

One of our great temporal curses is our consummate poverty. We are the poorest people, as a class, in the world of civilized mankind — abjectly, miserably poor, no one scarcely being able to assist the other. To this, of course, there are noble exceptions; but that which is common to, and the very process by which white men exist, and succeed in life, is unknown to colored men in general. In any and every considerable community may be found, some one of our white fellow-citizens, who is worth more than all the colored people in that community put together. We consequently have little or no efficiency. We must have means to be practically efficient in all the undertakings of life; and to obtain them, it is necessary that we should be engaged in lucrative pursuits, trades, and general business transactions. In order to be thus engaged, it is necessary that we should occupy positions that afford the facilities for such pursuits. To compete now with the mighty odds of wealth, social and religious preferences, and political influences of this country, at this advanced stage of its national existence, we never may expect. A new country, and new beginning, is the only true, rational, politic remedy for our disadvantaged position; and that country we have already pointed out, with triple golden advantages, all things considered, to that of any country to which it has been the province of man to embark.

Every other than we, have at various periods of necessity, been a migratory people; and all when oppressed, shown a greater abhorrence of oppression, if not a greater love of liberty, than we. We cling to our oppressors as the objects of our love. It is true that our enslaved brethren are here, and we have been led to believe that it is necessary for us to remain, on that account. Is it true, that all should remain in degradation, because a part are degraded? We believe no such thing. We believe it to be the duty of the Free, to elevate themselves in the most speedy and effective manner possible; as the redemption of the bondman depends entirely upon the elevation of the freeman; therefore, to elevate the free colored people of America, anywhere upon this continent; forebodes the speedy redemption of the slaves. We shall hope to hear no more of so fallacious a doctrine—the necessity of the free remaining in degradation, for the sake of the oppressed. Let us apply, first, the lever to ourselves; and the force that elevates us to the position of manhood's considerations and honors, will cleft the manacle of every slave in the land.

When such great worth and talents — for want of a better sphere — of men like Rev. Jonathan Robinson, Robert Douglass, Frederick A. Hinton, and a hundred others that might be named, were permitted to expire in a barber-shop; and such living men as may be found in Boston, New York, Philadelphia, Baltimore, Richmond, Washington City, Charleston, (S. C.) New Orleans, Cincinnati, Louisville, St. Louis, Pittsburg, Buffalo, Rochester, Albany, Utica, Cleveland, Detroit, Milwaukie, Chicago, Columbus, Zanesville, Wheeling, and a hundred other places, confining themselves to Barber-shops and waiterships in Hotels; certainly the necessity of such a course as we have pointed out, must be cordially acknowledged; appreciated by every brother and sister of oppression; and not rejected as heretofore, as though they preferred inferiority to equality. These minds must become "unfettered," and have "space to rise." This cannot be in their present positions. A continuance in any position, becomes what is termed "Second Nature;" it begets an *adaptation,* and *reconciliation* of *mind* to such condition. It changes the whole physiological condition of the system, and adapts man and woman to a higher or lower sphere in the pursuits of life. The offsprings of slaves and peasantry, have the general characteristics of their parents; and nothing but a different course of training and education, will change the character.

The slave may become a lover of his master, and learn to forgive him for continual deeds of maltreatment and abuse; just as the Spaniel would couch and fondle at the feet that kick him; because he has been taught to reverence them, and consequently, becomes adapted in body and mind to his condition. Even the shrubbery-loving Canary, and lofty-soaring Eagle, may be tamed to the cage, and learn to love it from habit of confinement. It has been so with us in our position among our oppressors; we have been so prone to such positions, that we have learned to love them. When reflecting upon this all important, and to us, all absorbing subject; we feel in the agony and anxiety of the moment, as though we could cry out in the language of a Prophet of old: "Oh that my head were waters, and mine eyes a fountain of tears, that I might weep day and night for the" degradation "of my people! Oh that I had in the wilderness a lodging place of way-faring men; that I might leave my people, and go from them!"

The Irishman and German in the United States, are very different persons to what they were when in Ireland and Germany, the countries of their nativity. There their spirits were depressed and downcast; but the instant they set their foot upon unrestricted soil; free to act and untrammeled to move; their physical condition undergoes a change, which in time becomes physiological, which is transmitted to the offspring, who when born under such circumstances, is a decidedly different being to what it would have been, had it been born under different circumstances.

A child born under oppression, has all the elements of servility in its constitution; who when born under favorable circumstances, has to the contrary, all the elements of freedom and independence of feeling. Our children then, may not be expected, to maintain that position and manly bearing; born under the unfavorable circumstances with which we are surrounded in this country; that we so much desire. To use the language of the talented Mr. Whipper, "they cannot be raised in this country, without being stoop shouldered." Heaven's pathway stands unobstructed, which will lead us into a Paradise of bliss. Let us go on and possess the land, and the God of Israel will be our God.

The lessons of every school book, the pages of every history, and columns of every newspaper, are so replete with stimuli to nerve us on to manly aspirations, that those of our young people, who will now refuse to enter upon this great theatre of Polynesian adventure, and take their position on the stage of Central and South America, where a brilliant engagement, of certain and most triumphant success, in the drama of human equality awaits them; then, with the blood of *slaves,* write upon the lintel of every door in sterling Capitals, to be gazed and hissed at by every passer by —

> Doomed by the Creator
> To servility and degradation;
> The SERVANT of the *white man,*
> And despised of every nation!

Frederick Douglass, a lifetime opponent of colonization and emigration, was even persuaded to take a friendly position toward departure for Haiti by those who could no longer reconcile themselves with life in the United States. In an editorial published in January, 1861, Douglass emphasized that he had not changed his mind on the emigration, but he could see some good reasons for leaving the United States and some good reasons for selecting Haiti as the place for settlement. He said,

> She [Haiti] offers the strongest inducements to emigration to her shores. Her mountain sides, her valleys, and her plains have been, by a wise and hospitable government, flung open to us, as will be seen by an official document elsewhere, on the most generous terms [the document will be printed below]. The doors are open, a warm welcome and a secure home are proffered to the industrious and upright colored man and his family, if he will but go forward and accept them.[9]

As a reason to leave the United States, Douglass could say this:

> . . . the United States is in great trouble. Slavery, vengeance and settled hate, frown on and threaten the free colored people in the slave States with bondage or exploitation, while evidences are abundant of a settled purpose to hold them as a servile and degraded casts in the freest of the free States. Every negro is looked upon as a hinderance to the peace and

harmony of the free and slave States, and as long as that harmony is thought desirable by the free States, they will hate and persecute the colored people.[10]

In the face of these circumstances, and the fact that free states were even then in the process of passing laws to deny the vote to free black citizens, Douglass drew this conclusion:

We do not wonder, therefore, at the readiness with which colored men are now preparing to leave the United States for Hayti — We should not be surprised to find thousands of them flocking to that country. While we have never favored any plan of emigration, and have never been willing to concede that this is a doomed country, and that we are a doomed race in it, we can raise no objection to the present movement towards Hayti. For years we have looked to such emigration as a possible necessity to our people; and though we do not think that necessity has yet fully come, we can no longer throw our little influence against a measure which may prove highly advantageous to many families, and of much service to the Haytian Republic.[11]

Douglass was obliged to admit that most of his old arguments against the American Colonization Society did not apply to the present case of emigrating to Haiti. There was no reason to charge that emigration was a sign of dealing with pro-slave interests, or a denial of assistance to the enslaved, or the concession that Africa was the only home for the black man. But Douglass refused to endorse Haitian emigration — he would only say that if one were to emigrate, Haiti, where one would still be close enough to the United States to continue the fight for abolition, would be the place to go.

To close this reluctant support for emigration, Douglass provided free advertising space in his paper for the Haitian representative. He said that he had gone to Boston and had seen the "Haytian Bureau of Emigration, and made the acquaintance of Mr. Redpath, the General Agent." This man convinced Douglass that he was to be trusted, was a full opponent of slavery, and in closing, Douglass gave the address to which interested parties could write. If all critics of emigration had been as generous as Frederick Douglass, pro-emigrationists would not have needed friends.

Probably no better evidence of the persuasiveness of the speakers for settlement in Haiti can be found than in this commentary by Douglass. To illustrate the more formal type of advertising then used, the circular to which Douglass alluded is printed below.

Haytian Advertisements

*Invitation**

Hayti will soon regain her ancient splendor. This marvelous soil that our fathers, blessed by God, conquered for us, will soon yield to us the wealth now hidden, in its bosom. Let our black and yellow brethren, scattered through the Antilles, and North and South America, hasten to co-operate with us in restoring the glory of the Republic. Hayti is the common country of the black race. Our ancestors, in taking possession of it, were careful to announce in the Constitution that they published, that all the descendants of Africans, and of the inhabitants of the West Indies, belong by right to the Haytian family. The idea was grand and generous.

Listen, then, all ye negroes and mulattoes who, in the vast Continent of America, suffer from the prejudices of caste. The Republic calls you; she invites you to bring to her your arms and your minds. The regenerating work that she undertakes interests all colored people and their descendants, no matter what their origin or where their place of birth.

Hayti, regaining her former position, retaking her ancient sceptre as Queen of the Antilles, will be a formal denial, most eloquent and peremptory, against those detractors of our race who contest our desire and ability to attain a high degree of civilization.

GEFFRARD

Circular — No. I

To the Blacks, Men of Color, and Indians in the United States and British North American Provinces:

Friends: I am authorized and instructed by the Government of the Republic, to offer you, individually and by communities, a welcome, a home, and a free homestead, in Hayti.

Such of you as are unable to pay your passage will be provided with the means of defraying it.

Two classes of emigrants are especially invited — laborers and farmers. None of either class, or any class, will be furnished with passports, who cannot produce, before sailing, the proofs of good character for industry and integrity.

To each family of emigrants, five carreaux (a carreau is 3 acres and 3⅓ rods) of fresh and fertile land, capable of growing all the fruits and staples of the tropics, will be gratuitously given, on the sole condition that they shall settle on it and cultivate it, and declare their intention of becoming citizens of Hayti. To unmarried men, on similar conditions, two carreaux will be granted.

Board and lodging, free of cost, will be furnished to the emigrants for at least eight days after their arrival in the island.

The government also will find remunerative work for those of you whose means will not permit you to begin immediately an independent cultivation.

---

*The *Douglass Monthly*, IX, No. 7 (December, 1861), 576.

Emigrants are invited to settle in communities.

Sites for the erection of schools and chapels will be donated by the State, without regard to the religious belief of the emigrants.

The same protection and civil rights that the laws give to Haytians are solemnly guaranteed to the emigrants.

The fullest religious liberty will be secured to them; they will never be called on to support the Roman Catholic Church.

No military service will be demanded of them, excepting that they shall form military companies and drill themselves once a month.

All the necessary personal effects, machinery and agricultural instruments introduced by emigrants shall be entered free of duty.

The emigrants shall be at liberty to leave the country at any moment they please; but those whose passage shall be paid by government, if they wish to return before the expiration of three years, will be required to refund the money expended on their account. A contract, fixing the amount, will be made with each emigrant before leaving the continent.

I have been commissioned to superintend the interests of the emigrants, and charged with the entire control of the movement in America, and all persons, therefore, desiring to avail themselves of the invitation and bounty of the Haytian Government, are requested to correspond with me. I shall at once, as directed by the Government, establish a bureau of emigration in Boston, and publish a Guide Book for the use of those persons of African or Indian descent who may wish to make themselves acquainted with the resources of the country and the disposition of its authorities.

I shall also appoint Agents to visit such communities as may seriously entertain the project of emigration.

Immediate arrangements, both here and in Hayti, can be made for the embarkment and settlement of one hundred thousand persons.

By order of the Government of the Republic of Hayti.

James Redpath,
General Agent of Emigration

Boston, Nov. 3, 1860

Haytian Bureau of Emigration, August 31, 1861
*Autumn Arrangements**

Arrangements will be made by which emigrants can sail from different ports during the autumn and winter. Due notice will be given of the days of sailing, through the columns of "The Pine and Palm."

---

*The *Douglass Monthly*, IX, No. 7 (December, 1861), 576.

Persons desiring to emigrate are requested to read carefully the circulars of this Bureau, and to follow the directions therein given, as it is impossible to provide for the comfort of passengers except by insisting on a strict compliance with our regulations.

I. Let it be understood, that all who can pay for their passage are expected to do so; and that a passage will be advanced to such farmers and laborers only as are unable to meet this expense.

II. All mechanics who intend to practice their trades in Hayti, must go at their own expense; the Government guarantees to find work for farmers and laborers only. It will welcome all colored emigrants; but it cannot agree to provide work for all classes of mechanics. Its demands for agricultural labor is unlimited; but for mechanical skill this is not the case.

III. Passengers will be charged at the rate of $18 each adult from United States ports; from Canada West, $25. Children under eight will be charged half price; infants under one year, free.

IV. Passengers, in all cases, should provide their own bedding. Mattresses must be four feet wide. Each passenger must be provided with a tin gallon can for water, a tin cup, a tin plate, knife and fork, a few pounds of soap, and towels, with such extra utensils as may be deemed necessary to hold the daily rations.

V. The amount of baggage allowed to every passenger is two trunks, or two barrels, or one trunk and one barrel. All freight over that amount will be charged for, separately from the passage ticket, at the rate of 75 cents per barrel or 15 cents per cubic foot from American ports; or 90 cents per barrel and 18 cents per cubic foot from British North American ports. This is exclusive of the bedding, which goes free. — All goods must be boxed up.

VI. The board provided for emigrants will be the navy rations of the United States, minus intoxicating spirits, which will not be allowed in our vessels. The following is the fare:

NAVY RATION FOR EACH DAY OF THE WEEK

Days	Bread	Beef	Pork	Flour	Rice	Dried Fruit	Pickles	Sugar	Tea (Choice of Either)	Coff (Choice of Either)	Butter	Cheese	Beans	Molasses	Vinegar	Water
	oz	lb	lb	lb	lb	lb	lb	oz	oz	oz	oz	oz	pt	pt	pt	gal
Sunday	14	1		½		¼		2	¼	1						1
Monday	14		1					2	¼	1			½			1
Tuesday	14	1			½			2	¼	1	2	2				1
Wednesday	14		1				¼	2	¼	1			½			1
Thursday	14	1		½		¼		2	¼	1						1
Friday	14	1	1		½			2	¼	1	2	2	½			1
Saturday	14						¼	2	¼	1				½	½	1
	98	4	3	1	1	½	½	14	1¾	7	4	4	1½	½	½	7

Emigrants are at liberty to carry, free of expense, additional provisions to be used on the voyage. Slight additions may be made to the navy rations; but the Bureau does not pledge itself to do so.

VII.   As efforts have been industriously made by unscrupulous men to misrepresent the conditions under which emigrants who do not prepay their passage, will accept the offers of the Government of Hayti, it is deemed advisable to publish below, in full, the contract to be made with them. The words in italic and within brackets (blank in the original) are filled 'up to how precisely the terms on which a single man can emigrate. It should be distinctly understood, that no barrier whatever will be put to any man's return, excepting that he shall pay the sum of eighteen dollars before embarking for the United States, if he did not pay for his own passage from this country to Hayti. The Government of Hayti, while they will welcome all visitors, cannot reasonably be expected to pay their passages. Hence this provision.

The following is the contract with the emigrants who do not prepay their passages:

ARTICLES OF AGREEMENT

This Agreement, made and entered into this (first) day of (January) A.D., 1861, by and between James Redpath, of Boston, General Agent of Emigration, on behalf of the Government of the Republic of Hayti, and (John Smith) late of (Detroit, Michigan) and an emigrant to Hayti;

Witnesseth: That said James Redpath, on behalf of the Government of Hayti aforesaid, agrees to provide a passage for said (John Smith) from the port of (Boston) to the port of (St. Mark) in said Hayti in the (Brig L'Ami d'Haiti) leaving the port of (Boston) on or about the (third) day of (January) 1861, upon the conditions hereafter following, viz:

First, said (John Smith) hereby acknowledges the receipt of (a) ticket of passage from said port of (Boston) to said port of (St. Mark) in Hayti, and agrees during the term of said voyage to provide (his) own bedding, and the necessary utensils for eating and drinking.

Secondly, in consideration of receiving the passage aforesaid, said (John Smith) further agrees, that if he accepts a grant of land from the Government of Hayti, under the provisions of the law of Emigration, approved by His Excellency, the President of the Republic of Hayti, September 1, 1860, he will repay to the Treasury of the Republic of Hayti the sum of (eighteen) dollars, American currency, with (three years) from the date of the contract.

Furthermore, that if from any cause said (John Smith) sees proper to leave Hayti before the expiration of the term of three years from the date of (his) arrival in the Island, (he) shall pay the Treasury of the Republic of Hayti the sum of (eighteen) dollars, American currency, as repayment of expenses incurred by the agents of the Government for (his) passage to Hayti; but, nevertheless, with this express provision: That if (he) does remain three years in the Island from the date of (his) arrival therein, and does not see fit to accept a grant of land from the Government of the Republic of Hayti, (he) shall not be required to repay to the Treasury of the

Republic of Hayti, or any agent of Government thereof, any sum whatever on account of said passage.

In Witness Whereof, the said parties have hereunto set their hands and seals the day and year above written.

L.S.   (John Smith)
L.S.   JAMES REDPATH

VIII.   Emigrants must pay their expenses to the port of embarkation.

IX.   To aid emigrants who wish to carry extra baggage, the Bureau will allow them (by giving a note payable to the Government of Hayti) to take such freight to the amount of $10 .

X.   The Bureau wishes it to be distinctly understood, however, that unless at least twenty days notice is given of intention to sail, with the amount of baggage to be taken, it will not hold itself responsible to secure a passage for any one.

XI.   All persons desiring information relative to the movement, are cordially invited to correspond with the General Bureau, or personally to visit it. The fullest information will be afforded them.

XII.   Usual length of voyage, from fourteen to twenty days.

A. E. Newton
Corresponding Secretary

The Haytian Central Bureau of Emigration has been removed from Boston to New York. Persons intending to emigrate, or desiring information respecting Hayti, should now address Mr. A.E. Newton, the Corresponding Secretary, New York City. The next emigrant vessel will leave New York for Hayti on the 18th of this month.

One of Douglass' most learned and professionally successful opponents in the emigration debate was Richard Theodore Greener. Although Greener had been associated with Douglass in the publication of the *New National Era,* they were opponents in a debate on emigration before the American Social Science Association. Douglass, who simply wrote a paper outlining his opposition to departure from the United States, was not present in person, which may have been a mistake. Greener was a successful and experienced orator who at one time had been compared with Douglass and Langston as one of the three leading speakers among black Americans.[12] During his undergraduate days at Harvard University, from which he graduated in 1870, Greener had won the Boylston Prize in oratory twice.[13] He had taught classics and international and constitutional law at the University of South Carolina for a while, and had completed his studies for the practice of law at the same time. During his lifetime, he was active in politics and held a variety of government positions concurrently with his practice of law.

Greener's speech is significant, first, because he concerns himself primarily with movement from the South to western parts of the United States. While this type of emigration is hardly in the spirit of Delany and the colonizationists who sought sanctuary for black people outside the jurisdiction of the United States, it is in the same direction and a particularly appealing alternative. At that time, the West was opening up to settlers, and vast quantities of land were available at little or no cost. What could be more logical than to form black communities in Kansas, Oklahoma, Washington, and other states? They would be out of reach of the former white oppressors in the South, and largely away from the interference of any powerful white interests.

The reader will be impressed with Greener's scholarly style, probably well suited to his audience from the American Social Science Association who had just heard Douglass' paper arguing the other side. Greener employs considerable evidence to support his ideas, which is consistent with persuasion theory in such a situation. His description of the oppression of the sharecropping system was clear and leaves the reader with a better understanding of why one might want to escape this situation. The speaker adjusted to the fact that his audience consisted of educated whites by showing them the motivations for the black exodus — by reducing the excessive supply of labor, economic benefits might be expected. He contrasts this argument with the notation that some southern landowners were resurrecting some of the old laws of serfdom.

Finally, revealing his legal background, Greener carefully itemized the arguments made by Douglass as well as other opponents of emigration and refuted them one-by-one. While the speech is, for the most part, without oratorical passion, Greener at times shows his feeling. When attacking Douglass' alleged statement that Massachusetts once was Mississippi, he calls Douglass incorrect, unkind, and unjust.

Also significant to the student of rhetoric is Greener's observation, toward the end of his speech, that emigration was a movement which has passed a first stage of talking to white people, and had entered a second stage in which black must communicate with black and seek the development of black initiative and organizations. The scholar does allow himself a peroration delivered with feeling, thus providing a good conclusion to this section on emigration.[14]

R.T. Greener

The Emigration of Colored Citizens from the Southern States*

The land question is no new one; at the present time there are difficulties in England, Ireland, Scotland and India with regard to this tenure of land; and when we come to study them, we find many analogous cases to those in America. There are remarkable coincidences and wonderful similarities of conditions, complaints and demands, which show conclusively that injustice and wrong, and disregard of rights and abuses of privilege are not confined to any one country, race or class. As a rule, capital takes advantage of the needs of labor. Landlords in every country oppress tenants, and sometimes disregard the welfare of the humbler agricultural laborer. The race in power lords it over the humbler; and if any change takes place from such normal condition, it only comes after a fierce outbreak of pent-up passion, or smouldering fires of wrong; or because some bold champion of the people rises to denounce oppression and demand redress. It has been fourteen years since the Confederacy collapsed, and eleven years since reconstruction. The South has now had for three years home rule, "Autonomy;" and yet, instead of the renewed prosperity, harmony of races, and absence of political violence and lawlessness, which we were promised, we find demoralized credit, shameless repudiation, and organized lawlessness—rendering the condition of the negro tenant class worse than at any period since slavery. So deplorable and abject indeed is it that expatriation and escape to Liberia, or the West, seems the only hope, as it is the continued dream of the negroes, old and young, in the six Southern States. We are accustomed to blame the Southern whites for the ultimate and approximate causes of this sad state of affairs. They are deeply responsible. I do not hesitate to place upon their shoulders all they deserve; but the North is not wholly innocent. We legislate for the interests of four million blacks just freed from bondage, demoralized by four years of war, and for two million rebellious whites, landless, hopeless, thankful at that time, even if their lives were spared, and we ignore all the precedents of history — the West Indies, Ireland, Russia and Germany. We threw the negro without anything, the carpet-bagger with his musket, the ex-Confederate disarmed, pell-mell together, and told them to work out the problem.

After the war it was difficult to purchase land because the old master was not disposed to sell. With the downfall of reconstruction a new lease of life was given to Southern barbarity and lawlessness. As usual, the negro was the principal sufferer. Negro representation went first; next the educational system, which the carget-bagger had brought to the South, was crippled by insufficient appropriations. Majorities were overcome by shot-gun intimidation, or secretly by the tissue ballot. Radical office-holders were forced to resign, robbed of their property by "due process of law," and driven North.

*R.T. Greener, "The Emigration of Colored Citizens from the Southern States," *Journal of Social Science,* No. 11 (May, 1880), pp. 22-35.

The jury-box and representation the negro was forced to give up; but after enduring all this, he found himself charged exorbitantly for the most necessary articles of food. His land was rented to him at fabulous prices. His cabin was likely to be raided at any time, whenever capricious lust, or a dreadful thirst for blood was roused. He saw his crop dwindling day by day; he saw himself growing poorer and getting into debt; his labor squandered between exacting landlords and rapacious store-keepers. It was then the negro resolved to give up the fruitless contest so long and hopelessly waged, and try his fortune in the great West, of which he had heard and read so much during the past ten years.

IMMEDIATE CAUSES OF THE EXODUS

To quote from the *St. Louis Memorial:* "The story is about the same, in each instance; great privation and want from excessive rent exacted for land; connected with the murder of colored neighbors and friends, and threats of personal violence to themselves; the tenor of which statement is that of suffering and terror. Election days and Christmas, by the concurrent testimony, seem to have been preferred for killing the 'smart man,' while robbery and personal violence, in one form and another, seem to have run the year around. Here they are in multitudes, not often alone, but women and children, old and middle-aged and young, and with common consent, leaving their old home for an unnatural climate, and facing storms and unknown dangers to go to northern Kansas. Why? Among them little is said of hope in the future; it is all of fear in the past. They are not drawn by the attractions of Kansas, they are driven by the terrors of Mississippi and Louisiana." The thriftless habits of work, engendered by southern life; the utter lack of foresight found in white and black alike, are powerful agents in bringing about the Exodus. The universal credit system is fostered by the planters, and kept up by the wily store-keeper; the insecurity of the holdings (long leases being unknown), is such that, if the negro succeeds in raising a good crop, he has no guaranty that he can keep his patch the next year. The prices charged for the necessities of life may be noticed. These are copied from the original documents brought by the refugees: $1.50 per lb. for tobacco; molasses, $1.50 per gallon; filling out a contract, $2.50; meal, per bushel, $2.00, not worth more than $1; pork, per barrel, $30.00.

Again, the political difference of opinion which exists in the South, is another important cause. There, political convictions rank with religious opinions in intensity. The over-production of cotton is another cause, by the low price of that staple. Then the fact that the negro owns neither land, nor presses, cotton-gin, and implements, but buys mules, rents land, and purchases his provisions at an advance, often of thirty and forty per cent., is sufficient cause for Exodus. If we add that the landlord has a first claim on the crop, a law which is identical with the Scotch law of hypotheca, we shall see reasons enough for a failure, and for the disposition to seek a happier home elsewhere. It can not be denied that there are instances where the negroes find themselves hopelessly involved; and seeing no prospect for any compensation, have at once repudiated their contracts and their country. This, of course, does not apply to those who have mules, carts, implements, and other utensils, which keep them attached closer to the soil. The law protects the landlord, and his claim always has the precedence. It is a punishable offence to remove any portion of the crop from the plantation before the landlord's claim is met. Next comes the store-keeper with his bill of six months. If anything were left for the negro when all these demands are satisfied, it would partake of the nature of a genuine miracle.

ADVANTAGES OF THE EXODUS TO THE NEGRO

This emigration will benefit the negro, who is now too much inclined to stay where he is put. At the South, he never knows his own possibilities. Then again, the South is a wretched place for any people to develop in, and this is especially true of the negro; because, like all subject races, he imitates the life about him. The negro at the South is in a demoralized condition, and no jury will convict for political offences committed against him. Chief Justice Waite, at Charleston, in the case of the Ellerton rioters, could not charge the jury in favor of liberty and protection. District attorneys are appointed at the recommendation of known rebels and sympathizers and assassins. Of course, they will not do their duty; hence, the negro dares not look for justice in the courts, — once proudly called the palladium of English liberty. The use of the military power to enforce any right, is repudiated at the North. But I remember it was employed quite efficaciously to return Anthony Burns and Simms, fugitive slaves, some years ago. I need not enumerate the demoralizing features of Southern life, the reckless disregard for human life, the lack of thrift, drinking customs, gaming, horse-racing, etc. The negro needs contact with all that is healthful and developing in modern civilization, and by emigration the negro will learn to love thrift, and unlearn many bad habits and improvident notions acquired from preceding generations.

The exclusive devotion of the negro to the culture of cotton and rice is demoralizing to him. They drag women and children into the field, with no commissioner of labor to look out for outraged childhood and impaired maternity. I do not expect this argument to find favor with those who think the negro has no other future before him than to cultivate sugar, cotton and rice. On the politico-economic side a partial Exodus will benefit those who remain, by raising the wage fund, increasing the demand, and insuring better treatment to those who are left; the fact of the Exodus being a preventive check, if I may borrow a phrase from Mr. Malthus. It will remove the negro from the incessant whirl of politics, in which, like all dark races, he is governed more by feeling than selfish interest.

At present the negro stands in the way of his own advancement, by reason of political fidelity, and the very excess of population, not diminished since the war, and yet not so systematically diffused and employed. Even Senator Butler, of South Carolina, says: "We have too much cheap negro labor in the South." As to wages, the average negro can earn higher wages and live more comfortably at the North, even if confined to humble employments, than he can at the South. When we add such trifles as protection, school privileges, free suffrage and Christian influences, we transcend the limits of legitimate comparison. That the departure of the few will benefit the many might be abundantly illustrated by the condition of Ireland after the famine of 1848, or England after the Lancashire distress, when Canon Girdlestone, Mr. Froude and Goldwin Smith counselled emigration.

I assume that the predominance of the negro in politics at the South is gone for a generation at least. The South will not have it and the North has exhibited no very marked disposition to enforce it. If it be ever desirable again, let it come when the children of the present black colonists go back to the mother land, improved in all that makes good citizens by a sojourn in the West.

OBJECTIONS TO THE EXODUS.

There are few opponents of the Exodus. Most of them are only negative objectors. The only class positively objecting is the planting class. At Vicksburg, and in Washington County (Miss.), they objected vehemently and loudly. Foreign labor, they say, would cost money. Not one planter in ten is able to make further outlay. During the change of laborers, even, they would go to rack and ruin. The negro is the only one who can do their work. To go now will ruin the cotton crop, and, hence, affect the North as well as the South.

No one disputes the right of the negro to go West, now that he is free. We accord to all men the right to improve their condition, by change of residence or employment. Nearly all of the objectors, white and black, have grave doubts as to our ability to stand this severe Northern climate. They fear we may not find work adapted to our limited and peculiar powers; may not meet with kind friends and genial sympathy. We must endure privations and meet with ostracism at the North. Mechanics will not work with negroes. The negro remembers Slavery, Black Codes, Ku-Klux, Sister Sallie's plan, tissue ballots, the murder of Dr. Dostie and Randolph in South Carolina, Caldwell and Dixon in Mississippi, and says "My relatives and friends who have gone North since the war tell a different story. They have held no offices, but they are free. They sleep in peace at night; what they earn is paid them, if not, they can appeal to the courts. They vote without fear of the shotgun, and their children go to school. It is true the Northern people do not love us so well as you did, and hence the intermixture of races is not so promiscuous there as here. This we shall try to endure, if we go North, with patience and Christian resignation. We have never heard of the people at the North paying in ten, twenty-five and fifty cent scrip, payable four years hence, nor charging $2.00 a plug for tobacco, and $2.50 for witnessing a contract. While we may not have so much social equality as with you, we shall have more political equality and man to man justice. You charge $15.00 and $25.00 per acre for worn-out land; we can buy better in Kansas and Nebraska at $2.50 an acre. We had rather die free at the North than live as paupers and pariahs here, only nominally free. You thought Kansas not too cold for us in 1854-5; we are not afraid to try it now."

The most important opponent of the Exodus is Marshall Frederick Douglass, my distinguished antagonist in this discussion, who, I sincerely regret, is not here, to lend to his able and ingenious argument the magic of his presence and the influence of his eloquent voice. The greatest negro whom America has produced, having suffered all that our race could endure, and having been elevated higher than any other negro, he cannot lack sympathy with any movement which concerns his race, and hence, any objection coming from him challenges attention, and demands to be answered. Age, long service, and a naturally keen and analytic mind, would presume a soundness of view on almost any topic of national importance or race interest. It is, therefore, with the highest regard for the honesty of Mr. Douglass's views that I venture to reply to some of his objections. Mr. Douglass has not been an inactive opponent. He has written elaborate resolutions, made at least six speeches, spoken at the Methodist Conference, and been interviewed on the Exodus. While time has modified his extreme views, and more recent events have blunted the edge of his sarcasm, and while most of his objections are of the negative rather than the positive order, against the methods and men who seek to help the movement, rather than against the Exodus itself, still the morale of his influence is in opposition. Mr. Douglass's arguments, as I have been able to find them in speeches, resolutions, and the paper just read, are briefly these: —

1.   Emigration is not the proper nor permanent remedy.

2.   The Government ought to protect colored citizens at the South; to encourage emigration gives the Government a chance to shirk its duty; while the advocates of the measure leave Equal Rights, Protection and Allegiance open questions.

3.   The colored race should be warned against a nomadic life and habits of wandering.

4.   African emigration and migration to the West are analogous; the failure of the one is prophetic of the other.

5.   The negro now is potentially able to elect some members of his race at the South to Congress; this is impossible at the North.

6.   At the South he has a monopoly of the supply of labor; at the West he would not have it. At the South, land owners must have laborers or starve; Western land owners are independent.

7.   The Exodus does not conform to "the laws of civilizing emigration," as the carrying of a language, literature, etc. of a superior race to an inferior; nor does it conform to "the laws of geography." These, according to Mr. Douglass, "require for healthy emigration that it proceed from East to West, not from South to North, and not far away from latitudes and climates in which the emigrants were born."

To these objections first, it may be said, no favorer of migration claims it as the sole, proper or only permanent remedy for the aggravated relation of landlord and tenant at the South. It is approved of as one remedy, thus far the most salutary, in stopping lawlessness and exactions. The reciprocity of allegiance and protection is granted; but it is asked, "How can the United States Government protect its black citizens while the fallacy of State rights and the

undefinable 'home rule' or 'autonomy,' prevent interference?" The Duke of
Argyle believes that "there is no abstract limit to the right of the State to do
anything." "In the interest of economy," says he, "it may pass sumptuary
laws, or regulate the wages of farm laborers." This is under a monarchy.
With us, neither Government nor courts may interfere with contracts, either
to enforce the terms or insure justice, when the local sentiment is opposed.
The Government does not protect the negro because it finds itself powerless to
do so. As a general rule, the negro may well be warned against a wandering
life; but in the present instance such advice is gratuitous.

The failure of the analogy drawn between African colonization and
migration to the West may be stated in this way: the one was worked up by
slave-owners in the interest of slavery; this one springs spontaneously, according to Mr. Douglass's view, from the class considering itself aggrieved; one
led out of the country to a comparative wilderness; the other directs to better
land and larger opportunities here at home. The one took the negro to contend with barbarism. This places him under more civilizing influences than
he has ever enjoyed, involving no change of allegiance nor serious differences
of climate. If the colored people are "potentially" able to elect one of their
own race to Congress, they cannot now make that potentiality possible. Emigration surely cannot lessen the potentiality, since the emigrants will remain
citizens. I am inclined to think it will not diminish the probability. If I remember correctly, Massachusetts first elected colored men to her General Court;
Ohio has nominated one, and Illinois has a colored representative.

Mr. Douglass is rather misleading and fails again in his analogy, when
he infers that the negro must go West as a civilizer or not go at all. He goes
out from the house of bondage up from the land of Egypt, directed, I am
inclined to think, by the same mighty hand which pointed out the way to
Israel: —

> "By day, along the astonished land,
> The cloudy pillar glided slow;
> By night, Arabia's crimsoned sand,
> Returned the fiery column's glow."

If by the laws of geography, to which, unfortunately, this new Exodus
does not conform, Mr. Douglass means that colonization, migration or civilization proceed best within the isothermal lines, we may concede the law,
but all history shows exceptions remarkable and instructive.

The Phoenicians sailed West and North; the Greek colonies were at all
known points; the Dutch and English have not been hindered by isothermal
lines, penetrating far away from the latitudes in which they were born. Magna
Graecia, in distinction from Hellas, and Mr. Dilke's "Greater Britain," are
pertinent illustrations of the unsoundness of this seeming historical statement.
If it were even philosophically correct, there is no analogy in the examples:
the Southern negro, if he emigrate to Washington Territory or Arizona,
would not be as far from home as the Aryan race now is by its excessive waves
of migration from the Black and Caspian Seas. When Mr. Douglass grants
in his paper that if the half is true of what the negro suffers, the Exodus is

justified, — he grants all that any advocate of it asks. It is from causes, which he condemns, denounces, deplores and considers disgraceful, that we say, "emigrate, and if you can, better your condition."

The Exodus is complained of as a "policy." We might answer, it is a result, not a policy in the ordinary sense, although, as a safe check to certain ulterior causes, we might well commend it to oppressed people anywhere as a measure of policy.

We are told, aphoristically, that the negro's labor made him free, and therefore, it can make him "free, comfortable, and independent." The assumed fact is not exactly clear, and the conclusion is scarcely warranted by the negro's statements of his condition, according to Mr. Douglass.

We are called upon to say whether we would remove a part, or all of the colored people from the South. "A part," we answer, "if that will insure protection and just treatment for the rest; the whole, if they can be protected in no other way." "But where will you get money to remove them?" is the new horn to the dilemma. "Congress cannot give it, because of the public debt," and yet Congress, [what Congress?] would rather spend $200,000,000 to *protect* them where they are." In short, Mr. Douglass grants the negro's misery, but tells him to wait, his present state is "exceptional and transient," his rights "will revive, survive and flourish;" but the poor frightened, half-starved negroes, crouching along the Mississippi, fear this will not happen until they have literally passed over. Mr. Douglass is not willing to have Congress nor the capitalists help these houseless wanderers, to whom we gave nothing when we freed them. We did better than that by fugitives forty years ago, and I see no good reason why Northern philanthropy should close its hand and ears now, to a cry which is as despairing as that which rang from Ireland in 1848, or from the yellow fever sufferers, a twelvemonth ago. We see capital employed to build better houses for the poor, to transport young children to the West; why shall we not try to help those who are trying as best they may, to help themselves? The statement that Massachusetts was once Mississippi, is a favorite one of Mr. Douglass, and has been reiterated so often as to lead the unwary to believe that the Marshal of the District of Columbia thinks it true. I am more inclined to ascribe it to the orator's love of antithesis; so incorrect, so unjust, and for Frederick Douglass, so unkind would such a remark be.

To say to the emigrants, "Better stay than go," is analogous to saying "Be ye warmed and filled, notwithstanding ye give not those things which are needful for the body." Nor do proverbs add protection to the one argument any more than food and raiment to the other.

The Exodus may be a failure and a mistake, but whether it is or not, it has no connection with the power of the Republican party, or the retention of political power by the negro. Both may be benefited, and it may fail; both may be injured by it, and it may nevertheless succeed. This is a specimen *non-sequitur,* very familiar in arguments against the present migration.

We are assured that there will be misery and want resulting from this "ill-timed" movement. Doubtless there will be; every movement having in it the elements of good, has brought some hardship: —

"Never morning wore
To evening, but some heart did break."

The crucial test, however, is whether there will be more misery and want by migrating than by remaining; we think not.

Another distinguished gentleman, a financier, a banker, a political economist, Ex-Secretary McCulloch, in his seventh Harvard lecture, thinks the Exodus unfortunate. He also has faith that all will be well. With a refinement of unconscious sarcasm, he quotes Charles Sumner, and says to the negroes, "stick," "fight it out" where you are, "if it takes not merely the present, but many other summers." But the Ex-Secretary, less cautious than Mr. Douglass, says, if they [the colored people] were forced to go, they should be returned, even with the aid of the Government. Here is much sympathy enclosed in a dubious sentence. We do not know whether financial aid, or bayonet aid is to return these refugees, and nothing is said of their possible condition after they are returned With such matters of detail the optimist and the doctrinaire have no concern. I shall call on Henry Jackson, to answer Mr. Douglass and Mr. McCulloch: "I left the South because I could not make a living. Year before last I made ten bales of cotton, and never got a cent for it. I sued for it but could not get anything; they wanted me to pawn my horse and begin over again; but I told them I was going to sell my horse to go away. I would not go back to the South again because I could not live; cannot live there and give $2 for meal, and $30 for a barrel of pork, $10 an acre for land, $5 for ginning cotton, and then being cheated out of everything after I made it. My wife is along with me. I reckon I have money enough to get to Kansas."

BEST TIME TO EMIGRATE.

The western lands are waiting for settlers, and are being rapidly filled up by Swedes, Norwegians, Mennonites, Icelanders and Poles, why should not the negro participate? 600,000 acres of public land have been taken up since June 30, 1878; 50,000 families have gone westward under the homestead law, exclusive of those who have small sums to invest. Why shall we debar the negro? Irish Catholics have raised a fund of $100,000 to assist their poor from the large cities. The Hebrews have also an excellent association for the same purpose. These aid societies hold meetings and solicit funds. No one denounces them or impugns the motives of their advocates. What will benefit Irish, Hebrew, Swede, and Norwegian, cannot be decidedly injurious to the colored race alone.

HOW WILL THEY BE TREATED IN THE WEST?

Governor St. John, of Kansas, is authority on this point. "Up to the present writing, about 3,000 destitute refugees have arrived, the most of whom have been cared for by our committee. We have been very successful in securing for them employment, and thus placed them in a position that they soon became self-sustaining, and no longer required aid. These people seem to be honest, and of good habits; are certainly industrious and anxious to work, and, so far as they have been tried, have proved to be faithful and excellent laborers." Sir George Campbell* says, "In Kansas City, and still more in the suburbs of Kansas proper, the negroes are much more numerous than I have yet seen. On the Kansas side, they form quite a large proportion of the population. They are certainly subject to no indignity or ill-usage. * * * Here the negroes seem to have quite taken to work at trades; I saw them doing building work, both alone and assisting white men, and also painting and other tradesmen's work. On the Kansas side, I found a negro blacksmith, with an establishment of his own; he was an old man and very 'negro.' He grumbled just like a white. * * * He came from Tennessee, after emancipation; had not been back there, and did not want to go. * * I also saw black women keeping apple stalls and engaged in other such occupations. In these States, which I may call intermediate between black and white countries [States], the blacks evidently have no difficulty."

What is true of Kansas is true of the Indian Territory. A recent traveller there, writes: "The cozy homes and promising fields were the property of freedmen; every ploughboy you see has been a slave. All the farms along our route today belong to freedmen, to whom the Creeks accord every right and privilege they enjoy themselves, — annuity lands, offices and honors. * * * Every home gives proof of thrift. New fences, addition to the cabins, new barns and out-houses, catch the eye on every hand, except the school-house and church; these appear to be going to decay, but it is only in the rude buildings that this is true. Both church and school are prosperous."

At the South the negro, under adverse conditions, is not a great land owner, but yet he is not wholly landless. In South Carolina he owns 20,000 acres; in Georgia pays taxes on $6,000,000, mostly in land; and in Mississippi and Louisiana, it is estimated he pays taxes on between $10,000,000 and $20,000,000, the greater portion in land.

Emigration is no new thing, beginning with Senator Windom's speech. It began in 1840 and has kept up ever since. You may remember some of the old pictures of the emigrant with bundle on his shoulder. He went alone formerly, and was often taken back at the Government's expense; now he takes his family, and cannot be taken back against his will. In Kansas there are now five or six colonies, some of them established since 1870; Baxter Springs, Nicodemus, Morton City and Singleton. The reports from all are favorable. The people are said to be thrifty, intelligent and willing to work. All are paying for their land by instalments, at prices from $1.25 to $6.00 per acre. If, dissatisfied with Kansas, they wish to "move on," no one interferes with them. Mississippi, in spite of her Constitution, which says, "No citizen shall be prevented from emigrating on any pretence whatever," attempts to keep them back by libelling the steamboats for carrying excessive numbers. The negroes are also detained by writs gotten up on spurious charges. In short, the Southern landlord now demands more than the lord paramount in the middle ages; the tenant must be a permanent fixture to the

*"Black and White in the U. S."

land. Georgia and South Carolina have already revived the law of Edward VI. (Act I, c. 3, 1381), and sell idle vagrants, or farm them out to service in gangs, as their prejudice dictates.

THE POLITICAL SIDE OF THE EXODUS.

We are told it is a political scheme. To insure success as a political move-ment, 60,000 colored voters should be distributed in certain States before November, 1879, the end of the period allowed for legal residence. If the Exodus were promoted by politicians, we should find 20,000 negroes going to Pennsylvania, 20,000 to New Jersey, 10,000 at least to New York, the same number for Indiana, and a spare 5,000 for Connecticut. This could not be done under $2,000,000, even had it begun six months ago. Thus far at the North, not $20,000 has been raised to help the refugees, notwithstanding $100,000,000 would not be idly spent to help the negro and end this vexed question. It is estimated that 15,000 have gone West within eight months; 150 leave New Orleans each week. All are not going to Kansas. Many are wisely pushing farther North. As a class, they differ from the West India negroes after their emancipation. The Southern negro did not relapse into barbarism; he manifests a disposition and an adaptability to work. That he is industrious is shown by the immense cotton crop, just reported as contributing to the exportable products of the nation, $189,000,000 per annum.

No view of the movement would be complete which did not notice the relation of the colored people of the country to this flight from oppression. The first stage is passed, the appeal to white philanthropists. My notion is the second is here, the appeal to ourselves. We must organize societies, con-tribute our dimes, and form a network of communication between the South and every principal point North and West. We should raise $200,000 to form a company; we should have a National Executive Committee, and have agents to buy land, procure cheap transportation, disseminate accurate information, and see to it that they are neither deluded nor defrauded. Such an organiza-tion, working through our churches and benevolent societies, would do more to develop our race than all the philanthropic measures designed to aid us since the war.

THE EXODUS WILL GO ON.

The little rill has started on its course toward the great sea of humanity. It moves slowly on by virtue of the eternal law of gravitation, which leads peoples and individuals toward peace, protection and happiness. Today it is a slender thread and makes way with difficulty amid the rocks and tangled growth; but it has already burst through serious impediments, showing itself possessed of a mighty current. It started in Mississippi, but it is even now being rapidly fed by other rills and streams from the territory through which it flows. Believing that it comes from God, and feeling convinced that it bears only blessings in its course for that race so long tossed, so ill-treated, so sadly misunderstood, I greet its tiny line, and almost see in the near future its mag-nificent broad bosom, bearing proudly onward, until at last, like the travel-worn and battle-scarred Greeks of old, there bursts upon its sight the sea, the broad sea of universal freedom and protection.

AFRICA FOR THE AFRICANS

To the reader who has followed this study for the past few chapters, the cyclical nature of the assimilationist-separationist debate should become apparent. Even during the Colonial Period, the argument went back and forth; sometimes the assimilationist rhetoric was more appropriate to the rhetorical situation. Sometimes, the combination of the exigence — the urgent need for black men to determine the course for the future — and the men and events of the day, seemed more susceptible to assimilationist ideas.[15] Later, the separatist rhetoric seemed a more appropriate response.

Critics have been unable to agree about strategy that was pursued during the period which has been described as the Age of Booker T. Washington. Previously, we interpreted Washington as an extreme assimilationist. In this chapter some additional mention should be made of Washington as a moderate separationist. If one were to re-read his Atlanta address, his statement of remaining as separate as the fingers on the hand could be heard as calling for just what it said — separation. Much of Washington's accommodationist rhetoric could be dismissed as nothing more than talk to appease white people, to keep the contributions flowing and give black people some relief while they obtained educational experience and opportunities to use it. It is a fact that Washington, while speaking to satisfy the white man, was at the same time forming the National Negro Business League which still exists; he organized the southern Negro farmers, sharecroppers, and small businessmen through regular conferences at his institution in Tuskegee; and he built up a successful all black educational institution.[16] Cruse, in arguing this interpretation, even states: ". . . the Black Power slogan today . . . *is* neo-Booker T-ism. . . ."[17]

How Washington should actually be evaluated is most likely to remain an unanswered question. But, there is no doubt that if the period from 1895 to 1915 is properly called the Age of Booker T. Washington, then the period immediately following that, and lasting until the late 1920's should be called the Age of Marcus Garvey, and there is no difference of opinion over the strategy this man represented — separatism. The discussion of Washington not only relates the two men in time, but it serves to introduce a relationship between the two. Garvey respected Washington, and felt that the concept of the black trade school was consistent with his notions of black consciousness. Garvey's wife said:

> Seamen travelling on Banana ships told him [Garvey] of opportunities in America; he also heard of the help Booker T. Washington got for his work in the Southern States, so he wrote him, and Washington encouraged him to come up. Garvey felt that if he could get funds, he would return and open a Trade School like Tuskegee. This would give practical help to the masses, who then had no such opportunity for training; at the same time he could inculcate in them Race-love, and strengthen his African programme in the entire Island. The Trade School would in time furnish competent men and women as Technical Missionaries to be sent to the Mother country — Africa.[18]

The Island to which Marcus Garvey would return was the place of his birth, Jamaica in the British West Indies. He was born in 1887; he was of unmixed black blood, of which he grew increasingly proud. He ended his formal education at the age of fourteen, but continued to learn all his life.

From the earliest recollection, Garvey seemed interested in advancing the lot of his fellow black men. He engaged in labor activities in Jamaica; he traveled to London to study the situation of black men throughout the Empire; and by 1914 he had returned to Jamaica and formed the Universal Negro Improvement and Conservation Association, and African Communities League for the purpose of bringing the black people of the world together.

It is interesting to note that while in London, Garvey read a copy of Washington's autobiography, *Up from Slavery,* and later testified that it motivated him to undertake a lifetime of activity for the black cause. Cronon remarks in his extensive study of Garvey: "The seeds of Garveyism had unwittingly been sown by the great compromiser and advocate of accommodation, the venerable Sage of Tuskegee!"[19] After reading Cruse's analysis, one must wonder if Washington's influence was all that unwitting. The mistake might not have been Washington's; it may be in the interpreters of him.

Garvey arrived in the United States in 1916, to spread the word of the Universal Negro Improvement Association (UNIA) in the area where the promise of financial support and the potential for members was greatest. He eventually spent his most productive years as a persuader in this country and became a major influence in the rhetoric of separation in America.

Although Garveyism is called a movement, and although he deserves a section in the chapter on separation alongside those devoted to groups of effective persuaders, Marcus Garvey's movement was essentially a one-man effort. The story of Garveyism can be adequately told through the speeches of Marcus Garvey.

Following his definitive work on the man, Edmund David Cronon concludes that, "Garvey is now universally acclaimed as a master propagandist and gifted leader of men."[20] Although Cronon found it almost impossible to make a reliable assessment of the membership of the UNIA at its peak, he asserts that it probably included at least the 20,000 to 80,000 members some have suggested, although it probably did not reach the millions Garvey claimed. In any event, thousands inside and outside the UNIA were influenced by the speaking of Marcus Garvey.[21]

The story of Garvey's adventure in shipping and other forms of black controlled commerce has been adequately told elsewhere. It would only distract from his chief accomplishment — his communication with the masses of black men in the United States and around the world. But, before turning to his message to black men, note how he addressed himself to the white people of the United States. Few separatists have sought to establish communication with the white community; it is almost impossible, and probably useless. Garvey made the attempt, and as the reader reads his appeal it is difficult to picture him as the buffoon the white press portrayed him to be. Follow along as he instructs, cautions, calms, and seeks to persuade the white man.

Marcus Garvey
An Appeal to the Soul of White America*

Surely the soul of liberal, philanthropic, liberty-loving, white America is not dead.

It is true that the glamour of materialism, has to a great degree, destroyed the innocence and purity of the national conscience, but, still, beyond our politics, beyond our soulless industrialism, there is a deep feeling of human sympathy that touches the soul of white America upon which the unfortunate and sorrowful can always depend for sympathy, help, and action.

It is to that feeling that I appeal at this time for four hundred million Negroes of the world, and fifteen million of America in particular.

---

*Marcus Garvey, *An Appeal to the Soul of White America* (New York: UNIA, 1923).

There is no real white man in America, who does not desire a solution
of the Negro problem. Each thoughtful citizen has probably his own idea of
how the vexed question of races should be settled. To some the Negro could
be gotten rid of by whole sale butchery, by lynching, by economic starvation,
by a return to slavery and legalized oppression; while others would have the
problem solved by seeing the race all herded together and kept some where
among themselves, but a few — those in whom they have an interest should
be allowed to live around as the wards of a mistaken philanthropy; yet, none
so generous as to desire to see the Negro elevated to a standard of real progress, and prosperity-welded into a homogeneous whole, creating of themselves
a mighty nation with proper systems of government, civilization, and culture,
to mark them admissable to the fraternities of nations and races without any
disadvantage.

I do not desire to offend the finer feelings and sensibilities of those white
friends of the race who really believe that they are kind and considerate to us
as a people; but I feel it my duty to make a real appeal to conscience and not
belief. Conscience is solid, convicting and permanently demonstrative; belief,
is only a matter of opinion, changeable by superior reasoning. Once the
belief was that it was fit and proper to hold the Negro as a slave, and in this
the Bishop, Priest and layman agreed. Later on they changed their belief or
opinion, but at all times the conscience of certain people dictated to them
that it was wrong and inhuman to hold human beings as slaves. It is to such
a conscience in white America that I am addressing myself.

Negroes are human beings — the peculiar and strange opinions of
writers, ethnologists, philosophers, scientists and anthropologists notwithstanding — they have feelings, souls, passions, ambitions desires, just as other
men, hence they must be considered.

Has white America really considered the Negro in the light of permanent
human progress? The answer is NO.

Men and women of the white race, do you know what is going to happen
if you do not think and act now? One of two things. You are either going to
deceive and keep the Negro in your midst until you have perfectly completed
your wonderful American civilization with its progress of art, science, industry, and politics, and then, jealous of your own success and achievements in
those directions, and with the greater jealousy of seeing your race pure and
unmixed, cast him off to die in the whirlpool of economic starvation, thus,
getting rid of another race that was not intelligent enough to live, or, you
simply mean by the largeness of your hearts to assimmilate fifteen million
Negroes into the social fraternity of an American race, that will neither be
white nor back. Don't be alarmed! We must prevent both consequences. No
real race loving white man wants to destroy the purity of his race, and no real
Negro conscious of himself, wants to die, hence there is room for an understanding, and an adjustment, and that is just what we seek.

Let white and black stop deceiving themselves. Let the white race stop
thinking that all back men are dogs and not to be considered as human beings.
Let foolish Negro agitators and so-called reformers, encouraged by deceptive
and unthinking white associates, stop preaching and advocating the doctrine

of "social equality," meaning thereby the social intermingling of both races, intermarriages, and general social co-relationship. The two extremes will get us nowhere, other than breeding hate and encouraging discord, which will eventually end disastrously to the weaker race.

Some Negroes in the quest of position, and honor, have been admitted to the full enjoyment of their constitutional rights, thus we have some of our men filling high and responsible Government positions, others on their own account, have established themselves in the profession, commerce and industry. This the casual onlooker, and even the men themselves, will say carries a guarantee and hope of social equality, and permanent racial progress. But this is the mistake. There is no progress of the Negro in America that is permanent, so long as we have with us the monster evil-prejudice.

Prejudice, we shall always have between black and white, so long as the latter believes that the former is intruding upon their rights. So long as white laborers believe that black laborers are taking and holding their jobs, so long as white artisans believe that black artisans are performing the work that they should do; so long as white men and women believe that black men and women filling the positions that they covet; so long as white political leaders and statesmen believe that black politicians and statesmen are seeking the same positions in the Nation's Government; so long as white men believe that black men want to associate with and marry white women, then we will have prejudice and not only prejudice, but riots, lynchings, burnings, and God to tell what next and to follow!

It is this danger that drives me mad. It must be prevented. We cannot allow white and black to drift along unthinkingly toward this great gulf and danger, that is nationally ahead of us. It is because of this, that I speak, and now call upon the soul of great white America to help.

It is no use putting off, the work must be done, and it must be started now.

Some people have misunderstood me. Some don't want to understand me. But I must explain myself for the good of America, and for the good of the world and humanity.

Those of the Negro race who preach social equality, and who are working for an American race that will in complexion be neither white nor black, have tried to misinterpret me to the white public, and create prejudice against my work. The white public, not stopping to analyze and question the motive behind criticisms and attacks, aimed against new leaders and their movements, condemn without even giving a chance to the criticised to be heard. Those who oppose me in my own race, because I refuse to endorse their program of social arrogance and social equality, gloat over the fact that by their misrepresentation and underhand methods, they were able to have me convicted and imprisoned for crime which they calculate will so discredit me as to destroy the movement that I represent, in opposition to their program of a new American race; but we will not now consider the opposition to a program or a movement, but state the facts as they are, and let deep souled white America pass its own judgement.

In another one hundred years white America will have doubled its population, in another one hundred years it will have trebled itself. The keen student must realize that the centuries ahead will bring us an overcrowded and over populated country; opportunities, as the population grows larger will be fewer; the competition for bread between the people of their own class will become keener, and so much more so will there be no room for two competitive races, the one strong and the other weak. To imagine Negroes as District Attorneys, Judges, Senators, Congressmen, Assemblymen, Aldermen, Government Clerks, and Officials, Artisans and laborers at work while millions of white men starve, is to have before you the bloody picture of wholesale mob violence, that I fear, and against which I am working.

No preaching, no praying, no presidential edict, will control the passion of hungry unreasoning men of prejudice when the hour comes. It will not come I pray in our generation, but it is of the future that I think and for which I work.

A generation of ambitious Negro men and women, out from the best Colleges, Universities, Institutions, capable of filling the highest and best positions in the nation, in industry, commerce, society and politics! Can you keep them back? If you do so they will agitate and throw your constitution in your faces. Can you stand before civilization and deny the truth of your constitution? What are you going to do then? You who are just will open up the door of opportunity and say to all and sundry "Enter in." But ladies and gentlemen, what about the mob, that starving crowd of your own race? Will they stand by, suffer and starve, and allow an opposite competitive race to prosper in the midst of their distress? If you can conjure these things up in your mind, then you have the vision of the race problem of the future in America.

There is but one solution, and that is to provide an outlet for Negro energy, ambition, and passion, away from the attraction of white opportunity and surround the race with opportunities of its own. If this is not done, and if the foundation for same is not laid now, then the consequences will be sorrowful for the weaker race, and be disgraceful to our ideals of justice, and shocking to our civilization.

The Negro must have a country, and a nation of his own. If you laugh at the idea, then you are selfish and wicked, for you and your children do not intend that the Negro shall discomode you in yours. If you do not want him to have a country and a nation of his own; if you do not intend to give him equal opportunities in yours; then it is plain to see that you mean that he must die, even as the Indian to make room for your generations.

Why should the Negro die? Has he not served America and the world. Has he not borne the burden of civilization in this Western world for three hundred years? Has he not contributed of his best to America? Surely all this stands to his credit, but there will not be enough room and the one answer is "find a place." We have found a place, it is Africa and as black men for three centuries have helped white men build America, surely generous and grateful white men will help black men build Africa.

And why shouldn't Africa and America travel down the ages as protectors of human rights and guardians of democracy? Why shouldn't black men help white men secure and establish universal peace? We can only have peace when we are just to all mankind; and for that peace, and for the reign of universal love I now appeal to the soul of white America. Let the Negroes have a Government of their own. Don't encourage them to believe that they will become social equals and leaders of the whites in America, without first on his own account proving to the world that they are capable of evolving a civilization of their own. The white race can best help the Negro by telling him the truth, and not by flattering him into believing that he is as good as any white man without first proving the racial, national constructive metal of which he is made.

Stop flattering the Negro about social equality, and tell him to go to work and build for himself. Help him in the direction of doing for himself, and let him know that self progress brings its own reward.

I appeal to the considerate and thoughtful conscience of white America not to condemn the cry of the Universal Negro Improvement Association for a nation in Africa for Negroes, but to give us a chance to explain ourselves to the world. White America is too big and when informed and touched, too liberal, to turn down the cry of the awakened Negro for a "place in the sun."

In the same year the appeal was written, Garvey sent out the following news release in an effort to communicate more effectively with the American people through the medium of the press. He shows himself to be a conscious user of what came to be called public relations, not only by frequently using the device of press releases, but also by using exaggeration in his assertion that the membership in his organization had reached 5,000,000.

The following is the complete text of the release, with occasional phrases deleted because of the illegibility of the manuscript.

Marcus Garvey
An Answer To His Many Critics*

IMMEDIATE RELEASE   January 1923

The following Letter is Released at the American Headquarters of the Universal Negro Improvement Association, 52-54-56 West 135th Street, New York City to the White Press of the World by MARCUS GARVEY as an

---

*Marcus Garvey, "An Answer To His Many Critics," a news release in January, 1923. Reprinted from the Schomburg Collection of the John E. Bruce Papers, Harlem branch of the New York Public Library, New York City, New York.

Explanation Of The Aims And Objects Of The Universal Negro Improvement Association of which he is President-General.

AN ANSWER TO HIS MANY CRITICS.

THE EDITOR.

Sir.

You have, for quite some time, been publishing news, letters and other
articles in your paper purporting to be information about the activities of the
Universal Negro Improvement Association, the "Back to Africa Movement,"
so named by critics, the Black Star Line Steamship Corporation and myself,
but you have never been fair enough to give the public and your readers the
other side of the story or the picture painted by you.

It has been my policy not to pay any attention to prejudiced and unfair
criticism, in that I always believed that truth of any kind cannot be permanently crushed; but whilst I personally still feel this way, a large number of
my friends and well wishers have for more than a thousand times endeavored
to have me place the Association I represent in a proper light before the
public so that the general misrepresentations of the Movement can be clari-
fied, I still would not have yielded but for the increasing demands made upon
me by those whose interest I serve, and because this misrepresentation has
been conveyed to a large number of your readers who seem to regard me as
some "hideous" person who hates all white people.

I am not blaming you for the stand you have taken against me and
against the Movement I represent because I know that you have arrived at
your conclusions through the misrepresentations made to you directly or indirectly by my enemies within my own Race who, being jealous of my success
in assembling together more members of my Race throughout this Country
and the world than any other person has done, have been and are endeavoring to so misrepresent me as to cause an oppostition sentiment to develop
that would eventually handicap and thwart the objects of the Organization
I am leading.

The real function of the press is public service without prejudice or
partiality to convey the truth as it is seen and understood without favoritism
or bias.

You have already by your many reports published one side of my activities; I feel you will be honest enough to now publish at least a part of the
other side. First of all let me say that all that have been published about the
Universal Negro Improvement Association and about me tending to show
that there is any hatred of other peoples, any scheme for personal gain, any
desire to stir up Race friction, are all false.

The following Preamble [speaks for itself]:

> The Universal Negro Improvement Association and African Com-
> munities' League is a social, friendly, humanitarian, charitable,
> educational, institutional, constructive and expansive society, and
> is founded by persons, desiring to the utmost, to work for the gen-

eral uplift of the Negro peoples of the world. And the members pledge themselves to do all in their power to conserve the rights of their noble race and to respect the rights of all mankind, believing always in the Brotherhood of Man and the Fatherhood of God. The motto of the organization is: "One God! One Aim! One Destiny!" Therefore, let justice be done to all mankind, realizing that if the strong oppresses the weak confusion and discontent will ever mark the path of man, but with love, faith and charity towards all the reign of peace and plenty will be heralded into the world and the generations of men shall be called Blessed.

[Manuscript indecipherable]

Surely you will not find hate or anything unworthy in the above declaration.

The oft repeated statement that the Movement is sponsored and supported by the ignorant and gullible is so frivolous as to need no comment. Our Movement reflects the highest intelligence of the Race and as proof of this, we have challenged and still challenge anyone within the Race to debate our differences. No one has been manly enough out of the critics to accept the challenge.

Among our bitterest critics and opponents are W. E. B. DuBois, James Weldon Johnson and their National Association for the Advancement of Colored People, yet, these persons have not the manhood to match the intelligence of their Association with that of the Universal Negro Improvement Association by accepting the challenge.

Our Organization stands for the highest in Racial ideals, yielding to all Races the right to ascend to the loftiest peak of human progress and demanding for ourselves a similar privilege.

Starting our Organization in New York four and one half (4½) years ago with Thirteen (13) members, we have now grown into an approximate membership of five million (5,000,000) people scattered all over the world, but principally to be found in the United States of America, Canada, South and Central America, the West Indies and Africa. [Manuscript indecipherable] ... Every effort among Negroes has been made and exhausted by my enemies to defeat me and yet they have failed, hence they resort to the Government and the white Press for the accomplishment of this purpose. To repeat, it is not because I fear defeat or the sting of unfriendly or unfair criticism that I write to you because I owe my success in organization to no one. Neither the Press nor my enemies made me, so neither can they break me. No influence, caring not how great, can defeat a righteous cause so I am not personally disturbed, but I would like the public to be correctly informed about the Movement I represent for the good of the members and those interested. The Negro problem in America and elsewhere must be solved. We cannot do this by postponing the issue or by side-tracking it. We might as well face it now. [Manuscript indecipherable] ... We of the Universal Negro Improvement Association believe in a pure black Race, just as now all self-respecting whites believe in a pure white Race as far as that can be.

We are conscious of the fact that slavery brought upon us the curse of many colors within our Race, but that is no reason why we of ourselves should perpetuate the evil, hence instead of encouraging a wholesale bastardy in the Race, we feel that we should now set out to create a Race type and standard of our own which could not, in the future, be stigmatized by bastardy but could be recognized and respected as the true Race type anteceding even our own time.

We believe that the Negro has at least, a social, cultural and political destiny of his own and any attempt to make a white man of him is bound to fail in the end. In like manner, we believe that you cannot successfully make a Negro out of a white man in that he too has at least a social, cultural and political destiny of his own. Therefore, the fullest opportunity should be given to both Races to develop independently a civilization of their own, meaning not to infer thereby that either Race could not, in a limited degree, become a part of the civilization of each without losing their respective Racial, cultural, social an (sic.) political identities.

If this can be done, then we feel that the Negro too should have a Government of his own and not remain in the Countries of whites to aspire for and to positions that they will never get under the rule of the majority group upon his merely asking for or demanding such positions by an accidental constitutional right.

If the Negro is to have a Government of his own of any importance, then there can be no better place than Africa, the land to which centuries ago he was born a Native. Admitting that this is right, is the reason why the Universal Negro Improvement Association of which I am President-General, raises the cry of: "Africa For the Africans at Home and Abroad." This, I see will be the only solution of the Negro problem not only in America but all over the world.

We have been brutally criticized for advancing this programme as a solution of the Race problem. Some critics have been honest enough to give their reasons for attacking us, others have done so, as I have already stated, through jealousy and prejudice.

Within the Negro Race, if I must repeat, there is as much prejudice, and I believe probably more, than is exercised against us by other races. Some mulattos and other types within the Race do not want to be classified with Negroes and hate to be identified with anything African in color or in spirit except for immediate personal benefit. Such persons are mainly responsible for the general opposition to the African programme in that they claim they are not to be personally benefitted; being the offsprings of black and white in America, they constitute the only true Americans.

How far the two Races will travel together socially, industrially and politically before a serious civil clash ensues is the speculation of all earnest thoughtful people. It is because I personally want to prevent such a clash that I am advocating the cause of the Universal Negro Improvement Association.

My interest in the Negro people of America and of the world is purely Racial, because I feel proud of my Race; I have the highest regard for the

Motherhood of the Race, and I see absolutely no reason why all Negroes should not be as proud of themselves as outher races are.

Now let us look at the Race problem reasonably:

We are educating the Negro, the slave of the last century. He is so advanced educationally that he claims scholastic recognition everywhere. Place him in any school, college or university and he comes out with honors. In Science, Music, Art and Literature, he is holding a place of equality with other Races everywhere. His ability fits him no longer for the farm, cotton field, or plantation as a Race. He seeks broader opportunities in every field. He is a Citizen. He pays Taxes. He observes the Law. He supports the Government. He applies for and seeks the position that attracts him.

"Why shouldn't I be President?" he asks himself. "I have the education and the ability."

"Why shouldn't I be a member of the Cabinet, a Postmaster-General, Attorney-General, Secretary of War or Secretary of State?

"Why shouldn't I be Governor of the State; Mayor of the City; a Judge of the Supreme Court; Police Commissioner or President of the Board of Aldermen?

"Why shouldn't I be a Conductor on the Railroad; or the Pullman Car or Tramp Car service?"

"Why shouldn't I be employed in all the useful and productive industries of the Nation?"

All these are positions and jobs sought by the majority group of whites in America and elsewhere. As the Negro becomes more insistent on these demands for Constitutional rights and privileges and threatens the more to compete with the white man for the job that the latter seeks and believes worth while having, then the inevitable conflict will come, and the group that is not strong enough to hold its own will go down, irrespective of the law and of the Government because the law and the Government are but executive expressions of the sober will of the people, but when the people, through prejudice or any mass opinion, become dissatisfied, the law and the Government are no longer able to [protect the black people from such reactions as were seen in] [manuscript indecipherable]

... the riots of East St. Louis and Chicago; the political riot of Washington and the commercial riot of Tulsa, Oklahoma. The things that the White majority want in their own countries they will not yield to the Negro or to ANY OTHER RACE and that is natural. The only sensible thing for the Negro to do, therefore, is to "BUILD" for himself. This can be done without friction or animosity between the Races and that is why the Universal Negro Improvement Association believes in the building up of Africa for the Negro Race.

Those Negroes who are too lazy to work and lay the foundation for such a Government are among those who criticize us.

Pilgrim Fathers we had in America before we enjoyed the delights of New York, Chicago or Boston. Pilgrim Fathers we must have if Africa is to rise from her slumber and darkness.

We of the Univeral Negro Improvement Association are satisfied to be called ignorant and gullible in working toward this end.

The Black Star Line's failure has been made much of by the Press and our critics. In another letter, I will explain to the public, through you, the cause of the failure of this Corporation.

Yours truly,

MARCUS GARVEY
PRESIDENT GENERAL

UNIVERSAL NEGRO IMPROVEMENT ASSOCIATION
56 West 135th St.
New York

An example of Garvey's effective persuasion is given in the testimony of John E. Bruce, a well-known New York journalist who published a column in the *Negro World* under the title, "Bruce Grit's Column." He regularly signed his name as Bruce Grit in other communications besides his news writing. When Garvey first came to New York, Bruce Grit was among those who wrote highly critical articles about him. Garvey was accused of being another spellbinding opportunist of which Harlem had seen more than enough. After a time, however, Bruce became so strong a supporter of the Garvey movement, that he was made a knight by the organization. At the time of Garvey's greatest popularity, in the early 1920's, Bruce could make these comments reflecting the influence of Marcus Garvey.

J. E. Bruce

Replies to the Claim the Goals of
*Black and White are Identical**

"Before entering upon the reading of the paper which I am about to submit for your consideration, I wish briefly to advert to some of the things which appear in our race press this week, touching upon the relations between the

---

*J. E. Bruce, "Replies to the Claim the Goals of Black and White are Identical." Handwritten notes reprinted from the Schomburg Collection of the John E. Bruce Papers, Harlem Branch of the New York Public Library, New York City, New York.

races and the ultimate outcome. It is reported that at a convention or conference of Negroes in a western city and state, a series of resolutions was adopted affirming that the destiny of the two races is identical-coordinate, etc. etc. I am unable to accept these rosy statements because they are not historically true and never have been — In the first place the status of the blacks and colored people from the beginning of the government down to the present hour has not been identical with that of the white race. Only things equal to the same thing are equal to each other.

The black and colored men who contributed their all to the greatness and glory of this republic never were *citizens*. They were not even good Hessian Soldiers for those were actually paid for their services as fighting men. These black and colored men fighting America's battles from the earlier Indian Wars down to the World War 1914 - 18: were not fighting as American *citizens* as were white men thus engaged, But [sic] as separate *units* under the direction of white men. And having no claim or interest or right to the spoils of the victory. He ought to have by virtue of his services But not having status as a citizen being a citizen on paper only, he can make no demands that will be heeded or respected. He can beg for, appeal to, plead and petition for these rights, and benefits but this is not the business of *equal citizens* of peers of the realm where everyman is a sovereign a king!

It is the apotheasis of folly for the Negro to assert and insist that he is an American citizen — when a *single* citizenship *right* is denied or withheld from him.

Negroes all over the country today are clammoring for these rights and trying to convince white men that they are entitled to them because the Constitution guarantees them — but the *nation* is too cowardly to enforce them. The reason is not too far to seek. The race feeling equality with the present dominant white race in America is a non assimilable [sic] race — being Negro and negroid and the question of granting to it relative position with the white race will be a long while pending. The longer it is delayed the more difficult its solution.

We deceive ourselves in believing a solution possible that will be advantageous to us as a race. So far as I have been able to learn there have been no gestures made by the white race to the Negro race for this union of which so many misguided Negro *leaders* dream. When Kipling wrote:

For East is East, and West is West
And never the twain shall meet

He wrote the sentiments of the white nations of the earth as they respect their relations toward the black, brown and yellow races of whom there are 9,47,000,000 [sic] struggling to reach their place in the social progression, and to play their parts in the great World drama, when the white man reluctantly releases his grip on world affairs and retires to return no more to power he so much loved and so arbitrarily exercised when he possessed it. The Pendulum is swinging the other way. The mills of the Gods grind slowly but they grind exceeding true."

It was, however, in speaking to the average black man, not the intellectual or the professional, that Garvey was most persuasive. Insight into this side of his nature can be found in the book of speeches and ideas prepared by his wife, Amy Jacques Garvey, *Philosophy and Opinions of Marcus Garvey.*[22] When she prepared the collection, she said:

> . . . in order to give to the public an opportunity of studying and forming an opinion of him; not from inflated and misleading newspaper and magazine articles, but from expressions of thoughts enunciated by him in defence of his oppressed and struggling race; so that by his own words he may be judged, and Negroes the world over may be informed and inspired, for truth, brought to light, forces conviction, and a state of conviction inspires action.[23]

Although Garvey's speeches were typically short, Mrs. Garvey chose to devote a large portion of her collection to a series of his ideas on various subjects organized by concept. For example, the following series of quotations appears on a single page.

> This is the day of racial activity, when each and every group of this great human family must exercise its own initiative and influence in its own protection, therefore, Negroes should be more determined to-day than they have ever been, because the mighty forces of the world are operating against non-organized groups of peoples, who are not ambitious enough to protect their own interests.

> Wake up Ethiopia! Wake up Africa! Let us work towards the one glorious end of a free, redeemed and mighty nation. Let Africa be a bright star among the constellation of nations.

> A man's bread and butter is only insured when he works for it.

> The world has not reached the stage when humanity is really at at the parting of the ways. It is a question of "MAN MIND THYSELF."

> The political readjustment of the world means that those who are not sufficiently able, not sufficiently prepared, will be at the mercy of the organized classes for another one or two hundred years.

> The only protection against INJUSTICE in man is POWER — Physical, financial, and scientific.

> The masses make the nation and the race. If the masses are illiterate, that is the judgment passed on the race by those who are critical of its existence.[24]

In other parts of the book, Garvey is quoted as saying, "NATION-HOOD is the only means by which modern civilization can completely protect itself." In words that have remained to the present day to inspire black nationalists such as Malcolm X, Garvey said, "Nationhood is the highest ideal of all peoples."

Garvey was a master of organization as well as a master of persuasion. In the quotation above, he observed the value of being organized to survive. Of his own efforts to bring organization to all the black men of the world, he said: "We of the Negro Race are moving from one state of organization to another, and we shall so continue until we have thoroughly lifted ourselves into the organization of GOVERNMENT." One goal of organization, which proved to be Garvey's downfall, was the amassing of capital. Again, a possible influence on modern spokesmen who argue that as long as the black man is in a state of poverty he will lack the capacity to participate in the decision-making that affects his life, Garvey showed no sympathy with poverty:

> To be prosperous in whatever we do is the sign of TRUE WEALTH. We may be wealthy in not only having money, but in spirit and health. It is the most helpful agency toward a self-satisfying life. One lives, in an age like this, nearer perfection by being wealthy than by being poor. To the contended [sic.] soul, wealth is the stepping stone to prefection [sic]; to the miser it is the nearest avenue to hell. I would prefer to be honestly wealthy, than miserably poor.[25]

Recognizing, as he did, the value of organization, Garvey perceived the damage wrought from the constant intra-racial disagreements and competition. He lamented the danger of the many black-oriented organizations failing to work together. He said, "the greatest weapon used against the Negro is DISORGANIZATION." He further said,

> PREPAREDNESS is the watch-word of this age. For us as a race to remain, as we have been in the past — divided among ourselves, parochializing, insularizing and nationalizing our activities as subjects and citizens of the many alien races and governments under which we live — is but to hold ourselves in readiness for that great catastrophe that is bound to come — that of racial extermination, at the hands of the stronger race — the race that will be fit to survive.[26]

The message of forthcoming race extermination is a powerful motivation for men to join the persuader and take concerted action. The message is used now with similar persuasive effect, and one of the most meaningful concepts to modern black Americans is "survival."

As we will see in the next section, the Black Muslims are so often accused of race hatred that a regular feature in their newspaper, *Muhammad Speaks,* is an explanation that their teachings are not of hate. Similarly, Marcus Garvey was accused of hating the white race. Perhaps, when white people hear someone arguing forcefully for black men, a feeling of guilt combines with a need to perceive the speaker as an undesirable person, and the term "hate," is ascribed. In reply to this charge, Garvey said, "I am not opposed to the white race as charged by my enemies. I have no time to hate any one. All my time is devoted to the up-building and development of the Negro Race." He also said,

> At no time within the last five hundred years can one point to a single instance of the Negro as a race of haters.
> The Negro has loved even under severest punishment. In slavery the Negro loved his master, he safe-guarded his home even when he further planned to enslave him. We are not a race of Haters, but Lovers of humanity's Cause.[27]

To those who perceived a physical threat in his rhetoric, Garvey answered that, "Mob violence and injustice have never helped a race or a nation . . . we as a people in this new age desire to love all mankind, not in the social sense, but in keeping with the Divine Injunction 'MAN LOVE THY BROTHER.' " But this rejection of physical violence did not prevent Garvey from anticipating what is now considered a modern slogan, "Black Power." He said this:

> Power is the only argument that satisfies man.
> Except the individual, the race or the nation has POWER that is exclusive, it means that that individual, race, or nation will be bound by the will of the other who possesses this great qualification.
> It is the physical and pugilistic power of Harry Wills that makes white men afraid to fight him.
> It was the industrial and scientific power of the Teutonic race that kept it for years as dictator of the economic and scientific policies of Europe.
> It is the naval and political power of Great Britain that keeps her mistress of the seas.
> It is the commercial and financial power of the United States of America that makes her the greatest banker in the world. Hence it is advisable for the Negro to get power of every kind. POWER in education, science, industry, politics

and higher government. That kind of power that will stand out signally, so that other races and nations can see, and if they will not see, then FEEL.

Man is not satisfied or moved by prayers or petitions, but every man is moved by that power of authority which forces him to do even against his will.[28]

Garvey was clearly inclined to use his powers of persuasion for his own race and realized the inability of persuasion to move the white man.

In the long-standing debate between the assimilationist and the separatist, Garvey made his position on the side of separation abundantly clear. His views are summarized in the statement included below.

Marcus Garvey

Race Assimilation*

Some Negro leaders have advanced the belief that in another few years the white people will make up their minds to assimilate their black populations; thereby sinking all racial prejudice in the welcoming of the black race into the social companionship of the white. Such leaders further believe that by the amalgamation of black and white, a new type will spring up, and that type will become the American and West Indian of the future.

This belief is preposterous. I believe that white men should be white, yellow men should be yellow, and black men should be black in the great panorama of races, until each and every race by its own initiative lifts itself up to the common standard of humanity, as to compel the respect and appreciation of all, and so make it possible for each one to stretch out the hand of welcome without being able to be prejudiced against the other because of any inferior and unfortunate condition.

The white man of America will not, to any organized extent, assimilate the Negro, because in so doing, he feels that he will be commiting racial suicide. This he is not prepared to do. It is true he illegitimately carries on a system of assimilation; but such assimilation, as practised, is one that he is not prepared to support because he becomes prejudiced against his own offspring, if that offspring is the product of black and white; hence, to the white man the question of racial differences is eternal. So long as Negroes occupy an inferior position among the races and nations of the world, just so long will others be prejudiced against them, because it will be profitable for

---

*From Amy Jacques Garvey, ed., *Philosophy and Opinions of Marcus Garvey*, Vol. I (New York: The Universal Publishing House, 1923), p. 26.

them to keep up their system of superiority. But when the Negro by his own initiative lifts himself from his low state to the highest human standard he will be in a position to stop begging and praying, and demand a place that no individual, race or nation will be able to deny him.

Some of our leaders in the Negro race flatter themselves into believing that the problem of black and white in America will work itself out, and that all the Negro has to do is to be humble, submissive and obedient and everything will work out well in the "Sweet bye and bye."

Some of us believe that this slave race of ours will live in the United States of America and in the future again become law makers [he observed the fury of whites during Reconstruction when black men had become law-makers] for the white race (our slave masters of sixty years ago). Nothing of the kind has happened in all human history. There is not one instance where a slave race living in the same country (within the same bounds as the race of masters that enslaved them and being in numbers less than the race of masters) has ever yet ruled and governed the masters. It has never been so in history, and it will never be so in the future. The hidden spirit of America is determined that it shall never be, caring not what hopes and promises we get.

But history has recorded where a race of slaves through evolution, through progress, has risen to the heights where they ruled and dominated those who once enslaved them, but that race of slaves has always had to betake itself to other habitats (usually their own native land) and there, apart from those who once enslaved them, developed a power of their own, a strength of their own, and in the higher development of that strength, and of that power, they, like others, have made conquests, and the conquests sometimes have enabled them to enslave those who once enslaved them. So for us to encourage the idea that one day Negroes will rise to the highest in the administration of this white government, is only encouraging a vain hope.

The only wise thing for us as ambitious Negroes to do, is to organize the world over, and build up for the race a mighty nation of our own in Africa. And this race of ours that can not get recognition and respect in the country where we were slaves, by using our own ability, power and genius, would develop for ourselves in another country in our habitat a nation of our own, and be able to send back from that country, — from that native habitat — to the country where we were once enslaved, representatives of our race, that would get as much respect as any other ambassadors from any other race or nation.

To a black man who had just returned from participation in World War I only to find he was still "boy" to the majority of his fellow American citizens, a voice like Marcus Garvey's, telling him to be a man, was inspiring. Even if Booker T. Washington was a brilliant tactician for race improvement through careful preparation, the average black man who lived in poverty with no apparent hope for any improvement in his lifetime, or even his children's, found it

difficult to be patient. Reasonably, he wanted to do something to improve his lot now, but everywhere he turned, he lacked the power to do anything for himself or his race. In the face of frustration, it would not be unreasonable for him to give up; to drop out, and feel fate was against him. Then came Marcus Garvey who rejected that attitude, and said some self-respect and organization would open the gates to anything.

Many times Garvey is perceived as a bombastic, highly oratorical speaker, probably because of the image left by the elaborate uniforms he wore, and the flashy parades he staged in connection with the conventions of the UNIA. In the passage published below, he reveals himself to be capable of a restrained, although inspiring, style. His message, in this case, is not designed to be logical; he does not feel the need to supply evidence. His audience consists of persons who have suffered from the incongruity between their central belief of themselves as human beings, and the peripheral beliefs derived from hundreds of daily experiences, telling them they were less than human; less than men — only "boys" or "girls." These peripheral beliefs, though individually inconsequential, combined to form such a contrast with the central beliefs as to make a significant impact on the behavior of black people in the United States. In seeking to modify these behaviors — deference to white men, acceptance of second-class citizenship, lack of personal initiative to improve oneself — Garvey related the central concept of "humanity" with peripheral beliefs regarding acceptable behavior in American society. In this sense, his persuasive campaign is quite consistent with the recommendations of Rokeach discussed in Chapter I.[29] In this sense, he was leading the way for modern persuaders who are seeking essentially the same rhetorical appeal. In the following statement, Garvey makes the appeal which probably characterizes his principal persuasive approach, and his major contribution to black rhetoric.

Marcus Garvey
Man Know Thyself*

For man to know himself is for him to feel that for him there is no human master. For him Nature is his servant, and whatsoever he wills in Nature, that shall be his reward. If he wills to be a pigmy, a serf or a slave, that shall he

---

*From Amy Jacques Garvey, ed., *Philosophy and Opinions of Marcus Garvey*, Vol. I (New York: The Universal Publishing House, 1923), pp. 38-39.

be. If he wills to be a real man in possession of the things common to man, then he shall be his own sovereign.

When man fails to grasp his authority he sinks to the level of the lower animals, and whatsoever the real man bids him do, even as if it were of the lower animals, that much shall he do. If he says, "go." He goes. If he says "come," he comes. By this command he performs the functions of life even as by a similar command the mule, the horse, the cow perform the will of their masters.

For the last four hundred years the Negro has been in the position of being commanded even as the lower animals are controlled. Our race has been without a will; without a purpose of its own, for all this length of time. Because of that we have developed few men who are able to understand the strenuousness of the age in which we live.

Where can we find in this race of ours real men. Men of character, men of purpose, men of confidence, men of faith, men who really know themselves? I have come across so many weaklings who profess to be leaders, and in the test I have found them but the slaves of a nobler class. They perform the will of their masters without question.

To me, a man has no master but God. Man in his authority is a sovereign lord. As for the individual man, so of the individual race. This feeling makes man so courageous, so bold, as to make it impossible for his brother to intrude upon his rights. So few of us can understand what it takes to make a man — the man who will never say die; the man who will never give up; the man who will never depend upon others to do for him what he ought to do for himself; the man who will not blame God, who will not blame Nature, who will not blame Fate for his condition; but the man who will go out and make conditions to suit himself. Oh, how disgusting life becomes when on every hand you hear people (who bear your image, who bear your resemblance) telling you that they cannot make it, that Fate is against them, that they cannot get a chance. If 400,000,000 Negroes can only get to know themselves, to know that in them is a sovereign power, is an authority that is absolute, then in the next twenty-four hours we would have a new race, we would have a nation, an empire, — resurrected, not from the will of others to see us rise, — but from our own determination to rise, irrespective of what the world thinks.

The selections which have been printed here from the *Philosophy and Opinions of Marcus Garvey* reflect both his message and his rhetorical method of disseminating it. Without trying to make a comparison along ideological lines, there is a similarity between this book and the little red book of *Quotations of Chairman Mao Tse tung,* which has become so much a part of the rhetoric of Communist China and many revolutionaries around the world including some black revolutionaries in America. It might be more appropriate for black Americans to use the quotations from Marcus Garvey.

To close this section on Garvey's United Negro Improvement Association, we have included his speech delivered at Liberty Hall in New York City during the second International Convention of Negroes, August, 1921. At this time, Garvey was near the peak of his popularity and strength. This speech, unlike some of the more restrained and inspirational ones already printed, is intended to suit a convention occasion, when ringing oratory is the order of the day. As the reader will see, Garvey is more than able to adjust to the situation.

Marcus Garvey
From *Philosophy and Opinions of Marcus Garvey**

Four years ago, realizing the oppression and the hardships from which we suffered, we organized ourselves into an organization for the purpose of bettering our condition, and founding a government of our own. The four years of organization have brought good results, in that from an obscure, despised race we have grown into a mighty power, a mighty force whose influence is being felt throughout the length and breadth of the world. The Universal Negro Improvement Association existed but in name four years ago, today it is known as the greatest moving force among Negroes. We have accomplished this through unity of effort and unity of purpose, it is a fair demonstration of what we will be able to accomplish in the very near future, when the millions who are outside the pale of the Universal Negro Improvement Association will have linked themselves up with us.

By our success of the last four years we will be able to estimate the grander success of a free and redeemed Africa. In climbing the heights to where we are today, we have had to surmount difficulties, we have had to climb over obstacles, but the obstacles were stepping stones to the future greatness of this Cause we represent. Day by day we are writing a new history, recording new deeds of valor performed by this race of ours. It is true that the world has not yet valued us at our true worth but we are climbing up so fast and with such force that every day the world is changing its attitude towards us. Wheresoever you turn your eyes today you will find the moving influence of the Universal Negro Improvement Association among Negroes from all corners of the globe. We hear among Negroes the cry of

---

*From Amy Jacques Garvey, ed., *Philosophy and Opinions of Marcus Garvey*, Vol. I (New York: The Universal Publishing House, 1923), pp. 93-97.

"Africa for the Africans". This cry has become a positive, determined one. It is a cry that is raised simultaneously the world over because of the universal oppression that affects the Negro. You who are congregated here tonight as Delegates representing the hundreds of branches of the Universal Negro Improvement Association in different parts of the world will realize that we in New York are positive in this great desire of a free and redeemed Africa. We have established this Liberty Hall as the centre from which we send out the sparks of liberty to the four corners of the globe, and if you have caught the spark in your section, we want you to keep it a-burning for the great Cause we represent.

There is a mad rush among races everywhere towards national independence. Everywhere we hear the cry of liberty, of freedom, and a demand for democracy. In our corner of the world we are raising the cry for liberty, freedom and democracy. Men who have raised the cry for freedom and liberty in ages past have always made up their minds to die for the realization of the dream. We who are assembled in this Convention as Delegates representing the Negroes of the world give out the same spirit that the fathers of liberty in this country gave out over one hundred years ago. We give out a spirit that knows no compromise, a spirit that refuses to turn back, a spirit that says "Liberty or Death", and in prosecution of this great ideal — the ideal of a free and redeemed Africa, men may scorn, men may spurn us, and may say that we are on the wrong side of life, but let me tell you that way in which you are travelling is just the way all peoples who are free have travelled in the past. If you want Liberty you yourselves must strike the blow. If you must be free you must become so through your own effort, through your own initiative. Those who have discouraged you in the past are those who have enslaved you for centuries and it is not expected that they will admit that you have a right to strike out at this late hour for freedom, liberty and democracy.

At no time in the history of the world, for the last five hundred years, was there ever a serious attempt made to free Negroes. We have been camouflaged into believing that we were made free by Abraham Lincoln. That we were made free by Victoria of England, but up to now we are still slaves, we are industrial slaves, we are social slaves, we are political slaves, and the new Negro desires a freedom that has no boundary, no limit. We desire a freedom that will lift us to the common standard of all men, whether they be white men of Europe or yellow men of Asia, therefore, in our desire to lift ourselves to that standard we shall stop at nothing until there is a free and redeemed Africa.

I understand that just at this time while we are endeavoring to create public opinion and public sentiment in favor of a free Africa, that others of our race are being subsidized to turn the attention of the world toward a different desire on the part of Negroes, but let me tell you that we who make up this Organization know no turning back, we have pledged ourselves even unto the last drop of our sacred blood that Africa must be free. The enemy may argue with you to show you the impossibility of a free and redeemed Africa, but I want you to take as your argument the thirteen colonies of America, that once owed their sovereignity to great Britain, that sovereignity has been destroyed to make a United States of America. George Washington was not God Almighty. He was a man like any Negro in this building, and if he and his associates were able to make a free America, we too can make a free Africa. Hampden, Gladstone, Pitt and Disraeli were not the representatives of God in the person of Jesus Christ. They were but men, but in their time they worked for the expansion of the British Empire, and today they boast of a British Empire upon which "the sun never sets." As Pitt and Gladstone were able to work for the expansion of the British Empire, so you and I can work for the expansion of a great African Empire Voltaire and Mirabeau were not Jesus Christs, they were but men like ourselves. They worked and overturned the French Monarchy. They worked for the Democracy which France now enjoys, and if they were able to do that, we are able to work for a democracy in Africa. Lenine and Trotzky were not Jesus Christs, but they were able to overthrow the despotism of Russia, and today they have given to the world a Social Republic, the first of its kind. If Lenine and Trotzky were able to do that for Russia, you and I can do that for Africa. Therefore, let no man, let no power on earth, turn you from this sacred cause of liberty. I prefer to die at this moment rather than not to work for the freedom of Africa. If liberty is good for certain sets of humanity it is good for all. Black men, Colored men, Negroes have as much right to be free as any other race that God Almighty ever created, and we desire freedom that is unfettered, freedom that is unlimited, freedom that will give us a chance and opportunity to rise to the fullest of our ambition and that we cannot get in countries where other men rule and dominate.

We have reached the time when every minute, every second must count for something done, something achieved in the cause of Africa. We need the freedom of Africa now, therefore, we desire the kind of leadership that will give it to us as quickly as possible. You will realize that not only individuals, but governments are using their influence against us. But what do we care about the unrighteous influence of any government? Our cause is based upon righteousness. And anything that is not righteous we have no respect for, because God Almighty is our leader and Jesus Christ our standard bearer. We rely on them for that kind of leadership that will make us free, for it is the same God who inspired the Psalmist to write "Princes shall come out of Egypt and Ethiopia shall stretch out her hands unto God". At this moment methinks I see Ethiopia stretching forth her hands unto God and methinks I see the Angel of God taking up the standard of the Red, the Black and the Green, and saying "Men of the Negro Race, Men of Ethiopia, follow me". Tonight we are following. We are following 400,000,000 strong. We are following with a determination that we must be free before the wreck of matter, before the crash of worlds.

It falls to our lot to tear off the shackles that bind Mother Africa. Can you do it? You did it in the Revolutionary War. You did it in the Civil War; You did it at the Battles of the Marne and Verdun; You did it in Mesopotamia. You can do it marching up the battle heights of Africa. Let the world know that 400,000,000 Negroes are prepared to die or live as free men. Despise us as much as you care. Ignore us as much as you care. We are coming 400,000,000 strong. We are coming with our woes behind us, with the memory of suffering behind us — woes and suffering of three hundred years — they shall be our inspiration. My bulwark of strength in the conflict for freedom in Africa, will be the three hundred years of persecution and hardship left behind in this Western Hemisphere. The more I remember the suffering of my fore-fathers, the more I remember the lynchings and burnings in the Southern States of America, the more I will fight on even though the battle seems doubtful. Tell me that I must turn back, and I laugh you to scorn. Go on! Go on! Climb ye the heights of liberty and cease not in well doing until you have planted the banner of the Red, the Black and the Green on the hilltops of Africa.

THE NATION OF ISLAM

The various separatist rhetorics examined thus far have concentrated on the idea that the white man can never be expected to give equal status in his society to his former slaves. They have stressed the inherent value in accepting and praising their identity as black people; they have sought refuge from the white man on this continent. They have tried to return to Mother Africa; they have even considered rejecting the white man's religion and adopting an essentially African theology. Edward W. Blyden recommended the Muslim religion as more suited to black men. The emergence of an organization which embraces all these rhetorical sub-strategies should, therefore, not be surprising.

By 1930, a black separatist leadership vacuum existed. Garvey had been exiled ostensibly because of difficulties with his many business ventures but possibly because he had worried those in positions of power. No other organizations had yet generated leaders of his capacity. The United Negro Improvement Association was in a state of confusion and dissension that caused a split between Garvey, then in Jamaica, and the leaders of the American branch of the UNIA. Two separate organizations were created; neither as powerful as before, and the Americans had no one to succeed Garvey.

It was in that year, 1930, that a strange man by the name of Wallace D. Fard appeared in the black community of Detroit. He mysteriously avoided answering questions about himself, and allowed all sorts of speculation to arise. He suggested that he had come from Mecca to save the black people of America from the white man. Fard established an organization called the Nation of Islam, and one of his early followers was a man born to the name Elijah Poole, who took the name Elijah Muhammad after joining the Nation of Islam and rejecting his slave-name, Poole. Mr. Muhammad became fully devoted to the organization and to Fard.

So devoted to Fard was Elijah Muhammad that he established him as a deity come to earth to lead the black man. Elijah Muhammad was also responsible for perpetuating the Muslim group when Fard disappeared, never to return, in 1934.

The premises upon which the Black Muslims, as they later came to be called, advanced themselves to the black men of America have already been indicated. First, as with all separatist groups, they argued that the white man will never grant the blacks equal status in this country. Lincoln, in his study of the Muslims, suggests that this idea meets with ready acceptance among black Americans.

> There is a widespread belief that the white man will *never* of his own accord accept non-whites as his equals in status and opportunity, in America or elsewhere. There is a surprisingly broad conviction that — as the Muslims insist — the white man has deliberately "written the Negro out of history," refusing to recognize the Black Man's contribution to the great Afro-Asian civilizations and, especially, to the development of America.[30]

This claim can be advanced simply by recounting a series of factual statements which most black men accept at once, because they have lived through similar experiences. These statements are familiar to the reader because they have been used by most of the separatist persuaders discussed in this chapter. The black man provided the free labor on which this nation was founded, but he has had no share in that success. The black man has fought in wars for the freedom of America, but he has no freedom in America. The black man was a better Christian than the white man, but the whites show no sign of Christian behavior in return; he is not even allowed to worship with whites. The list goes on; it does not need to be exaggerated. From these facts, the claim is drawn that the white man will never grant equality. The obvious warrant for the claim is this: since the white men have shown no sign of granting equality for over 300 years, they will never do so. It does not need to be stated — most black audiences recognize it implicitly, and on this warrant they either accept or reject the Muslim appeal. Considerable rhetorical effort is required to convince blacks that there is no hope for true integration and that it is acceptable to *want* to live with others of their own kind. So much has been done in America to establish the value of integration, and to oppose any sign of segregation, that many blacks hesitate to agree publicly that separation is a positive good. Notice below Elijah Muhammad's words designed to free his black audience from the dissonance this idea of separation generates.

Elijah Muhammad

Separation Is A Must*

Why not a united Black Nation? Have the white people not been a united white people all their days? Have they not lived in their own quarters and countries under their own white rulers, kings, queens, and presidents?

What is all the excitement over the Black Man wanting to live to himself? We have lived under segregation forced upon us up until today. Now, why think living apart, out of the white man's society, is something that we should not think about doing?

Black people and white people are used to living apart from each other. It is the nature of us both and we are better off living apart than trying to mix together (which is against the nature of Black and white). We are two different people.

Black ants do not try living with red ants, white ants, or any color but their own color. Even black birds will not try mixing with yellow, red, and white birds. Everything abides by the law of nature in which it was created but the white man and his Black slave.

White people want to mix with every color of people on earth. And, they have nearly mixed up the entire population of the earth in various colors. They did not want to destroy their color. They do not even want to destroy it today but they want to force their color into other people.

Now, many of the Black slaves desire to live with their Black selves, after living under a forced mixture of our slavemaster's children.

Now, today, the very nature of us is being taught by God, Who Knows all of us. This teaching of self from God makes us desire, as never before, to be ourselves.

To further advance the acceptability, even the necessity, of separation, Elijah Muhammad shows a point of view consistent with modern psychology. He recognizes the importance of a sense of identity. As discussed in Chapter I, Rokeach includes one's identity as a central, primitive belief which is important to one's entire belief system and potentially damaging if it is negatively modified. Muhammad claims that the white man stole the black's sense of identity, and that he now is "mentally dead." He cannot become a white man; he has not recovered his identity as a black man. He is lost but can be found through the Nation of Islam. To find oneself, says Elijah Muhammad, the black man must reject the non-identity given him by whites: the name "Negro" or "nigger"

*Elijah Muhammad, "Separation Is A Must," *Muhammad Speaks,* VIII, No. 32, April 25, 1969, 20.

must be rejected along with the slave-name. In the passage that follows, note how Muhammad uses both universally accepted facts about the attitude of white men and the analogies to things in the world of animals and other natural phenomena to encourage acceptance. As with all his rhetoric, Muhammad includes the assertion that he is merely reporting the facts as God or Allah has given them to him — an additional effort to establish authority.

Elijah Muhammad

*Negro**

WE ARE NOT NEGROES. That is, those of us who have awakened into the knowledge of self. WE ARE BLACK ORIGINAL PEOPLE.

THERE IS NO RACE OR NATION, which has been called from their BEGINNING . . . NEGROES. This is a slang that the slave-master and his children have given to the American Black Slave after they had been success-ful in depriving our fathers of the knowledge of self. They made us neutral. We were not respected as a member of the societies of the earth nor by him because of the lack of knowledge of self and others.

THEY MADE US A SPIRITUALLY BLIND, DEAF AND DUMB PEOPLE. It is PITIFUL even to write it. They used our fathers whom the slave-masters had made helpless by the robbery of the knowledge of ourselves.

ALLAH (GOD), WHO CAME IN THE PERSON OF MASTER FARD MUHAMMAD, to WHOM Praises are Due forever, said to me, that there cannot be a worse robbery than to rob a man of the knowledge of self. This is why it is associated with physical blindness. It is awful, even for one to go and rob a man of his eyes with which he sees the way in going forth and coming in. The blind man depends on others to lead him, and the support of canes to help him to get around among the people. He cannot see. His eyes have been put out. PITIFUL.

AFTER THE WHITE SLAVE-MASTERS, put our fathers in this con-dition, robbed of the knowledge of self they called them Negroes, meaning something that is mentally dead and is neutral and cannot go of itself, in such condition.

A NEGRO, BEING MENTALLY DEAD, is not a part of civilization. He is subject to be taken and put into service to anyone who desires him.

IF YOU DO NOT LEAD HIM TO THE WORK, tell him what to do and how to do it, he will stand, sit or lay down and work not. He becomes a servant in the hands of civilization.

---

*Elijah Muhammad, "Negro," *Muhammad Speaks*, VIII, No. 32, April, 25, 1969, 21.

HIS MENTAL BLINDNESS is compared with PHYSICAL BLIND-NESS. A person who is physically blind has to be lead and guided everywhere he goes or he feels his way with a walking cane, or is lead by one who sees where he is going. So it is with the mentally dead Black Man of America.

NEGRO . . . He prides himself in whatever slang names and service made of him by his now mocking slave-master. He does not know his own name. He is proud of being called by a name of his slave-master or whatever the slave-master calls him; he will answer to it. They feel proud to answer to meaningless and disgraceful names and nicknames that the white man calls him.

IF YOU TRY TO MAKE HIM SEE that he is disgracing himself by answering to nick-names given to him by his master, he will dismiss you and say, "What is in a name. A name does not mean anything." This is silliness. He makes himself meaningless. Regardless to what he is called he means nothing after all. THIS IS OUR POOR PEOPLE.

BLACK EDUCATORS, Black business men and Black ministers refuse to accept the Honorable and Independent Names of God that would give them respect. He refuses because he loves and worships his master's name which keeps him a slave to his master.

THE WHITE SLAVE-MASTERS AND THEIR CHILDREN call them Negroes or Nigger after having neutralized them so that they are unable to join and become a member of the civilized society of the Nations.

HE CALLS HIMSELF A NEGRO. Let us see what this Negro (nigger) actually means. In log mills there is a large piece of iron that is powered by steam, that turns the logs for sawing boards from it, by what we call, the sawyer. The piece of iron is called the 'nigger.' The sawyer makes the piece of iron (nigger) to turn the log in whatever way he wants it to be turned. I have worked in saw mills when I was a young man.

THIS PIECE OF IRON (nigger) which is used to turn the heavy log, is neutral. It cannot move of itself.

THE BLACK MAN, so-called Negro, uneducated and deprived of the knowledge of self was given this name by the white man, meaning that "he is now a neutral man. He is not one of us nor is he able to call himself one of the members of his own people, for he has lost the knowledge of both and he now awaits someone to put him into action toward the knowledge of self."

THIS IS THE AMERICAN SO-CALLED NEGRO. SO ALLAH (GOD) TAUGHT ME.

Muslim rhetoric is not based on a separation of equals: it is not a case of two distinct but equal groups feeling the need to exist apart from each other. Rather, as Elijah Muhammad advances the message, the black man has the opportunity to return to the original status of the select people of God, from which he was taken by the inferior white man. In this the black man is allowed to practice a form of exclusion — he can become a part of a religion that is not open to white men; he can even adopt a name which is virtually unavailable to white men, but reflects the superior status of the black. This carries the notion of Crummell and others that God has chosen the black race for a superior position a step further. In the message below, which is regularly published by the Black Muslims, the names of whites, which do not praise God, are ridiculed, and the selectivity of Muslim names is developed.

Elijah Muhammad
*Why Black Man Should Be Called By the Names of God**

THE BLACK man from the root beginning is from a Black Father. Therefore, he should go in the Name of his BLACK FATHER.

As I have said, as long as the so-called American Negro is blind to the knowledge of self, he does not know by what name he should be called. You could call him anything and he would answer to it, for he does not know his True Name.

The white man calls the so-called American Negro by many nick-names. The so-called American Negro, then re-nick names for himself, the nick-names of the white man, although he does not even know what they mean.

The black man (so-called American Negro) is a member of the family and a direct descendant of the Creator Who made the Heavens and the Earth. Therefore the son should be called by the Name of his Father and not called by the name of an alien. The white race is an alien people to the Black Man.

So many times you have heard that God has ninety-nine (99) Names or Attributes (That Which Is Attributed to God). The 100th Name or Attribute of God is the Name, Allah, Which Represents that He is ALL IN ALL, of every Good name. His Name Begins with the Name CREATOR and Ends with THE FIRST AND THE LAST, THE ETERNAL. Many of His Attributes refer to such Names as POWER, FORCE, THE MIGHTY, THE WISE. THE MOST MERCIFUL, THE MAKER, THE FASHIONER, THE BEST KNOWER, THE ALL-HEARING ONE, THE ALL-SEEING ONE.

THE HOLY QUR-AN says that He has the Best Names and the Most Beautiful Names. So many of these Names that we should have, are pertaining to Our Father.

His Names of Praise and One worthy of Praise, are just a few of the Great Names Which Belong to God, and He Wants to Give Them to us. The Bible teaches us, that He will Give His Names to those who believe in Him. According to the Bible, Rev. 7:3, the Judgment cannot take place

---

*Elijah Muhammad, "Why Black Man Should Be Called By the Names of God," *Muhammad Speaks*, VIII, No. 32, April 25, 1969, 21.

until those Who Believe in Him are Given His Name, (sealed in their forehead).

Will you turn down a Great Name which will Live Forever, Bible Is. 56:5, in exchange for the nick-names of your very enemies? They have no meaning as to a human being, such as Mr. Fish. We are human beings and should not be called Mr. Fish. They name you Mr. Hog. You are not a Hog. They call you Mr. Bird. We should not be called bird. We are not winged fowl. They are names which are worthless to human beings.

The only white people who are allowed to use One of the Names of Allah (God) is one who has accepted Islam. These Names are given to them because of their faith in the religion of Allah (God). However, this does not mean that by nature, these Names belong to them.

IT IS ONLY YOU, Black Brother, that by nature should be called by the Names of your God and Father, the Creator of the Heavens and the Earth.

THIS IS WHAT ALLAH HAS TAUGHT ME. BELIEVE IT OR LET IT ALONE!

Elijah Muhammad's rhetorical style is distinctive in that he teaches the strongest of doctrines in a most gentle fashion. He does not rant about the white man; he does not shout words of hate. In polite language, he almost reluctantly seems forced to report the truth as Allah has given it. His expression, "This is what Allah has taught me. Believe it or let it alone," implies that he has no particular need to have people believe him. He merely tells the truth; one does not perceive him as a highly motivated persuader, but one who might allow you to see the truth as he does. Another well-known black speaker, Dick Gregory, is inclined to use the same technique in his addresses to college audiences. He says he does not care if you (the audience) believe him; he merely comes to tell the truth. Notice here how Elijah Muhammad politely rejects the "hate teacher" label, but does not draw back an inch from his attitude toward the white man.

Elijah Muhammad
Accusations Of Teaching Hate*

I AND MY FOLLOWERS, are ever being accused of teaching hate. I am sorry that you have gotten so many contrary answers from some of my

*Elijah Muhammad, "Accusations Of Teaching Hate," Muhammad Speaks, VIII, No. 29, April 4, 1969, 19.

followers, who are not qualified in knowledge, to answer such questions of whether or not we are teaching hate.

BY NO MEANS SHOULD THE TEACHINGS BE CONSIDERED the teachings of hate. It does not deny that truth is not accepted by a race of people who are made contrary to the nature and practice of truth. I am not surprised that they call me a hate teacher, due to the fact they they were not made of truth. They were made just the opposite, See Bible, John 8:44.

IF TRUTH OF THE WORLD IS CLASSIFIED as hate teaching, then I am a friend of God, for in the very beginning, according to the Bible, God hated one brother and loved the other (Gen., God loved Jacob and hated Esau). The cause of God's hatred was due to one brother's works of evil and envy of his brother, whom God Loved.

ACCORDING TO THE DESCRIPTION given by Esau and Jacob, one was hairy and the other of smooth skin. This has a great significance of truth. THE WHITE MAN became a hairy man until the birth of Moses because of the beast life he lived due to being deprived of the knowledge of self. They actually lived the life of beasts and acquired much of their characteristics. This is why the Revelator of the Bible, refers to them as beasts.

THEY ARE NOT four-footed beasts, but due to these 2,000 years in the hills and cavesides of Europe before the birth of Moses, they acquired the characteristics of beasts instead of human beings. They were reduced to the status of apes and monkeys.

WE HAVE IN THE HOLY QUR-AN, which is the most true Book in the hands of human beings, a Surah or Chapter entitled, THE CAVE (Chap. 18). This Chapter teaches a portion of the history of the white race in those 2,000 years before Moses.

IN THE NEW TESTAMENT, Jesus demanded this specific qualification (hate) of whomever would become his follower. (Luke 14:26), although it was not given in a very intelligent way. The truth of it is, he cares nothing about disbelieving parents, disbelieving brothers, or disbelieving sisters. He considered them as his enemies and the Believers should consider them as their enemies regardless to the closeness of kin. This is a Law. The Holy Qur-an teaches you that you will not see a Believer befriend a disbelieving people though they be their near of kin. This is commonly practiced by all of civilization whether they be religious or not.

IT IS THE NATURE OF PEOPLE, that if you do not like what they like or believe as they do, hatred of each other is seen between them. Here Jesus bears witness to the God's hatred of even a brother of a brother who is not a Believer.

THE CHRISTIANS BACK UP THE MINISTRY and teachings of Jesus by saying he taught love. They leave out the fact that he taught hate too. They left in the things with which they could quickly enslave the Black Man.

THE WHITE MAN DID NOT TEACH the Black Preachers the true theology of the Bible. Jesus classified the priest and the preacher as being blind, scripturally: 'the blind leading the blind and they both fall in the ditch (hell).' Bible, Rev. 19:20.

ALLAH (GOD) Who Came in the Person of Master Fard Muhammad, To Whom Praises are Due forever, has taught me the knowledge of the Bible and now the Holy Qur-an, translated by the Muslim Scientists.

IT IS THE VERY NATURE OF PEOPLE, TO HATE ONE ANOTHER WHEN THEY ARE NOT UNITED TO EACH OTHER.

Elijah Muhammad, unrestrained by Christian doctrine, is able to carry his pro-black rhetoric farther than nearly all the separatists who preceded him. Even Crummell, who preached that the black race was selected by God for superior things, was not able to draw an image of God as a black man; of the original man as black, and whites as a weak and undesirable derivative from cast-off blacks. When Elijah counsels his people not to be ashamed of their blackness, he supports his appeal with a black-oriented theology that is virtually unique.

As he admits, the label, "Black Muslims," was one applied by the press and not chosen by Elijah Muhammad and his followers. However, he turns a potentially derisive label to his own uses, much as the American Revolutionaries turned the name, "Yankee," to their own advantage.

The article published here is a regular feature of the newspaper *Muhammad Speaks.*

Elijah Muhammad
Are We the Black Muslims?*

SURE, WE ARE BLACK MUSLIMS! As white people call themselves white Christians, we are Black Muslims!

OF COURSE IT STARTED at first from the press. But we do not get indignant about being called Black for that is what we are.

WE WERE BLACK IN THE VERY BEGINNING of the Creation of the Father, who was Black. Black is what we prefer to be called. There is no white scholar or scientist of history and religion that will dare say otherwise.

---

*Elijah Muhammad, "Are We The Black Muslims?" *Muhammad Speaks,* VIII, No. 32, April 25, 1969, 19.

WHY SHOULD YOU FEEL OFFENDED when you are called a Black Muslim? The white people are not offended if you call them white Christians.

IT IS DUE TO THE FACT that the so-called American Negro has been mocked by the white slave-master, after the white slave-master, attracted them with the power of unalike. He attracted the slave so much so, that he desired to be white instead of his own nature color, Black, in which he was created. White is a made color and not a created color.

THE WHITE PEOPLE WHO ENSLAVED our fathers had an unrestrained hand and power over the Black slave. They could beat and force the slave to believe, answer to and obey anything they taught the Black slave without hindrance for we had no teachers among our slave-parents. The poor slave had no help here or there for centuries. I should say until today, on The Coming of Our God and Saviour, In the Person of Master Fard Muhammad, To Whom Praises are Due forever.

BUT I SAY, BROTHERS AND SISTERS, be happy that you are Black. It is the first color, original of man, in the sun. It is honorable, durable and lasting. It is not easy to be changed even under climatic conditions.

ALLAH (GOD) is the Father of the Creation of the Heavens and the Earth. His Color is Black. It is the best and purest of all the colors. It is Unchangable as His Wisdom, which is Superior over All.

IT IS TRUE WE ARE BLACK MUSLIMS. Our very Nation is Black People. Our Creator was a Black God.

SO DO NOT BE ASHAMED TO ACCEPT YOUR OWN BLACK SELF. It is an honorable color. IT IS THE FIRST AND THE LAST.

Elijah's rhetorical position is well summarized in his regularly published statement of the Muslim program. The reader can see that the statement covers almost every complaint the black man has raised against white American society. Although the demand for a separate land in which to reside is still prominent, the claim has not been pushed. As item seven indicates, the Muslims are willing to recognize that full separation is a thing of the future (if ever) and in the meantime, they intend to push for satisfaction of their grievances within the United States government. No evidence is presented; little argument is given. A series of demands is presented in language that communicates both strength and determination. The regular use of "we" suggests concerted action — one of the major persuasive tools of the Muslims. Their occasional demonstrations of group solidarity have been used effectively to recruit new members.

Read, then, the Muslim Program as given by "The Messenger of Allah."

Elijah Muhammad

The Muslim Program*
What the Muslims Want

This is the question asked most frequently by both the whites and the blacks. The answers to this question I shall state as simply as possible.

1. We want freedom. We want a full and complete freedom.

2. We want justice. Equal justice under the law. We want justice applied equally to all, regardless of creed or class or color.

3. We want equality of opportunity. We want equal membership in society with the best in civilized society.

4. We want our people in America whose parents or grandparents were descendants from slaves, to be allowed to establish a separate state or territory of their own — either on this continent or elsewhere. We believe that our former slave masters are obligated to provide such land and that the area must be fertile and minerally rich. We believe that our former slave masters are obligated to maintain and supply our needs in this separate territory for the next 20 to 25 years — until we are able to produce and supply our own needs.

Since we cannot get along with them in peace and equality, after giving them 400 years of our sweat and blood and receiving in return some of the worst treatment human beings have ever experienced, we believe our contributions to this land and the suffering forced upon us by white America, justifies our demand for complete separation in a state or territory of our own.

5. We want freedom for all Believers of Islam now held in federal prisons. We want freedom for all black men and women now under death sentence in innumerable prisons in the North as well as the South.

We want every black man and woman to have the freedom to accept or reject being separated from the slave master's children and establish a land of their own.

We know that the above plan for the solution of the black and white conflict is the best and only answer to the problem between two people.

6. We want an immediate end to the police brutality and mob attacks against the so-called Negro throughout the United States.

We believe that the Federal government should intercede to see that black men and women tried in white courts receive justice in accordance with the laws of the land — or allow us to build a new nation for ourselves, dedicated to justice, freedom and liberty.

7. As long as we are not allowed to establish a state or territory of our own, we demand not only equal justice under the laws of the United States, but equal employment opportunities — NOW!

We do not believe that after 400 years of free or nearly free labor, sweat and blood, which has helped America become rich and powerful, that so

---

*Elijah Muhammad, "The Muslim Program," *Muhammad Speaks,* VIII, No. 32, April 25, 1969, 40.

many thousands of black people should have to subsist on relief, charity or live in poor houses.

8. We want the government of the United States to exempt our people from ALL taxation as long as we are deprived of equal justice under the laws of the land.

9. We want equal education — but separate schools up to 16 for boys and 18 for girls on the condition that the girls be sent to women's colleges and universities. We want all black children educated, taught and trained by their own teachers.

Under such schooling system we believe we will make a better nation of people. The United States government should provide, free, all necessary text books and equipment, schools and college buildings. The Muslim teachers shall be left free to teach and train their people in the way of righteousness, decency and self respect.

10. We believe that intermarriage or race mixing should be prohibited. We want the religion of Islam taught without hinderance or suppression.

These are some of the things that we, the Muslims, want for our people in North America.

WHAT THE MUSLIMS BELIEVE

1. WE BELIEVE in the One God Whose proper Name is Allah.

2. WE BELIEVE in the Holy Qur-an in the Scriptures of all the Prophets of God.

3. WE BELIEVE in the truth of the Bible, but we believe that it has been tampered with and must be reinterpreted so that mankind will not be snared by the falsehoods that have been added to it.

4. WE BELIEVE in Allah's Prophets and the Scriptures they brought to the people.

5. WE BELIEVE in the resurrection of the dead — not in physical resurrection—but in mental resurrection. We believe that the so-called Negroes are most in need of mental resurrection; therefore, they will be resurrected first.

Furthermore, we believe we are the people of God's choice, as it has been written, that God would choose the rejected and the despised. We can find no other persons fitting this description in these last days more than the so-called Negroes in America. We believe in the resurrection of the righteous.

6. WE BELIEVE in the judgement; we believe this first judgement will take place as God revealed, in America ...

7. WE BELIEVE this is the time in history for the separation of the so-called Negroes and the so-called white Americans. We believe the black man should be freed in name as well as in fact. By this we mean that he should be freed from the names imposed upon him by his former slave masters. Names which identified him as being the slave master's slave. We believe that if we are free indeed, we should go in our own people's names — the black peoples of the earth.

8. WE BELIEVE in justice for all, whether in God or not; we believe as others, that we are due equal justice as human beings. We believe in equality — as a nation — of equals. We do not believe that we are equal with our slave masters in the status of "freed slaves."

We recognize and respect American citizens as independent peoples and we respect their laws which govern this nation.

WE BELIEVE that the offer of integration is hypocritical and is made by those who are trying to deceive the black peoples into believing that their 400-year-old open enemies of freedom, justice and equality are, all of a sudden, their "friends." Furthermore, we believe that such deception is intended to prevent black people from realizing that the time in history has arrived for the separation from the whites of this nation.

If the white people are truthful about their professed friendship toward the so-called Negro, they can prove it by dividing up America with their slaves.

We do not believe that America will ever be able to furnish enough jobs for her own millions of unemployed, in addition to jobs for the 20,000,000 black people as well.

10. WE BELIEVE that we who declared ourselves to be righteous Muslims, should not participate in wars which take the lives of humans. We do not believe this nation should force us to take part in such wars, for we have nothing to gain from it unless America agrees to give us the necessary territory wherein we may have something to fight for.

11. WE BELIEVE our women should be respected and protected as the women of other nationalities are respected and protected.

12. WE BELIEVE that Allah (God) appeared in the Person of Master W. Fard Muhammad, July, 1930; the long-awaited "Messiah" of the Christians and the "Mahdi" of the Muslims.

We believe further and lastly that Allah is God and besides HIM there is no God and he will bring about a universal government of peace wherein we all can live in peace together.

Muslim rhetoric, and the overall strategy of its campaign to win converts, shows many of the characteristics usually associated with effective persuasive efforts, such as Christian evangelism and political mass movements. Recalling the discussion of Hoffer on mass movements in Chapter I, one will remember that those who engaged in a movement are probably intensely discontented, yet not destitute. They are set to discredit the prevailing society, and to perceive some "devil" in it. They also have "the feeling that by the possession of some potent doctrine, infallible leader or some new technique they have access to a source of irresistible power.[31]

Lincoln's study of the Black Muslims records that eighty percent of the members are between the ages of 17 and 35; they are predominantly male Americans; they come from the lower economic levels of society; and are largely ex-Christians.[32] The message, which is adjusted for the educational level of audiences, is aimed at this group of young males who have faced the frustrations of being unable to earn enough to establish self-respect in their family or society, but are not ready to give up and simply survive. Muhammad's relation to Allah gives a source of irresistible power, which, when combined with the organized strength of their movement, they hope, will bring the desired ends in their lives.

Much religious symbolism is associated with the recruitment process into the Muslim organization. Perhaps the most symbolic is the rejection of the slave-name in favor of "X" and later of a Muslim name.

> The symbol X has a double meaning: implying "ex" it signifies that the Muslim is no longer what he was; and as "X," it signifies as unknown quality or quantity. It at once repudiates the white man's name and announces the rebirth of Black Man. . . .[33]

Muslims go into the street to find their converts. They go to the most degraded ghetto areas; they go into prisons; they go wherever they are likely to find promising converts. Much persuasion for conversion takes place in an interpersonal setting before the new man attends a formal service for the first time. The sermons themselves are similar to Christian evangelical efforts as those who have been persuaded are asked to come forward at the end of the service to join the group. One unusual characteristic of the service occurs toward the end. Questions and disagreements are accepted, and the minister strives to answer the objections on the spot.[34] The Muslims also exploit mass media through regular publications of their own, feature articles in other newspapers, and regular broadcasts over radio and television.

The most articulate and well-known of all the Muslim Ministers was Malcolm X. He was particularly responsible for spreading the doctrine throughout the country, bringing the message to great numbers of blacks. At the same time, he was the chief spokesman of the Muslims to the white community. Although Malcolm X was a frequent and effective public speaker in a formal situation, he probably did as much or more of his persuading in a dialogue situation. He was adept at an interchange of ideas with those who would challenge his, or rather, Muhammad's, ideas. He had quick and cutting answers. He usually could handle challenges. He frequently was found spreading the Muslim message through radio and television. In the interview presented below, prepared for National Educational Television in Boston, Malcolm X demonstrates his typical quick-answer style. Both the interviewer, Kenneth B. Clark, and Malcolm X himself give some information on his life and personality which helps to introduce this important speaker.

Malcolm X
Malcolm X Talks with Kenneth B. Clark*

Malcolm X is a punctual man. He arrived at the television studio, with two of his closest advisors, at the precise time of our appointment. He and his friends were immaculately dressed, with no outward sign of their belonging either to a separate sect or the ministry. Minister Malcolm X (and he insists upon being called "Minister Malcolm") is a tall, handsome man in his late thirties. He is clearly a dominant personality whose disciplined power seems all the more evident in contrast to the studied deference paid him by his associates. He is conscious of the impression of power which he seeks to convey, and one suspects that he does not permit himself to become too casual in his relations with others.

Although Minister Malcolm X seems proud of the fact that he did not go beyond the eighth grade, he speaks generally with the vocabulary and the tone of a college-educated person. Happy when this is pointed out to him, he explains that he has read extensively since joining the Black Muslim movement. His role as the chief spokesman for this movement in the New York-Washington region is, he insists, to raise the level of pride and accomplishment in his followers.

Malcolm X has been interviewed on radio, television, and by newspapermen probably more than any other Negro leader during the past two years. He shows the effects of these interminable interviews by a professional calm, and what appears to be an ability to turn on the proper amount of emotion, resentment, and indignation, as needed. One certainly does not get the impression of spontaneity. On the contrary, one has the feeling that Minister Malcolm has anticipated every question and is prepared with the appropriate answer, and answer which is consistent with the general position of the Black Muslim movement, as defined by the Honorable Elijah Muhammad.

We began the interview by talking about Malcolm X's childhood:

I was born in Omaha, Nebraska, back in 1925, that period when the Ku Klux Klan was quite strong in that area at that time — and grew up in Michigan, partially. Went to school there.

CLARK: What part of Michigan?

MALCOLM X: Lansing. I went to school there — as far as the eighth grade. And left there and then grew up in Boston and in New York.

CLARK: Did you travel with your family from Omaha to Michigan to Boston?

MALCOLM X: Yes. When I was born — shortly after I was born — the Ku Klux Klan gave my father an ultimatum — or parents an ultimatum — about remaining there, so they left and went to —

CLARK: What was the basis of this ultimatum?

MALCOLM X: My father was a Garveyite, and in those days, you know, it wasn't the thing for a black man to be outspoken or to deviate from the accepted stereotype that was usually considered the right image for Negroes to fulfill or reflect.

CLARK: Of all the words that I have read about you, this is the first time that I've heard that your father was a Garveyite. And, in fact, he *was* an outspoken black nationalist in the nineteen-twenties?

MALCOLM X: He was both a Garveyite and a minister, a Baptist minister. In those days you know how it was and how it still is; it only changed in the method, but the same things still exist: whenever a black man was outspoken he was considered crazy or dangerous. And the police department and various branches of the law usually were interwoven with that Klan element, so the Klan had the backing of the police, usually the police had the backing of the Klan, same as today.

CLARK: So in effect your father was required, or he was forced —

MALCOLM X: Yes, they burned the house that we lived in in Omaha, and I think this was in 1925, and we moved to Lansing, Michigan, and we ran into the same experience there. We lived in an integrated neighborhood, by the way, then. And it only proves that whites were as much against integration as they are now, only then they were more openly against it. And today they are shrewd in saying they are for it, but they still make it impossible for you to integrate. So we moved to Michigan and the same thing happened; they burned our home there. And he was — like I say — he was a clergyman, a Christian; and it was Christians who burned the home in both places — people who teach, you know, religious tolerance and brotherhood and all of them.

CLARK: Did you start school in Michigan?

MALCOLM X: Yes.

CLARK: How long did you stay in Michigan?

MALCOLM X: I think I completed the eighth grade while I was still in Michigan.

CLARK: And then where did you go?

MALCOLM X: To Boston.

CLARK: Did you go to high school in Boston?

MALCOLM X: No, I have never gone to high school.

CLARK: You've never gone to high school?

MALCOLM X: The eighth grade was as far as I went.

CLARK: That's phenomenal.

MALCOLM X: Everything I know above the eighth grade, I've learned from Mister Muhammad. He's been my teacher, and I think he's a better teacher than I would have had had I continued to go to the public schools.

CLARK: How did you meet Mister Muhammad?

MALCOLM X: I was — when I was in prison, in 1947, I first heard about his teaching; about his religious message. And at that time I was atheist, myself. I had graduated from Christianity to agnosticism on into atheism.

CLARK: Were the early experiences in Nebraska and Michigan where, as you say, Christians burned the home of your father who was a Christian minister — were these experiences the determinants of your moving away from Christianity?

MALCOLM X: No, no, they weren't, because despite those experiences, I, as I said, lived a thoroughly integrated life. Despite all the experiences I had in coming up — and my father was killed by whites at a later date — I still thought that there were some good white people; at least the ones I was associating with, you know, were supposed to be different. There wasn't any experience, to my knowledge, that opened up my eyes, because right up until the time that I went to prison, I was still integrated into the white society and thought that there were some good ones.

CLARK: Was it an integrated prison?

MALCOLM X: It was an integrated prison at the prison level, but the administrators were all white. You usually find that in any situation that is supposed to be based on integration. At the low level they integrate, but at the administrative or executive level you find whites running it.

CLARK: How long did you stay in prison?

MALCOLM X: About seven years.

CLARK: And you were in prison in Boston. And this is where you got in touch with —

MALCOLM X: My family became Muslims; accepted the religion of Islam, and one of them who had spent pretty much — had spent quite a bit of time with me on the streets of New York out here in Harlem had been exposed to the religion of Islam. He accepted it, and it made such a profound change in him. He wrote to me and was telling me about it. Well, I had completely eliminated Christianity. After getting into prison and having time to think, I could see the hypocrisy of Christianity. Even before I went to prison, I had already become an atheist and I could see the hypocrisy of Christianity. Most of my associates were white; they were either Jews or Christians, and I saw hypocrisy on both sides. None of them really practiced what they preached.

CLARK: Minister Malcolm —

MALCOLM X: Excuse me, but despite the fact that I had detected this, my own intellectual strength was so weak, or so lacking, till I was not in a position to really see or come to a conclusion concerning this hypocrisy until I had gotten to where I could think a little bit and had learned more about the religion of Islam. Then I could go back and remember all of these experiences and things that I had actually heard — discussions that I had participated in myself with whites. It had made everything that Mister Muhammad was saying add up.

CLARK: I see.

MALCOLM X: He was the one who drew the line and enabled me to add up everything and say that this is this, and I haven't met anyone since then who was capable of showing me an answer more strong or with more weight than the answer that the Honorable Elijah Muhammad has given.

CLARK: I'd like to go back just a little to your life in prison. What was the basis — how did you —

MALCOLM X: Crime. I wasn't framed. I went to prison for what I did, and the reason that I don't have any hesitation or reluctance whatsoever to point out the fact that I went to prison: I firmly believe that it was the Christian society, as you call it, the Judaic-Christian society, that created all of the factors that send so many so-called Negroes to prison. And when these fellows go to prison there is nothing in the system designed to reform them. All it does is — it's a breeding ground for more professional type of criminal, especially among Negroes. Since I saw, detected, the reluctance on the part of penologists, prison authorities, to reform men and even detected that — noticed that after a so-called Negro in prison trys to reform and become a better man, prison authorities are more against *that* man than they were against him when he was completely criminally inclined, so this is again hypocrisy. Not only is the Christian society itself religious hypocrisy, but the court system is hypocrisy, the entire penal system is hypocrisy. Everything is hypocrisy. Mister Muhammad came along with his religious gospel and introduced the religion of Islam and showed the honesty of Islam, showed the justice in Islam, the freedom in Islam. Why naturally, just comparing the two, Christianity had already eliminated itself, so all I had to do was accept the religion of Islam. I know today what it has done for me as a person.

CLARK: I notice that the Black Muslim movement has put a great deal of time, effort and energy in seeking recruits within the prisons.

MALCOLM X: This is incorrect.

CLARK: It is incorrect?

MALCOLM X: It is *definitely* incorrect.

CLARK: Eric Lincoln's book —

MALCOLM X: Well, Lincoln is incorrect himself. Lincoln is just a Christian preacher from Atlanta, Georgia, who wanted to make some money, so he wrote a book and called it *The Black Muslims in America*. We're not even Black Muslims. We are black people in a sense that "black" is an adjective. We are black people who are Muslims because we have accepted the religion of Islam, but what Eric Lincoln shrewdly did was capitalize the letter "b," and made "black" an adjectival noun and then attached it to "Muslim," and now it is used by the press to make it appear that this is the name of an organization. It has no religious connotation or religious motivation or religious objectives.

CLARK: You do not have a systematic campaign for recruiting or rehabilitating?

MALCOLM X: No, no.

CLARK: What about rehabilitation?

MALCOLM X: The reason that the religion of Islam has spread so rapidly in prison is because the average so-called Negro in prison has had experiences enough to make him realize the hypocrisy of everything in this society, and he also has experienced the fact that the system itself is not designed to rehabilitate him or make him turn away from crime. Then when he hears the religious teaching of the Honorable Elijah Muhammad that restores to him his racial pride, his racial identity, and restores to him also the desire to be a man, to be a human being, he reforms himself. And this spreads so rapidly among the so-called Negroes in prison that, since the sociologist and the psychologists and the penologist and the criminologist have all realized their own inability to rehabilitate the criminal, when Mr. Muhammad comes along and starts rehabilitating the criminal with just the religious gospel, it's a miracle. They look upon it as a sociological phenomenon or psychological phenomena, and it gets great publicity.

CLARK: You do not, therefore, have to actively recruit.

MALCOLM X: The Honorable Elijah Muhammad has no active effort to convert or recruit men in prison any more so than he does Negroes, period. I think that what you should realize, is that in America there are twenty million black people, all of whom are in prison. You don't have to go to Sing Sing to be in prison. If you're born in America with a black skin, you're born in prison, and the masses of black people in America today are beginning to regard our plight or predicament in this society as one of a prison inmate. And when they refer to the President, he's just another warden to whom they turn to open the cell door, but it's no different. It's the same thing, and just as the warden in the prison couldn't rehabilitate those men, the President in this country couldn't rehabilitate or change the thinking of the masses of black people. And as the Honorable Elijah Muhammad has been able to go behind the prison walls — the physical prison walls — and release those men from that which kept them criminals, he likewise on a mass scale throughout this country — he is able to send his religious message into the so-called Negro community and rehabilitate the thinking of our people and made them conquer the habits and the vices and the evils that have held us in the clutches of this white man's society.

CLARK: I think, Minister Malcolm, what you have just said brings me to trying to hear from you directly your ideas concerning the philosophy of the Black Muslim movement. Among the things that have been written about this movement, the things which stand out are the fact that this movement preaches hatred for whites; that it preaches black supremacy; that it, in fact, preaches, or if it does not directly preach, it accepts the inevitability of violence as a factor in the relationship between the races. Now —

MALCOLM X: That's a strange thing. You know, the Jews here in this city rioted last week against some Nazi, and I was listening to a program last night where the other Jew — where a Jewish commentator was congratulating what the Jews did to this Nazi; complimenting them for it. Now no one mentioned violence in connection with what the Jews did against these Nazis. But these same Jews, who will condone violence on their part or hate someone whom they consider to be an enemy, will join Negro organizations and tell Negroes to be non-violent; that it is wrong or immoral, unethical, unintelligent for Negroes to reflect some kind of desire to defend themselves from the attacks of whites who are trying to brutalize us. The Muslims who follow the Honorable Elijah Muhammad don't advocate violence, but Mister Muhammad does teach us that any human being who is intelligent has the right to defend himself. You can't take a black man who is being bitten by dogs and accuse him of advocating violence because he trys to defend himself from bite of the dog. If you notice, the people who are sicking the dogs on the black people are never accused of violence; they are never accused of hate. Nothing like that is ever used in the context of a discussion when it's about them. It is only when the black man begins to explode and erupt after he has had too much that they say that the black man is violent, and as long as these whites are putting out a doctrine that paves the way to justify their mistreatment of blacks, this is never called hate. It is only when the black man himself begins to spell out the historic deeds of what whites have been doing to him in this country that the shrewd white man with his control over the news media and propaganda makes it appears that the black people today are advocating some kind of hate. Mr. Muhammad teaches us to love each other, and when I say love each other — love our own kind. This is all black people need to be taught in this country because the only ones whom we don't love are our own kind. Most of the Negroes you see running around here talking about "love everybody" — they don't have any love whatsoever for their own kind. When they say, "Love everybody," what they are doing is setting up a situation for us to love white people. This is what their philosophy is. Or when they say, "Suffer peacefully," they mean suffer peacefully at the hands of the white man, because the same non-violent Negroes are the advocates of non-violence. If a Negro attacks one of them, they'll fight that Negro all over Harlem. It's only when the white man attacks them that they believe in non-violence, all of them.

CLARK: Mister X, is this a criticism of the Reverend Martin Luther King?

MALCOLM X: You don't have to criticize Reverend Martin Luther King. His actions criticize him.

CLARK: What do you mean by this?

MALCOLM X: Any Negro who teaches other Negroes to turn the other cheek is disarming that Negro. Any Negro who teaches Negroes to turn the other cheek in the face of attack is disarming that Negro of his God-given right, of his moral right, of his natural right, of his intelligent right to defend himself. Everything in nature can defend itself, and is right in defending itself except the American Negro. And men like King — their job is to go among Negroes and teach Negroes "Don't fight back." He doesn't tell them, "Don't fight each other." "Don't fight the white man." is what he's saying in essence, because the followers of Martin Luther King will cut each other from head to foot, but will not do anything to defend themselves against the attacks of the white man. But King's philosophy falls upon the ears of only a small minority. The majority or masses of black people in this country are more inclined in the direction of the Honorable Elijah Muhammad than Martin Luther King.

CLARK: Is it not a fact though —

MALCOLM X: *White* people follow King. *White* people pay King. *White* people subsidize King. *White* people support King. But the masses of black people don't support Martin Luther King. King is the best weapon that the white man, who wants to brutalize Negroes, has ever gotten in this country, because he is setting up a situation where, when the white man wants to attack Negroes, they can't defend themselves, because King has put this foolish philosophy out — you're not supposed to fight or you're not supposed to defend yourself.

CLARK: But Mister X, is it not a fact that Reverend King's movement was successful in Montgomery —

MALCOLM X: You can't tell me that you have had success — excuse me, sir.

CLARK: Was it not a success in Birmingham?

MALCOLM X: No, no. What kind of success did they get in Birmingham? A chance to sit at a lunch counter and drink some coffee with a cracker — that's success? A chance to — thousands of little children went to jail; they didn't get out, they were bonded out by King. They had to *pay* their way out of jail. That's not any kind of advancement or success.

CLARK: What *is* advancement from the point of view of the Muslims?

MALCOLM X: Any time dogs have bitten black women, bitten black children — when I say dogs, that is four-legged dogs and two-legged dogs have brutalized thousands of black people — and the one who advocates himself as their leader is satisfied in making a compromise or a deal with the same ones who did this to these people only if they will offer him a job, one job, downtown for one Negro or things of that sort. I don't see where there's any kind of success, sir; it's a sellout. Negroes in Birmingham are in worse condition now than they were then because the line is more tightly drawn. And to say that some moderate — to say that things are better now because a different man, a different white man, a different southern white man is in office now, who's supposed to be a moderate, is to tell me that you are better off dealing with a fox than you were when you were dealing with a wolf. The ones that they were dealing with previously were wolves, and they didn't hide the fact that they were wolves. The man that they got to deal with now is a fox, but he's no better than the wolf. Only he's better in his ability to lull the Negroes to sleep, and he'll do that as long as they listen to Doctor Martin Luther King.

CLARK: What would be the goals, or what are the goals of the Black Muslim movement? What would the Black Muslim movement insist upon in Birmingham, in Montgomery and in Jackson, Mississippi, et cetera?

MALCOLM X: Well, number one, the Honorable Elijah Muhammad teaches us that the solution will never be brought about by politicians, it will be brought about by God, and that the only way the black man in this country today can receive respect and recognition of other people is to stand on his own feet; get something for himself and do something for himself; and the solution that God has given the Honorable Elijah Muhammad is the same as the solution that God gave to Moses when the Hebrews in the Bible were in a predicament similar to the predicament of the so-called Negroes here in America today, which is nothing other than a modern house of bondage, or a modern Egypt, or a modern Babylon. And Moses' answer was to separate these slaves from their slave master and show the slaves how to go to a land of their own where they would serve a God of their own and a religion of their own in which they could feed themselves, clothe themselves, and shelter themselves.

CLARK: In fact then, you're saying that the Black Muslim movement —

MALCOLM X: It's not a Black Muslim movement.

CLARK: All right then —

MALCOLM X: We are black people who are Muslims because we believe in the religion of Islam.

CLARK: — this movement which you so ably represent actually desires separation.

MALCOLM X: Complete separation; not only physical separation but moral separation. This is why the Honorable Elijah Muhammad teaches the black people in this country that we must stop drinking, we must stop smoking, we must stop committing fornication and adultery, we must stop gambling and cheating and using profanity, we must stop showing disrespect for our women, we must reform ourselves as parents so we can set the proper example for our children. Once we reform ourselves of these immoral habits, that makes us more godly, more godlike, more righteous. That means we are qualified then, to be on God's side, and it puts God on our side. God becomes our champion then, and makes it possible for us to accomplish our aims.

CLARK: This movement then, is not particularly sympathetic with the integrationist goals of the N.A.A.C.P., C.O.R.E., Martin Luther King, and the student non-violent movement.

MALCOLM X: Mister Muhammad teaches us that integration is only a trick on the part of the white man today to lull Negroes to sleep, to lull them into thinking that the white man is changing and actually trying to keep us here; but America itself, because of the seeds that it has sown in the past against the black man is getting ready to reap the whirlwind today, reap the harvest. Just as Egypt had to pay for its crime that it committed for enslaving the Hebrews, the Honorable Elijah Muhammad teaches us that America has to pay today for the crime that is committed in enslaving the so-called Negroes.

CLARK: There is one question that has bothered me a great deal about your movement, and it involves just a little incident. Rockwell, who is a self-proclaimed white supremacist and American Nazi, was given an honored front row position at one of your —

MALCOLM X: This is incorrect.

CLARK: Am I wrong?

MALCOLM X: This is a false statement that has been put out by the press. And Jews have used it to spread anti-Muslim propaganda throughout this country. Mister Muhammad had an open convention to which he invited anyone, black and white. (And this is another reason why we keep white people out of our meetings.) He invited everyone, both black and white, and Rockwell came. Rockwell came the same as any other white person came, and when we took up a collection, we called out the names of everyone who made a donation. Rockwell's name was called out the same as anybody else's, and this was projected to make it look like Rockwell was financing the Muslims. And secondly, Rockwell came to another similar meeting. At this meeting Mister Muhammad gave anyone who wanted to oppose him or congratulate him an opportunity to speak. Rockwell spoke; he was not even allowed up on the rostrum; he spoke from a microphone from which other whites spoke at the same meeting. And again the Jewish press, or the Jewish who are a part of the press — Jewish *people* who are part of the press — used this as propaganda to make it look like Rockwell was in cahoots with the Muslims. Rockwell, to us, is no different from any other white man. One of the things I *will* give Rockwell credit for: he preaches and practices the same thing. And these other whites running around here posing as liberals, patting Negroes on the back — they think the same thing that Rockwell thinks, only they speak a different talk, a different language.

CLARK: Minister Malcolm, you have mentioned the Jews and the Jewish press and Jewish propaganda frequently in this discussion. It has been said frequently that an important part of your movement is anti-Semitism. I have seen you deny this.

MALCOLM X: No. We're a —

CLARK: Would you want to comment on this?

MALCOLM X: No, the followers of Mister Muhammad aren't anti-anything but anti-wrong, anti-exploitation and anti-oppression. A lot of the Jews have a guilty conscience when you mention exploitation because they realize that they control ninety per cent of the business in every Negro community from the Atlantic to the Pacific and that they get more benefit from the Negro's purchasing power than the Negro himself does or than any other white or any other segment of the white community does, so they have a guilt complex on this. And whenever you mention exploitation of Negroes, most Jews think that you're talking about them, and in order to hide what they are guilty of, they accuse you of being anti-Semitic.

CLARK: Do you believe the Jews are more guilty of this exploitation than are —

MALCOLM X: Jews belong to practically every Negro organization Negroes have. Arthur T. Spingarn, the head of the N.A.A.C.P., is Jewish. Every organization that Negroes — When I say the head of the N.A.A.C.P., the *president* of the N.A.A.C.P. is Jewish. The same Jews wouldn't let you become the president of the B'nai B'rith or their different organizations.

CLARK: Thank you very much. You have certainly presented important parts of your movement, your point of view. I think we understand more clearly now some of your goals, and I'd like to know if we could talk some other time if you would tell me a little about what you think is the future of the Negro in America other than separation.

MALCOLM X: Yes. As long as they have interviews with the Attorney General and take Negroes to pose as leaders, all of whom are married either to white men or white women, you'll always have a race problem. When Baldwin took that crew with him to see Kennedy, he took the wrong crew. And as long as they take the wrong crew to talk to that man, you're not going to get anywhere near any solution to this problem in this country.

While he was in prison, Malcolm X participated in a debate program devised by consultants from the speech field. In his autobiography he indicates that this particular experience meant much to him. In the same way that thousands of high school and college students before him have found their greatest excitement in the intellectual combat of debate, Malcolm X, convict, discovered debating:

> ... debating, speaking to a crowd, was as exhilarating to me as the discovery of knowledge through reading had been. Standing up there, the faces looking up at me, the things in my head coming out of my mouth, while my brain searched for the next best thing to follow what I was saying, and if I could sway them to my side by handling it right, then I had won the debate — once my feet got wet, I was gone on debating.³⁵

Whether in a debate or speaking alone, Malcolm's speech was characterized by a debater's style. His presentation was rapid; his sentences generally were short and pointed. He seemed to enjoy the attack — he was at his best when discrediting the white society, the integrationists, or an opponent's arguments. Although lacking in formal education, his word choice was broad, and his capacity to call forth specific data for use as evidence in support of a contention was greater than the capacity of many noted men of affairs who are accustomed to bare assertions supported only by their own authority.

Also typical of the debater's style is his exposure and denial of an opponent's major premise. In the debate published here, he attacks the assumption that if integration is achieved, the black man will achieve human dignity. First, he observes that, ". . . oft times we make the mistake of confusing the objective with the means by which the objective is to be obtained," directly opposing James Farmer's speech in which progress in integration was discussed in detail, but little was said of "human dignity."

Malcolm agrees that both groups — integrationists and separationists — have the same goals of freedom, justice, equality, human dignity, or "the good life." However, he challenges the likelihood of achieving the goal through the route of integration. In a clear, logical argument, Malcolm X argues either integration will bring human dignity or another method will have to be tried.

As a minor premise, he argues that integration has had ample time to achieve its goal and has failed; there is no reason to expect it to do better in the future for it will never be more than a white-oriented, token integration that will continue to enslave the black man mentally if not physically. The conclusion, by the method of residue, is separation.

In good debater's form, the final portion of his constructive speech is given to a statement of his proposed plan for separation, based upon the teachings of Elijah Muhammad. As Mr. Farmer charges in his rebuttal, the plan for separation is not specific, nor are the many questions of practicality answered. This seems to be characteristic of Muslim rhetoric. Malcolm rests his case upon an indictment of integrationist strategy as inherently demeaning to black men and thus inherently incapable of achieving the human dignity which is the ultimate goal. If this line of reasoning is accepted, separation is about the only alternative remaining. It will either become practical, or all will be lost. This debate constitutes a summary, in modern terms, of the entire controversy which has been revealed in the last four chapters.

James Farmer and Malcolm X
Separation or Integration*

JAMES FARMER

When the Freedom Riders left from Montgomery, Alabama, to ride into the conscience of America and into Jackson, Mississippi, there were many persons who said to us, "Don't go into Mississippi, go anyplace you like, go to the Union of South Africa but stay out of Mississippi." They said, "What you found in Alabama will be nothing compared to what you will meet in Mississippi. I remember being told a story by one minister who urged us not to go. He said, "Once upon a time there was a Negro who had lived in Mississippi, lived for a long time running from county to county. Finally he left the state, and left it pretty fast, as Dick Gregory would put it, not by Greyhound, but by bloodhound, and he went to Illinois to live, in Chicago. And unable to find a job there, after several weeks of walking the street unemployed, he sat down and asked God what he should do. God said, "Go back to Missis-

*James Farmer and Malcolm X, "Separation or Integration," *Dialogue Magazine*, (May, 1962), pp. 13-18; a debate before students of Cornell University United Religious Work.

sippi." He said, "Lord you surely don't mean it, you're jesting. You don't mean for me to go back to Mississippi. There is segregation there!" The Lord said, "Go back to Mississippi." The man looked up and said, "Very well, Lord, if you insist, I will do it, I will go. But will you go with me?" The Lord said "As far as Cincinnati."

The Freedom Riders felt that they should go all the way because there is something wrong with our nation and we wanted to try to set it right. As one of the nation's scholars wrote at the turn of the century, "The problem of the twentieth century will be the problem of the color-line, of the relations between the lighter and the darker peoples of the earth, Asia and Africa, in America, and in the islands of the sea." What prophetic words, indeed. We have seen the struggle for freedom all over the world. We have seen it in Asia; we have seen it in the island of the sea; we have seen it in Africa, and we are seeing it in America now. I think the racist theories of Count DeGobineu, Lothrop Stoddard and others have set the pattern for a racism that exists within our country. There are theories that are held today, not only by those men and their followers and successors, but by Ross Barnett, John Patterson devotees and followers of the Klan and the White Citizens Councils, and Lincoln Rockwell of the American Nazi Party.

These vicious racist theories hold that Negroes are inferior and whites are superior innately. Ordained by God, so to speak. No more vicious theory has existed in the history of mankind. I would suggest to you that no theory has provided as much human misery throughout the centuries as the theory of races — The theories that say some people are innately inferior and that others are innately superior. Although we have some of those theories in our country, we also have a creed of freedom and of democracy. As Pearl Buck put it, "Many Americans suffer from a split personality. One side of that personality is believing in democracy and freedom, as much as it is possible for a man so to believe. The other side of this personality is refusing, just as doggedly, to practice that democracy and that freedom, in which he believes." That was the split personality. Gunnar Myrdal, in his book, *The American Dilemma,* indicated that this was basically a moral problem, and that we have this credo which Americans hold to, of freedom, and democracy, and equality, but still we refuse to practice it. Gunnar Myrdal indicated that this is sorely troubling the American conscience.

All of us are a part of this system, **all** a part of it. We have all developed certain prejudices, I have mine, you have yours. It seems to me that it is extremely dangerous when any individual claims to be without prejudice, when he really does have it. I'm prejudiced against women drivers. I think they are a menace to civilization, and the sooner they are removed from the highways, the safer we will all be, but I know that's nothing but a prejudice. I have seen women drivers who are better drivers than I am, but does that destroy my prejudice? No. What I do then, is to separate her from the group of women drivers and say, "Why she is an exception." Or maybe I say she is driving very well because she feels guilty. She knows that other women in the past have had accidents, and so she drives cautiously.

I remember several years ago when I was a youth, attending a church youth conference, and a young fellow from Mississippi and I became very good friends. The last day of the conference as we walked along the road he put his arm an my shoulder and said, "Jim, I have no race prejudice." "No." said I. "Absolutely not," said he. I raised my eyebrows. "As a matter of fact," he went on, "I was thirteen years old before I knew I was any better than a Negro." Well sometimes a supposed absence of racial prejudice runs quite along those lines. Now prejudice is a damaging thing to Negroes. We have suffered under it tremendously. It damages the lives of little children. I remember when I first came into contact with segregation; It was when I was a child in Mississippi when my mother took me downtown, and on the way back this hot July day I wanted to stop and get a coke, and she told me I couldn't get a coke. I had to wait until I got home. "Well why can't I, there's a little boy going in" said I, "I bet he's going to get a coke." He was. "Well, Why can't I go?" "Because he's white," she said, "and you're colored." Its not important what happened to me, the fact is that the same thing over and over again happens to every mother's child whose skin happens to be dark.

If the damage that is done to Negroes is obvious, the damage that is done to whites in America is equally obvious, for they're prejudiced. I lived in Texas a large part of my life; remember driving through the state, and after dusk had fallen being followed by cars of whites who forced me off the road and said to me. "Don't you know that your kind is not supposed to be in this town after sundown." I wondered what was happening to these people; how their minds were being twisted, as mine and others like me had had our minds twisted by this double-edged sword of prejudice. It is a disease indeed. It is an American disease. It is an American dilemma.

THE NATION SUFFERS FOR SEGREGATION

The damage to Negroes is psychological, it is also economic. Negroes occupying the bottom of the economic ladder, the poorest jobs, the lowest paying jobs. Last to be hired, and first to be fired, so that today the percentage of unemployed Negroes is twice as high as that of whites. There has been political damage as well. In the south we find that comparatively few Negroes are registered to vote. Many are apathetic even when they could register. The percentage who are registered in the north is almost equally as low. As a result, comparatively few Negroes are elected to political office. Thus, the damage to the Negroes, as a result to the disease of segregation has been psychological, economic, social, and political. I would suggest to you that the same damages have occurred to whites. Psychological damages are obvious. Economic — the nation itself suffers economically, as a result of denying the right of full development to one-tenth of its population. Skills, talents, and abilities, are crushed in their cradle, are not allowed to develop. Snuffed out. Thus, the nation's economy has suffered. People who could be producing are instead walking the streets. People who could be producing in better jobs and producing more are kept in the lower jobs, sweeping the floors and serving other persons. The whole nation has been damaged by segregation. Now, all of us share the guilt too. I myself am guilty. I am guilty because I spent half my life in the South. During those years I participated in segregation, cooperated with it, and supported it.

We are all intricately involved in the system of segregation. We have not yet extricated ourselves. Negroes are involved, and guilty, and share the blame to the extent they themselves have, by their deeds and their acts, allowed segregation to go on for so long. I do not believe that guilt is a part of my genes or your genes. It hinges upon the deeds that you have done. If you have supported segregation, then you are guilty. If you continue to support it, then your guilt is multiplied. But that is your guilt, that is mine. We share the guilt for the disease of segregation, and its continued existence. All too long, Negro Americans have put up with the system of segregation, North and South. Incidentally, it is not a Southern problem, it is a Northern one as well. Segregation exists in housing and in jobs, and in schools. We have put up with it, have done nothing about it.

The day before the Freedom Riders left Washington, D.C. to ride into the South, I visited my father who was in the hospital on what proved to be his deathbed. I told him I was going on a freedom ride in to the South. He wanted to know what it was and I told him. "Where are you going?" he asked, and I told him. He said, "Well, I'm glad that you're going, son, and I hope you survive. I realize you may not return, but," said he, "I'm glad you're going because when I was a child in South Carolina and Georgia, we didn't like segregation either, but we thought that's the way things always had to be and the way they always would be, so we put up with it, took part in it, decided to exist and to stay alive. I am glad," said he, "that there are lots of people today who are no longer willing to put up with the evil of segregation, but want to do something about it and know that something can be done." How right he was indeed.

The masses of Negroes are through putting up with segregation; they are tired of it. They are tired of being pushed around in a democracy which fails to practice what it preaches. The Negro students of the South who have read the Constitution, and studied it, have read the amendments to the Constitution, and know the rights that are supposed to be theirs — they are coming to the point where they themselves want to do something about achieving these rights, not depend on somebody else. The time has passed when we can look for pie in the sky, when we can depend upon someone else on high to solve the problem for us. The Negro students want to solve the problem themselves. Masses of older Negroes want to join them in that. We can't wait for the law. The Supreme Court decision in 1954 banning segregated schools has had almost eight years of existence, yet, less than eight percent of the Negro kids are in integrated schools. That is far too slow. Now the people themselves want to get involved, and they are. I was talking with one of the student leaders of the South only last week; he said, "I myself desegregated a lunch counter, not somebody else, not some big man, some powerful man, but me, little me. I walked the picket line and sat in and the walls of segregation toppled. Now all people can eat there." One young prize fighter was a cellmate of mine in the prisons of Mississippi as a

freedom rider; he had won his last fight and had a promising career. I saw
him three weeks ago, and asked him, "How are you coming along?" He
said, "Not very well, I lost the last fight and I am through with the prize
ring, I have no more interest in it". "The only fight I want now, said he, "is
the freedom fight. Because, I a little man can become involved in it, and can
help to win freedom." So that's what's happening; you see, we are going
to do something about freedom now, we are not waiting for other people
to do it. The student sit-ins have shown it; we are winning. As a result of
one year of the student sit-ins, the lunch counters were desegregated in more
than 150 cities. The walls are tumbling down.

DIRECT ACTION BRINGS RESULTS

Who will say that lunch counters, which are scattered all over the country
are not important? Are we not to travel? Picket lines and boycotts brought
Woolworth's to its knees. In its annual report last year, Woolworth's indicated that profits had dropped and one reason for the drop was the nationwide boycott in which many Northern students, including Cornellians participated. The picketing and the nationwide demonstrations are the reason
that the walls came down in the south, because people were in motion with
their own bodies marching with picket signs, sitting in, boycotting, withholding their patronage. In Savannah, Georgia, there was a boycott, in which
ninety-nine percent of the Negroes participated. They stayed out of the
stores. They registered to vote. The store owners then got together and
said, "We want to sit down and talk; gentlemen, you have proved your
point. You have proved that you can control Negroes' purchasing power
and that you can control their votes. We need no more proof, we are ready
to hire the people that you send." Negroes are hired in those stores now as
a result of this community-wide campaign. In Lexington, Kentucky, the theatres were opened up by CORE as a result of picketing and boycotting.
Some of the theatres refused to admit Negroes, others would let Negroes sit
up in the balcony. They boycotted that one, picketed the others. In a short
period of time, the theatre owners sat down to negotiate. All of the theatres
there are open now. Using the same technique, they provided scores of jobs
in department stores, grocery stores, and more recently as city bus drivers.
Then came the freedom rides. 325 people were jailed in Jackson, Mississippi, others beaten, fighting for freedom non-violently. They brought down
many many barriers. They helped to create desegregation in cities throughout
the South. The ICC order was forthcoming as a result of the freedom rides
and a more recent Supreme Court ruling. CORE sent test teams throughout
the South after the ICC order went into effect. The test teams found that in
hundreds of cities throughout the South, where terminals had been previously
segregated, they now were desegregated and Negroes were using them.
Mississippi is an exception, except for two cities; Louisiana is an exception,
except for one pocket of the state; but by and large the Rides were successful.
And then on Route 40. How many Negroes and interracial groups have
driven route 40 to Washington or to New York and carried their sandwiches,

knowing that they could not eat between Wilmington and Baltimore. The freedom rides there, and some Cornell students participated in those freedom rides, brought down the barriers in more than half of those restaurants and each weekend, rides are taking place aimed at the others. By Easter we will have our Easter dinner in any place we choose on Route 40. At least 53 out of the 80 are now desegregated. In voter registration projects, we have registered 17,000 Negroes in South Carolina, previously unregistered. The politicians, segregationists, it's true, now call up our leaders and say, "I would like to talk to you because I don't believe in segregation as much as my opponent," or, "We would like to sit down and talk," or, "Can you come by my house and let's talk about this thing." Because they are realizing that now they have to be responsible to the votes of Negroes as well as the handful of whites, these are the things that are being done by people themselves in motion. Not waiting for someone else to do it, not looking forward to pie in the sky at some later date, not expecting a power on high to solve the problem for them; but working to solve it themselves and winning.

INTEGRATION REPUDIATES RACIST THEORIES

What are our objectives; segregation, separation? Absolutely not! The disease and the evils that we have pointed to in our American culture have grown out of segregation and its partner, prejudice. We are for integration, which is the repudiation of the evil of segregation. It is a rejection of the racist theories of DeGobineu, Lothrop Stoddard and all the others. It matters not whether they say that whites are superior to Negroes and Negroes are inferior, or if they reverse the coin and say that Negroes are superior and whites are inferior. The theory is just as wrong, just as much a defiance of history. We reject those theories. We are working for the right of Negroes to enter all fields of activity in American life. To enter business if they choose, to enter the professions, to enter the sciences, to enter the arts, to enter the academic world. To be workers, to be laborers if they choose. Our objective is to have each individual accepted on the basis of his individual merit and not on the basis of his color. On the basis of what he is worth himself.

This has given a new pride to large number of people. A pride to the people in Mississippi, who themselves saw others, white and Negro, joining them in the fight for freedom; 41 local citizens went into the jails of Mississippi joining the freedom riders. They have come out now and they have started their own non-violent Jackson movement for Freedom. They are sitting in. They are picketing, they are boycotting, and it is working. In Macomb, Mississippi, local citizens are now seeking to register to vote, some of them registering. In Huntsville, Alabama, as a result of CORE's campaign there (and we are now under injunction), for the past six weeks local Negro citizens have been sitting in every day at lunch counters. One of the white CORE leaders there in Huntsville was taken out of his house at gun point, undressed and sprayed with mustard oil. That's the kind of treatment they have faced, but they will not give up because they know they are right and they see the effects of their efforts; they see it in the crumbling walls in inter-state transportation and in other public facilities.

We are seeking an open society, an open society of freedom where people will be accepted for what they are worth, will be able to contribute fully to the total culture and the total life of the nation.

Now we know the disease, we know what is wrong with America, we know now that the CORE position is in trying to right it. We must do it in interracial groups because we do not think it is possible to fight against caste in a vehicle which in itself is a representative of caste. We know that the students are still sitting in, they are still fighting for freedom. What we want, Mr. X, the representative of the Black Muslims and Elijah Muhammed, to tell us today, is what his program is, what he proposes to do about killing this disease. We know the disease, physician, what is your cure? What is your program and how do you hope to bring it into effect? How will you achieve it? It is not enough to tell us that it may be a program of a black state. The Communists had such a program in the thirties and part of the forties, and they dropped it before the fifties as being impractical. So we are not only interested in the terminology. We need to have it spelled out, if we are being asked to follow it, to believe in it, what does it mean? Is it a separate Negro society in each city? As a Harlem, a South Side Chicago? Is it a separate state in one part of the country? Is it a separate nation in Africa, or elsewhere? Then we need to know how is it to be achieved. I assume that before a large part of land could be granted to Negroes or to Jews or to anybody else in the country it would have to be approved by the Senate of the United States.

You must tell us, Mr. X, if you seriously think that the Senate of the United States which has refused or failed for all these years to pass a strong Civil Rights Bill, you must tell us if you really think that this Senate is going to give us, to give you, a black state. I am sure that Senator Eastland would so vote, but the land that he would give us would probably be in the bottom of the sea. After seeing Alabama and Mississippi, if the power were mine, I would give you those states, but the power is not mine, I do not vote in the Senate. Tell us how you expect to achieve this separate black state.

Now it is not enough for us to know that you believe in black businesses, all of us believe that all Americans who wish to go into business, should go into business. We must know, we need to know, if we are to appraise your program, the kind of businesses, how they are to be established; will we have a General Motors, a General Electric? Will I be able to manufacture a Farmer Special? Where I am going to get the capital from? You must tell us if we are going to have a separate interstate bus line to take the place of Greyhound and Trailways. You must tell us how this separate interstate bus line is going to operate throughout the country if all of us are confined within one separate state.

You must tell us these things, Mr. X, spell them out. You must tell us also what the relationship will be between the black businesses which you would develop and the total American economy. Will it be a competition? Will it be a rival economy, a dual economy or will there be cooperation between these two economies?

Our program is clear. We are going to achieve our goals of integration by non-violent direct action on an interracial level with whites and Negroes jointly cooperating to wipe out a disease which has afflicted and crippled all of them, white and black alike. The proof of the pudding is the eating. We have seen barriers fall as the result of using these techniques. We ask you, Mr. X, what is your program?

MALCOLM X

In the name of Allah, the Beneficent, the Merciful, to whom all praise is due whom we forever thank for giving America's 20 million so-called Negroes the most honorable Elijah Muhammad as our leader and our teacher and our guide.

I would point out at the beginning that I wasn't born Malcolm Little. Little is the name of the slave master who owned one of my grandparents during slavery, a white man, and the name Little was handed down to my grandfather, to my father and on to me. But after hearing the teachings of the Honorable Elijah Muhammad and realizing that Little is an English name, and I'm not an Englishman, I gave the Englishman back his name; and since my own had been stripped from me, hidden from me, and I don't know it, I use X; and someday, as we are taught by the Honorable Elijah Muhammad, every black man, woman and child in America will get back the same name, the same language, and the same culture that he had before he was kidnaped and brought to this country and stripped of these things.

I would like to point out in a recent column by James Reston on the editorial page of the New York Times, December 15, 1961, writing from London, Mr. Reston, after interviewing several leading European statesmen, pointed out that the people of Europe, or the statesmen in Europe, don't feel that America or Europe have anything to worry about in Russia,; that the people in Europe foresee the time when Russia, Europe, and America will have to unite together to ward off the threat of China and the non-white world. And if this same statement was made by a Muslim, or by the honorable Elijah Muhammad, it would be classified as racist; but Reston who is one of the leading correspondents in this country and writing for one of the most respected newspapers, points out that the holocaust that the West is facing is not something from Russia, but threats of the combined forces of the dark world against the white world.

Why do I mention this? Primarily because the most crucial problem facing the white world today is the race problem. And the most crucial problem facing white America today is the race problem. Mr. Farmer pointed out beautifully and quoted one writer actually as saying that the holocaust that America is facing is primarily still based upon race. This doesn't mean that when people point these things out that they are racist; this means that they are facing the facts of life that we are confronted with today. And one need only to look at the world troubles in its international context, national context, or local context, and one will always see the race problem right there, a problem that it is almost impossible to duck around.

It so happens that you and I were born at a time of great change, when changes are taking place. And if we can't react intelligently to these changes, then we are going to be destroyed. When you look into the United Nations set-up, the way it is, we see that there is a change of power taking place, a change of position, a change of influence, a change of control. Wherein, in the past, white people used to exercise unlimited control and authority over dark mankind, today they are losing their ability to dictate unilateral terms to dark mankind. Whereas, yesterday dark nations had no voice in their own affairs today, the voice that they exercise in their own affairs is increasing, which means in essence that the voice of the white man or the white world is becoming more quiet every day, and the voice of the non-white world is becoming more loud every day. These are the facts of life and these are the changes that you and I, this generation, have to face up to on an international level, a national level, or a local level before we can get a solution to the problems that confront not only the white man, but problems that confront also the black man, or the non-white man.

When we look at the United Nations and see how these dark nations get their independence — they can out-vote the western block or what is known as the white world — and to the point where up until last year the U. N. was controlled by the white powers, or Western powers, mainly Christian powers, and the secretaryship used to be in the hands of a white European Christian; but now when we look at the general structure of the United Nations we see a man from Asia, from Burma, who is occupying the position of Secretary, who is a Buddhist, by the way, and we find the man who is occupying the seat of President is a Moslem from Africa, namely Tunisia. Just in recent times all of these changes are taking place, and the white man has got to be able to face up to them, and the black man has to be able to face up to them, before we can get our problem solved, on an international level, a national level, as well as on the local level.

In terms of black and white, what this means is that the unlimited power and prestige of the white world is decreasing, while the power and prestige of the non-white world is increasing. And just as our African and Asian brothers wanted to have their own land, wanted to have their own country, wanted to exercise control over themselves and govern themselves — they didn't want to be governed by whites or Europeans or outsiders, they wanted control over something among the black masses here in America. I think it would be mighty naive on the part of the white man to see dark mankind all over the world stretching out to get a country of his own, a land of his own, an industry of his own, a society of his own, even a flag of his own, it would be mighty naive on the part of the white man to think that same feeling that is sweeping through the dark world is not going to leap 9000 miles across the ocean and come into the black people here in this country, who have been begging you for 400 years for something that they have yet to get.

In the areas of Asia and Africa where the whites gave freedom to the non-whites a transition took place, of friendliness and hospitality. In the areas where the non-whites had to exercise violence, today there is hostility between them and the white man. In this, we learn that the only way to solve a problem that is unjust, if you are wrong, is to take immediate action to correct it. But when the people against whom these actions have been directed have to take matters in their own hands, this creates hostility, and lack of friendliness and good relations between the two.

AN ERA OF GREAT CHANGE

I emphasize these things to point up the fact that we are living in an era of great change; when dark mankind wants freedom, justice, and equality. It is not a case of wanting integration or separation, it is a case of wanting freedom, justice, and equality.

Now if certain groups think that through integration they are going to get freedom, justice, equality and human dignity, then well and good, we will go along with the integrationists. But if integration is not going to return human dignity to dark mankind, then integration is not the solution to the problem. And oft times we make the mistake of confusing the objective with the means by which the objective is to be obtained. It is not integration that Negroes in America want, it is human dignity. They want to be recognized as human beings. And if integration is going to bring us recognition as human beings, then we will integrate. But if integration is not going to bring us recognition as human beings, then integration "out the window," and we have to find another means or method and try that to get our objectives reached.

The same hand that has been writing on the wall in Africa and Asia is also writing on the wall right here in America. The same rebellion, the same impatience, the same anger that exists in the hearts of the dark people in Africa and Asia is existing in the hearts and minds of 20 million black people in this country who have been just as thoroughly colonized as the people in Africa and Asia. Only the black man in America has been colonized mentally, his mind has been destroyed. And today, even though he goes to college, he comes out and still doesn't even know he is a black man; he is ashamed of what he is, because his culture has been destroyed, his identity has been destroyed; he has been made to hate his black skin, he has been made to hate the texture of his hair, he has been made to hate the features that God gave him. Because the honorable Elijah Muhammad is coming along today and teaching us the truth about black people to make us love ourselves instead of realizing that it is you who taught us to hate ourselves and our own kind, you accuse the honorable Elijah Muhammad of being a hate teacher and accuse him of being a racist. He is only trying to undo the white supremacy that you have indoctrinated the entire world with.

I might point out that it makes America look ridiculous to stand up in world conferences and refer to herself as the leader of the free world. Here is a country, Uncle Sam, standing up and pointing a finger at the Portuguese, and at the French, and at other colonizers, and there are 20 million black people in this country who are still confined to second-class citizenship, 20 million black people in this country who are still segregated and Jim-Crowed, as my friend, Dr. Farmer has already pointed out. And despite the fact that 20 million black people here yet don't have freedom, justice and equality, Adlai Stevenson has the nerve enough to stand up in the United Nations and point the finger at South Africa, and at Portugal and at some of these other countries. All we say is that South Africa preaches what it practices and practices what it preaches; America preaches one thing and practices another. And we don't want to integrate with hypocrites who preach one thing and practice another.

The good point in all of this is that there is an awakening going on among whites in America today, and this awakening is manifested in this way: two years ago you didn't know that there were black people in this country who didn't want to integrate with you; two years ago the white public had been brainwashed into thinking that every black man in this country wanted to force his way into your community, force his way into your schools, or force his way into your factories; two years ago you thought that all you would have to do is give us a little token integration and the race problem would be solved. Why? Because the people in the black community who didn't want integration were never given a voice, were never given a platform, were never given an opportunity to shout out the fact that integration would never solve the problem. And it has only been during the past year that the white public has begun to realize that the problem will never be solved unless a solution is devised acceptable to the black masses, as well as the black bourgeoisie — the upper class or middle class Negro. And when the whites began to realize that these integration-minded Negroes were in the minority, rather than in the majority, then they began to offer an open forum and give those who want separation an opportunity to speak their mind too.

MIDDLE-CLASS SETTLES FOR INTEGRATION

We who are black in the black belt, or black community, or black neighborhood can easily see that our people who settle for integration are usually the middle-class so-called Negroes, who are in the minority. Why? Because they have confidence in the white man; they have absolute confidence that you will change. They believe that they can change you, they believe that there is still hope in the American dream. But what to them is an American dream to us is an American nightmare, and we don't think that it is possible for the American white man in sincerity to take the action necessary to correct the unjust conditions that 20 million black people here are made to suffer morning, noon, and night. And because we don't have any hope or confidence or faith in the American white man's ability to bring about a change in the injustices that exist, instead of asking or seeking to integrate into the American society we want to face the facts of the problem the way they are, and separate ourselves. And in separating ourselves this doesn't mean that we are anti-white or anti-American, or anti-anything. We feel, that if integration all these years hasn't solved the problem yet, then we want to try something new, something different and something that is in accord with the conditions as they actually exist.

The honorable Elijah Muhammad teaches us that there are over 725 million Moslems or Muslims on this earth. I use both words interchangeably. I use the word Moslem for those who can't undergo the change, and I use the word Muslim for those who can. He teaches us that the world of Islam stretches from the China Seas to the shores of West Africa and that the 20 million black people in this country are the lost-found members of the nation of Islam. He teaches us that before we were kidnaped by your grandfathers and brought to this country and put in chains, our religion was Islam, our culture was Islamic, we came from the Muslim world, we were kidnaped and brought here out of the Muslim world. And after being brought here we were stripped of our language, stripped of our ability to speak our mother tongue, and it's a crime today to have to admit that there are 20 million black people in this country who not only can't speak their mother tongue, but don't even know they ever had one. This points up the crime of how thoroughly and completely the black man in America has been robbed by the white man of his culture, of his identity, of his soul, of his self. And because he has been robbed of his self, he is trying to accept your self. Because he doesn't know who he is, now he wants to be who you are. Because he doesn't know what belongs to him, he is trying to lay claim to what belongs to you. You have brain-washed him and made him a monster. He is black on the outside, but you have made him white on the inside. Now he has a white heart and a white brain, and he's breathing down your throat and down your neck because he thinks he's a white man the same as you are. He thinks that he should have your house, that he should have your factory, he thinks that he should even have your school, and most of them even think that they should have your woman, and most of them are after your woman.

SO-CALLED NEGROES ARE LOST SHEEP

The honorable Elijah Muhammad teaches us that the black people in America, the so-called Negroes, are the people who are referred to in the Bible as the lost sheep, who are to be returned to their own in the last days. He says that we are also referred to in the Bible, symbolically, as the lost tribe. He teaches us in our religion, that we are those people whom the Bible refers to who would be lost until the end of time. Lost in a house that is not theirs, lost in a land that is not theirs, lost in a country that is not theirs, and who will be found in the last days by the Messiah who will awaken them and enlighten them, and teach them that which they had been stripped of, and then this would give them the desire to come together among their own kind and go back among their own kind.

And this, basically, is why we who are followers of the honorable Elijah Muhammad don't accept integration: we feel that we are living at the end of time, by this, we feel that we are living at the end of the world. Not the end of the earth, but the end of the world. He teaches us that there are many worlds. The planet is an earth, and there is only one earth, but there are many worlds on this earth, the Eastern World and the Western World. There is a dark world and a white world. There is the world of Christianity, and the world of Islam. All of these are worlds and he teaches us that when the book speaks of the end of time, it doesn't mean the end of the earth, but it means the end of time for certain segments of people, or a certain world that is on this earth. Today, we who are here in America who have awakened to the knowledge of ourselves; we believe that there is no God but Allah, and we believe that the religion of Islam is Allah's religion, and we believe that it is Allah's intention to spread his religion throughout the entire earth. We believe that the earth will become all Muslim, all Islam, and because we are in a Christian country we believe that this Christian country will have to accept Allah as God, accept the religion of Islam as God's religion, or otherwise God will come in and wipe it out. And we don't want to be wiped out with the American white man, we don't want to integrate with him, we want to separate from him.

SEPARATION IS THE BEST SOLUTION

The method by which the honorable Elijah Muhammad is straightening out our problem is not teaching us to force ourselves into your society, or force ourselves even into your political, economic or any phase of your society, but he teaches us that the best way to solve this problem is for complete separation. He says that since the black man here in America is actually the property that was stolen from the East by the American white man, since you have awakened today and realized that this is what we are, we should be separated from you, and your government should ship us back from where we came from, not at our expense, because we didn't pay to come here. We were brought here in chains. So the honorable Elijah Muhammad and the Muslims who follow him, we want to go back to our own people. We want to be returned to our own people.

But in teaching this among our people and the masses of black people in this country, we discover that the American government is the foremost agency in opposing any move by any large number of black people to leave here and go back among our own kind. The honorable Elijah Muhammad's words and work is harassed daily by the F.B.I. and every other government agency which use various tactics to make the so-called Negroes in every community think that we are all about to be rounded up, and they will be rounded up too if they will listen to Mr. Muhammad; but what the American government has failed to realize, the best way to open up a black man's head today and make him listen to another black man is to speak against that black man. But when you begin to pat a black man on the back, no black man in his right mind will trust that black man any longer. And it is because of this hostility on the part of the government toward our leaving here that the honorable Elijah Muhammad says then, if the American white man or the American government doesn't want us to leave, and the government has proven its inability to bring about integration or give us freedom, justice and equality on a basis, equally mixed up with white people, then what are we going to do? If the government doesn't want us to go back among our own people, or to our own people, and at the same time the government has proven its inability to give us justice, the honorable Elijah Muhammad says if you don't want us to go and we can't stay here and live in peace together, then the best solution is separation. And this is what he means when he says that some of the territory here should be set aside, and let our people go off to ourselves and try and solve our own problem.

Some of you may say, Well, why should you give us part of this country? The honorable Elijah Muhammad says that for 400 years we contributed our slave labor to make the country what it is. If you were to take the individual salary or allowances of each person in this audience it would amount to nothing individually, but when you take it collectively all in one pot you have a heavy load. Just the weekly wage. And if you realize that from anybody who could collect all of the wages from the persons in this audience right here for one month, why they would be so wealthy they couldn't walk. And if you see that, then you can imagine the result of millions of black people working for nothing for 310 years. And that is the contribution that we made to America. Not Jackie Robinson, not Marian Anderson, not George Washington Carver, that's not our contribution; our contribution to American society is 310 years of free slave labor for which we have not been paid one dime. We who are Muslims, followers of the honorable Elijah Muhammad, don't think that an integrated cup of coffee is sufficient payment for 310 years of slave labor.

REBUTTAL

JAMES FARMER

I think that Mr. X's views are utterly impractical and that his so-called 'black state' cannot be achieved. There is no chance of getting it unless it is to be given to us by Allah. We have waited for a long time for God to give us other things and we have found that the God in which most of us happen to believe helps those who help themselves. So we would like you to tell us, Mr. X, just what steps you plan to go through to get this black state. Is it one that is going to be gotten by violence, by force? Is it going to be given to us by the Federal government? Once a state is allocated, then are the white people who happen to live there to be moved out forcibly, or Negroes who don't want to go to your black state going to be moved in forcibly? And what does this do to their liberty and freedom?

Now Mr. X suggests that we Negroes or so-called Negroes, as he puts it, ought to go back where we came from. You know, this is a very interesting idea. I think the solution to many of the problems, including the economic problem of our country, would be for all of us to go back where we came from and leave the country to the American Indians. As a matter of fact, maybe the American Indian can go back to Asia, where I understand the anthropologists tell us he came from, and I don't know who preceded him there. But if we search back far enough I am sure that we can find some people to people or populate this nation. Now the overwhelming number of Negroes in this country consider it to be their country; their country more than Africa: I was in Africa three years ago, and while I admire and respect what is being done there, while there is certainly a definite sense of identification, and sympathy with what is going on there, the fact is that the cultures are so very different. Mr. X, I am sure that you have much more in common with me or with several people whom I see sitting here than you do with the Africans, than you do with Tom Mboya. Most of them could not understand you, or you they, because they speak Swahili or some other language and you would have to learn those languages.

I tell you that we are Americans. This is our country as much as it is white American. Negroes came as slaves, most of us did. Many white people came as indentured servants; indentured servants are not free. Don't forget it wasn't all of you who were on that ship, The Mayflower.

Now separation of course has been proposed as the answer to the problem, rather than integration. I am pleased however that Malcolm, oh pardon me, Mr. X, indicated that if integration works, and if it provides dignity, then we are for integration. Apparently he is almost agreeing with us there. He is sort of saying as King Agrippa said to St. Paul, "Almost Thou Persuadest Me." I hope that he will be able to come forth and make the additional step and join me at the integrationist side of this table. In saying that separation really is the answer and the most effective solution to this problem, he draws a distinction between separation and segregation, saying that segregation is forced ghettoism while separation is voluntary ghettoism. Well now, I would like to ask Mr. X whether it would be voluntary for Negroes to be segregated as long as we allow discrimination in housing throughout our country to exist. If you live in a black state and cannot get a house elsewhere, then are you voluntarily separated, or are you forcibly segregated?

BLACK MEN AND WHITE WOMEN

Now Mr. X suggests that actually the Negroes in this country want the white man's women. Now this is a view, of course, which is quite familiar to you; I've heard it before, there are some Negroes who are married to white people, and I, just before I came up, was looking over a back issue of the paper of the Muslims, and saw in there an indication that I myself have a white wife. And it was suggested that therefore I have betrayed my people in marrying a white woman. Well you know I happen to have a great deal of faith in the virtues and the abilities and capacities of Negroes. Not only Negroes, but all of the people too. In fact, I have so much faith in the virtues of Negroes that I do not even think those virtues are so frail that they will be corrupted by contact with other people.

Mr. X also indicated that Negroes imitate whites. It is true, we do, he is right. We fix our hair and try to straighten it; I don't do mine, I haven't had a conk in my life, I think they call it a process now, etc. But this is a part of the culture of course. After the black culture was taken away from us, we had to adapt the culture that was here, adopt it, and adapt to it. But it is also true that white people try to imitate Negroes, with their jazz, with their hair curlers, you know, and their man-tans. I think, Mr. X, that perhaps the grass is always greener on the other side of the fence. Now when we create integration, perhaps it won't be so necessary for us to resort to these devices.

The black bourgeoisie — is it only the middle class that wants integration. Were the sit-in students black bourgeoisie? They didn't fit into the definition in E. Franklin Frazier's book on the black bourgeoisie. Quite to the contrary, these students were lower class people. Many of them were workers working to stay in school. In the Freedom Rides, were they black bourgoisie? No, we didn't have exceptions there, we had some people who were unemployed. These are not the black bourgeoisie who want integration. Quite to the contrary, very frequently, the middle class developed a vested interest in the maintenance of segregation. Because if they have a store, and if segregation is eliminated, then I'll be in open competition with the white stores. And thus it is most often true as Frazier pointed out in his book, that the middle class tends to be opposed to desegregation. Now I would wonder also in the building of black businesses if we are not going to be building another black bourgeoisie? If Negroes may not perhaps be giving up one master for another, a white one for a black one? Are we going to build a new Negro middle class, and say that no matter how tyrannical it may prove to be it is my own and therefore, I like it?

Now we of course know that the Negro is sick, the white man is sick, we know that psychologically we have been twisted by all of these things; but still, Mr. X, you have not told us what the solution is except that it is separation, in your view. You have not spelled it out. Well, now, this sickness, as I tried to indicate in my first presentation, springs from segregation. It is segregation that produces prejudice, as much as prejudice produces segregation. In Detroit, at the time of the race riot, the only rioting, the only fighting, was in the all-Negro and all-white sections of the city, where separation was complete. In those several sections of the city where Negroes and whites lived together, next door to each other, there was no fighting because there the people were neighbors or friends. Now you propose separation as the solution to this problem, as the cure to the disease. Here we have a patient that is suffering from a disease caused by mosquitoes, and the physician proposes as a cure that the man go down and lie in a damp swamp and play with wiggletails.

REBUTTAL

MALCOLM X

I hadn't thought, or intended anyway, to get personal with Mr. Farmer in mentioning his white wife; I thought that perhaps it would probably have been better left unsaid, but it's better for him to say than for me to say it, because then you would think I was picking on him. I think you will find if you were to have gone into Harlem a few years back you would have found on the juke boxes, records by Belafonte, Eartha Kitt, Pearl Bailey, all of these persons were very popular singers in the so-called Negro community a few years back. But since Belafonte divorced Marguerite and married a white woman it doesn't mean that Harlem is anti-white, but you can't find Belafonte's records there; or maybe he just hasn't produced a hit. All of these entertainers who have become involved in intermarriage, and I mean Lena Horne, Eartha Kitt, Sammy Davis, Belafonte, they have a large white following, but you can't go into any Negro community across the nation and find records by these artists that are hits in the so-called Negro community. Because, sub-consciously, today the so-called Negro withdraws himself from the entertainers who have crossed the line. And if the masses of black people won't let a Negro who is involved in an inter-marriage play music for him, he can't speak for him.

The only way you can solve the race problem as it exists, is to take into consideration the feelings of the masses, not the minority; the majority not the minority. And it is proof that the masses of white people don't want Negroes forcing their way into their neighborhood and the masses of black people don't think it's any solution for us to force ourselves into the white neighborhood, so the only ones who want integration are the Negro minority, as I say, the bourgeoisie and the white minority, the so-called white liberals. And that same white liberal who professes to want integration whenever the Negro moves to his neighborhood, he is the first one to move out. And I was talking with one today who said he was a liberal and I asked him where did he live, and he lived in an all-white neighborhood and probably might for the rest of his life. This is conjecture, but I think it stands true. The Civil War was fought 100 years ago, supposedly to solve this problem. After the Civil War was fought, the problem still existed. Along behind that, the thirteenth and fourteenth Amendments were brought about in the Constitution supposedly to solve the problem; after the Amendments, the problem was still right here with us.

Most Negroes think that the Civil War was fought to make them citizens; they think that it was fought to free them from slavery because the real purpose of the Civil War are clothed in hypocrisy. The real purpose of the Amendments are clothed in hypocrisy. The real purpose behind the Supreme Court Desegregation decision was clothed in hypocrisy. And any time integrationists, NAACP, CORE, Urban League, or what you have, will stand up and tell me to spell out how we are going to bring about separation, and here they are integrationists, a philosophy which is supposed to have the support of the Senate, Congress, President, and the Supreme Court, and still with all of that support and hypocritical agreeing, eight years after the desegregation decision, you still don't have what the court decided on.

So we think this, that when whites talk integration they are being hypocrites, and we think that the Negroes who accept token integration are also being hypocrites, because they are the only ones who benefit from it, the handful of hand-picked high-class, middle-class Uncle Tom Negroes. They are hand-picked by whites and turned loose in a white community and they're satisfied. But if all of the black people went into the white community, over night you would have a race war. If four or five little black students going to school in New Orleans bring about the riots that we saw down there, what do you think would happen if all of the black people tried to go to any school that they want, you would have a race war. So our approach to it, those of us who follow the honorable Elijah Muhammad, we feel that it is more sensible than running around here waiting for the whites to allow us inside their attic or inside their basement.

ANTI-DISCRIMINATION GROUPS DISCRIMINATE

Every Negro group that we find in the Negro community that is integrated is controlled by the whites who belong to it, or it is led by the whites who belong to it. NAACP has had a white president for 53 years, it has been in existence for 53 years; Roy Wilkins is the Executive Secretary, but Springarn, a white man has been the president for the past 23 years, and before him, his brother, another white man was president. They have never had a black president. Urban League, another so-called Negro organization, doesn't have a black president, it has a white president. Now this doesn't mean that that's racism, it only means that the same organizations that are accusing you of practicing discrimination, when it comes to the leadership they're practicing discrimination themselves.

The honorable Elijah Muhammad says, and points out to us that in this book ("Anti-Slavery") written by a professor from the University of Michigan, Dwight Lowell Dumond, a person who is an authority on the race question or slave question, his findings were used by Thurgood Marshall in winning the Supreme Court Desegregation decision. And in the preface of this book, it says that second-class citizenship is only a modified form of slavery. Now I'll tell you why I'm dwelling on this; everything that you have devised yourself to solve the race problem has been hypocrisy, because the scientists who delved into it teach us or tell us that second-class citizenship is only a modified form of slavery, which means the Civil War didn't end slavery and the Amendments didn't end slavery. They didn't do it because we still have to wrestle the Supreme Court and the Congress and the Senate to correct the hypocrisy that's been practiced against us by whites for the past umteen years.

And because this was done, the American white man today subconsciously still regards that black man as something below himself. And you will never get the American white man to accept the so-called Negro as an integrated part of his society until the image of the Negro the white man has is changed, and until the image that the Negro has of himself is also changed.

TWO AMERICAS

In 1962, Malcolm X could accurately observe that two years ago the white man didn't know that there were black people in this country who didn't want to integrate. Because of the widely publicized speeches of Malcolm X, a series of "long, hot summers," the Report of the National Advisory Commission on Civil Disorders, and a number of magazine and newspaper articles, white Americans are now fully aware of the existence of a group of blacks who wish to remain separate in some way or another. Although the extent of the effect of separatist rhetoric on modern blacks remain in question, the white members of the so-called establishment are showing signs of concern. The statement in the Kerner Report suggesting the coming of two Americas, separate and unequal, one black and the other white, shocked many. In January of 1969, one Congressman, Mr. Rarick, felt the need to inform the public about the threat of a concerted program to obtain five states for the establishment of a separate black nation. He was particularly distressed to note the apparent intention of bringing this matter to the attention of the United Nations, a proposal originally advanced by Marcus Garvey with regard to the League of Nations, and later by Malcolm X and Stokely Carmichael with regard to the United Nations. The Congressman said:

> The conclusion can be but publicized treason and sedition against the American people along with demands against the U.S. State Department to negotiate for peaceful settlement and petitions — as if from an established government — to the United Nations.[36]

In a reaction that seems to typify whites, the Congressman confessed that he knew little about this movement, but he seemed confident that it was Communist inspired. "The real danger and threat to our national security," he said, "comes from those who are the guiding intelligence and supplying the financial aid." He pointed to an article in what he called "the theoretical magazine of the Communist Party of the U.S.A." discussing the right of black America to create a nation, and demanded to know "what, if anything, has been done to protect the sovereignty of the Union and protect them [the American people] from this openly publicized threat against our lives and property?" He could not believe that black Americans were willing and able to generate their own separatist movement. Perhaps if he had read the history of black rhetoric, he would not have found the idea so surprising.

One communication that particularly upset Congressman Rarick and his constituents was a letter to Secretary of State Dean Rusk from Milton R. Henry, First Vice President of the Republic of New Africa.

Milton R. Henry

The Republic of New Africa*

Hon. Dean Rusk   May 29, 1968
Department of State, The United States of
America, Washington, D.C.

GREETINGS: This note is to advise you of the willingness of the Republic of New Africa to enter immediately into negotiations with the United States of America for the purpose of settling the long-standing grievances between our two peoples and correcting long-standing wrongs.

The wrongs to which we refer are those, of course, which attended the slavery of black people in this country and the oppression of black people, since slavery, which continues to our own day. The grievances relate to the failure of the United States to enter into any bilateral agreements with black people, either before or after the Civil War, which reflect free consent and true mutuality. Black people were never accorded the choices of free people once the United States had ceased, theoretically its enslavement of black people, and this constitutes a fatal defect in the attempt to impose U.S. citizenship upon blacks in America.

The existence of the Republic of New Africa poses a realistic settlement for these grievances and wrongs. We offer new hope for your country as for ours. We wish to see an end to war in the streets. We wish to lift from your country, from your people, the poorest, most depressed segment of the population, and, with them, work out our own destiny, on what has been the poorest states in your union (Mississippi, Louisiana, Alabama, Georgia, and South Carolina), making a separate, free, and independent black nation.

Our discussions should involve land and all those questions connected with the prompt transfer of sovereignty in black areas from the United States to the Republic of New Africa. They must also involve reparations. We suggest that a settlement of not less than $10,000 per black person be accepted as a basis for discussion. We do assure you that the Republic of New Africa remains ready instantly to open good faith negotiations, at a time and under conditions to be mutually agreed. We urge your acceptance of this invitation for talks in the name of peace, justice, and decency.

MILTON R. HENRY
First Vice President.

Milton R. Henry, speaking in an interview published in *Esquire,* emphasized that his movement was essentially peaceful — he did not want a war, but his group was determined to engage in self-

---

*Congressional Record, 91st Congress, 1st Session, January 6, 1969, p. H79.

defense even to the extent of calling on their ally, China, to protect them from the United States Army. As with other separatists, he would be pleased to remain in the United States if fundamental changes leading to real equality were to occur, but, "this country won't make those changes. . . . It'd be easier to give me five states."[37]

Henry shows his knowledge of Hoffer on mass movements, and his influence by the Black Muslims in his need to characterize the white man as a devil.

> Eric Hoffer said you cannot build a movement without a devil, but you can build a movement without angels. And you see the essential is to build a movement. . . . We have to paint the picture, to create the mythology, to give life to it. We have to enlarge it. There's no terms you can think up that would be any better than to say the white man is a devil. That term embraces the conception of the destruction of life.[38]

In another interview, Henry described the rhetorical objectives of his movement as two-fold. First, they aim to engineer consent among all black people living in the United States, and second, to create an "atmosphere of support and toleration of the Republic among the white as well as the black population of the U.S. and the world." He continued, "Our strategic purpose is to neutralize the negative attitudes of the U.S."[39]

Quite clearly, the debate between the assimilationists and the separationists continues, perhaps stronger than ever, in the present day. This chapter reveals a long history of separatist rhetoric. It has included messages of racial pride, unity, and self-help. The rhetoric has been predicated upon the need to discover an acceptable identity for the black man living in a white and hostile nation. The persuasion has arisen from a basic premise that white men will never grant a kind of equality that would allow black men a dignified, and full participation in this society. The arguments for separation have ranged from direct efforts to return to Africa, through demands for a separate territory within the present area of the United States, to a social-cultural separation in which the two races withdraw from each other while continuing to live side-by-side. Institutions from which the call for separation has come have included both Christian and Muslim churches, social organizations, socio-political organizations such as the United Negro Improvement Association, and fully political arrangements such as the Republic of New Africa. They have been characterized by a desire to let black men take care of themselves without the interference — either friendly or hostile — of white men.'

It is easy, and to an extent, perhaps, accurate, to dismiss the rhetoric of separation as a minority position — there is no reason to believe that the appeal has ever attracted as many as half the black population at any one time. But the consistently strong voice given to this message suggests it deserves attention as a significant strategy of black rhetoric. As separation takes its strength from the presumed failure of assimilation, each year that passes without real (not token) success, gives greater strength to the rhetoric of separation, and its co-alternative, revolution.

As a summary to this study of separation, the following article outlining a scholarly case for two Americas is included. The article is significant in several ways. First, by appearing in the leading newspaper of the United States — *The New York Times* — instead of a black-oriented paper or one devoted to dissent, the separatist appeal is given a dignity rarely achieved. Second, the article is a calm, well-reasoned case, addressed to well-informed persons of all races. It contains no bombastic or agitational rhetoric which has often been associated with separatist appeals.[40] It does not rest upon mystery or religious faith, but upon reasoned social, ethnic, economic, and cultural arguments. But for all that, the lines of reasoning in this 1968 essay are not new. They will, on the contrary, be quite familiar to one who has just read this chapter.

Robert S. Browne
*The Case for Two Americas — One Black, One White**

A growing ambivalence among Negroes is creating a great deal of confusion both within the black community itself and within those segments of the white community that are attempting to relate to the blacks. It arises from the question of whether American Negroes are a cultural group significantly distinct from the majority culture *on an ethnic* rather than a socio-economic basis.

If one believes the answer to this is yes, one is likely to favor the cultural distinctiveness and to vigorously oppose efforts to minimize or submerge

---

*Robert S. Browne, "The Case for Two Americas — One Black, One White," *The New York Times Magazine,* August 11, 1968, pp. 10, 13, 50, 51, 56, 60, 61. © 1968 by The New York Times Company.

the differences. If, on the other hand, one believes there are no cultural differences between blacks and whites or that the differences are minimal or transitory, then one is likely to resist emphasis on the differences and to favor accentuation of the similarities. Those two currents in the black community are symbolized, perhaps oversimplified, by the factional labels of separatists and integrationists.

The separatist would argue that the Negro's foremost grievance cannot be solved by giving him access to more gadgets — although this is certainly a part of the solution — but that his greatest need is of the spirit, that he must have an opportunity to reclaim his group individuality and have that individuality recognized as equal with other major cultural groups in the world.

The integrationist would argue that what the Negro wants, principally, is exactly what the whites want — that is, to be "in" in American society — and that operationally this means providing the Negro with employment, income, housing and education comparable to that of the whites. Having achieved this, the other aspects of the Negro's problem of inferiority will disappear.

The origins of this dichotomy are easily identified. The physical characteristics which distinguish blacks from whites are obvious enough; the long history of slavery and the post-emancipation exclusion of the blacks from so many facets of American society are equally undeniable. Whether observable behavioral differences between blacks and the white majority are attributable to this special history of the black man in America or to racial differences in life style is arguable. What is not arguable, however, is that at the time of the slave trade, the blacks arrived in America with a cultural background and life style quite distinct from that of the whites. Although there was perhaps as much diversity among these Africans from widely scattered portions of their native continent as there was among the settlers from Europe, the differences between the two racial groups was unquestionably far greater, as attested by the different roles they were to play in the society.

Over this history there seems to be little disagreement. The dispute arises from how one views what happened after the blacks reached this continent. The integrationist would focus on their transformation into imitators of the European civilization. European clothing was imposed on the slaves, eventually their languages were forgotten, the African homeland receded ever further into the background.

Certainly after 1808, when the slave trade was officially terminated, thus cutting off fresh injections of African culture, the Europeanizing of the blacks proceeded apace. With emancipation, the Federal Constitution recognized the legal manhood of the blacks, citizenship was conferred on the ex-slave, and the Negro began his arduous struggle for social, economic and political acceptance into the American mainstream.

The separatist, however, takes the position that the cultural transformation of the black man was not complete. Whereas the integrationist more or less accepts the destruction of the original culture of the African slaves as a *fait accompli* — whether he feels it to have been morally reprehensible or not — the separatist is likely to harbor a vague resentment toward the whites for having perpetrated this cultural genocide; he would nurture whatever vestiges may have survived the North American experience and would encourage a renaissance of these lost characteristics. In effect, he is sensitive to an identity crisis which presumably does not exist in the mind of the integrationist.

The separatist appears to be romantic and even reactionary to many observers. On the other hand, his viewpoint squares with mankind's most fundamental instinct — the instinct for survival. With so powerful a stimulus, and with the oppressive tendencies of white society, one could have almost predicted the emergence of the black separatist movement. Millions of black parents have been confronted with the poignant agony of raising black, kinky-haired children in a society where the standard of beauty is a milk-white skin and long, straight hair. To convince a black child that she is beautiful when every channel of value formation in the society is telling her the opposite is a heart-rending and well-nigh impossible task.

It is a challenge which confronts all Negroes, irrespective of their social and economic class, but the difficulty of dealing with it is likely to vary with the degree to which the family leads an integrated existence. A black child in a predominantly black school may realize that she doesn't look like the pictures in the books, magazines and TV advertisements, but at least she looks like her schoolmates and neighbors. The black child in a predominantly white school and neighborhood lacks even this basis for identification.

This identity problem is, of course, not peculiar to the Negro, nor is it limited to questions of physical appearance. Minorities of all sorts encounter it in one form or another —the immigrant who speaks with an accent, the Jewish child who doesn't celebrate Christmas, the vegetarian who shuns meat. But for the Negro the problem has a special dimension, for in the American ethos a black man is not only "different," he is classed as ugly and inferior.

This is not an easy situation to deal with, and the manner in which a Negro chooses to handle it will be both determined by, and a determinant of, his larger political outlook. He can deal with it as an integrationist, accepting his child as being ugly by prevailing standards and urging him to excel in other ways to prove his worth; or he can deal with it as a black nationalist, telling the child that he is not a freak but rather part of a larger international community of black-skinned, kinky-haired people who have a beauty of their own, a glorious history and a great future.

In short, he can replace shame with pride, inferiority with dignity, by imbuing the child with what is coming to be known as black nationalism. The growing popularity of this latter viewpoint is evidenced by the appearance of "natural" hair styles among Negro youth and the surge of interest in African and Negro culture and history.

Black Power may not be the ideal slogan to describe this new self-image the black American is developing, for to guilt-ridden whites the slogan conjures up violence, anarchy and revenge. To frustrated blacks, however, it symbolizes unity and a newly found pride in the blackness with which the Creator endowed us and which we realize must always be our mark of identification. Heretofore this blackness has been a stigma, a curse with which we were born. Black Power means that this curse will henceforth be a badge of pride rather than of scorn. It marks the end of an era in which black men devoted themselves to pathetic attempts to be white men and inaugurates an era in which black people will set their own standards of beauty, conduct and accomplishment.

Is this new black consciousness in irreconcilable conflict with the larger American society? In a sense, the heart of the American cultural problem has always been the need to harmonize the inherent contradiction between racial (or national) identity and integration into the melting pot which was America. In the century since the Civil War, the society has made little effort to afford the black minority a sense of racial pride and independence while at the same time accepting it as a full participant. Now that the implications of this failure are becoming apparent, the black community seems to be saying, "Forget it! We'll solve our own problems." Integration, which never had a high priority among the black masses, is now being written off by them as not only unattainable but actually harmful, driving a wedge between them and the so-called Negro élite.

To these developments has been added the momentous realization by many of the "integrated" Negroes that, in the U.S., full integration can only mean full assimilation — a loss of racial identity. This sobering prospect has caused many a black integrationist to pause and reflect, even as have his similarly challenged Jewish counterparts.

Thus, within the black community there are two separate challenges to the traditional integration policy which has long constituted the major objective of esablished Negro leadership. There is general skepticism that the Negro will enjoy full acceptance into American society even after having transformed himself into a white blackman; and there is the longer-range doubt that complete integration would prove to be really desirable, even if it should somehow be achieved, for its price might be the total absorption and disappearance of the race — a sort of painless genocide.

Understandably, it is the black masses who have most vociferously articulated the dangers of assimilation, for they have watched with alarm as the more fortunate among their ranks have gradually risen to the top only to be promptly "integrated" into the white community — absorbed into another culture, often with undisguised contempt for all that had previously constituted their racial and cultural heritage.

Also, it was the black masses who first perceived that integration actually increases the white community's control over the black one by destroying black institutions, absorbing black leadership and making its interests coincide with those of the white community. The international "brain drain" has its counterpart in the black community, which is constantly being denuded of its best-trained people and many of its natural leaders. Black institutions of all sorts — colleges, newspapers, banks, even community organizations — are all losing their better people to the newly available openings in white establishments. This lowers the quality of the Negro organizations and in some cases causes their demise or increases their dependence on whites for survival. Such injurious, if unintended, side effects of integration have been felt in almost every layer of the black community.

If this analysis of the integrationist-separatist conflict exhausted the case, we might conclude that the problems have all been dealt with before by other immigrant groups in America. (It would be an erroneous conclusion, for while other groups may have encountered similar problems, their solutions do not work for us, alas.) But there remains yet another factor which is cooling the Negro's enthusiasm for the integrationist path — he is becoming distrustful of his fellow Americans.

The American culture is one of the youngest in the world. Furthermore, as has been pointed out repeatedly in recent years, it is essentially a culture which approves of violence, indeed enjoys it. Military expenditures absorb roughly half of the national budget. Violence predominates on the TV screen, and toys of violence are best-selling items during the annual rites for the much praised but little imitated Prince of Peace. In Vietnam the zeal with which America has pursued its effort to destroy a poor and illiterate peasantry has astonished civilized people around the globe.

In such an atmosphere the Negro is understandably apprehensive about the fate his white compatriots might have in store for him. The veiled threat by President Johnson at the time of the 1966 riots, suggesting that riots might beget pogroms and pointing out that Negroes are only 10 per cent of the population, was not lost on most blacks. It enraged them, but it was a sobering thought.

The manner in which Germany herded the Jews into concentration camps and ultimately into ovens was a solemn warning to minority peoples everywhere. The casualness with which America exterminated the Indians and later interned the Japanese suggests that there is no cause for the Negro to feel complacent about his security in the U.S. He finds little consolation in the assurance that if it does become necessary to place him in concentration camps it will only be to protect him from uncontrollable whites. "Protective incarceration," to use governmental jargon.

The very fact that such alternatives are becoming serious topics of discussion has exposed the Negro's already raw and sensitive psyche to yet another heretofore unfelt vulnerability — the insecurity which he suffers as a result of having no homeland which he can honestly feel is his own. Among the major ethno-cultural groups in the world, he is unique in this respect.

As the Jewish drama during and following World War II painfully demonstrated, a national homeland is a primordial and urgent need for a people, even though its benefits are not always readily measured. For some, the homeland is a vital place of refuge from the strains of a life led too long in a foreign environment. For others, the need to live in the homeland is considerably less intense than the need for merely knowing that such a homeland exists. The benefit to the expatriate is psychological, a sense of security in knowing that he belongs to a culturally and politically identifiable community. No doubt this phenomenon largely accounts for the fact that both the West Indian Negro and the Puerto Rican exhibit considerably more self-assurance than the American Negro, for both West Indian and Puerto Rican have ties to identifiable homelands which honor and preserve their cultural heritage.

It has been marveled that we American Negroes, almost alone among the cultural groups of the world, exhibit no sense of nationhood. Perhaps it is true that we lack this sense, but there seems little doubt that the absence of a homeland exacts a severe if unconscious price from our psyche. Theoretically our homeland is the U.S.A. We pledge allegiance to the Stars and Stripes and sing the national anthem. But from the age when we first begin to sense that we are somehow "different," that we are victimized, these rituals begin to mean less to us than to our white compatriots. For many of us they become form without substance; for others they become a cruel and bitter mockery of our dignity and good sense; for relatively few of us do they retain a significance in any way comparable to their hold on our white brethren.

The recent coming into independence of many African states stimulated some speculation among Negroes that independent Africa might become the homeland they so desperately needed. A few made the journey and experienced a newly found sense of community and racial dignity. For many who went, however, the gratifying racial fraternity which they experienced was insufficient to compensate for the cultural estrangement accompanying it. They had been away from Africa too long and the differences in language, food and custom barred them from the "at home" feeling they were eagerly seeking. Symbolically, independent Africa could serve them as a homeland; practically, it could not. Their search continues — a search for a place where they can experience the security which comes from being a part of the majority culture, free at last from the inhibiting effects of cultural repression, from cultural timidity and shame.

If we have been separated from Africa for so long that we are no longer quite at ease there, we are left with only one place to make our home, and that is in this land to which we were brought in chains. Justice would indicate such a solution in any case, for it is North America, not Africa, into which our toil and effort have been poured. This land is our rightful home and we are well within our rights in demanding an opportunity to enjoy it on the same terms as the other immigrants who have helped to develop it. Since few whites will deny the justice of this claim, it is paradoxical that we are offered the option of exercising this birthright only on the condition that we abandon our culture, deny our race and integrate ourselves into the white community.

The "accepted" Negro, the "integrated" Negro are mere euphemisms which hide a cruel and relentless cultural destruction that is sometimes agonizing to the middle-class Negro but is becoming intolerable to the black masses. A Negro who refuses to yield his identity and to ape the white model finds he can survive in dignity only by rejecting the entire white society, which must ultimately mean challenging the law and the law-enforcement mechanisms. On the other hand, if he abandons his cultural heritage and succumbs to the lure of integration, he risks certain rejection and humiliation along the way, with absolutely no guarantee of ever achieving complete acceptance. That such unsatisfactory options are leading to almost continuous disruption and dislocation of our society should hardly be cause for surprise.

A formal partitioning of the United States into two totally separate and independent nations, one white and one black, offers one way out of this tragic situation. Many will condemn it as a defeatist solution, but what they see as defeatism may better be described as a frank facing up to the realities of American society. A society is stable only to the extent that there exists a basic core of value judgments that are unthinkingly accepted by the great bulk of its members. Increasingly, Negroes are demonstrating that they do not accept the common core of values which underlies America, either because they had little to do with drafting it or because they feel it is weighted against their interests. The alleged disproportionately large number of Negro law violators, of unwed mothers, of illegitimate children, of nonworking adults *may* be indicators that there is no community of values such as has been supposed, although I am not unaware of racial socio-economic reasons for these statistics also.

But whatever the reason for observed behavioral differences, there is clearly no reason *why* the Negro should not have his own ideas about what the societal organization should be. The Anglo-Saxon system of organizing human relationships has certainly not proved itself to be superior to all other systems, and the Negro is likely to be more acutely aware of this fact than are most Americans.

Certainly partition would entail enormous initial hardships. But these difficulties and these hardships should be weighed against the prospects of prolonged and intensified racial strife stretching for years into the future. Indeed, the social fabric of America is far more likely to be able to withstand the strains of a partitioning of the country than those of an extended race war.

On the other hand, if it happened that the principle of partition were accepted by most Americans without a period of prolonged violence, it is possible that only voluntary transfers of population would be necessary. No one need be forced to move against his will.

This unprecedented challenging of the "conventional wisdom" on the racial question is causing considerable consternation within the white community, especially the white liberal community, which has long felt itself to be the sponsor and guardian of the blacks. The situation is further confused because the challenges to the orthodox integrationist views are being projected by persons whose roots are authentically within the black community — whereas the integrationist spokesmen of the past have often been persons whose credentials were partly white-bestowed. This situation is further aggravated by the classical intergenerational problem — with black youth seizing the lead in speaking out for nationalism and separatism whereas their elders look on askance, a development which has at least a partial parallel in the contemporary white community, where youth is increasingly strident in its demands for thoroughgoing revision of our social institutions.

If one inquires about the spokesmen for the new black nationalism, or for separatism, one discovers that the movement is locally based rather than nationally organized. In the San Francisco Bay area the Black Panther party is well known as a leader in winning recognition for the black community. Its tactic is to operate via a separate political party for black people, a strategy I suspect we will hear a great deal more of in the future. The work of the Black Muslims is well known and perhaps more national in scope than that of any other black-nationalist group. Out of Detroit there is the Malcolm X Society, led by attorney Milton Henry, whose members reject their U.S. citizenship and are claiming five Southern states for the creation of a new black republic. Another major leader in Detroit is the Rev. Albert Cleage, who is developing a considerable following for his preachings of black dignity and who has also experimented with a black political party, thus far without success.

The black students at white colleges are one highly articulate group seeking for some national organizational form. A growing number of black educators are also groping toward some sort of nationally coordinated body to lend strength to their local efforts to develop educational systems better tailored to the needs of the black child. Under the name of Association of Afro-American Educators, they recently held a national conference in Chicago which was attended by several hundred public school teachers and college and community workers from all over the country.

This is not to say that every black teacher or parent-teacher group which favors community control of schools is necessarily sympathetic to black separatism. Nevertheless, the move toward decentralized control over public schools, at least in the larger urban areas, derives from an abandoning of the idea of integration in the schools and a decision to bring to the ghetto the best education that can be obtained.

Similarly, a growing number of community-based organizations are being formed to facilitate the economic development of the ghetto, to replace absentee business proprietors and landlords with black entrepreneurs and resident owners. Again, these efforts are not totally separatist, for they operate within the framework of the present national society, but they build on the separatism which already exists in the society rather than attempt to eliminate it.

To a black who sees salvation for the black man only in a complete divorce of the two races, these efforts at ghetto improvement appear futile, perhaps even harmful. To others, convinced that coexistence with white America is possible within the national framework if only the whites permit the Negro to develop as he wishes (and by his own hand rather than in accordance with a white-conceived and white-administered pattern), such physically and economically upgraded black enclaves will be viewed as desirable steps forward.

Finally, those blacks who still feel that integration is in some sense both acceptable and possible will continue to strive for the color-blind society. When, if ever, these three strands of thought will converge, I cannot predict. Meanwhile, however, concerned whites wishing to work with the black community should be prepared to encounter many rebuffs. They should keep in mind that the black community does not have a homogenous vision of its own predicament at this crucial juncture.

REFERENCES

1*Frederick Douglass' Paper,* March 11, 1852, p. 2. Note that the contemporary spelling "Hayti" will be used in direct quotations.

2*Ibid.,* p.3.

3*Ibid.*

4*Ibid.*

5*Ibid.*

6*Frederick Douglass' Paper,* May 6, 1852, p. 3, and May 20, 1852, p. 1.

7This information was reported in a rhetorical analysis by Arthur Smith, "Back to Africa: The Rhetoric of Physical and Spiritual Emigration," a paper presented at the Central States Speech Association Conference, 1970, Chicago, Illinois, April 10, 1970. It is consistent with comments in Richard Bardolph, *The Negro Vanguard* (New York: Vintage Books, 1959), pp. 106, 111.

8Martin R. Delany, *The Condition, Elevation, Emigration, and Destiny of the Colored People of the United States Politically Considered* (N.Y.: Arno Press Inc., and The New York Times, 1968, reprint of 1852 edition), p. 169.

9*Douglass Monthly,* III, No. 8, January 1, 1861, p. 386.

10*Ibid.*

11*Ibid.*

12William J. Simmons, *Men of Mark* (New York: Arno Press Inc., and *The New York Times,* 1968 reprint of 1887 edition), p. 327.

13Richard Bardolf, *The Negro Vanguard* (N.Y.: Vintage Books, 1959), p. 117.

14Greener, a professor at Howard University at this time, delivered this paper at the 1879 meeting of the American Social Science Association held at Saratoga Springs, New York. Carter Woodson, in his *Negro Orators and Their Orations,* incorrectly dates Greener's speech as 1874. It was, in fact, presented to the same group which heard the Douglass paper read, and on the same day.

15See the discussion of Bitzer on the rhetorical situation in Chapter I.

16Harold Cruse, *Rebellion Or Revolution* (New York: William Morrow & Co., Inc., 1968), pp. 204-07.

17*Ibid.,* p. 206.

18Amy Jacques Garvey, *Garvey and Garveyism* (Jamaica, W.I.: Amy J. Garvey, 1963), pp. 13-14.

19Edmund David Cronon, *Black Moses* (Madison, Wis.: The University of Wisconsin Press, 1955), p. 16.

20*Ibid.,* p. 203.

21*Ibid.,* p. 205.

22Amy Jacques Garvey, ed., *Philosophy and Opinions of Marcus Garvey,* Vol. 1 (New York: The Universal Publishing House, 1923).

23*Ibid.,* p. vii.

24*Ibid.,* p. 5.

25*Ibid.,* p. 9.

26*Ibid.,* p. 12.

[27]*Ibid.*

[28]*Ibid.,* pp. 21-22.

[29]See the discussion of Rokeach, *Beliefs, Attitudes, and Values,* in Chapter I.

[30]C. Eric Lincoln, *The Black Muslims in America* (Boston: Beacon Press, 1961), p. 253.

[31]Eric Hoffer, *The True Believer* (New York: Harper & Row, Publishers, 1951), p. 20.

[32]Lincoln, *op. cit.,* pp. 22-26.

[33]*Ibid.,* p. 110.

[34]*Ibid.,* pp. 111-26.

[35]Malcolm X and Alex Haley, *The Autobiography of Malcolm X* (N.Y.: Grove Press, Inc., 1964), p. 184. Reprinted with permission of Grove Press. Copyrighted © 1964 by Alex Haley and Malcolm X. Copyrighted © 1965 by Alex Haley and Betty Shabazz.

[36]Congressional Record, 91st Congress, 1st Session, January 6, 1969, p. H 79.

[37]Robert Sherrill, "We Also Want Four Hundred Billion Dollars Back Pay," *Esquire,* Vol. LXXVI, No. 1 (January, 1968), cited in *Congressional Record, ibid.,* p. H 85.

[38]*Ibid.*

[39]*Esquire,* Vol. LXXI, No. 1 (January, 1969), reprinted in *Congressional Record, ibid.*

[40]Robert S. Browne is assistant professor of economics at Fairleigh Dickinson University, and this article derives from a debate with Bayard Rustin before the National Community Relations Advisory Council.

Chapter 6

THE RHETORIC OF REVOLUTION

The third major strategy used by black Americans may be classified under the broad heading of revolution. More difficult to define than either assimilation or separatism, the concept of revolution is both elusive and, to some extent, non-rhetorical. Indeed, revolution is antagonistic to persuasion as a method of instituting social change. When a movement relies primarily on coercion, power, or revolt, it has essentially discarded freedom of choice, which is an integral element of rhetoric. Nevertheless, there are several compelling reasons for including a chapter on revolution. First, the ambiguity inherent in the term "revolution" has had, in itself, a profound effect on the civil rights campaign structure, and the response engendered by it. Particularly in recent years, spokesmen have employed the concept without desiring to communicate all the actions that might be associated with the term. In the case of black Americans, the entire movement of black men to achieve a good life has often been called a revolution. Martin Luther King, Jr.'s behavior, for example, represented to many observers a non-violent revolution. Other essentially moderate, persuasion-oriented, black speakers have used the term with no intention of suggesting Molotov cocktails and snipers in the ghetto. Equally significant in understanding the effect of this ambiguity is the fact that the laws of the United States concerning free speech are not altogether clear. Speakers may be charged with criminal behavior for inciting a riot or encouraging the violent otherthrow of the government, or for constituting a clear and present danger. One of the results of this pervasive ambiguity, therefore, is a vagueness in discussing the specific methods of achieving revolution. Malcolm X might say, as he did in the South, "I don't want to encourage you to do anything you *wouldn't have done anyway."* Similarly, Dick Gregory may say that he does not necessarily advocate the use of violence and riot, but it is not for him to suggest how people should go about obtaining the goals they seek. He simply tells his listeners of the goals, and encourages them to go after them in *any way they deem necessary.*

When the ambiguity associated with revolution is removed and the speaker and audience share a similar understanding of the recommended strategies of coercion, power, and revolt, the role of rhetoric as a catalyst for these approaches cannot be ignored easily. A policy of revolution based on the theory of higher law, for instance, may derive its preliminary thrust from a rhetorical effort calling for a majority vote in support of violence. It is this pattern which made Henry Highland Garnet's 1843 convention address, recommending official support for a possible slave insurrection, historically significant. For the most part, however, movements do not often meet in parliamentary session, propose a motion urging the group henceforth to utilize coercion, force, and revolutionary strategies to achieve its ends; nor do they often debate the motion, and pass it by majority rule. Rather, as Killian suggests, the strategy of revolution emerges gradually out of the failure of other approaches which are chosen first.[1] Nor does rhetoric even under revolution play an unimportant role. It was through the written and spoken word that David Walker couched his persuasive appeals for a slave revolt in 1828 and Rap Brown initiated his philosophy of defensive violence in the 1960's.

Rhetoric is a significant corollary of revolution, or fanaticism as Hoffer terms it, because it is one phase in a mass movement which has been essentially persuasive in the past, and will be again when practical men of action are called in to establish a new order, or return the old order. Finally, for a movement to become revolutionary, as Killian, Hoffer, and others indicate, a charismatic and fanatical leader must emerge to direct the movement. Even though the leader is the epitome of the failure and rejection of persuasion as a strategy of change, he must necessarily utilize rhetoric to establish himself as the head of the movement and organize his people into a unified, revolutionary force. How this was achieved by men like Denmark Vesey and Nat Turner in the 1820's and early 1830's, for example, will be discussed later in this chapter.

It would appear, then, that a chapter on revolutionary rhetoric must not describe the planning and activities of revolutionists as they create terror and disorder in the society they wish to destroy. Rather, it should analyze the role of rhetoric, first, as its breakdown gives rise to the need and motivation for revolution; second, as it is used by potential leaders of the revolution to establish themselves; and third, as it is used *within the revolutionary group* to organize for the coming battle. The latter function—the rhetoric of organization for revolution — is perhaps the most critical in the black experience. This study suggests, and the testimony of Killian and others confirms, that the greatest single failure of black rhetoric has been its inability to establish unity of purpose and cohesive organization among all black Americans, or even a majority of them. The one man who perhaps perceived this need most clearly, and came the closest to achieving it, was Marcus Garvey, but he was deported before he could accomplish his goals. The only other recent figure with a sense of organization and the charismatic talents to equal Garvey was Malcolm X, and he was assassinated just as he began his effort. Presently, the two most likely candidates for leader of the black revolution — Stokely Carmichael and Eldridge Cleaver — are in serious conflict over the basis of organization.

In the strategies of assimilation and separation, it was possible to find a continual thread of development from colonial times to the present. While they competed with each other and still do, while one would, at times, overshadow the other and still does, they represent long-term rhetorical strategies containing historical development. This cannot be said about the strategy of revolution. First, the character of the anti-slavery revolutionary struggle was different from that of the present day. Comparisons between the two, therefore, should be made hesitantly. They are alike in the sense that both involved the effort to free an enslaved people of black color, and they both emerge out of the failure of persuasion to achieve the goal. But beyond these two similarities, comparisons are difficult. From the end of the Civil War until about 1954, there is relatively little evidence of revolutionary rhetoric. The situation simply did not call for it; leaders did not feel the need to advocate it; nor did the audience seem ready to respond to calls for revolution. Thus the study of the rhetoric of revolution is, in fact, two studies — one occurring prior to the Civil War; the other starting from the time of the 1954 Supreme Court decision on school segregation and continuing to the present. In the first revolution the goal was clear and singular: free the slaves. In the second the goals are ambiguous, multiple, and in a constant state of change.

Finally, as a preliminary observation, the term "nationalism" must once again be treated. In Chapters IV and V this term was not employed because it was less useful in grouping the rhetoric to be studied. Although the concepts "Black Power" and "Black Nationalism" are relevant to the current chapter, they have been rejected in favor of the more universal concept, "revolution." As interpreted in this discussion, revolution need not imply violence; it does describe a social movement seeking to bring about change in the locus of power within a political unit. Moreover, it comes to be regarded, states Killian, "by a significant portion of society as *dangerous*," and "is therefore opposed with force, legal and illegal." Revolution "is compelled to rely on illegitimate means to achieve its objectives."[2] The term, "black power," has been used so frequently that it has relatively little specific meaning for either blacks or whites. "Black Nationalism" is used to strike an analogy to the colonial resistance of the Third World and reflects the influence of Frantz Fanon who wrote not so much for black Americans as for those living in actual colonized countries. Therefore, the Black Nationalism concept represents only one, albeit significant, thrust of black revolutionary rhetoric.

RHETORIC OF REVOLUTION IN THE ANTE-BELLUM PERIOD

Two forms of revolutionary rhetoric characterized the speaking of a select group of black Americans during the antebellum era. The first, initiated by slaves and free Negroes in the South, involved charismatic leaders who not only recommended the need for revolt but also organized and participated in the uprisings. The second consisted of revolutionary appeals by abolitionist speakers in the North who grew impatient with the democratic pattern of conflict-negotiation-compromise which too frequently prolonged suppression of blacks or, at best, led to tokenism. This section will provide some insight into these distinctive types of pre-Civil War rhetoric.

THE RHETORIC OF REVOLT BY SLAVES AND FREE NEGROES IN THE SOUTH

Tradition has pictured southern slaves and free negroes as contented and submissive people who happily yielded to their inferior status, and, indeed, risked their own lives while protecting the families of masters dedicated to perpetuating slavery. This was true in many instances, for the uneducated slave may have either experienced overpowering fear, or may have understandably mistaken paternalism for love and compassion. Yet, there is another and less familiar side marked by reckless courage and militancy, deriving its strength from Biblical passages and a sense of historical and heavenly mission. Concerned with their lack of freedom and occasionally motivated by visions, some southern blacks struck down their oppressors with sudden acts of violence. It is difficult to determine the full scope of their disobedience because of the inadequate historical data in the early days of the American Republic, and the tendency of political leaders to suppress "news of actual conspiracies . . . lest publication stimulate further unrest."[3] Extant statistics from the state of Virginia, however, reveal that resistance by slaves caused alarm through the white South. From 1783 to 1834, in Virginia alone there were 432 slaves executed for alleged murders, poisoning, and arson.[4] Although this unrest seldom involved large numbers and tended to be spontaneous, it sometimes reached the level of planned revolt. In the late summer of 1800, "General" Gabriel, a tall and commanding slave, persuaded a group of Richmond Negroes to collect whatever arms they could find and march on the capital. Subsequent testimony in the trial that followed described the rhetoric of preparation that preceded the event. A key participant, "Ben alias Ben Woolfolk," told how he had used the Bible to instruct and inspire the conspirators. "I told them that I had heard in the days of old, when the Israelites were in service to King Pharoah they were taken from him by the power of God, and were carried away by Moses."[5] This reliance upon the Scriptures for guidance and inspiration was to become a trademark in the persuasive communications of later insurrectionists.

In 1822, Denmark Vesey, a free Negro who worked as a successful carpenter in Charleston, South Carolina,[6] created "the most elaborate insurrectionary project ever formed by American slaves."[7] Laying plans to capture the city of Charleston, he patiently enlisted over a period of several years the support of approximately 9,000 Negroes in South Carolina and sought additional help from St. Domingo. Vesey's careful and detailed approach constitutes a remarkable instance of the rhetoric of preparation for revolutionary action. The first element of his strategy was to win respect for himself as a man fully committed to the task of achieving liberty for all of his comrades. He therefore made it known that he had refused to go to Africa on the grounds that he was needed at home. The fact that he lived in comfortable circumstances and yet expressed concern for the unfortunate plight of the slaves added to his appeal. Possessing enormous physical strength and energy, an impetuous and domineering personality, and articulate speech, he was viewed with awe bordering on reverence by most Negroes who came in contact with him.

But Vesey's persuasive power was not due primarily to the force of his ethos and image. Rather, it was the result of his skillful campaign to convey the message of revolt through interpersonal communication and dialectic. He sought every available opportunity of addressing, either directly or indirectly, the members of his race. When he could see, for example, that Negroes were in hearing range, he would cleverly introduce the subject of slavery and civil rights to white acquaintances standing near. He rebuked black companions when he saw them bow in the streets of Charleston to whites as they passed by. More significantly, he frequently held meetings in his home for the purpose of telling his guests about their abominable lives.[8]

What Vesey said to his black listeners always adhered to a standard pattern. He first sketched the inherent problem in the status quo, and then suggested that the only solution would be the immediate and total extermination of slavery. Those who feared such drastic measures were told that their unhappy situation was analagous to that of the ancient Israelites whose acts of violence on behalf of freedom had the endorsement of God. As Vesey unfolded his argument he buttressed his revolutionary thesis by quoting the following Scriptures from the Old Testament:

> Behold, the day of the Lord cometh, and thy spoil shall be divided in the midst of thee. For I will gather all nations against Jerusalem to battle; and the city shall be taken, and the houses rifled, and the women ravished; and half of the city shall go forth into captivity, and the residue of the people shall not be cut off from the city. Then shall the Lord go forth, and fight

against those nations, as when he fought in the day of battle. (*Zechariah*, XIV, 1-3.)

And they utterly destroyed all that was in the city, both man and woman, young and old, and ox, and sheep, and ass, with the edge of the sword. (*Joshua*, VI, 21.)

With the aid of this rhetoric Vesey's plot resembled a holy crusade which placed the higher law of God above human life. If murders were to take place, these violent acts would be committed not as deeds of vengeance or retribution but rather as action to achieve the ultimate goal of freedom and equality for all men. This, he was careful to point out, was merely a repetition of the history of the Israelites.

Although Vesey drew heavily upon the Bible to support his cause, he did not ignore other source material. He made certain that the anti-slavery literature coming into Charleston would be placed into the hands of blacks whenever possible. Another of his favorite rhetorical tactics was to read aloud extensive excerpts from the congressional debates delivered during the Missouri Compromise struggle to his followers. In all, he effectively used the constituent elements of dialectic — a statement of proposition defining the issue, and a dialogue containing clearly stated arguments and forms of proof.[9]

Despite the fact that Vesey's plot was well conceived and formulated and generated enthusiastic support from many blacks, the revolution he envisoned never took place. A slave who, in the end, felt indebted to a kind master betrayed Vesey who, with many of his followers, was put to death. South Carolina and other southern states responded to the threat of widespread slave insurrection by instituting a rigid set of black codes. These acts of reprisal, however, did not prevent Vesey from becoming a symbol of the black American's campaign for freedom. Within nine years another charismatic leader, inheriting the mantle of Vesey, precipitated the most celebrated slave revolt of the antebellum period. Nat Turner did what Vesey could not do; he went beyond the rhetoric of preparation and participated as the central agent in the revolution he had designed.[10]

Turner's early experiences led him to believe that he was a man of destiny and an instrument of God's will. Taught by his mother from early childhood that he was born to be a prophet, preacher, and deliverer, he educated himself for his mission. Soon he saw visions and heard what appeared to be divine revelations.

At twenty-five he began to preach to slaves in his locale. Three years later he had new visions and further communications with God. After receiving his last vision in February, 1831, he felt the time had come to launch his campaign to free the slaves, but it was not until August 21 of the same year that the revolt occurred. Despite the fact that Turner often kept his ideas to himself and remained to some degree a man cloaked in mystery, he had to rely on rhetoric to communicate the meaning of his visions and to detail the plan of action for carrying out God's design. On the night of the attack, he addressed his four closest confidantes and conspirators with these words:

> Friends and brothers: We are to commence a great work to-night. Our race is to be delivered from slavery, and God has appointed us as the men to do his bidding, and let us be worthy of our calling. I am told to slay all the whites we encounter, without regard to age or sex. We have no arms or ammunition, but we shall find these in the houses of our oppressors, and as we go on others can join us. Remember that we do not go forth for the sake of blood and carnage, but it is necessary that in the commencement of this revolution all the whites we meet should die, until we shall have an army strong enough to carry on the war upon a Christian basis. Remember that ours is not a war for robbery and to satisfy our passions; it is a struggle for freedom. Ours must be deeds, and not words. Then let's away to the scene of action.[11]

In the uprising that ensued, Turner and his men killed sixty whites within twenty-four hours. Not until the group of conspirators were met and overpowered by federal and state militia did the revolt end.

Most of what is known about Turner's historic venture comes from his *Confessions,* edited by Thomas Gray, a contemporary who interviewed him and summarized his testimony.[12] The extensive excerpt from these *Confessions* included below contains an autobiographical sketch of Turner and the method he used in conceiving and executing his plan. It is instructive to note that Turner, unlike his predecessor Vesey, drew his principal inspiration from the New Testament. Identifying his cause with that of Christ, he was prepared to pick up the yoke that Christ had laid down and use it in the fight to release the slaves from bondage. Although there is much in the *Confessions* that reveals a man who was obsessed with mysticism, signs, and fantaticism, Turner's forthright remarks clearly show that he was intelligent, courageous, and sincere.[13] More than any other antebellum document, this work symbolizes the present revolutionary spirit that characterizes some of the rhetoric in the current civil rights movement.

Nat Turner

From *The Confessions of Nat Turner**

Agreeable to his own appointment, on the evening he was committed to prison, with permission of the jailer, I visited NAT on Tuesday the 1st November, when, without being questioned at all, he commenced his narrative in the following words:—

Sir,—You have asked me to give a history of the motives which induced me to undertake the late insurrection, as you call it—To do so I must go back to the days of my infancy, and even before I was born. I was thirty-one years of age the 2nd of October last, and born the property of Benj. Turner, of this county. In my childhood a circumstance occurred which made an indelible impression on my mind, and laid the ground work of that enthusiasm, which has terminated so fatally to many, both white and black, and for which I am about to atone at the gallows. It is here necessary to relate this circumstance —trifling as it may seem, it was the commencement of that belief which has grown with time, and even now, sir, in this dungeon, helpless and forsaken as I am, I cannot divest myself of. Being at play with other children, when three or four years old, I was telling them something, which my mother overhearing, said it had happened before I was born—I stuck to my story, however, and related somethings which went, in her opinion, to confirm it— others being called on were greatly astonished, knowing that these things had happened, and caused them to say in my hearing, I surely would be a prophet, as the Lord had shewn me things that had happened before my birth. And my father and mother strengthened me in this my first impression, saying in my presence, I was intended for some great purpose, which they had always thought from certain marks on by head and breast—[a parcel of excrescences which I believe are not at all uncommon, particularly among negroes, as I have seen several with the same. In this case he has either cut them off or they have nearly disappeared]—My grandmother, who was very religious, and to whom I was much attached—my master, who belonged to the church, and other religious persons who visited the house, and whom I often saw at prayers, noticing the singularity of my manners, I suppose, and my uncommon intelligence for a child, remarked I had too much sense to be raised, and if I was, I would never be of any service to any one as a slave—To a mind like mine, restless, inquisitive and observant of everything that was passing, it is

---

*From Thomas R. Gray, *The Confessions of Nat Turner* (Baltimore: Thomas Gray, 1831), pp. 7-12.

easy to suppose that religion was the subject to which it would be directed, and although this subject principally occupied my thoughts—there was nothing that I saw or heard of to which my attention was not directed—The manner in which I learned to read and write, not only had great influence on my own mind, as I acquired it with the most perfect ease, so much so, that I have no recollection whatever of learning the alphabet—but to the astonishment of the family, one day, when a book was shewn to me to keep me from crying, I began spelling the names of different objects—this was a source of wonder to all in the neighborhood, particularly the blacks—and this learning was constantly improved at all opportunities—when I got large enough to go to work, while employed, I was reflecting on many things that would present themselves to my imagination, and whenever an opportunity occurred of looking at a book, when the school children were getting their lessons, I would find many things that the fertility of my own imagination had depicted to me before; all my time, not devoted to my master's service, was spent either in prayer, or in making experiments in casting different things in moulds made of earth, in attempting to make paper, gunpowder, and many other experiments, that although I could not perfect, yet convinced me of its practicability if I had the means.* I was not addicted to stealing in my youth, nor have ever been—Yet such was the confidence of the negroes in the neighborhood, even at this early period of my life, in my superior judgment, that they would often carry me with them when they were going on any roguery, to plan for them. Growing up among them, with this confidence in my superior judgment, and when this, in their opinions, was perfected by Divine inspiration, from the circumstances already alluded to in my infancy, and which belief was ever afterwards zealously inculcated by the austerity of my life and manners, which became the subject of remark by white and black.—Having soon discovered to be great, I must appear so, and therefore studiously avoided mixing in society, and wrapped myself in mystery, devoting my time to fasting and prayer—By this time, having arrived to man's estate, and hearing the scriptures commented on at meetings, I was struck with that particular passage which says: "Seek ye the kingdom of Heaven and all things shall be added unto you." I reflected much on this passage, and prayed daily for light on this subject—As I was praying one day at my plough, the spirit spoke to me, saying "Seek ye the kingdom of Heaven and all things shall be added unto you. *Question*—what do you mean by the Spirit. *Ans.* The Spirit that spoke to the prophets in former days—and I was greatly astonished, and for two years prayed continually, whenever my duty would permit—and then again I had the same revelation, which fully confirmed me in the impression that I was ordained for some great purpose in the hands of the Almighty. Several years rolled round, in which many events occurred to strengthen me in this my belief. At this time I reverted in my mind to the remarks made of me in my childhood, and the things that had been shewn me—and as it had been said of me in my childhood by those by whom I

---

*When questioned as to the manner of manufacturing those different articles, he was found well informed on the subject.

had been taught to pray, both white and black, and in whom I had the greatest confidence, that I had too much sense to be raised, and if I was, I would never be of any use to any one as a slave. Now finding I had arrived to man's estate, and was a slave, and these revelations being made known to me, I began to direct my attention to this great object, to fulfill the purpose for which, by this time, I felt assured I was intended. Knowing the influence I had obtained over the minds of my fellow servants, (not by the means of conjuring and such like tricks—for to them I always spoke of such things with contempt) but by the communion of the Spirit whose revelations I often communicated to them, and they believed and said my wisdom came from God. I now began to prepare them for my purpose, by telling them something was about to happen that would terminate in fulfilling the great promise that had been made to me—About this time I was placed under an overseer, from whom I ranaway—and after remaining in the woods thirty days, I returned, to the astonishment of the negroes on the plantation, who thought I had made my escape to some other part of the country, as my father had done before. But the reason of my return was, that the Spirit appeared to me and said I had my wishes directed to the things of this world, and not to the kingdom of Heaven, and that I should return to the service of my earthly master—"For he who knoweth his Master's will, and doeth it not, shall be beaten with many stripes, and thus have I chastened you." And the negroes found fault, and murmured against me, saying that if they had my sense they would not serve any master in the world. And about this time I had a vision—and I saw white spirits and black spirits engaged in battle, and the sun was darkened—the thunder rolled in the Heavens, and blood flowed in streams—and I heard a voice saying, "Such is your luck, such you are called to see, and let it come rough or smooth, you must surely bare it." I now withdrew myself as much as my situation would permit, from the intercourse of my fellow servants, for the avowed purpose of serving the Spirit more fully—and it appeared to me, and reminded me of the things it had already shown me, and that it would then reveal to me the knowledge of the elements, the revolution of the planets, the operation of tides, and changes of the seasons. After this revelation in the year 1825, and the knowledge of the elements being made known to me, I sought more than ever to obtain true holiness before the great day of judgment should appear, and then I began to receive the true knowledge of faith. And from the first steps of righteousness until the last, was I made perfect; and the Holy Ghost was with me, and said, "Behold me as I stand in the Heavens"—and I looked and saw the forms of men in different attitudes —and there were lights in the sky to which the children of darkness gave other names than what they really were—for they were the lights of the Saviour's hands, stretched forth from east to west, even as they were extended on the cross on Calvary for the redemption of sinners. And I wondered greatly at these miracles, and prayed to be informed of a certainty of the meaning thereof—and shortly afterwards, while laboring in the field, I discovered drops of blood on the corn as though it were dew from heaven— and I communicated it to many, both white and black, in the neighborhood— and I then found on the leaves in the woods hieroglyphic characters, and numbers, with the forms of men in different attitudes, portrayed in blood, and representing the figures I had seen before in the heavens. And now the Holy Ghost had revealed itself to me, and made plain the miracles it had shown me —For as the blood of Christ had been shed on this earth, and had ascended to heaven for the salvation of sinners, and was now returning to earth again in the form of dew—and as the leaves on the trees bore the impression of the figures I had seen in the heavens, it was plain to me that the Saviour was about to lay down the yoke he had borne for the sins of men, and the great day of judgment was at hand. About this time I told these things to a white man, (Etheldred T. Brantley) on whom it had a wonderful effect—and he ceased from his wickedness, and was attacked immediately with a cutaneous eruption, and blood ozed from the pores of his skin, and after praying and fasting nine days, he was healed, and the Spirit appeared to me again, and said, as the Saviour had been baptised so should we be also—and when the white people would not let us be baptised by the church, we went down into the water together, in the sight of many who reviled us, and were baptised by the Spirit—After this I rejoiced greatly, and gave thanks to God. And on the 12th of May, 1828, I heard a loud noise in the heavens, and the Spirit instantly appeared to me and said the Serpent was loosened, and Christ had laid down the yoke he had borne for the sins of men, and that I should take it on and fight against the Serpent, for the time was fast approaching when the first should be last and the last should be first. *Ques.* Do you not find yourself mistaken now? *Ans.* Was not Christ crucified. And by signs in the heavens that it would make known to me when I should commence the great work— and until the first sign appeared, I should conceal it from the knowledge of men—And on the appearance of the sign, (the eclipse of the sun last February) I should arise and prepare myself, and slay my enemies with their own weapons. And immediately on the sign appearing in the heavens, the seal was removed from my lips, and I communicated the great work laid out for me to do, to four in whom I had the greatest confidence, (Henry, Hark, Nelson, and Sam)—It was intended by us to have begun the work of death on the 4th July last — Many were the plans formed and rejected by us, and it affected my mind to such a degree, that I fell sick, and the time passed without our coming to any determination how to commence—Still forming new schemes and rejecting them, when the sign appeared again, which determined me not to wait longer.

Since the commencement of 1830, I had been living with Mr. Joseph Travis, who was to me a kind master, and placed the greatest confidence in me; in fact, I had no cause to complain of his treatment to me. On Saturday evening, the 20th of August, it was agreed between Henry, Hark and myself, to prepare a dinner the next day for the men we expected, and then to concert a plan, as we had not yet determined on any. Hark, on the following morning, brought a pig, and Henry brandy, and being joined by Sam, Nelson, Will and Jack, they prepared in the woods a dinner, where, about three o'clock, I joined them.

Q. Why were you so backward in joining them.

A. The same reason that had caused me not to mix with them for years before.

I saluted them on coming up, and asked Will how came he there, he answered, his life was worth no more than others, and his liberty as dear to him. I asked him if he thought to obtain it? He said he would, or loose his life. This was enough to put him in full confidence. Jack, I knew, was only a tool in the hands of Hark, it was quickly agreed we should commence at home (Mr. J. Travis') on that night, and until we had armed and equipped ourselves, and gathered sufficient force, neither age nor sex was to be spared, (which was invariably adhered to.)

The South, as noted in an earlier chapter, reacted predictably to the Turner insurrection. State legislatures convened to strengthen the Black Codes. Reports of the uprising, combined with the awareness that Negroes often outnumbered whites in key areas throughout the South, produced alarm among the white populace, many of whom lay awake at night fearful of another attack. Less frightened political leaders and plantation owners attempted to play down the significance of the event by asserting that Turner was a religious fanatic and atypical slave who represented only a small degree of discontent. Yet, even they were baffled and disturbed by Turner's forthright claim that his master had treated him well. What made Turner's rebellion historically important, therefore, is the fact that it "was not against particular abuses of the Peculiar Institution," observes Boorstin, "but against the Institution itself; not against a harsh master but against all masters. Turner was a man . . . 'in whom came to focus the restless passions of a race condemned to enforced servitude.' "[14]

Apart from the development of more stringent measures designed to control slavery, make emancipation more difficult, and restrict the privileges of free Negroes, other influences were either directly or indirectly attributable to the Turner insurrection. In the early winter of 1832, just four months after the bloody uprising in Southampton County, legislators in Virginia met in state convention and held public debates on the subject of slavery. Although this freedom of expression was not repeated in subsequent years, the debates were unusually significant. This historic occasion marked the first time that free and open public discussion of the merits of slavery occurred in the South. Similarly, "it offered," as Boorstin suggests, "a preview of arguments for and against slavery that were to be advanced in the next three decades, and it was a turning point in Southern attitudes to the Peculiar Institution."[15]

A second influence stemming from the revolt had more effect on the attitudes of Negroes in the South. Almost immediately

Turner became a symbol for oppressed members of his race. As many of them reflected on his courageous attempt to free the slaves and the eloquent words of his *Confession,* they expressed their antipathy toward slavery by precipitating further uprisings. Between 1835 and 1856 slaves revolted in Georgia, Mississippi, Alabama, Louisiana, and North Carolina.[16] These episodes, demonstrating the deep-seated resentment that Negroes held for slavery, did not compare in their range or scope with the dramatic performances of Vesey and Turner.

THE RHETORIC OF REVOLT BY BLACK AMERICANS IN THE NORTH

The call for revolt on the part of southern Negroes was echoed in the addresses of influential northern spokesmen in the decades preceding the Civil War. One of these early champions of revolutionary rhetoric was David Walker, a free Negro who had emigrated to Boston from his native state of North Carolina in 1827.[17] As a correspondent for the *Freedom's Journal* and an occasional civil rights speaker in Massachusetts, he started as an assimilationist but shifted rapidly to a more militant stance.[18] He was pained by what he had seen on the slave plantations in North Carolina and disturbed by the treatment that Garrison had received in the North because of his abolitionist views. These events caused him to write his famous *Appeal* in 1829. With this publication, called injudicious by some northern abolitionists and incendiary by most white southerners, Walker was suddenly thrust into the national arena. His work, which was published at his own expense and distributed freely throughout the country, is an anguished cry, intoning the wretchedness of slavery. It is divided into four chapters portraying the miserable condition of Negroes in general and slaves in particular because of their bondage and ignorance, the propaganda of Christian ministers, and the colonization movement. In expressing his outrage that the Negro was treated not as a man but as a "talking ape," Walker accused the whites of keeping blacks ignorant so that they could be dominated. He further condemned those Christian ministers who condoned slavery and preached the need for obedience. Nor did he spare revered political leaders whose conservative civil rights philosophy hampered progress toward emancipation. He rebuked Jefferson for claiming that Negroes, despite their occasional exemplary accomplishments, were inferior to whites. Moreover, he suggested that Henry Clay's attempts to colonize black Americans by sending them to Africa was nothing more than a carefully constructed scheme to get rid of the free Negro. These circumstances of oppression even at the hands of enlightened white leaders, who doubtlessly were familiar with the teachings of the New Testament and the natural rights philosophy of the Declaration of Independence, gave to Negroes, in Walker's opinion, the challenge to break the manacles that enslaved them.

The appeal, in short, was a devastating and eloquent portrait of all the wrongs Negroes had suffered, and it constituted an unmistakable call for violence and revolt. Current historical scholarship tends to support the following analysis presented by Dumond:

> Walker's mind was not trained, perhaps not disciplined, but that is precisely what made his *Appeal* one of the greatest pieces of antislavery literature. It was the primitive cry of anguish from a race oppressed. It was precisely what would have come from a million throats could they have been articulate and have been heard. It may have caused Walker's death. If so, no man ever died more nobly, because he left a legacy of raging hatred for slavery, for the degradation, wretchedness, and ignorance of his people, and for colonization, which was designed to rob them of their natural leaders.[19]

Within one year Walker's *Appeal* went through three editions, but the central message in each was essentially the same. Of the four articles included in his pamphlet, the first, entitled "Our Wretchedness in Consequence of Slavery," perhaps best summarizes the depth of despair experienced by concerned free Negroes in the North as they examined the plight of their brethren who were enslaved in the South. The full manuscript of the article that follows is a compelling rhetorical document that may be studied with interest.[20] Lacking refinement in style and a cohesive structure, and containing excessive hyperbole, it nevertheless has the saving merit of convincing evidence and refutation and strong pathetic proof. Note how Walker ranges with ease over classical and European history and the Bible, and shows a keen awareness of the political issues of the day. His adeptness in refuting the contentions of Jefferson reveals a sensitive and penetrating mind. "Walker's analysis of the Negro mind and personality," observes Eaton, "was perceptive and has largely been confirmed by the progress of the race within recent years.[21]

David Walker

Our Wretchedness in Consequence of Slavery.*

My beloved brethren:—The Indians of North and of South America—the Greeks—the Irish, subjected under the king of Great Britain—the Jews, that ancient people of the Lord——the inhabitants of the islands of the sea—in fine, all the inhabitants of the earth, (except however, the sons of Africa) are called *men,* and of course are, and ought to be free. But we, (coloured people) and our children are *brutes!!* and of course are, and *ought to be* SLAVES to the American people and their children forever!! to dig their mines and work their farms; and thus go on enriching them, from one generation to another with our *blood* and our *tears!!!!*

I promised in a preceding page to demonstrate to the satisfaction of the most incredulous, that we, (coloured people of these United States of America) are the *most wretched, degraded* and *abject* set of beings that *ever lived* since the world began, and that the white Americans having reduced us to the wretched state of *slavery,* treat us in that condition *more cruel* (they being an enlightened and christian people,) than any heathen nation did any people whom it had reduced to our condition. These affirmations are so well confirmed in the minds of all unprejudiced men, who have taken the trouble to read histories, that they need no elucidation from me. But to put them beyond all doubt, I refer you in the first place to the children of Jacob, or of Israel in Egypt, under Pharaoh and his people. Some of my brethren do not know who Pharaoh and the Egyptians were—I know it to be a fact, that some of them take the Egyptians to have been a gang of *devils,* not knowing any better, and that they (Egyptians) having got possession of the Lord's people, treated them *nearly* as cruel as *christian Americans* do us, at the present day. For the information of such, I would only mention that the Egyptians, were Africans or coloured people, such as we are—some of them yellow and others dark—a mixture of Ethiopian and the natives of Egypt—about the same as you see the coloured people of the United States at the present day.—I say, I call your attention then, to the children of Jacob, while I point out particularly to you his son Joseph, among the rest, in Egypt.

"And Pharoah, said unto Joseph, thou shalt be "over my house, and according unto thy word "shall all my people be ruled: only in the throne "will I be greater than thou."**

"And Pharoah said unto Joseph, see, I have set "thee over all the land of Egypt."†

"And Pharaoh said unto Joseph, I am Pharaoh, "and without thee shall no man lift up his hand or "foot in all the land of Egypt."‡

Now I appeal to heaven and to earth, and particularly to the American people themselves, who cease not to declare that our condition is not *hard,*

---

*From David Walker, *Walker's Appeal, in Four Articles, Together with a Preamble to the Colored Citizens of the World, but in Particular, and Very Expressly to those of the United States Of America* (Boston: D. Walker, 1830), pp. 9-21.
**See Genesis, chap. xli, v. 40. †v. 41, ‡v. 44. §v. 45.

and that we are comparatively satisfied to rest in wretchedness and misery, under them and their children.—Not, indeed, to shew me a coloured President, a Governor, a Legislator, a Senator, a Mayor, or an Attorney at the Bar.— But to show me a man of colour, who holds the low office of a Constable, or one who sits in a Juror Box, even on a case of one of his wretched brethren, throughout this great Republic!—But let us pass Joseph the son of Israel a little farther in review, as he existed with that heathen nation.

"And Pharaoh called Joseph's name Zaphnath-"paaneah; and he gave him to wife Asenath the "daughter of Potipherah priest of On. And Joseph "went out over all the land of Egypt."§

Compare the above, with the American institutions. Do they not institute laws to prohibit us from marrying among the whites? I would wish, candidly, however, before the Lord, to be understood, that I would not give a *pinch of snuff* to be married to any white person I ever saw in all the days of my life. And I do say it, that the black man, or man of colour, who will leave his own colour (provided he can get one, who is good for any thing) and marry a white woman, to be a double slave to her, just because she is *white,* ought to be treated by her as he surely will be, viz: as a NIGER!!!! It is not, indeed, what I care about inter-marriages with the whites, which induced me to pass this subject in review; for the Lord knows, that there is a day coming when they will be glad enough to get into the company of the blacks, notwithstanding, we are, in this generation, levelled by them, almost on a level with the brute creation: and some of us they treat even worse than they do the brutes that perish. I only made this extract to show how much lower we are held, and how much more cruel we are treated by the Americans, than were the children of Jacob, by the Egyptians.—We will notice the sufferings of Israel some further, under heathen Pharaoh, compared with ours under the christians of America.

"And Pharaoh spake unto Joseph, saying, thy "father and thy brethren are come unto thee:"

"The land of Egypt is before thee: in the best "of the land make thy father and brethren to dwell; "in the land of Goshen let them dwell: and if thou "knowest any men of activity among them, then "make them rulers over my cattle."*

I ask those people who treat us so *well,* Oh! I ask them, where is the most barren spot of land which they have given unto us? Israel had the most fertile land in all Egypt. Need I mention the very notorious fact, that I have known a poor man of colour, who laboured night and day, to acquire a little money, and having acquired it, he vested it in a small piece of land, and got him a house erected thereon, and having paid for the whole, he moved his family into it, where he was suffered to remain but nine months, when he was cheated out of his property by a white man, and driven out of door!—And is not this the case generally? Can a man of colour buy a piece of land and keep it peaceably? Will not some white man try to get it from him, even if it is in a *mud hole?* I need not comment any farther on a subject, which all, both black and

---

*Genesis, chap. xlvii. v. 5, 6.

white, will readily admit. But I must, really, observe that in this very city, when a man of colour dies, if he owned any real estate it most generally falls into the hands of some white person. The wife and children of the deceased may weep and lament if they please, but the estate will be kept snug enough by its white possessor.

But to prove farther that the condition of the Israelites was better under the Egyptians than ours is under the whites. I call upon the professing christians, I call upon the philanthropist, I call upon the very tyrant himself, to show me a page of history, either sacred or profane, on which a verse can be found, which maintains, that the Egyptians heaped the *insupportable insult* upon the children of Israel, by telling them that they were not of the *human family*. Can the whites deny this charge? Have they not, after having reduced us to the deplorable condition of slaves under their feet, held us up as descending originally from the tribes of *Monkeys* or *Orang-Outangs?* O! my God! I appeal to every man of feeling—is not this insupportable? Is it not heaping the most gross insult upon our miseries, because they have got us under their feet and we cannot help ourselves? Oh! pity us we pray thee, Lord Jesus, Master.— Has Mr. Jefferson declared to the world, that we are inferior to the whites, both in the endowments of our bodies and of minds? It is indeed surprising, that a man of such great learning, combined with such excellent natural parts, should speak so of a set of men in chains. I do not know what to compare it to, unless, like putting one wild deer in an iron cage, where it will be secured, and hold another by the side of the same, then let it go, and expect the one in the cage to run as fast as the one at liberty. So far, my brethren, were the Egyptians from heaping these insults upon their slaves, that Pharaoh's daughter took Moses, a son of Israel for her own, as will appear by the following.

"And Pharaoh's daughter said unto her, [Moses' "mother] take this child away, and nurse it for me, "and I will pay thee thy wages. And the woman "took the child [Moses] and nursed it.

"And the child grew, and she brought him unto "Pharaoh's daughter and he became her son. And "she called his name Moses: and she said because "I drew him out of the water."*

In all probability, Moses would have become Prince Regent to the throne, and no doubt, in process of time but he would have been seated on the throne of Egypt. But he had rather suffer shame, with the people of God, than to enjoy pleasures with that wicked people for a season. O! that the coloured people were long since of Moses' excellent disposition, instead of courting favor with, and telling news and lies to our *natural enemies,* against each other—aiding them to keep their hellish chains of slavery upon us. Would we not long before this time, have been respectable men, instead of such wretched victims of oppression as we are? Would they be able to drag our mothers, our fathers, our wives, our children and ourselves, around the world in chains and hand-cuffs as they do, to dig up gold and silver for them and theirs? This question, my brethren I leave for you to digest; and may God Almighty force it home to your hearts. Remember that unless you are united, keeping your

---

*See Exodus, chap. ii. v 9, 10.

tongues within your teeth, you will be afraid to trust your secrets to each other, and thus perpetuate our miseries under the *christians!!!!!!* [☞ADDITION.— Remember, also to lay humble at the feet of our Lord and Master Jesus Christ, with prayers and fastings. Let our enemies go on with their butcheries, and at once fill up their cup. Never make an attempt to gain our freedom or *natural right,* from under our cruel oppressors and murderers, until you see your way clear—when that hour arrives and you move, be not afraid or dismayed; for be you assured that Jesus Christ the king of heaven and of earth who is the God of justice and of armies, will surely go before you. And those enemies who have for hundreds of years stolen our *rights,* and kept us ignorant of Him and His divine worship, he will remove. Millions of whom, are this day, so ignorant and avaricious, that they cannot conceive how God can have an attribute of justice, and show mercy to us because it pleased Him to make us black—which colour, Mr. Jefferson calls unfortunate!!!!!! As though we are not as thankful to our God, for having made us as it pleased himself, as they, (the whites,) are for having made them white. They think because they hold us in their infernal chains of slavery, that we wish to be white, or of their colour—but they are dreadfully deceived—we wish to be just as it pleased our Creator to have made us, and no avaricious and unmerciful wretches, have any business to make slaves of, or hold us in slavery. How would they like for us to make slaves of, and hold them in cruel slavery, and murder them as they do us?—But is Mr. Jefferson's assertions true? viz. "that it is unfortunate for us that our Creator has been pleased to make us *black."* We will not take his say so, for the fact. The world will have an opportunity to see whether it is unfortunate for us, that our Creator *has made us* darker than the *whites.*

Fear not the number and education of our *enemies,* against whom we shall have to contend for our lawful right; guaranteed to us by our Maker; for why should we be afraid, when God is, and will continue, (if we continue humble) to be on our side?

The *man* who would not fight under our Lord and Master Jesus Christ, in the glorious and heavenly cause of freedom and of God—to be delivered from the most wretched, abject and servile slavery, that ever a people was afflicted with since the foundation of the world, to the present day—ought to be kept with all of his children or family, in slavery, or in chains, to be butchered by his cruel enemies.☜].

I saw a paragraph, a few years since, in a South Carolina paper, which, speaking of the barbarity of the Turks, it said: "The Turks are the most bar-"barous people in the world—they treat the Greeks "more like *brutes* than human beings." And in the same paper was an advertisement, which said:— "Eight well built Virginia and Maryland *Negro "fellows* and four *wenches* will positively be *sold* "this day, to the *highest bidder!"* And what astonished me still more was, to see in this same humane paper!! the cuts of three men, with clubs and budgets on their backs, and an advertisement offering a considerable sum of money for their apprehension and delivery. I declare, it is really so *funny* to hear the Southerners and Westerners of this country talk about *barbarity,* that it is positively, enough to make a man *smile.*

The sufferings of the Helots among the Spartans, were somewhat severe, it is true, but to say that theirs, were as severe as ours among the Americans, I do most strenuously deny—for instance, can any man show me an article on a page of ancient history which specifies, that, the Spartans chained, and hand-cuffed the Helots, and dragged them from their wives and children, children from their parents, mothers from their suckling babes, wives from their husbands, driving them from one end of the country to the other? Notice the Spartans were heathens, who lived long before our Divine Master made his appearance in the flesh. Can Christian Americans deny these barbarous cruelties? Have you not Americans, having subjected us under you, added to these miseries, by insulting us in telling us to our face, because we are helpless, that we are not of the human family? I ask you, O! Americans, I ask you, in the name of the Lord, can you deny these charges? Some perhaps may deny, by saying, that they never thought or said that we were not men. But do not actions speak louder than words?—have they not made provisions for the Greeks, and Irish? Nations who have never done the least thing for them, while *we,* who have enriched their country with our blood and tears— have dug up gold and silver for them and their children, from generation to generation, and are in more miseries than any other people under heaven, are not seen, but by comparatively, a handful of the American people? There are indeed, more ways to kill a dog, besides choaking it to death with butter. Further—The Spartans or Lacedemonians, had some frivolous pretext, for enslaving the Helots, for they (Helots) while being free inhabitants of Sparta, stirred up an intestine commotion, and were, by the Spartans subdued, and made prisoners of war. Consequently they and their children were condemned to perpetual slavery.*

I have been for years troubling the pages of historians, to find out what our fathers have done to the *white Christians of America,* to merit such condign punishment as they have inflicted on them, and do continue to inflict on us their children. But I must aver, that my researches have hitherto been to no effect. I have therefore, come to the immoveable conclusion, that they (Americans) have, and do continue to punish us for nothing else, but for enriching them and their country. For I cannot conceive of any thing else. Nor will I ever believe otherwise, until the Lord shall convince me.

The world knows, that slavery as it existed among the Romans, (which was the primary cause of their destruction) was, comparatively speaking, no more than a *cypher,* when compared with ours under the Americans. Indeed, I should not have noticed the Roman slaves, had not the very learned and penetrating Mr. Jefferson said, "when a master was "murdered, all his slaves in the same house, or "within hearing, were condemned to death."*—Here let me ask Mr. Jefferson, (but he is gone to answer at the bar of God, for the deeds done in his body while living,) I therefore ask the whole American people, had I not rather die, or be put to death, than to be a slave to any tyrant, who takes not only my own, but my wife and children's lives by the

---

*See Dr. Goldsmith's History of Greece — page 9. See also Plutarch's Lives. The Helots subdued by Agis, king of Sparta.

inches? Yea, would I meet death with avidity far! far!! in preference to such *servile submission* to the murderous hands of tyrants. Mr. Jefferson's very severe remarks on us have been so extensively argued upon by men whose attainments in literature, I shall never be able to reach, that I would not have meddled with it, were it not to solicit each of my brethren, who has the spirit of a man, to buy a copy of Mr. Jefferson's "Notes on Virginia," and put it in the hand of his son. For let no one of us suppose that the refutations which have been written by our white friends are enough—they are *whites*—we are *blacks*. We, and the world wish to see the charges of Mr. Jefferson refuted by the blacks *themselves,* according to their chance; for we must remember that what the whites have written respecting this subject, is other men's labors, and did not emanate from the blacks. I know well, that there are some talents and learning among the coloured people of this country, which we have not a chance to develope, in consequence of oppression; but our oppression ought not to hinder us from acquiring all we can.—For we will have a chance to develope them by and by. God will not suffer us, always to be oppressed. Our sufferings will come to an *end,* in spite of all the Americans this side of *eternity*. Then we will want all the learning and talents among ourselves, and perhaps more, to govern ourselves.—"Every dog must have its day," the American's is coming to an end.

But let us review Mr. Jefferson's remarks respecting us some further. Comparing our miserable fathers, with the learned philosophers of Greece, he says: "Yet notwithstanding these and other discouraging circumstances among the Romans, "their slaves were often their rarest artists. They "excelled too, in science, insomuch as to be usually employed as tutors to their master's children; "Epictetus, Terence and Phædrus, were slaves,—"but they were of the race of whites. It is not "their *condition* then, but *nature,* which has produced the distinction."* See this, my brethren!! Do you believe that this assertion is swallowed by millions of the whites? Do you know that Mr. Jefferson was one of as great characters as ever lived among the whites? See his writings for the world, and public labors for the United States of America. Do you believe that the assertions of such a man, will pass away into oblivion unobserved by this people and the world? If you do you are much mistaken— See how the American people treat us—have we souls in our bodies? are we men who have any spirits at all? I know that there are many *swell-bellied* fellows among us, whose greatest object is to fill their stomachs. Such I do not mean—I am after those who know and feel, that we are MEN, as well as other people; to them, I say, that unless we try to refute Mr. Jefferson's arguments respecting us, we will only establish them.

But the slaves among the Romans. Every body who has read history, knows, that as soon as a slave among the Romans obtained his freedom, he could rise to the greatest eminence in the State, and there was no law instituted to hinder a slave from buying his freedom. Have not the Americans instituted laws to hinder us from obtaining our freedom? Do any deny this charge? Read

See his Notes on Virginia, page 210.
*See his Notes on Virginia, page 211.

the laws of Virginia, North Carolina, &c. Further: have not the Americans instituted laws to prohibit a man of colour from obtaining and holding any office whatever, under the government of the United States of America? Now, Mr. Jefferson tells us, that our condition is not so hard, as the slaves were under the Romans!!!!!!

It is time for me to bring this article to a close. But before I close it, I must observe to my brethren that at the close of the first Revolution in this country, with Great Britain, there were but thirteen States in the Union, now there are twenty-four, most of which are slave-holding States, and the whites are dragging us around in chains and in handcuffs to their new States and Territories to work their mines and farms, to enrich them and their children— and millions of them believing firmly that we being a little darker than they, were made by our creator to be an inheritance to them and their children for-ever—the same as a parcel of *brutes!!!*

Are we MEN!!—I ask you, O my brethren! are we MEN? Did our creator make us to be slaves to dust and ashes like ourselves? Are they not dying worms as well as we? Have they not to make their appearance before the tribunal of heaven, to answer for the deeds done in the body, as well as we? Have we any other master but Jesus Christ alone? Is he not their master as well as ours?—What right then, have we to obey and call any other master, but Himself? How we could be so *submissive* to a gang of men, whom we cannot tell whether they are *as good* as ourselves or not, I never could con-ceive. However, this is shut up with the Lord and we cannot precisely tell— but I declare, we judge men by their works.

The whites have always been an unjust, jealous, unmerciful, avaricious and blood-thirsty set of beings, always seeking after power and authority.— We view them all over the confederacy of Greece, where they were first known to be any thing, (in consequence of education) we see them there, cutting each other's throats—trying to subject each other to wretchedness and misery —to effect which, they used all kinds of deceitful, unfair, and unmerciful means.—We view them next in Rome, where the spirit of tyranny and deceit raged still higher.—We view them in Gaul, Spain and in Britain—in fine, we view them all over Europe, together with what were scattered about in Asia and Africa, as heathens, and we see them acting more like devils than account-able men. But some may ask, did not the blacks of Africa, and the mullattoes of Asia, go on in the same way as did the whites of Europe. I answer, no— they never were half so avaricious, deceitful and unmerciful as the whites, according to their knowledge.

But we will leave the whites or Europeans as heathens and take a view of them as christians, in which capacity we see them as cruel, if not more so than ever. In fact, take them as a body, they are ten times more cruel, avari-cious and unmerciful than ever they were; for while they were heathens, they were bad enough it is true, but it is positively a fact that they were not quite so audacious as to go and take vessel loads of men, women and children, and in cold blood, and through devilishness, throw them into the sea, and murder them in all kind of ways. While they were heathens, they were too ignorant for such barbarity. But being christians, enlightened and sensible, they are completely prepared for such hellish cruelties. Now suppose God were to give them more sense, what would they do? If it were possible would they not *dethrone* Jehovah and seat themselves upon his throne? I therefore, in the name and fear of the Lord God of heaven and of earth, divested of prejudice either on the side of my colour or that of the whites, advance my suspicion of them, whether they are *as good by nature* as we are or not. Their actions, since they were known as a people, have been the reverse, I do indeed suspect them, but this, as I before observed, is shut up with the Lord, we cannot exactly tell, it will be proved in succeeding generations.—The whites have had the essence of the gospel as it was preached by my master and his apostles— the Etheopians have not, who are to have it in its meridean splendor—the Lord will give it to them to their satisfaction. I hope and pray my God, that they will make good use of it, that it may be well with them.

Walker's militant and radical philosophy caused dissonance among the black assimilationists who were anxious to maintain rapport with the white community in the North. While these blacks supported his goals and shared his antipathy toward slavery, they preferred a solution based on persuasion rather than revolution. An important exception to this general reaction was the attitude expressed by Henry Highland Garnet who proved to be one of the most eloquent assimilationists in the antebellum period. Throughout much of his career, Garnet was an aggressive moderate and a faithful advocate of the democratic process. Yet in 1843, he delivered the most memorable revolutionary speech ever given in the first half of the nineteenth century. The occasion was the convention of the Liberty Party, meeting in Buffalo, New York from August 15-19, 1843. The setting, the issues, and the audience gave Garnet the kind of challenge he needed to stimulate his imagination and trigger his eloquence. It was, observes Brewer, "the first time in American history that Negro citizens were actively in the leadership of a political convention."[22] Among those present were Charles Lenox Remond, Frederick Douglass, and Samuel Ward.

The attitudes and motives of the audience formed an important aspect of the rhetorical situation. All of them were dedicated abolitionists who wanted an early end to slavery. But they adhered to a conservative-liberal philosophy that gave precedence to moral suasion over revolutionary action. In short, they had little desire to endorse resolutions or addresses that might jeopardize their security, particularly in the border states. Garnet was fully aware of the prevailing sentiments of his listeners, but thought the exigencies of the situation required a drastic solution by the delegates. The time had come, he felt, to cast aside expedient circumstances — however compelling they appeared to be — and adopt a course of action rooted in definition or the essential nature of things. Within this philosophical framework, he developed his dramatic "Address to the Slaves of the United States of America."[23] Speaking first to the free Negroes of the North, he argued that it was not enough for them to continue their practice of rendering moral support to an enslaved people who for more than two hundred years had waited patiently for deliverance, only to see their wretchedness steadily increase. In language that transcended the primitive cry of Walker, Garnet next turned to the slaves, urging them to rise up against the institution that for so long had degraded them. "It is your solemn and imperative duty," he asserted, "to use every means, both moral, intellectual, and physical, that promises success." He then translated this generalized appeal into revolutionary language that few could misunderstand. "If you must bleed, let it all come at once — rather, *die freemen than live to be slaves.*" In his closing remarks Garnet importuned all slaves to accept the motto of "Resistance," and like Patrick Henry, Denmark Vesey, and Nat Turner seek liberty even if it meant death.

Garnet hoped that his rhetorical effort would cause the assembly to formally approve the revolutionary policy delineated in his address. He soon learned that the convention was deeply divided on the issue. Douglass, who strongly opposed any militant sentiments, rose to offer a refutation. He developed his reply around two major objections. First, the address was a war-like message that would encourage insurrection that perhaps would fail. Second, if it were adopted by the convention, delegates from the border states would be unable to return to their homes with safety. And this, added Douglass, "was what he wished in no way to have any agency in hurrying about and what we were called upon to avoid."[24] Others began to take the floor, reiterating Douglass' concern for the security of many of the delegates. When the vote for approval of Garnet's address was taken, the measure was defeated nineteen to eighteen. Later in the convention Douglass presented a report on abolition in which he included the words "moral suasion." Garnet immediately moved to strike the phrase from the report. But Douglass again prevailed on the motion.

In this dramatic encounter between two former slaves, Douglass was victorious; and for the next two decades he became the leading symbol of the abolition movement. Yet, in the long view, Garnet's address to the slaves turned out to be one of the most influential and durable documents in the history of the rhetoric of black Americans. One enthusiastic commentator wrote to the editor of the *Buffalo Commercial Advertiser,* saying:

> Here, Mr. Editor, was true eloquence — the ridiculous, the pathetic, the indignant, all called into irresistible action; and I cannot but think, that had it been one of our white orators instead of Garnet, he would have been lauded to the skies.[25]

More significant was the impact of the address on John Brown who printed and distributed it at his own expense. It is interesting to note that the Harper's Ferry Raid sixteen years later "was a concrete attempt to test the possibilities of liberating the slaves."[26]

Garnet himself was overjoyed by the persistent popularity of his plea. In 1848, he edited a volume containing Walker's *Appeal* and his own address to the slaves. He said in the Preface:

> The Address was rejected by a small majority; and now in compliance with the earnest request of many who heard it, and in conformity to the wishes of numerous friends who are anxious to see it, the author now gives it to the public, praying God that this little book may be borne on the four winds of heaven, until the principles it contains shall be understood and adopted by every slave in the Union.[27]

Later testimonials by blacks who knew Garnet confirmed the judgment of those who urged its publication in 1848. William Wells Brown in 1863 called it "one of the most noted addresses ever given by a colored man in this country. . . ."[28] Even more laudatory was Alexander Crummell's claim that "the Buffalo speech . . . was equal, as an oratorical effort, to anything which has ever been heard on the American continent. . . . Opinion is unanimous that nothing like it had fallen upon the ears of its auditory in this generation."[29]

If the Garnet address stands as a landmark in the abolition movement, it also has meaning for the contemporary revolutionary emphasis sometimes used in the current civil rights struggle. A close reading of this speech included below shows that the rhetorical exigencies facing Garnet in 1843 have, despite the formal elimination of slavery, persisted through the years.

Henry Highland Garnet
Address to The Slaves of The U. S.*

BRETHREN AND FELLOW CITIZENS:
Your brethren of the north, east, and west have been accustomed to meet together in National Conventions, to sympathize with each other, and to weep over your unhappy condition. In these meetings we have addressed all classes of the free, but we have never until this time, sent a word of consolation and advice to you. We have been contented in sitting still and mourning over your sorrows, earnestly hoping that before this day, your sacred liberties would have been restored. But, we have hoped in vain. Years have rolled on, and tens of thousands have been borne on streams of blood, and tears, to the shores of eternity. While you have been oppressed, we have also been partakers with you; nor can we be free while you are enslaved. We therefore write to you as being bound with you.

Many of you are bound to us, not only by the ties of a common humanity, but we are connected by the more tender relations of parents, wives, husbands, children, brothers, and sisters, and friends. As such we most affectionately address you.

Slavery has fixed a deep gulf between you and us, and while it shuts out from you the relief and consolation which your friends would willingly render, it afflicts and persecutes you with a fierceness which we might not expect to see in the fiends of hell. But still the Almighty Father of Mercies has left to us a glimmering ray of hope, which shines out like a lone star in a cloudy sky. Mankind are becoming wiser, and better—the oppressor's power is fading and you, every day, are becoming better informed, and more numerous. Your grievances, brethren, are many. We shall not attempt, in this short address, to present to the world, all the dark catalogue of this nation's sins, which have been committed upon an innocent people. Nor is it indeed, necessary, for you feel them from day to day, and all the civilized world look upon them with amazement.

Two hundred and twenty-seven years ago, the first of our injured race were brought to the shores of America. They came not with glad spirits to select their homes, in the New World. They came not with their own consent, to find an unmolested enjoyment of the blessings of this fruitful soil. The first dealings which they had with men calling themselves Christians, exhibited to them the worst features of corrupt and sordid hearts; and convinced them that no cruelty is too great, no villainy, and no robbery too abhorrent for even enlightened men to perform, when influenced by avarice, and lust. Neither did they come flying upon the wings of Liberty, to a land of freedom. But, they came with broken hearts, from their beloved native land, and were doomed to unrequited toil, and deep degradation. Nor did the evil of their bondage end

---

*From Henry Highland Garnet, *Walker's Appeal with a Brief Sketch of his Life by Henry Highland Garnet and also Garnet's Address to the Slaves of the United States of America* (New York: J.H.Tobitt, 1848), p. 90-96.

at their emancipation by death. Succeeding generations inherited their chains, and millions have come from eternity into time, and have returned again to the world of spirits, cursed, and ruined by American Slavery.

The propagators of the system, or their immediate ancestors very soon discovered its growing evil, and its tremendous wickedness, and secret promises were made to destroy it. The gross inconsistency of a people holding slaves, who had themselves "ferried o'er the wave," for freedom's sake, was too apparent to be entirely overlooked. The voice of Freedom cried, "emancipate your Slaves." Humanity supplicated with tears, for the deliverance of the children of Africa. Wisdom urged her solemn plea. The bleeding captive plead his innocence, and pointed to Christianity who stood weeping at the cross. Jehovah frowned upon the nefarious institution, and thunderbolts, red with vengeance, struggled to leap forth to blast the guilty wretches who maintained it. But all was vain. Slavery had stretched its dark wings of death over the land, the Church stood silently by—the priests prophesied falsely, and the people loved to have it so. Its throne is established, and now it reigns triumphantly.

Nearly three millions of your fellow citizens, are prohibited by law, and public opinion, (which in this country is stronger than law), from reading the Book of Life. Your intellect has been destroyed as much as possible, and every ray of light they have attempted to shut out from your minds. The oppressors themselves have become involved in the ruin. They have become weak, sensual, and rapacious. They have cursed you—they have cursed themselves—they have cursed the earth which they have trod. In the language of a Southern statesman, we can truly say, "even the wolf, driven back long since by the approach of man, now returns after the lapse of a hundred years, and howls amid the desolations of slavery."

The colonists threw the blame upon England. They said that the mother country entailed the evil upon them, and that they would rid themselves of it if they could. The world thought they were sincere, and the philanthropic pitied them. But time soon tested their sincerity. In a few years, the colonists grew strong and severed themselves from the British Government. Their Independence was declared, and they took their station among the sovereign powers of the earth. The declaration was a glorious document. Sages admired it, and the patriotic of every nation reverenced the Godlike sentiments which it contained. When the power of Government returned to their hands, did they emancipate the slaves? No; they rather added new links to our chains. Were they ignorant of the principles of Liberty? Certainly they were not. The sentiments of their revolutionary orators fell in burning eloquence upon their hearts, and with one voice they cried, LIBERTY OR DEATH. O, what a sentence was that! It ran from soul to soul like electric fire, and nerved the arm of thousands to fight in the holy cause of Freedom. Among the diversity of opinions that are entertained in regard to physical resistance, there are but a few found to gainsay that stern declaration. We are among those who do not.

SLAVERY! How much misery is comprehended in that single word. What mind is there that does not shrink from its direful effects? Unless the image of God is obliterated from the soul, all men cherish the love of Liberty. The nice discerning political economist does not regard the sacred right, more than the untutored African who roams in the wilds of Congo. Nor has the one more right to the full enjoyment of his freedom than the other. In every man's mind the good seeds of liberty are planted, and he who brings his fellow down so low, as to make him contented with a condition of slavery, commits the highest crime against God and man. Brethren, your oppressors aim to do this. They endeavor to make you as much like brutes as possible. When they have blinded the eyes of your mind—when they have embittered the sweet waters of life—when they have shut out the light which shines from the word of God—then, and not till then has American slavery done its perfect work.

To such degradation it is sinful in the extreme for you to make voluntary submission. The divine commandments, you are in duty bound to reverence, and obey. If you do not obey them you will surely meet with the displeasure of the Almighty. He requires you to love him supremely, and your neighbor as yourself—to keep the Sabbath day holy—to search the Scriptures —and bring up your children with respect for his laws, and to worship no other God but him. But slavery sets all these at naught, and hurls defiance in the face of Jehovah. The forlorn condition in which you are placed does not destroy your moral obligation to God. You are not certain of Heaven, because you suffer yourselves to remain in a state of slavery, where you cannot obey the commandments of the Sovereign of the universe. If the ignorance of slavery is a passport to heaven, then it is a blessing, and no curse, and you should rather desire its perpetuity than its abolition. God will not receive slavery, nor ignorance, nor any other state of mind, for love, and obedience to him. Your condition does not absolve you from your moral obligation. The diabolical injustice by which your liberties are cloven down, NEITHER GOD, NOR ANGELS, OR JUST MEN, COMMAND YOU TO SUFFER FOR A SINGLE MOMENT. THEREFORE IT IS YOUR SOLEMN AND IMPERATIVE DUTY TO USE EVERY MEANS, BOTH MORAL, INTELLECTUAL, AND PHYSICAL, THAT PROMISE SUCCESS. If a band of heathen men should attempt to enslave a race of Christians, and to place their children under the influence of some false religion, surely, heaven would frown upon the men who would not resist such aggression, even to death. If, on the other hand, a band of Christians should attempt to enslave a race of heathen men and to entail slavery upon them, and to keep them in heathenism in the midst of Christianity, the God of heaven would smile upon every effort which the injured might make to disenthral themselves.

Brethren, it is as wrong for your lordly oppressors to keep you in slavery, as it was for the man thief to steal our ancestors from the coast of Africa. You should therefore now use the same manner of resistance, as would have been just in our ancestors, when the bloody foot prints of the first remorseless soul thief was placed upon the shores of our fatherland. The humblest peasant is as free in the sight of God, as the proudest monarch that ever swayed a sceptre. Liberty is a spirit sent out from God, and like its great Author, is no respector of persons.

Brethren, the time has come when you must act for yourselves. It is an old and true saying, that "if hereditary bondmen would be free, they must themselves strike the blow." You can plead your own cause, and do the work of emancipation better than any others. The nations of the old world are moving in the great cause of universal freedom, and some of them at least, will ere long, do you justice. The combined powers of Europe have placed their broad seal of disapprobation upon the African slave trade. But in the slave holding parts of the United States, the trade is as brisk as ever. They buy and sell you as though you were brute beasts. The North has done much—her opinion of slavery in the abstract is known. But in regard to the South, we adopt the opinion of the New York Evangelist—"We have advanced so far, that the cause apparently waits for a more effectual door to be thrown open than has been yet." We are about to point you to that more effectual door. Look around you, and behold the bosoms of your loving wives, heaving with untold agonies! Hear the cries of your poor children! Remember the stripes your fathers bore. Think of the torture and disgrace of your noble mothers. Think of your wretched sisters, loving virtue and purity, as they are driven into concubinage, and are exposed to the unbridled lusts of incarnate devils. Think of the undying glory that hangs around the ancient name of Africa:— and forget not that you are native-born American citizens, and as such, you are justly entitled to all the rights that are granted to the freest. Think how many tears you have poured out upon the soil which you have cultivated with unrequited toil, and enriched with your blood; and then go to your lordly enslavers, and tell them plainly, that YOU ARE DETERMINED TO BE FREE. Appeal to their sense of justice, and tell them that they have no more right to oppress you, than you have to enslave them. Entreat them to remove the grievous burdens which they have imposed upon you, and to remunerate you for your labor. Promise them renewed diligence in the cultivation of the soil, if they will render to you an equivalent for your services. Point them to the increase of happiness and prosperity in the British West Indies, since the act of Emancipation. Tell them in language which they cannot misunderstand, of the exceeding sinfulness of slavery, and of a future judgment, and of the righteous retributions of an indignant God. Inform them that all you desire, is FREEDOM, and that nothing else will suffice. Do this, and for ever after cease to toil for the heartless tyrants, who give you no other reward but stripes and abuse. If they then commence the work of death, they, and not you, will be responsible for the consequences. You had far better all die—*die immediately,* than live slaves, and entail your wretchedness upon your posterity. If you would be free in this generation, here is your only hope. However much you and all of us may desire it, there is not much hope of Redemption without the shedding of blood. If you must bleed, let it all come at once—rather, *die free-men, than live to be slaves.* It is impossible, like the children of Israel, to make a grand Exodus from the land of bondage. THE PHARAOHS ARE ON BOTH SIDES OF THE BLOOD-RED WATERS! You cannot remove en masse to the dominions of the British Queen—nor can you pass through Florida, and overrun Texas, and at last find peace in Mexico. The propagators of American slavery are spending their blood and treasure, that they may plant the black flag in the heart of Mexico, and riot in the halls of the Montezumas. In the language of the Rev. Robert Hall, when addressing the volunteers of Bristol, who were rushing forth to repel the invasion of Napoleon, who threatened to lay waste the fair homes of England, "Religion is too much interested in your behalf, not to shed over you her most gracious influences."

You will not be compelled to spend much time in order to become inured to hardships. From the first moment that you breathed the air of heaven, you have been accustomed to nothing else but hardships. The heroes of the American Revolution were never put upon harder fare, than a peck of corn, and a few herrings per week. You have not become enervated by the luxuries of life. Your sternest energies have been beaten out upon the anvil of severe trial. Slavery has done this, to make you subservient to its own purposes; but it has done more than this, it has prepared you for any emergency. If you receive good treatment, it is what you could hardly expect; if you meet with pain, sorrow, and even death, these are the common lot of the slaves.

Fellow-men! patient sufferers! behold your dearest rights crushed to the earth! See your sons murdered, and your wives, mothers, and sisters, doomed to prostitution! In the name of the merciful God! and by all that life is worth, let it no longer be a debateable question, whether it is better to choose LIBERTY or DEATH!

In 1822, Denmark Veazie, of South Carolina, formed a plan for the liberation of his fellow men. In the whole history of human efforts to overthrow slavery, a more complicated and tremendous plan was never formed. He was betrayed by the treachery of his own people, and died a martyr to freedom. Many a brave hero fell, but History, faithful to her high trust, will transcribe his name on the same monument with Moses, Hampden, Tell, Bruce, and Wallace, Touissaint L'Overteur, Lafayette and Washington. That tremendous movement shook the whole empire of slavery. The guilty soul thieves were overwhelmed with fear. It is a matter of fact, that at that time, and in consequence of the threatened revolution, the slave states talked strongly of emancipation. But they blew but one blast of the trumpet of freedom, and then laid it aside. As these men became quiet, the slaveholders ceased to talk about emancipation: and now, behold your condition to-day! Angels sigh over it, and humanity has long since exhausted her tears in weeping on your account!

The patriotic Nathaniel Turner followed Denmark Veazie. He was goaded to desperation by wrong and injustice. By Despotism, his name has been recorded on the list of infamy, but future generations will number him among the noble and brave.

Next arose the immortal Joseph Cinque, the hero of the Amistad. He was a native African, and by the help of God he emancipated a whole ship-load of his fellow men on the high seas. And he now sings of liberty on the sunny hills of Africa, and beneath his native palm trees, where he hears the lion roar, and feels himself as free as that king of the forest. Next arose Madison Washington, that bright star of freedom, and took his station in the constellation of freedom. He was a slave on board the brig Creole, of Richmond, bound to New Orleans, that great slave mart, with a hundred and four others. Nineteen struck for liberty or death. But one life was taken, and the whole were emancipated, and the vessel was carried into Nassau, New Providence.

Noble men! Those who have fallen in freedom's conflict, their memories will be cherished by the true hearted, and the God-fearing, in all future generations; those who are living, their names are surrounded by a halo of glory.

We do not advise you to attempt a revolution with the sword, because it would be INEXPEDIENT. Your numbers are too small, and moreover the rising spirit of the age, and the spirit of the gospel, are opposed to war and bloodshed. But from this moment cease to labor for tyrants who will not remunerate you. Let every slave throughout the land do this, and the days of slavery are numbered. You cannot be more oppressed than you have been—you cannot suffer greater cruelties than you have already. RATHER DIE FREEMEN, THAN LIVE TO BE SLAVES. Remember that you are THREE MILLIONS.

It is in your power so to torment the God-cursed slaveholders, that they will be glad to let you go free. If the scale was turned, and black men were the masters, and white men the slaves, every destructive agent and element would be employed to lay the oppressor low. Danger and death would hang over their heads day and night. Yes, the tyrants would meet with plagues more terrible than those of Pharaoh. But you are a patient people. You act as though you were made for the special use of these devils. You act as though your daughters were born to pamper the lusts of your masters and overseers. And worse than all, you tamely submit, while your lords tear your wives from your embraces, and defile them before your eyes. In the name of God we ask, are you men? Where is the blood of your fathers? Has it all run out of your veins? Awake, awake; millions of voices are calling you! Your dead fathers speak to you from their graves. Heaven, as with a voice of thunder, calls on you to arise from the dust.

Let your motto be RESISTANCE! RESISTANCE! RESISTANCE!—No oppressed people have ever secured their liberty without resistance. What kind of resistance you had better make, you must decide by the circumstances that surround you, and according to the suggestion of expediency. Brethren, adieu. Trust in the living God. Labor for the peace of the human race, and remember that you are three millions.

Samuel Ringgold Ward,[30] who was present when Garnet delivered his provocative convention address, was not ready to condone revolutionary action that might lead to increased tension and impede the progress of civil rights. A former slave and successful Presbyterian minister to a predominantly white congregation in New York, he, like Douglass, was an abolitionist committed to assimilation. During the decades of the 1840's he projected his doctrine of freedom and equality "in every church, hall, or school house in Western and Central New York."[31] In the winter and spring of 1850, however, he viewed with consternation the provisions of the compromise measures being debated in the United States Senate. He was particularly distressed about the proviso requiring the return of fugitive slaves, for it meant that he and other escapees would be returned to their southern masters. Such precipitous action, he believed, was contrary to the laws of God and to the inherent rights of man, and would, if sanctioned, dampen the hope for emancipation. He was pained, therefore, when Daniel Webster — an orator to whom Ward was often compared — gave his Seventh of March Speech supporting the compromise. These events convinced Ward that resistance to the pending fugitive slave law must, if necessary, take the form of open revolt.

With his newly acquired militant stance, Ward began a campaign to heighten the zeal of abolitionists, encouraging them to revolt rather than submit to injudicious acts passed by Congress. On April 3, 1850, he condemned the orthodox churches in America for lacking the courage to take a Biblical stand on the subject of slavery and segregation:

> I grieve to say, but the truth must be plainly spoken. . . . The church in the present day . . . has refused to be what the Corinthian church was, a laborer together with God on this great subject, and as there is no medium ground betwixt the two; that very refusing makes her the co-worker of Satan.[32]

Two days later Ward went to Boston and addressed a protest rally at Faneuil Hall comprised largely of New England abolitionists who had become disenchanted with Webster. His reputation as a convincing orator added to the receptivity of the audience. Many of his listeners who had known him through the years regarded him as "the black Daniel Webster."[33] Standing over six feet and possessing a manly, resonant voice and energetic gestures, he appealed to the intellect, rather than to the emotions.[34] Of all the black orators he had ever heard, Frederick Douglass ranked Ward as the most impressive. Shortly after Ward's death, Douglass observed:

> As an orator, and thinker he was vastly superior, I thought, to any of us, and being perfectly black and of unmixed African descent, the splendors of his intellect went directly to the glory of race. In depth of thought, fluency of speech, readiness of wit, logical exactness, and general intelligence, Samuel R. Ward has left no successor among the colored men amongst us, and it was a sad day for our cause when he was laid low in the soil of a foreign country.[35]

All of his talents as an orator were present as Ward spoke on this occasion. The brief speech, published in its entirety below, is a ringing indictment against the Fugitive Slave Bill. Observe how

Ward disarms his audience at the outset by meeting them on common ground. Then, building his case slowly against the bill, he weaves into his discourse a strong attack on the issue at hand. At the same time, he cleverly uses ridicule to weaken the ethos of Webster. It is especially instructive to note that not until his closing line does he offer as a potential solution, the need for revolution. The feedback, measured by the reporter's marginal statements on the manuscript, suggests that Ward created a strong favorable response.

Samuel R. Ward
Speech on the Fugitive Slave Bill*

I am here tonight simply as a guest. You have met here to speak of the sentiments of a Senator of your State whose remarks you have the honor to repudiate. In the course of the remarks of the gentleman who preceded me, he has done us the favor to make honorable mention of a Senator of my own State— Wm. H. Seward. [Three hearty cheers were given for Senator Seward.]

I thank you for this manifestation of approbation of a man who has always stood head and shoulders above his party, and who has never receded from his position on the question of slavery. It was my happiness to receive a letter from him a few days since, in which he said he never would swerve from his position as the friend of freedom. [Applause.]

To be sure, I agree not with Senator Seward in politics, but when an individual stands up for the rights of men against slaveholders, I care not for party distinctions. He is my brother. [Loud cheers.]

We have here much of common cause and interest in this matter. That infamous bill of Mr. Mason, of Virginia, proves itself to be like all other propositions presented by Southern men. It finds just enough of Northern doughfaces who are willing to pledge themselves, if you will pardon the uncouth language of a backwoodsman, to lick up the spittle of the slavocrats, and swear it is delicious. [Applause]

You of the old Bay State—a State to which many of us are accustomed to look as to our fatherland, just as well look back to England as our mother country—you have a Daniel who has deserted the cause of freedom. We, too, in New York, have a 'Daniel who has come to judgment,' only he don't come quite fast enough to the right kind of judgment. [Tremendous enthusiasm.] Daniel S. Dickinson represents some one, I suppose in the State of New York;

---

*Samuel R. Ward, "Speech on the Fugitive Slave Bill." From *The Liberator*, April 5, 1850.

God knows, he doesn't represent me. I can pledge you that our Daniel will stand cheek by jowl with your Daniel. [Cheers.] He was never known to surrender slavery, but always to surrender liberty.

The bill of which you most justly complain, concerning the surrender of fugitive slaves, is to apply alike to your State and to our State, if it shall ever apply at all. But we have come here to make a common oath upon a common altar, that that bill shall never take effect. [Applause.] Honorable Senators may record their names in its behalf, and it may have the sanction of the House of Representatives; but we, the people, who are superior to both Houses and the Executive, too [hear! hear!], we, the people, will never be human bipeds, to howl upon the track of the fugitive slave, even though led by the corrupt Daniel of your State, or the degraded one of ours. [Cheers.]

Though there are many attempts to get up compromises—and there is no term which I detest more than this, it is always the term which makes right yield to wrong; it has always been accursed since Eve made the first compromise with the devil. [Repeated rounds of applause.] I was saying, sir, that it is somewhat singular, and yet historically true, that whensoever these compromises are proposed, there are men of the North who seem to forsee that Northern men, who think their constituency will not look into these matters, will seek to do more than the South demands. They seek to prove to Northern men that all is right and all is fair; and this is the game Webster is attempting to play.

'Oh,' says Webster, 'the will of God has fixed that matter, we will not re-enact the will of God.' Sir, you remember the time in 1841, '42, '43 and '44, when it was said that Texas could never be annexed. The design of such dealing was that you should believe it, and then, when you thought yourselves secure, they would spring the trap upon you. And now it is their wish to seduce you into the belief that slavery never will go there, and then the slave-holders will drive slavery there as fast as possible. I think that this is the most contemptible proposition of the whole, except the support of that bill which would attempt to make the whole North the slave-catchers of the South.

You will remember that that bill of Mr. Mason says nothing about color. Mr. Phillips, a man whom I always loved [applause], a man who taught me my horn-book on this subject of slavery, when I was a poor boy, has referred to Marshfield. There is a man who sometimes lives in Marshfield, and who has the reputation of having an honorable dark skin. Who knows but that some postmaster may have to sit upon the very gentleman whose character you have been discussing tonight? [Hear! Hear!] 'What is sauce for the goose is sauce for the gander.' [Laughter.] If this bill is to relieve grievances, why not make an application to the immortal Daniel of Marshfield? [Applause.] There is no such thing as complexion mentioned. It is not only true that the colored man of Massachusetts—it is not only true that the fifty thousand colored men of New York may be taken—though I pledge you there is one, whose name is Sam Ward, who will never be taken alive. [Tremendous applause.] Not only is it true that the fifty thousand black men in New York may be taken, but any one else also can be captured. My friend Theodore Parker alluded to Ellen Crafts. I had the pleasure of taking tea with her, and accompanied her here to-night. She is far whiter than many who come here slave-catching. This line of distinction is so nice that you cannot tell who is white or black. As Alexander Pope used to say, 'White and black soften and blend in so many thousand ways, that it is neither white nor black.' [Loud plaudits.]

This is the question, Whether a man has a right to himself and his children, his hopes and his happiness, for this world and the world to come. That is the question which, according to this bill, may be decided by any backwoods postmaster in this State or any other. Oh, this is a monstrous proposition; and I do thank God that if the Slave Power has such demands to make on us, that the proposition has come now—now, that the people know what is being done—now that the public mind is turned toward this subject—now that they are trying to find what is the truth on this subject.

Sir, what must be the moral influence of this speech of Mr. Webster on the minds of young men, lawyers and others, here in the North? They turn their eyes towards Daniel Webster as towards a superior mind, and a legal and constitutional oracle. If they shall catch the spirit of this speech, its influence upon them and upon following generations will be so deeply corrupting that it never can be wiped out or purged.

I am thankful that this, my first entrance into Boston, and my first introduction to Faneuil Hall, gives me the pleasure and privilege of uniting with you in uttering my humble voice against the two Daniels, and of declaring, in behalf of our people, that if the fugitive slave is traced to our part of New York State, he shall have the law of Almighty God to protect him, the law which says, 'Thou shalt not return to the master the servant that is escaped unto thee, but he shall dwell with thee in thy gates, where it liketh him best.' And if our postmasters cannot maintain their constitutional oaths, and cannot live without playing the pander to the slave-hunter, they need not live at all. Such crises as these leave us to the right of Revolution, and if need be, that right we will, at whatever cost, most sacredly maintain.

With the passage of the compromise measures in the fall of 1850, Ward and other fugitives escaped to Canada where they continued their abolitionist activities. The compromise had blunted the thrust of the revolutionists. For the next decade black Americans waited while the assimilationists held center stage. The advent of the war in 1861, however, was an event that altered the perception of free Negroes in the North. The conflict moved the idea of revolution from an unfavorable to favorable position on the attitude scale. Thus, William Wells Brown, in the conclusion of his portrait on Nat Turner in 1863, was able to say:

Thirty years' free discussion has materially changed public opinion in the non-slaveholding states, and a negro insurrection, in the present excited state of the nation, would not receive the condemnation that it did in 1831. The right of man to the enjoyment of freedom is a settled point; and where he is deprived of this, without any criminal act of his own, it is his duty to regain his liberty at every cost. If the oppressor is struck down in the contest, his fall will be a just one, and all the world will applaud the act. This is a new era, and we are in the midst of the most important crisis that our country has yet witnessed. And in the crisis the negro is an important item. Every eye is now turned towards the south, looking for another Nat Turner.[36]

But the superior strength of the Union Army obviated the need for another Nat Turner. Within four years the war was over, and the dream of the black revolutionists — the permanent elimination of slavery — had become a reality.

BLACK RHETORIC AND THE MODERN REVOLUTION

The emancipation and physical, social, economic, and political punishment of white men in the South gave extraordinary force to the rhetoric of the black assimilationists. Never before had the arguments predicting the ultimate integration of black men into the mainstream of America had such substantial evidence. As the preceding chapter suggests, however, there remained a significant group of black Americans who were unconvinced of the possibility or desirability of life intertwined with the whites. There were others, few at first and many today, who felt the revolt had not gone far enough. They observed the speed with which white exploiters rushed into the vacuum created by the war, seeking profit wherever it might be found. With incredible speed the white man re-established his control, through terror, violence, and finally through legal channels. Franklin advances this conclusion:

> Peace had not yet come to the South. The new century opened tragically with 214 lynchings in the first two years. Clashes between the races occurred almost daily, and the atmosphere of tension in which people of both races lived was conducive to little more than a struggle for mere survival, with a feeble groping in the direction of progress. The law, the courts, the schools, and almost every institution in the South favored the white man. This was White Supremacy.[37]

To some black men these were ominous signs. There was evidence to suggest that assimilation was out of the question under the conditions of white supremacy, and even separation would amount to little more than acceptance of a caste system with the black man at the level of the untouchables. The evil, it seemed to some, was a system which allowed these power relationships to exist; which, indeed, was designed to reward the man who could take advantage of his fellowmen. The indicated remedy for this evil, they thought, is revolution—the overturning of the power structure and the establishment of new values, power relationships, and rewards; in other words, a new approach to humanity.

To contemporary Americans who are shocked and dismayed to discover strong socialist and communist ideologies among black citizens, it may be comforting to learn that these beliefs did not require the inspiration of the Soviet Union. On the contrary, during the last half of the nineteenth century, T. Thomas Fortune perceived the role of the black man in America as similar to laboring and peasant classes everywhere who were also oppressed by a tyranny of "land monopoly" and "corporation greed." James M. McPherson, professor of History at Princeton University, describes Fortune as a follower of Marx, and Henry George, born in 1856 and founder of the leading black newspaper, the New York *Age,* during the 1880's and 90's.[38]

Setting a pattern which will be useful in studying contemporary revolutionists, Fortune identified white oppression as the key factor behind an evil system. What he called a "spirit of injustice inborn in the Caucasian nature" led persons of African descent to be considered aliens within this country and like the American Indian, suitable for exploitation. Even at the time of emancipation, believed Fortune, a majority of whites did not desire to see the slave freed.[39] The white man, however, was not the ultimate evil. To remove him and leave the system which made it possible for landlords or owners to grow rich through the labor of their tenants, and capitalists to gain by making their useless capital valuable through the labor of the poor, would be to stop short of full remedy.[40] Fortune directly attacked a capitalistic materialism which was to become an increasingly typical part of American culture.

> A people's greatness should be measured, not by its magnificant palaces, decked out in all the gaudy splendors of art and needless luxuries . . . not in the number of colossal fortunes accumulated out of the stipend of the orphan and widow and the son of toil; . . . not in the vast aggregations of capital in the coffers of the common treasury. . . . A people's greatness should not be measured by these standards, for they are the parasites which eat away the foundations of greatness and stability. On the contrary, such greatness is to be found in the general diffusion of wealth, the comparative contentment and competency of the masses, and the general virtue and patriotism of the *whole* people.[41]

Thus, Fortune envisioned the establishment of a socialist state. His means of achieving it began with his idea that it could be best accomplished through a coalition between blacks and oppressed whites, a point of conflict among contemporary revolutionaries. The idea was unpopular even then as this comment indicates:

> I may stand alone in the opinion that the best interests of the race and the best interests of the country will be conserved by building up a bond of union between the white people and the negroes of the South — advocating the doctrine that the interests of the white and the interests of the colored people are one and the same . . .[42]

Beyond the coalition, of course, lay revolution. In stating this clearly and without flinching, Fortune set a rhetorical pattern frequently used today: he spoke what he believed to be the truth; i.e., he told it "like it is." He observed that telling the truth was not popular among economic writers, but he felt that when "the wail of distress encircles the world" those who hate injustice and sympathize with the "distressed, the weak, and the friendless . . . [are] morally bound to tell the truth. . . ."[43] The truth he told was of the inevitability of violent revolution: "The fires of revolution are incorporated into the *Magna Charta* of our liberties, and no human power can avert the awful eruption which will eventually burst upon us. . . . It is too late for America to be wise in time. *'The die is cast.' "*[44]

In the two fragments of revolutionary rhetoric included below, Fortune presents two fundamental ideas — that revolution is necessary and inevitable, and that revolution is justifiable, even desirable. His idea is simple, but it is the essential rationale of revolution. Nature and society are in such a constant state of process that there necessarily will be positive advancement or positive decline. In the course of this process, Fortune claims, it is inevitable that conflict will occur, for without the conflict that comes from the clashing of those seeking opposite paths, no growth is possible. Fortune even suggests that all positive advancement has come from revolution.

The agitator is an inextricable part of the process of revolution. Thus, Fortune defines his own rhetorical role. His review of the agitators of the past shows a broad study, and a willingness to associate great white activists with great black heroes such as Nat Turner. In much of what he says, Fortune shows a remarkable capacity for anticipating the rhetoric of contemporary America. His use of the prestige and moral character of Jesus Christ to justify revolution is similar to the rhetoric of the Reverend Albert

B. Cleage, Jr. today. Even his observation that an agitator must never be in advance of his times is extraordinary in that he apparently described himself: in spite of all his rhetoric, Fortune did not bring on a revolution. In fact, the Era of Booker T. Washington emerged, and the next significant surge of revolutionary rhetoric did not come until the present day. But before turning to that, note T. Thomas Fortune's arguments in justification of revolution and agitation.

T. Thomas Fortune
The Logic of Revolutions*

Revolutions are of many sorts. They are either silent and unobservable, noiseless, as the movement of the earth on its axis, or loud and destructive, shaking the earth from centre to circumference, making huge gaps in the map of the earth, changing the face of empires, subverting dynasties and breaking fetters asunder or rivetting them anew. Agitators are inevitable. They are as necessary to social organism as blood is to animal organism. Revolutions follow as a matter of course. Each link in the long chain of human progress is indelibly marked as the result of a revolution. The thunder-storm clarifies the atmosphere and infuses into the veins of all animal life new vigor and new hope. Revolutions clarify the social and civil atmosphere. They sober the nation; they sharpen the wits of the people; they make rights and privileges which have been the bone of contention all the more precious, because of the labor severe which consecrated them anew to ourselves and our posterity. The benefits that come to us as rewards of our genius, untiring industry, and frugality are more highly and justly prized than benefits that come to us by indirection and without our seeking. The aspirations of the human soul, like the climbing vine, are forever in the line of greater freedom, fuller knowledge, and ampler possessions. These aspirations find always opposing aspirations. It is true of nations seeking greater reforms. To accomplish these, agitations are necessary. The revolutionary institutions of mankind are fundamental and sleepless. It is the discontent, the restlessness, the sleepless aspiration of humanity, voiced by some braver, some more far-seeing member of society, some man ready to be a martyr to his faith or wear a crown of victory, which keep the world in a ferment of excitement and expectancy, and which force the adoption of those reforms which keep society from retrograding to the

---

*T. Thomas Fortune, "The Logic of Revolutions." This statement and the following one are reprinted from the Alexander Crummell Scrapbook in the Schomburg Collection, Harlem Branch, New York Public Library, New York City, New York. Neither statement is dated, and there are no indications that they were published in written form. They probably represent Fortune's most radical period, around 1890.

conditions of savage life from which it has slowly and painfully moved forward. There can be no middle ground in social life. There must be positive advancement or positive decline.

The Agitator and his Mission

"The world has been rocked in the cradle of agitation from Moses to Gladstone. The normal condition of mankind is one of perpetual change, arrest, and aspiration—a contention of the virtues against the vices of mankind. The great moving and compelling influence in the history of the world is agitation, and the greatest of agitators was He, the despised Nazarene, whose doctrines have revolutionized the thought of the ages. The progress of mankind has been greatest in eras of most unrest and innovation. Iconoclasm has always been the watchword of progress. It is a narrow and perverted philosophy which condemns as a nuisance agitators. Demosthenes, thundering against the designs of Philip of Macedon upon the liberties of Greece; Cicero holding up to scorn and ridicule the schemes of Cataline against the freedom of Rome; Oliver Cromwell baring his sturdy breast to the arrows of royalty and nobility to preserve to Englishmen the rights contained in the Magna Carta; Patrick Henry, fulminating against the arrogant and insolent encroachments of Great Britain upon the rights of the American Colonies; Nat Turner, rising from the dust of slavery and defying the slave oligarchy of Virginia and John Brown resisting the powers of the United States in a heroic effort to break the chains of the bondsman—these are some of the agitators who have voiced the discontent of their times at the peril of life and limb and property. Who shall cast the stone of reproach at these children of the race? Who shall say they were not heroes born to live forever in the annals of song and story? A portion of mankind remains always conservative, while the other portion is moved by the spirit of radicalism' and no man can predict where the conflict may lead when once the old idea and the new one conflict, and must needs appeal to the logic of revolution to arbitrate between them. Few Romes are large enough to hold a Caesar and a Brutus. The old idea and the new idea, the spirit of freedom and the spirit of tyranny and oppression cannot live together without friction. The agitator must never be in advance of his times. The people must be prepared to receive the message that he brings them. The harvest must be ripe for the sickle when the reaper enters the field."

THE ROLE OF RHETORIC IN REVOLUTION

Fortune's ideas on the role of the agitator suggest only a part of the rhetorical functions necessarily connected with revolution. In moving to an examination of contemporary black revolutionary rhetoric, some additional observations on the role of rhetoric must be made. First, those who generate the messages must consider what their objectives are. Earlier chapters have analyzed the "rhetoric of preparation" in which revolutionary and violent talk is used to move society — the white man — to make concessions peacefully without revolution. If this is, indeed, the object of the rhetoric, then to be successful it must be presented so that the white man feels that he is eavesdropping on actual battle plans. He certainly must hear them if they are to move him to action. If, however, the rhetoric is generated by those genuinely committed to revolution; if the battle plans are meant to be carried to conclusion, then the enemy must not know them. As James Forman said, "The man has an intelligence file on everybody."

> And he has gotten that information in part because we have been running off at the mouths cooperating with some research project about a rebellion. You don't make a rebellion and describe it until after it's all over.[45]

Julius Lester, who is both an articulate spokesman of black revolution and an astute rhetorical critic, makes the same observation. He commends some of the talk of the black revolutionists, but goes on to say:

> But much of the rhetoric has been of therapeutic value only to those in need of therapy. One can understand and feel the anger which gives rise to the cry of "Free Huey or the sky's the limit!" But on the level of revolutionary strategy it makes little sense. One never tells the enemy what he is going to do.[46]

In fact, talk may become a serious impediment to effective revolution. If tough talk takes the place of tough action, it may simply dissipate the anger and motivation that drives revolution. There will be no actual accomplishments. Lester has little use for the so-called militant, and observes that the black movement has had a tendency toward "militant-sounding rhetoric." "Militant rhetoric," he says, "has its place, but it is not a substitute for revolutionary principle. Sometimes militant rhetoric is nothing more than a cover-up for a lack of revolutionary thought.[47] Developing this theme, Lester goes on to say,

> Militant rhetoric has its place. In the initial stages, it is invaluable as an awakener of the people. The enunciation of the concept of black power did just that. However, militant rhetoric is always a dangerous tool, for it can so quickly and so easily begin to devour all who use it and all who listen. It feels so good when it comes from the tongue and it sounds so good as it enters the ear. If used without discretion, it can become a thing to be loved for itself. Thus, because of their militant rhetoric and personal charisma, some radical black leaders have become "happenings," not revolutionaries.[48]

Even though there is a potential conflict between rhetoric and revolution, without rhetoric, revolution is unlikely. Moreover, when the established order has control over most avenues of communication, it becomes necessary for revolutionaries, to develop their own media. The emergence of many so-called underground newspapers, the widespread use of handbills, and the increasing instance of small group and person-to-person "rap" or discussion sessions as well as the many mass rallies is evidence of revolutionary communication networks emerging to compete with the established ones. As Lester observes, the established channels of communication are working constantly to counter the revolutionary message, thereby challenging the revolutionists to work harder. The contest can be won, says Lester, ". . . if we begin to understand the immense power that people have when their political ideology is correct and when they know the best way to communicate it.[49]

The following message is an illustration of Lester's use of the handbill. It was distributed under his name at Washington University, St. Louis. The theme developed in this handbill is one of the basic justifications for revolution — genocide. No greater motive can be found for violent reaction to the government than the revelation that the government intends to eliminate a race, just as Hitler's Germany sought to destroy the Jews. If a rhetorical appeal can be made to raise even a substantial suspicion that some, if not all, parts of government desire the extermination of black Americans, a valid case for armed self-defense follows easily. In the short space of a single handbill, Lester develops a basically logical case for suspecting genocidal tendencies within white Americans. Further, he recognizes the likely disbelieving reaction of his predominantly white audience, and rejects the charge of paranoia by instructing his readers to look to their own past. Finally, he has incorporated a specific plan for retaliation which his audience can follow. This is not rhetoric of preparation. It is a clear call to action.

Julius Lester
From the Other Side of the Tracks*

Let there be no doubt about it. There is going to be violence in the ghetto this summer.

---

*Julius Lester, "From the Other Side of the Tracks" Handbill distributed on July 1, 1968 at Washington University, St. Louis, Missouri. Reprinted from U.S. Congress, Senate Committee on Government Operations, Permanent Subcommittee on Investigations, Hearings, Riots, Civil and Criminal Disorders, 91st Congress, First Session, 1969, pp. 4135-36.

Even if all blacks stay inside, eat watermelon and watch TV from March until October, there is going to be violence. The police and the military have made that inevitable. The Pentagon announced last week that it has supplied weapons and heavy artillery to every major city where there is a likelihood of violence. The Attorney General has announced that the army will stand ready all summer to back up the National Guard. The government has made extensive preparations for the coming summer. If necessary they'll hire somebody to go throw a rock through the window of a ghetto store. Anyway, you go, there is going to be violence this summer.

From these extensive preparations made by the government, it appears that their concern is not "riot control", but the extermination of blacks. This may sound paranoid, but when one hears public officials and the press referring to a "Hostile minority" that must be dealt with, that which appears to be paranoia is only sober realism. When Time and Newsweek report that white housewives in Kansas City, Missouri and Dearborn, Michigan, are being given free lessons in pistol shooting by the police at the police station, it is all too reminiscent of the South African government's training and arming of white women, and we all know where South Africa is at.

So it's not going to be a "long, hot summer." The days of sweating it out until first frost are over. It's going to be "Bloody Summer" and the likelihood is that black undertakers may ask for a mid-summer cease-fire so they could have a few days to recuperate from overwork.

America's relationship to blacks is very clear. Blacks were brought here because they were an asset to the economy. Now the economy no longer needs them. Not only are there no jobs for blacks, there aren't even enough for whites. It's a big enough job trying to figure out what to do with unemployed white workers who are being displaced by automation. The second factor is that blacks are a hostile minority. They're like the Vietnamese, in that you really aren't sure whether or not that black working behind the counter at Nedick's (a New York hot dog chain) can really be trusted. He may get off work and go straight to some kind of black power meeting. And what about that black who works next to you on the job? Was he really telling the truth when he said he didn't like Rap Brown or was he just saying what you wanted to hear? Eartha Kitt proved you can't trust blacks. The story out of Washington is that she was thoroughly checked by the FBI before being invited to the White House, and they said she was O.K. And then look what she did. One congressman said, "We can't even trust our Toms anymore."

So faced with a hostile minority that can be trusted and is totally useless, the solution is evident. Exterminate them.

Of course, this will not all take place this summer, but the wheels are clearly in motion. The government thinks in a long-range perspective—10, 20, 50 years. This is their long-range program for their "hostile minority." It points up the necessity for those of us who oppose this government to begin thinking, also, in a long-range perspective. At the present time, however, many people on the left think only in terms of issues—Vietnam, anti-draft activity, Latin America—and they move from issue to issue without ever coming to grips with the roots of the various issues. (And the roots of all the issues are the same.) It is necessary for us to begin to project what the government is going to do and what our response to that will be. To do that, it is necessary to (1) know our enemy and what he is capable of, and (2) know what we stand for. This calls for a level of political understanding and commitment that is not yet evident.

Faced with the prospect of extermination, blacks are arming themselves, and saying thereby, if you are marked for death, just don't die without knowing that some honky is going to be buried the same day you are. And preferably, two or three. The question then becomes, what will be the response of the white radical to the government's extermination program for blacks? James Forman of the Student Nonviolent Coordinating Committee (SNCC) is asking white revolutionaries for the following in the event that he is assassinated:

Ten war factories destroyed.
Fifteen police stations blown up.
Thirty power plants demolished.
No flowers.
One Southern governor, two mayors and 500 racist white cops dead.
A generous sustaining contribution to SNCC.

And for the assassination of Stokely and/or Rap, he is asking that the above figures be doubled.

That is one effective answer. For those whites who eschew violence, but still think of themselves as radicals or revolutionaries, there are other effective answers. But the time to think of what to do is not on the morning you pick up the paper and through half-awake eyes read that 10,000 blacks were shot down the night before. The time to prepare now, so that when 10,000 are shot down, a response from the American white revolutionary community will be swift and effective.

For those who read this and can only view it as extreme paranoia, reflect on the history of this country—the rape of Africa for black slaves, the extermination of the Indian, the atomic bomb dropped on Hiroshima and Nagasaki, the war in Vietnam. America's history shows that its capacity to murder is unfathomable. Hitler is held up to us as the example supreme of a madman, but only so that attention will be drawn away from our own history. That history is an unending record of madness and insanity. Blacks are taking up arms to respond to this madness. It is not the role of whites to argue against this. Their role is merely to decide what their effective response to the madness will be.

H. Rap Brown further reinforces the idea that genocide may constitute a basic justification of revolution and the value of rhetoric to the effort. He states that revolution need not be restricted to residents of the ghetto. Even the middle-class, well educated black man can serve a rhetorical function.

> You don't have to throw a Molotov cocktail to be a revolutionary. One thing which the Black college student can do is to begin to legitimatize the brother's actions — begin to articulate

his position, because the college student has the skills that the blood doesn't have.[50]

Beyond developing these and other arguments to justify revolution, rhetoric serves other, related, functions. Before examining in greater detail the justifications of revolution, it will be useful to analyze these additional rhetorical goals: destruction of white cultural values, development of a black nationalist culture, generation of unity and organization among black Americans, and the popularization of slogans.

The steps to destroy, within the black community, commitment to white cultural values began with overt measures, such as discontinuing hair straightening and skin bleaching, and the adoption of African-inspired styles in hair, jewelry, clothing, and even modes of address or greeting taken from African languages. Other overt, non-verbal behaviors have been used to challenge white values. For example, a strong heritage, probably derived from the British codes of fair play, demands that when two men meet, even though they are adversaries, they will treat each other in a "civil" manner. Thus, if two enemies meet off the field of battle, they will at least shake hands. Some black Americans have refused to shake hands with white men, even in the most formal of social occasions. One white man whose hand had been left untouched in mid-air returned from the experience enraged and confused. He had, he felt, always held favorable views toward black people, and he had always been willing to help them. Now, he could not understand why he had been treated in this shabby way, and most of his good will toward black men was gone. Some would ask why it will help the black cause to antagonize potential friends, but the black man claims that they must realize that this was done, not for or against the white man, but to help the black man who refused to shake hands reject his identification with white values. As the furious white man stalked away, not only had he felt the anger of the black man, but the black man had taken a small step toward creating a new identity for himself. As Jean-Paul Sartre says in his Preface to Fanon's The Wretched of the Earth, to shoot down a European (either literally or through some symbolic act) is ". . . to kill two birds with one stone, to destroy an oppressor and the man he oppresses at the same time: there remains a dead man, and a free man. . . ."[51]

Frantz Fanon, the ideological inspiration for much revolutionary rhetoric, argues that one strategy of colonial powers is the insistence that the subjugated people acknowledge the supremacy of the oppressor's values. Therefore, in ". . . the period of decolonization, the colonized masses mock at these very values, insult them, and vomit them up."[52] Taking the premise that the black Americans constitute a colonized people, H. Rap Brown advises following Fanon's decolonization plan. In doing so, he cites Mao Tse tung as authority.

> If white folks say it's more cultured to whisper, you talk loud. If white folks say gray suits are fashionable, you go buy a pink one. If they say america [sic.] is great, you say america ain't shit. Chairman Mao says, "Whatever the enemy supports, we oppose. Whatever the enemy opposes, we support."[53]

Eldridge Cleaver and Rap Brown are two men who have shown more willingness to launch attacks on the verbal values of the white society. The refusal to accept what is advanced as "correct" grammar, and use instead the idiom of the typical black American, even in such formal situations as a public speech or published book, are perceived as particularly effective weapons.

Several instances can be seen in the passage taken from Brown's book. Most obvious are his choices of an ungrammatical and obscene word which by white standards is totally inappropriate in a formal publication. More subtle is his refusal to capitalize "America" and, in other parts of the book, his insistence upon capitalizing the first letter in "black." Cleaver, speaking before an audience at Stanford University in 1968, showed his sensitivity to this device. In his opening statements, he used an obscenity, and then said, "Some people told me when I came down here that I shouldn't use any four-letter words." In reply, he said,

> I want to couple my basic response to that with my response to Ronald Reagan. I guess people are getting more and more permissive in this society, because I think people are ready to hear someone say Fuck Ronald Reagan, or Fuck the private money at Stanford University. Fuck Stanford University if that's necessary, dig it? That may or may not be the limit of my vocabulary, I don't know. I don't go around counting words. Because we're reaching the point today where words are becoming more and more irrelevant.[54]

Of course, Cleaver's extensive writing, in which he conforms totally to the expected grammatical and rhetorical conventions of white society, thoroughly demonstrates that four-letter words do not constitute the limit of his vocabulary. When he claims that words are becoming irrelevant, he means that using the words expected by the white society is becoming less relevant. Cleaver by no means suggests he considers verbal behavior irrelevant.

In a speech only a few months later, in San Francisco, he observed,

> There's something more dangerous about attacking the pigs of the power structure verbally than there is in walking into the Bank of America with a gun. . . . Bankers hate armed robbery, but someone who stands up and directly challenges their racist system, that drives them crazy.[55]

The violent reaction of many whites to the term "pig" is good evidence of this assertion.

The corollary of destroying the white man's value system is the erection of a black culture and national identity. Benny Stewart, chairman of the Black Student Union at San Francisco State College, described the status of the black liberation movement in this way in 1959.

> The movement is beginning to solidify, making that step which makes clear just who the oppressor is. During the civil rights era we dealt primarily with the moral conscience of the racist oppressor, and later we developed some cultural identity. Now, through the vanguard leadership of the Black Panther Party, we are beginning to move, at least, as we see it, to understanding a revolutionary nationalism.[56]

Here, again, the inspiration of Frantz Fanon is clear. In his analysis of wars of liberation, Fanon observes the development of men of culture who work alongside politicians; the former deal in history while the latter face present-day events. He charges that colonial powers pervert history and logic to hold people in bondage. Therefore, the oppressed people's claim to a national culture in the past ". . . does . . . rehabilitate that nation and serve as a justification for the hope of a future national culture. In the sphere of psycho-affective equilibrium it is responsible for an important change in the native."[57] In this respect, much of the separatist rhetoric, calling for black history studies and seeking to bring to the public attention the accomplishments and heroics of black men, constitutes an integral step in the revolutionary development.

Perhaps the most critical rhetorical function other than establishing the revolution itself, is the creation of a sense of unity and organization. The reader will recall the speech of Maria Stewart within the discussion of separation in which she contrasted the black man with the American Indian. She noted that the Indian had a sense of nationhood which held that to attack one man was to attack thousands; the black man, on the other hand, might join in the attack on one of his fellows.

Mrs. Stewart spoke during the early abolition period when black Americans were still in slavery. Today, more than one hundred years later, black men are still making the appeal: "We've got to make the white man understand that there are 20 million black people in this country and that when they mess with one black man they got to mess with 20 million black people."[58] Fanon argues that another colonialist strategem is to instill a sense of individualism in colonized people. Whether it was done intentionally or not, whether it establishes the colonialist character of the black American or not, this had apparently come to pass in the United States. H. Rap Brown joins Stewart and Cleaver in decrying this state of affairs in this statement: "There are nationalist groups that won't accept light-complexioned Blacks. What they're doing is helping the white man, because they're creating the potential for a divisive fight inside the Black community."[59] Huey P. Newton, Minister of Defense of the Black Panther Party, develops the point still further and describes the essential nature of organization to revolution in an editorial in *The Black Panther* newspaper of 1967.

> The slaves have always outnumbered the slavemasters. The power of the oppressor rests upon the submission of the people. When Black people really unite and rise up in all their splendid millions, they will have the strength to smash injustice. We do not understand the power in our numbers. . . .
>
> We, with all our numbers, are recognized by no one. In fact, we do not even recognize our own selves. We are unaware of the potential power latent in our numbers . . . we are still so blind to our critical fight for our very survival that we are continuing to function in petty, futile ways. Divided, confused, fighting among ourselves, we are still in the elementary stage of throwing rocks, sticks, empty wine bottles, and beer cans at racist cops who lie in wait for a chance to murder unarmed Black people.[60]

Eldridge Cleaver, in 1967, was determined to develop a means of putting ". . . an end to the archipelago of one-man showcase groups that plagued the black community with division."[61] He, like Fanon, felt that individualism is the first thing that must disappear if de-colonization is to take place. "Brother, sister, friend— these are words outlawed by the colonialist bourgeoisie. . . ." said Fanon.[62] Cleaver saw that a sense of black brotherhood must be a first step to revolution. Indeed, one of the most simple, but pervasive, of all rhetorical techniques has been the development of "brother" and "sister" as inevitable modes of address among black Americans. In this way, a bond is created among perceived equals that even transcends the concept of "comrade" utilized by socialists and communists.

In his rhetoric, Cleaver develops the ultimate appeal for organization. He seeks to overcome the defeatist attitude arising from black Americans who perceive themselves as a helpless minority by showing their relation to the non-white peoples of the world. Two parallel, persuasive goals are sought. First, to instill in the black audience this sense of identity as part of the world's majority; second, to show the determination of white people to prevent their successful organization. Again, the argument seeks to portray the white man as the aggressor, the one who is already taking steps to hold down the black man. This gives a moral justification for organization, and develops a sense of urgency. Cleaver argues that at no time in the past has there been such a mass awareness of black unity, and the time is short before white men will have effectively stopped any real chances of unity. It is an old, but persuasive message—act now, or it will be too late.

> We live today in a system that is in the last stages of the protracted process of breaking up on a worldwide basis. The rulers perceive the greatest threat to be the national liberation movements around the world. . . . In order for them to wage wars of suppression against these national liberation movements abroad, they must have peace and stability and unanimity of purpose at home. But at home there is a Trojan Horse, a black Trojan Horse that has become aware of itself and is now struggling to get on its feet. It too, demands liberation. . . . a Black Trojan Horse within white America. . . . in excess of 23,000,000 strong. That is a lot of strength. But it is a lot of weakness if it is disorganized. . . . The need for one organization that will give one voice to the black man's common interest is felt in every bone and fiber of black America.[63]

The only way black Americans can be confident of their strength, claims Cleaver, is to look for their one organization in common with their brothers around the world. To prevent this, he says, the white American is trying to bring the hate which those in other lands feel for the white "ugly" American down upon the black American as well. This is to be accomplished by sending black troops to Vietnam to kill the Asians with whom they should be working. Today, asserts Cleaver, there is great love among the peoples of the world for black Americans, and this love must be turned into power through organization. It must not be destroyed through black participation in the Vietnam war.

Slogan development, as a part of revolutionary rhetoric, is relatively obvious, and requires little elaboration. However, it is significant to note the extent to which the formula outlined by Fanon is followed by black Americans, particularly the Black Panther Party. Fanon said that when the colonized people finally set out to destroy the system through violence, they ". . . very soon find themselves with the barren, inert slogan 'Release X or Y.' "[64] If the imprisoned man is indeed a recognized spokesman of the people, the organization may be able to use his period of imprisonment to launch new leaders. The constantly heard slogan of the Black Panther Party is, "Free Huey," in reference to Huey Newton, Minister of Defense of the party. During his period of detention, he has been used as the symbol of the repression by whites, and his lost freedom gives a specific goal around which others can rally. Of course, several other leaders have emerged during this time.

In outlining a plan to organize the youth of the ghetto, the Revolutionary Action Movement (RAM) reveals an awareness of the value of generating slogans. The problem as perceived by this group was not how to motivate the ghetto youth to accept violence as a method. The problem, rather, was to instill in them a sense of victory — to make the prospect of success real and meaningful. They sought to build an idea of strength through organization, pride and anger.

> The slogans of the army should be, "We will win by any means necessary." The colors of the army should be red, black and green, an army song should be established and a blood oath should be taken to avenge the murder of Brother Malcolm, using Brother Malcolm and Garvey as prophets. Train the troops to have a sense of retribution, or physical retaliation. The doctrine should use the assassination of Brother Malcolm as an example to show what the troops are up against; finks, uncle toms, and whiteys. Developing them to a fanatical point of striking the one physical blow in the name of Malik Shabazz that could bring the oppressor to his knees.
> The doctrine must have the sense of ultimate destiny to discipline the troops not to move prematurely but for the unleashing of the final blow. This means the doctrine must have the total prospective of the Black revolution including the new world society and Black dictatorship in this country. The Marxian concept of destiny of the dictatorship of the proletariat must be replaced by Black dictatorship of the world.[65]

With this discussion of the general role of rhetoric in revolution, it becomes more meaningful to examine the rhetoric itself. In making the examination, it will be useful to study the apparent goals sought, the intended audience, and whether or not the rhetoric embraces actual appeals for revolutionary action rather than merely an infatuation with tough talk. The material that follows includes an analysis of revolutionary persuasion and will be organized according to the main themes that have emerged from the discussion. The sequence in which the themes will be examined reflects a general pattern of development within the broad persuasive campaign and many single messages. Revolutionary speakers and writers seem to utilize a sequence of topics designed to carry the audience from the attitudes of typical Americans to the attitudes of violent revolutionaries. The rhetorical campaign, moreover, seems to have followed the same pattern — as the general audience internalizes one concept, the next is stressed, and so on until they are convinced. Since the sequence of topics represents a broad generalization of steps, the following pattern will be discussed: exposure of the inherent evil of whites; the inherent evil of capitalism; the identification of black Americans as a colonized people; the failure of integration; inevitability of revolution; the question of coalition with whites; the moral justification of violence; and finally the visualization of the goal of a socialist state.

THE INHERENT EVIL OF WHITES

If black men are to be mobilized into a revolutionary army, they first must be convinced of the inherent evil of the white man. While most black people are quite ready to accept the fact of basic evils within the white race, they are still inclined, in many cases, to acknowledge that not all whites are bad, and even the bad ones might be redeemed. Furthermore, it is one thing to despise a man or his race, but still another to accept the necessity of fighting and killing him. Therefore, most wars are accompanied by propaganda designed to build hate for the enemy. Stories of atrocities and information about the determination of the enemy to destroy a people and what they stand for help to create a concept of hate sufficient to move them to war. Black revolutionary propagandists utilize the same approach. The white man is pictured as ready to commit genocide. To overcome the willingness to accept individual whites, the argument is advanced that the causes of white and black are diametrically opposed. It is not necessary to believe that each white individual is evil; it is enough to know that his identity and well-being are in conflict with yours.

Stokely Carmichael, an ardent advocate of this philosophy, is one of the most eloquent and active of all the black revolutionaries. Born in Trinidad, and educated in New York City and Washington, D.C., Carmichael has been an active speaker, writer, and organizer since his college days at Howard. He was a member of the organizing group of the Student Nonviolent Coordinating Committee in 1960, and was elected its chairman in 1966. He has divided his time between political action, organization within black ghettos, particularly Washington D. C., and touring the country to speak to various groups. Although he has spoken to white audiences, he spends much of his time speaking to black college students. He makes no pretense about his intention of bringing them into the revolutionary movement.

Carmichael is, perhaps, the most consistently anti-white of all the black speakers. Speaking to the student body of St. Augustine College in Raleigh, North Carolina in November, 1968, he identified himself with the black people throughout the world who seek some way to survive. He then said, "My major assumption is that white people are preparing to commit genocide against black people." Acknowledging that white men deny this ambition, Carmichael said they told the same thing to the Indians. Then, recognizing the difficulty many find in accepting this proposition, he said, "Even if it's not true, it wouldn't hurt if we were prepared."

Developing his theme of the need for all black people to accept an African heritage, Carmichael attacked the "evil" white man. "Africans. We are Africans. And we have been scattered all over the Western Hemisphere by the malicious design of the powers of white Western society in order that our unity cannot come about."[66] He clearly charges the white man with separating blacks in order to prevent their unified challenge to his control. Carmichael said, toward the end of his speech: "I do not think the white institutions will allow equality with the black man, because just as they have taught us to be inferior, they have taught themselves to be superior." The white man must dominate, and "what he cannot dominate, he destroys."

Carmichael, possessing little mercy for the black man who does not hate whites, refuses to shrink from distinguishing between love and hate. He says if one knows love, he must know hate; otherwise he would have no concept of love. Thus, if we love someone, and another man threatens or kills him, we must hate that person. "When black people say, 'I don't hate white folk,' Carmichael adds, "they do not hate white folk because they do not love their people." He then concludes: "If we loved our people, we would have to hate the institution of white Western society for what it has done to us and to our people. . . ." The disjunction is clearly set up—if you love your brothers, you would hate whites. If you don't hate whites, you don't love your brothers. In this way, maximum social pressure is applied to the college student who is trying to walk the middle ground of loving his black brothers without harboring hate for whites. Carmichael will not let him do it, nor will other leaders who hold similar views. Observe, for instance, how the singular evil of the white American is expressed in this summary statement by Grier and Cobbs in their analysis of *Black Rage:*

> America has waxed rich and powerful in large measure on the backs of black laborers. It has become a violent, pitiless nation, hard and calculating, whose moments of generosity are only brief intervals in a ferocious narrative of life, bearing a ferocity and an aggression so strange in this tiny world where men die if they do not live together.[67]

In this kind of rhetoric, the first step — hate for the white man — is established by revealing his inherent evil.

THE INHERENT EVILS OF CAPITALISM

"As I left the auditorium," said Eldridge Cleaver after listening to a speech by Robert Kennedy, "I said to myself: We don't need a War on Poverty. What we need is a war on the rich."[68] In the rhetoric of black revolutionaries, white men, their system of capitalism, and human misery are so intertwined that in order to change one, the others must change as well. While the white man, and his agents — the police — are the overt object of black hatred, the actual battle is against their system, ". . . which has created political and economic institutions whose sole aims are the oppression, degradation and exploitation of everyone.[69] H. Rap Brown puts the idea this way:

> . . . the truth of the matter is that we cannot end racism, capitalism, colonialism and imperialism until the reins of state power are in the hands of those people who understand that the wealth, the total wealth of any country and the world, belongs equally to all people. Societies and countries based on the profit motive will never insure a new humanism or eliminate poverty and racism.[70]

Using a more lurid style designed to arouse a more popular audience than Brown was addressing, James Forman wrote the fol-

lowing words in a pamphlet distributed by the Student Nonviolent
Coordinating Committee:

> Our liberation will only come when there is final destruction of
> this mad octopus—the capitalistic system of the United States
> with all its life-sucking tenacles of exploitation and racism that
> choke the people of Africa, Asia, and Latin America.[71]

George Mason Murray, Minister of Education of the Black Panther
Party, carried the rhetoric further along the path to the propa-
gandistic form that has come to typify the persuasion of socialist-
communist countries. His frequent use of the term, "imperialist
dogs," recalls the repetition of the label, "imperialist warmongers,"
used by the Soviet Union and its associated countries. The speech
seems to be without the logical structure that has characterized
most of the black rhetoric studied. Instead, the speaker moves
almost randomly from point to point, often repeating themes. He
does strongly relate capitalism and imperialism with white-
controlled United States. The fact that he speaks from Cuba and
can use it as an example of a successful revolution, gives credibility to his words of certain victory. Murray, who was for a time
a graduate assistant at San Francisco State College, reveals, in
this speech, no commitment to scholarly methods of documenta-
tion of assertions and restraint in generalizations. Here he is
speaking as a revolutionary orator exhorting his people to action.

George Mason Murray
Black Panther Leader Calls for Armed Struggle*

[Message from the Black Panther Party Minister of Education George Mason
Murray, currently visiting Cuba—voice with American accent]

HAVANA.—This is George Murray, minister of education of the Black Panther
Party of the United States, representing the Central Committee of the Black
Panther Party; our Minister of Defense Huey Newton, who is imprisoned and
being tried by the racist dogs at Oakland, California; our Comrade Bobby
Seale; our Minister of Information Elridge Cleaver; and the entire Central
Committee.

---

*George Mason Murray, "Black Panther Leader calls for Armed Struggle,"
monitored Cuban broadcast. Reprinted from U.S. Congress, Senate Committee on
Government Operations, Permanent Subcommittee on Investigations, Hearings,
Riots, Civil and Criminal Disorders, 91st Congress, First Session, 1969, pp. 3739-44.

For our brothers in the United States, we would like to say that the Cuban people are on our side. Our comrades in Cuba, in the liberated territory of Cuba, have shown us the correct way to put an end to Yankee imperialism and racism throughout the world. While here in Cuba, we have met with brothers —people of Africa, Asia and Latin America—and they have told us that they are on our side; that they are beginning to understand every day the exactness of our present and the necessity for us to resist by guerrilla armed warfare.

Brothers and sisters, we must not misunderstand the nature of the capitalist beast; any man who would—any man, any system, any organization— that would kill our dear brother Martin Luther King or our brother Medgar Evers, our brother in Africa Patrice Lumumba, our comrade in South America Che Guevara, our brothers and sisters in Vietnam, and then send our black youth between the ages of 17 and 22 over to Vietnam to die fighting a group of yellow people who have never called us nigger while the imperialist dogs of the United States harass us, murder us, and beat us every day.

BLACK PANTHER TACTICS

Brothers and sisters, we must understand that we must put an end to the racism, neocolonialism, and colonialism that the United States is carrying on throughout the world. Today, in the United States—in Oakland, California— our minister of defense and leader of the struggle in the United States, Huey P. Newton, is on trial. To the black people of the South, the North, the East, and the West, we would like to say that in the Black Panther Party, we say to the American imperialist, "The sky is the limit if you kill Huey P. Newton." To those people in the United States who do not know of our brother Minister of Defense Huey P. Newton nor the Black Panther Party, we would like to say that the Black Panther Party is an armed political organization of black people who have realized that the imperialist dogs are trying to wipe us out; to do us the way the Indians were done and arrest the few of us that survive and put us in concentration camps with gas chambers—on reservation camps as they have done with the Indians.

With this realization, the Black Panther Party was formed first in Oakland, California, where it began troop patrols against the police, and every night it would go out in the streets with shotguns and rifles and pistols to make sure that no more black people were murdered. The result is that many of our comrades were killed. No later than last week in Los Angeles, six members of the Black Panther Party in Los Angeles, California, were shot down—ambushed—by the imperialist dog police of L.A. [Los Angeles].

We want you to know that black people are responding correctly throughout the United States. For instance, last week our brothers in Cleveland, Ohio, showed the proper sentiment to resist oppression.

They ambushed the police and killed three police and wounded 27. We are very happy with this political consciousness that the racists of Cleveland, Ohio, suffered. In New York, two police were shot; in Chicago, seven police were shot; in Peoria, Illinois, nine police were shot; in Little Rock, Arkansas, three police were shot; in Seattle, Washington, two police were shot.

So you see, brothers and sisters in the United States, we cannot end our situation, the situation of colonialism—and we are a colony, because we are oppressed, we are crowded into ghettos where we die, we are crowded into ghettos where our children are born dead, we are crowded into ghettos where black people, where black people, babies die three times as fast at birth as white people. We are crowded into ghettos where many of our young brothers and sisters are forced out of school and are sent to the army and die in Vietnam. Many of us are 18, 19, and 20 years old—unless we begin to resist oppression, to resist capitalism, to resist racism in the United States—we will not survive to become 21 or 22, because imperialists will send us to fight against people of color in Vietnam, or send us to fight against our own brothers in Africa in order to kill us and to kill them.

DEMOCRATIC PARTY

Concerning the Democratic convention that will be starting soon. You must not be deceived by the Democratic Party. It was the Democratic Party (?that was in office when our dear brother Malcolm X was assassinated.) The Democratic Party was in office when our great leader Dr. Martin Luther King was assassinated. And it is the Democratic Party, the Oakland Police, the CIA and all the imperialists in America who are trying our minister of defense and leader, Huey P. Newton, and they hope to send him to the gas chamber and to make him die as a dog would die, strangling him to death on gas.

Brothers, we must not let the imperialists make us misunderstand the situation of the people in Cuba. The people in Cuba are our comrades; the people in Cuba are our brothers. Fidel Castro is our brother; Ernest Che Guevara is our brother; the Central Committee of the Communist Party of Cuba are our comrades. All the peoples of Asia, Africa, and Latin America belong to the family of Afro-Americans in the United States. We cannot afford to (?disavow) ourselves from the Cuban people. We cannot afford to turn our backs on the Cuban people, because they have supplied us with a correct example of how to resist racism. The Cuban people were robbed by racism, just as we are robbed and sold poison and rotten food in stores of the black community.

In the United States, we are one—we are one people, we are flesh of the same flesh and blood of the same blood. But American brothers and sisters, black people of United States, we would like to say to you again that victory will be ours. We understand our brother Dr. Martin Luther King who said to the dogs in Washington, D.C. in March, in LOOK magazine—he stated this: He said we were going to go to Washington, D.C. on the poor people's march and that if this march was not successful, this was the last time that he was going to petition the American Government in a peaceful manner. Afterward, he would return to the South and organize black people to take care of (? righteous business of those dogs.)

The imperialists know that. They knew also that they did not intend to pay. They did not intend to stop killing black people in the United States.

They did not intend to stop bombing people of color in Vietnam. They did not intend to stop raining napalm on the black or Indians or Spanish-speaking people in Latin America who are resisting the ownership of their countries by fools such as Rockefeller, and MacNamara and Johnson and the Kennedys, and because they have done this they have died.

So brothers and sisters do not be deceived by the Democratic Party convention that is going on now. They are doing nothing but choosing another racist who is going to oppress us for the next 4 years. We feared Johnson; in 1964 we feared Goldwater. And because we feared Goldwater, we voted for Johnson and when Johnson came into power, he didn't do anything but send the Marines in on our people in Detroit. They shot young black people 12 years old. He didn't do anything but send the Marines in on our people in Newark and to shoot black people down at 12 years of age and run through the houses and tried shooting every black person whose face was in the window. We elected Johnson, and he sent in the police on 90 and a 100-year-old people at the poor people's march who were living in mud and slop, and eating bacon fat.

So you look at this brothers and sisters and you will understand the Democratic Party is the enemy of mankind. The Republican Party we already know is the enemy of mankind. All the racists and imperialists in the United States must die. We will not be saved until all the people like Johnson have been dismissed from the world.

Another thing, brothers and sisters, we must not be deceived by cries of black power, and misunderstand black power and misinterpret black power. Agreed, we need black power, but when we say black power we do not mean— we mean—if our black people are controlling stores and exploiting and robbing black people. [sentence as heard] For instance, if a black mayor calls in the national guard on black people, and he knows that the national guard is only going to murder black people, then that black mayor is an enemy of the black community, even though he is black. We must understand this. For instance, had Mayor Stokes of Cleveland, Ohio, been a righteous brother, he would not have called in the national guard on black people, or the police. The national guard and police are our enemies, we understand that. And if [name indistinct] called in the national guard and the police on the black people, then that means that he loves his position as mayor more than he loves black people. Therefore, he is an enemy of black people.

Brothers and sisters, please understand, we have a long struggle ahead of us. We have—many of us will die in the struggle, but dying is but a small price to pay because we know that our children and many of the young black people of today will enjoy the fruit of the struggle, which will be freedom, and justice, and equality for people of color throughout the world.

Our experience here in Cuba has taught us that it is worth a struggle. It is very beautiful to see farmers' daughters from the farming section of the Cuban territory on scholarships in schools in Havana, Cuba. We know that in the United States the children of black farmers have no hope. They cannot go to school. They may go to school for the sixth grade or for the ninth grade, but in terms of a college education, there is none. In Cuba, our brothers are doing a wonderful job.

They are taking care of the Cuban people. The Cuban people's needs are being met. Whereas in the United States the capitalist dogs tell us to turn our backs on the Cuban people because they are communists. At the same time, we flunk out of every school in the United States because the American educators are not interested in teaching black people.

Therefore, we say that the only way—the only correct way—that we can [?reject] the imperialist dogs is through guerrilla warfare. Brothers and sisters, understand that we are not advocating violence for the sake of violence. The issue confronting black people in the United States is not one of nonviolence or violence. Dr. Martin Luther King did not die for nonviolence. Dr. Martin Luther King died because he was resisting oppression and racism in the world today. Malcolm X did not die because he said that we must begin a long struggle, he died because he demanded that we have human rights.

IMPERIALIST TRICKS

Again, do not be confused by the imperialists. The imperialists use a vain . . . ah . . . strange trick on black people. Strange in the sense that they had not done it before. The imperialists killed Macolm X, and the excuse that they gave for killing Malcolm X was that he was militant and violent, and that he was a black (?man) and a separatist. They gave orders to us not to resist them —listen, black people—not to resist them throwing teargas grenades on black people, not to resist them when they attempt to kill our minister of defense and leader of the Black Panther Party, Huey P. Newton.

The Democratic Party, the CIA, the U.S. [words indistinct] racist dogs; they killed Martin Luther King because they knew that most of us would be (?for him) and (?what) he asked us to do. That is what we said earlier, that Martin Luther King had promised the imperialists over in the United States that if the colored people's march did not produce a guaranteed annual income that he would return to the South and organize and prepare for guerrilla warfare against the dogs that run this country.

Realizing that they did not intend to change, they killed Martin Luther King. And there were more revolts and rebellions in one week, the week of 3 [through 10], the week that Martin Luther King was assassinated, there were more riots, more revolts, more rebellions. There (?were) 127 that the white press counted. 127 revolts and rebellions in one week—because (?our dear one was killed) and we knew that it was right and correct and proper to (?ask) for struggle and violent means against racism and imperialism.

But to confuse us, realizing that more black people were turning toward the Black Panther Party for our armed guerrilla struggle and for the correct (?political) indoctrination, realizing that the black people were turning toward the Black Panther Party, the U.S. Government then decided to kill . . . ah . . . the liberal, the racist dog, liberal Robert Kennedy, who a lot of us were (?forced toward). When they killed him, they tried to [words indistinct] by killing that they had confused our people. How? They said, oh, "violence,

violence, violence! Violence is the cause for Martin Luther King's dying, and violence is the cause of Robert Kennedy dying." And if they [words indistinct] Robert Kennedy and they used violence to destroy him—that is, they used a gun—then we will not pick up the gun to defend ourselves.

So you see how (?foolish) the imperialists are. They say that violence killed Robert Kennedy and that violence is wrong, but at the same time they drop tons of bombs everyday on people of color in Vietnam. They say violence is wrong, but they have blown up a church in Birmingham and murdered (?three men there)." They say violence is wrong, but they assassinated Martin Luther King. They say violence is wrong, but in Oakland, California, the Oakland police killed at least two black people (?5 April), when it murdered two members of the Black Panther Party. They say violence is wrong, but (?last week) six members of the Black Panther Party were shot down like dogs by the Los Angeles racist police.

So they killed this fellow Kennedy, they killed this racist named Kennedy. That fellow Kennedy claimed that he was for black people, and a lot of us in the South, even the brother of Medgar Evers—our friend and martyr, our brother who was shot down like a dog in Mississippi—even [Charles] Evers claims that Robert Kennedy is a friend of the black people. But black people in the southern part of the United States—listen to this: Kennedy is a multi-millionaire. Kennedy had 400 million dollars. If Kennedy was on the side of the poor people, why did he not take the 400 million dollars that he owned and distribute it among the black people of the south who are starving to death, who are kicked off the farms of racist (?crackers) like James O. Eastland, who is one of the highest members of the United States Government—a leader of a Senatorial committee? If Kennedy was for black people, why did he not take it (?out of) his family and distribute it to black people? So we see he was not for black people. He was for imperialism. He was dividing up South America and taking part of it from [words indistinct] the lives of our brothers in South America.

His brother, John Kennedy, was President when the air force of the United States was used to bomb and attack people of color in Cuba and to murder and destroy the Cuban people in their strugle for freedom. So the imperialist dogs used a trick on us. They killed one of our greatest leaders and then turned around and assassinated one of their leaders in order to make us feel sorry and feel that violence is not the way.

ENEMIES OF BLACK PEOPLE

We do not advocate violence, we advocate armed resistance. As we said earlier, the issue for black people is not whether we will be violent or non-violent. Those terms are meaningless. They have no meaning in a country where the imperialists kill people of color in every quarter of the world. They murdered our brother Patrice Lumumba and they say that violence is wrong. But the issue is not violence; the issue is war, the war of armed struggle. The Democratic Party is an enemy of the black people in the United States; the Supreme Court is an enemy of black people in the United States; the Congress is an enemy of black people in the United States; and all the governors of the states of the United States are racist dogs.

Rockefeller is a racist dog. He is not for black people. If he was for black people, he would not be taking all the (?ores) and the minerals from South America, from the Latin American people, and bringing them to the United States. If Rockefeller was for black people, he would not let Harlem, New York exist. Harlem is the largest ghetto in the United States. A million black people crowded into rooms that are only fit for two black people to live in—two—where you find families of black people, as many as 10 persons in a single two-room house in the state that Rockefeller is the governor of. If he was the friend of black people, he would change that situation. Rockefeller is such a dog that he owns oilfields in South Africa. He owns diamond mines in South Africa where black men die every year a mile deep in the ground bringing out diamonds as big as our hand, and imperialists sell tiny pieces of diamonds for 3 and 4 and 5 and 6,000 dollars to us.

PLAN OF ACTION

Brothers and sisters, we must be aware of the imperialist dogs. We must understand that the emperialists murdered Martin Luther King and murdered Malcolm X that they will definitely murder any of us. Now with this understanding, what we must do is to collect our arms. To arm ourselves with guns and force in an organized manner to resist racists' oppression. Brothers and sisters throughout the United States, let us say this: Concerning our leader Huey P. Newton, the leader of the Black Panther Party. Our (?plan) is this: If Huey is killed, the sky is the limit.

No business, no American business, factory, (?base) or industry will be spared (?by us), nor will be spared the lives of the U.S. senators, the mayors of cities, the governors of states, the presidential candidates, ex-presidents, or any imperialist dog anywhere in the United States. Black people of America, we must not allow the imperialists to kill Huey P. Newton.

They think that if they kill Huey Newton, that they will be putting an end to guerrilla warfare. What do we mean by guerrilla warfare? We mean to organize the black people in two's and three's and four's and five's (?to) assassinate the police who kill us. When we speak of guerrilla warfare, we mean the opening of schools for black people throughout the United States where we can be taught our true (?cause) and our true history and our true way of life. When we speak of guerrilla warfare, we mean the opening of hospitals in the black community where more black people can be born without dying from being born at home, or without dying from malnutrition or without dying from starvation. And when we speak of guerrilla warfare, we mean the opening up of farms for black people where black youths can be trained, where black people can produce their own food, where black people in the United States can live in peace. And when we speak of guerrilla warfare, we mean sending black men in the United States to resist (?racism) in their homes, rather than being sent 10,000 miles away to die fighting the Vietnamese who have never called us niggers, (?for some crackers) who will call us niggers and shoot us down any day or any hour in the United States.

Again brothers and sisters, I am George Murray, the minister of education of the Black Panther Party, here in the liberated free territory of Cuba enjoying the truth of the people's rebellion.

It is wonderful, it is glorious, and its is something that all black people in the United States should behold. We know that the imperialist dogs in the United States will attempt to arrest us—maybe even kill us—for coming here and spreading our truth to our Asian, African, and Latin American brothers, but we want you to know this: If we die tonight, we can say like Martin Luther King: we've been to the mountain top, we've seen the promised land, we've seen the truth of struggle. And we would like to say to black people, ever onward to victory. We know that we will be free, we know that we shall overcome, and as our brothers say in Spanish, "venceremos."

We understand that we shall conquer without a doubt, as our brother (Ethan Dyer) said. Why? Because the truth is on our side. What is the truth? The truth is the people of Africa, Asia, and Latin America who are resisting U.S. imperialism throughout the world. The police must be stopped. The national guard must be stopped. The U.S. Army must be stopped. The U.S. Marines must be stopped. The only way you can stop them, brothers and sisters, is not by being on our knees and praying and asking them to leave us alone. Martin Luther King understood this. The only way they will be stopped is for us to arm ourselves for trouble. They have (?guards) that can be blown up; they have bridges that can be blown up; they have airports that can be blown up; they have IBM schools that can be blown up; they have factories that can be burnt to the ground; they have public buildings that can be blown up; they have people walking the streets who are mayors and governors, and senators whose lives can be taken in exchange for the lives of black people that they have taken.

Brothers and sisters, the U.S. Government admits that between 75 and 100 million Africans—our brothers—were made in the slave trade. We are the only surviving Africans in the United States. It is necessary for us to resist—and to resist firmly, wholly, completely, and absolutely. The only way we can do this is to unite together and have a true revolutionary black power, which means the end of capitalism, which means the end of exploitation, which means the beginning of the world struggle in every state, on every inch of American soil. We shall conquer without a doubt. To our brothers in the Black Panther Party throughout the United States, we would like to say: Power to the people, black power for black people, and panther power to the vanguards in the USA.

BLACK AMERICANS AS A COLONIZED PEOPLE

The status of people of African descent in the United States is singular in many ways. Their arrival here as slaves, and their lives in a system of oppression and segregation as a minority sets them apart from their black brothers and sisters living in their native lands. Even Fanon draws this conclusion from what happened at congresses of the African Cultural Society. He notes that, "... little by little the American Negroes realized that the essential problems confronting them were not the same as those that confronted the African Negroes." Developing the idea, Fanon continues, "The test cases of civil liberty whereby both whites and blacks in America try to drive back racial discrimination have very little in common in their principles and objectives with the heroic fight of the Angolan people against the detestable Portuguese colonialism."[72] However, black analysts realized that the strong precedent for revolution, the established examples and justifications, involved colonized people throwing off their oppressors. If, therefore, black analyists continued, the black Americans could be perceived as a similarly colonized people, there would follow a justification for revolution in this country. This required a redefinition of the civil rights struggle into the anti-colonial concept of seeking to drive out (from government, from power, even from land) white colonialists.

The theme has already been illustrated in the rhetorical documents printed above. However, some additional examples might be of value. H. Rap Brown quoted one of his own speeches to this effect:

> Today I will talk about two things—colonialism and revolution. In other words, sickness and cure. The United States redefined colonialism. It not only went to Africa and exploited the land and its people; it brought Black people here and continues its exploitation; and it drove the native American Indians by murder and wholesale genocide onto reservations. . . .[73]

James Forman, who was executive secretary of the Student Non-violent Coordinating Committee from 1961 to 1966, and currently director of international affairs of SNCC, also elaborated on this theme of anti-colonialism in the keynote speech at the Western Regional Black Youth Conference in Los Angeles, California, on November 23, 1967. In this address he observed:

> To view our history as one of resistance is to recognize more clearly the colonial relationship that we have with the United States. Traditionally, when one thinks of colonialism, images of foreign powers occupying another land and subjecting its people are the kinds of mental pictures we frame. But our own

colonial status is unique in that we are the descendants of people enslaved and transplanted into a colonial status. The rhetoric, the false claims, the meaningless phrases, all these try to tell us that we are citizens. We are Americans. I will not dwell on the absurdity of that, for we all know too well that the internal rebellions in this country, led by Watts, would not occur if in fact that was the case.

The serious condition in which we find ourselves as a people demands that we begin talking more of the colonized and the colonizer.[74]

INTEGRATION IS UNACCEPTABLE

When one hypothesizes that black Americans are, in fact, a colonized people, the next logical step is to reject completely any ideas favoring integration. Such a conclusion follows clearly from the first three themes. If one finds himself a black man living in a land controlled by evil white men, within an evil capitalist system, holding the status of colonial subject, he certainly cannot hold any hope or desire of integrating with these people. Fanon rejects any compromise with the former colonial master, alleging that it can signal ultimately only tighter rein. Failing to read history, he feels, leads leaders to enter into undefined compromises. To Fanon's way of thinking, therefore, the moderate black American who seeks and accepts compromise with the white man can be, at best, ignorant of history.

The basic argument against integration is the charge of the inherent incapacity of the white-controlled system to provide what the black man must have. Lester suggests that the federal government could provide every black man in the United States with a color TV and a guaranteed annual income, and "...the fundamental racism in this country would remain untouched. The American system is incapable of touching it."[75] If the white man is inherently an oppressor, and if the only way of satisfying the black man is to stop oppression, then, concludes Lester, there is no way to solve the problem within the context of the present system. Cleaver advances much the same line of reasoning. He argues that advocates of integration fail to realize that the black people in America are a colonized people, and it is historically impossible for the colonizer and the colonized to merge.

Many revolutionists have adopted a creative approach to the discrediting of integration. Their strategy is to reject the idea that integration or assimilation has ever been the goal of most black people. They follow two lines of thought. First, they will go to the speeches and writings of black leaders of the past, such as Frederick Douglass, and select the most militant of their statements, quoting them as evidence that they never seriously sought assimilation with whites. Similar to the arguments used to show Booker T. Washington as a separatist, it is suggested that any talk of assimilation was solely for the benefit of white men. Second, it may be argued that while some leaders may have sought assimilation, the great masses of black people did not. James Forman asserts that while many so-called black leaders have accommodated to the capitalistic system, the great masses of blacks have never done so.[76]

In his editorials in *The Black Panther,* Minister of Defense, Huey P. Newton shows the influence of Fanon in his ideas about the established system. He defines a triangle consisting of the oppressor, the white man, the endorsed spokesman, black leaders who have been selected by the white man to speak for the black population, and the implacables, or groups such as the Black Panthers who reject the concept of integration.

> The oppressor, the endorsed spokesman, and the implacables form the three points of a triangle of death. The oppressor looks upon the endorsed spokesmen as a tool to use against the implacables to keep the masses passive within the acceptable limits of the tactics he is capable of containing. The endorsed spokesmen look upon the oppressor as a guardian angel who can always be depended upon to protect them from the wrath of the implacables, while he looks upon the implacables as dangerous and irresponsible madmen who, by angering the oppressor, will certainly provoke a blood bath in which they themselves might get washed away. The implacables view both the oppressors and the endorsed leaders as his deadly enemies. If anything, he has a more profound hatred for the endorsed leaders than he has for the oppressor himself. . . ."[77]

The implacable's argument is developed more explicitly in an interview broadcast from Cuba in 1968. When asked what he thought would be the outcome of his pending trial, Newton said,

> I think the jury will acquit, will deliver a verdict of not guilty on the first vote. I think any verdict other than acquittal would be embarrassing. The current court structure is operated and controlled by a small imperialist and racist ruling class. This in no way represents the people, especially the Negro population of many ghettoes across the length and breadth of the country. This is only a weapon of the power structure for enforcing its

laws, which are against the people and which keep them in a state of captivity.

He was next asked by the interviewer what he believed would be the best way to commemorate the anniversary of the Watts rebellion:

> Che Guevara said that we need not only a Watts but many Watts throughout the United States, throughout the World. I think we can celebrate and commemorate this anniversary by resisting and escalating our resistance against North American imperialism.

Finally, Newton was asked to link the objectives of the struggle supported by Che Guevara with those of the Negro movement in the United States:

> Che Guevara was an internationalist who felt deeply for all the peoples of the world. He told all the peoples to consider the imperialists from the United States as world enemy number one. The Negroes in this country are suffering because of imperialism, and we are identified with all the colonized peoples and with the peoples who are suffering neocolonialism. And now we are increasing our resistance, and we are taking a position of placing ourselves at the side of all peoples in order to resist the world's number one criminal, U.S. imperialism.
>
> Che Guevara called on all colonized peoples to resist the racist and bureaucratic North American imperialism's assault troops. Therefore, we consider ourselves an integral part of the army of resistance that is being mobilized all over the world.

REVOLUTION IS THE ONLY WAY

Still continuing the sequential development of the rhetorical campaign, the next step after discrediting the white man, the capitalist system, the colonialist methods, and the deceitful plan of integration, is to prove that the only way the black man will improve his lot is through revolution. In this effort, the black revolutionary rhetorician has a ready-made persuasive appeal. If revolution is a repugnant idea today, to persuade people to accept it requires, among other strategies, the association of the unacceptable idea with an idea that is highly valued. In this case, the obvious choice is the American Revolution, for all Americans, white and black, have learned to revere the heroes who fought in 1776. Note how Huey P. Newton developed this argument by showing that the plight of modern black Americans is the same as the one faced by our forefathers.

Before 1776, white people were colonized by the English. The English government had certain laws and rules that the colonized Americans viewed as not to their best interests but as a colonized people. At that time the English government felt that the colonized Americans had no right to establish laws to promote the general welfare of the people living here in America. The colonized American felt he had no choice but to raise the gun in defense of the welfare of the colonized people. At this time, he made certain laws insuring his protection from external and internal aggressions from governments and agencies. One such form of protection was the Declaration of Independence . . . .

Now these same colonized white people, these ex-slaves, robbers, and thieves, have denied the colonized black man the right to even speak of abolishing this oppressive system which colonized Americans created.[78]

Beyond this relatively unique line of justification for revolution, the arguments advanced are not particularly original. Essentially they are a collection of ideas taken from such revolutionaries as Mao Tse tung, Stalin, Lenin, Ho Chi Minh, Frantz Fanon, Leon Trotsky, Ernesto Che Guevara, with Malcolm X supplying the essentially black arguments.

ON COALITION WITH WHITES

Much more distinctly black-oriented is the debate within revolutionary groups themselves over the question of whether a coalition with white people is desirable. Stokely Carmichael has become a leading exponent of no coalition with whites. His reasoning rests upon the assumption that whites, no matter what their class, profit from the capitalistic society. "Unfortunately, they do not recognize that if they smashed that system they could build a better system for themselves, but they are so afraid of giving up the dollars that they now have, that they hang on to it and fight to keep the system going."[79] Because of this, reasons Carmichael, when black men attack the system, all white groups become a "monolithic structure." "When faced with demands from black people, the multi-faction whites unite and present a common front."[80]

The Reverend Albert B. Cleage, Jr., who will be discussed in greater detail later, agrees with Carmichael's analysis. In the opening sermon of a collection published under the title *The Black Messiah*, Cleage makes this statement:

We are the revolution. There are some white people who are poor, who are exploited but they are white. There are some white people who are liberal, but they are white. There are some white people who are radical, but they are white. And in the final analysis all these white people stand together.[81]

Perhaps the most unyielding of all black positions is that taken by the Revolutionary Action Movement (RAM). This group envisions a world under black domination, whereas Carmichael allows the possibility that ultimately whites may legitimately join the revolution. The following statement in a RAM publication makes their position clear.

Revolutionary Black Inter-Nationalism is the philosophy of co-operation, unity of Black Nationalists throughout the world to bring about a world revolution in which Black culture dominates and rules the planet. Revolutionary Black Inter-Nationalism is the philosophy that black people of the world (black, yellow, brown, and red) are all enslaved by the same forces. Revolutionary Black Inter-Nationalism is the philosophy of a common international cultural heritage and identity among all non-European people, that is African, Asian and Latin American people all have similar if not the same cultural histories and have a common destiny.

Revolutionary Black Inter-Nationalism is the philosophy of a world black revolution of the black underclass rising up against their slavemasters.[82]

H. Rap Brown seems inclined to agree with Carmichael, while still allowing some recognition that other oppressed people may usefully join the revolution. In the concluding pages of his book, Brown exhorts the reader to see that the struggle is for all oppressed people including Mexican-Americans, Puerto Ricans, American Indians, Japanese-Americans and even poor whites. However, earlier in the book he notes that poor whites always feel themselves to be superior to blacks no matter how ignorant, hungry, and dirty they may be. And, he says, "As long as they got that attitude, I don't want nobody talking to me about coalitions with poor whites."[83]

The Black Panther Party speaks unanimously for the inclusion of other oppressed people. Developing a much more Marxist-Leninist line of reasoning, spokesmen for the BPP argue that the revolution is a class war and must include all oppressed peoples. Eldridge Cleaver entered a debate by published letter with Stokely Carmichael over this question. In a strong denunciation, Cleaver wrote in the September, 1969 issue of *Ramparts* that Carmichael's opposition to coalition with whites stems from his experience in SNCC which was, indeed, controlled by whites. This leads to an excessive fear of white people bordering on the fear of the white slavemaster. Such a fear, says Cleaver, belittles the intelligence of black people. Carmichael suggests, as indicated in the discussion above, that coalition with whites, if it ever comes, must await the development of a true revolutionary conscience. Of this, Cleaver says, "Your talk and fears about premature coalition are absurd, because no coalition against oppression by forces possessing revolutionary integrity can ever be premature."[84] The very disunity which comes from positions such as Carmichael's, Cleaver charges, gives strength to the forces of counter-revolution. In summary, Cleaver develops the philosophical justification of his position by stating that the revolution must fight racism, but only to develop a higher conception of humanity, and "an undying love for black people that denies the humanity of other people is doomed."[85] This kind of racist thinking, concludes Cleaver, is precisely what caused the white man to hate blacks and thereby lose his own humanity.

MORAL JUSTIFICATION OF VIOLENCE

Probably the most difficult persuasive task of the entire revolutionary movement is bringing people to a point of taking violent action. Earlier in this discussion the problem of allowing tough rhetoric to take the place of tough behavior was revealed. As Fanon observes, if the last shall be first, if the oppressed are to achieve power and control, a violent struggle with those now in power is inevitable. Therefore, the revolution can never become a reality until the people accept, and act upon, the acceptability of violence. But when one is dealing with a population strongly influenced by the Christian religion and based on peace, love, and turning the other cheek, the persuasive task is tremendous. When the substantial influence of Christianity is added to generations of experience which show that any violent act against the white man leads to quick and terrible retaliation, the persuasive problem is even greater.

Revolutionary speakers have sought to meet the persuasive problem of violence in a variety of ways. A first message takes advantage of the idea of the inherent evil of white men. The white man. and white America, are the most violent of all creatures on earth; as H. Rap Brown has said many times, "Violence is as American as cherry pie." Going more deeply into this concept, white men are pictured as a savage race of people. While the black and yellow men were developing culture, religion, and science in Africa and the eastern nations, the white man in Europe was still a beast. Albert B. Cleage Jr., pastor of the 1,000 member Shrine of the Black Madonna in Detroit, Michigan, develops this idea. The Reverend Mr. Cleage is a graduate of Wayne State University and Oberlin Graduate School of Theology. He has served as a social case worker with the Detroit Department of Public Welfare, and is now very much identified with the concept black power. Cleage, in his sermons and in public speeches, notes that the Jews of the time of Jesus Christ and before, were black men who had a long history of culture and religion, whereas the white man has a history of violence and power used cruelly, brutally, ruthlessly.

> His [the white man] whole experience from the time the white man climbed down out of the tree and stopped licking bugs and eating raw meat was complete brutality, feelings of the complete human animal exposed. He thought only in terms of brutality — he had a gun and he had no civilization. He was a retarded race of people, as well. But other people, the black people, the dark people, the non-white people were developing philosophy, developing history, had libraries, had culture, had religion. The white man was still living in trees and in caves and eating raw meat and drinking blood. He had developed nothing but he did develop the instrument of power and having no culture, no religion to speak of, he had a concept of religion as an extension of his own power. . . .[86]

This picture of the white man as a primitive beast pleases the black audiences tremendously and lays the foundation for legitimizing violence against white people. Following logically from this idea is the assertion that it is fruitless to talk of peaceful and traditional means of change — the white man simply will not allow it.

> To talk about conventional warfare, to talk about peace movements when those whom we face do not understand what peace is all about, what tranquility is all about, is foolish and even redundant. I think Malcolm X pointed this out when he said the students should be nonviolent with those who are nonviolent with them; but that the first law of nature (? is that everyone must defend himself, defend his right to survive.) Anyone who does not understand this, anyone who does not want to employ this tactic, is doing nothing more than committing suicide, putting his life into the hands of the aggressor.[87]

Two major lines of reasoning emerge from these messages. First, as suggested above, the law of nature calls for self-defense when faced with a violent and brutal attack. Second, when the white man assumes the role of a power-using animal who used his guns to enslave and oppress other peoples, he relinquishes any rights he might have had to be dealt with peacefully. The slogan emerges, "the oppressor has no rights which the oppressed are bound to observe."

A similar line of argument used to legitimize violence is the observation that man has not condemned all violence. Those in power are in the position to define what violence will be considered undesirable. Thus, argues Stokely Carmichael, if I kill a yellow man in the United States, I will be put in jail, but if I kill thirty of them in Vietnam, I will be called a hero. Carmichael states that the black man must assume for himself the privilege of defining his own enemies; of deciding what violence will be undesirable, and that if this is done, the black man will realize that the North Vietnamese are not his enemies; they are the white man's enemies. It is the white man who is the enemy of blacks. Similarly, when black people utilize violent means to advance their values, they are considered criminals. When, on the other hand, the white police use guns, gas, dogs, and water hoses to uphold their values, it is called law and order.

Robert Williams, President of the Republic of New Africa, wrote a newsletter from exile in which he developed this idea.

> The racist power structure is attempting to cloak mass lynching, unmitigated police violence, racial emasculation and extermination in a viciously hypocritical crusade disguised as "law and order."
>
> There has been no implemented concern for law and order for protection of the human rights for Black Americans throughout the history of violently racist America. Now what is the cause for this sudden concern and pious sounding devotion to "law and order" and safety on the streets? Under the new Hitlerites order who will defend the rights of the disinherited victims whose eternal abuse is considered an accepted peculiarity of the American way of life? No sensible person can take exception to the just and impartial application of law and order. The most sinister and repulsive factor in the whole affair is the cruel fact that white man's "law and order" to Black America means racist license to rape, maim, plunder, dehumanize and massacre the most abused and unprotected element of the heartless society.
>
> Who can have any faith in the demagogic utterances of a brigand whose entire history indicts him as a lawless savage whose very sadistical nature seems to condemn him to the hopeless region of human society dominated by the incorrigible? Can a leopard change its spots? Can a rabid wolf become

a lamb? Can Black America rely on a viciously racist cop to justly enforce impartial law and order?[88]

Following a similar line Julius Lester suggests that violence is neither good nor evil; it simply is. If black men must humanize America by beginning a revolution, they must go about their task without concerning themselves with questions of the morality of violence. If the white man responds with violence; if the white man seeks to kill the black, "he is, in effect, giving me permission to try and take his life."[89]

Stokely Carmichael has given much of his rhetorical energy over many years to the development of a justification of violence. His efforts have included the idea of power to define for oneself who his enemies will be, and the violent, racist character of white America necessitating a violent response. In the interview published below, Carmichael develops these and other themes which have characterized his speaking. While he is pictured in this document in a non-public speaking situation, he does reveal in the answers, the ways in which each idea is expressed in speech after speech. For this reason, the interview effectively reveals the broad scope of Carmichael's public speaking and is printed below in its entirety.

Stokely Carmichael
Stokely Carmichael Interviewed by Sucesos Magazine*

Havana in English to South America 2106 GMT 9 Sep 67 E
Excerpts of undated recorded interview given by Stokely Carmichael to Mario Menendez, editor of Mexican Magazine SUCESOS, during Carmichael's stay in Havana

Question. What is the Student Nonviolent Coordinating Committee?
Answer. The Student Nonviolent Coordinating Committee is the organization for which I work and is a group of young black people in the United States who decided to come together to fight racial and economic exploitation.
Question. When and why was it founded?
Answer. The Student Nonviolent Coordinating Committee was founded in 1960 by a group of young black students who felt the need to come together

*Stokely Carmichael Interviewed by Sucesos Magazine. Reprinted from U.S. Congress, Senate Committee on Government Operations, Permanent Subcommittee on Investigations, Hearings, Riots, Civil and Criminal Disorders, 91st Congress, First Session, 1969, pp. 4005-13.

and actively fight against racial segregation in the United States. They came together because they felt the older organizations were not doing an effective job and were not actively participating. Most of them were taking their troubles to the courts and we felt that you could not take a problem of the whites' injustice to black people to the courts if those courts were all white. You would be taking an unjust problem to people who themselves were unjust.

It could not be solved that way. The only way to solve it was in the streets. We used the name nonviolent because at that time Martin Luther King was the central figure of the black struggle and he was still preaching nonviolence, and anyone who talked about violence at that time was considered to have committed treason, so we decided that we would use the name nonviolent, but in the meantime we knew our struggle was not about to be nonviolent, but we would just wait until the time was right for the actual (word indistinct) name. We came together, we would coordinate activities between the students whenever we have a nonviolent demonstration.

But after one year many of us decided that demonstrations were not the answer. The only answer was organizing our people. So we moved into the worst state, Mississippi, and began to organize our people to fight. And we are now at the front where we are encouraging people to pick up arms and fight back.

Question. What are the political, social, and economic goals pursued by your organization.

Answer. Politically, we want black people in the United States to be free of oppression. We also want the peoples of the third world to be free from oppression, particularly Africa, Asia, and Latin America. We see that our freedom, our liberation, depends on these people and vice versa, their liberation depends on us, so we must wage the same struggle.

Politically speaking (words indistinct) in the United States we want the right to politically control the communities in which we live. In the United States we cannot do that. The communities in which we live, which they call ghettos, are politically controlled by whites. So in a real sense, we have colonialism inside the United States, just like colonialism in Latin American countries, or I should probably say all the Latin American countries, with the exception of Cuba, are controlled politically from the outside by the United States. Politically, we seek to free those colonies of any political intervention from the outside.

Economically speaking, we want our people to be able to enjoy life and to get all the things they need for a decent life without having to struggle as hard as they now do because they are economically exploited by the imperialist power structure of the United States, just as the colonies outside are economically exploited. We want to be able not only to control the resources inside our communities, but also we want to be able to divide those resources among the people of the (?backward) communities. We do not want to set up, for example, a black capitalist system. We want to economically destroy capitalism because capitalism goes hand in hand with racism and exploitation. Wherever capitalism has gone, those two characteristics are sure to follow, racism and exploitation, so we must destroy the capitalistic system which enslaves us on the inside and the people of the third world on the outside.

Socially, I guess we want what most people want out of life: people who are happy and free and who can live (?better) than they now live and who make and participate in decisions that affect their lives, and never feel ashamed of the color of their skin or ashamed of their culture. In order for capitalism to exist it must make the people they conquer feel ashamed of themselves, ashamed of their culture, and what we want to do is to make our people ashamed (word indistinct) so that they can feel that they are equal to any-body else psychologically, physically, and morally.

Question. In particular, what are the relations between the colored people of the north and of the south, and, in general, in the whole United States of America?

Answer. The black people who are living in the north are first-generation people, that is to say, it is the first generation of black people that has been born in the north. Most of the people in the north migrated from the south right after World War II. They migrated from the south because racial dis-crimination was the (worst) and most brutal in the south and they were told that in the north people did not care about the color of your skin. It did not matter, there were opportunities and a good job if you just worked hard.

And we believed that nonsense and packed our bags and went north. But what we found when we got north was that life was the same. So the [word indistinct] that we found in the north was that there is nowhere in the United States where you can go under the capitalistic system and enjoy a decent way of life. So what you have now are people without faith in any of the legal systems [words indistinct]. So the relationship has become very strong because people from the south no longer look to the north as an escape, and we now see that the only way that we are going to get out of the capitalistic system and gain our liberatoin is that both of us join hands and see ourselves as one people.

What you have now across the United States is a feeling of solidarity among black people wherever we are, and our saying is that when they touch one, they have to touch all. That saying is more than a slogan because it now has meaning. Every time a racist police dog shoots one of us they have to fight the entire city, and now it is not only one city, they have to fight several cities, so the black feeling of solidarity is very, very near.

Question. Some persons think Negroes in the United States only think of the fight as a racial conflict against the whites instead of interpreting it as a class struggle. What do you have to say on this matter?

Answer. Well, that is very, very important, because in the United States racism is so strong it is almost impossible to get white people to struggle against it, and there are many reasons for that. Most of the poor whites, the white working class in the United States, when they organize, their fight is never a fight for the redistribution of land. Their fight is a fight for more money. All they want is more money. They do not have any concept of the distribution of wealth because they are so capitalistic in their own approach.

So what happens is that the ruling class in America then begins to exploit other countries in the third world to make more money. When they get more of those profits, they share those profits with the white working class.

But the ruling class never cuts down on its profits. As a matter of fact, it makes more. Once it begins to share its profits with the working class, the working class becomes part and parcel of the capitalist system and they enjoy blood money. They enjoy so much the money that is exploiting other people that they are then incapable of fighting the system, because they are a part of it from accepting the blood money. So it is hard to develop a white working class revolutionary consciousness. What you have then is white people who are fighting to save their money.

For example, that is why you cannot find white working class people in the United States who oppose the war in Vietnam, because it is from the war in Vietnam that they enjoy the life they are living and the luxuries they have. If they opposed the war in Vietnam, they would be smashing the system. Unfortunately, they do not recognize that if they smashed that system they could build a better system for themselves, but they are so afraid of giving up the dollars that they now have, that they hang on to it and fight to keep the system going. So what you do have at this point, unfortunately, is black people waging the fight and interpreting it as a black-white struggle, which it does, in fact, become because the white working class begins to attack us, because they are afraid that we will destroy their way of life.

We believe that the only way to develop white working class revolutionary consciousness is for the United States to begin losing its profits that it gets from the third world. Once it begins to lose that and its profits are cut down and it must begin to turn inward for the means of livelihood, then and only then will the white working class develop a revolutionary consciousness. What that means is that at this time we will struggle. We would like white working class people to struggle with us. Whether they do or not does not make any difference; we will struggle. When they finally join the fight, we will welcome them, but until that time we will struggle.

And another reason why it is (?so) is because the white ruling class in America recognizes Marx' concept of the inevitable class conflict. In order to avoid an inevitable class conflict in the United States they exploit the third world and bring the money from the third world into the United States and share it with the working class.

So what you now have is just a postponement of inevitable class conflict. What has developed around the world is that the third world has become the proletariat and the white Western society has become the bourgeoisie. So when you have lines drawn along lines of color, it is also class because of the way white Western society has incorporated most of its working class. What is precisely what Europe did when it sat down and divided up Africa and Latin America. It avoided inside its countries the inevitable class conflict. But that cannot be postponed anymore; the confrontation is here.

And finally, I think that people outside the United States recognize, unlike any other people, that we were the only people who were made slaves inside the continent by the people who were exploiting us. Other people were slaves in their own countries, so that when they fought they could develop a nationalistic concept as a point of unity. We were brought to the United States, which is the most vicious thing that the United States could have done. So we cannot develop a nationalistic concept, our concept must be around our color, because it was our color which was the deciding factor in making us slaves. So our color is, in a sense, our nationality, because what the white man has done is to scatter black people from Africa throughout the United States, through the Caribbean into Cuba, into Brazil, and all the way up through South America, and we are just (?planted) all over these countries without any nationality.

Now in Cuba the African has a concept of nationality because they were exploited along with the whites in Cuba. So they called themselves Afro-Cubans and can feel a part of the Cuban system, especially since the revolution. Unfortunately, for us in the United States that cannot be done because for 400 years we have been the victims of brutal fascism and no white man has ever come to our defense, real defense, except John Brown. All of the others talk, they talk, but none of them are actually willing to fight to destroy the system of which they are a part.

Question. What relations exist between the Student Nonviolent Coordinating Committee and the Puerto Rican Pro-Independence Movement? How do you see the interrelation between the struggle of the Puerto Rican people for their independence and the fight of the Negroes in the United States? How do you see the fight of the Negro people of the United States as they help the Puerto Rican, and the unity between the two organizations?

Answer. Now, Brother Malcolm taught us that we must internationalize our struggle. In an effort to follow some of his teachings, we started with Puerto Rico. We started with Puerto Rico for many reasons. Number one, it is very close to the United States in terms of geographic position. Number two, it is a real U.S. colony in every sense. And thirdly, a large number of people who live in the ghettos of the United States with us are Puerto Ricans.

And what we find happening is that we were fighting Puerto Ricans. Instead of joining hands with our Puerto Rican brothers and fighting the system that oppresses both of us, we were made to fight each other while the white policeman sat around and laughed. So we thought one of the ways to start raising the political consciousness of our people to join hands with the Puerto Ricans was to physically go to the island of Puerto Rico and raise questions of independence. That worked very, very well, because prior to this year if the police attacked the Puerto Ricans, blacks would not do anything. As a matter of fact, we were likely to join sides with the police and help beat the Puerto Ricans. And if a policeman attacked a black man, the Puerto Ricans would not anything, they would probably join hands with the police and beat us.

But this year, because we have been able to raise the question and raise the political consciousness of both groups, when the police attacked Puerto Ricans in New York, blacks and Puerto Ricans took to the streets together to fight the police. The same thing happened in Newark, and the same thing is happening in Chicago. So that trip enabled us to raise political consciousness, and we were able to sit down and bring both groups together and begin to talk about fighting the system that oppresses both of us.

Question. What sort or type of fight will develop in the United States against the imperialist policy? Do you think that the armed way is the only way left for the North American people to obtain the government? What is your opinion on revolutionary violence as compared with reactionary violence?

Answer. When we say that we insist, we say very clearly that the only solution is black revolution and that we are not concerned with peaceful coexistence. Armed struggle, for a number of reasons, is the only way, not only for us but for all oppressed people around the world. People who talk about peaceful coexistence are talking about maintaining the status quo. The only way that you can disrupt an imperialistic system is by force. You do not disrupt it with talk. That has been crystal clear to us. It has been crystal clear to us especially because for 400 years the majority of African-Americans in the United States have been talking, talking, and talking, and the reason is because whey you talk you play the imperialist game. They invented the game of talk, and when you talk, you talk in their language.

But now we have a new game. It is called guerrilla warfare. They cannot play our game, and if you want to win a game, you have to make the rules. If somebody else makes the rules, they will always win. The imperialists have made the rules of talk, so when you sit down to talk with them you can not possibly win. They will always find a reason why they cannot do this now, or why they could not do it then, and they will seem very rational and you will sit there and try to reason with them on their grounds, in their terms, but they cannot do that. In the first place, they have no right to oppress people, so there is no need to talk about oppression. They have absolutely no right to oppress and to exploit anybody else, so to begin talks about freeing yourself from exploitation and oppression from the people who oppress you is ridiculous. It is like a slave sitting down with his master and talking to his master about when his master is going to set him free. That is nonsense. The master has no business enslaving him. So all the slave has to do is get up and kill the master if the master refused to stop enslaving him. That is the only solution.

So it is crystal clear, as far as we are concerned: armed struggle, that is all, no time for talk. We have talked and talked and talked and talked for too long. You must disrupt the system by any means necessary.

Now, secondly, reactionary violence can be legitimatized by people in power. For example, if I were to shoot a man who had slanted eyes, it depends if I shot him in the United States or if I shot him in Vietnam, there would be two different reactions. If I shot 30 men who had slanted eyes in Vietnam and they happened to be Vietnamese, I would get a medal, because I would be in the army. If I shot 30 people who had slanted eyes or one person who had slanted eyes in the United States, in New York, I would get the chair, the electric chair for murder.

So it is never a question of violence, it is a question of who can legitimatize violence, that is all. A policeman can shoot and kill anybody he wants to kill for any reason and go to court and say "I did it in line of duty," and they will let him go. But a man who shoots a policeman is automatically going to jail, so you never discuss violence as far as we are concerned. It is whether or not you can legitimatize it.

And the oppressed people of the world must legitimatize violence in their own minds as the way to solve their problems. Once they have legitimatized violence, then there is no question, there is no answer, it is just a course of taking what belongs to them. The reactionaries only stay in power by violence. That is the only way they stay in power. However, they legitimatize their violence, and they tell everybody else that violence is not the way. Take away the guns from the imperialist forces and see how many people would listen to them. Take away the bases in Santo Domingo, take away the bases in Venezuela, take away the bases in Brazil, take away the bases in Chile, take away the bases all over South America, get the guns out of their hands, and you would see nobody would listen. But it is because of the guns that people are forced to listen, and so the only thing you can do is get yourself guns and the will to fight, and then the answer is clear.

For example, we want you to look at people who are pacifists, and all this nonsense about pacifism. The United States, Britain, France, and Russia developed the atomic and the hydrogen bombs. After they developed the atomic and the hydrogen bomb, then all four of them got together and said "let us stop nuclear tests, there will be no more testing of bombs." And everybody was sitting there and falling for this nonsense because they would say to the people, "We do not want any more bombs and if more people would get bombs it would just mean violence." But what they were doing was that they had the bomb and they were stopping other people from developing the bomb. So they were keeping other people unequal. If everybody is to be equal, everybody must have the bomb. That is the only answer. If some people have the bomb and others do not it is inequality. That is just one example of how the West uses violence as a way to stop other people.

It is crystal clear that the West has developed the best weapons, but weapons can never defeat the will of men to fight, and that is precisely where the world is today. The oppressed people have the will to fight and they are fighting the people who oppress them, and they have weapons. A good example of that would be Vietnam, where the United States, with all of its weapons, cannot defeat a nation so small as Vietnam because they have the will to fight and they are willing to fight to the death rather than let the United States enslave them. That is very important.

And the discussion is never about that, the discussion is of the right of people to defend themselves against aggression. When the United States talked about bombing Cuba and missiles in Cuba, they said that Cuba did not have the right to defend itself. They said that Cuba should not even get antimissiles and the rest of the world was supporting Cuba rather than the United States because the United States had no business (?committing) aggression against Cuba, just as they have no business (?committing) aggression against Vietnam, and what happens is that the people of Vietnam are fighting not only a defensive war but defensive propaganda, if in fact they begin to accept that definition.

The people of Vietnam have every right to send a bomber over the United States and start bombing the United States. That would be real equality in terms of a fight. That would be real equality, but instead they are now forced to fight a defensive war, and that was the position Cuba was in with the missiles, they were also fighting a defensive war. And people have been telling me about Debray's book, which I have not had a chance to read yet. "Revolution Within a Revolution." Debray points out that we must begin to move beyond defensive wars, and I think that is the next step for the peoples of the third world, to move beyond defensive wars.

Question. What do you think of guerrilla warfare in the American continent to obtain its liberation? What do you think of this sort of fight being developed by the colored people in the country and cities of the United States?

Answer. It is crystal clear to us that the way the imperialists take everything is by force. The only way it has conquered all the countries here is by force. They made the Indian population of Cuba, for example, extinct. They took their land by force. The only way you can remedy that is by force. The only way to use force is to start guerrilla warfare. Guerrilla warfare should never be discussed as to whether it is right or wrong. It is the only way. It is the only way to stop exploitation and oppression. To wage a discussion as to whether it is right or wrong is to play the game of the imperialists. When you are waging a war, there is no right, there is no wrong, it is just what you feel is necessary to obtain your goals, and that is what we must understand, those of us who are in the oppressed world.

There is no question, guerrilla warfare is the only way. We will not raise the question of whether it is right or whether it is wrong, we will only raise a tactical question of when do we use it. That is the only question we should be concerned with. Guerrilla warfare is where we are moving to in the United States, we are going to develop an urban guerrilla warfare, and we are going to beat them in urban guerrilla warfare, because there is one thing the imperialists do not have. Their men do not have the will to fight. They do not have the will to fight. What they call guerrilla warfare is in fact hand to hand combat.

See, their men are cowards. White America is the most cowardly nation in the world. It could send a million troops into Vietnam and they could not kill the Vietnamese people. The Vietnamese people in hand to hand combat would wipe them out. So what they do is say, "In Vietnam they are fighting guerrilla warfare," and you think that guerrilla warfare is dirty, it is not clean, it is not supposed to be done. And they said, "To beat guerrilla warfare we will now send men and planes to drop bombs," and nobody asked, "Is it not more disgusting to send a man in a plane who can drop 50 or 60 bombs on defenseless women and children or use napalm and burn them to death than to fight them hand to hand combat? Which is more honorable?" So that is the question, it is just when we use it. Urban guerrilla warfare is the only way we will beat the United States because they cannot use bombs on us, because we are inside their country. They will have to fight us hand to hand combat. We will win, we will win.

The counterpart of that will be in the south in the countryside where we know the land, where we know the terrain, where we have worked it for years, where the white man is in [word indistinct] with sweat from us.

He has enjoyed us walking all over the countryside. Well, we have walked over it so much so that when we take to the hills there, he does not know it. He will be unable to find us. We will (?hit him), we will be able to beat him in guerrilla warfare. The only way that you can bring white men to their knees is through guerrilla warfare, because guerrilla warfare is the one warfare they cannot fight with their big guns and their big bombs. And that is the one place you beat them because they do not have any guts.

Question. What do you think of solidarity between all countries that fight for their liberation?

Answer. It is the only answer. I think that what we do not recognize, or we have not recognized in the past, is that capitalism has become international, and that we are fighting international capitalism. In order to fight international capitalism, you must wage an international fight. What has happened in the past, for example, is that if one nation was struggling everybody wished that nation good luck, but nobody (served) as part of that same fight. Although they could see that the same countries were oppressing their countries, they still did not make the connection in their minds that that was their common enemy.

Today we have made the connection in our minds. We see a common enemy, so it is crystal clear to us that we are fighting an international structure that enslaves us all. The only way we can beat it is to internationalize our struggle. So you have an international power fighting an international power. That is the only way we can win. If we do what Che says we should do, that is, create two, three, many Vietnams, we will have them fighting on all fronts at the same time and they cannot win.

When we isolate the struggle, they can bring all their power to bear on one country. And once they do that, that country is lost. However, they cannot fight us all at the same time. So even if we do not have the same goals, even if we do not have the same ideas, the same political ideology, we have the same common enemy, and that, if nothing else, is what is going to bring us together.

Question. What do you think of the solidarity organization for Asian, African, and Latin American countries? What does an organization such as yours expect from the AALAPSO?

Answer. Well, one thing is that we are now beginning to more firmly establish our relationship with those groups because we have found out that we must establish firm relations and must do so on an international level. So the first thing we want to do is (?to meet) all the fighters that we read about, to sit down and talk with them, and exchange our ideas. Once we have done that, we can begin to move together, to plot together how to fight for our liberation.

For example, when they start bombing a country or when they start assassinating a liberation, let us say they assassinate a leader of the liberation struggle. A few months ago, they assassinated Ben Bark. See what the rest of us, if we had been together, should have done was to take Johnson, or to take De Gaulle, and put a gun to his head and say "if Ben Barka is not freed in 24 hours, De Gaulle is dead, or Johnson is dead, or Harold Wilson is dead." And not many—any—[interrupts self] But the only way we can do that is to internationalize our struggle, because they have their systems of the CIA and all the other intelligence agencies which are international and work hand in hand with each other, so they can assassinate and carry out coups against governments when they begin to move for their libertion. To protect those governments for inspiration and aid, we must begin to do the same thing to develop them. So I think that is one of the concrete areas in which we can begin to move.

But more important is that once we have seized power, as we will, the question is to begin to develop an international system that will not give vent to capitalism, where we can trade with each other on the basis of our needs, on what we need and on what each country has, rather than fight to control the world market where we would set prices for goods by profits and not by the needs of humanity. And that is the concept that we must begin to talk more and more about, because we will find out that as we seize power, unless we have the spirit, the will, and the intelligence of the leaders in Cuba, most of us will end up the way all other countries that have coups or that seize power end up: they will accept the entire bureaucratic structure that the imperialists have imposed on their countries and will not be able to fight it. So we must begin to do that.

The other thing is that we must begin to do is to exchange fighters so that we can understand different areas where the imperialists live. For example, we should begin to exchange fighters with people of Africa and Latin America who are fighting for their liberation so we can set up an international system of guerrilla warfare, and, for example, when we start fighting the real war in the United States, if there are people from other countries who are willing to come to the United States and help us fight, that is well and good, and we will be willing to reciprocate.

We will be willing to go and fight because that is what the capitalists do. Whenever one of their countries is in trouble they send aid to help that country. That is clearly what happened in Israel. Israel is an imperialist country backed by the imperialist West, and when it was in trouble all of them stood behind it and supported it, including France. Every one of them supported it. What we have to do is recognize that once the fight starts, we must also be willing to back up the liberation forces with our men, because they are willing to back them up with their guns, their money, and their men, and we must begin to do the same.

Question. What do you think of the solidarity organization for Latin America? What does an organization as yours expect from LASO?

Answer. Well, this is the First LASO Conference and we are more than honored, happy, and pleased to be here and to be able to share in LASO and to be part of this for many, many reasons. Number one is that Latin America is very close to us geographically. Latin America is one of the areas that the United States really exploits. Many Latin Americans come into the United States. All of those reasons and the closeness of Latin America makes it a necessity that we begin to move.

More importantly, Cuba is part of Latin America, and the United States really wants to crush Cuba, and Cuba is an inspiration to others, not only to blacks in the United States but also to all Latin American countries to begin to struggle and to begin to fight. So it is fitting and proper that LASO should be held in Cuba and that we should come to show our solidarity, not just by talk but also by our willingness to put our life on the line for the struggle in Latin America.

We want to be able to explain to the Latin American countries what our struggle is about, because their only way of getting an explanation now is from UPI and AP, which is the controlled communications system of the imperialists. Vice versa, we cannot get any news about Latin American countries except from UPI and AP, which is again controlled by the imperialists. So what we get is that there are bandits or there is a group of rebel forces or communists fighting in Venezuela or rebel forces took to the streets in Guatemala, Santo Domingo, or Panama. And only through our political awareness to know those groups who really fighting for their country are we able to read through the lies and propaganda that is [word indistinct]. So number one, it is the first time we have had a chance to meet sincere people who are fighting for their liberation struggles and listen to explanations of their idealogies so we can see where the common ground is and understand their struggle and explain to them what our struggle is, without having the propaganda of the imperialist interpreting our struggles to each other. This is the first thing.

The second thing is that, concretely, we must unite our struggles, and that is done just by our mere presence. And thirdly, to begin to counteract the OAS; and the mere fact that we have a conference here is already doing that. It will counteract the OAS and begin to minimize its importance in the minds of our peoples, which is very, very important because the imperialists control the propaganda and can win the minds of our people. And one of the most important fights today is the fight to win the minds of our people, because when we have won the minds of our people there will be no question, they will be ready to fight, and begin setting up systems and ways of helping and aiding each other.

Question. What do you think about the guerrilla leaders like Douglas Bravo from Venezuela, Fabio Vasquez from Columbia, Marulanda from Columbia, Cesar Montes from Guatemala, and the leaders of the Bolivian guerrillas?

Answer. We want to say to our brothers, or comrades, that while they may not know it, that there are many of us who are actually morally pulling for them, who listen very closely and very attentively to any news we can get about their struggles. And we know they are waging a victorious, valiant, and good fight, and that while we do not control the communications system so that we would be able to tell them this, we want them to know that they should never despair and never feel that their fight is in vain or that nobody knows about it.

We know about it and we are 150 percent behind them, and the day is not far off when they can come out in the open and together we can join hands and build a world that we are working to build. Our only word to them is to not despair and keep up the fight because there are many of us out here who are depending on them. We look to them for inspiration and hope.

Question. What do you think of the Vietnam aggression?

Answer. I think it is the most disgusting aggression in the world today. I think it is the height of cowardice displayed by the United States. I think that today it is the filthiest war that has ever been, and I think, because of that and along with the will of the Vietnamese people, the United States is going to lose the war.

Question. What made you come to Cuba?

Answer. Well, when the Cuban revolution was being waged I was a young boy but we were very interested in it. My interest was heightened by the fact that when the prime minister of Cuba, Fidel Castro, came to the UN he lived in Harlem with black people. He came to the hotel Theresa, and that meant that our connection with Cuba became a real one in the sense that their prime minister, unlike all other prime ministers who come to the country, came to live in a ghetto with us while he stayed in the United States. And we have always felt that we owed something to Cuba, at least that same visit which they bestowed on us by their prime minister.

Secondly, we have always known that the Cuban revolution is a good revolution. And, unlike most of the people in the United States—white United States—who question the Cuban revolution, we never questioned it, we know it is good. We just came to Cuba to learn, and, in the few days that we have been here, what we have gotten out of the Cuban revolution we could never get out of books, movies, or anything else. By just being able to be here, to live among a free people, and to understand and see how they are solving their problems is beyond comprehension. That is what we came to do, we came to learn. We have learned quite a bit.

Question. What do you think of the prime minister of Cuba, Fidel Castro?

Answer. He is the greatest man I have ever met.

Question. What do you think of Che Guevara and what he has said about the revolution in America and Latin America and the whole world?

Answer. We agree 150 percent with Che. He is becoming one of the most widely read men in black United States today. Black people are reading Che wherever you go, and not only that, Che is being read around the world. One of the reasons I think that people appreciate and respect Che because he has not only talked about revolution but has gone and helped make one. Even after winning a revolutionary struggle for power in his country, he did not settle back in his country, but left his wife and went on to other countries to help wage the fight, to sacrifice his very life. You do not find men like that every day.

Question. The fight you are developing in the United States signifies for people, for outsiders, that you have signed your death sentence. What do you think, or have to say, about that?

Answer. Brother Malcolm used to tell us that there were several types of death. I think a dehumanized people who do not fight back are a dead people. That is what the West has been able to do to most of us. They dehumanized us to the point where we would not even fight back. Once you have begun to fight back, you are alive, you are alive, and bullets do not kill you. If you do not fight back, you are dead, you are dead, and all the money in the world cannot bring you alive. So we are alive today, we are alive all over the world. All of our black people are coming alive because they are fighting back. They are fighting for their humanity. They are doing the type of thing that Fidel talks about. When you become alive, you want to live so much that you fight to live. See, when you are dead, when you do not rebel, you are not fighting to live, you are already dead. Well, we are alive and we love life so much that we are willing to die for it. So, we are alive. Death cannot stop us.

The Reverend Albert B. Cleage, Jr. has developed an entire Christian theology that justifies revolution and violence. Using Biblical and other historical information, Cleage traces the movements of the various peoples who made up the Jews at the time of Jesus Christ. He asserts that they were entirely African people — black people. Modern Jews with white skins are derived from European peoples and are of much later origin. Following logically, Jesus was a black man, the son of a black woman, and a leader of black people.

Moreover, at the time of Christ, the Jews were under the oppressive control of white men from Rome. Jesus acted as a revolutionary leader of black people seeking to overthrow the control of white men. With this interpretation, Cleage explains, he hopes to re-establish the Christian religion as relevant to the young black revolutionary. Cleage puts it this way:

> The Black Messiah Jesus did not build a Church, but a movement. He gathered together people to follow him and he sent them out to change the world. He sent out the seventy two-by-two, and he himself went from place to place. He built a Movement, not a Church. Like today's young black prophets, he rejected the institutionalization of religion. He rejected the Church deliberately because he said, "It's wrong, it's hypocritical, and it's opposed to the will of God." He rejected the morality of his time. He rejected the Church of his time. He was a prophet.[90]

Carrying the justification further to include violence, Cleage alleges that the time of the black man's greatest strength in America occurred during the slave insurrections when men such as Nat Turner believed that when they killed white slave owners they were following the will of God. Black men must have that same faith today, states Cleage. "We must believe that our struggle is a revolutionary struggle designed to change the world and to establish us in our rightful position." Continuing, he says, "We must have faith that we are doing the will of God who created us in his own image."[91] Completing the argument, Cleage states, "There is no halfway revolution. When it starts, it is going to go to its logical conclusion. Either we get free or we end up in concentration camps."[92] Cleage does not shrink from stating explicitly that revolution includes violence of whatever kind is necessary. Thus, he has sought to provide the deepest of all moral justifications for violent revolution — carrying out the will of God as manifest in the life of His prophet Jesus Christ.

THE GOAL OF A SOCIALIST STATE

Viewed in terms of traditional rhetorical theory, the final step in black revolutionary efforts is the "visualization" step or the picturing of the dawn of a new day. In other words, the audience must be brought to see what it is they are being asked to fight for. In this step, the revolutionaries are not totally clear. Some see the revolution as the path to the establishment of separate, black nations throughout the world, and within the North American continent. Their views, exemplified by Robert Williams, are separatist and have been discussed in the preceding chapter.

However, many of the black revolutionaries advocate a new form of humanity which can be developed only in a socialist environment. Lester observes that a revolutionary is one who loves humanity and hates injustice. Lester is very sensitive to the fact that a revolution may well end in another, perhaps worse, form of oppression. "As we destroy," he says, "let us not forget that it is only so we may be more human." Further, he says, "We must destroy in order to live, but let us never enjoy the destroying more than the New Life."[93] Stokely Carmichael speaks of liberating all the peoples of the Third World and "struggle for true humanity."[94] Eldridge Cleaver defines the new humanity in socialist terms:

> The goal must be to make possible a more equitable distribution of goods and services — but also to have a different set of values, so that things themselves don't become a substitute for life itself. In order to achieve that dual goal, we're going to have to move toward a new form of socialism.[95]

During 1969, the one rhetorical effort of black revolutionaries that seemed to have the most immediate and tangible effect was the so-called Black Manifesto of James Forman. At the National Black Economic Development Conference held on the campus of Wayne State University in Detroit, Michigan, on April 25, 1969, Forman presented his statement for consideration and adoption. Since that time, he has presented it forcibly to the congregations of white churches, and it has been considered by church conventions. Some, according to newspaper accounts, have decided to give substantial sums of money to Forman and his cause. Perhaps they do this with the hope of disarming the revolution and settling the differences peacefully. Perhaps they do so because of the morality of the appeal. To anyone who reads the Manifesto, it is clear that the demands come not as a substitute to revolution, but as one of the early demands of the revolution. Because of its comprehensive statement of the revolutionary demands, and because it has achieved wide attention and response, the Manifesto is printed here as a summary to this study of black revolutionary rhetoric. The reader may decide for himself the basis and end of the appeal.

James Forman

*To the White Christian Churches and the Jewish Synagogues in the United States of America and all other racist institutions Black Manifesto**

TOTAL CONTROL AS THE ONLY SOLUTION TO THE ECONOMIC PROBLEMS OF BLACK PEOPLE

Brothers and Sisters:
We have come from all over the country, burning with anger and despair not only with the miserable economic plight of our people, but fully aware that the racism on which the Western World was build dominates our lives. There can be no separation of the problems of racism from the problems of our economic, political, and cultural degradation. To any black man, this is clear.

But there are still some of our people who are clinging to the rhetoric of the Negro and we must separate ourselves from those Negroes who go around the country promoting all types of schemes for Black Capitalism.

Ironically, some of the most militant Black nationalists, as they call themselves, have been the first to jump on the bandwagon of black capitalism. They are pimps; Black Power Pimps and fraudulent leaders and the people must be educated to understand that any black man or Negro who is advocating a perpetuation of capitalism inside the United States is in fact seeking not only his ultimate destruction and death, but is contributing to the continuous exploitation of black people all around the world. For it is the power of the United States Government, this racist, imperialist government that is choking the life of all people around the world.

---

*James Forman, "Black Manifesto," delivered and adopted by the National Black Economic Conference in Detroit, Michigan on April 26, 1969.

We are an African people. We sit back and watch the Jews in this country make Israel a powerful conservative state in the Middle East, but we are not concerned actively about the plight of our brothers in Africa. We are the most advanced technological group of black people in the world, and there are many skills that could be offered to Africa. At the same time, it must be publicly stated that many African leaders are in disarray themselves, having been duped into following the lies as laid out by the Western Imperialist governments.

Africans themselves succumbed to and are victims of the power of the United States. For instance, during the summer of 1967, as the representatives of SNCC, Howard Moore and I traveled extensively in Tanzania and Zambia. We talked to high, very high, governmental officials. We told them there were many black people in the United States who were willing to come and work in Africa. All these government officials who were part of the leadership in their respective governments, said they wanted us to send as many skilled people that we could contact. But this program never came into fruition and we do not know the exact reasons, for I assure you that we talked and were committed to making this a successful program. It is our guess that the United States put the squeeze on these countries, for such a program directed by SNCC would have been too dangerous to the international prestige of the U.S. It is also possible that some of the wild statements by some black leaders frightened the Africans.

In Africa today, there is a great suspicion of black people in this country. This is a correct suspicion since most of the Negroes who have left the States for work in Africa usually work for the Central Intelligence Agency (CIA) or the State Department. But the respect for us as a people continues to mount and the day will come when we can return to our homeland as brothers and sisters. But we should not think of going back to Africa today, for we are located in a strategic position. We live inside the U.S. which is the most barbaric country in the world and we have a chance to help bring this government down.

Time is short and we do not have much time and it is time we stop mincing words. Caution is fine, but no oppressed people ever gained their liberation until they were ready to fight, to use whatever means necessary, including the use of force and power of the gun to bring down the colonizer.

We have heard the rhetoric, but we have not heard the rhetoric which says that black people in this country must understand that we are the Vanguard Force. We shall liberate all the people in the U.S. and we will be instrumental in the liberation of colored people the world around. We must understand this point very clearly so that we are not trapped into diversionary and reactionary movements. Any class analysis of the U.S. shows very clearly that black people are the most oppressed group of people inside the United States. We have suffered the most from racism and exploitation, cultural degradation and lack of political power. It follows from the laws of revolution that the most oppressed will make the revolution, but we are not talking about just making the revolution. All the parties on the left who consider themselves revolutionary will say that blacks are the Vanguard, but we are saying that not only are we the Vanguard, but we must assume leadership, total control and we must exercise the humanity which is inherent in us. We are the most humane people within the U.S. We have suffered and we understand suffering. Our hearts go out to the Vietnamese for we know what it is to suffer under the domination of racist America. Our hearts, our souls and all the compassion we can mount goes out to our brothers in Africa, Santa Domingo, Latin America and Asia who are being tricked by the power structure of the U.S. which is dominating the world today. These ruthless, barbaric men have systematically tried to kill all people and organizations opposed to its imperialism. We no longer can just get by with the use of the word capitalism to describe the U.S., for it is an imperial power, sending money, missionaries and the army throughout the world to protect this government and the few rich whites who control it. General Motors and all the major auto industries are operating in South Africa, yet the white dominated leadership of the United Auto Workers sees no relationship to the exploitation of black people in South Africa and the exploitation of black people in the U.S. If they understand it, they certainly do not put it into practice which is the actual test. We as black people must be concerned with the total conditions of all black people in the world.

But while we talk of revolution which will be an armed confrontation and long years of sustained guerilla warfare inside this country, we must also talk of the type of world we want to live in. We must commit ourselves to a society where the total means of production are taken from the rich people and placed into the hands of the state for the welfare of all the people. This is what we mean when we say total control. And we mean that black people who have suffered the most from exploitation and racism must move to protect their black interest by assuming leadership inside of the United States of everything that exists. The time has passed when we are second in command and the white boy stands on top. This is especially true of the Welfare Agencies in this country, but it is not enough to say that a black man is on top. We must be committed to building the new society, to taking the wealth away from the rich people such as General Motors, Ford, Chrysler, the DuPonts, the Rockefellers, the Mellons, and all the other rich white exploiters and racists who run this world.

Where do we begin? We have already started. We started the moment we were brought to this country. In fact, we started on the shores of Africa, for we have always resisted attempts to make us slaves and now we must resist the attempts to make us capitalists. It is in the financial interest of the U.S. to make us capitalists, for this will be the same line as that of integration into the mainstream of American life. Therefore, brothers and sisters, there is no need to fall into the trap that we have to get an ideology. We HAVE an ideology. Our fight is against racism, capitalism and imperialism and we are dedicated to building a socialist society inside the United States where the total means of production and distribution are in the hands of the State and that must be led by black people, by revolutionary blacks who are concerned about the total humanity of this world. And, therefore, we obviously are different from some of those who seek a black nation in the United States, for there is no way for that nation to be viable if in fact the United States remains in the hands of white racists. Then too, let us deal with some arguments that we should share power with whites. We say that there must be a revolutionary black Vanguard and that white people in this country must be willing to accept black leadership, for that is the only protection that black people have to protect ourselves from racism rising again in this country.

Racism in the U.S. is so pervasive in the mentality of whites that only an armed, well-diciplined, black-controlled government can insure the stamping out of racism in this country. And that is why we plead with black people not to be talking about a few crumbs, a few thousand dollars for this cooperative, or a thousand dollars which splits black people into fighting over the dollar. That is the intention of the government. We say . . . think in terms of total control of the U.S. Prepare ourselves to seize state power. Do not hedge, for time is short and all around the world the forces of liberation are directing their attacks against the U.S. It is a powerful country, but that power is not greater than that of black people. We work the chief industries in this country and we could cripple the economy while the brothers fought guerrilla warfare in the streets. This will take some long range planning, but whether it happens in a thousand years is of no consequence. It cannot happen unless we start. How then is all of this related to this conference?

First of all, this conference is called by a set of religious people, Christians, who have been involved in the exploitation and rape of black people since the country was founded. The missionary goes hand in hand with the power of the states. We must begin seizing power wherever we are and we must say to the planners of this conference that you are no longer in charge. We the people who have assembled here thank you for getting us here, but we are going to assume power over the conference and determine from this moment on the direction in which we want it to go. We are not saying that the conference was planned badly. The staff of the conference has worked hard and have done a magnificent job in bringing all of us together and we must include them in the new leadership which must surface from this point on. The Conference is now the property of the people who are assembled here. This we proclaim as fact and not rhetoric and there are demands that we are going to make and we insist that the planners of this conference help us implement them.

We maintain we have the revolutionary right to do this. We have the same rights, if you will, as the Christians had in going into Africa and raping our Motherland and bringing us away from our continent of peace and into this hostile and alien environment where we have been living in perpetual warfare since 1619.

Our seizure of power at this conference is based on a program and our program is contained in the following MANIFESTO:

A Black Manifesto to the white Christian churches and the Jewish synagogues in the United States of America and all other racist institutions.

We, the Black people, assembled in Detroit, Michigan for the National Black Economic Development Conference, are fully aware that we have been forced to come together because racist white America has exploited our resources, our minds, our bodies, our labor. For centuries we have been forced to live as colonized people inside the United States, victimized by the most vicious, racist system in the world. We have helped to build the most industrial country in the world.

We are therefore demanding of the White Christian churches and Jewish synagogues which are part and parcel of the system of capitalism, that it begin to pay reparations to Black people in this country. We are demanding $500,000,000 from the Christian white churches and the Jewish synagogues. This total comes to $15.00 per nigger. This is a low estimate for we maintain there are probably more than 30,000,000 Black people in this country. $15.00 a nigger is not a large sum of money and we know that the churches and synagogues have a tremendous wealth and its membership, white America, has profited and still exploits Black people. We are also not unaware that the exploitation of colored peoples around the world is aided and abetted by the white Christian churches and synagogues. This demand for $500,000,000 is not an idle resolution or empty words. $15.00 for every Black brother and sister in the United States is only a beginning of the reparations due us as people who have been exploited and degraded, brutalized, killed and prosecuted. Underneath all of this exploitation, the racism of this country has produced a psychological effect upon us that we are beginning to shake off. We are no longer afraid to demand our full rights as a people in this decadent society.

We are demanding $500,000,000 to be spent in the following way:

1.   We call for the establishment of a Southern land bank to help our brothers and sisters who have to leave their land because of racist pressure, a people who want to establish cooperative farms, but who have no funds. We have seen too many farmers evicted from their homes because they have dared to defy the white racism of this country. We need money for land. We must fight for massive sums of money for this Southern land bank. We call for $200,000,000 to implement this program.

2.   We call for the establishment of four major publishing and printing industries in the United States to be funded with ten million dollars each. These publishing houses are to be located in Detroit, Atlanta, Los Angeles, and New York. They will help to generate capital for further cooperative investments in the Black community, provide jobs an alternative to the white dominated and controlled printing field.

3.   We call for the establishment of four cable T.V. networks to be located in Detroit, Chicago, Cleveland and Washington, D.C. These cable T.V. networks will provide an alternative to racist propaganda that fills the current television networks. Each of these T.V. cable networks will be funded by ten million dollars each.

4.   We call for a research skills center which will provide futuristic research on the problems of Black people. This center must be funded with no less than thirty million dollars.

5.   We call for the establishment of a training center for the teaching of skills in community organization, photography, movie making, television making and repair, radio building and repair and all other skills needed in com-

munication. This training center shall be funded with no less than ten million dollars.

6.   We recognize the role of the National Welfare Right Organization and we intend to work with them. We call for ten million dollars to assist in the organization of welfare recipients. We want to organize the welfare workers in this country so that they may demand more money from the government and better administration of the welfare system of this country.

7.   We call for $20,000,000 to establish a National Black Labor Strike and Defense Fund.

8.   We call for the establishment of a Black University to be funded with $130,000,000 to be located in the South.

9.   We call for the establishment of the United Black Appeal. This operation will be funded with no less than $20,000,000. The United Black Appeal is charged with producing more capital for the establishment of cooperative businesses in the United States and in Africa, our Motherland. The United Black Appeal is one of the most important demands that we are making for we know that it can generate and raise funds throughout the United States. We recognize that IFCO has incorporated the name of the United Black Appeal and we plan to work closely with it in implementing the United Black Appeal.

10.   We demand that IFCO allocate all unused funds in the planning budget to implement the demands of this conference.

In order to win our demands we are aware that we will have to have massive support, therefore:

1.   We call upon all Black people throughout the United States to consider themselves as members of the National Black Economic Development Conference and to act in unity to help force the racist white Christian churches and Jewish synagogues to implement these demands.

2.   We call upon all the concerned Black people across the country to contact Black workers, Black women, Black students and the Black unemployed, community groups, welfare organizations, teachers organizations, church leaders and organizations explaining how these demands are vital to the Black community of the United States. Pressure by whatever means necessary should be applied to the white power structure of the racist white Christian churches and Jewish synagogues. All Black people should act bolding in confronting our white oppressors and demanding this modest reparation of $15.00 per Black man.

3.   Delegates and members of the National Black Economic Development Conference are urged to call press conferences in the cities and to attempt to get as many Black organizations as possible to support the demands of the conference. The quick use of the press in the local areas will heighten the tension and these demands must be attempted to be won in a short period of time, although we are prepared for protracted and long range struggle.

4.   We call for the total disruption of church sponsored agencies operating anywhere in the United States and the world. Black workers, Black women, Black students and the Black unemployed are encouraged to seize the offices,

telephones, and printing apparatus of all church sponsored agencies and to hold these in trusteeship until our demands are met.

5. We call upon all delegates and members of the National Black Economic Development Conference to stage sit-in demonstrations at selected Black and white churches.

6. We call upon Black people to commence the disruption of racist churches on Sunday, and for all Black people to commence seizing and holding churches beginning on May 4, 1969 throughout the United States.

7. We call upon IFCO to serve as a central staff to coordinate the mandate of the conference and to reproduce and distribute en masse literature, leaflets, news items, press releases and other material.

8. We call upon all delegates to find within the white community those forces which will work under the leadership of Blacks to implement these demands whatever means necessary. By taking such actions white Americans will demonstrate concretely that they are willing to fight the white skin privilege and the white supremacy and racism which has forced us as Black people make these demands.

9. We call upon all white Christians and Jews to practice patience, tolerance, understanding and non-violence as they have encouraged, advised and demanded that we as Black people should do throughout our entire enforced slavery in the United States. The true test of their faith and belief in the cross and the words of the prophets will certainly be put to a test as we seek legitimate and extremely modes reparations for our role in developing the industrial base of the Western world through our slave labor. But we are no longer slaves, we are men and women, proud of our African heritage, determined to have our dignity.

10. We are so proud of our African heritage and realize concretely that our struggle is not only to make revolution in the United States, but to protect our brothers and sisters in Africa and to help them rid themselves of racism, capitalism and imperialism by whatever means necessary, including armed struggle. We are and must be willing to fight the defamation of our African image wherever it rears its ugly head. We are therefore charging the Steering Committee to create a Black Anti-Defamation League to be funded by money raised from the United Black Appeal.

11. To implement these demands we must have a fearless leadership. We must have a leadership which is willing to battle the church establishment to implement these demands. To win our demands we will have to declare war on the white Christian churches and this means we may have to fight the total government structure of this country. Let no one here think that these demands will be met by our mere stating them. For the sake of the churches and synagogues we hope that they have the wisdom to understand that these demands are modest and reasonable. But if the white Christians and Jews are not willing to meet our demands through peace and good will, then we declare war and we are prepared to fight by whatever means necessary. We are, therefore, proposing the election of the following Steering Committee:

Lucius Walker—Executive Director of the Inter-religious Foundation for Community Organizations

Renny Freeman

Luke Tripp—Conference coordinator of the National Black Economic Conference

Howard Fuller

James Forman

John Watson—Editor of South End

Dan Aldridge—Chairman Black United Front

John Williams—School Principal

Ken Cockrel—Lawyer

Chuck Wooten—League of Revolutionary Black Workers

Fannie Lou Hamer—Southern Activist

Julian Bond—Georgia Legislature

Mark Comfort—Oakland Defense Action Committee

Earl Allen—Houston, Texas, Vice President of IFCO

Robert Browne—Farleigh-Dickinson

Vincent Harding, Director—Martin Luther King Project

Mike Hamlin—League of Revolutionary Black Workers

Len Holt

Peter Bernard

Michael Wright, student—San Francisco State

Muhammed Kenyatta—Activist from Jackson, Mississippi

Mel Jackson—Dayton

Harold Homes—Chicago

Howard Moore

Brothers and sisters, we no longer are shuffling our feet and scratching our heads. We are tall, black and proud.

And we say to the white Christian churches and Jewish synagogues, to the government of this country and to all the white racist imperialist who compose it, there is only one thing left that you can do to further degrade Black people and that is to kill us. But we have been dying too long for this country. We have died in every war. We are dying in Vietnam today fighting the wrong enemy.

The new Black man wants to live and to live means that we must not become static or merely believe in self-defense. We must boldly go out and attack the white Western world at its power centers. The white Christian churches and the Jewish synagogues are another form of government in this country and they are used by the government of this country to exploit the people of Latin America, Asia and Africa, but the day is soon coming to an end. Therefore, brothers and sisters, the demands we make upon the white Christian churches and the Jewish synagogues are small demands. They represent $15.00 per Black person in these United States. We can legitimately demand this from the church power structure. We must demand more from the United States government.

But to win our demands from the church which is linked up with the United States government, we must not forget that it will ultimately be by force and power that we will win.

We are not threatening the churches. We are saying we know the churches came with the military might of the colonizers and have been sustained by the military might of the colonizers. Hence, if the churches in colonial territories were established by military might, we know deep within our hearts that we must be prepared to use force to get our demands. We are not saying that this is the road we want to take. It is not, but let us be very clear that we are not opposed to force and we are not opposed to violence. We were captured in Africa by violence. We were kept in bondage and politician servitude and forced to work as slaves by the military machinery and the Christian church working hand in hand.

Our demands are negotiable, but they cannot be minimized, they can only be increased and the church is asked to come up with larger sums of money than we are asking. Our slogans are all roads must lead to revolution unity with whomever you can unite, neutralize wherever possible, fight our enemies relentlessly, victory to the people! Life and good health to mankind! Resistance to domination by the white Christian churches and the Jewish synagogues and their racist membership! Revolutionary Black Power and we shall win without a doubt!

In the studies of assimilation and separation, it was possible to assess, at least partially, the effect of the rhetoric on both black and white audiences. This is almost impossible to do in the rhetoric of black revolution. As indicated at the first of the chapter, true revolutionary rhetoric is sufficiently concealed to allow for the planning of anti-system actions. Furthermore, as discussed under the rhetoric of separation, public opinion polls inherently show a bias toward pro-establishment attitudes. That is to say, when a pollster asks a black citizen whether or not he approves of revolution or violence, self-interest dictates that the black man reply in the negative. A similar instance can be found in efforts to assess the strength of communist revolutionary efforts in the United States. Loyalty oaths and other public declarations were set up, ostensibly to expose those who endorse the violent overthrow of the government. Of course, the true revolutionary was the first to sign a declaration of loyalty. Reasoning still further, success of revolutionary rhetoric cannot be measured in gross numbers of people accepting the ideas. Revolution in the United States, should it come, would probably proceed from relatively small but totally dedicated groups who would engage in acts which would step-by-step disarm the established society and increase the willingness of more people to join the movement when the time is right. Rhetorical success, then, most suitably would be measured in the degree of ego-involvement in the revolution on the part of a selected small group. Of course, this group is unavailable for audience analysis. In conclusion, the success or failure of black revolutionary rhetoric will be measured, if at all, in terms of the success or failure of the revolution itself. No polls will be needed.

REFERENCES

[1]Lewis M. Killian, *The Impossible Revolution?* (New York: Random House, Inc., 1968), pp. 65-91.

[2]*Ibid.,* p. 7.

[3]Winthrop D. Jordan, *White Over Black: American Attitudes Toward the Negro, 1550-1812* (Chapel Hill: The University of North Carolina Press, 1968), p. 392.

[4]*Ibid.*

[5]*Ibid.,* p. 393.

[6]Vesey was born in 1781 on the island of St. Thomas. After serving as a slave, he purchased his freedom and became a carpenter in Charleston, South Carolina.

[7]T. W. Higginson, "Denmark Vesey," *Atlantic Monthly*, VII, No. 54 (June, 1861), 730.

[8]*Ibid.,* 731.

[9]For a detailed analysis of Vesey's strategy see *ibid.,* 728-44.

[10]Turner was born in Virginia in 1800 and became the property of Benjamin Turner. With the help of his master's son, he educated himself, and began preaching at the age of twenty-five. Six years later he led the insurrection.

[11]William Wells Brown, *The Black Man, His Antecedents, His Genius, and His Achievements* (New York: Thomas Hamilton, 1863), p. 64.

[12]Thomas R. Gray, *The Confessions of Nat Turner* (Baltimore: Thomas Gray, 1831).

[13]Both the *Richmond Whig* and the *Petersburg Intelligencer* praised Turner as a shrewd, intelligent and courageous man. See William C. Nell, *The Colored Patriots of the American Revolution* (Boston: Robert

W. Wallcut, 1855), pp. 224-25. Gray corroborates this view in *The Confessions*, p. 18.

[14]Daniel Boorstin, *The Americans: The National Experience* (New York: Random House, Inc., 1965), p. 184.

[15]*Ibid.*, p. 185.

[16]John Hope Franklin, *From Slavery to Freedom*, 3rd ed. (New York: Alfred A. Knopf, Inc., 1967), p. 213.

[17]Walker was born in Wilmington, North Carolina in 1785, the son of a free woman and a slave father. In 1827, after emigrating to Boston, he entered the clothing business and became a part time correspondent for *Freedom's Journal*. He died mysteriously in 1830, only a short while after the publication of the third edition of his *Appeal*.

[18]His speech before the General Colored Association of Boston in December, 1828 was forceful and aggressive, yet moderate in emphasis. See *Freedom's Journal*, December 19, 1828.

[19]Dwight L. Dumond, *Antislavery: The Crusade for Freedom in America* (Ann Arbor: University of Michigan Press, 1961), p. 329. For similar views see Louis Filler, *The Crusade Against Slavery, 1830-1860* (New York: Harper & Row, Inc., 1960), p. 23; and Clement Eaton, *The Mind of the Old South*, Rev. ed. (Baton Rouge: Louisiana State University Press, 1967), p. 179.

[20]Among those who later were to feel the impact of Walker's rhetoric was Henry Highland Garnet.

[21]Eaton, *The Mind of the Old South*, p. 181.

[22]W. M. Brewer, "Henry Highland Garnet," *Journal of Negro History*, Vol. XIII (January, 1928), pp. 44-45.

[23]The document used here is taken from *Walker's Appeal with a Brief Sketch of his Life by Henry Highland Garnet and also Garnet's Address to the Slaves of the United States of America* (New York: J. H. Tobitt, 1848).

[24]*Minutes of the National Convention of Colored Citizens, Buffalo, New York, August, 1843*, cited in Brewer, Henry Highland Garnet," p. 46.

[25]Cited in Charles H. Wesley, "The Participation of Negroes in Antislavery Political Parties," *Journal of Negro History*, Vol. XXIX (January, 1944), pp. 43-44.

[26]Brewer, "Henry Highland Garnet," 45.

[27]Henry Highland Garnet, *Walker's Appeal with a Brief Sketch of his Life by Henry Highland Garnet and also Garnet's Address to the Slaves of the United States of America.*

[28]Brown, *The Black Man*, p. 149.

[29]Alexander Crummell, *Africa and America* (Springfield, Mass.: Wiley & Co., 1891), p. 294.

[30]Ward served for years as a Presbyterian minister in New York. With the passage of the Fugitive Slave Law in 1850 he fled to Canada. Later he visited England where he was regarded as an eloquent advocate of his race. He then moved to Kingston, Jamaica.

[31]Brown, *The Black Man*, p. 284.

[32]Cited in Carter G. Woodson, ed., *The Mind of the Negro as Reflected in Letters Written During the Crisis 1800-1860* (Washington, D.C.: The Associated Publishers, 1926), p. 284.

[33]Brown, *The Black Man*, p. 284.

[34]Crummell observed: "There was Samuel R. Ward, that mighty master of speech, that giant of intellect, called in his day 'the ablest thinker on his legs' . . . ." *Africa and America*, p. 291.

[35]Frederick Douglass, *The Life and Times of Frederick Douglass* (New York: Collier Books, 1962), p. 277.

[36]Brown, *The Black Man,* pp. 74-5.

[37]John Hope Franklin, *From Slavery to Freedom* (New York: Alfred A. Knopf, Inc., 1965), p. 338.

[38]James M. McPherson, writing an introduction to the re-publication of Timothy Thomas Fortune, *BLACK AND WHITE: Land, Labor, and Politics in the South* (New York: Arno Press and The New York Times, 1968).

[39]T. Thomas Fortune, *BLACK AND WHITE: Land, Labor, and Politics in the South* (N.Y.: Fords, Howard, & Hulbert, 1884); re-printed by Arno Press and The New York Times, 1968) pp. 11, 17, 22.

[40]*Ibid.*, pp. 34-35; 147.

[41]*Ibid.*, pp. 64-65.

[42]*Ibid.*, p. 116.

[43]*Ibid.*, p. 234.

[44]*Ibid.*, p. 233.

[45]James Forman, "Liberation Will Come From A Black Thing," Text of a speech delivered at the Western Regional Black Youth Conference in Los Angeles, California, November 23, 1967, reprinted in U.S. Congress, Senate Committee on Government Operations, Permanent Subcommittee on Investigations, Hearings, Riots, Civil and Criminal Disorders, 91st Congress, First Session, 1969, p. 4069.

[46]Julius Lester, *Revolutionary Notes* (New York: Richard W. Baron Publishing Co., Inc., 1969), p. 179. © by Julius Lester. Reprinted by permission of Richard W. Baron Publishing Co., Inc.

[47]*Ibid.*, pp. 93-94.

[48]*Ibid.*, p. 101.

[49]*Ibid.*, pp. 53-54.

[50]Reprinted from *Die Nigger Die!*, copyright © 1969 by Lynne Brown. Used by permission of the publishers, The Dial Press. p. 67

[51]Jean-Paul Sartre, "Preface," in Frantz Fanon, *The Wretched of the Earth*, Translated by Constance Farrington, (New York: Grove Press, Inc., 1968), p. 22.

[52]Frantz Fanon, *The Wretched of the Earth*, *ibid.*, p. 43.

[53]H. Rap Brown, *op. cit.*, p. 55.

[54]Robert Scheer, ed., *Eldridge Cleaver Post-Prison Writings and Speeches* (New York: Random House, Inc., 1969), p. 114.

[55]*Ibid.*, p. 150.

[56]"An Interview — Black Student Union's Move to Revolutionary Nationalism," *People's World*, February 15, 1959, reprinted in Hearings, *op cit.*, p. 3775.

[57]Fanon, *op. cit.*, p. 210.

[58]Scheer, *op. cit.*, p. 49, quoting Cleaver.

[59]H. Rap Brown, *Die Nigger Die!*, p. 13.

[60]Huey P. Newton, "In Defense of Self Defense," *The Black Panther*, June 20, 1967.

[61]Scheer, *op. cit.*, p. 28.

[62]Fanon, *op. cit.*, p. 47.

[63]Eldridge Cleaver, "The Black Man's Stake in Vietnam," *The Black Panther,* III, No. 22, (September 20, 1969), 13.

[64]Fanon, *op. cit.*, p. 72.

[65]RAM, "On Organization of Black Ghetto Youth," reprinted in Hearings on Riots, Civil and Criminal Disorders, *op. cit.*, p. 4223.

[66]The recorded transcript of this speech was made by radio station WSHA, Shaw University, Raleigh, North Carolina.

[67]William H. Grier and Price M. Cobbs, *Black Rage* (New York: Bantam Books, Inc., 1968), p. 172.

[68]Scheer, *op. cit.*, p. 22.

[69]Lester, *Revolutionary Notes, op. cit.*, p. 139.

[70]H. Rap Brown, *op. cit.*, p. 128.

[71]James Forman, 1967: *High Tide of Black Resistance*, (Student Nonviolent Coordinating Committee, 1968).

[72]Fanon, *op. cit.*, p. 216.

[73]H. Rap Brown, *Die Nigger Die!*, p. 135.

[74]James Forman, "Liberation Will Come From A Black Thing," *op. cit.*, p. 4066.

[75]Lester, *Revolutionary Notes, op. cit.*, p. 72.

[76]Forman, *op. cit.*

[77]Huey P. Newton, monitored by the United States Government broadcast from Cuba, August 18, 1968, reprinted in Hearings, *op. cit.*, pp. 3736-37.

[78]Huey P. Newton, "In Defense of Self Defense," *The Black Panther*, July 3, 1967.

[79]Stokely Carmichael Interviewed by *Sucesos Magazine*, Broadcast in English from Havana, Monitored by the United States Government on September 9, 1967, printed in Hearings, *op. cit.*, p. 4006.

[80]Stokely Carmichael and Charles V. Hamilton, *Black Power, The Politics of Liberation in America* (New York: Vintage Books, 1967), p. 7.

[81]Albert B. Cleage, Jr., *The Black Messiah* (New York: Sheed and Ward, 1968), p. 15.

[82]RAM, printed in Hearings, *op. cit.*

[83]Brown, *op. cit.*, p. 57.

[84]Eldridge Cleaver, "An Open Letter to Stokely Carmichael," *Ramparts*, VIII, No. 3 (September, 1969), 31-32.

550   THE RHETORIC OF REVOLUTION

[85]*Ibid.*, p. 32.

[86]Albert B. Cleage, Jr., Speech on "Black Power," delivered at Ohio State University, October 14, 1969.

[87]Irving Davis, deputy administrator and acting director of international affairs of the Student Nonviolent Coordinating Committee, Monitored by the United States Government from a broadcast from Cuba on October 2, reprinted in Hearings, *op. cit.*, p. 4205.

[88]Robert F. Williams, "1969: A Season of Terror," *The Crusader Newsletter*, X, No. 1 (November, 1968), printed in *Hearings, op. cit.*, 4205.

[89]Lester, *Revolutionary Notes, op. cit.*, p. 42.

[90]Albert B. Cleage, Jr., *The Black Messiah, op. cit.*, pp. 44-45.

[91]*Ibid.*, p. 54.

[92]Cleage speaking at Ohio State, *op. cit.*

[93]Lester, *Revolutionary Notes, op. cit.*, pp. 108, 129.

[94]Stokely Carmichael, "Where SNCC Now Is," May 1967, reprinted in Hearings, *op. cit.*, p. 4014.

[95]Scheer, *op. cit.*, p. 207.

INDEX

INDEX